Protest, Defiance and Resistance in the Channel Islands

Protest, Defiance and Resistance in the Channel Islands

German Occupation, 1940–45

Gilly Carr, Paul Sanders and Louise Willmot

Bloomsbury Academic
An imprint of Bloomsbury Publishing Plc

BLOOMSBURY
LONDON • NEW DELHI • NEW YORK • SYDNEY

Bloomsbury Academic
An imprint of Bloomsbury Publishing Plc

50 Bedford Square   1385 Broadway
London   New York
WC1B 3DP   NY 10018
UK   USA

www.bloomsbury.com

BLOOMSBURY and the Diana logo are trademarks of Bloomsbury Publishing Plc

First published 2014

Paperback edition published 2015

© Gilly Carr, Paul Sanders and Louise Willmot, 2015

Gilly Carr, Paul Sanders and Louise Willmot have asserted their right under the Copyright, Designs and Patents Act, 1988, to be identified as Authors of this work.

All rights reserved. No part of this publication may be reproduced or transmitted in any form or by any means, electronic or mechanical, including photocopying, recording, or any information storage or retrieval system, without prior permission in writing from the publishers.

No responsibility for loss caused to any individual or organization acting on or refraining from action as a result of the material in this publication can be accepted by Bloomsbury or the authors.

British Library Cataloguing-in-Publication Data
A catalogue record for this book is available from the British Library.

ISBN: HB: 978-1-4725-0920-8
      PB: 978-1-4725-3624-2
      ePDF: 978-1-4725-0813-3
      ePub: 978-1-4725-1296-3

Library of Congress Cataloging-in-Publication Data
A catalog record for this book is available from the Library of Congress.

Typeset by Newgen Knowledge Works (P) Ltd., Chennai, India

*This book is dedicated to all Channel Islanders who committed
acts of protest, defiance and resistance during the German occupation,
all those who were imprisoned and deported for such actions,
and those who made the ultimate sacrifice*

Contents

List of Illustrations	viii
List of Graphs and Tables	x
Acknowledgements	xi
Introduction *Gilly Carr, Paul Sanders and Louise Willmot*	1
1 Symbolic Resistance *Gilly Carr*	19
2 The V-sign Campaign and the Fear of Reprisals *Gilly Carr*	43
3 Radio Days *Paul Sanders*	65
4 Humanitarian Resistance: Help to Jews and OT Workers *Louise Willmot*	97
5 Defiance and Deportations *Gilly Carr*	127
6 Institutional Resistance: Political Groups, Clergy and Doctors *Louise Willmot*	153
7 Women and Resistance *Louise Willmot*	183
8 Sabotage, Intelligence-gathering and Escape *Louise Willmot*	213
9 The Peculiarities of Being under the Swastika and the Crown: Officials and Their Resistance *Paul Sanders*	243
10 Economic Resistance and Sabotage *Paul Sanders*	277
11 Heritage, Memory and Resistance in the Channel Islands *Gilly Carr*	307
12 Conclusion *Gilly Carr, Paul Sanders and Louise Willmot*	339
Bibliography	355
Index	367

List of Illustrations

1.1	Crest badge	32
1.2	Two trench art German helmets, painted with images originally by Bert Hill	36
1.3	Stone de Croze cartoon by Alan Guppy	38
2.1a	Alf Williams flashing his V-sign badge	51
2.1b	Image of V-sign badge	51
2.2	Pencil sketch of Monty Manning by Eric Sirett	55
2.3	Plaque commemorating the fiftieth anniversary of the arrival of the Vega in December 1994	57
3.1	Frank Falla listening to the BBC, cartoon by Bert Hill	77
4.1	Albert Bedane, who sheltered Mary Erica Richardson	102
4.2	Robert Le Sueur, a young Jerseyman who found safe houses for Russian fugitives	110
4.3	Ivy Forster, who sheltered a Russian fugitive, George Koslov, in the family home	112
5.1	Union Jack from a Colman's mustard tin	143
5.2	Photo from the August Bank Holiday fancy dress cavalcade in Biberach, 1943	144
5.3	V-mug made by Byll Balcombe in Biberach camp, in private ownership	145
6.1	Norman Le Brocq, a founder member of the Jersey Communist Party	156
6.2	Arthur Halliwell, consultant surgeon at Jersey General Hospital	171
6.3	Noel McKinstry, Medical Officer of Health in Jersey	171
7.1	Sketch made by Suzanne Malherbe in prison, showing the view through the cell keyhole	188
7.2	Lucy Schwob (Claude Cahun) – self-portrait (with Nazi badge between her teeth), 1945	190
7.3	Louisa Gould, whose decision to shelter Fyodor Burriy was to cost her life	195
7.4	Marie Ozanne in Salvation Army uniform	198

List of Illustrations

8.1	Peter Painter	219
8.2	William Gladden, who gathered intelligence as well as sheltering a Russian OT fugitive	222
8.3	The master mariner George Sowden	229
8.4	Patriotic watercolour painted in Gloucester Street by the political prisoner Dennis McLinton, showing 'Britannia' escaping from Jersey	231
10.1	The legal team of the eight policemen who took their case to the Privy Council on a flying visit to Guernsey, February 1952	291
10.2	Frank Tuck and Eric Goldrein at the time of the Privy Council appeal, ca. 1951–2	292
11.1	Political prisoner certificate	314
11.2	Image from nurse Renee Griffin's autograph book	315
11.3	Evelyn Janvrin's political prisoner badge	318
11.4	Painting of Joe Miere by Andrew Tift	321
11.5	Photo of the twenty-first annual reunion of political prisoners, Guernsey 1966	322
11.6	Photo of Frank Falla's briefcase, in which his letters, testimonies and newspaper cuttings were kept	325
11.7	Lighthouse Memorial, St Helier, Holocaust Memorial Day	328
11.8	Memorial cross to Joseph Gillingham at the Guernsey War Memorial	330

List of Graphs and Tables

Graphs

3.1	Guernsey radio offences: correlation between age groups A and sex	68
3.2	Guernsey radio offences over time	69
3.3	Jersey radio offences: correlation between age groups A and sex	69
3.4	Jersey radio offences: correlation between age groups B and sex	70
3.5	Jersey trials for radio offences over time	70
3.6	Radio offences: age groups B in Jersey and Guernsey	71
12.1	Convictions over time in Guernsey and Jersey	347

Tables

3.1	Analysis of German police files, wireless cases, July 1945	84
3.2	German court files: radio offences in Guernsey, 1944	85
3.2.1	Source leading to arrest: German Military	85
3.2.2	Source leading to arrest: House search	85
3.2.3	Source leading to arrest: Anonymous letter	86
3.2.4	Source leading to arrest: Confidential source	86
3.2.5	Source leading to arrest: Other	86
9.1	Billeting of German soldiers (1942)	253

Acknowledgements

This book would not have been possible had we not been given complete access to all records, open and closed, at Guernsey and Jersey archives. We would like to thank the staff there who went above and beyond the call of duty to help us. They include: Darryl Ogier, Nathan Coyde and Lawrence West at the Island Archives in Guernsey, and Linda Romeril, Stuart Nicolle and all the staff at Jersey Archives. We would like to take this opportunity to thank the Law Officers' Department in Jersey, the Police Service in Guernsey and Jersey, the Guernsey Greffe, and the Bailiff's and Lieutenant-Governor's offices in Guernsey and Jersey.

We would also like to thank Chris Addy for all of the help he gave us when we examined the archives and collections at Jersey War Tunnels; Amanda Bennett, Sue Laker, and all of the staff at the Priaulx Library, Guernsey, for helping us find all the Occupation-related diaries relevant to this project; Val Nelson, Doug Ford, Jon Carter and staff at Jersey Heritage; Jason Monaghan, Matt Harvey and other staff at Guernsey Museum; Richard Heaume, Director of the German Occupation Museum in Guernsey, for allowing us access to his archives and objects, and for his kindness and many cups of tea and Occupation-related conversations; and to Peter and Paul Balshaw, owners of the Vallette Underground Military Museum in St Peter Port, for access to their collections.

A number of friends in the Channel Islands helped us in our archival data collection, and they include Gillian Lenfesty, Ken Tough and Fay Warrilow. We would also like to thank Annie Corbitt, our research assistant in 2011 who helped analyse the statistical data; Mark Lamerton, who was his usual helpful self in feeding us useful press cuttings and emails; Jose Day, who allowed us to peruse her father's diary; and most of all, to Rebecca Montague, who had the onerous job of compiling and editing the primary and secondary bibliographies, and who made the referencing styles of three academics consistent. Thank you Rebecca! You are a star.

We would also like to thank the staff at The National Archives in Kew, the Imperial War Museum, the International Tracing Service in Arolsen, and at the Military Archive in Freiburg. Our thanks also to Rachel O'Flynn and Mary Pring at the Foreign Office, who have been more helpful than they realize.

Channel Islanders from Jersey, Guernsey and Sark have been helpful, supportive, generous and open in allowing us to consult their cherished family archives, diaries, and other relevant papers. We have received letters, emails and phone calls weekly from the Channel Islands, the United Kingdom and further afield since the project began in 2010, with people coming forwards with offers of family information. This has been incredibly important in helping the project be as comprehensive as it has.

Our chief thanks must go jointly to the families of Frank Falla and Joseph Gillingham for their generosity, kindness, support and trust in our project. We would also like to thank other former political prisoners and their families from across the Channel Islands who were interviewed for this project, including: William Ozanne and the rest of the Ozanne clan, Francis Harris, Leo Harris, Alf Williams, Peter Gray, Wendy Tipping, Richard Ahier, Mickey Neil, Basil Le Brun, Mavis Lemon, Victor Webb, the Sowden and Hamon families and Bernard Turpin. In addition, we are deeply grateful to other islanders who opposed the Germans but were never arrested, including Robert Le Sueur.

We would like to thank former Bailiffs, Sir Philip Bailhache, Sir Geoffrey Rowland and Sir de Vic Carey, who have granted us interviews for this project.

Members of the Guernsey Deportee Association and former Jersey ex-Internee Association and their families have kindly allowed Gilly Carr to interview them for this project. We thank them warmly and list them here: Tom Remfrey, Michael Ginns, Moggie Hill, Ursula Dingle, John Green, Yvonne Osborn, Peter Sirett, Barry Webber, Sylvia Diamond, Heather Duggan, John Goodwin, Godfrey Le Cappelain, David Skillett, David Barrett, Sheila Legg, Mary Cornish, Peter Levitt, Irene Barrett and Christine Bailey.

Throughout this volume we have quoted from or referenced aspects of many unpublished and archival Occupation diaries and papers. We have tried to track down all of the individuals and families concerned but this has not proved possible. Those who have given their permission include, with our grateful thanks: Peter Gray, Michael Elstob, Nigel Lewis, Joyce Le Ruez, the legal owners of the diaries of Gertrude Corbin and Ella Frampton, Margaret Le Vesconte, Arnold Bennett, Bernard Cavey, Gordon Duquemin, the families of Albert Chardine, Arthur Mahy, Charles Albert Friend, Adèle Lainé, the Reverend Ord, Bert Williams, Kingston George Bailey and the family of René Havard. Violet Carey's unpublished diaries were quoted with the kind permission of Patricia Paxton.

We would welcome contact from the families of other diarists whose work we referenced in the bibliography and who we have tried to track down without success.

To those who have given us permission to reproduce photographs, we would like to thank: Christine Bailey, Peter and Paul Balshaw, Jonathan Bartlett, Damien Horn, the family of Frank Falla, Eric Goldrein, Mr and Mrs A. T. Green, Mark Guppy, Richard Heaume, Jersey Heritage Collections, William Ozanne, Peter Sirett, the Société Jersiaise, Andrew Tift and Wendy Tipping. The wonderful image on the front cover is of a crystal radio set owned by Mrs A. M. Le Quesne; we thank her grandson for permission to use it.

We would also like to thank the editors of the Guernsey Press and the Jersey Evening Post for their continued help in allowing us to publicize the project. This has encouraged islanders to come forwards, which has been of immeasurable help to us. Our editors at Bloomsbury Academic have also been a pleasure to work with, and we would especially like to thank Emily Drewe and Frances Arnold.

Gilly Carr would like to thank Taylor and Francis for permission to reproduce an adapted part of the book chapter 'God save the King!' Creative modes of protest, defiance and identity in Channel Islander internment camps in Germany, 1942–1945' in *Cultural Heritage and Prisoners of War: Creativity Behind Barbed Wire*, edited by Gilly Carr and Harold Mytum (2012). Paul Sanders would like to thank Inga and Eric Goldrein, and Jacques Semelin, for interviews granted in 2011 and 2013.

This project was made possible with the generous financial support of the British Academy, the Société Jersiaise and the family of Joseph Gillingham.

Introduction

Gilly Carr, Paul Sanders and Louise Willmot

This book fills a gap that has become noticeably wider over the last 20 years. Such have been the repeated misinterpretations of this lacuna in scholarship that, in 2009, the authors decided to take on the rewriting of this particular history. As the only three university academics in Europe to specialize in the German Occupation of the Channel Islands, we realized that we were the people to tackle this task. Although we were aware of each other's existence, we had not worked together before. In 2010 we secured funding from the British Academy, the Société Jersiaise, and the family of Joseph Gillingham, a man who had, during the Occupation, been a member of an underground news network, the Guernsey Underground News Service (GUNS).

That year, we discovered the excitement of working together as a team, and were spurred on and inspired by each other's discoveries and insights. Sitting together while we worked at a table in the archives in Guernsey and Jersey, we were able to have many conversations which began, 'Have you noticed …?', which went on to trigger important observations of patterning which we would not have taken seriously enough had we worked alone. We also experienced together the frustrations of missing archival documents; those which had been destroyed by the Germans or had simply never been deposited in the archives or had gone missing over the last 70 years. The lack of a prison log from Guernsey was a hindrance to inter-island comparison, but we found ways to continue our research without it.

That year we were also handed the Frank Falla files by a member of Falla's family. Falla, another member of GUNS who, like Gillingham, had been deported to a Nazi prison, had helped islanders seek compensation, in 1965, from the German government, for victims of Nazi persecution. His file was full of correspondence and testimonies from other Channel Islanders who had suffered in prisons and camps. This file showed us that a substantial part of Channel Islands Occupation-era history had yet to be written, and that this book would be just the start.

In this volume, we begin by suggesting that, since 1945 there has been no detailed academic study of resistance in the German-occupied Channel Islands, because historians considered that there was insufficient evidence of it to warrant their attention. The neglect had its roots in two incontrovertible facts: no German soldier was killed or seriously injured by a Channel Islander during the Occupation, and the islands were liberated by the surrender of German armies on the European continent and not by any fighting in the islands themselves. The facts of geography, the scale of the German presence, the lack of weapons and outside encouragement, it was thought, had made significant resistance impossible, and left islanders with little choice but to wait for liberation from outside. Once it was established that *military* resistance was minimal or non-existent, the incentive to search for evidence of other forms of opposition to German rule was correspondingly reduced.

This volume is testimony to the fact that we do not accept the suggestion that island resistance is not worth studying; we think there are distinct problems in ignoring it. Its neglect has left the field open to a tendentious collaboration narrative – the accusation that islanders collaborated proactively during the Occupation and did not resist enough – and prevented a fruitful comparison of conditions in the islands with those in other flat, densely populated areas of Western Europe. We accept that open *military* resistance was never possible in the Channel Islands, but argue that its inhabitants and their governments did have some 'margin' for action against the occupiers. For example, they could assert their sense of patriotism through symbols and artefacts; they could protest against specific German policies, either individually or in large gatherings; they could defy German orders altogether, for example by withholding sets after the confiscation of radios in June 1942; they could attempt to raise morale by circulating the BBC news; they could plan for a more democratic future after the liberation, which entailed not only attacking German rule, but also taking a critical attitude to the democratic legitimacy of the local administrations; they could aid victims of persecution by feeding and hiding them; and they could attempt to contribute to Allied military victory even without engaging in partisan warfare, by means of intelligence-gathering, petty sabotage and military larceny, and escape. Although the islands were liberated without a shot being fired, it could not be known at the time whether the German garrison in the islands would make a last stand. It is no use to argue with the benefit of hindsight; the context prevailing at the time needs to be factored in. And this tells us that the Allies, for their part, had included the eventuality of a last stand in their contingency planning and that the help given to them by Channel Islanders in making preparations was inestimable. Islanders took these opportunities in varying degrees in the two islands and were motivated by different sentiments, but they were not 'choiceless' between 1940 and 1945.

Definitions

In this volume we discuss protest, defiance and resistance, but we do not use these terms interchangeably. Instead we treat them as different and sometimes overlapping forms of opposition to German rule, rather than as mutually exclusive spheres of action. At an individual level, people could enact different forms of opposition at different times, as can be seen in the case of Marie Ozanne, for example, who wrote letters to the Feldkommandant to protest against the German treatment of foreign labourers and Jews but also defied German orders against the wearing of the Salvation Army uniform. Jersey's Medical Officer of Health, Noel McKinstry, made private protests against German policies towards OT workers and the mentally ill, but also engaged in clandestine resistance to the regime by giving aid to fugitive slave workers and helping smuggle military intelligence off the island.

The boundaries between protest, defiance and resistance were blurred at times; the same act at different times constituted a different form of anti-German action. The V-sign, for example, started out as a patriotic sentiment and a protest against German occupation. After the Germans declared that it was a punishable offence, its continued appearance can be classed as defiance. It was also, arguably, a form of symbolic resistance, and was recognized as such all over Europe. By expressing faith in an allied victory, it attempted to boost the morale of islanders and to damage that of the Germans, which can be seen as part of a wider intention to thwart German aims of victory.

Definitions are not always easy, although publicly or privately protesting against German orders by writing letters, singing patriotic songs in a public place or through group demonstrations, are easily labelled. Defiance of the rules of the occupying forces can be identified by people continuing to do what has been forbidden – it is, in other words, disobedience. However, the definition of 'resistance' is not so obvious; no longer is it restricted simply to military action which furthered the allied war effort. As Semelin[1] found, it is a complex phenomenon that does not tolerate rigid categorization; the nature of resistance and the motivations of those involved are many and various.[2] Although many have argued that any activity which thwarted German plans or worked against their interests could be defined as resistance,[3] it is easier instead to define resistance in the context of where it took place rather than finding a one-size-fits-all definition which applies to all occupied countries – a notoriously difficult task. While military resistance, which included intelligence gathering and sabotage operations, can unquestionably be included in the definition, we can also consider the many civilian forms of resistance that are included in this book. Perhaps the best way to understand 'resistance' is as an umbrella term under which other specific forms, such as defiance and protest, might shelter. There were many different forms: moral, religious, spiritual, ideological, political, symbolic and humanitarian, but forming an exhaustive list or even a water-tight definition is not necessarily a useful exercise.

In analysing resistance in the Channel Islands, we wanted to know what forms existed, when during the war they took place, what motivations or triggers could be identified, whether any patterns related to demography or social class could be observed among the kinds of people who carried out certain forms, and, finally, how resistance changed between 1940 and 1945. Often, only statistical information could provide the kind of insight we sought, and it is this level of information that has been lacking in previous accounts of the Occupation, so preoccupied have people been with the human stories of known individuals, which inevitably stand out more in small and close-knit societies such as are to be found in the Channel Islands. We hope that this book unites both the individual stories with the wider picture and insights provided from studying police and prison records.

The historiography of resistance

For 50 years after the Liberation, resistance in the Channel Islands was never the subject of academic study in its own right, but was discussed only as a part of the overall experience of the Occupation. In the immediate aftermath of the Liberation, as Gilly Carr demonstrates elsewhere in this book, Channel Islanders had taken pride in their defiance of the Germans through memoirs and film.[4] Only ten years later, however, Alan Wood and Mary Seaton Wood detected a sea-change in attitudes there. Although their own lively popular history gave due weight to defiance and resistance and explained the rationale of the island administrations in opposing it, the authors noted a 'strange disposition' among the inhabitants to forget the recent Occupation altogether, except as a useful and anodyne addition to the tourist trade.[5] Collaboration was not discussed, and resisters had apparently been forgotten: the island authorities had not even compiled a Roll of Honour of the men and women whose opposition to the Germans had cost them their lives. The British government, they thought, had reinforced this selective amnesia by opting not to insist on an investigation of cases of alleged collaboration, and by hurrying to hand out honours to high-ranking members of the wartime administrations, including knighthoods for Alexander Coutanche, John Leale and Victor Carey. With one exception, none of the residents who had risked their lives to oppose the occupiers had been honoured.[6] Controversial aspects of the Occupation, it seemed, were deliberately ignored.

Whatever the reason for the silence, the impact on the historiography of the Occupation and the treatment of resistance was profound. When Charles Cruickshank's official history of the Occupation, commissioned by the States of Jersey and Guernsey, was published in 1975, it focused on the details of everyday life, on the conduct of the local and German administrations and on the fate of the various British commando operations there. Apart from very brief references to the V-sign campaign, help to OT workers, petty sabotage and escapes, Cruickshank hardly mentioned resistance.[7] There had been, he thought, 'not the slightest hope' that it could achieve anything of significance: the islands were tiny, densely populated with German troops and lacked escape routes.[8] If the inhabitants had been unwise enough to attempt sabotage against military installations, reprisals would have been unavoidable and could have been catastrophic. Although the island governments occasionally seemed to go beyond the bounds of purely passive co-operation with the occupiers, their decision to oppose all acts of resistance had been 'plain commonsense', and ordinary Channel Islanders had demonstrated their own good sense in choosing not to engage in it.[9] The small minority who did take part, though sometimes courageous, had failed 'to see the harm it could do to their fellow islanders'.[10]

Cruickshank's assessment of the value of resistance in the islands was based primarily on an analysis of its ability – or, rather, inability – to contribute to Allied *military* victory. A distinctly more critical note, however, was sounded by Norman Longmate in his brief survey of the Occupation in 1971. For Longmate the issue was the absence of an *organized resistance movement*: the Channel Islands had been 'the only enslaved country' [sic] not to create one, which was 'hardly a matter of pride' for British observers even though it had spared the islands from the massacres and reprisals that marked German rule elsewhere.[11] Nor had there been any general strikes or major demonstrations of the kind that had occurred elsewhere in occupied Europe, though hundreds had gathered to show patriotic solidarity during the deportations of British-born islanders in 1942. Otherwise, apart from defiance of the radio ban and occasional outbursts of abuse by isolated individuals, islanders had done little more than display patriotic symbols and had remained passive in the face of the persecution of Jews and the ill-treatment of forced labourers. Longmate was careful to balance his remarks by commenting that there had been little active collaboration, either, with the exception of the 'many' local girls who went out with German soldiers. Although few Channel Islanders had been heroes, he argued, fewer still were traitors.[12]

It was in the prelude to the fiftieth anniversary celebrations of the Liberation that critical assessments of the conduct of islanders and their governments reached their peak. In their popular histories of the Occupation, both Peter King and Madeleine Bunting devoted chapters to island resistance and acknowledged the courage of those who engaged in it, but in both cases the dominant narrative was of the passivity and even collaboration of the islanders and, especially, their governments. In *The Channel Islands War 1940–1945*, published in 1991, King repeated the criticisms made by Alan Wood and Mary Seaton Wood almost 40 years before: even now, the island governments had yet to honour the 'army of Unknown Warriors' who had resisted the Occupation.[13] His definition of resistance was more broadly drawn than Cruickshank's had been, and included protests and demonstrations as well as defiance of the radio ban, intelligence-gathering, escape and help to forced and slave labourers. King also accepted that the scope for active resistance was limited by the geography of the islands and the scale of the German presence. Like Longmate, however, he was troubled by the absence of an organized resistance movement: the Resistance historian Henri Michel, he wrote, had been wrong to claim that every occupied European country had its 'clandestine resistance', since the Channel Islands had produced none of their own.[14] King's main criticisms, however, were reserved for the conduct of the island governments, which had continued to receive the 'perks and privileges' of office under the Germans and, in return, had obeyed their orders almost without question. Their attitude towards resistance had been shaped by the conviction that they could best protect the interests of the inhabitants by remaining in post, which depended on outright condemnation of all opposition to Occupation. As a result, they had urged Channel Islanders to obey the Germans, report law-breakers, hand over escaped prisoners, oppose escapers and refrain from sabotage.[15] What Cruickshank had seen as 'passive co-operation' was, to King, more like collaboration: the island authorities, he wrote, 'seem sometimes to have forgotten who were the enemy'.[16] Three years later, these arguments were repeated in a work by the French historian J. Y. Ruaux, *Vichy Sur Manche*.[17]

However, it was the publication of *The Model Occupation* (1995), by journalist and history graduate Madeleine Bunting, that brought the experiences of Occupation to the attention of a wider public. Based on interviews with survivors as well as documentary material, the book was well received in Britain but was greeted with dismay, even outrage, in the islands themselves.[18] Significant sections of it – and the parts that received most publicity – were devoted to aspects that belonged squarely in the domain of 'collaboration': to informers, to women who had relationships with German soldiers, to fraternization, and to the conduct of the island governments in working for 'correct relations'. Bunting did not deny that there had been some resistance to the Occupation, nor that its protagonists had demonstrated a 'bravely defiant spirit'.[19] As King had done, she outlined a broad spectrum of activity in her chapter on resistance, including protests and demonstrations as well as escapes, intelligence-gathering and aid to slave labourers. Nevertheless, the fact that the chapter was titled 'Resistance? What Resistance?' gives an idea of its overall belittling tone. Islanders, she argued, had done nothing to compare with the Resistance heroes of France, Belgium or Greece. With a small number of honourable exceptions, adults had demonstrated no more than a 'passive patriotism' – for instance in displaying patriotic symbols – and though teenagers and young adults had been bolder, much of their defiance had been little more than 'childish mischievousness and teenage delinquency' dressed up as patriotic resistance.[20]

Bunting offered some thoughtful and reasonable explanations for islanders' passivity, of which the most important were the constraints of geography, the lack of traditions of political opposition and resistance and the relative mildness of German conduct. Yet even when these were taken into account, she argued, they had been 'more quiescent' and less likely to resist than other Europeans.[21] Their governments had failed lamentably to protect the islands' Jews or to protest against the ill-treatment of forced and slave workers, while the inhabitants themselves had remained passive even after the confiscation of radios and during the deportations of British-born residents in 1942. Strikes and collective action had been conspicuous by their absence. Now, decades later, islanders were still reluctant to discuss the few cases of genuine resistance that had taken place. Their silence was easily explained, she thought: to acknowledge the courage of a few would only draw embarrassing attention to the inadequacies of the rest, and to the conduct of the islands' leaders.[22] It was hardly surprising that Channel Islanders felt they had been judged and condemned.

The controversy aroused by *The Model Occupation* generated a great deal more heat than light. In mainland Britain, reviewers emphasized the extent of collaboration and the relative absence of resistance, while also suggesting that the experience of the islands provided a salutary and unflattering indication of how the rest of the country would have behaved in the event of a German invasion.[23] *The Model Occupation* also did very little to advance the study of resistance. On the other hand, a Madeleine Bunting was probably necessary in order to rattle islanders out of their complacency in believing that their special relationship to Britain would forestall critical scrutiny of the war years of the kind that had become increasingly common elsewhere in Europe since the early 1980s. It was also an effective antidote against the commonly held view that Charles Cruickshank had 'exhausted' the topic of the Channel Islands occupation, that there was nothing controversial about it and that no further historiographical work – and certainly not on resistance – was necessary. Bunting also demonstrated that a wealth of information was still available, either through interviews or in the form of documentary evidence, and that this could also be tapped by other researchers.

What the discussion of resistance still lacked was a detailed analysis of the possibilities and limitations, nature and extent of resistance in the islands, but situated squarely within the context of the European resistance *as a whole* to provide the necessary comparisons and interpretative framework. The problem was that, in the half century since 1945, historians of the European resistance had failed to include the Channel Islands in their analyses at all. A British contributor, M. R. D. Foot, explained his own approach in 1976. The Channel Islands, he wrote, were 'an embarrassment' (that word again!) to British writers because 'there was virtually no resistance there': the lack of young men of military age, the high garrison-to-population ratio and the absence of hiding places or escape routes meant that the conditions for it simply did not exist.[24] His analysis was shaped by the over-riding emphasis in early resistance historiography on the *military* value of resistance and its contribution to eventual Allied victory through underground armies, sabotage, intelligence-gathering and escape networks. With these as the reference point, it was easy to dismiss the experience of the islands as irrelevant and the contribution of their inhabitants as negligible.[25]

The exclusion of the Channel Islands from comparative studies had significant consequences: as well as reinforcing the view that there had been no real resistance, it also detached them from mainstream developments in the historiography of European resistance. By the early 1970s, this historiography was moving beyond a narrow early focus on the contribution of resistance to Allied military victory – chiefly through sabotage, intelligence-gathering and partisan warfare – towards a broader and more flexible interpretation of its nature and extent that could usefully have been applied to the islands' experience. A key role in this development was played by the French historian Henri Michel in *The Shadow War*, published in English in 1972. Although still devoting much of his work to strikes, escape networks, sabotage, assassinations and partisan warfare, Michel's analysis also included passive and administrative resistance, for example by postal workers who were able to divert letters of denunciation directed to the Germans.[26] Equally important for the future analysis of resistance, Michel identified three overlapping phases common to its development across Europe: an early *phase of refusal to submit*, characterized by small-scale leafleting, petty sabotage and acts of solidarity with persecuted individuals or groups; an *organization phase* which saw the emergence of underground newspapers, co-ordinated strikes, escape lines and the systematic collection of intelligence; and a *phase of battle*, in which resistance was directed towards achieving national liberation, usually in cooperation with Allied armies (whether or not resistance groups did any fighting).[27] Everywhere resistance had increased in response to several factors, chief among them the increase in internal repression by the occupiers, Allied military successes, and direct encouragement from outside forces based in London or Moscow. Notwithstanding these common features, the nature of resistance had varied greatly from region to region, depending on 'the attitude of the occupying power, the nature of the country, the assistance provided by the Allies and the country's strategic importance'.[28]

The development of a flexible typography of resistance was further advanced in 1975 by Steven Hawes and Ralph White's edited volume *Resistance in Europe 1939–1945*, based on the proceedings of a symposium at the University of Salford two years before.[29] In his introductory chapter on the unity and diversity of resistance, White confirmed the common pattern of development outlined by Michel. Everywhere resistance had begun with small gestures or 'pinpricks' – defacing German posters, for example – that did little to damage the occupiers but served to boost morale and suggest the possibility of more organized activity. Only gradually did resistance become more 'corporate' or group-based, and included patriotic gatherings on 'national' days, the staging of demonstrations, the exchange of radio news and the planning of escapes. Crucial for its further development, however, was the emergence of specific organizations and movements that could co-ordinate action effectively.[30]

The emergence of resistance depended in no small part on the actions of the occupiers themselves. In Western Europe – in stark contrast to the East – it grew only slowly, largely because German conduct had been *relatively* restrained and limited forms of self-government often permitted. When it did emerge, its character was determined by the unique political, social and cultural circumstances of each state. These included its political traditions, the nature of its wartime government and the inescapable facts of geography, which made partisan operations possible in France and Yugoslavia but made them more difficult, for example, in Denmark.[31] White also demonstrated how far resistance historiography had progressed since the early emphasis on its military aspects. As well as an attempt to contribute to the Allied war effort, it was also to be understood as a patriotic struggle for national liberation and/or an ideological struggle against Nazism, and as an expression of hostility to local collaborators and their organizations.[32]

The volume was also notable for a revisionist contribution by the economic historian Alan Milward, who challenged the view that major sabotage attacks by organized resistance groups had significantly damaged Germany's forces or war effort. With very few exceptions, he argued, such direct attacks had been ineffective, either because they chose the wrong targets or because they had no impact on production in the long-term. What damaged the Germans in the occupied territories far more was declining labour productivity in industry and widespread evasion of the Service du Travail Obligatoire (STO), the forced drafting of labour to work in German factories. Both of these were the product of countless individual decisions that demonstrated the 'social effectiveness' of resistance in certain psychological and political conditions.[33] Otherwise, however, resistance was more valuable for its moral and psychological dimension, as an affirmation of human values and spirit, than for any achievements of co-ordinated resistance movements.[34] Some years later, Jacques Semelin's *Unarmed against Hitler* switched the focus away from armed resistance, or preparations for it, altogether. His subject was civilian resistance to occupation, or 'the civil society's spontaneous struggle, by unarmed means, against the aggression of which it is victim'.[35] The definition of what constituted resistance now broadened perceptibly to include strikes, demonstrations, church or court protests, civil disobedience movements, aid to victims of Nazi persecution and the actions and declarations of medical, religious and educational organizations. Even symbolic actions – the display of national colours, flowers or badges – were weapons in the struggle, acting as a permanent challenge to the Nazi order and showing the determination of a society to affirm the legitimacy of its own values and loyalties.[36] The term 'passive resistance', often applied to opposition of this kind, was too negative, failing to recognize the risks run by those who took part.[37]

Civilian resistance, according to Semelin, could be offered both by institutions and by the broad mass of the population. In its institutional form, it referred to actions taken by representatives of the 'legitimate political power' – the local, non-Nazi government and administration – and by organized representatives of political parties, churches, unions and associations. Popular resistance, on the other hand, included grass-roots mobilizations in the form of strikes, go-slows, demonstrations and civil disobedience.[38] The pre-condition for the emergence of effective civilian resistance was social cohesion, or the strength of the ties that bound individuals and groups to each other and to the values and institutions of their society. Where social cohesion was strong – as in Norway in 1940 – civilian resistance had emerged and developed more quickly. On the other hand, in societies where the prewar period had seen bitter social and political divisions, there was less social cohesion and civilian resistance had more limited scope, at least until the Germans' own conduct forged a new consensus. Previous assessments of resistance – of its military effectiveness, its internal political significance, or the moral courage of those who engaged in it – thus needed to be supplemented by another, which analysed resistance movements against the background of the society and culture in which they emerged and grew.[39]

In his wide-ranging introduction and conclusion to the edited volume *Resistance in Western Europe*, which contained a series of country-by-country case-studies and was published in 2000, Bob Moore outlined common elements in the approach taken by contributors. All now included both organized and non-organized activities, including acts by lone individuals as well as social protest and passive defiance, but gave particular weight to the emergence of resistance organizations and movements and investigated their size, political allegiances and social composition in relation to the population as a whole.[40] Working with a nuanced version of Michel's concept of resistance development as a series of phases, Moore emphasized the changing war situation and the growing harshness of German rule as the key factors stimulating the growth of resistance. In Western Europe, the vast majority of the population remained passive until German orders and demands began to disrupt everyday life and infringe against the accepted norms and values of society. Ordinary citizens now found themselves criminalized for behaviour that had once been entirely unremarkable – such as keeping a radio set and listening to BBC news broadcasts.[41] By the latter stages of the war, he argued, large numbers of people in the occupied territories had been driven to disobey their occupiers – especially in the mass evasion of the STO, or forced labour service, by hundreds of thousands of ordinary men and women. By greatly hindering German economic objectives, Moore argued, this had to be regarded as a form of resistance.[42] Other forms of disobedience, especially the back market, were more difficult to fit into a resistance framework because these could involve self-interest and profit as much as a desire to damage German interests. It was thus essential for historians to examine the 'grey areas' of behaviour in order to establish an accepted definition of resistance appropriate to each country.[43]

Until the last months of the war, the number of people in *organized* resistance movements in Western Europe remained small – perhaps no more than 2 per cent of the population in each country, at least according to the narrow definitions generally adopted by resistance historians. However, Moore was wary of accepting these estimates as definitive, emphasizing that the number of sympathizers and passive resisters who surrounded the activists was several times larger.[44] Furthermore, a focus on the *membership* of resistance organizations rather than on the infrastructures and activities that *supported* them could be counter-productive. For instance, it had done much to obscure the role of women in the resistance. Only a small proportion of the members of organized movements were women – and they were even less well represented when honours were handed out after the Liberation – but they formed an indispensable element in resistance infrastructures, as couriers and liaison agents and in the provision of food and shelter to resisters, Jews and forced labour evaders.[45] In most countries, the 'lesser known and unsung heroines of the resistance' were still awaiting their historians.[46] And in any case, most Europeans – the 'muddled majority' – were neither resisters nor collaborators, but adjusted to the new realities of occupation while longing for liberation. Recent works continue to question the usefulness of simplistic paradigms of resistance and collaboration in explaining the conduct of Europeans under occupation. In a recent work on France, for example, Julian Jackson has emphasized the contradictory attitudes and behaviours manifested even by single individuals: in German-occupied France, there were resisters who were anti-Semitic, but also Vichy officials who tried to protect Jews.[47]

By the time Moore's study appeared, the interpretative framework of resistance was sufficiently flexible to be applied to the Channel Islands.[48] Even before its publication, Paul Sanders had adopted an explicitly comparative analysis in his study of the Jersey offenders who were deported to the continent for offences against the occupiers and never returned.[49] The question that had to be answered in the islands, he argued, was why the undoubted 'disposition' for more active forms of resistance there – which was probably on the same relative scale as in France – had never developed into significant collective action but had remained in an 'embryonic' stage.[50] The answer was to be found in the unique demographic, geographic, social, strategic and historical factors that shaped the identity of the islands and influenced the Germans' attitudes towards them, and which play a significant part in this book. He developed this approach in his chapter on resistance, repression and persecution in his detailed study of the occupation in 2005, a broad survey that included a section on administrative resistance and an analysis of the conduct of the island authorities.[51] A similarly comparative approach was attempted by another contributor to this volume, Louise Willmot, in a chapter in Moore's book. This, too, argued that the extent of resistance in the islands had been underestimated, and that it had, like resistance elsewhere, developed in phases as a response to the Germans' own policies and the changing war situation: the summer and autumn 1942, which saw the confiscation of radios, the arrival in Jersey of large numbers of OT workers and the deportation of British-born islanders, had been the catalyst for greater numbers of islanders to defy the Germans and for the emergence of the limited forms of collective action that existed.[52] Although there had been no resistance 'movement', personal contacts between islanders had done something to compensate for the lack of resistance organizations and had allowed for at least some forms of collective action.[53] Although open battles with firearms were never fought between islanders and occupiers, the analysis of artefactual evidence by a contributor to this volume, Gilly Carr, suggests that there was no shortage of non-military battles fought between the two sides, below the radar, with 'weapons of the weak'[54] such as V-sign graffiti and the use of the islands' crests.[55]

In planning and writing this book, we have consciously adapted the insights of the historiography in order to re-integrate the Channel Islands into the history of European Resistance. So, for example, we look for signs of the development of resistance over time, in response to the Germans' own conduct and to Allied military progress, and we seek to apply Michel's concept of its development as a series of consecutive or overlapping phases. We look for evidence of social cohesion and for German efforts to erode it, and examine the ways this impacted on the conduct of the inhabitants and their governments. We take account of the geography and topography of the islands and of wartime population structures in order to understand the different responses to occupation in Guernsey and Jersey. We try, as White and Semelin suggested, to assess resistance activity in several ways: as an intended contribution to Allied military victory; as a patriotic struggle against Germany or an ideological struggle against Nazism; as an internal political struggle against local administrations and their alleged collaboration; and as a reflection of the society in which they emerged and developed. We attempt to analyse and understand the activities of different social groups – of women, of the island governments, of teenagers and young men, for example – in the light of the circumstances they faced and the limited opportunities open to them. As Moore suggested, our definition of resistance includes both organized and non-organized actions designed to damage the German war effort, hinder German objectives and raise the morale of the inhabitants.

Book structure

We begin, as Channel Islanders did, with symbolic forms of resistance by individuals in Chapter 1, and with the V-sign protests examined in Chapter 2, which began in 1941, then changed in form and went underground before emerging again at the time of Liberation. In Chapter 3, we then move on to discuss what we term 'radio resistance'. This was the mass private and entirely unspoken defiance of German orders which banned listening to the BBC coupled with the requisitioning of all radios in June 1942. In addition to a significant number of households defying orders and hanging on to their radio set, a small number of underground news sheets also sprang up after this period. These included both Guernsey Active Secret Press (GASP) and GUNS in Guernsey.[56] While huge numbers were involved in secret listening to the radio and reading the news sheets, the consequences for those who were caught listening or disseminating the news were extremely serious and cost several Channel Islanders their lives. Of the 29 islanders who did not return from camps and prisons on the continent after the war, 9 were deported for radio-related resistance.[57]

Other acts of defiance against German orders can also be seen in Chapter 4, where we consider the humanitarian aid given to slave and forced workers, but also, to a lesser extent, to the islands' Jews. In this chapter we highlight the vital role played by such men as Noel McKinstry and Norman Le Brocq, who helped to organize some of the assistance given to Russian workers on the run, while also noting that some of the most remarkable acts of rescue – of Jews as well as slave workers – were undertaken by men and women who acted alone or in family groups.

Staying with the theme of mass or group action for Chapter 5, but this time of people who knowingly acted together to achieve their aims, we examine the period of the deportations of September 1942 and February 1943, and the role played by the local government, doctors and young people in protesting against the deportations and in trying to wangle exemptions. We also follow islanders on their journey to the internment camps and examine the forms of resistance which took place there.

The year 1942 marked a turning point in the Occupation, both in terms of the severity of the German grip and the intensified reaction of local people. Now that the gloves were off, less ambiguous and more daring acts of resistance became more common and a small number of rudimentary resistance organizations emerged. At the same time, German punishments for islanders caught in acts of resistance were more severe, and those who were caught and deported into the maelstrom of the German prison and camp system were less likely to return. No longer content with merely 'testing the water' with symbolic resistance, islanders began to be more outspoken, whether from their pulpits or within newly cemented political groups. In Chapter 6, we examine the role of the Jersey Democratic Movement and the Jersey Communist Party and the attempts of their members to influence the island's political development both during and after the Occupation and we discuss the factors that hampered the development of organized resistance in the islands. In Chapter 7, we turn to the long-overlooked and marginalized role of women. As well as assessing the ways in which women's participation was shaped by political, economic and social factors, we shine the spotlight on three women whose courage was remarkable by any standards: Salvationist Major Marie Ozanne from Guernsey, and Lucy Schwob and Suzanne Malherbe in Jersey, a two-woman resistance organization who remained undetected for so long because they were women.

In Chapter 8, we move from the realm of women to that of men, and consider the actions of teenage boys in stealing weapons and forming resistance units, and of older men who had fought in WWI and contributed by collecting intelligence and helping young people escape from the islands. Together, their actions constituted military resistance, and we consider how these actions facilitate the placing of Channel Islands resistance into a European framework.

Chapters 9 and 10 move into the territory of the 'double gamers', islanders in official positions who delayed, diverted or 'diluted' the Occupation regime, in what they held to be the public interest. The past over-emphasis on a narrative of collaboration in the historiography of the Occupation has clouded perception of those who learned to do their jobs while obeying the Germans, but who also used the limited means at their disposal to resist when the Germans looked the other way. Although the number of such resisters was small, it was not insignificant. Of particular interest in view of Scott's 'hidden transcripts' (discussed below) is the way resistance-minded officials could sometimes be shielded by their superiors, but also the format they adopted: this had more in common with what German historian Martin Broszat named *Resistenz* than with the post-war myth of *Résistance*, the dominant influence on all subsequent representations of resistance (for a detailed discussion of the terminology please refer to Chapter 9). Chapter 9 also contains a long-overdue assessment of the ambiguities and dilemmas of holding an official position during the Occupation. It asks us what we are to make of the efforts of public servants who made important contributions to the survival of their communities, but who, at the same time, 'dirtied their hands'. The chapter indicates where to draw the moral line, by using novel concepts such as legitimacy and ethical leadership, and it challenges the status quo in the historiographical debate surrounding the action of officials in occupied countries.

Chapter 10 continues on the same footing of ambiguity, by detailing the double meaning of 'economic crimes' (such as theft, receiving stolen items, pilfering or black marketeering) prosecuted during the Occupation. It argues that some of these offences were little different to current-day common law offences, but that many others had a political motivation. The case discussed at great length in this chapter is the still highly controversial 'sabotage' of German and civilian supplies by members of the Guernsey police, in 1941–2. The discussion of this case demonstrates how difficult it is to determine the legitimacy of 'sabotage', but also what principles can be employed in order to arrive at a more adequate portrayal of such activities. The Guernsey policemen have never been rehabilitated, as their Privy Council appeal lodged in the early 1950s was unsuccessful. The chapter then also serves to redress a historical injustice in as far as this is possible.

Chapters 9 and 10 profile in particularly intricate detail the 'weapons of the weak' referred to by James Scott in his seminal study of 'everyday resistance among rural peasants in Malaysia'. Scott identified a mode of non-confrontational resistance and defiance against those who would extract taxes, labour and rent from them, or who would expect them to adhere to onerous new laws. This resistance included 'a struggle over the appropriation of symbols', 'foot dragging, dissimulation, desertion, false compliance, pilfering, feigned ignorance, slander, arson, sabotage, and so on'.[58] Scott labelled these sorts of actions as the 'weapons of the weak' – the 'ordinary weapons of relatively powerless groups'. The 'weapons' that these people wielded were critiques of power designed to nibble away at the authority of those in positions of power over them.

Despite the obvious differences in time and space between Malaysia in the late 1970s (when Scott carried out his fieldwork) and the Channel Islands during the 1940s, Scott's work strikes a strong chord with the different forms of resistance known to have taken place in the islands and with those identified here. In analysing more closely the various weapons of the weak and behaviours of the dominated in different arenas, Scott developed his concept of the 'hidden' and 'public transcripts'. The 'hidden transcript' he defined as the 'critique of power spoken behind the back of the dominant', a 'discourse that takes place 'offstage', beyond direct observation by power holders', fuelled by 'anger, indignation, frustration and swallowed bile'. The public transcript is a 'subordinate discourse in the presence of the dominant';[59] in the context in which we are working in the Channel Islands, the public transcript was what an islander was prepared to say to the face of a German soldier. It is clear that each transcript is produced for a different audience. Again, public and private transcripts are to be found in abundance in the anecdotes, memoirs, diaries and archives of the Channel Islands relating to the occupation.

Scott also proposed a third realm of 'subordinate group politics that lies strategically between the first two. This is a politics of disguise and anonymity that takes place in public view but is designed to have a double meaning or to shield the identity of the actors'.[60] This is the very kind of 'double game' which is explored in Chapters 9 and 10.

Before we conclude the book by drawing our data together and presenting our observations, models, statistics and hypotheses, we present a chapter which deals with the period from 1945 to the present day. No book on protest, defiance and resistance in the Channel Islands would be complete without an analysis of how those who protested, defied and resisted the Germans were treated and remembered after the war. Chapter 11 assesses the long-term memory and memorialization of resisters, political prisoners and those who suffered in Nazi prisons and camps; it also discusses the important role of 'guardians of memory' such as Joe Mière in Jersey and Frank Falla in Guernsey. Finally, it highlights the long period of silence in the heritage arena of the Channel Islands of resistance, drawing attention to the differences between the Channel Islands and continental Europe in this regard.

Our aim in writing this book was to produce something accessible, which could be enjoyed equally by both the average intelligent person and the academic reader alike. While we hope that many of our readers will be able to bear with us from cover to cover (and we believe that the investment of time will be worthwhile), we realize that for many people, this volume will act primarily as a reference work. For this reason, there will inevitably be a slight overlap between chapters. If nothing else, this illustrates the similarly overlapping nature of different kinds of resistance; the interrelationship of individual islanders within a small community; and the impact of one kind of resistance upon the lives of others. As each of the chapters has been written by a different one of us, we hope that you, the reader, will not find the inevitable difference of writing style an impediment; rather, we hope that it will give you something to savour, and perhaps an enticement to sample another chapter.

We have inevitably been constrained by missing and incomplete archival records, but have resisted the use of anecdotal evidence in their stead. We are wholeheartedly grateful to Channel Islanders, archivists, the law offices, the prison service and the Bailiff's offices for allowing us, as researchers, full access to all surviving archives and papers in the Channel Islands. While some records in the UK archives remain closed, such as the Foreign Office files of testimonies of victims of Nazi persecution, we were able to gain an insight into these through the Frank Falla files. As the discovery of these files made the news headlines, we are aware that readers have inevitably been waiting to read more within the pages of this volume. Indeed, the wider context of Frank Falla, his work, and the compensation claims of 1965 can be found in Chapter 11.

Over three years of research, we have consulted every record, diary and paper we could find and which was made available to us. We are indebted to islanders who wrote to us with stories of their parents and grandparents, who gave us access to previously unseen diaries, and who were prepared to trust us with their precious paperwork. In writing this volume, we were determined to write a definitive work which would stand the test of time. The book has been produced despite the three of us juggling research with our full university posts and teaching loads. We hope that the book provides the reader with the satisfaction it has given us in learning about protest, defiance and resistance in the Channel Islands between 1940 and 1945.

Gilly Carr, Paul Sanders and Louise Willmot, July 2013

Government Structures and Key Personnel during the Occupation

On the outbreak of war, Jersey and Guernsey had long-established representative bodies, in Jersey the Assembly of the States and in Guernsey the States of Deliberation, presided over in each case by a Bailiff appointed by the Crown. In both islands, a significant proportion of States representatives were not elected directly by the inhabitants, but were either parish rectors appointed by the Crown or unpaid jurats who combined judicial functions with law-making and were elected for life by the ratepayers (Jersey) or an electoral college (Guernsey). On the eve of invasion, however, streamlined emergency cabinets were established in both islands – a Superior Council in Jersey and a Controlling Committee in Guernsey – to allow for more rapid and flexible responses to the coming crisis than the States were likely to provide. During the Occupation these cabinets were composed as follows:

Superior Council, Jersey

President	Alexander M. Coutanche, Bailiff
Attorney General	Charles W. Duret Aubin
Solicitor General	C.S. Harrison
Essential Commodities	Jurat E.P. Le Masurier
Transport and Communications	Jurat J.M. Norman
Agriculture	Jurat T.J. Brée
Public Health	Jurat P.M. Baudains
Essential Services	Deputy W.S. Le Masurier
Public Instruction	Jurat P.E. Brée
Labour	Deputy E. Le Quesne

Controlling Committee, Guernsey

President	Major Ambrose Sherwill until October 1940; Jurat the Rev. John Leale, Acting President from October 1940, President from January 1941.
Vice President and Essential Commodities	Jurat Sir Abraham Lainé
Health Services Officer	Dr A. N. Symons
Horticulture	Dr A. M. Drake, to May 1941; P. Dorey to May 1945.
Agriculture	R. O. Falla
Labour	Deputy R. H. Johns
Information	Deputy Stamford Raffles, d. 1942
H. M. Comptroller	G. P. Ridgway, from December 1940 (d. September 1942)
Acting Attorney General	J. E. L. Martel, from March 1943.

Ambrose Sherwill attended meetings of the Committee as Attorney General from July 1942 until his deportation early in 1943.

During the Occupation, the emergency cabinets dealt with a German military administration that was part of the *Département de la Manche* based in France. Within this structure, *Feldkommandantur 515* (FK 515) was established in Jersey with responsibility for all the islands, and with three subordinate posts – a *Nebenstelle* or branch on Guernsey, an *Aussenstelle* or outpost on Alderney, and a stores assembly point at Granville in France. Reflecting the organization of the military administration in France, FK 515 liaised with the German armed forces, and comprised a civil affairs branch responsible for the administration of the civil government in the islands. The senior German officials during the Occupation were:

Inselkommandant (military affairs)	Major-General Rudolf Graf von Schmettow, September 1940–February 1945; Vice-Admiral Friedrich Hüffmeier.
Feldkommandant (civil affairs)	Colonel Friedrich Schumacher, until October 1941; Colonel Friedrich Knackfuss, October 1941–February 1944; Major Heider, Captain von Cleve (as Platzkommandant)

- Jersey administration: Chief administrator Wilhelm Casper until 1943, then Baron Hans Max von Aufsess – and staff.
- Guernsey branch: Kratzer, Brosch, Reich
- Alderney outpost: Herzog, Richter

According to Charles Cruickshank, FK 515 functioned as 'a secretariat responsible for ensuring that the government of the islands was carried on efficiently', following the pattern set in France.[61]

Notes

1 Jacques Semelin, *Unarmed against Hitler: Civilian Resistance in Europe, 1939–1943*, Westport CT and London, Praeger, 1993, p. 25.
2 Bob Moore, *Resistance in Western Europe*, Oxford and New York: Berg, 2000, p. 1.
3 Ibid., p. 2.
4 See the chapter on heritage, memory and resistance in the Islands, elsewhere in this book.
5 Alan Wood and Mary Seaton Wood, *Islands in Danger: The Fantastic Story of the German Occupation of the Channel Islands 1940–1945*, London, First Four Square edn, 1966, first published 1955, pp. 1, 303.
6 Ibid., pp. 303–4, 312–13. The British Empire Medal was awarded to Bill Bertram, who helped parties of escapers to get away from Fauvic. In fact, another resister – Noel McKinstry – was awarded the Order of the British Empire, but this was for his work as Jersey's Medical Officer of Health and not for his many resistance activities.

7   Charles Cruickshank, *The German Occupation of the Channel Islands: The Official History of the Occupation Years*, Guernsey, Guernsey Press Co./Trustees of the Imperial War Museum, 1975, pp. 152, 156–61. The book devotes seven pages to it out of 350 – and almost 50 pages to the British commando operations against the islands.
8   Ibid., pp. 160, 156.
9   Ibid., p. 156.
10 Ibid., p. 157.
11 Norman Longmate, 'Appendix 1: Our Dear Channel Islands', in *How We Lived Then: A History of Everyday Life during the Second World War*, London, Arrow, 1971, pp. 512–22, here p. 513.
12 Ibid., p. 515.
13 Peter King, *The Channel Islands War 1940–1945*, London, Robert Hale, 1991, pp. 172–3.
14 Ibid., p. 83.
15 Ibid., pp. 51–2.
16 Ibid., p. 53.
17 JeanYves Ruaux, *Vichy Sur Manche*, Rennes, Éditions Ouest France, 1994.
18 See Louise Willmot, 'The Channel Islands', in Moore, pp. 65–91, here p. 83.
19 Madeleine Bunting, *The Model Occupation: The Channel Islands under German Rule 1940–1945*, London, Pimlico edn 2004, first published 1995.
20 Ibid., p. 199.
21 Ibid., p. 330.
22 Ibid., p. 193.
23 Here see Willmot, 'The Channel Islands', p. 83; Paul Sanders, *The British Channel Islands under German Occupation*, Jersey, Société Jersiaise and Jersey Heritage Trust, 2005, pp. 58–9, 258–9.
24 Michael. R. D. Foot, *Resistance: European Resistance to Nazism 1940–45*, London, Eyre Methuen, 1976, p. 5.
25 See the dictionary definition in the Shorter OED, 3rd edn 1969, quoted by Foot, *Resistance*, p. 5, defining resistance as an 'organised underground movement' with an armed wing. The emphasis on resistance contribution to Allied victory is perceptible in two books that emerged from two international conferences, in 1958 and 1960, devoted to the history of the resistance: *European Resistance Movements 1939–1945: First International Conference on the History of the Resistance Movements*, London, Pergamon, 1960 and *European Resistance Movements: Second International Conference on the History of the Resistance Movements*, London, Pergamon, 1964. Elements of this approach survived, however, in Jorgen Haestrup, *European Resistance Movements, 1939–1945: A Complete History*, Westport and London, 1981.
26 Henri Michel, *The Shadow War: Resistance in Europe 1939–1945*, London, The History Book Club, 1972, pp. 211ff. He also pointed out that the Communists had encouraged this kind of petty sabotage.
27 Ibid., pp. 13–14.
28 Ibid., p. 13.
29 Steven Hawes and Ralph White (eds), *Resistance in Europe: 1939–1945*, London, Allen Lane, 1975.
30 Ralph White, 'The Unity and Diversity of European Resistance', in Hawes and White, p. 10.
31 Ibid., p. 18.
32 Ibid., p. 8.

33 Alan S. Milward, 'The Economic and Strategic Effectiveness of Resistance', in Hawes and White, pp. 186–203, here pp. 197–200.
34 Ibid., p. 202.
35 Semelin, *Unarmed against Hitler*, p. 27.
36 Ibid., p. 162.
37 Ibid., p. 1, also pp. 28–9.
38 Ibid., p. 28.
39 Ibid., pp. 25–7.
40 Moore, *Resistance in Western Europe*, p. 8. See also W. Neugebauer, J. Zamojski, J. Gotovitch, M. Skodvin and T. Ferenc, 'Gesichtpunkte fur eine vergleichende Untersuchung des Widerstandes: Scheme und Erlaüterung', in Ger van Rood (ed.), *Europaischer Widerstand im Vergleich. Die Internationalen Konferenzen Amsterdam*, Berlin, Siedler Verlag, 1985, pp. 38–41.
41 Moore, *Resistance in Western Europe*, p. 254.
42 Ibid.
43 Ibid., p. 3.
44 Ibid., quoting Robert Paxton, *Vichy France. Old Guard and New Order*, New York, Knopf, 1972, p. 260.
45 Ibid., p. 261.
46 Ibid.
47 See, for example, Julian Jackson, *France: the Dark Years 1940–1944*, Oxford, Oxford University Press, 2001, p. 4.
48 Willmot, 'The Channel Islands', pp. 65–91.
49 Paul Sanders, *The Ultimate Sacrifice. The Jersey Islanders Who Died in German Prisons and Concentration Camps, 1940–1945*, Jersey, Jersey Heritage Trust, 2nd edn, 2004, pp. 122–34. See for example his references to social cohesion and German efforts to undermine it.
50 Ibid., pp. 127–8.
51 Paul Sanders, *The British Channel Islands under German Occupation*, here pp. 122–4.
52 Willmot, 'The Channel Islands', pp. 68–9. See also by the same author, '"Nothing Was Ever the Same Again": Public Attitudes in the Occupied Channel Islands, 1942', *The Local Historian: Journal of the British Society for Local History*, Vol. 35, 2005, 9–20.
53 Willmot, 'The Channel Islands', pp. 84–5.
54 James C. Scott, *Weapons of the Weak: Everyday Forms of Peasant Resistance*, New Haven and London, Yale University Press, 1985.
55 Gillian C. Carr, 'Of Coins, Crests and Kings: Symbols of Identity and Resistance in the Occupied Channel Islands', *The Journal of Material Culture*, Vol. 17 (4), 327–44.
56 The Guernsey Active Secret Press and the Guernsey Underground News Service.
57 Joseph Gillingham, Charles Machon and Percy Miller from Guernsey; John Soyer, Frederick Page, John Nicolle, Joseph Tierney, Arthur Dimmery and Clifford Cohu from Jersey.
58 Scott, *Weapons of the Weak*, pp. xvi–xvii, 29.
59 James C. Scott, *Domination and the Arts of Resistance: Hidden Transcripts*, New Haven and London: Yale University Press, 1990, pp. xii, 4, 111.
60 Ibid., p. 19.
61 Cruickshank, *The German Occupation*, pp. 106–9, also appendices I, II. See also King, *The Channel Islands War*, pp. 38–42.

1

Symbolic Resistance

Gilly Carr

In this chapter, I take as my point of departure the work of Jacques Semelin who, in his study of non-military forms of resistance against the Germans, noted the importance of symbolic resistance. 'Symbols are the prime 'weapon' of civilian resistance', he argued. '[They] are the language through which an occupied society still expresses its independence of spirit. Whether in the form of a flower, a sign, or colours, symbols were a permanent challenge to the Nazi order ... [they] are the rallying points for all those who refuse to bow their heads.'[1]

Taking Semelin's cue, I explore here the multiple forms of symbolic resistance in the Channel Islands. My primary argument is that, as in other occupied countries, this form of defiant behaviour acted not only to boost the morale of those who saw it, but also to create bonds of solidarity and fellow-feeling among others. Further, I also argue that it gave some people the courage to go on to commit acts of more daring or dangerous resistance and defiance. By observing that those around them felt as patriotic or anti-German as they did, the illusion (real or not) of a safety net of support for the resister could thus be created.

Symbolic resistance was, for the most part, non-confrontational by nature. It did not require the resister to face the occupier at any point. This is partly because the intended primary audience of this form of defiance was not the occupier, but other islanders. The form of the defiance was sometimes in a coded language that only other islanders could understand. Where the form of symbolism was more obvious both to occupiers and the occupied, such as in the use of patriotic colours, it was still primarily intended to boost morale and create solidarity among fellow islanders. It enabled them to 'thumb their noses' at the Germans during the period when such behaviour was tolerated without repercussions. When penalties began to be enacted and grew more severe for symbolic resistance, it is likely that forms of resistance grew more obscure, more encoded and less frequent. This, however, must remain supposition as it is extremely difficult to document the real frequency or dates of occurrence of most forms of symbolic resistance. Only in its more well-documented forms, such as the V-sign campaign, is enough data available to be able to draw accurate conclusions. As it is, we must rely upon easily overlooked references in diaries and often unidentified objects in Occupation museums in order to gain some insight into the range of opportunities for symbolic resistance in the Channel Islands.

The primary source for this chapter is, thus, the Occupation diary, which also acts as a method of contextual interpretation for understanding resistant artefacts. Through examining as many published and unpublished diaries as possible, we can begin to gauge the frequency with which islanders both used and observed symbolic resistance. While the aim in this chapter is not to catalogue every example of such resistant behaviour – an impossible task – the intention is to sample its range. For the most part, resistant symbols were worn unobtrusively on the body or clothing; unobtrusive, perhaps, to a German soldier who might not have understood their meaning, but decipherable among other islanders who knew how to read culturally-specific symbols.

While there are those who might be inclined to dismiss such small and insignificant aspects of resistance,[2] I would argue that the fact that they are commented upon in diaries and caused the wearer of such symbols to be arrested, both in the Channel Islands and in other occupied countries, demonstrates that these 'insignificant' signs and codes were nothing of the sort. Neither were they deemed to be without value or significance by the occupier.

The V-sign campaign is perhaps the most notorious, well-known and best-documented of all the acts of symbolic resistance and, because of this, it has been given a chapter to itself elsewhere in this volume in order to fully explore its trajectory.

While the V became internationally recognized as a defiant symbol across Europe and was so dangerous that the Germans quickly adopted and adapted it for themselves, many lesser known symbols were culturally specific. In Norway, for example, one of the most effective anti-Nazi demonstrations was the wearing of the traditional red woollen stocking cap during the winter of 1940–1.[3] These hats, known as *nisselue* in Norwegian, were not only pro-Norwegian but also, as they were red, were supportive of their allies, the Russians. The Nazis saw all red clothing as suspect during Hitler's invasion of Russia in June 1941. The wearing of any red clothing could lead to arrest.[4] But it was not only the more 'obvious' symbols redolent of patriotism or political support to which the Nazis objected in Norway; Kathleen Stocker informs us of other symbols used in a particularly clever or punning way. For example, it was common to stick one's coat or jacket lapel through its button hole in order to 'stick out one's tongue' at the Germans. To suggest that they were 'enlightened' and could not be fooled by German propaganda, some men wore matches in their hat bands. In Norwegian, *opplyst* means both 'lit up' and 'enlightened', and thus the match signified this play on words.[5]

Dozens of similar examples of symbolic colours, clothes and objects can be found all over Europe. In occupied Holland, for example, the colour orange was important for obvious reasons, and badges of orange trees bearing fruit were worn. Queen Wilhelmina of the House of Orange managed to evacuate to London before the Germans arrived, and coins bearing her image were particularly important to the Dutch to express their loyalty to their Queen and their faith in the return of the royal family. Examples in the *Verzetsmuseum* (Resistance Museum) in Amsterdam show coins made into souvenir spoons, bracelets, brooches, cuff-links and necklaces. Badges showing the letters 'OZO' (meaning 'so there!'), also an acronym for *Oranje zal Overwinnen* (Orange Shall Triumph), became popular, especially those painted either orange, or in red, white and blue (the colours of the Dutch flag).

Like the Norwegians, the Dutch also liked to pun and play with words. The Reichskommissar in the Netherlands was Arthur Seyss-Inquart. The Dutch made a joke out of his name by making cigarette extinguishers out of soldered together six-and-a-quarter cent coins (the half-cent coin being cut in half as part of the design). *Zes-en-een-kwart* is the Dutch for 'six-and-a-quarter', which not only worked as a nickname, but also made a verbal and visual reference to Seyss-Inquart's lame leg.

Whether we think of the *Croix de Lorraine* (the Cross of Lorraine), the symbol worn by the French to show solidarity with the Free French forces led by General de Gaulle, or, indeed, that arch-symbol of the Nazis, the swastika itself, we see that symbols can be extremely potent. They can generate despair or hope; fear or courage; and loathing or patriotism and loyalty in those who see or wear them. The Channel Islanders were no different to other occupied peoples in Europe at this time, and references to symbolic flowers, patriotic colours and the flag are both hinted at and stated boldly in comments in personal diaries. Such symbols can also be observed, in artefactual form, in the Occupation museums of the Channel Islands today.

We can divide actions and behaviours which come under the banner of 'symbolic resistance' into two groups: those which were anonymous (e.g. the V-sign campaign) and those which could not be because they were attached to the clothing or body of individuals, and included patriotically coloured clothing, flowers and badges. These latter examples I term 'buttonhole resistance'. Some of these were hidden and some were on full display. Some were encoded and others made more obvious statements. I also divide symbolic resistance into that which was tangible and that which was intangible. Among the latter category I include the telling of patriotic or anti-German jokes, and the singing of patriotic songs. While jokes will be discussed in this chapter, I include discussion of the role of patriotic songs within the chapter on resistance and the deportations, as it was on this occasion that it was used as an effective form of resistance. It also illustrates well the penalties which could be incurred by such actions.

How might we understand the need for and value of such symbols to occupied peoples? They are classified here as the kinds of 'weapons of the weak' referred to by James Scott,[6] and as discussed in the introduction of this volume. Such 'weapons' of non-confrontational resistance are used by relatively powerless groups against those in positions of authority over them; they are intended to nibble away at that authority. Such resistance includes the 'struggle over the appropriation of symbols', making it highly appropriate for the topic in discussion in this chapter. Scott believed that an important aspect of defiance was a shared worldview of the meaning and value behind the acts carried out.[7] Certainly in the Channel Islands, islanders knew that the meaning of the display of Vs or patriotic colours or symbols was to express wordlessly to others one's patriotic stance and anti-German world view; it was an appeal to solidarity.

Red, white and blue: The use of patriotic colours

Quite the most popular, not to say comforting, way of voicing a silent protest was to wear the patriotic colours of red, white and blue. In the early days of the Occupation, this appeared not to be accorded too much value by the Germans – or at least, not enough to warrant arrest. It seems that islanders who dared to wear such colours for patriotic reasons were testing the boundaries of the Orders that related to relating to associations, meetings, distinctive emblems and beflagging, dated 28 August 1940. The third Order of this series forbade the population from wearing 'distinctive apparel and uniform emblems'. In the fourth Order, the beflagging of property, the display of streamers, standards and other emblems on vehicles was forbidden. While these orders did not specify that patriotic colours were not to be worn in clothing, it seems clear that people preferred to observe the letter of the law rather than its spirit. All the same, the penalties for contravention of these Orders were imprisonment and/or a fine, but for some this was not enough of a deterrent, in the early days of the Occupation, to make them adhere to German commands.

In 1940 and 1941, the use of patriotic colours gave islanders a simple thrill and allowed them to hold their chins high and maintain their pride despite military occupation. Izett Croad in Jersey remarked that, at the 1941 Harvest Thanksgiving, the font in her local church was decked out in red, white and blue. She wrote that 'A lot of us wear the three colours whenever we can; I had a navy and white dress and hat and a small red brooch.' By December of that year, Izett was proud to note in her diary that her friend Enid had given her a brooch decorated with gold, red, white and blue, 'so now I am quite patriotic'.[8] Eight months later, in late August 1942, Izett again remarked in her diary about a recent patriotic purchase: 'Actually bought a new blouse this morning *and* a pair of shoes … The shoes have wooden soles and heels painted red, canvas navy and white uppers, so I shall be quite patriotic.'[9] As Beryl Ozanne remarked in her memoirs, 'Anything British, or red, white and blue, meant so much to us as it was 'verboten'.'[10]

While not everyone who wore or used patriotic colours did so knowingly or intending to make a statement, those who saw the use of such colours sometimes chose to interpret it in a way that would give them a boost. An example can be seen in the case of Dorothy Langlois, a well-known ballet dancer who formed the Guernsey Co-optimist dance company. In early February 1942, Dorothy choreographed and performed her dance 'On Parade' as part of the show 'Tit-bits'. Dorothy performed a military dance wearing a red-lined cape, a white skirt and a blue top without thinking at all about its significance; she had choreographed the dance and had the costume made before the Occupation. Perhaps unsurprisingly, after her performance she had an absolutely rousing reception, despite the presence of German soldiers in the audience. The following day she went into town, hoping to bump into people who had seen the show and who would tell her what they thought of it. The first person she met expressed surprise that she was not in prison. Alarmed, Dorothy exclaimed that she hadn't done anything. 'Yes you have!' they retorted, 'everybody's talking about it!' It seemed that everyone was talking about her military dance in patriotic colours done *in front of the Germans*, as if to deliberately provoke them. As neither dance nor costume had been intended as a deliberately defiant act, it had not occurred to Dorothy that she might be in trouble. In the event, nothing happened to her; the soldiers attending the performance had obviously been ballet lovers first and foremost. 'But', said Dorothy, 'I never did it again. You just wouldn't do that' (i.e. go out wearing patriotic colours).[11]

Dorothy was adamant that she would not deliberately have put dancers on stage in patriotic colours as she was not the kind of woman to court danger and did not want to get the theatre or her dance company closed down. However, it is interesting to note that by February 1942, not only was it still possible to wear patriotic colours and not get arrested, but it was possible to wear these colours without noticing the implications of what you were doing. People were not yet being as vigilant as they were to become at a later date.

We can contrast Dorothy's experience with one that was almost identical and took place in Jersey eight months later. Donald Journeaux, a dancer, had choreographed a ballet called 'Knave among the Hearts'. He wrote in his memoirs of the Occupation years that 'The finale of the first part of the show was devoted to sea songs and shanties … the costumes were simple but effective, with the girls in white shorts wearing matelot caps and the men in white slacks, blue shirts and caps kindly lent by the Yacht club. A grand scene including the numbers 'Join the Navy' and 'Crest of a Wave' caused a small riot. The applause was tremendous and some of the audience were so excited that they stood on the seats, clapping and singing 'Join the Navy'. We were amazed and delighted by the effect of this …'.[12] Unlike Dorothy, Donald was later called up to appear before the Feldkommandant on 12 October 1942 for 'demonstration during an entertainment' because of his display of 'uniforms resembling those of the British Navy'. He was requested not to display such uniforms again. In the space of less than a year, the Germans were growing aware of the effect on the population of patriotic colours and clothing and beginning to apply pressure on those who were deemed to be courting provocation.

One can chart the growing danger of the use of patriotic colours by examining entries in diaries, from which we can learn that such acts were outlawed at the height of the occupation. On 30 June 1943, for example, the Reverend Ord in Guernsey recorded in his diary that the Gestapo 'have been arresting people for wearing patriotic insignia, particularly the 'V'-sign brooches, the wearing of red, white and blue colours – even in dress'. It seems that earlier on, however, people (such as Dorothy Langlois) could get away with such daring. On 23 January 1942, for example, Violet Carey wrote that 'for the first time a German soldier noticed and remarked on my gay red, white and blue gaiters last Friday! I am now knitting myself gay red, white and blue and brown stockings.' Six months later, on 5 June 1942, she commented again about this patriotic defiance. 'I had quite a thrill when I noticed in some of the shops little red, white and blue bouquets … I also saw several girls in red, white and blue dresses, and had even a greater thrill when I realized that subconsciously I was wearing a red hat and a blue and white cotton frock!'

As 1942 progressed, people became well aware of the value of patriotic colours and were thrilled to see them publically worn. It is likely that as this feeling grew, so did German irritation over its use. It is apparent that the grip of the Occupation became more severe in this respect between June 1942 and June 1943 as the Germans attempted to stamp out ever smaller details of defiance. The second half of 1942, from June onwards, was also the time of the radio ban, the arrival of the Russian slave workers in Jersey, and the deportation of many civilians to German internment camps; the grip of the occupiers was tightening during this period.[13] By the beginning of July 1943, Ord wrote about a display in a shop window in St Peter Port, Guernsey's capital which, 'in direct defiance of the Gestapo' was decorated 'in red, white and blue – red cloth basis, blue vase, and ivory elephants. This required great courage and has spoken a message to all who pass by. Nor has it been ignored.' Ord implied that the use of patriotic colours, visible to all, acted to incite others to greater, more courageous and perhaps more risky acts of resistance. This, and the boosting of morale, was perhaps the greatest value of symbolic and patriotic defiance enacted through material culture.

One of the most widespread public uses of patriotic colours was seen in November 1943, well into the danger zone chronologically speaking. On the night of 23/24 October of that year, the British light cruiser HMS *Charybdis* was sunk by German torpedoes. By November, 41 bodies of Royal Naval personnel had been washed up on the beaches of Guernsey, Jersey and Sark. These were buried with full military honours. In Guernsey around 5,000 islanders – more than 20 per cent of the population – decided to attend the funerals at the Foulon cemetery as a display of loyalty to Britain and as a passive demonstration of where their true feelings lay.[14] This kind of group or 'corporate' resistance has been identified by White,[15] who suggested that it emerged during the German occupation of Western Europe after an initial phase of small 'pinpricks' on the part of would-be resisters, and was provoked by or emerged because of the less restrained actions of the occupiers themselves. Large numbers of islanders sent flowers for the *Charybdis* funerals and these were tied with patriotically coloured ribbons. As so many people attended, or visited the cemetery afterwards, there is no shortage of private diaries which record the event to draw upon for eye-witness accounts. Frank Falla, who covered the story for the Evening Press, counted a final total of 900 wreaths in all. He thought that there would have been more had the supply of flowers in the island not given out. He believed that, despite their sadness, people had an air of satisfaction in having a chance to show their true feelings at last.[16] Although the censors prevented Falla, at the time, from recording the patriotic sentiments expressed by the inscriptions attached to the wreaths, there were others who recorded them in their diaries. More interestingly for our purposes, many made reference to the patriotically coloured ribbons which were attached to the wreaths and bunches of flowers.

In the unabridged and unpublished version of Violet Carey's diary,[17] the entry for 19 November 1943 recorded that Violet's friend, Mrs Hazell, took a spray of flowers to the cemetery, tied up with red, white and blue ribbon. The Reverend Ord in Guernsey also remarked in his diary entry for 17 November both of the crowds who attended the funerals, and the carpet of flowers.[18] He wrote that 'It was an extraordinary manifestation of patriotic feeling – the first the Island had had a chance to show – when the vast area covered by wonderful floral tributes was viewed. The inscriptions on the cards attached and the abundance of red, white and blue ribbons and rosettes showed what people felt after three years and more of foreign repression ... Apart from the sorrow of the occasion, the Island has benefitted by the opportunity of letting its feelings shew [sic].'

The Germans were very much taken by surprise by the public demonstration of British loyalty in Guernsey and so did what they could to downplay the subsequent funerals through a 'hush-hush policy' in Jersey,[19] where a private service was held. This did not stop individuals from sending wreaths and visiting the graves later in the day and in the days following. In his diary-memoir, Arthur Kent observed that 'Few chances came to express outwardly patriotism for the Allied cause, but no opportunity was missed'; thus 'many thousands' of people lined the route to the cemetery at funerals of British and American sailors and airmen whose bodies had been washed ashore by the sea, and a 'mountain of wreaths was laid on the graves in colours of red, white and blue'.[20]

Kent was commenting on more than just the Charybdis funerals; other funerals of Allied military personnel had taken place earlier in 1943. In early June, the bodies of two Royal Air Force (RAF) airmen were washed ashore in Jersey and the private service was held at 7 a.m. on 6 June 1943; no members of the public were allowed into the cemetery during the burial, although Leslie Sinel records that 'hundreds of people had gathered in the vicinity and all along the route leading to the Mont-à-L'Abbé cemetery.[21] Izett Croad noted in her diary that 'the florist shops today are full of red, white and blue wreaths'.[22] The day after the funerals, Izett visited the cemetery. 'Again there was a queue, yesterday afternoon thousands went. The Bailiff placed a wreath on behalf of the king. There must have been well over a hundred wreaths, mostly red, white and blue.'[23] Mrs Attenborough of Jersey also noted in her diary that 'At 2pm the public was allowed entry, most of whom carried wreaths, sheaves, bunches of flowers, or the tiny posies of the children ... The huge mass of blooms was a medley of red, white and blue.'[24]

Clearly, islanders were prepared to take risks when there was deemed to be safety in numbers and when sizeable percentages of the population were involved. In another example, both Arthur Kent and policeman Bert Chardine, also in Jersey, commented on a football match (the final of the Occupation Cup), which took place on 29 May 1944 between the Corinthians (for whom Bert Chardine played, and whose colours were red and white) and St Clements (whose colours were blue and white). This was such a significant match (or perhaps, such a fine opportunity for defying the Germans) that Leslie Sinel commented that between four and five thousand people attended[25] (a number also estimated by Chardine, who probably used Sinel as a reference for his memoirs).

Chardine recalled that even though the Germans had decreed that it was an offence for crowds to gather, thousands turned up to watch the match in vans and horses and traps, all decked out in their team's colours.[26] Kent adds to this detail, noting that '... a score or more of farmers drove their vans in from the country, each one armed with enthusiasts and the horses trailing ribbons of either team. Now there was much excitement and considerable noise at the final – rattles sounded, bugles blared, bells were rung and motor horns wailed, the whole contributing to the noisiest, gayest assembly in the four years of Occupation.'[27]

The Germans knew defiant behaviour when they saw it, and labelled the gathering at the football match a patriotic demonstration, and forbade the *Jersey Evening Post* from advertising any sporting fixtures in the press likely to induce crowds to gather.

While both Kent and Chardine suggest that the Germans thought that people had found the courage to demonstrate because Rome had fallen to the Allies 'the same day' (Kent) or 'the day before' (Chardine), Rome was not, in fact, taken until 5 June 1944. As both Kent and Chardine's texts were written after the Occupation, based on diary entries (Kent) and reminiscences (Chardine), it is likely that either both used a faulty source when compiling their papers, or else both recalled (quite correctly) that acts of defiance were apt to be triggered by positive advances in the war news, as discussed elsewhere in this volume. In any case, we might observe that occasions such as funerals and football matches were attractive to Channel Islanders for patriotic displays, given the lack of any kind of national day (such as Bastille Day) to make feelings known. Such days were well-used by other occupied countries.[28]

Patriotic colours were not confined to clothing. Houses were similarly decked on special occasions as a form of defiant interior decoration. In his diary entry for Christmas Day 1941, Ambrose Robin described the decorations, writing that he 'hoisted a Union Jack across the dining room' and 'therefore had our Christmas dinner under the good old flag'.[29] Later on, 'we then had ... a Christmas cake upon which was a small Union Jack – this was set in the middle of the window in the front room and attracted the attention of passing German soldiers'. While Robin wrote, on Christmas Day a year later, that his dinner was served 'under the Union Jack', the time for safely displaying such symbols in the windows of houses had passed and, if not, was fast running out.

Ambrose Robin was not alone in his patriotic interior design. It is likely that it became increasingly popular after the wearing of such colours in public became too dangerous. For example, on Christmas Day 1944, Violet Carey wrote in her diary that 'James and I had a wonderful dinner. I found one of my gay paper tablecloths and I had a Union Jack in a centre piece.'[30]

In December 1944, the arrival of the Red Cross ship, the Vega, heralded the return to the stage of the covert display of patriotic colours. Its contents seemed to fuel the courage as well as the bodies of Channel Islanders. As he recounted to his daughter during his reminiscences in 1995, Bert Chardine was guarding the Red Cross parcel store after a return visit of the Vega in February. During the night, he observed that some Germans had painted swastikas with tar all over the store and up the street. As revenge, he and three auxiliary policemen took some tins of red, white and blue paint and painted V-signs, Union Jacks and French flags around St Helier.[31] This was not just an idle boast in his old age. Arthur Kent also noted this event, stating that 'During the night of February 21st [1945], almost every house in practically every street in the island capital St Helier, besides hundreds in the country, was daubed in tar with swastikas, big and small. This curious act is credited to the naval elements who must have been out in strength to complete their self-imposed task before daybreak. Four nights later many Union Jacks, meticulously painted in red, white and blue and dozens of 'V' signs mysteriously appeared overnight in conspicuous centres of the town.'[32] Leslie Sinel also notes the event in his diary, but said that many householders 'tried to remove these swastikas or paint over them, and some turned them into Union Jacks'. While the admission of Chardine, who also implicated his fellow policemen, must be taken at face value, we cannot know how many other householders (if any) painted over the swastikas with Union Jacks.

Such patriotic defiance was not to be repeated for another month. Donald Journeaux, also in Jersey, noted that on 23 March 1945, two Union Jacks had been suspended during the night between the towers of Victoria College, but were immediately taken down.[33] Journeaux also noted that children had been wearing red, white and blue favours under their coats in the closing months of the war.[34] This is confirmed by Leslie Sinel's diary entry for 31 March 1945; Sinel also added that the positive war news had 'prompted a rush for flag-staffs and red-white-and-blue ribbon'.

In Guernsey, Violet Carey wrote that, on 12 April 1945, the Easter decorations at the Forest Church for that year were lovely: 'Several windows with red, white and blue, and the V-sign on the pulpit, in freesias.' This was daring indeed, but although adults were generally still circumspect about openly displaying such patriotic sentiments on clothing in March and April 1945, it seems that children felt less at risk from the Germans; by 7 April they were wearing them openly in Jersey[35] and from the very beginning of May, they were joined by the adults. By then, the final outcome of the war was so obvious that Leslie Sinel saw some shops in St Helier 'openly selling Union Jacks and other patriotic emblems, and people were carrying these through the streets with the Germans looking on'.[36] On 4 May, Sinel reports that there were queues to buy flags and favours in patriotic colours and, on the following two days, people were prematurely carrying or hoisting flags and wearing emblems. In Guernsey, Reverend Ord noted, of 7 May, that 'As the day wore on, young people began to bring out their red, white and blue insignia – a little like cutting the cake before the bride has signed the register.' The following day, he remarked that 'one [German] was actually seen wearing a red, white and blue rosette'.[37] Adèle Lainé, also in Guernsey, corroborated Ord's observations. Her diary for 7 May 1945 records that 'We are all preparing our flags. Already on Saturday the shops were sold out of any flags they had left, and numerous small boys were parading their little flags under the very noses of the Germans.'[38]

On 8 May, Bailiff Coutanche announced that after Churchill's speech, it would (officially) be appropriate to raise flags, and 'from that moment', Sinel recorded, 'we never looked back'. Although in black and white, photographs from the time of liberation in both Guernsey and Jersey confirm both the number of flags on buildings, and the rosettes, emblems and favours attached to almost every person's clothing. Arthur Kent in Jersey noted that, on Liberation Day, people '… looked magnificent with scarves, hats and even dresses of red, white and blue'.[39] At last it was truly safe for people to wear what they wanted.

Making a point: 'buttonhole' resistance

Wearing patriotic colours in clothing or using flags to good effect was not the only way that islanders were able to express their feelings (often at their peril) in front of the occupier. Some resorted to the slightly less obvious forms of making their point by displaying symbols that were physically small and were therefore unlikely to be noticed or were easily overlooked. These symbols were those that would have been more meaningful to islanders than occupiers; they communicated a message that was predominantly meant for a specific audience. As many of these symbols were encapsulated in brooches, badges and flowers, worn on the button hole or jacket lapel, we might refer to them collectively as 'buttonhole resistance'. An example from the occupied Netherlands shows us how effective this practice could be.

On 29 June 1940, at a time when the Channel Islands were on the very brink of occupation, Prince Bernhard celebrated his twenty-ninth birthday. The Prince was the consort of Juliana, who was the only child of Queen Wilhelmina, and he had left the Netherlands to seek refuge in London with Wilhelmina during the war. Although the German Order of 25 June 1940 had forbidden the display of national or orange-coloured flags from public buildings, the Dutch public decided to wear emblems of national allegiance that day: orange bows, or red, white and blue insignia. As white carnations had been the Prince's favourite flower at his public engagements, people wanted to wear this flower to mark his birthday. When word got around that members of the Dutch Nazi Party were ripping these flowers and insignia from lapels and buttonholes, people inserted fragments of razor blades in the carnations, causing badly cut Nazi fingers.[40] By 1 August 1940, the Germans had prohibited any kind of demonstration in favour of the House of Orange: no flags, insignia or anything of an orange colour, including flowers which would be considered tokens of loyalty to the Dutch monarchy. As Wilhelmina's sixtieth birthday was on 31 August 1940, the Germans were anxious to be well prepared, so that even the display of a carnation could be classed as a 'criminal act'.[41]

The value and importance of emblems, insignia and flowers in resistance was lost on neither the occupiers nor the occupied, and there are a number of instances of the use of 'buttonhole resistance' in the Channel Islands that are worth discussing here. They can broadly be divided into badges which depicted symbols of monarchy, and which were often associated with Vs; badges displaying Channel Island crests (which may have had associations with the armed forces); and the wearing of flowers on certain key national dates.

While flower-related resistance campaigns were not as popular in the Channel Islands as in the Netherlands, there are at least two dates on which some people made a particular effort to wear them in their buttonhole. On 24 May 1941 Izett Croad in Jersey recorded that some people were taking pride in wearing daisies in their button holes on Empire Day,[42] thus making a simple statement of solidarity with the rest of the British Empire. The daisy, with its many petals within a single flower, represented both a united empire and the mother country surrounded by colonies. The second date was 23 April (St George's Day), when people were normally apt to wear a red rose. Both Leslie Sinel and Donald Journeaux remark that in 1945, many people were wearing them openly,[43] suggesting that this practice had become private or had been discontinued at earlier dates during the Occupation.

Symbols of past, exiled and current monarchy were extremely popular throughout occupied Europe. Mrs Dorothy Monkton in Jersey commented in her diary entry for 19 October 1941 that she constantly wore her silver jubilee brooch (which, if anything like the silver jubilee medal for George V, was produced in 1935 and featured the King and Queen on one side and the royal cipher of George Rex Imperator (GRI) surmounted by an imperial crown on the reverse), 'but if a German ordered me to take it off I would rather do so than that either Cecil or I should have to go to Germany'.[44]

Coins usually provided a ready source of monarchic symbols and I have already noted how coins of Queen Wilhelmina were used in the Netherlands during her exile. One-*öre* coins showing Haakon VII's 'H7' insignia were also worn in Norway,[45] and in Denmark people wore badges made up of four coins which together came to nine øre (100 øre = 1 *krone*). It was considered best if the coins were minted in 1940. This symbolism of '9.4.1940' is the date on which Denmark was occupied. Danes would also proudly wear the '*Kongemærke*' (the 'King's badge'), which was issued on 26 September 1940, King Christian X's seventieth birthday,[46] and displayed the King's monogram, CX.[47]

In the Channel Islands, badges were made out of coins displaying the King, although this was not the only important symbol on display. The letter V for victory was also carefully carved underneath, and these were deemed to be 'V-sign badges' rather than 'King's badges'. The V-sign was thus the predominant symbol, but this is not to play down the importance of the monarch, because the combined meaning was, of course, a British victory.

In the spring and summer of 1941, the V-sign campaign was at its height in the Channel Islands, as discussed in more detail elsewhere in this volume. At around this time, two young Guernseymen, Alf Williams and Roy Machon, met Guy Guillard, a young Belgian *Organisation Todt* (OT) worker. The OT were a paramilitary engineering auxiliary of the German armed forces, which brought thousands of foreign labourers to the Channel Islands to build the concrete fortifications of the Atlantic Wall. Guillard showed them an English penny, which he had crudely clipped so that the King's profile was cut out with a 'V'-shape carved underneath. Williams and Machon both decided that they would start making versions of this V-sign coin, but would file them down to make a finer version which could be worn as a badge. Machon, who worked as a projector operator at the local cinema, made his badges in the projection room while the Germans watched films. Alf made his badges in his workshop in the dairy at his father's farm.

Alf and Roy wore their badges on the inside lapel of their jackets, so that they could not be seen by any passing German soldier or anyone else who might have reported them. Soon, trusted friends were asking for their own badges, and Alf estimated that he and Roy made around 300–400 badges between them, worn secretly, or just kept as souvenirs and mementoes by men and women alike. When worn, the wearer could flash the inside of their lapel to trusted friends as they passed them in the street. In this way, islanders could signal to each other not only their exclusive membership of an unofficial and impromptu patriotic 'resistance group', but also could communicate group solidarity.

People who wanted a badge would bring along their own pennies, sixpences, shillings, florins and half-crowns, and they paid one Occupation Reichmark to Williams or Machon for the finished product. A small safety pin was usually soldered to the back of the coin to make it into a badge. While Williams continued to make V-sign badges, undetected, until the end of the war, Roy was caught wearing one openly on his lapel by the Germans in 1942. He was sentenced to six months in a camp in Munich, where he was persistently maltreated by his guards by being hit about the head, and was then deported to the male civilian internment camp of Laufen until the end of the war.[48]

Around a dozen of these badges still survive in Guernsey museums and, delightfully, they are referred to in at least three Occupation diaries, all dating from 1942 and 1943, showing the longevity of the popularity of the badges. The first reference is to be found in the diary of Violet Carey, in her entry for 23 October 1942. Violet wrote, 'I met Mabel Kinnersly who gave me my 'Kings Head'. She knows a mysterious boy who cuts out the King's head in an English shilling and also cuts out a beautiful 'V' under the King's head and mounts a pin on it. He does it with a fretsaw. It is lovely; I wear my marquisite crown and G.R. [George Rex] on top of it. We have to provide the shilling and pay him a mark. We all wear them under our coats. Mabel wears hers openly, but it is rather silly because if the Gestapo spot it they will take it from her'.[49]

The following month, on 16 November 1942, Reverend Ord wrote that 'Brooches are being sold for a Mark. They are fashioned out of a shilling by cutting out the King's head in relief and the rest of the coin to make a 'V'. The Gestapo are on the watch for any who wear them and for the maker. If they caught a wearer they would, if necessary, use third-degree methods to track down the maker. This job is ruinous to the little saws used. Like everything else they wear out and cannot be replaced.'[50] This comment suggests that it is likely that the Reverend Ord saw the badges being made or spoke to Machon or Williams.

Carey and Ord both mention the Gestapo in their diary entries. While they actually meant the 'Gefepo', the *Geheime Feldpolizei* (the Secret Field Police), they were acutely aware that the Germans were increasingly cracking down on symbolic resistance by this date. By 1943, Ambrose Robin noted the first arrests of V-sign badge wearers in his diary. Islanders had clearly been extremely careful and clever not to have been caught earlier. His entry for 2 July 1943 noted that 'several other people have been locked up for wearing victory brooches and badges made out of 1/- s and 6ds with a V and the King's head.'[51] Perhaps one of these people had confessed where they purchased the badge. Machon was convicted on 17 July and, by 28 September 1943, Robin commented that '... Machon the Regal operator [is to be sent to a camp in Germany] for making 2,000 V brooches out of coins with the King's head in the centre.'[52]

While V-sign/King badges were popular in Guernsey but did not seem to spread to other islands, other kinds of badges which had associations with the armed forces were popular in Jersey as well. Before we explore these, it is worth noting that these were worn not just by men. Alan and Mary Wood[53] described the case of Mrs Ferrers[54] in Jersey, who lived with her husband, a retired Indian judge, in the Ommaroo Hotel. She often wore a jewelled brooch shaped in the form of an RAF pilot's wings, given to her by her airman son the first time that he had flown solo. While the Woods say that a woman who lunched in the hotel pointed the brooch out to the Germans, Leo Harris, whose parents were friends with Mr and Mrs Ferrers, says that a young Luftwaffe pilot, also quartered in the hotel, happened to notice it and asked her to remove it, saying that it was 'offensive to German forces'.[55] Either way, Mrs Ferrers refused, as did Mr Ferrers when he arrived on the scene. He grew angry, the Feldgendarmerie was called, and he was taken for questioning. Ralph Mollet, who was the secretary to Bailiff Coutanche in Jersey, noted in his diary of 26 September 1941 that Mr Ferrers was court martialled and sentenced to 12 months' imprisonment.[56] Both the Woods and Harris report that Mr Ferrers was sent to prison in France. It seems that he briefly returned to the island,[57] but was then sent away with the February 1943 deportations (which targeted, among other groups, those who were deemed to be trouble makers and who had previously spent time in prison). Ferrers was sent to Compiègne and later to Biberach internment camp.[58] His wife died while he was away.

In her diary, Violet Carey hints at a different form of military badge form, which I have suggested elsewhere was worn by ex-servicemen.[59] On 7 September 1942, she wrote that '… we are not allowed to wear badges of any kind. That order dates from the time those boy spies came over and to help them, all the British Legion wore their badges to show they were the British Legion and were ready to help them at any time.'[60]

The 'boy spies' to which Carey was referring were the commandoes who took part in the raids of summer 1940.[61] While there is no documentary evidence to corroborate the story which Carey relates, there is further artefactual evidence which suggests that ex-servicemen were locked in a different sort of battle with the occupiers. This evidence resides in the recycled coin badges which exist in very small numbers in three different Occupation museums in Jersey and Guernsey.[62] Rather than using the King's head, these badges used different symbols: the Guernsey and Jersey crests. These two crests are very similar to each other, differing mainly in the sprig of foliage which blossoms from the top of the Guernsey crest, and the way that the shield of the crest was drawn on coins from each island. Both crests, like that of Normandy, features three leopards *passant guardant*. The obverse of the Jersey coins featured the king, always depicted crowned, while coins from Guernsey did not depict the monarch until 1985. Instead, during the Occupation, they showed the value of the coin in 'doubles', of which eight made a penny, and which could be subdivided into denominations of one, two, four and eight. These coins were also decorated with laurel wreaths on the bottom halves. Jersey copper coins were issued in fractions of a penny. The copper coinage of both islands was used alongside British silver coinage. Coins featuring the crest were used in trench art[63] by German soldiers and locals alike, but for different reasons.

The contents of the Occupation museums in the Channel Islands make it clear that German soldiers appropriated the islands' crests from the earliest days of occupation. Many of the items made by soldiers (ranging from candlesticks to bread bowls, and cigarette lighters and ash-trays to tobacco boxes) display the islands' crests, making it clear that their attitude was that now they 'owned' the islands, the crests were theirs to use as they pleased.

It is likely that certain segments of the population were aware of what the other was making and using, if only because they traded with each other or lived and worked in close proximity, sometimes in the same house or building. It seems that some islanders were well aware of the occupiers' appropriation of the crest because an attempt was made to reclaim it, with some success.

A small number of items of jewellery depicting the crest exist in the Valette Military Museum in Guernsey. Made from trimmed and filed-down coins showing the island crest, or that of the British royal family taken from the reverse of the florin, these badges, brooches and rings proudly display a message of identity and pride, and were most likely made by islanders as a form of symbolic resistance (Figure 1.1). It was a

Figure 1.1 Crest badge, courtesy of La Vallette Military Museum, Guernsey. Photo copyright Gilly Carr

statement of identity, reclaimed from the occupiers, and quietly worn unobtrusively on the body or on clothing, quite probably hidden from view.

A further level of interpretation is possible. These crested badges are highly reminiscent of the Royal Guernsey (and Jersey) Militia cap badges and lapel badges worn during the First World War. It is probable that crested coin badges were gendered objects, worn by veterans, to signal their former membership of the military in a way that would have invoked what Nicholas Saunders[64] calls the 'memory bridge'.

> The memory bridge is one way of conceptualising the effects of the materiality of the First World War on those who lived during the inter-war years. Objects, ideas and attitudes linked the two World Wars during a period of dramatic social, economic and cultural change, forming a bridge composed of materiality, emotion and memory.

For islanders, wearing the crest-badge would have indicated the continuation of the 1914–18 fight with the Germans through material culture. The act of attaching the badge to their clothes would have evoked in the veteran memories of the act of dressing for battle. In this context, the coin badge would have metonymically stood for the whole uniform or battledress, and would have been recognized as such by other veterans. As Doyle and Foster[65] remind us, soldiers were taught to love their regiment. To wear the cap badge, with its embodied symbols, was to appropriate for the veterans' own use the 'heroic and historic actions' of their forebears. Because the cap badge represented in miniature 'a compressed time capsule of the achievements of the regiment', the veteran wearing it during the German Occupation would have been continuing the ethos and tradition of his regiment.

If badges made from coins were used in this way, some of the meanings of one type of object were carried forward, via the 'memory bridge', into a different object that was similar in appearance. While in one sense, the context had changed entirely; in another, this was still war, fought against the same enemy. Only the site, form and weapons of the battle had changed.

Intangible symbolic resistance: The role of anti-German jokes

While most aspects of symbolic resistance discussed in this chapter were expressed through objects, dress or flags (i.e. something tangible and material) there was also a form of resistance which left no trace at all because it was verbal. This is not to say that it was not eventually or occasionally written down in diaries and memoirs; indeed, if it had not been, we would not know about it today. But the beauty of verbal, oral or 'intangible' symbolic resistance is that it left no trace and so the 'perpetrator' of such actions could not get into trouble or be arrested – unless, of course, they were overheard by the wrong people. The 'wrong people' included a group wider than just German soldiers; there were those who might denounce for personal gain or to even old scores. In speaking or singing such 'intangible symbolic resistance', one had to be very sure of one's audience, and often telling jokes was a way of gauging this.

Such forms of resistance are to be contrasted with those who shouted at German soldiers: those who lost their temper and spoke their minds directly to the occupiers. While shouting or speaking one's mind is also intangible, it is confrontational unlike other forms of symbolic resistance. It is not done behind the back of the occupier, and neither does it have a symbolic element. While the symbolism of patriotic songs, discussed elsewhere in this volume, is obvious (redolent as they are with references to monarchy, country and nationality), that of jokes is, perhaps, less so. The evidence that we have suggests that this form of humour drew upon certain stereotyped images or caricatures, such as the dim-witted soldier, the rabid Nazi, the local girl who fraternized, or even key events in the war, all of which were, or were to become, symbols of war (albeit sometimes short-lived) in their own way.

In Kathleen Stokker's study of humour in occupied Norway,[66] she observed that when a joke was told, the political views of the hearer could be gauged by noting their reaction. This accords with the work of Christopher Wilson, who suggested that 'the ambiguity of the joke, in being both serious and trivial, allows the joker to test for fellow feelings of rebelliousness. If others signal their approval in smiling or laughter, the joker can reassure himself that he is among like-minded people, and he and the group may graduate to the more satisfying expression of direct disparagement.'[67] This has clear value in an occupation situation. Like the display of patriotic symbols, the telling of jokes was a way of testing fellow-feeling among friends and acquaintances as a prelude to more direct anti-German speech and behaviour. Humour was a weapon which provided a forum for 'communicating courage and censored opinion, solidarity and hope'. Stokker argued that by convincingly portraying the Norwegians as unanimously engaged in a fearless degradation of the Nazi regime, the jokes created a wartime feeling of solidarity that assisted the resistance effort.[68] Jokes, like patriotic symbols, broke down isolation among individuals. Solidarity and courage are powerful weapons indeed, and it is possible that they provided the necessary boost to other islanders who committed more dangerous or more courageous acts of resistance. While the perceived threat of denunciation was always present, it would have receded if all around appeared like-minded.

It is worth noting that some of the anti-German jokes that circulated in the Channel Islands seem to be remarkably similar to those which were told in Norway; Stokker suggests that they travelled in a variety of ways, including via the BBC.[69] Island diaries suggest that the occupying soldiers themselves and OT workers[70] were other modes by which the jokes travelled between countries. While compilations of Channel Island occupation jokes do not survive or may never have been made, there is a smattering to be found in many diaries. As Wilf Renouf observed of 1941 in his diary, 'Many were the stories, verses and lampoons which went the round those days about the Nazis and the Controllers.'[71]

The jokes seem to fall into a number of different categories; some were used to make clear the moral standards that were expected or to note behaviours that were frowned upon. Most of these seem to relate to girls who fraternized with German soldiers. An example was related by the Reverend Ord in his diary entry for 17 February 1943: 'a local girl had a child to a German, as was well-known to the father's fellow soldiers. The child lay in its pram yelling lustily as the troops marched by. One of the men shouted to the column: 'Germany calling.'[72] It is perhaps telling that this joke was related by a clergyman.

Other jokes made fun of German intelligence, portraying them as stupid and easy to fool. Examples of this kind are noted by both the Reverend Ord and by Ambrose Robin in June 1942 and March 1943 respectively. Ord described his joke as a 'delightful story', which related the tale of 'a German official who knew no English being sent out to make a list of houses he thought suitable for billets. He was to put down the names of the residences. When the return was examined it was found he had included such names of houses as 'Tradesmen's entrance', 'Shut this gate', and 'Beware of dog'. Perhaps he thought these were patois.'[73] Robin's entry described the 'yarn that Goering ordered his pilot to take him over London to see the destruction. After flying for an hour or so he leaned out and exclaimed "Ah, completely destroyed". The pilot – "Mein Herr – that is not London; that is Wilhemshaven".'[74]

Another popular form of jokes constituted punning or simple plays on words, often in a way that allowed the venting of true feelings. For example, Ambrose Robin related the 'tale of the day' in his diary entry for 30 July 1941: 'there is no more soap but the 'suds' are still here.'[75] There were also jokes which were topical and drew upon minor local or major international news, as related by Ruth Ozanne in Guernsey and Arthur

Kent in Jersey respectively. Ozanne wrote, on 9 December 1940, that the 'latest local riddle' was 'Why are the Germans going to close St Joseph's church? Because there is a canon in the pulpit'.[76] Arthur Kent related a 'famous pun' which circulated after the final German defeat in the Crimea in May 1944: "The Gestapo are going." "Why?" "No Crimea [crime here]."[77] Anything which drew attention to German defeats was bound to make a popular joke.

Finally, we see another strand of joking which offered opportunities for the teller – and the key protagonist of the story – to demonstrate their patriotism. Stokker argues that jokes which portrayed resisters as positive role models were crucial for keeping people on the right path.[78] In his diary entry for 12 June 1941, Ambrose Robin wrote down a story which had 'circulated some months ago – that a German officer entered a department store with 'Heil Hitler – which way is the gents dept?' A lady assistant replies 'God save the King – first turn on the left.'[79]

It is likely that, while many jokes would simply have been topical and would have corresponded to the latest war news and opportunities that provided for all and any form of witticism, we can observe a certain chronological patterning to others. The longer the occupation lasted, the more islanders needed an opportunity to vent their feelings about or make fun of their occupiers and so the more savage the jokes.

Cartoons

Closely allied to jokes, and drawing upon a similar repertoire of symbols (although clearly not intangible), are cartoons. While their inclusion in this chapter stretches the definition of symbolic resistance per se, their relationship to jokes warrants a discussion of their value here. I see their role as one of defiance or protest; they were a vehicle for free speech at a time when it was not possible. Of course, none of the cartoons discussed here received a public audience during the Occupation. Channel Islanders did not use cartoons in their underground newspapers, although they did employ them in private cards to each other and in formats that were published after the war. While our stock of such cartoons is limited, the names of three artists/cartoonists are known and can be discussed: Albert ('Bert') Hill, Edmund Blampied and Alan Guppy. The latter was a cartoonist who achieved local fame in the 1970s, but his work alluded to the Occupation in a way that educated a post-war generation. This type of wartime reference can still be observed in modern newspaper cartoons in the *Guernsey Press* and *Jersey Evening Post* today.

A cartoonist on *The Star* newspaper in Guernsey (and in a number of other UK penny comics before and after the war[80]), Bert Hill (1901–86) is best known today for his iconic liberation image of a Guernsey donkey kicking a German soldier out of the island, the soldier depicted with hoof prints on his backside. The original is now on display at the German Occupation Museum in Guernsey. Although Hill first drew the image on a greetings card during the Occupation accompanied by the caption 'Any minute now!', the liberation version (which features a much plumper-looking German and a large V for victory) has since been made into postcards, tea towels, fridge magnets, mugs and cuff-links, and from time to time still crops up in newspaper cartoons today illustrating some aspect of Guernsey or typically 'donkeyish' stubborn behaviour. Although the symbol of the kicking donkey is recognized and used throughout the Channel Islands today, Hill also drew another less well-known image at the time of liberation. This featured a whole host of iconic symbols: a lion in British army uniform cutting the chains of a Guernsey donkey who is shackled to a large swastika, with Winston Churchill looking on in the background, all standing on the outline of a map of Guernsey. The cartoon is captioned 'Freedom!', and the dates of the start of the Occupation and VE Day are given.

Recently, a pair of German helmets, said to have originated in a private collection in the United Kingdom, appeared in the militaria collectors' market painted with these two classic Bert Hill images (Figure 1.2). They provoked instant controversy among collectors in the Channel Islands. Were they painted by Bert Hill? Were the images identical in style and content to the paper versions? And had the value of the helmets been increased or decreased by such artwork?

While the helmets quickly changed hands a number of times within the islands, coming to rest in the German Occupation Museum in Guernsey, I would argue that the originality (or not) of the artwork and its resulting financial value is not the most important aspect of these helmets. Instead, we should see them as examples of trench art. Trench art has been defined by Nicholas Saunders as 'any item made by soldiers, prisoners of war and civilians, from war matériel directly, or any other material, as

Figure 1.2 Two trench art German helmets, painted with images originally by Bert Hill. Courtesy of Richard Heaume, German Occupation Museum, Guernsey. Photo: Gilly Carr

long as it and they are associated temporally and/or spatially with armed conflict *or its consequences*.'[81] As a consequence of the Occupation, somebody (whether or not it was Bert Hill) has painted the most iconic symbols of freedom and victory upon the most iconic symbols of suppression and Nazism, changing the overall resulting meaning of the German helmet and all that it stood for in the psyche of occupied peoples.

The second artist who is perhaps best known in the Channel Islands for his wartime artwork, despite having a successful career both before and after the war, is Edmund Blampied of Jersey (1886–1966). Although he was capable of being both political and subversive (as can be seen in his designs on stamps and banknotes, as discussed elsewhere in this volume), it is his cartoons and sketches that depicted the realities of the Occupation, often with a humorous touch, that are of interest here. This is best exemplified in *Jersey in Jail* by Horace Wyatt, illustrated by Blampied, and first published in 1945. The volume contains harsh images of singing occupying soldiers, slave workers being kicked and beaten by their guards, and islanders being deported. There are also gentler, humorous illustrations featuring two girls drawing V-signs on a wall, a farmer's wife keeping watch from the top of a ladder while her menfolk listen to an illicit radio hidden in a hay loft, and islanders waving excitedly at Allied planes flying overhead at the time of the D-Day landings. Resistance is thus depicted to balance out the horror and brutality.

The third artist I consider here is Alan Guppy, who died in 1980, and whose much-loved character, 'Stone de Croze, the original Guernseyman', is still thought of with great fondness among a certain generation. Guppy's Stone de Croze had a weekly strip cartoon in the Guernsey Evening Press and Star throughout the 1970s. Set in the Stone Age, dressed only in a traditional knitted Guernsey, and always carrying a granite stone hammer, Stone de Croze spoke with a Guernsey accent. Characters from other islands often appeared in the comic strips alongside sunburnt and sunglasses-wearing tourists from England, and square-and-stubble-headed, rotund, duel-scarred visitors from Germany. While the depiction of the Stone Age Germans, who spoke in a stereotyped German accent, was not exactly politically correct, they were used as a device to introduce the Occupation to a younger generation. The most well-known cartoon shows Stone de Croze in conversation with two Germans. Stone de Croze expresses some consternation at seeing them again. The tallest German tells Stone de Croze that they have come to warn him that they will one day return and occupy him. As the two men depart in their coracle in the next image, Stone de Croze seeks the advice of the Sarkman, asking what 'occupy' means. 'Occupy?' says the Sarkman. 'It's the plural of octopus I think!' (Figure 1.3). In three short images, Guppy has both punctured the taboo of the subject of the Occupation and lampooned the image of the feared German.

When the Germans next appear in the comic strip, announcing that they are well armed and intend to occupy by force, Stone de Croze hits them over the head with his stone hammer and the Germans depart in their coracle, deciding that they will probably stand a better chance once they have invented the tin hat. Stone de Croze thus manages to single-handedly prevent an Occupation several thousand years early. Other cartoon strips show the Germans treading in cow pats and their accents being misunderstood

Figure 1.3 Stone de Croze cartoon by Alan Guppy. Courtesy and copyright Mark Guppy.

in comical ways by the islanders.[82] Stone de Croze's cartoons, like many of the wartime jokes, let Channel Islanders get the upper hand over the German enemy.

As most of the cartoons drawn during the Occupation were published after the war, their subsequent and long-term role has been to educate the next generation. Sometimes the images used in those cartoons have become symbols of occupation in their own right and have common currency today (e.g. the kicking donkey, used to represent the true Guernseyman). Others, such as the sketches by Blampied, have been used as stock images of the brutality – and the humour – of the war years, and subsequently used in many books on the Occupation. The repertoire of symbols and images of war have had a long afterlife in the Channel Islands.

Conclusion: The longevity of symbols

This chapter has discussed the range of non-confrontational symbolic resistance in the Channel Islands, comprising the role of patriotic colours, 'buttonhole resistance', 'intangible symbolic resistance' in the form of jokes, and the cheekily defiant Channel Islands voice which found its medium in cartoon form. I have discussed the importance of such defiance and resistance for individual and community morale, for group solidarity, and for its potential value in boosting the courage in those who might go on to carry out more dangerous acts of resistance.

Many of these symbols have acquired a status and currency in the Channel Islands which has only grown with time. On Liberation Day each year, islanders once again wear patriotic colours and symbols in memory of 9 May 1945, when they were freely able to wear such symbols for the first time in five years.

A number of these symbols have become what Pierre Nora calls '*lieux de mémoire*', or realms or sites of memory. Nora intended a *lieux de mémoire* to mean 'any significant entity, whether material or non-material in nature, which by dint of human will or the work of time has become a symbolic element of the memorial heritage of any community'.[83] Such an entity can be almost anything which has become 'invested with a symbolic aura' by the imagination.[84] In the Channel Islands, examples of Occupation-related *lieux de mémoire* include dates (e.g. 9 May); monuments (such as the Liberation monuments in the centre of St Helier and St Peter Port); diaries (a good example of which is the Jersey Occupation diary by Leslie Sinel); people (and here I could mention certain members of the Occupation generation who have become locally well-known for a combination of their longevity, their good memory of the Occupation years and their frequent appearance on local TV and radio). Similarly, resistant symbols have also acquired the status of sites of memory over the years: the V-sign is probably the prime example of this, but so is the kicking donkey. On an individual scale, other symbols such as the crest or the image of the King may also have been sites of memory for an older generation.

The resistance value of many of these examples has been previously dismissed because they did not further the British war effort, or because they were not military in nature, or did not involve a confrontation with the occupiers. I have argued here, however, that we must expand our understanding of the range and definition of resistance and defiance and the important role that it can play during occupation.

Notes

1 Jacques Semelin, *Unarmed against Hitler: Civilian Resistance in Europe, 1939–1943*, Westport, CT, Praeger, 1993, p. 162.
2 For example Bob Moore, 'Comparing Resistance and Resistance Movements', in B. Moore (ed.), *Resistance in Western Europe*, Oxford and New York, Berg, 2000, p. 254.
3 Kathleen Stokker, *Folklore Fights the Nazis: Humour in Occupied Norway 1940–1945*, Madison, University of Wisconsin Press, 1997, p. 72.
4 Ibid.
5 Ibid., p. 71.
6 James Scott, *Weapons of the Weak: Everyday Forms of Peasant Resistance*, New Haven and London, Yale University Press, 1985.
7 Ibid., p. 38.
8 JAS.I./C/77/A/1–8, Izett Croad, Occupation Diary.
9 Ibid.
10 Beryl S. Ozanne, *A Peep behind the Screens: 1940–1945*, Guernsey, Guernsey Press Co. Ltd., 1994, p. 91.
11 Interview with Dorothy Hurrell Langlois, Guernsey, 27 January 2011.
12 Donald P. Journeaux, *Raise the White Flag: A Life in Occupied Jersey*, Leatherhead, Ashford, Buchan and Enright, 1995, pp. 36–7.
13 Louise Willmot, '"Nothing Was Ever the Same Again": Public Attitudes in the Occupied Channel Islands, 1942', *The Local Historian: Journal of the British Association for Local History*, Vol. 35 (1), 2005, 9–20.
14 Charles Cruickshank, *The German Occupation of the Channel Islands: The Official History of the Occupation Years*, London, Sutton Publishing, 2004, pp. 263–4.
15 Ralph White, 'The Unity and Diversity of European Resistance', in S. Hawes and R. White (eds), *Resistance in Europe: 1939–1945*, London, Allen Lane, 1975, pp. 7–23.
16 Frank Falla, *The Silent War: The Inside Story of the Channel Islands under the Nazi Jackboot*, Guernsey, Burbridge Ltd., 1994, p. 71.
17 IA.AQ 0368/01–11. Violet Carey, Occupation Diaries 1940–1945.
18 PL.LF940.53 ORD. Reverend R. Douglas Ord, Occupation Diary.
19 Leslie Sinel, *The German Occupation of Jersey: A Complete Diary of Events from June 1940–June 1945*, Jersey, The Evening Post, 1945, p. 161.
20 JWT.2004/134/12–16. Arthur Kent, Draft of Occupation Memoirs, 1983.

21 Sinel, *The German Occupation of Jersey*, p. 141.
22 JAS.L/C/77/A/1-8. Izett Croad, Occupation Diary, 5 June 1943.
23 Ibid., 7 June 1943.
24 IWM.Documents.11646 02/17/1. Mr and Mrs G. Attenborough, papers.
25 Sinel, *The German Occupation of Jersey*, 29 May 1944.
26 SJ.OCC 942 CHA. Albert Alfred Chardine, reminiscences taped by his daughter Colette Chardine and transcribed, 1995.
27 JWT.2004/131/41-73. Arthur Kent, Diary, 1945.
28 For example Semelin, *Unarmed against Hitler*, pp. 73-6.
29 PL.LF940.53 ROB. Ambrose C. Robin, Occupation Diaries 17 June 1940-18 May 1945.
30 IA.AQ 0368/01-11. Violet Carey, Occupation Diaries 1940-1945.
31 SJ.OCC 942 CHA. Albert Alfred Chardine, reminiscences taped by his daughter Colette Chardine and transcribed, 1995, pp. 40-3.
32 JWT.2004/131/48-73. Arthur Kent, Diary, 1945.
33 Journeaux, *Raise the White Flag*, p. 120.
34 Ibid., p. 121.
35 Sinel, *The German Occupation of Jersey*, 7 April 1945.
36 Ibid., 1 May 1945.
37 PL.LF940.53 ORD. Reverend R. Douglas Ord, Occupation Diary.
38 PL.LF940.53 LAI. Adèle Lainé, 'The German Occupation of Guernsey, 1940-1945'.
39 JWT/2004/131/58-73. Arthur Kent, Diary, 1945.
40 L. De Jong and Joseph W. F. Stoppelman, *The Lion Rampant: The Story of Holland's Resistance to the Nazis*, New York, Querido, 1943, pp. 28-9.
41 Ibid., p. 29.
42 JAS.L/C/77/A/1-8. Izett Croad, Occupation Diary.
43 Sinel, *The German Occupation of Jersey*; Journeaux, *Raise the White Flag*, p. 124.
44 SJ.GO Box 10/27. Mrs Dorothy Monckton, Diary letter.
45 Stokker, *Folklore Fights the Nazis*, p. 74.
46 Museum of Danish Resistance 1940-1945.
47 This badge can be seen at http://en.wikipedia.org/wiki/File:Kongem%C3%A6rker.jpg, accessed 4 January 2013.
48 Gillian Carr and Richard Heaume, 'Silent Resistance in Guernsey: The V-sign Badges of Alf Williams and Roy Machon', *Channel Islands Occupation Review*, Vol. 32, 2004, 51-5.
49 Violet Carey, *Guernsey under Occupation. The Second World War Diaries of Violet Carey*, ed. A. Evans, Chichester, Phillimore, 2009), p. 107.
50 PL.LF940.53 ORD. Reverend R. Douglas Ord, Occupation Diary.
51 PL.LF940.53 ROB. Ambrose C. Robin, Occupation Diaries 17 June 1940-18 May 1945.
52 Ibid.
53 Alan Wood and Mary Wood, *Islands in Danger: The Story of the German Occupation of the Channel Islands, 1940-1945*, New York, Macmillan, 1955, pp. 117-18.
54 There seems to be some disagreement in the literature over the spelling of Mrs Ferrers' name. While some, including the Woods, refer to her as Ferris, her husband's internment records make clear that the surname was Ferrers.
55 Leo Harris, *A Boy Remembers*, Jersey, Channel Island Publishing, 2004, pp. 55-6.
56 JAS.M/28/2. Ralph Mollet, *Occupation Diary, Volume 2*, 1 February 1941-6 June 1943.
57 Wood and Wood, *Islands in Danger*, p. 118.
58 Roger E. Harris, *Islanders Deported* (Part I), Ilford, Essex, Channel Islands Specialists Society Publishing, 1979, p. 152.

59 Gillian Carr, 'Of Coins, Crests and Kings: Symbols of Identity and Resistance in the Occupied Channel Islands', *The Journal of Material Culture*, Vol. 17 (4), 2012a, 327–44.
60 IA.AQ 0368/01–11. Violet Carey, Occupation Diaries 1940–1945.
61 For example Barry Turner, *Outpost of Occupation: How the Channel Islands Survived Nazi Rule 1940–1945*, London, Aurum Press Ltd., 2010, pp. 84–99.
62 The German Occupation Museum and the Valette Military Museum in Guernsey, and Jersey War Tunnels.
63 As defined by Nicholas Saunders, *Trench Art: Materialities and Memories of War*, Oxford and New York, Berg, 2003, p. 11.
64 Nicholas Saunders, 'Apprehending Memory: Material Culture and War, 1919–1939', in P. Liddle, J. Bourne and I. Whitehead (eds), *The Great World War 1914–45. Volume 2, The Peoples' Experience*, London, Hammersmith: HarperCollins, 2001, pp. 476–88.
65 Peter Doyle and Chris Foster, *British Army Cap Badges of the First World War* (Oxford: Shire Publications Ltd., 2010), p. 24.
66 Stokker, *Folklore Fights the Nazis*.
67 Christopher Wilson, *Jokes: Form, Content, Use and Function*, European Monographs in Social Psychology, no. 16, London, Academic Press, 1979, p. 277.
68 Stokker, *Folklore Fights the Nazis*, pp. 210–12.
69 Ibid., p. 3.
70 PL.LF940.53 BRO. Mrs Peggy Brock, 'The Second Diary of the Occupation', October 1940–January 1942, 30 November 1941.
71 GOMG. Wilfred Renouf, Occupation Diary.
72 PL.LF940.53 ORD. Reverend R. Douglas Ord, Occupation Diary.
73 Ibid., 27 June 1942.
74 PL.LF940.53 ROB. Ambrose C. Robin, Occupation Diaries 17 June 1940–18 May 1945, 30 March 1943.
75 Ibid., 30 July 1941.
76 Ruth Ozanne, *Life in Occupied Guernsey: The Diaries of Ruth Ozanne 1940–1945*, ed. W. Parker, Stroud, Amberley, 2011, p. 56.
77 JWT.2004/131/31–73. Arthur Kent, Diary, 1945.
78 Stokker, *Folklore Fights the Nazis*, p. 18.
79 PL.LF940.53 ROB. Ambrose C. Robin, Occupation Diaries 17 June 1940–18 May 1945.
80 'Bert Hill (1 December 1901–86, UK)' Lambik Comiclopedia, http://www.lambiek.net/artists/h/hill-bert.htm, accessed 25 February 2013.
81 Saunders, *Trench Art*, p. 11, my italics.
82 Alan Guppy, *Stone de Croze! The Original Guernseyman*, Vol. 2, Guernsey: The Guernsey Press Co. Ltd, 1979.
83 Pierre Nora, 'From lieux de mémoire to Realms of Memory', in D. Kritzman (ed.), *Realms of Memory: Rethinking the French Past. Volume I: Conflicts and Divisions*, (English language edition with a foreword by L. D. Kritzman, trans. Arthur Goldhammer), New York, Columbia University Press, 1996, p. xvii.
84 Pierre Nora, 'Between Memory and History: les lieux de mémoire', *Representations*, Vol. 26, 1989, 19.

2

The V-sign Campaign and the Fear of Reprisals

Gilly Carr

The V-sign campaign which swept through occupied Europe in the summer of 1941 is one of the most well-known, widespread and successful examples of what might be considered 'resistant graffiti' of the twentieth century. So strongly did it catch the popular imagination that it still holds currency today in the Channel Islands, as can be seen on Liberation Day each year. What is less well known is that the V-sign campaign continued throughout the war in Guernsey and Jersey. This chapter charts the trajectory of the campaign, showing how it changed in form and medium as the war progressed, how it dipped below the radar after 1941 but resurfaced towards liberation and how it was reclaimed as a symbol of pride in achieved (as opposed to desired) victory in 1945, a position it has held ever since. This chapter also argues that a fear of reprisals lay at the heart of the authorities' attitudes towards the V-sign campaign and prevented them from protecting those who were denounced, imprisoned and deported for their actions.

V-for-victory: A pan-European campaign

The idea for a resistance movement in German-occupied Europe which would be co-ordinated by BBC broadcasts out of London was first mooted by Douglas Ritchie in 1940, who at the time was assistant director of the European News Department of the BBC. In early May 1941, Ritchie put forward his ideas in a confidential document titled *Broadcasting as a New Weapon of War*. In it he proposed that London take a central role in uniting occupied peoples through radio broadcasts and encouraging them to sabotage the German war effort by all means possible. This would involve populations in different countries carrying out synchronized acts calculated to make things difficult for occupying troops. The use of the V-sign was mooted as a symbol, and it was suggested that broadcasts take place in co-operation with the Ministry of Economic Warfare.[1] Ritchie predicted far-reaching military and political implications for his broadcasts; his suggestions seemed sensational yet were feasible.

Ritchie's inspiration for the role of the V-sign in broadcasts came from Victor de Lavelaye of the BBC Belgian service. Observing that in Belgium children were chalking 'RAF' on walls, de Lavelaye suggested that the letter 'V' should be used as it was the first letter of the word 'victory' in nearly every European language except German.[2] As he explained, V was the first letter of:

> '*Victoire*' in French and '*Vrijheid*' in Flemish: two things which go together, as Walloons and Flemings are at the moment marching hand in hand: two things which are the consequence of one of the other, the victory which will give us back our freedom, the victory of our good friends the English. Their word for Victory also begins with V. As you see, things "fit" all round. The letter V is the perfect symbol of Anglo-Belgian understanding.[3]

De Lavelaye had first broadcast the V-sign on Free Belgian radio in London on 14 January 1941. In this broadcast, he asked the occupied peoples to 'let the occupier, by seeing this sign, always the same, infinitely repeated, understand that he is surrounded, encircled, by an immense crowd of citizens'.[4] The BBC extended the V-campaign to France and, within weeks, people were chalking Vs on walls in Belgium and France and, by April, it was being employed in Czechoslovakia, Yugoslavia and Holland. The same month, the Germans announced that anyone caught chalking up Vs would be prosecuted. In case the occupiers were in any doubt as to what was going on in the occupied countries, in May 1941 the BBC broadcast on their German service to tell the Germans about the V-sign campaign, telling them that it was a 'Symbol of defiance. A symbol of hate. Above all, symbol of final victory'.[5]

The success of de Lavelaye's V-sign, coupled with Ritchie's document on the new role of broadcasting, led to the appointment of a 'V-Committee', of which de Lavelaye was a member and Ritchie was chairman. It convened for the first time on 26 May 1941, almost three weeks after its proposal by Ritchie.

At this meeting it was decided that the function of the committee should be threefold. First, it would encourage a feeling of solidarity among the occupied peoples of Europe so that they would feel united as an underground army. Second, it would instruct the army to act in unison as a way of boosting morale. Third, it would direct occupied peoples in a manner which would cause economic difficulties to the Germans. It was also decided that the V-sign should be central to the early campaign in uniting Europe, through weekly broadcasts, in a synchronized anti-German campaign.[6]

Douglas Ritchie undertook to write the weekly messages to Europe,[7] the first of which he broadcast to English-speaking listeners on 5 June 1941 in the guise of 'Colonel Britton'. These were then translated and adapted for broadcasting in other languages the following day.[8] The first broadcast introduced listeners to the V-sign and V-sound and the number of ways it could be written, scratched, planted in flower beds, saluted through hand gestures, tapped, clapped, played and generally used all over Europe in order to make the Germans 'extremely nervous'. The V-sign was to mark the beginning of a 'war of nerves'.[9]

The V-sound was the rhythm of the Morse letter V (three dots and a dash), and the European service broadcast this from 20 July 1941. It was played on an African kettledrum by percussionist James Blades, followed by the 'da-da-da-dum' opening theme of Beethoven's Fifth Symphony, which preceded the news. It became the station identification and interval signal, allowing it to be identified under difficult circumstances.[10]

Throughout June and July, Colonel Britton cemented the use of the V-sign and sound with repeated broadcasts on its value and use, telling occupied peoples that it was a sign of 'resistance to tyranny'. On 5 July, he asked people to hold fire until 14 July, the day declared as 'V-day', inspired by the French Bastille Day, when unarmed French people marched against the 'Gestapo of the 18th century'. On that day, people were asked to surround the Germans with V-sounds and signs. However, with just two days to go, V-day was changed to 20 July,[11] and people were asked to produce Vs in increasing intensity until that day.[12] It is likely that Bastille Day was considered to be too explicitly French for Europe-wide unity. On 20 July, Winston Churchill was deployed to give a speech to emphasize, boost and add gravitas to the V-campaign. He declared that:

> The V-sign is the symbol of the unconquerable will of the occupied territories, and a portent of the fate awaiting the Nazi tyranny. So long as the peoples of Europe continue to refuse all collaboration with the invader, it is sure that his cause will perish, and that Europe will be liberated.[13]

Although the BBC directed its broadcasts to the occupied peoples of Europe and translated Colonel Britton's speeches so that people in a variety of countries could join the 'underground V-army', there is no archival reference to suggest that the Channel Islanders were considered as possible conscripts,[14] perhaps because of the precariousness of their position. Despite this, islanders heard the broadcasts and joined in the campaign.

The V-sign campaign in the Channel Islands

At the beginning of July 1941, Islanders began to paint V-signs on street signs and walls as Colonel Britton had requested. His broadcasts caused great excitement: Mrs Bullen wrote in her diary how she 'stayed up till midnight last night to hear Colonel Brittain [sic] on the wireless.'[15] There is no shortage of personal diaries written at the time which record the campaign; for example, Nan Le Ruez in Jersey wrote on 5 July that 'This morning we heard a recording of a broadcast made by Col. Britain [sic] last night to occupied countries, again about the V-sound and sign. He told people in occupied countries to keep quiet until July 14th, then, on that day to let Germans see V-signs everywhere.'[16] In Sark, Julia Tremayne considered indulging in V-sign graffiti, but was put off by the potential repercussions.[17] Ken Lewis, a clerk of the Controlling Committee in Guernsey, noted that 'latterly in Guernsey the 'V' campaign was in full swing, everybody giving the V-knock, that is, three soft and one hard knock, and also on all the walls one could see the 'V'-sign chalked up.'[18] V-signs were so much on the mind that people began to see them everywhere; on

29 June Louis Guillemette, Victor Carey's secretary, reported having seen a British plane writing a V in the sky.[19]

Diarist Leslie Sinel in Jersey also recorded the presence of V-signs painted on houses and walls in St Helier from 1 July, noting that the Germans saw such actions as sabotage. They announced that if the responsible people did not give themselves up, then penalties on the affected district would mean the confiscation of radio sets, a fine, and a civilian guard that would be required nightly to prevent a recurrence.[20] The first and last of these penalties were carried out, although Countanche wrote to the Germans asking for exemptions for some of the more elderly and infirm inhabitants of the affected districts.[21]

On 4 July the Feldkommandantur wrote to Victor Carey threatening 'severe reprisals against all the inhabitants of the respective parishes' if the culprits could not be identified.[22] The same day, Carey issued a warning to the population via the local press, saying that 'these foolish acts ... accomplish nothing but merely bring grave consequences in their train.'[23]

The same day the local police reported that a group of seven schoolboys at the Castel school, aged between 6 and 12, were accused of painting V-signs in the parish.[24] Headmaster Peter Girard later recalled that John Leale, President of the Controlling Committee, had telephoned him to explain that as the Germans were threatening to take hostages from among prominent citizens unless the V-sign culprits were found, it would be necessary to report the children. He guaranteed that no harm would befall the children or anyone else involved, as long as the incident was reported. In the event, the children were taken away for questioning by the Germans but returned 'full of smiles' after being fed with chocolate and cakes. The parents of the children and the school staff were lectured by a 'delegation from the secret police'.[25]

On 8 July, the Bailiff received an urgent letter from the Feldkommandantur reporting more anti-German graffiti and V-signs, stating that 'an adequate punishment cannot be foregone', and that the perpetrators must be 'identified without delay'. This led to one of the most controversial acts of the V-sign campaign and of Carey's occupation-period career – the request for denunciations. The same day Carey issued a reward of £25 to:

> ... the person who first gives to the Inspector of Police information leading to the conviction of anyone (not already discovered) for the offence of marking on any gate, wall or other place whatsoever visible to the public the letter 'V' or any other sign or any word or words calculated to offend the German authorities or soldiers.[26]

Violet Cortvriend reported that Carey had told her that the Germans had threatened to 'deport a number of residents, including several Jurats, to Germany unless the culprits were discovered, and that it seemed to him in the best interests of the population that the notice should be published.'[27] Canon Frossard, too, stated that the Germans had 'threatened to deport 25 leading islanders to a concentration camp if the culprits were not discovered or denounced', adding that the reward was never earned.[28] The rumour of deportations to concentration camps also reached Ralph Durand, librarian of the Priaulx Library and curator of the island museum.[29] So many contemporary sources registered the threat of hostage taking that either this threat was genuine but never put down in writing, or else Carey acted on his own initiative out of a real fear of worst-case scenario repercussions but immediately afterwards circulated the story of deportations to excuse an ill-judged move.

While we cannot know which of these is correct, the lack of documentary evidence of any German threat of deportations does not necessarily imply that the threat was never made. Violet Carey made an intriguing entry in her diary earlier that year after having tea with Victor Carey. Victor told her that if he had to write to the Germans, 'they never answer back in writing, always verbally'.[30] This reveals that the Germans sometimes preferred there not to be a documentary record of proceedings. On the other hand, we must balance this with a letter written by Victor Carey to the Germans on 8 July, the same day as the notice in the paper, which includes the phrase 'I am causing an advert to be put in the local papers offering a reward'. Because such a step was not requested by the Germans in their letter to him earlier in the day, it suggests that this was entirely his own idea, unless there had been verbal exchanges as well as written ones.

Violet Carey also noted that Victor Carey had told her that every little misdemeanour had to be reported to Berlin, and that Berlin had the final say. 'If they are satisfied with the measures taken by the Command here', she wrote, 'well and good, but they can order any punishment, even 'death', for anything.'[31] Ambrose Sherwill, President of the Controlling Committee until he was removed from the post by the Germans for his role in the Nicolle-Symes affair, also gave his opinion in his memoirs about Carey's actions. He wrote that Carey believed that the notice would 'deter people from doing foolish things and incurring condign punishment and would serve to warn them that the Germans would exact the extreme penalty in certain cases'. He also noted that the Germans 'were surprised at the appearance of the reward notice'. He made no mention of threatened deportations,[32] although perhaps he was not kept abreast of this threat, having been removed from office. The best spin we can put on the situation is that perhaps Carey, worried sick, made what he judged to be the right decision, even if the local population – and history – was then to judge him in turn. On the other hand, it is difficult to understand why Carey needed to protect the islanders from the German threat of deportation; it surely would have persuaded them, better than a request for denunciations, to refrain from making V-signs.

His incitement to people to denounce their fellow islanders provoked a cartoon of Carey as Judas Iscariot, copies of which were put through letterboxes during this period. It depicted Carey hanging from the V-shaped branch of a tree, the ermine on his official robes marked with Vs and a bird on the other branch whistling a V in Morse code. The caption reads '£25 Reward', with the 'w' in 'reward' looking like a 'v'.

The day after Carey's notice in the paper, Inspector Sculpher wrote to the Bailiff to report that another child from the Castel School had been caught writing a V-sign.[33] On 15 July in Jersey, the police reported a 6-year-old boy who was found playing with paper Vs in Royal Square; days later the police reported a pupil of Jersey Girls' College, who had been seen chalking up red, white and blue Vs.[34] The willingness to offer up children as culprits[35] was a gamble that paid off in so far as their parents were not punished, even though Carey was afraid that this would happen in Guernsey.[36]

However, as V-signs continued, the German desire to find more perpetrators had not yet abated. Anxious to avoid reprisals against prominent citizens, people of the parish, or inhabitants of the island as a whole, the police of both islands were seemingly assiduous in reporting to the authorities every V-sign that they found, and these were passed to the Germans.[37]

Paul Sanders has argued that the authorities in the Channel Islands operated utilitarian doctrines in a manner that was not always appropriate. Such doctrines meant operating in a way which argued, for example, that it was more important to favour the community over the individual (the 'greater good' logic) so that fewer people ultimately might suffer. When the police submitted reports on V-signs and V-sign graffiti artists, which were then passed along to the Germans, the outcome was more or less certain for the offender. Sanders argues that rather than trying to work out whether the moral dilemma here lay with the police in reporting the offence, or the authorities in passing the report along to the Germans, it is more important to observe that the activity in question should never have been allowed to become a punishable offence by the authorities. They should have refused to have anything to do with this measure against 'V-sign propaganda' and its implementation. Sanders further argues that in situations such as this, the authorities not only failed to live up to their reputation of acting as a 'buffer' between the Germans and the population, but they also failed to foresee the consequences of their actions. The only way to avoid being 'dragged further into the quagmire of doing the occupier's work' would have been to resist the Germans from the beginning.[38] The authorities failed to take a principled stand.

Children were not the only ones who produced V-signs. A number of policemen in Guernsey, who were allowed out after curfew, later admitted proudly that they had been active in chalking V-signs across the island. In affidavits sworn after the war, Kingston George Bailey, Jack Harper, Charles Friend and Archibald Tardif all testified to being inspired by Colonel Britton's instructions and carrying out V-sign graffiti, particularly on the fronts of hotels where German soldiers were stationed.[39] Having been dissuaded or restrained from enlisting in the armed forces by their superior, Inspector Sculpher,[40] the young men in the Guernsey police force felt frustrated at their powerlessness. However, by joining Colonel Britton's underground army, they felt that they could still fight the enemy. As Jack Harper wrote:

> In the circumstances that followed [the arrival of the Germans] I welcomed the opportunity of banding together to take subversive action against the enemy and of forming one more link in the great chain of underground forces being set up all over Europe and receiving guidance from London. We received much inspiration from Col. Britton's broadcasts and felt that he was talking to us and inciting us to action. After all, he was speaking to us in English, and we were the only part of the realm occupied.... . I retained my radio when they were called in as reprisals ... in order to listen to Col. Britton and BBC news. We circulated the BBC news bulletins in all manner of ways. We conducted a V-sign campaign with energy.[41]

V-signs appeared not just as graffiti, but in other, less noticeable forms. Vs were chalked onto the bicycle seats of German soldiers[42] and traced in the dusty windows of unoccupied houses and shops; people also cut Vs out of pieces of newspaper and scattered them in the streets.[43] Other recorded examples of Vs from this time include the act of breaking matches in the form of a V and throwing them in the road; leaving knives and forks on tables in the shape of a V after a meal in a café;[44] the use of the algebraic fraction '22/G', which meant 'Victory over Germany' (as V is the 22nd letter of the alphabet); signs proclaiming 'VVanted Rabbits And Fowls', which meant 'Victory—RAF';[45] and the use of the Morse V to knock at the door of trusted friends.[46] Ralph Durand recorded that a Mr Robilliard 'planted sunflowers in the form of huge Vs with a background of other crops, thus making a sign that could plainly be seen from the air'.[47]

The 'underground V-army' did not, however, have it all their own way; the day before Colonel Britton's 'V-day', scheduled for 20 July, the Germans began to appropriate the V-sign in the Channel Islands. Nan Le Ruez recorded in her diary entry for 20 July, '… we have been hearing a lot about the 'V' lately. Today was to be the mobilisation of the V-army all over Europe! We don't quite understand what it all means. Here in Jersey, this week, the Germans have been painting huge Vs on the houses where they are and on cars, etc. They want it to mean Victory for them!'[48] Ella Simon in Jersey noted on 18 July that the 'Germans [are] unable to check V campaign in occupied countries so they have decided to do the same by putting V on cars here, and there is a huge V decorated with flowers and circles on the Pomme D'Or and Southampton Hotels.' The following day she added that 'all the cars which the Germans are using have also been decorated with the famous V'.[49] In Guernsey, too, many noticed that the German V was painted with victory laurels underneath,[50] thus clearly marking it out from Colonel Britton's V. Ralph Durand noted that the Guernsey Underground News Service (GUNS) informed local people that the German V stood for 'Verminous'.[51]

Colonel Britton himself responded to the German theft of the V throughout Europe, tauntingly remarking in his broadcast that it would not be long before they would be stealing other European symbols, mottos and acronyms, and even appropriating portraits of European monarchs and pretending that they were members of the Nazi party. He reassured listeners that people all over Europe were laughing at the Germans;[52] indeed, diarist Ruth Ozanne wrote that the German V-sign gave her 'the best laugh of the war',[53] and Adèle Lainé thought it 'too funny for words'.[54]

The Guernsey Press ran an article five days later which proclaimed 'German victories on all fronts'. It stated that 'V' stood for 'Viktoria' (victory), the 'sign of the certainty of the German victory in the struggle for Europe; also a sign which can only be attributed to those whose colours have never borne a retreat, but only victories … 'V' is the sign worn and displayed with the certain confidence of a German victory on all fronts.'[55] In August 1941, in Jersey, the Germans issued a postcard that soldiers placed in the windows of German barracks and billets, which read '*Victoria – von den Ahnen begonnen, von den Enkeln vollendet*' (Victoria – begun by the ancestors, completed by the grandchildren).[56]

In Sark, too, the German V made an appearance. Ken Lewis noted in his diary that the entrance to the tunnel at the harbour had been painted with two large Vs and the words '*Deutschland Seig an allen Fronten*' (German victory on all fronts). He also spotted a V on the cliffs when he left the island.[57]

As a response to the German V, more graffiti was produced across Guernsey and Jersey, as reported by the police.[58] Variations on the V and other pro-British, pro-Allied and anti-German graffiti and cartoons[59] were also widespread, such as 'EV' (English Victory), 'Deutschland unter alles', 'RAF',[60] 'British victory is certain, down with the Germans', and 'Heil Moscau'.[61]

Despite these reactions from some, others were highly dispirited by the German appropriation. Winifred Harvey wrote in her diary, 'I think that they have cleverly won that round. And when I heard Colonel Britten [sic] on the 20th morning appealing for a flood of 'V's, the point was gone. It was no longer funny or amusing.'[62] Violet Cortvriend recalled that the German action 'was certainly effective and succeeded in completely killing this branch of Britain's 'war of nerves', as far as Guernsey was concerned.'[63] Cruickshank, too, suggested that 'before long both bailiwicks returned to the sensible role of patient, passive cooperation'.[64] They were all wrong.

Although the Germanified V could have taken the wind out of the sails of the V-army, it did not. Instead, the campaign soon moved underground and became more subtle and creative. The potential to be part of an 'underground resistance army' was a powerful and attractive inducement to the Channel Islanders who felt loyalty to Colonel Britton. As well as resorting to publically visible graffiti, the V-signs continued to appear in other less noticeable forms. After the transience of the painted and chalked signs of the first phase, and the ephemerality and vulnerability of the cut-out newspaper Vs and broken match sticks, the campaign moved into new territory and, paradoxically, into less ephemeral media as the movement went underground and the penalties continued. During this next phase, Vs became smaller, more mobile and more ambiguous to escape detection. Examples appeared on bank notes, stamps, cigarette lighters and badges.

Because of a shortage of coinage, in December 1941 it was decided to print Jersey notes in small denominations. The Jersey artist, Edmund Blampied, was commissioned to design the notes in denominations of £1, 10/-, 2/-, 1/- and 6d, all but the last bearing a Jersey scene on the back. The 6d note had the word 'sixpence' written across the back in such a way that, when the note was folded horizontally, a large V, the top section of the 'X' in 'sixpence', was visible, and Jersey people would pass each other notes folded in this fashion.[65] Blampied's designs obviously met with approval as, by May 1942, a month after the new banknotes were issued, Blampied was asked to design a set of pictorial stamps as stocks were running out. Again, he used well-loved Jersey scenes in his designs, and beneath each of these he introduced inverted Vs[66] which remained undetected by the Germans.

Guernseymen Roy Machon and Alf Williams made V-sign badges throughout this period and until the end of the war, as described elsewhere in this volume. They and others wore their badges underneath the lapel of their jackets so that they could not be seen by any passing German soldier or anyone else who might have reported them (Figures 2.1a and 2.1b). They would lift their lapels to flash the badge at friends they passed in the street. Williams estimated that he and Machon made 300–400 badges between them, worn secretly, or just kept as souvenirs and mementoes by men and women alike.[67] The badges were even remarked upon by several island diarists in 1942

The V-sign Campaign and the Fear of Reprisals

Figure 2.1a Alf Williams flashing his V-sign badge. Photo copyright Gilly Carr

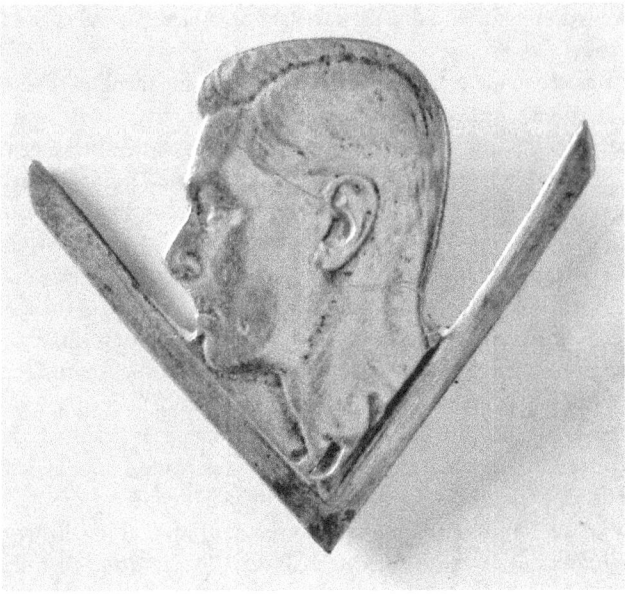

Figure 2.1b Image of V-sign badge. Photo copyright Gilly Carr

and 1943, showing the longevity of their appeal after the popularly perceived end of the V-sign campaign.[68]

In addition to badges, island men also made trench art cigarette lighters which they sold to Germans, probably in exchange for cigarettes or food. They are very similar to the ones made by Allied soldiers in the trenches in the First World War, and the men who made them could well have fought in that conflict. What is remarkable about these items is the way in which they were decorated. Like the earlier examples, they had coins pressed into the sides as decoration; however, more often than not, the coins chosen to decorate the lighters made for Germans were those depicting George V.[69] The more inventive the V-campaign became, the less it was recognized, such that eventually these small items of resistance, including stamps, bank notes and cigarette lighters, were seen and used by the enemy without being recognized for what they were.

V-signs continued to appear throughout the Occupation; in fact, if the lack of comment by diarists is to be taken as evidence, it seems that it was the Germanified V which first fell out of use and became a passing phase of the summer of 1941. Reports of Colonel Britton's V, on the other hand, continued throughout the Occupation in one form or another. In Jersey, Feldkommandant Knackfuss wrote to Coutanche throughout the autumn and winter of 1941 and 1942 to request inquiries into the continued graffiti.[70] Other forms of the V appeared now and again thereafter, but perhaps without the intensity of the summer of 1941. They were still not far from the forefront of people's minds; they appeared everywhere, from Jersey jail[71] to the cliff paths of Guernsey, where Violet Carey 'noticed the V-sign everywhere, but whether Dame Nature writes it herself I don't know. Bent brambles, hay stalks and thorns were all over the paths'.[72]

When it was originally conceived, Douglas Ritchie intended the V-sign campaign to be used at special anniversaries, suggesting 1 September 1941 (the anniversary of the Battle of the Marne) and Armistice Day as times when the V-army might be mobilized.[73] While other acts were, in the event, requested from Colonel Britton on these dates, islanders were capable of being creative and acting independently from the Colonel, choosing their own triggers and dates for V-signs. While Colonel Britton broadcast for the last time on 8 May 1942,[74] the V-army continued its work.

One of the better-known and more audacious V spin-offs in Jersey was a Christmas card created by teenage siblings Maurice, Leslie and Esme Green, children of the cinema projectionist Stanley Green, who was later sent to Buchenwald for possession of a radio.[75] Leslie and Esme designed the card and Maurice printed it. In his memoirs, Leslie described how the card was made with a tracing paper insert which was folded in half and placed in the middle. A diagonal line was made along the length of each side of tracing paper such that when the two halves of the insert were closed, a V-sign could clearly be seen. Inside an appropriate verse was printed, originally written by John Greenleaf Whittier during the American civil war.[76] The card was first made in 1941. After Leslie was deported to Laufen, Maurice continued to produce it annually. In 1944 it was sold through gift shop owner Mr Blackmore, who got a thrill out of selling it even to German customers. In the event, neither Maurice nor Blackmore was caught.[77]

As amusing and satisfying as the V-sign campaign undoubtedly was to many, it could also be extremely dangerous. The Germans carried out their threats of punitive action and deportation, although in the end this was meted out to individual offending citizens rather than prominent members of the community. In addition to both compulsory guard duty for men and the confiscation of radios in the area where offending Vs were discovered, there were four well-publicized deportations for V-sign offences and a fifth where the use of the V made matters worse for the offender. In Guernsey, a 57-year-old Frenchman who was disabled in one leg, Xavier de Guillebon, was the first to be sent away. He was informed upon by two neighbours in Cobo who claimed to have observed him writing V-signs.[78] One reported to the police that 'he deserves to be punished otherwise all the island will suffer'.[79] He was convicted on 17 July 1941[80] and served only 8 months of a 12-month sentence in the Maison D'Arrêt, the Nazi prison in Caen, after his wife appealed for his pardon.[81] Dr Albert Bisson was able to speak to de Guillebon's wife after the trial and was told that the local advocate who defended him before a court of German officers had spoken to her afterwards with the words 'Oh well, Madame, it's very unfortunate but it's better for one man to be punished than for the whole island to suffer'.[82]

Six days later, on 23 July, two young Jersey sisters, 21-year-old Kathleen Norman and 24-year-old Lilian Kinnard, were also convicted of the 'anti-German demonstration' of 'V propaganda', as the Germans termed it.[83] Izett Croad noted in her diary that they had stuck a scrap of paper, showing a V-sign and Union Jack, onto a German notice board, a version of events corroborated by Leslie Sinel.[84] Mrs Iris Bullen wrote that the German reaction had been 'deeply felt by all of us to think that for such a small crime these women have to be brutally dealt with'.[85]

The Jersey sisters, too, went to the same prison in Caen. Also joining them in the same cell during their nine-month sentence was Winifred Green. She was given a six-month sentence in September 1941[86] for being disrespectful to a pro-Nazi Swiss chef in the hotel where she worked, shouting 'Heil Churchill' in retaliation for his daily 'Heil Hitler', and giving him the V-sign.[87] She served four-and-a-half months in the prison and, while there, embroidered a handkerchief with the words 'Heil Churchill', 'Caen Prison', 'RAF', and, of course, the letter 'V'.[88]

Roy Machon suffered a worse experience than the others, perhaps because the Vs that he made were neither ephemeral graffiti nor produced as a single fleeting example of defiance. As one of the young men who made V-sign badges, when he was caught in June 1943 and convicted on 17 July, he was initially imprisoned locally for one month. Six weeks after his release he was suddenly re-arrested and deported, not to Caen prison, but to Laufen internment camp, where he joined other island men who had been deported the previous September. Two months later he was informed that he had been tried in his absence for holding forbidden political meetings (which is how the Germans had perceived his goodbye party before he left the island, which they had gate-crashed), and was sentenced to five months' solitary confinement with hard labour at Stadelheim Prison in Munich. While in prison he was hit about the head and neck by the guards so frequently that he went permanently deaf.[89] After his release he was sent back to Laufen.

While Chief Inspector Albert Lamy reputedly gained both de Guillebon and Machon a lighter sentence by telling the Germans that both men were 'soft in the head',[90] he was the only person in authority who tried to help V-sign makers. The lack of sympathy was no doubt due both to the fear of repercussions on the island as a whole and the desire to maintain 'correct relations' with the Germans. In his memoirs, Sherwill wrote that Carey 'deplored – as we all did – the stupid things like putting up V-signs'.[91] Deputy Edward Le Quesne in Jersey described them as one of 'those silly incidents which jeopardise our liberty ... whether we agree with the sentiments is beside the point. The facts are that Jerry is furious ... a great deal of harm is done by this silly type of patriotism'.[92] Violet Carey, whose husband James was a Jurat, wrote in her diary:

> I don't see much to admire in people who scribble 'EV's when they are quite sure no-one sees them, and then allow the parish to be penalised. Many people think that these 'EV' scribblers are very careful not to do it in their own parish. The exception is poor Monsieur de Guillebon who has been so severely punished and who said at his trial, 'Punish me but don't penalise the island'. I admire him *enormously*.[93]

Those in positions of authority with responsibility for the safety of the population were understandably more nervous and condemnatory about the V-sign campaign. Violet Carey's admiration was not for de Guillebon's graffiti; it was for his desire to save the population from reprisals.

The response of other members of the population towards the V-sign campaign was more mixed. While Frank Falla, perhaps predictably, spoke warmly of it,[94] and the Reverend Ord relayed, revealingly, only anti-German anecdotes about people's responses to the Germanification of the V's,[95] Mr L'Amy in Jersey called it 'good psychological propaganda ... [which] led to instant reprisals against the innocent rather than the guilty', adding that 'certain irresponsible individuals ... [even] painted their signs in a district other than their own by way of ensuring their own immunity from collective punishment'.[96] Peggy Brock in Guernsey was clearly supportive of V-signs, wishing 'Good luck to the chalkers thereof' in her diary.[97] While R. E .H. Fletcher in Jersey initially thought that V-sign artists were 'acting foolishly', nearly three weeks later he described the German Vs as 'a very feeble attempt to thwart the efforts of the allies' unseen army'.[98] There is no doubt that while the sheer volume written about the V-sign campaign by diarists showed their intrigue and interest in the outcome of this 'battle', their support for the cause of Colonel Britton was outweighed by their fear of punishment.

The V-sign campaign in the camps

As discussed elsewhere in this volume, the V-sign campaign continued in the civilian internment camps in Germany where islanders were sent in 1942 and 1943. As the frightened and hungry deportees were taken through war-torn France and Belgium by train, the local civilians gave them the V-sign gesture behind the backs of the German guards to express their sympathy and empathy.[99] After their arrival in the camps, any feeling of temporary immunity brought on by the act of their 'punishment' in the form of deportation dissipated. While the V-sign campaign continued in the camps, it did not take the form of V-sign graffiti – or at least such graffiti was not reported by any deportee. Instead, the V-sign campaign continued in an artefactual form, much as it was doing back in the Channel Islands. The deportees were expressing not just their solidarity with their friends and family left behind in the islands, but were expressing a subtle statement of resistance to internment and a source of pride at being unbroken in spirit despite living behind barbed wire.

To what extent the camp guards noticed these Vs is unknown. It has been suggested that as long as the guards were slipped a piece of soap or cigarettes from a Red Cross parcel, they could be persuaded to turn a blind eye to various activities in the camp.[100] What we can observe, through studying artefactual and artistic archives from the internment camps, is that all the Vs made in these locations were either very cleverly hidden and often highly ambiguous in design, or else circulated tightly among internees.

Among such examples we might include the facial hair of Biberach internee Monty Manning. A pencil sketch of him by fellow internee Eric Sirett shows Manning sporting a beard and moustache cut into a V; the caption makes it clear that this was deliberate.[101] To German guards, Manning was probably seen as an eccentric Englishman, but to other internees, Manning was a walking V-sign and his appearance must have provoked much laughter and good cheer in camp (Figure 2.2). A similar example can be seen on

Figure 2.2 Pencil sketch of Monty Manning by Eric Sirett. Copyright and courtesy Peter Sirett

a woman's rope-soled shoe made in Wurzach camp which has a V-sign made from plaited Red Cross parcel string on its sole.[102] This would have left the most marvellous footprints around camp, especially when wet. The evidence of this resistance would soon dry and disappear, preferably before the guards had seen it.

Vs were also used to create camaraderie between fellow inmates. In Laufen, a group of islanders made a gift for the Greek contingent in their camps: a 'decorated box containing the Greek and British national colours in silk and a large V-sign with the year 1943 set in between'.[103] Camaraderie and friendships were also cemented and celebrated by the exchange of greeting cards on special occasions, which was clearly a widespread craze and pastime in all camps judging by the large number of these that survive today. Several depict V-signs, often in patriotic colours.[104]

Sometimes V-signs were on display in barrack rooms, clearly a more daring activity. However, artwork shows that these were placed above the doorway on the inside of the room; thus, any guard standing in the doorway looking in would not have seen the V.[105] V-signs were used with circumspection in the camps. While the internees had already suffered the ultimate reprisal by being deported, there were other ways in which the guards could punish them. Red Cross parcels could have been withheld, and the internees remembered only too well the early days of malnourishment and hunger when they first arrived in the camp, before the Red Cross had started their regular delivery. There was thus still an ongoing need for caution.

V for Victory! 1945 and beyond

Back in the Channel Islands, the situation deteriorated considerably after June 1944. However, as the war entered its final months and the likelihood of a German defeat started to become increasingly obvious, islanders began to throw their earlier caution to the wind. On 3 March, Jersey diarist Leslie Sinel recorded that 'someone has been busy during the night, for Union Jacks, French Tricolours and V-signs have been painted in red, white and blue in many parts of town'.[106] Many years later, policeman Bert Chardine wrote in his memoirs that he, along with two other policemen, was responsible.[107]

Less than a month before the eventual liberation, Violet Carey noticed that the Forest parish church in Guernsey had been decorated for Easter with red, white and blue flowers, and a V-sign had been picked out on the pulpit in fresias.[108] A little earlier in the spring in Jersey, work was being carried out by stonemason Joseph Le Guyader, who was relaying the paving in Royal Square in St Helier. A certain section of it was covered in a heap of sand that was being used as a foundation for the paving slabs. A few days after liberation, the sand was removed and the paving brushed clean. The reaction of the crowd was noted by Mr L'Amy: 'There were shouts of triumphant laughter. For there, incorporated in the paving in imperishable Jersey granite, was a permanent memorial to Colonel Britton's campaign in the form of a huge V in dressed stone and with the year '1945' in cut stonework embedded firmly below it.'[109] L'Amy, who had been critical of the 'despicable cowards' who had made the earlier V-signs, praised the artists of the Royal Square V-sign as 'courageous men

Figure 2.3 Plaque commemorating the fiftieth anniversary of the arrival of the Vega in December 1994. Copyright Gilly Carr

with a keen sense of humour'.[110] Now that the threat of reprisals was over, attitudes changed radically.

On 9 May, liberation day itself, a number of photographs were taken of the rejoicing crowds. Close scrutiny of these today show a number of islanders giving the V-salute, or wearing home-made Vs stuck on to their hats.[111] The V was fully embraced with pride. Rather than standing for an aspired victory, the V-sign could at last claim its desired meaning: a victory realized; a victory to be celebrated.

Today the V has retained that meaning and is used as the primary symbol of celebration in the islands on Liberation Day each year. It has shed any previous negative connotations or associations that it might once have held. It, like other aspects of the Occupation, is today remembered with pride in the Channel Islands. In 1985, on the 40th anniversary of the liberation, the Duchess of Kent visited the Channel Islands and unveiled a special slate border that had been made around the Royal Square V-sign by the descendants of Joseph Le Guyader. In December 1994, to commemorate 50 years since the arrival of the Red Cross ship, the Vega, a large golden V-for-Vega-and-for-Victory was carved into the wall of the Albert Pier in St Helier, next to an inlaid red cross and a plaque to mark the event (Figure 2.3).

Such is the value that is now accorded to the V (and all remnants of the Occupation), some old Vs still visible in the island have not been removed. There is a house in St Peter Port in Guernsey, once lived in by German soldiers, which still bears the German V, complete with green laurels. It has clearly been repainted and renewed through time; fading has not been an option here.

Even today, the V-sign retains its currency in the Channel Islands. It is one of the few symbols of Occupation era known and understood by almost all islanders and continues to be used on 9 May to decorate houses, shop windows, bunting across the islands, and the liberation day commemorative programme of events. The letter V is now a symbol of pride and identity.

Conclusion

The V-sign campaign, the polarized responses to it, and the change in attitudes through time all throw into sharp relief the overwhelming fear of reprisals which lay at the heart of stance taken by the islands' authorities. The campaign captured the rapt attention of both the occupied and the occupiers during the summer of 1941, and the events were eagerly recorded by excited observers. However, the fear of reprisals led to people reporting or informing on each other, as happened to Roy Machon,[112] Xavier de Guillebon and Winifred Green. There was a detectable appetite for offering victims to the Germans to appease their wrath and avert reprisals falling upon everybody else, even if those victims were children, women or disabled members of the community.

We can put this into context for men like Victor Carey: he had seen Ambrose Sherwill and others deported to Cherche-Midi prison in Paris the previous year and had no doubt heard Sherwill's experiences upon his return. German threats were real and were carried out, and Carey had no desire to experience such reprisals himself, even less to see them carried out on his fellow islanders for whom he felt great responsibility. Fear lay at the core of his actions – a fear shared by islanders, who themselves were eager to avoid mass reprisals. To sacrifice members of the community to avert group punishment was clearly deemed perfectly acceptable, even if the deportation of those individuals was shocking. As Sanders has argued, the utilitarian doctrines adopted by the authorities were not always appropriate, and it would have been better if they had not conducted the occupier's business for them in the first place.

Ultimately, looking back on the summer of 1941, we cannot help but ask: what was the value of the V-sign campaign? What did it achieve? Undoubtedly many islanders felt ambivalent about the V-campaign: on the one hand they were entirely supportive of the allies and the morale boost that the campaign gave; on the other, they were entirely at the mercy of the goodwill of their occupiers and they knew it. It is clear that painting a V obviously acted as a release for pent-up frustration and anger, such as that felt by Guernsey and Jersey policemen and other men, women and children, many of whom resented not being able to join the armed forces whether or not they were eligible. Judging by the number of police reports, V-sign graffiti (as opposed to the V-sound or other V-related objects) was not as widespread as might be thought, and yet it had a disproportionate effect. Vs undoubtedly boosted the morale of many who saw them, and who perceived them as a tiny victory scored against the enemy. They were also an excellent visual way to communicate a subversive message and encourage defiant behaviour among a large number of people. The real value of this form of symbolic resistance was thus solidarity; it gave a feeling of security in numbers. As the Vs multiplied, the more people became assured that others shared their anti-German feelings. To signal or express approval of a V was a way of signalling to others that one belonged to an anti-German, patriotic club. While the perceived threat of denunciation was always present, that perception would have receded if all around appeared like-minded. Just as the Vs may have invited denunciation, paradoxically they may also have lowered the chances of them actually happening.

It is ironic that what started out as defiant and anonymous graffiti, beginning as the most ephemeral and transient symbol of the Occupation, drawn in dust, ripped out of newspapers or existing only as a sound, was, at the same time, a powerful symbol which fostered social cohesion and solidarity against the occupiers, and has also become the most durable and long-lived of all wartime symbols. The V-sign links the community of islanders back to their wartime legacy, which is such an integral part of their identity today.

Notes

1. CAC.GBR/0014/NERI 2/2/3. Douglas Ritchie, 'Broadcasting as a New Weapon of War', 4 May 1941.
2. CAC.GBR/0014/NERI 2/2/3. Letter from Douglas Ritchie to Emilio G. Peruzzi, 25 September 1945.
3. Quoted in C. J. Rolo, *Radio Goes to* War, London, Faber and Faber, 1943, p. 136.
4. Ibid., p. 137.
5. Edward Tangye Lean, *Voices in the Darkness: The Story of the European Radio* War, London, Secker and Warburg, 1943, p. 82.
6. CAC.GBR/0014/NERI 2/1/2. V-committee meeting minutes, 26 May 1941.
7. CAC.GBR/0014/NERI 2/2/3. Untitled document dated June 1945.
8. CAC.GBR/0014/NERI 2/2/3. Document dated 10 October 1942.
9. CAC.GBR/0014/NERI 2/2/2. Script for first broadcast, 5 June 1941.
10. James Blades, *Drum Roll: A Professional Adventure from the Circus to the Concert Hall*, London, Faber and Faber, 1977, p. 179.
11. CAC.GBR/0014/NERI 2/1/2. V-committee meeting minutes, 14 July 1941: available evidence suggests that this change of date was due to objections having been raised by the Ministry of Information.
12. CAC.GBR/0014/NERI 2/2/2. Scripts for broadcasts on 23 June and 5 July 1941.
13. Winston Churchill, *The War Speeches of the Rt. Hon. Winston S. Churchill, Volume 2*, ed. Charles Eade, London, Cassell, 1952, p. 31.
14. However, Cecil de Sausmarez, Seigneur of the parish of St Martin in Guernsey, worked as a member of the Political Warfare Executive during the Second World War. He is described as being 'one of the originators of the V-sign campaign' (L. James Marr, *Guernsey People*, Chichester, Phillimore and Co. Ltd., 1984, p. 145). While his precise role is unknown (his name does not appear on the V-sign committee minutes), it seems unlikely that he would not have drawn attention to the position of the Channel Islands at some point during proceedings.
15. IWM.Documents.9775 P324. Mrs I. M. Bullen, Diary, 20 July 1941.
16. Nan Le Ruez, *Jersey Occupation Diary: Her Story of the German Occupation, 1940–45*, Bradford-on-Avon, Seaflower Books, 2003, 5 July 1941.
17. Julia Tremayne, *War on Sark: The Secret Letters of Julia Tremayne*, Exeter, Webb and Bower, 1981, 1 July 1941.
18. IA.AQ 1212/098. K. G. Lewis, 'Diary of Events 1940–1945'.
19. Louis Guillemette, Diary, 29 June 1941, in private ownership.

20 Leslie Sinel, *The German Occupation of Jersey: A Complete Diary of Events from June 1940–June 1945*, Jersey, The Evening Post, 1945, 1 July 1941; see also JAS.B/A/W50/24. Notice from C. W. Duret Aubin, C. J. Cuming and G. J. Mourant to the population, published in the *Evening Post*, 2 July 1941.
21 JAS.B/A/W50/33. File on V-sign propaganda; requests by Coutanche for exemptions from radio confiscations.
22 IA.CC 09–02. Letter from Fürst Öttingen, Rittmeister, to Victor Carey, 4 July 1941.
23 IA.CC 09–02. Document signed by Victor Carey, dated 4 July 1941.
24 IA.CC 09–02. Report titled 'Letter "V" on sign posts etc', signed by Inspector Sculpher on 4 July 1941.
25 IWM.Documents.10992 P338. Peter Girard, 'My Occupation Memories, June 1940–May 1945', pp. 6–7.
26 IA.CC 09–02, Document titled 'Reward of £25', signed by Victor Carey on 8 July 1941.
27 Violet V. Cortvriend, *Isolated Island*, London, Streamline Publications Ltd., 1960, p. 102.
28 IWM.Documents.1806 91/5/1. Canon E. L. Frossard, Dean of Guernsey 1945–1968, 'The German Occupation of Guernsey', 1969, p. 397.
29 Ralph Durand, *Guernsey under German Rule*, London, The Guernsey Society, 1946, p. 74.
30 IA.AQ 0368/01–11. Violet Carey, Occupation Diaries 1940–1945, 1 March 1941.
31 Violet Carey, *Guernsey under Occupation. The Second World War Diaries of Violet Carey*, ed. A. Evans, Chichester, Phillimore, 2009, 26 July 1941.
32 Ambrose Sherwill, *A Fair and Honest Book: The Memoirs of Sir Ambrose Sherwill*, Lulu.com, 2006, pp. 186–7.
33 IA.CC 09–02. Letter from Inspector Sculpher to Victor Carey, 'Marking the letter "V" on signposts, buildings etc', 9 July 1941.
34 JAS.D/Z/H5/186. Police report dated 24 July 1941, submitted by Attorney General to the Court of the Field Command 515 on 25 July 1941.
35 My thanks to Graham Smyth for this observation.
36 IA.AQ 0368/01–11. Violet Carey, Occupation Diaries 1940–1945, 25 July 1941.
37 JAS.D/Z/H5/186. Correspondence relating to V-signs; IA.CC 09–02. Correspondence with the German Authorities, 18.3.41–5.11.41; IA.PC 175–04. V-Sign Correspondence.
38 Paul Sanders, *The British Channel Islands under German Occupation, 1940–1945*, Jersey, Jersey Heritage Trust and Société Jersiaise, 2005, pp. 65–6, 77.
39 IA.AQ 1214/30. Affidavits sworn by Kingston George Bailey, signed in front of James W. Ozanne, Notary Public, 10 February 1951; Jack Harper, signed in front of Robert Denoon, Notary Public, New York, 10 January 1950; Charles A. Friend, signed in front of P. J. Ozaine, Notary Public, 13 February 1951; Archibald Lloyd Tardif, signed in front of H. Ogier, Notary Public, Guernsey, 9 February 1951.
40 IA.AQ 1214/30. Affidavits sworn by Jack Harper, signed in front of Robert Denoon, Notary Public, New York, 10 January 1950; Charles A. Friend, signed in front of P. J. Ozaine, a Notary Public, 13 February 1951.
41 IA.AQ 1214/30. Affidavits sworn by Jack Harper, signed in front of Robert Denoon, Notary Public, New York, 10 January 1950.
42 Alf Williams, pers. comm., June 2004.
43 Some red paper Vs survive in the archives of Jersey War Tunnels: JWT.2002/486/5.
44 JAS.R/07/F1/15. Sound archive, BBC Radio Jersey Occupation Tapes, Part 15, V-sign interviews.

45 Winifred Harvey, *The Battle of Newlands: The Wartime Diaries of Winifred Harvey*, Guernsey, Rosemary Booth, 1995, p. 83.
46 Frank Falla, *The Silent War: The Inside Story of the Channel Islands under the Nazi Jackboot*, Guernsey, Burbridge Ltd., 1994, pp. 57–9.
47 Durand, *Guernsey under German Rule*, p. 74.
48 Le Ruez, *Jersey Occupation Diary*, p. 33.
49 IWM.Documents.13251 05/14/1. Ella Simon, 'The Diary of Ella Simon during the German Occupation of Jersey, 10 May 1940–11 September 1941'.
50 For example IA.AQ 0368/01–11. Violet Carey, Occupation Diaries 1940–1945, 25 July 1941; Harvey, *The Battle of Newlands*, p. 83.
51 Durand, *Guernsey under German Rule*, p. 75.
52 CAC.GBR/0014/NERI 2/2/2. Scripts for broadcasts on 18 July 1941.
53 Ruth Ozanne, *Life in Occupied Guernsey: The Diaries of Ruth Ozanne 1940–1945*, ed. W. Parker, Stroud, Amberley, 2011, 16 August 1941.
54 PL.LF940.53 LAI. Adèle Lainé, 'The German Occupation of Guernsey, 1940–1945', p. 33.
55 '"V" – German Victories on all Fronts', *Guernsey Evening Press*, 23 July 1941.
56 JAS.L/D/25/M2/3. German answer to the V-sign, from the scrapbook compiled by Mr E. J. de Ste Croix.
57 IA.AQ 1212/098. K. G. Lewis, 'Diary of Events 1940–1945', 26 August 1941.
58 IA.CC 09–02. Correspondence with the German Authorities, 18.3.41–5.11.41; IA.PC 175–04. Police reports on V-signs to President of Controlling Committee; JAS.D/Z/H5/186. Police reports on V-signs.
59 Falla, *The Silent War*, p. 56.
60 IA.PC 175–04. Police reports to President of Controlling Committee, 24 July and 14 August 1941; IA.CC 09–02. Correspondence with the German Authorities 18.3.41–5.11.41.
61 JAS.D/Z/H5/186. Police report dated 21 July 1941, submitted by Attorney General to the Court of the Field Command 515 on 22 July 1941; also police report dated 20 July 1941.
62 Harvey, *The Battle of Newlands*, p. 83.
63 Cortvriend, *Isolated Island*, p. 102.
64 Charles Cruickshank, *The German Occupation of the Channel Islands: The Official History of the Occupation Years*, London, Sutton Publishing, 2004, p. 169.
65 Marguerite Syvret, *Edmund Blampied: A Biography of the Artist 1886–1966*, London, Robin Garton for Société Jersiaise, 1986, p. 126.
66 Syvret, *Edmund Blampied*, pp. 126–7.
67 Gillian Carr and Richard Heaume, 'Silent Resistance in Guernsey: The V-sign Badges of Alf Williams and Roy Machon', *Channel Islands Occupation Review*, Vol. 32, 2004: 51–5.
68 IA.AQ 0368/01–11. Violet Carey, Occupation Diaries 1940–1945, 23 October 1942; PL.LF940.53 ORD. Reverend R. Douglas Ord, Occupation Diary, 16 November 1942; PL.LF940.53 ROB. Ambrose C. Robin, Occupation Diaries 17 June 1940–18 May 1945, 2 July 1943.
69 Gillian Carr, 'Of Coins, Crests and Kings: Symbols of Identity and Resistance in the Occupied Channel Islands', *The Journal of Material Culture*, Vol. 17 (4), 2012a: 327–44.
70 JAS.B/A/W50/33. Correspondence on V-sign propaganda.
71 IWM.Sound Archive.Interview 10683/Tape 4480. Joseph Arthur Mière, 1989.

72　IA.AQ 0368/01–11. Violet Carey, Occupation Diaries 1940–1945, 21 May 1942.
73　CAC.GBR/0014/NERI 2/1/2. V-committee meeting minutes, 14 July 1941.
74　CAC.GBR/0014/NERI 2/2/3. Letter from Douglas Ritchie to Emilio G. Peruzzi, 25 September 1945.
75　Madeleine Bunting, *The Model Occupation: The Channel Islands under German Rule, 1940–1945*, London, BCA/HarperCollins, 1995, pp. 210–11.
76　SJ.OCC 942 GRE. Leslie Green, 'My War Years', p. 13. The verse reads 'If we have whispered truth, whisper no longer / Speak as the tempest does, sterner and stronger; / Still be the tones of truth, louder and firmer, / Startling the haughty one with the deep murmur / God and our charter's right, freedom for ever! / Truce with oppression, never, oh! Never!'
77　IWM.Sound Archive.Interview 10716. Maurice Edwarde Green, 1989.
78　IA.CC 09–02. Letter to Bailiff. 'Marking the letter "V" on sign posts – buildings etc.', 5 July 1941.
79　IA.PC 175–04. Police report dated 4 July 1941.
80　GPHQ. Guernsey Police records, German convictions of civilians, 2 vols., 1940–1945; IA.FK 04–09. List of prison sentences 1940–1942.
81　IA.FK 13–01. Deportation exemption request from M. Le Guillebon, dated 4 February 1943.
82　PL.LF940.53 BIS. Albert Ogier Bisson, 'The Diary of Dr Albert Ogier Bisson in Guernsey during the German Occupation of the Channel Islands in the Second World War, 1940–1945', 4 September 1941.
83　JAS.D/AG/B7/1. 'Names of Political Prisoners August 1940' prison log book.
84　JAS.L/C/77/A/1–8. Izett Croad, Occupation Diary, 23 July 1941; Sinel, *The German Occupation of Jersey*, 28 July 1941.
85　IWM.Documents.9775 P324. Mrs I. M. Bullen, Diary, 27 July 1941.
86　GPHQ. Guernsey Police records, German convictions of civilians, 2 vols, 1940–1945.
87　'She defied the Germans with her embroidery … and it nearly got her shot', Island Sun, 20 April 1969.
88　On display in the German Occupation Museum, Guernsey. A second handkerchief embroidered with the word 'Caen' was also made by Winifred Green; this is on display in the Vallette Military Museum, Guernsey.
89　IA. Frank Falla Archive. Testimony of Roy Machon, 10 April 1965.
90　Falla, *The Silent War*, pp. 57, 59.
91　Sherwill, p. 187.
92　Edward Le Quesne, *The Occupation of Jersey Day by Day. The Personal Diary of Deputy Edward Le Quesne*, Jersey, La Haule Books, 1999, 29 June 1941.
93　Carey, *Guernsey under Occupation*, 25 July 1941.
94　Falla, *The Silent War*, pp. 56–9.
95　PL.LF940.53 ORD. Reverend R. Douglas Ord, Occupation Diary, 19 and 23 July 1941.
96　SJ.*OCC 942 L'AM. J. H. L'Amy, 'The German Occupation of Jersey', undated but written in 1945/46, pp. 30–31.
97　PL.LF940.53 BRO. Mrs Peggy Brock, 'The Second Diary of the Occupation', October 1940–January 1942.
98　IWM.Documents.2986. R. E. H. Fletcher, Diary.
99　IA.AQ 0078/10. Gerald Webb, Internment Diary, 28 and 29 September 1942; SJ.*OCC 942 DOI. David Doig, Diary, 17 September 1942.

100 Michael Ginns (former internee in Wurzach camp), pers. comm., 2008.
101 Eric Sirett, Portrait of Monty Manning, in private ownership.
102 JAS.L/D/25/E1/4. Sole of a sandal made from Red Cross parcel string.
103 IA.AQ 0078/10. Gerald Webb, Internment Diary, 31 December 1942.
104 For example, JAS.L/C/01/B/A/19. Card depicting V-sign.
105 GM.1979/314a. Sketch by John Merry of room 15, barrack 6 in Biberach camp; this same view is also rendered as an embroidery by Edna Dorrian, and is on display in the German Occupation Museum, Guernsey.
106 Sinel, *The German Occupation of Jersey*, 3 March 1945.
107 SJ.OCC 942 CHA. Albert Alfred Chardine, reminiscences taped by his daughter Colette Chardine and transcribed, 1995, pp. 40–43.
108 IA.AQ 0368/01–11. Violet Carey, Occupation Diaries 1940–1945, 12 April 1945.
109 SJ.*OCC 942 L'AM. J. H. L'Amy, 'The German Occupation of Jersey', undated but written in 1945/46, p. 32.
110 Ibid.
111 Mark Lamerton Archive, Jersey; IWM.Photograph Archive.D 24598: 'Liberation: Jubilant Crowds in St Peter Port, Guernsey.'
112 IA. Frank Falla Archive. Testimony of Roy Machon, 10 April 1965.

3

Radio Days

Paul Sanders

If one had to choose an iconic symbol of resistance during the Occupation, it would be hard to find a more fitting one than the radio. Radio listening was often the only pastime left to alleviate the distress of a particularly dark period in the lives of islanders. How fundamental morale was in keeping people going and how high an incidence it had on other forms of well-being appears in V. V. Cortvriend's comments on the causes of mental and physical breakdowns.[1] However, the radio was a lot more than a source of entertainment. What radio reception did above all was to neutralize German propaganda. Radio also countermanded the demoralizing effect of rumours, many of which were 'planted' among the population by the German police and their paid informers. Channel Islanders owed their relative moral sanity and stamina to the fact that they had access to alternative sources of information. The Revered Douglas Ord in occupied Guernsey described the wireless as a 'lifeline':

> (E)ach item of news obtained at risk from proscribed wireless sets constituted a milestone on our journey and has a definite relation to the varying moods of depression or elation.[2]

Even after their radios were confiscated in June 1942, Channel Islanders remained among the best-informed people in the whole of occupied Europe. This information advantage was perhaps the decisive factor in the battle of wits between islanders and their occupiers. The reception of outside news underpinned islanders' ability to form a counternarrative. Radios came to embody the very idea of freedom, as through them islanders could evade 'thought control' and were able to formulate alternative viewpoints. This information superiority formed the basis for other types of thought resistance. Seemingly harmless conversations with individual Germans could veer off in unexpected directions, where the Germans did not always get the upper hand. Karl-Heinz Pfeffer, a high-profile Nazi think-tanker touring the islands on an official mission in 1941, described the islanders he came across as being stuck in the 'irksome ways' he had observed as a frequent visitor to prewar Britain. He put much of this obstinacy down to the influence of the British radio.³ This German visitor also noticed the surreal situation that the occupiers' early radio tolerance had created:

> The permission to listen to the British wireless was exploited so that they placed loudspeakers at the open windows. Often in face of German demands there was an impudent appeal to the Hague land warfare rules or something of that sort.⁴

This was not an isolated incident.⁵ Probably the most fascinating question then is why the Germans tolerated the psychological irritant of radio reception for two long years. There were few places in Europe where listening to foreign broadcasts was not banned. The exceptions to the rule were Denmark, Sweden and Switzerland, but practically everywhere else in Nazi-dominated Europe listeners to enemy or neutral broadcasts were liable to prosecution and sometimes – as in Germany, Poland or Norway – even to capital punishment.⁶

Confiscation

On 30 May 1942 the commander of the 319th Infantry Division informed Knackfuss, the *Feldkommandant*, that 7th Army Command had decided to confiscate civilian wireless sets, instructing him that he was to implement the measure.⁷ The *Feldkommandantur* officials were not enthusiastic about this measure initiated by troop commanders in the islands, as they felt that it would rock relations with the islanders, who were bound to consider it a drastic violation of the 1940 guarantee. Nevertheless, within a week, both Bailiffs were informed of the decision and requested to prepare the execution of the order. Both Coutanche and Carey protested against the measure,⁸ but then complied. The population was notified about the collection procedure in the local press within days. A fortnight later 10,050 wireless sets were collected in Jersey⁹ and 8705 in Guernsey¹⁰ How many were retained by the population, in spite of the ban, is impossible to say, but the numbers were significant enough to keep them supplied with news throughout the Occupation.¹¹

Previous wireless confiscations had been motivated by a reprisal logic, in particular the confiscations that occurred in reaction to the 1941 V-sign campaign. But on each of these occasions the radios were returned to the population. The outward justification for the 1942 confiscation was new. First, there was security, namely the idea that islanders might receive instructions through radio messages and, likewise, that details of troop deployments, fortification work and other sensitive information could reach the United Kingdom through wireless receivers which had been converted into transmitters. This perception of the potential dangers of wireless reception was not shared by all Germans, such as the *Feldkommandantur* in Jersey, but the radicalization of the Occupation in the wake of the fortification of the islands, begun in 1941, would see to it that these moderate voices were soon silenced.¹²

Following unfavourable security assessments, events began to accelerate in spring 1942, when several high-level meetings were called on the wireless issue. Among the topics emerging during these discussions was the *idée fixe* of a substantial difference in character between native and non-native (British-born) Channel Islanders.[13] The inference from the constant allusions to the 'dangerousness' of the British-born is that they were also considered more susceptible to the British radio than native islanders. While the German security appraisals were not entirely exaggerated, the case of William Symes shows that native Guernseymen were no less dangerous to German interests than mainlanders. In 1941 Symes started passing on intelligence, on the Occupation and on the fortification of the islands, via a courier who came to the island in a small boat from Granville. The courier then went on to Bayonne, where he mailed the information to a receiver in San Sebastian. Symes was arrested in Guernsey on 10 November 1941, taken to Jersey, Paris, Bayonne and finally Biarritz, where he stood trial before a military court in 1942. He was sentenced to detention in a concentration camp for the duration of war, passing through Compiègne, Romainville and, finally, Buchenwald, where he arrived on 24 January 1944. He was released on 6 November 1944, ostensibly in anticipation of a prisoner exchange negotiated through the Swiss, and then sent to Laufen, the internment camp for Channel Islanders, via Biberach. He had lost almost half his body weight, and was never to regain it. In a statement in 1964 he said that he had suffered no apparent illness or disability in the years since, but that he had never recovered from the psychological torment.[14] Stanley Green, a Jersey cinema projectionist and radio offender also suspected of espionage activities, went through the same ordeal of Gestapo interrogation in France and transfer to Buchenwald, in August 1944. And, as Symes, he was released to Laufen, in January 1945.[15]

The second rationale for confiscation was that the access to 'enemy news' was undermining troop morale. In his analytical history *Why the Allies Won* Richard Overy dedicated an entire chapter to what he called the 'moral contest', the importance of a sense of moral purpose to winning the war. In his view the Allies were superior to the Axis in mobilizing their populations to the full. They achieved this, and 'won', because they had a better understanding of what they were fighting for than the Axis powers. By contrast, the Axis fought its war with 'much less moral certainty or popular commitment'.[16] It would lead too far to resolve the contradiction between this inferiority and the generally superior fighting capacity of the German armed forces. Suffice it to say that what the Germans lacked in conviction, they made up for through artificial consent, manufactured in Goebbels's propaganda factory. As Orwell described so aptly in *1984*, dictatorships fear nothing more than the truth, and they deploy prodigious efforts to prevent it from reaching the masses. The German spinmeisters of the day knew that this was their Achilles heel. Even in the army of occupation one could find men who had a hearty dislike, sometimes even hatred, of the Nazis.

Although, before June 1942, Channel-Islands-based Germans were subject to a formal ban on the reception of enemy broadcasts, contacts with the local population provided them with open access to British news items.[17] This was the greatest single attraction of being posted to the islands. This ease of access had corrosive effects on troop discipline, as some soldiers started to listen collectively to enemy broadcasts in their billets. One German contact of the Reverend Douglas Ord in Guernsey, a Lutheran minister by the name of Heinrich Bödeker, confided in March 1942 that his entire battery were listening to the BBC, after sounding out the trustworthiness of each new arrival.[18] The morale factor emerged in even starker profile once the 1942 wireless ban became effective. The German hunger for truth was such that, in October 1942, the radio sets of Germans billeted in private properties in Guernsey were either padlocked or removed entirely, to prevent the communal listening of islanders and Germans.[19] Two Guernsey escapees arriving in England in August 1943 corroborate this general view. They stated that by the time of their escape most Germans no longer entertained illusions about the eventual outcome of the war.[20] Realizing that little to nothing could be gained from relying on their own news outlets, many sought contact with the local population, in order to get the 'real' picture.[21] One of the two escapees stated that German soldiers would approach him for the news on his way to work in the morning.[22] Similar on-goings were reported by a German security source in Guernsey, who stated that local youths spread BBC news among German soldiers and that this led to 'growing unrest'.[23]

Radio reception as an authentic means of civilian resistance

This German Achilles heel was the reason why radio resistance became so significant. The confiscation of the radios in June 1942 sparked the most idiosyncratic, the most easily identifiable and the most frequent form of resistance tried by German courts during the Occupation. Turning to the figures first, it needs to be stressed that they relate to convictions for radio offences committed after June 1942.[24] Arrest and trial usually equalled conviction.[25]

The total number of these convictions in Guernsey is 64. Of these convictions 60.9 per cent, i.e. 39 out of 64, concerned adult men in their twenties and thirties (Graph 3.1).

As Graph 3.2 shows, there is a noticeable lack of convictions from May to July 1944, but they then pick up again around the time of the Liberation of Paris. The greatest numbers of radio-related convictions occurred in January and February 1945.

In Jersey, there were a total of 178 convictions for radio offences. Of these, 144 were for males (80.9 per cent) and 34 were for females (19.1 per cent) (Graph 3.3). This is

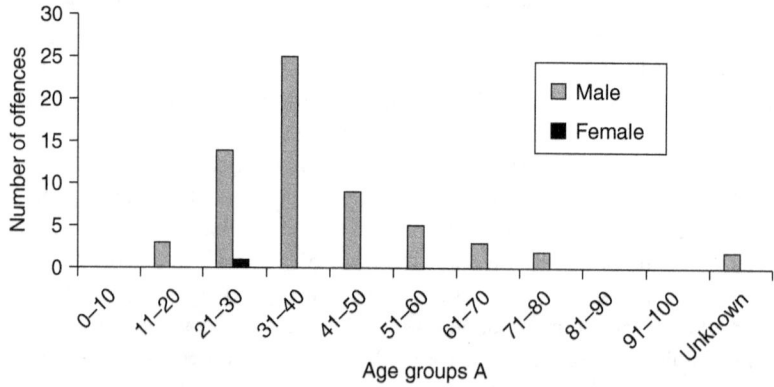

Graph 3.1 Guernsey radio offences: correlation between age groups A and sex

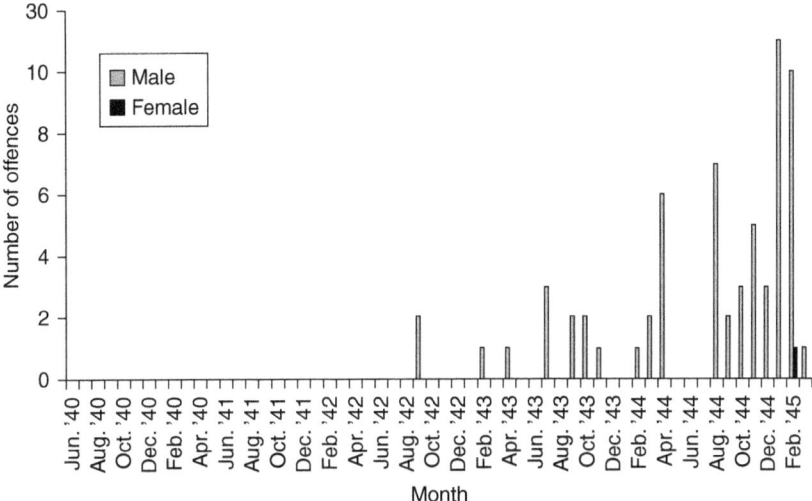

Graph 3.2 Guernsey radio offences over time

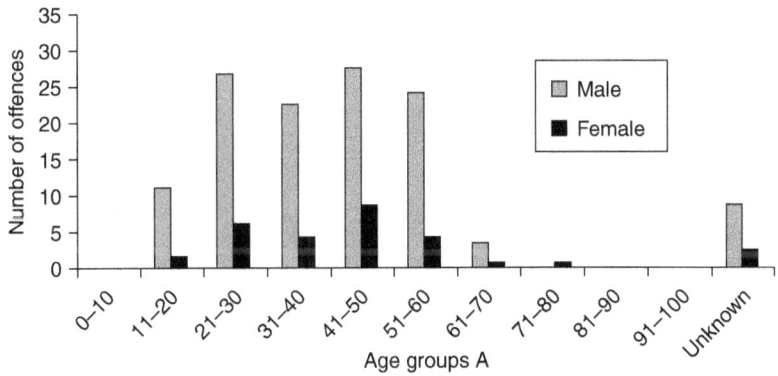

Graph 3.3 Jersey radio offences: correlation between age groups A and sex

the first significant difference; for female radio offenders are virtually absent from the Guernsey records.[26] The other surprise is that radio offences convictions concerned all age groups from 21 to 60, with only a relative preponderance of age groups 41–50 and 21–30.

When the Jersey data is aggregated, the older generation (age 40–65) even has a slight lead over the young (age 17–39), with 81 as against 80 convictions respectively (Graph 3.4).

The number of convictions peaked in the following six months: May 1943 (11), July 1943 (10), July 1944 (14), August 1944 (18), December 1944 (10), and January 1945 (15). Similar to Guernsey, there is a slump in repression in spring 1944 (March–June) (Graph 3.5).

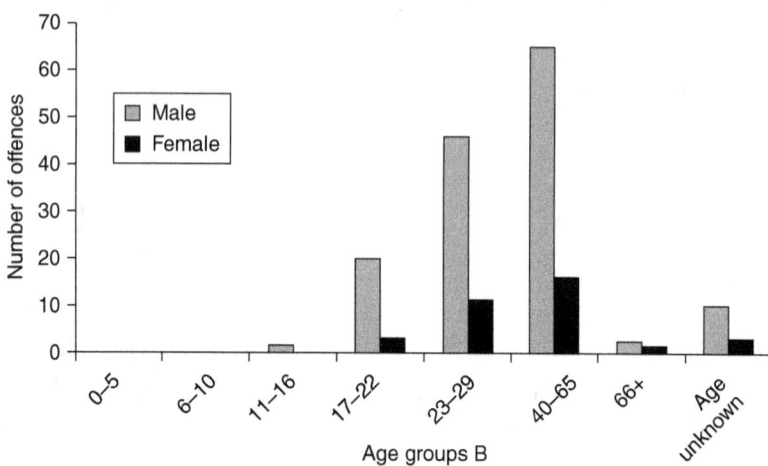

Graph 3.4 Jersey radio offences: correlation between age groups B and sex

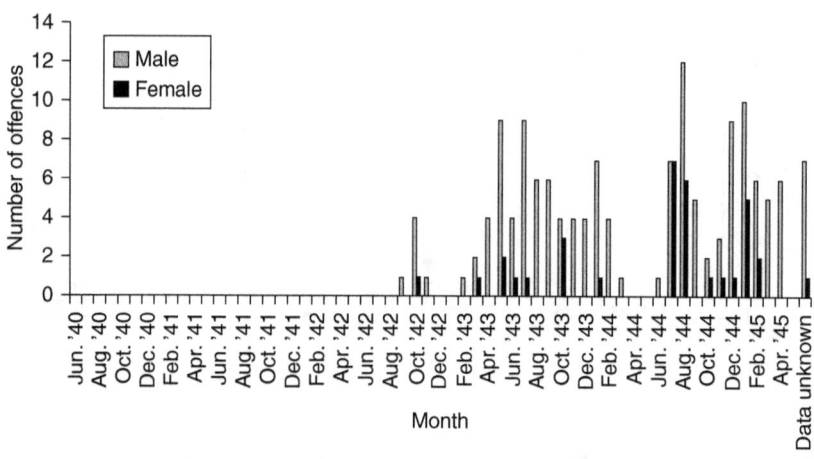

Graph 3.5 Jersey trials for radio offences over time

In absolute as well as in relative terms, radio offences seem to have been more 'popular' in Jersey than in Guernsey. They make up about 21 per cent of all trials before German courts in Jersey and about 14 per cent of the convictions for offences against the occupying authority in Guernsey (Graph 3.6).[27]

The very first of these offences were committed in defiance of the wireless confiscation order itself, in June 1942. The view that this measure constituted a point of no return in the occupier–occupied relationship was well understood by ordinary people, many of whom were dissatisfied with the soft attitude of their authorities in the face of what they considered excessive German demands. William Gladden, a Jersey building contractor and head warden of the parish of St Martin, wrote to Bailiff

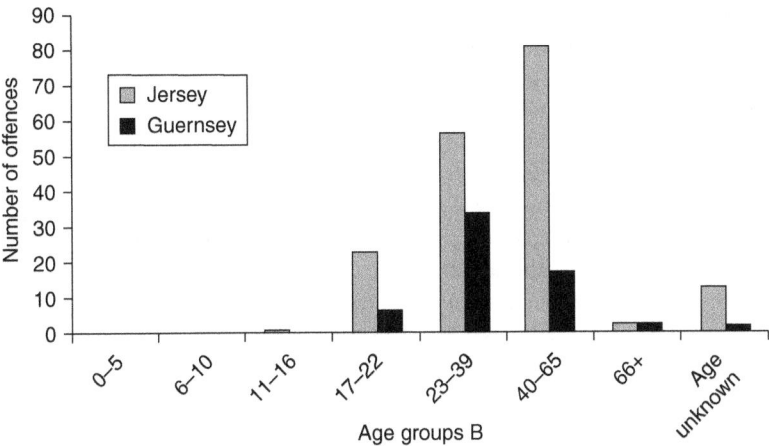

Graph 3.6 Radio offences: age groups B in Jersey and Guernsey

Coutanche on 9 June 1942. In his letter he reported that the temper of the people was rising dangerously high as a result of the wireless confiscation order, and that many were 'prepared to go to jail rather than comply with the order.' This indicated that the population was prepared to offend en masse. Generally, the order was considered a 'FLAGRANT BREACH of the Proclamation of the German Commandant [*sic*], of the beginning of July 1940' guaranteeing the life and property of Channel Islanders. Many thought that the Bailiff and the administration 'should refuse to collaborate in carrying out the order, even to the extent of going to jail'.[28] Similar outpourings of public anger were voiced in pamphlets distributed by a group called 'The British Patriots'. Their bulletin no. 1, distributed in Jersey on 15 June 1942, made the same argument as Gladden in his letter to the Bailiff. The German reaction in this case was harsh, as they took ten hostages, urging the culprits who had written the leaflets to surrender to the German authorities. Herbert and George Gallichan, two brothers, then came forward and were deported to long prison terms on the Continent.

Clandestine practices

The Germans soon understood that their June 1942 confiscation had not solved the problem and that prison sentences of up to six weeks and heavy fines of up to 30,000 marks (£3,000) were not a sufficient deterrent against continued reception. In November 1942 Knackfuss reported this unsatisfactory state of affairs to his superior authority, the German military governor in France. Under pressure from General Müller, the commander of the 319th Infantry Division and highest military authority in the islands, Knackfuss asked his hierarchy to issue an order threatening the death penalty for continued non-surrender of wireless sets or, alternatively, to give the FK 515 *carte blanche* to hand out longer prison sentences. A provision penalizing wireless retention and the dissemination of news was therefore included in the 'Order for the

Protection of the Occupying Authority' issued on 18 December 1942 by the military governor. If the maximum sentence was never passed on an islander, the FK, whose court had authority over the wireless cases, could now vary the prison sentences in a way that would provide a more effective deterrent.[29]

Radio resistance came in two forms: the reception of news on an individual basis; and the deliberate spreading of news, in the form of typed or handwritten newssheets or through oral transmission. The German authorities launched occasional campaigns against these practices (one is documented for November 1944). They also gave wide publicity to the sentences meted out to islanders caught red-handed, but they never tackled the problem. Among the many factors that can account for this failure, one is the ambiguity of many Germans themselves, who were not all in one mind about the desirability of the punishment of individual radio listening. Even among people in authority this practice could be viewed with sympathy.[30]

One of the many small-scale 'news exchanges' in the Channel Islands was the house of the Reverend Douglas Ord in Guernsey. It was here that information from trusted German contacts was collated with items from the Nazi-controlled local press and from wirelesses operating illegally in the island. The result was a half-way accurate picture that benefitted all Ord's visitors. While Ord had no illusions about the limited impact of subversion on the outcome of the war, he believed in the all-embracing power of the truth.[31] Not all attempts at incremental 'subversion' were as successful as Ord's. The tragedy of not making a careful choice of one's words (and one's counter-propaganda target) is demonstrated through the case of William Marsh, a Jerseyman employed on a German worksite. Marsh was known for spreading BBC news among the British workers and advocating a 'go slow' attitude, but this was only tolerated as long as he didn't involve Germans in his 'political discussions'. Once he crossed the Rubicon, however, he outed himself as too well-informed to escape the suspicion that he was receiving news from an illegal wireless. In spring 1944 he was denounced by his superiors, tried and deported to Germany (where he died one year later), for 'insulting the German forces, disturbing the work peace and disseminating anti-German information'.[32]

The St Saviour's wireless case

It was the collective practices which became the prime objective of the German clamp-down. The most heinous 'radio crime' of all was the deliberate spreading of news through news-sheets, a practice the Germans likened to sabotage. Culprits apprehended in this were severely dealt with, and some sentenced in show-trials.

The earliest of these 'wireless affairs' in the Channel Islands was the case involving the Reverend Clifford Cohu and three of his parishioners in St Saviour's, Jersey: John Nicolle, Joseph Tierney and Arthur Dimmery. Cohu had retired to Jersey in 1937 and during the Occupation he spread the news rather openly, including at the General Hospital where he served as chaplain. Cohu's source of information was the parish cemetery worker Joseph Tierney, who handwrote the news he received from John Whitley Nicolle and his father, two farmers. They retained a radio set loaned to them by a Mrs Bathe. On the basis of this information, news-sheets were produced by Tierney and another man, Arthur Wakeham, which were then carried to Canon Cohu and to Henry Coutanche, at St Saviour's Parish Hall.[33] Joseph Tierney was the first member of the network to be seized on 3 March 1943, followed by a number of other arrests, including Tierney and Cohu, over the ensuing fortnight.[34] A total of 18 people were roped in altogether, most of them for receiving or disseminating BBC news.[35] The number of victims could have been higher, had Cohu not managed to pass a warning to two other clergymen, who were also spreading the news.[36] The ensuing trial demonstrated the German occupiers' increasing apprehension about the flaunting of the wireless confiscation order. They made sure that the trial – which took place from 9 to 14 April 1943 – received the necessary publicity, and large crowds thronged Royal Square outside the States building where the trial was being held. The sentencing made a clear departure from any previous leniency and Cohu received a 18-month jail sentence. His principal helpers, Tierney and Nicolle (branded the 'chief culprit'), received two years and three years respectively.[37] The third line of attack targeted the English-born, such as Arthur Dimmery, a gardener whose 'crime' constituted in having dug up Mrs Bathe's wireless set, before it was handed over to Mr Nicolle. Dimmery's low sentence of three months and two weeks would normally have been served in the island prison, but he was sent to the Continent.[38] After completing his short term, he was sent to Neuengamme concentration camp, outside Hamburg.[39] How Dimmery came to be admitted to Laufen remains a mystery. He died there on April 4, 1944 and lies buried at Salzach Municipal Cemetery.[40]

Cohu was transported off the island on 13 July 1943, and then sent to Dijon (Fort Hauteville).[41] Tierney, who in the meantime had been allowed to attend the christening ceremony of his new-born daughter, followed him there on 18 September 1943, with John Nicolle and Frederick Page, also a radio offender.[42] Page had faced charges with four other men – James Davey, Davey's brother Isaac, Owen Dore and George Louis Sty – for a 'wireless offence' committed at James Davey's home. Sty later stated that three groups of radio listeners took turns in the loft of the house, but that he never knew who the members of the other two groups were. Page, an agricultural labourer born in Portsmouth in 1900, was an unassuming and calm man, practically indistinguishable from the other listeners. As in the St Saviour's Wireless Case, the listeners were not caught in the act, but hauled out of their beds, one morning at 6 a.m., and taken to *Feldgendarmerie* HQ, where each one was interrogated separately for three hours. On 19 July 1943 the group, together with nine other people, was summoned before the court. During the trial Page was the only one to not adopt a low profile, making it no secret that he was English-born and that he had served in the Great War.[43] Page had already been exempted from the 1942 deportation, and his sentence of 21 months – the toughest of the entire group – automatically earmarked him for transportation to the Continent.[44]

In late 1943 the Channel Islanders doing time at Dijon were sent to Saarbrücken prison, in Germany. As the 'chief culprit' of the St Saviour's wireless case, John Nicolle was now singled out and sent to Zweibrücken, on 27 December 1943.[45] Three-and-half months later he was sent to Bochum, and then to Dortmund, where he arrived on 21 April.[46] As one survivor later recounted, Bochum was 'bad, but it was a palace compared to Dortmund'. John Nicolle's journey was to end at Dortmund, where he perished from starvation and overwork, on 14 February 1945.[47] The other Channel Islands prisoners had been sent from Saarbrücken to Frankfurt-Preungesheim, where they arrived on 6 January 1944. By this time Preungesheim had become the principal detention centre for Channel Islands offenders in Germany.[48] As a rule, all Channel Islanders sentenced by German courts to longer prison terms were transferred to penitentiaries in Germany, usually after first serving time in the Channel Islands and in France.[49] Until 1942 people serving shorter sentences in France could be sent back to the Channel Islands, but this practice became increasingly uncommon later that year. The principal routes into the German prison system were, for men, the prisons in Saarbrücken and Wolfenbüttel (via Freiburg or Karlsruhe) and, for women, Cologne.[50] Because of overcrowding in Saarbrücken, Channel Islanders with sentences up to two years were sent to Preungesheim,[51] from December 1943.[52] Preungesheim had four five-floor blocks, filled with 850 prisoners of all European nationalities. These blocks led onto a central building which the Guernsey journalist Frank Falla described as 'a kind of platform and enclosed cabin in which worked the prison administrators, complete with Nazi uniform, Iron Cross, other medals, sword and all the trappings that were supposed to impress us.'[53]

Preungesheim was administered by the Gestapo. The warders were old or invalided ex-soldiers, sprinkled with Gestapo officers. The prisoners themselves wore blue dungarees with JV, for *Justizverwaltung* (penitentiary administration), written in red letters on the back, and an ID disc and number on strings around their necks.[54] After the war Canon Cohu's wife testified that her husband had remained in solitary confinement at Preungesheim, but that up to the D-Day landings he had been able to communicate with her once a month. The last time she had heard from him was in July 1944. In his letters to his wife he frequently referred to the gruelling conditions in prison, particularly the cold and the hunger. On a weekly bread ration of four-and-a-half pounds,[55] emaciation had already taken its toll: Cohu's weight had dropped from 10st. 3lb. when he left the island to 7st. in May 1944.[56]

When Saarbrücken prison suffered heavy bomb damage and Preungesheim became overcrowded, 11 of the Channel Islands prisoners[57] were transferred to Naumburg-on-Saale[58], in early July 1944.[59] Naumburg, holding 350 prisoners, was smaller than Preungesheim, but, if anything, conditions were even worse here than in the previous prison. Over the next months the Jersey prisoners wasted away. Cohu's sentence officially ended on 24 September 1944 and the sentence of Joseph Tierney on 25 March 1945. During their imprisonment in Preungesheim both men had appealed for an early release[60] and Cohu's efforts seemed to have borne fruit in late August, when he was discharged on the grounds of a 'suspension of sentence'.[61] Expecting, no doubt, to be sent to an internment camp, he was taken by the Gestapo to a 'work education camp' under SS authority, in Zöschen, 22 miles from Naumburg. He arrived there with a group of 50 prisoners, on 13 September 1944.[62] 'Work education camps' were punishment camps, specifically targeting those prisoners who refused to do their bit for the Nazi war effort. Conditions in these camps were primitive and reputedly worse than those in most concentration camps. At the time of Cohu's arrival the camp population had swollen to 500. Small round paper tents were erected into which 30 men each were crammed, with nothing to sleep on but the straw on the bare soil. Being British and a clergyman, Cohu attracted attention and provoked the guards' perverse ingenuity, the minute he set foot inside the camp. Feeble and thin, he was unable to lift a shovel, which earned him the direst of abuse and continual beatings. The camp SS were bent on bringing about one guard's ominous prognosis that he would not last longer than a week, and their brutality prevailed on 20 September 1944.[63]

Even less information has survived on Joe Tierney's ultimate fate, but it was no doubt similar to Cohu's. Tierney appears to have served his sentence in full and was discharged from Naumburg, on 25 March 1945.[64] He was killed during a forced march, near Celle in April 1945, having been recaptured after an escape attempt.[65]

GASP

If anything, organized news-sheeting seems to have been even more pronounced in Guernsey than in Jersey. One such endeavour was the Guernsey Active Secret Press (GASP), edited by the elderly L. E. Bertrand. A veteran of the Great War, Bertrand's health was frail, but his doctor had not been able to talk him out of the venture. When the radios were confiscated in 1942 Bertrand handed in one set, but retained a small one-valve radio which was easier to transport and hide. Betrand took details of broadcasts and another man, Reginald Warley, typed them out. Betrand had 12 distributors ('agents') who spread the news-sheets among reliable and trustworthy civilians.[66] One of these also recruited a number of foreign sub-agents, through whom the news reached labourers. They would meet at a local bicycle shop, a place camouflaged by the continuous hustle-and-bustle of customers whose bikes needed attention.

The sheets were in great demand. Their value lay not only in boosting morale, but also in the indications they provided to fishermen as to avoiding certain zones where military engagements were likely to take place. One of the most sought-after items, the BBC Editors 'Survey of the Week', broadcast on Sundays at 3 p.m., even reached the Bailiff, through Madeleine Simms, a States employee and the wife of one of Bertrand's agents.[67] Bertrand was not a complacent observer of the Guernsey scene and he was well aware of the disturbing fate of other news circuits such as GUNS, the Guernsey Underground News Service. He himself experienced many close calls with fate that could have turned nasty. Like many Channel Islanders, Bertrand had maps pinned to the walls showing the Allied positions. One day these maps were spotted by a German who had come to collect fruits in a nearby garden. When the man asked Bertrand whether he had a radio, he denied it, claiming that it was all made on the basis of the communiqués available in the German-controlled press. Although the German did not believe him, the thought of denouncing Bertrand did not occur to him. Later the same man brought some of his comrades along to study the map. Bertrand and the Germans even went to the point of having arguments about who was going to win the war until, one day, the flags on the map disappeared. Bertrand surmised that this had been done by one of his own people who had decided to put an end to the fun.

Among the other delicate problems in keeping the news cycle running was how to obtain replacement batteries for the radio. After much agonizing over whom he could trust, Bertrand took the risk of exchanging his cigarette ration with an unknown man offering a battery, and whose behaviour he did not find 'quite British'. Another close call with fate occurred at the time when electricity was running scarce. The man responsible for charging Bertrand's battery was already exceeding his supply and Bertrand, in an act of desperation, decided to 'borrow' a battery from a German car, which he returned to its proper place after every usage. Fortunately, a few weeks into this exceedingly dangerous daily routine instructions arrived through the BBC on how to make crystal sets. Later, when electricity was cut, Bertrand was caught siphoning off diesel oil, which he needed to provide light, from a German tank at the Electric Station. His ID card was confiscated by the man in charge, a Frenchman, and Bertrand was convinced that surely his time had come to pay a visit to the local gaol. But things took a different turn, for the next day he was handed back his ID card, by the same Frenchman. The latter had been pressurized, under a pretext, by the second-in-charge, a Pole by the name of 'Alex' who happened to be one of Bertrand's radio news recipients.[68]

GUNS

The perhaps even better-known Guernsey newsletter was GUNS, animated by the journalist Frank Falla. In contrast to Bertrand's seven lives, Falla's luck, and that of his colleagues Charles Machon, Cecil Duquemin, Joseph Gillingham and Ernest Legg, ran out in spring 1944, when they were arrested, tried and deported to German prisons. Two of the GUNS men, Machon and Gillingham, died while in captivity and the three survivors had to contend with the lasting effects of their detention in subsequent decades. Falla's story is well-known, as he wrote *The Silent War*, one of the earliest and most resonant occupation memoirs, and the only one dealing specifically with resistance at the time of its publication. The recent discovery of his private papers, discussed in the last chapter of this volume, allows us to add some fresh perspective.

The news-sheet was the 'brainchild' of Charles Machon, a linotype operator at the *Guernsey Star*.[69] The canonic version has it that GUNS appeared daily, except Sundays, between May 1942 and February 1944, but getting GUNS to 'market' may not always have been as smooth as this. GUNS summarized the highlights of the war's progress through an outline of the BBC evening news, a summary of the morning news bulletin and, occasionally, the full text of Churchill and Roosevelt speeches (Figure 3.1). It averaged about 800 words per issue and, typically, three sets of eight copies, on thin tomato-packing paper, that were handed to recipients, for oral transmission. Even if the actual number of copies was small, word-of-mouth reached 300 people, and probably many more.[70] The news-sheets were supposed to be destroyed after reading, but these recommendations were not always followed. In some cases news-sheets was even re-typed. According to Falla, GUNS to the people of Guernsey was something that 'money could not buy':

> This news-sheet [...] was the means, through many dark and dismal days, of doing more to maintain the morale of a subject people than any other one thing I know of for it kept up the spirits of the pessimist and helped the optimist to cheer on the thousands who, in Guernsey alone, were squirming under the Nazi heel.[71]

Figure 3.1 Frank Falla listening to the BBC, cartoon by Bert Hill, courtesy of the family of Frank Falla

The enterprise came to an abrupt end on 11 February 1944, when Machon and his then news-supplier, Cecil Duquemin, were arrested by the *Feldgendarmerie*, on indications given to them by a *V-Mann* (infiltrator) of Irish nationality, Peter Doyle. The descent on Machon was a scoop, as they found his typewriter ready set with copies and carbon for the receipt of the morning news, as well as back issues of the news bulletin stretching over several months, which should have been destroyed. When the German Secret Field Police (GFP) took over the investigation, they were convinced that GUNS was a large island-wide underground movement with some 'big people' at its head. A 51-year-old linotype operator suffering from a stomach ulcer did not fit this description; and neither did Duquemin, who was equally considered 'small fry'. The frantic search had to continue until the ringleaders were apprehended. The inability of the GFP to countenance a grassroots effort and their obsession with British espionage and subversion led to a 'pathetic and deluded eagerness to discover the ramifications of an omnipotent Secret Service in the most innocent circumstances'.[72] This disposition was nurtured by the reading of crime novels such as Dennis Wheatley's *File on Bolitho Blane*, a copy of which was later found on the bedside table of Einert, a prewar businessman and the team's ace in the hunting of illegal radios, during a search of Mon Plaisir, the GFP den in Guernsey, by British investigators in 1945.[73]

The names of Falla, Legg and Gillingham did not emerge immediately in the investigation. Peter Doyle was only able to denounce Machon and Duquemin, but not the other suppliers, as they had stopped operating in February 1944. The only person in the know was Machon, who managed to keep their names quiet for some time.

Considering that Machon was denied the special diet he needed to relieve his stomach condition, he held out surprisingly long. In a statement dated 21 February he denied his suppliers and newsletter recipients. Only four days later, in another statement, did he name Legg and Falla.[74] According to Falla, Machon 'broke' when the GFP showed him additional back issues of GUNS extending over several months, supplied to them by Doyle, and threatened to imprison his mother.[75] Falla also said that Machon suffered 'the ultimate in physical and mental torture',[76] and that the Germans 'pumped' two other people, on the understanding that their own skins would be saved.[77] Legg and Gillingham were questioned by German police in March 1944 respectively,[78] but then allowed to go home.[79] Gillingham (but not Legg[80]) was even allowed to return to his home after the trial, when he was told that the Germans would come for him. This they did on 3 June, when he was told to report at 7 p.m., to be transported to the Continent.[81] No other explanation for this lenient treatment, other than that no evidence had been discovered during the search of Gillingham's home, exists. This was different for Falla, whose house search, conducted by Einert on 3 April 1944, almost two months after the first arrests, produced another radio set. Falla was therefore remanded in custody.

A preliminary conclusion will find that the GUNS operation did not emerge suddenly, in one set piece, but went through several stages and evolved, as a practice, over an extensive period of time. GUNS had more than one supplier of its news, and these suppliers could take turns (or 'dry up'), when it got 'too hot'. The news-sheet was also typed up by various people, who did not necessarily know of each other's existence. Machon was the only relay and the only common link between the various members of the group. Prior to his arrest and trial, Falla did not know the other members of GUNS, apart from Machon. He got to know Duquemin only when he was taken to the GFP headquarters for questioning,[82] and he probably discovered the identities of Legg and Gillingham for the first time at their trial. The number and location of radios and written materials discovered provide further evidence. The Germans found radios belonging to Cecil Duquemin, in February 1944, and to Frank Falla, in April 1944, but none belonging to the other three. Machon had never kept a radio of his own, as he had depended on others for his supply of information. The first suppliers for his news-sheet are likely to have been Ernest Legg and Joseph Gillingham, but there could, of course, have been others. It is not entirely clear when Falla joined the effort, but this is also likely to have been fairly early on, as the news-sheet needed an expert hand. To begin with, Machon relied on the infrastructure he could find at the *Star*. Falla indicates that, for some time, the typing up was done at the offices of the *Star*; in emergencies the copy for GUNS was even set up in linotype, but this was risky, as it could be traced.[83] At some point the managing director of the *Star* put an end to this 'association'. Having called Falla into his office, he told him that his activities were too dangerous. Falla then worked from his home,[84] where he sub-edited and added to the news brought in from other suppliers, before supplying it in full when the initial flow of information 'dried up', sometime in late 1943.[85] All in all, Falla stated that he provided direct copy for 280 issues.[86]

There are various versions as to why Legg and Gillingham quit the effort in 1943. For one thing, they may have felt that Machon was 'overdoing it', as the news-sheet was initially intended for trusted friends and neighbours only.[87] The most likely reason, however, was the fact that Henrietta Gillingham, who took down the news for Legg,[88] was pregnant. She gave birth to a baby daughter on 27 December 1943.[89] In view of the fact that the Germans never found Gillingham's radio, it is quite likely then that what he told the German investigators was true; namely that he and Legg had continued to listen in for a while, after having discontinued their association with Machon, before finally destroying the radio in November 1943.[90] Falla also downscaled his involvement, when, to his dismay, he discovered a GUNS sheet on open display at a 'barter mart', a grey market shop run by Steve Picquet, an unsavoury character who was no stranger to the law.[91] To make things worse the particular copy on display was an original, in Falla's own handwriting. Falla then took Machon to task, saying that he would henceforth limit his activities to 'production'.[92] While it is unclear when exactly Cecil Duquemin started his association with GUNS, there is little doubt that he was Machon's last supplier of news.

When GUNS stopped circulating in February 1944, the readers of GUNS feared being drawn into the net.[93] One month after the initial arrests the Germans were still interrogating Machon's work colleagues. Those questioned generally admitted having read the news-sheet, but said that they had burnt it after reading.[94] Hubert Lanyon, the baker of Sark, a Methodist lay preacher and one of the GUNS recipients, minimized his contribution to news dissemination.[95] In a statement to the German police, he explained how Machon had come to Sark on a vacation in October 1942, and that Machon had asked him to recommend lodgings where he could be provided with food adapted to his stomach problems. During one conversation he opened himself up to Lanyon and offered to send him his news-sheets on a regular basis, a proposition that Lanyon accepted. Asked as to whether he had spread the news, he denied it, pretending that there were too many people who envied him and who could not be trusted.[96] Lanyon was then sentenced to five months' imprisonment in Guernsey, a sentence that was later cut to three months, due to 'good behaviour'.[97] The other recipients and distributors[98] roped in received similar sentences, but were also spared the fate dreaded most of all, transfer to a continental prison. Others, such as Bill Taylor, a shorthand note-taker who jotted down Churchill's speeches,[99] were never bothered. To be sure, many people covered up for each other, thereby avoiding dragging others into the morass. Hubert Lanyon shielded Cyril Wakely, the only civilian carrier in Sark allowed into the harbour. He stated that he had received the news through the postal service, when, in fact, it was Wakely who brought him the news-sheet, hidden among merchandise arriving from Guernsey by boat.[100] A particularly lucky escape was that of Henrietta Gillingham, the wife of Joseph Gillingham and sister of Ernest Legg. During their interrogations Legg and Gillingham managed to hide the fact that it was she who had taken down the news from the radio in longhand.[101]

The other thing that emerges, of course, is that once the German police understood that this was a grassroots effort, and not a sophisticated secret intelligence operation (*Nachrichtenzentrale*), they contented themselves with making an example of the key protagonists. John Crossley Hayes, an elementary school teacher from Manchester who had arrived in Guernsey during the Phoney War, stated that the German police were overwhelmed by the Sisyphean task of preventing the civilian population from gaining access to British news. Like so many others in Guernsey jail in 1944, Hayes had been apprehended for possession of a wireless and was sentenced to six months. Hayes later wrote a memoir in which he explained that he never discussed the news with anyone; somehow he also knew that he hadn't been denounced. He later found out that his name had slipped out, possibly inadvertently, during the interrogation of a third person (whom he does not name).[102] One of the more surprising things he says is that the way he – a wireless listener who did not spread the news – was treated by the German police indicated that they would have preferred to have let him off the hook, but that this was impossible.[103] They realized only too well that 'in hundreds of German billets all over the Island [sic], including their own, Guernseymen and Guernseywomen employed there as domestic helps had constant access to wireless sets and with only a little circumspection could have listened-in daily.'[104] German policing was clearly more interested in the suppliers and disseminators of news-sheets than in the consumers. Individual listeners who kept the news to themselves were considered relatively harmless, although their fate could, of course, be tragic.

Falla described his time in Guernsey prison as having been occupied with digging slit trenches, sweeping roads, peeling potatoes and podding peas for the German army. Duquemin shared his cell with Hayes, working with him in the garden of GFP headquarters, overseen by Einert, and in the garden of the vicarage of St James's, where they prepared the ground for growing potatoes. Duquemin was a professional grower who discoursed on the techniques of horticulture. In later years Hayes would try to emulate his practical skills, but without ever being able to match his digging expertise.[105] The GUNS trial eventually took place on 26 April 1944. The sentences handed down reflected Machon's status as the 'ringleader' (he received the longest sentence), the material evidence the German investigators had uncovered during the searches, and whether any attempts at dissemination could be proven.[106] Machon was dispatched to Rheinbach prison in May 1944, and from there to Hameln on 16 September 1944. He died a month later, on 26 October 1944.[107] The other GUNS men followed on 4 June, but were sent to the prison of Frankfurt-Preungesheim, where they arrived three days later. On their arrival they found a dozen other Channel Islanders languishing there, a large majority of whom had been sentenced for wireless offences. Prisoners were frequently assigned to work-parties clearing rubble or removing unexploded bombs from the devastated streets of Frankfurt. Falla himself was detailed to work on an air raid shelter for prison staff. Meanwhile, no air-raid shelters existed for prisoners and the frequent air bombardments on Frankfurt sent waves of terror through the prisoners who were confined to their crowded cells.[108] One of the earliest casualties in the group of Channel Islands prisoners was Percy Miller, a retired detective sergeant from Guernsey. He had been sentenced to 15 months for a wireless offence in July 1943.[109] When he was caught in the attempt to pass a note to another prisoner, he was confined to the punishment cell and put on bread and water for two weeks. Already starving at this point, this proved too much. Norman Dexter, another Guernsey prisoner at Preungesheim, later stated that he could hear him 'raving for several days' from his cell,[110] before he died on 16 July 1944.[111]

In early July 1944 the GUNS men were transferred to Naumburg prison with seven Jersey prisoners, none of whom survived the war.[112] The high death toll was attributable to the lack of sanitation and heating, physical maltreatment and starvation diet, consisting, in the main, of a few ounces of bread, watery vegetable soup and pig potatoes cooked in their jackets.[113] In Naumburg the GUNS men worked in a shed where they made wooden clogs, but where they were often surrounded by prisoners who welcomed death as a relief from 'the desperate struggle to survive'. As they made it into 1945, the question that haunted the survivors was 'who will be next'. Having seen so many die around them, it was doubtful whether any of the prisoners would still be alive when the Allies finally arrived.[114] In a draft newspaper article Falla later wrote that the only thing keeping him and Legg alive in those last days was the grapevine news of the Allied advance. Their hopes were rekindled when the overcrowded prison was overwhelmed by an influx of hundreds of concentration camp prisoners. From this Falla assumed that freedom was within their grasp. He also wrote that 'after seeing some of the walking skeletons sent out from these camps [...] I was lucky to survive'.[115] Falla appreciated this all the more, as fate could have easily caught up with him in the last two days before Liberation. On 12 April the guards asked for 50 men to come forward, for *Arbeit*, on the promise of extra food, and Falla and Legg were among them. The consolation of seeing the open sky for the first time in ten months was to be short-lived, however, for the group was sent to what once had been a synthetic oil plant, near Krumpa. On arrival, four men were delegated to each crater, dealt picks and shovels, and told to dig out unexploded bombs. Falla would later describe the experience as having been 'no fun [...] one just didn't know how deep the lethal object lay, a misplaced hit with a pickaxe or over-enthusiastic dig with a spade might spell the end'. A Frenchman on Falla's team was causing particular concern, as he was 'losing his cool and becoming a bit reckless, to the point where even the German guard told him to be more careful'. Although the men hardly had any 'strength left in their frames', and 'the promised extra food never materialised', they somehow got through the gruelling experience alive.[116]

When Falla was finally liberated on 14 April 1945, he weighed a mere 8 stone, down 3 stone from a previous 11. This was not all, for doctors later also detected a spot on one lung and a cloud on the other, the result of pneumonia contracted in prison, and for which he had been denied all medical assistance. Falla was advised to move to Switzerland by his Guernsey doctor, but this was not feasible as he had to support his widowed mother. All he could do was to avoid activities that put a strain on his lung. He also gave up his job as editor and became a freelance journalist, as this afforded him more time in the fresh air. Ernest Legg was in even worse shape on Liberation. He had developed a life-threatening case of dropsy and had buckets of water drained from his body.[117] He had also sustained a permanent injury to his leg, the result of a fall down a flight of stairs, deliberately provoked by the overseer of the clog workshop at Naumburg. In his 1964 application for compensation he stated that his leg had shortened by one inch, that he had developed a 'bad limp' and that he was in continuous pain.[118] Both men returned to Guernsey in summer 1945, but as the title of one of the last chapters in Falla's book makes clear ('Home – to disillusionment'), the joy of being reunited with their loved ones was short-lived. Falla was particularly gutted when he realized that neither the islands authorities nor the British government had any intention of seeking retribution against the 'disloyal two per cent' of collaborators whom he held responsible for his predicament and that of his fellow prisoners. This disillusionment later became the lifeblood of his later efforts to champion the cause of Channel Islands political prisoners.

Of the other two GUNS men sent to Naumburg, Cecil Duquemin survived. He was singled out in October 1944 and taken to an armaments factory, about 30 kilometres from Naumburg and not far from the Leuna synthetic oil plant, where he had to make shell cases. In December 1944 the factory was destroyed by Allied bombing and he was then taken to Halle prison, where one guard introduced him to the workings of the prison guillotine. After an interlude in another labour camp, the inmates were then taken on a railroad journey to Sudetenland and moved around aimlessly, to elude the advancing Allied armies. In a place that he named as 'Lesny', Duquemin and nine other prisoners were ordered to a cemetery, given spades and picks, and told to inter 42 bodies, ostensibly forced labourers or concentration camp prisoners, taken from a heap of bodies in the vicinity. They were then put back on the train, but when rumours spread that Hitler was dead, Duquemin and some other men took their chances and jumped from the open carriage, making their way to a nearby village. The next day Duquemin was liberated by Russian troops. After some serious altercations with an erratic Russian soldiery, he finally made his way back home.[119]

Joseph Gillingham, who had received the shortest term of all the GUNS men, was less lucky. Like Cohu, he was taken from prison by the Gestapo, exactly three weeks before the end of his term, on 2 February 1945, and swallowed by the fog of war. Henrietta Gillingham's attempts to trace her husband appear in a first letter to the Red Cross dated 12 June 1945. The search for him ended in 1947, when the Red Cross received an inconclusive letter from the police administration in Naumburg, now in the Soviet zone of occupation, and his search file was marked 'no further action – unsolved'.[120] He was officially declared dead some years after the war, but the location of his final burial place has remained elusive to this day.[121]

The three Channel Islands prisoners who were not dispatched to Naumburg in July 1944 – Norman Dexter, Walter Lainé and Gerald Domaille – survived, but otherwise their experience only varied to a degree.[122] Dexter and Lainé had been convicted in 1943 for wireless offences; Domaille in 1944 for a rationing offence. At Preungesheim, they worked for 11 hours a day, on nuts and bolts used for the construction and repair of tanks, but, despite the often inhuman treatment, they survived. Lainé completed his sentence in October 1944, but was then taken to the police prison in Frankfurt. Dexter remained in Preungesheim until March 1945, and was then taken with several thousands of prisoners on what he called an 'indescribable journey' in open trucks, which later continued on foot. On one occasion the prisoners were taken to a disused military training facility and made to kneel down facing the wall, ready to be shot, with SS parading in the centre, but that '(l)uckily [...] the order to fire never came'. He reached Straubing, in Bavaria, in April, where he stayed for two weeks. In Straubing, Lainé, who was on the same forced march, witnessed a line-up of 4800 prisoners in the prison yard. From among these the worst cases of illness and weakness were being selected and marched away. One of these 'wretched-looking' prisoners was Sidney Ashcroft, another Guernseyman, convicted for 'serious theft and resistance to officials' in 1942, and with whom Lainé had obviously been in touch at some point during his detention. It was the last he was to see of him, for

Ashcroft died in Straubing on 15 May 1945. The prisoners still able to lift a foot were then supposed to continue on to Dachau, and during this forced march Dexter was reunited with Lainé and Domaille. As he was to write later, this provided a modicum of 'moral and […] physical support'. Eventually the three survivors broke away from the column and spent the night in a barn. The next day, 30 April 1945, they were liberated by American forces.[123]

An assessment

A comparison between GUNS and GASP is *de rigueur*. Why did the fate of two groups of people engaged in the same illegal activity differ so much? The first reason why GASP was never unravelled is that it resembled a subscription newspaper, with a restricted readership and therefore less risk. GASP also enjoyed better protection,[124] for a member of the island police force, Inspector Banneville, tipped off Betrand in case of danger.[125] When GASP's first base, the bicycle shop, was being talked about too much as the place to get the 'real news', he told Bertrand to 'go easy'. Banneville also provided tipped-offs about German plans to raid particular districts. An interesting point is that these raids often followed broadcasts which were particularly popular with islanders: Churchill's speeches, the Editors' reports and anything which bore a connection to the Channel Islands. A second factor was Bertrand's camouflage. This was one of the craftier things in his approach, as he operated his wireless in a garden shed located right under the noses of a German anti-aircraft battery HQ. Finally, luck was also of the essence.

GUNS, it seems, had neither luck nor a reliable guardian angel. More than anything, however, the GUNS story demonstrates the vital importance of security precautions. How trusting many islanders still were, as late as 1943, emerges in the Reverend Ord's comments on 'loose talk' at a Guernsey shop: 'We have evidently failed after two-and-a-half years of living among spies and sneaks to acquire the technique of self-adjustment to such amenities.'[126] Charles Machon did not follow the established security protocol. As Frank Falla writes, he was 'over-confident', conserving material at his home that provided incontrovertible evidence of his activities.[127] The thought that he might one day be apprehended obviously never crossed his mind. At the trial the Germans were able to produce past issues of GUNS four inches high,[128] some the result of the search of Machon's house, the remainder supplied by the graces of Peter Doyle. Which brings us to the next issue: why share the news with a man such as Doyle, whose reputation was not sound? Frank Falla thought that denouncers were generally 'unscrupulous types who, to spite a relative or neighbour whom they knew had retained their radio-set, would inform anonymously either the local police or the *Feldgendarmerie*'.[129] Falla's motif, 'to spite a neighbour' was certainly not inaccurate, but neither does it tell the whole story. Peter Doyle had no personal motif. In the German files he appears as a *V-Mann* (paid informer), and one may ask how he got into this position. One could of course point towards his nationality. This was a popular theme in the post-war Channel Islands, where much of the popular ire concerning collaboration was directed against the Irish. Frank Falla himself thought the Germans had taken a particular liking to the members of neutral states, and that they were particularly willing recruits to their cause. But does his nationality or the lure of money explain his actions?

We do not know exactly when Doyle started out as an informer, but we do know that he had, previously, worked in German employ in another capacity. According to a pass, dated 30 December 1941 and confiscated by the *Feldgendarmerie*, who caught him out after curfew on 23 August 1943, he had worked for the German military administration in Alderney since 21 April 1941. It is safe to assume that this activity continued well into 1942. Doyle's job in Alderney was to supervise food deliveries to the island and the pass described him as 'absolutely reliable'.[130] Considering that a significant proportion of the food delivered to Alderney was misappropriated, it is only a short step to surmise that Doyle could have learnt the 'tricks of the trade' during his time there. The 1943 brush with the *Feldgendarmerie*, and the blackmail potential this entailed, probably spelt the beginning of his association with German law enforcement. In any case, by the time of the dismantling of GUNS, Doyle was involved in black market business[131] and in other activities requiring him to be out after curfew, a verdict borne out by two records against him lodged in the Guernsey Greffe.[132] Doyle was a particular type of black market operator, one who facilitated his illegal trading by signalling to the German police other matters that could be of interest to them. The practice itself is well-documented for occupied France and other countries. The Doyle case was not an exception, for the files also reveal the case of another informer swopping facilities in illegal slaughtering (and protection against prosecution by the island authorities) for information on radio listeners.[133]

How many other cases such as these could there have been? Of the sources leading to the apprehension of wireless offenders documented in the Freiburg (Ost Spezial) files[134] (mostly from the 1944–5 siege period), only a few were anonymous, but the majority tell a different story. A second set of files, a British analysis of German police records in Jersey, conducted in 1945, point in a similar direction.

The pattern that emerges for police methods in Jersey in the latter part of the Occupation is that 44 per cent of wireless arrests were the result of 'V person' activity, confidential or reliable sources, whereas 35 per cent were the result of tips-offs received

Table 3.1 Analysis of German police files, wireless cases, July 1945[135]

Date range: Late 1943 to 1945
Provenience: Jersey; GFP (Secret Field Police), Harbour police, *Feldgendarmerie*
Total number of cases: 140 (of which wireless offences: 43)

Source leading to arrests of wireless offenders	GFP	Harbour police	Feldgendarmerie
Military and Navy personnel	1	1	13
V person, confidential or reliable source	17	2	
Snap house search	2	1	
Anonymous letter	1		1
Loose talk		1	
Witness interrogation	1		
No information available	1	1	
TOTAL	23	6	14

from soldiers and sailors. Tip-offs from German military personnel and tip-offs from local and foreign civilians then were the principal weapon to hunt down radio offenders in Jersey. A further breakdown reveals the division of labour, principally between the GFP and the *Feldgendarmerie* (the executive arm of the *Feldkommandantur*): the GFP specialized in 'V person' activity, confidential or reliable sources (74 per cent of GFP cases relied on this method); the *Feldgendarmerie* specialized in tip-offs by military and navy personnel (93 per cent of *Feldgendarmerie* cases relied on this method).

An extraction of the Freiburg files revealed 23 radio offence cases (out of a total of 60 case files relating to offences against the occupying authorities in the Channel Islands), all from 1944, the majority post-dating D-Day, all (except one) relating to Guernsey, and concerning 32 individual offenders.[136] The first thing one notices in these files is the absence of the *Feldgendarmerie* from the process in Guernsey, as most of the investigations are initiated by a GFP intervention. Radio offences in Guernsey therefore were in the exclusive domain of the GFP. In the more militarized environment of Guernsey, the GFP, who were directly subordinate to the military (and not to the *Feldkommandantur*), would have been at an advantage in terms of honing their skills and establishing a division of labour with the *Feldgendarmerie*. This is what the Peter Doyle case suggests: Doyle is first apprehended by the *Feldgendarmerie* for a minor offence, and then passed on to and recruited by the GFP.

Table 3.2 German court files: Radio offences in Guernsey, 1944[137]

(Note: The analysis has been broken down according to sources leading to the arrest of wireless offenders).

Table 3.2.1 Source leading to arrest: German Military

Case number	Case opened	Location	Particulars	Type of radio found
V4714	12/1944	Guernsey	1–583	Detector
V4717	10/1944	Guernsey	319 ID intelligence officer	Detector
V4716	8/1944	Guernsey	3–584	Apparatus
V4706	8/1944	Guernsey	1–583	Apparatus
E2402	8/1944	Guernsey	1–583	Detector
V4718	6/1944	Guernsey	2–583	Apparatus

Table 3.2.2 Source leading to arrest: House search

Case number	Case opened	Location	Particulars	Type of radio found
V4713	12/1944	Guernsey	Related to other matter	Detector
V4708	12/1944	Guernsey	Ditto	Detector
V4705	12/1944	Guernsey	Ditto	Apparatus
V4719	11/1944	Guernsey	Related to other matter (black market)	Detector
V4791	8/1944	Guernsey	No information	Detector
V4707	6/1944	Guernsey	Related to other matter (burglary by military personnel)	Apparatus

Table 3.2.3 Source leading to arrest: Anonymous letter[138]

Case number	Case opened	Location	Particulars	Type of radio found
E2403	9/1944	Guernsey	Unknown	Detector
V1635	8/1944	Guernsey	ditto	Apparatus
V4702	6/1944	Guernsey	ditto	Apparatus
V4703	2/1944	Guernsey	ditto	Apparatus
E2404	2/1944	Guernsey	ditto	Apparatus

Table 3.2.4 Source leading to arrest: Confidential source

Case number	Case opened	Location	Particulars	Type of radio found
V4715	12/1944	Guernsey	A woman living in St Sampson's always has latest BBC news, probably from milk-man	Detector
V4721	10/1944	Guernsey	GFP notified on nightly gatherings of young people in King's Road, in St Peter Port, ostensibly to share out news; area then searched for radios.	Detector
V4701	7/1944	Guernsey	Unknown	Apparatus
V4459	2/1944	Guernsey	V person	Apparatus

Table 3.2.5 Source leading to arrest: Other

Case number	Case opened	Location	Particulars	Type of radio found
V4709	10/1944	Guernsey	Loose talk	Apparatus (previously destroyed)
V2366	3/1944	Sark	Witness statement in other enquiry	None

What conclusions can be drawn from these tables? First of all the GFP in Guernsey seems to have been even more methodical than their counterparts in Jersey. The rubrics demonstrate that they had a good understanding of the type of clues not directly related to wirelesses ('other matters'), but which could lead to the apprehension of wireless offenders. Secondly, almost half of the radios discovered at this later stage of the Occupation were radio detectors ('crystal sets'). These sets became the standard after D-Day, once radio signals from liberated France could be picked up at ease. Relatively easy to dissimulate, the discovery of crystal sets was often the result of carelessness. In one of the Freiburg cases soldiers passing by a house in a remote area of Guernsey, and peeking in through the window, perceived a man wearing headphones, whom they immediately reported to the GFP. The battalion to which these soldiers belonged (1st Battalion/583rd Grenadier Regiment) was particularly active in initiating house searches and tracking down radio offenders. In general, the files convey that German commanders were particularly irritable after D-Day, when illegal news about the Allied advance through France started to trickle through to the troops. Some commanders felt that official efforts to curb radio listening among the well-informed islanders were not sufficient and took things into their own hands.

Crystal sets

Provided one respected basic security precautions, operating a crystal set was safer than the alternative, which required keeping a bulky wireless set out of the sight of curious neighbours or passers-by. Frank Falla talked of crystal set manufacture as a thriving cottage industry, which included repair services.[139] Apart from earphones, taken from public telephone boxes across the islands, 'so that the crystal-set owner could twiddle his "whiskers" and hear the news', the other components needed were an aerial, crystals and wiring.[140] One of the many workshops catering to the demand in Guernsey was run by one Harry Capper, in an underground depot located in a house, the upstairs premises of which were being used by the *Feldgendarmerie* – perfect camouflage. His 'technical assistant' was a Norman Body, who installed crystal sets in many an islander's home.[141] Jerseyman George Sty also became an adept of crystal sets after a brush with German law enforcement and a short sojourn in Jersey prison, following his apprehension as a member of a regular 'listening party', in 1943. After his release he built a dozen sets for himself and others, using brass-beds as aerials.[142] Another noted crystal set manufacturer was the Jesuit padre Charles Rey, a seismologist of international renown who worked at the Highlands observatory, in Jersey. Born in Senegal in 1897, Rey had studied at the Jesuit seminary Maison Saint Louis in Jersey from 1917 and had returned there after some years in Madagascar as a missionary and scientific observer. Rey was one of the few padres to have remained in occupied Jersey, in order to safeguard the valuable 200,000-volume library at Maison Saint Louis. This was all the more necessary as part of the establishment was requisitioned by the Germans as a training college and could have become subject to pilfering. Naturally, as Rey was a Jesuit, the Germans would have had a dossier on him. He was burgled once by German soldiers and had a brush with the GFP who quizzed him over his African crystal collection, but things seem to have rested there. The reason for this was that Rey was running the only meteorological station in the island. Ironically, he was therefore allowed to retain his radio set after the June 1942 confiscation, as this was required to pick up the time signals sent by stations all over the world on special wave bands. Not that Rey would have used this set to listen to the British radio, as he had learnt how to build and dissimulate crystal sets through special dedicated programmes on the BBC. Rey put these skills to a wider use, supplying people across the island with crystal sets built to specifications. Some people wanted them built in the back of their watches, others in tins or in matchboxes, and again others in their telephone.[143]

Conclusions

Although no statistical records exist permitting to get to grips with the total number of islanders who retained their sets or operated crystal sets, everything points in the direction that radio resistance was, on aggregate, the most widely practiced type of resistance. About 19,000 radio sets were confiscated in June 1942, a figure that corresponds to about one-third of the population of the Channel Islands during the Occupation, or, very roughly, one radio per household. Nothing is known about the diffusion rate of radio apparatuses in the islands; but assuming that a minority of islanders were too poor to possess a radio set, that some had only one, but that an at least equally large number of households had multiple sets, it is fair to assume that a substantial number of households would have retained a set. This is exactly what French artists Suzanne Malherbe and Lucille Schwob did in Jersey: they handed in two sets in June, and retained one, which had never been registered, until their arrest in 1944.[144] It is these 'spares' that nourish the anecdotal evidence and the testimonies of Falla,[145] Ord, Crossley Hayes and other diarists and memorialists. As a result of the continued operation of these 'spares', the news was fairly abundant throughout the Occupation; and, in any case, it never 'dried up'. Towards the end of the Occupation, by which time crystal sets had become the norm, the availability of Allied war news grew into a torrent. Even in the holy of holies of Germans repression in Jersey, the prison, the news could not be kept from the inmates. At the time of their trial, in November 1944, Malherbe and Schwob were perfectly aware of the military situation on the Western front (a knowledge they used in their defence), despite having been imprisoned for three months.[146] On Liberation, radio sets are reputed to have appeared on the window sills of every third house in Jersey,[147] a ratio that is confirmed by other anecdotal evidence.[148]

The number of people arrested and imprisoned for such offences stands at 242 (out of 1309),[149] i.e. 18.5 per cent of the total number of offences committed against the occupying authority in the Channel Islands (see above). Among the group of islanders who died in camps and prisons on the Continent the percentage of radio resisters was even larger (34.5 per cent).[150] Despite many similarities, two noticeable differences emerge between Jersey and Guernsey: proportionately more people were convicted for radio offences in Jersey than in Guernsey (21 per cent vs 14 per cent). As there is no evidence to suggest that the German police in Guernsey was any laxer on the issue of pursuing radio offenders than their Jersey counterparts, the difference was most likely due to the actual discovery of larger numbers of radio apparatuses in Jersey. On the other hand, news-sheeting was apparently more developed in Guernsey than in Jersey. What this suggests is that, compared to Jersey, less people in Guernsey retained radios, perhaps because of the hard official line against resistance; but also that the resulting shortfall in demand for information was met by underground newsletters such as GASP and GUNS, of which there was no equivalent in Jersey.

Finally, if a very significant number of islanders were partaking in this activity, couldn't it be assumed to have involved relatively less risk? And how could it be that this very common act of defiance, regarded with a degree of sympathy and even covert complicity by some Germans, was responsible for the highest death toll among deported Channel Islands offenders? This core paradox in the Nazi prosecution of radio crimes, between terror and deterrence, on the one hand, and leniency, on the other, was noted by Michael Hensle, in his doctoral thesis. Referring to the prosecution of radio crimes in Germany, Hensle concluded that this was not an arbitrary or linear process, but that criteria applied which explained variations within the process of prosecution. The intensity of prosecution depended on chronology (particular periods or phases witnessed heightened activity), on the directives of the Berlin Gestapo Headquarters, on local initiatives or interpretations, or on whether offenders belonged to specific racial or political groups (e.g. Jews, Communists, Christian activists or foreign labourers).[151] Similar criteria also apply to radio resistance in the Channel Islands. The most important of these is the red line between listening and spreading the news. Six out of the ten Channel Islands radio offenders who died in captivity had committed the offence of spreading the news; the remaining four were listeners or communal listeners whose cases were aggravated by other circumstances.[152] It is this difference that accounts for the discrepancy between the lower proportion of radio offences in the overall statistics of offences and the higher proportion of radio offenders in the group of deported Channel Islands offenders who died in prisons and concentration camps. Secondly, the German occupying authority was interested in keeping in check antagonistic aspirations among the population, nurtured through the radio, and to maintain its narrative of a frictionless occupation. Although the islands were small, they were not insignificant. Any deterioration in the relationship between islanders and Germans had the potential to backfire on the Germans, in terms of prestige, propaganda and diplomacy. The prosecution of radio offences was ideally suited to strengthening social control, precisely because they were so ubiquitous. The need to maintain momentum and initiate periodic campaigns of intimidation became even stronger once the stakes had been raised in June 1942. Thereafter continued reception of British radio news was a political statement, in fact, the embodiment of the relative superiority of British radio news over German propaganda, and a slap in the face which the occupier could not possibly tolerate.

Notes

1   V. V. Cortvriend, *Isolated Island. A History and Personal Reminiscences of the German Occupation of the Island of Guernsey, June 1940–May 1945*, Guernsey, Guernsey Star and Gazette, 1945, pp. 124, 147.
2   JAS.L/C/144. Diary of The Reverend Douglas Ord 1940–1945, entry of 9 October 1942.
3   Paul Sanders, *The British Channel Islands under German Occupation 1940–1945*, Jersey, Jersey Heritage Trust, 2005, pp. 185–9.
4   TNA.HO.45/24756. Report of Professor Karl Heinz Pfeffer on research visit to the Channel Islands, from 10 to 25 September 1941, n.d.
5   JAS.D/Z/H5/97. Duret Aubin to Constable of St Helier, 28 November 1940; Duret Aubin to Constable of St Helier, 7 July 1941.
6   Michael Hensle, *Rundfunkverbrechen. Das Hören von 'Feindsendern' im Nationalsozialismus*, Berlin, Metropol, 2003, pp. 60–3.
7   BA-MA.RW.35/537. Reception of enemy broadcasts, 319th I.D. to FK 515, 30 May 1942.
8   Victor Carey voiced his 'great disappointment' in a letter to the Feldkommandant (8 June 1942), particularly as 'the local authorities have always endeavoured to act strictly in accordance with the rules laid down by the Hague Convention', JAS. B.A.W30/94. Papers relating to the order to surrender wireless sets, 1942-3.

9   Ibid.
10 William Bell, *I Beg to Report. Policing in Guernsey during the German Occupation*, Guernsey, Guernsey Press, 1995, p. 194.
11 Francis Falla, *The Silent War. The Inside Story of the Channel Islands under the Nazi Jackboot*, Guernsey, Guernsey Press, 1967, p. 97; for the relative facility of access to wireless news see JAS.L/C/144. Diary of the Reverend Ord, entries of 21 August 1942; 4 September to 8 September 1943; 29 December 1943.
12 Paul Sanders, *The Ultimate Sacrifice. The Jersey Islanders who died in German Prisons and Concentration Camps during the Occupation 1940–1945*, Jersey, 2004, pp. 108–12.
13 BA-MA.RW.49/97. Abwehr Command France (F/IIIc), Channel Islands – Commitment of labour resources, Protective security measures 1942–1944. Note on meeting of 6–7 May 1942; suggestions of Foreign Section/Abwehr, III, 11 May 1942; the other entities present at the 6–7 May meeting were Abwehr Command France, High Command of the 15th Army, Army Group D and the military governor in France.
14 IA. Falla papers, Statement by William Symes, Guernsey, October 1964; ITS. Doc. Nr. 7228068, Buchenwald registry records, William Symes, 1944.
15 Madeleine Bunting, *The Model Occupation: The Channel Islands under German Rule, 1940–1945*, London, HarperCollins, 1996, pp. 210–12; ITS. Doc. No. 6001784, Buchenwald registry records, Häftlingspersonalkarte, Stanley Green, 1944.
16 Richard Overy, *Why the Allies Won*, London, Pimlico, 1996, p. 298.
17 Sanders, *The Ultimate Sacrifice*, pp. 104–21.
18 JAS.L/C/144. Diary of The Reverend Douglas Ord, entry of 4 March 1942.
19 JAS.L/C/144. Diary of The Reverend Douglas Ord, entry of 9 October 1942.
20 TNA.HO.144/22834. Report MI19/1742, 'Channel Islands Guernsey, Interrogation of Two Channel Islands Escapees', 1943.
21 JAS.L/C/144. Diary of The Reverend Douglas Ord, entry of 24 August 1942; passim.
22 TNA.HO.144/22834. Report MI19/1742, 'Channel Islands Guernsey, Interrogation of Two Channel Islands Escapees', 1943.
23 IWM.Documents.13409.Dening 9. Document signed W, Einert re. 'Confiscation of Wireless Sets', 20 May 1945.
24 The data for the graphs was collated through an exploitation of the following two sources: JAS.D/Z/H6. Sentences and prosecutions by the Field Command and Troop Courts in Jersey; Guernsey Police records, German convictions of civilians, 2 vols., 1940–1945.
25 In the course of his research the author came across only one acquittal, BA-MA.I/10/Ost Spezial/V4718. Verfahren gegen Gosselin, Hannis und Burgess, Guernsey.
26 There was only one female, as opposed to 63 male radio offenders in Guernsey.
27 Respectively 178 of 857 and 64 of 447.
28 JAS.D/Z/H5/208. W. Gladden, Glencairn, St Martin, Jersey to Bailiff Coutanche, 9 June 1942.
29 BA-MA.RW.35/537. Reception of enemy broadcasts, Chief of administrative zone A of the military government in France, concerning the confiscation of radio sets in the Channel Islands, 7 November 1942.
30 Jerseyman Bob Le Sueur stated that the Germans took a very dim view on escaping and the smuggling of military intelligence, but that wireless retention was considered a less serious offence. German technicians at the power station commented the flickering of the consumption dial at the time of the nine o'clock news with comments

such as: 'There are your friends listening to Mister Churchill', Interview between author and Bob Le Sueur, 30 June 1997.
31 JAS.L/C/144. Diary of The Reverend Douglas Ord, passim.
32 Sanders, *The Ultimate Sacrifice*, pp. 28-30.
33 Falla, *The Silent War*, pp. 124-5.
34 Alex Glendinning, 'Canon Clifford John Cohu: A Victim of the Occupation – Part One', *Sunday Island Times*, 27 February 1994.
35 The other people who received prison sentences in connection with the St Saviour's wireless case were: Marguerite Alexander, Alfred Henry Coutanche, Harold Alexander Leneghan, Maud Alice Bathe, Arthur William Downer, Donald Journeaux, his wife Irene, Agnes Maria Sarah Newland (Mrs Journeaux's mother), Frederick John Nicolle (John Nicolle's father), Mabel Rubina Nicolle (John Nicolle's wife), John Whitley Starck, Arthur Stanley Wakeham, Edward John Gideon Mourant, Thomas Philip Mourant, see JAS.D/Z/H6. Sentences and prosecutions by the Field Command and Troop Courts in Jersey; Journeaux, Donald, *Raise the White Flag – A Life in Occupied Jersey*, Leatherhead, Ashford, Buchan and Enright), 1995, p. 66.
36 Alex Glendinning, 'Canon Clifford John Cohu: A Victim of the Occupation – Part Two', *Sunday Island Times*, 6 March 1994; that the German police considered clergymen a prime target can be inferred from the case of the Methodist Reverend Mylne whose family was 'framed' in early 1943, as they were receiving news, JAS.L/C/20/D/9. 'Under the Crooked Cross, Jersey 1940-1945: German Justice', by the Reverend Mylne, post-war.
37 Sanders, *The Ultimate Sacrifice*, pp. 21-5.
38 JAS.D/Z/H6. Sentences and prosecutions by the Field Command and Troop Courts in Jersey; Journeaux, *Raise the White Flag*, pp. 46-71.
39 JAS.L/C/24/A/5. Joe Mière Collection, List of political prisoners in the Channel Islands 1940-1945.
40 JAS.B/A/W85/5. War Graves of Civilians in Enemy or Enemy Occupied Territory, post-war.
41 Sanders, *The Ultimate Sacrifice*, p. 25.
42 List provided by the French Ministry of Veterans and War Victims, 31 July 1997 (in possession of author).
43 Interview between author and George Sty, 1 November 1997.
44 JAS.D/Z/H6. Law Officer's Department, Sentences and convictions by German courts.
45 List provided by the French Ministry of Veterans and Victims of War, 31 July 1997.
46 Ibid.
47 According to a letter written by Mr Verbene Amart to Ruby Nicolle after the war and cited by J. H. L'Amy in his unpublished occupation memoirs. The German Occupation of Jersey (in custody of the Société Jersiaise); ITS.Digitales Archiv. Hinweiskarte aus der Zentralen Namenkarte, John Whitley Nicolle, n.d.
48 BA-R.22/RMJ/1341. Army Notification Bulletins 1944, 10th edition, 18 May 1944.
49 BA-R.22/RMJ/1342 (Microfilms). OKW Memo re. transfer of Belgians and French to German penitentiaries, 13 May 1942.
50 BA-R.22/RMJ/1341. Army Notification Bulletins 1944, 10th edition, execution of sentences in the area of the military governor in France, 18 May 1944.
51 BA-R.22/RMJ/1341. Military government in France, Sec. Ib (Kommandostab)-Group 3, Order concerning the execution of sentences, 21 October 1943.

52 Sentences over two years were executed at Bochum prison, BA-R.22/RMJ/1341. Army Notification Bulletins 1944, 10th edition, 18 May 1944.
53 Falla, *The Silent War*, p. 114.
54 IA. Frank Falla papers, Statement by Frank Falla, Guernsey, October 1964.
55 Falla, *The Silent War*, p. 122.
56 JAS.B/A/L15/6. Enquiries for relatives, letter of Mrs Cohu to Lt-Col. J. W. Taylor, British Military Authority, Military HQ, Jersey, 18 May 1945.
57 Clifford Cohu, Joseph Tierney, Clifford Querée, Frederick Page, Emile Paisnel, William Marsh, George Fox, Frank Falla, Cecil Duquemin, Joseph Gillingham, Ernest Legg.
58 State Archives Hesse, Wiesbaden.Preungesheim prison records.Reference 409.4.File 2. Letter of Chief Prosecutor in Frankfurt to the Prosecutor at Frankfurt District Court, re. Order of the Reich Ministry of Justice of 8 October 1943, 4 January 1944.
59 ITS.Digitales Archiv. Hinweiskarten aus der Zentralen Namenkartei, Cecil Duquemin, Frank Falla, Joseph Gillingham, Ernest Legg, n.d.
60 On 11 October 1944 Tierney sent a plea for clemency to the court of FK 515, State Archives Hesse, Wiesbaden.Preungesheim prison records.Reference 461.18894.2.
61 Ibid., reference 461.18894.1.
62 TNA.FO.950/766. 'Index to names of British subjects in enemy concentration camps and statistical survey of camps', 1965.
63 For an account of Cohu's seven days at Zöschen, see Przemysl Polacek's letter to the British Embassy in Prague, 25 October 1945, TNA.WO.311/105. G. C. Allchin, Foreign Office, to Treasury Solicitor's Office, 27 March 1946.
64 IA. Falla papers, loose notes, n.d.
65 After the war a letter from a Belgian prisoner, René Vandenterghen, told Eileen, Tierney's wife, of the circumstances of her husband's death, see J. H. L'Amy, The German Occupation of Jersey, unpublished memoirs (in custody of Société Jersiaise).
66 Betrand's agents were: Deputy Inspector Banneville (police); his doctor, W. B. Fox; Charles Taylor, who also made his crystal set; Matron Finch, Sr Clayton and Sr Marquand for the Emergency Hospital; William Nant, George Wingate, Claude Trachy, Mr H. S. Snell, for St Peter Port; Fred Wellington for St Stephen's District; Mr H. R. Bichard for Vale; Mr E. Pill for St Martin's; Mr E. Bisson for St Peter Port; Mr W. Blatchford for St Peter Port; Mr J. Le Garff and Mr A. Bonathan for Vale and St Sampson's; Mr Frank Le Vallée for St John's; Mr P. W. Warley for the Post Office; Mr A. L. J. Bertrand for the Foreign Workers and PoWs; Mr A. V. Dorey for St Sampson's. Betrand also thanked the Fruit Export Co Ltd, T. Robin & Co Ltd and the GUB for their loyalty.
67 After Liberation Carey voiced his deep appreciation of the risk GASP had run and that he looked forward 'most eagerly' to the Editors Weekly Survey, see L. E. Bertrand, *A Record of the Work of the Guernsey Active Secret Press 1940-1945*, published by the Guernsey Star & Gazette Company, 1945.
68 Ibid.
69 Falla, *The Silent War*, p. 98.
70 Ibid., pp. 98–9.
71 IA. Frank Falla papers, loose notes, n.d.
72 IWM.Documents.13409.Dening 9. Force 135, I(b), 'GFP in Guernsey', 20 May 1945.
73 Ibid.
74 BA-MA.I/10/Ost Spezial/V4459. Untersuchungsakten in der Strafsache gegen Charles Machon, Cecil Duquemin, Ernest Legg, Joseph Gillingham, Francis Falla, George Collivet, Bericht vom 29. März 1944.

75 Falla, *The Silent War*, pp. 101–2.
76 IA. Frank Falla papers, Statement by Frank Falla, Guernsey, October 1964.
77 IA. Frank Falla papers, loose notes, n.d.
78 Legg on 8 March, Gillingham on 31 March.
79 In Gillingham's case the questioning amounted to filling in dates as to when he had supplied news to Machon, IA. Frank Falla papers, Statement by Henrietta Gillingham, Guernsey, October 1964.
80 BA-MA.I/10/Ost Spezial/V4459. Untersuchungsakten in der Strafsache gegen Charles Machon, Cecil Duquemin, Ernest Legg, Joseph Gillingham, Francis Falla, George Collivet, passim.
81 IA. Frank Falla papers, Statement by Henrietta Gillingham, Guernsey, October 1964. The boat was delayed by heavy fog and eventually left 24 hours later.
82 Falla, *The Silent War*, p. 104.
83 Ibid., pp. 98–9.
84 Ibid., p. 100.
85 IA. Frank Falla papers, loose notes, n.d.
86 Ibid.
87 IA. Frank Falla papers, Statement by Henrietta Gillingham, Guernsey, October 1964.
88 IA. Falla papers, Statement by Ernest Legg, Guernsey, October 1964.
89 IA. Frank Falla papers, Statement by Henrietta Gillingham, Guernsey, October 1964.
90 BA-MA.I/10/Ost Spezial/V4459. Untersuchungsakten in der Strafsache gegen Charles Machon, Cecil Duquemin, Ernest Legg, Joseph Gillingham, Francis Falla, George Collivet, Vernehmung Joseph Gillingham, 31 March 1944.
91 Bell, *I Beg to Report*, p. 257.
92 Falla, *The Silent War*, p. 100. Falla's private papers contain the phrase 'I supplied copy for 280 issues before giving up', IA. Frank Falla papers, loose notes, n.d.
93 IA. Frank Falla papers, loose notes, n.d.
94 Ibid.
95 BA-MA.I/10/Ost Spezial/V2366, Untersuchungsakten in der Strafsache gegen Hubert Lanyon, Sark wegen Verbreitung deutschfeindlicher Nachrichten, Vernehmung Lanyon, 11 April 1944.
96 According to Mavis Lemon, the daughter of Cyril Wakely, Lanyon circulated the news among his closest friends, but did not make it common knowledge, telephone interview between author and Mavis Lemon, July 2010.
97 BA-MA.I/10/Ost Spezial/V2366. Untersuchungsakten in der Strafsache gegen Hubert Lanyon, Sark wegen Verbreitung deutschfeindlicher Nachrichten, 1944.
98 The names mentioned in a 1945 newspaper article and in Frank Falla's papers are Hubert Lanyon, Rex Cowley, Edward Lihou (proof reader at the *Star*), L. C. Castel (also of the *Star*), F. N. Robin, S. Piquet, Gerald Hamon and a Mr McAuliffe, IA. Frank Falla papers, loose notes, n.d.; 'Man who gave his life for news. G.U.N.S. operator, betrayed, died in Germany', *The Star*, 17 May 1945.
99 Falla, *The Silent War*, p. 99.
100 BA-MA.I/10/Ost Spezial/V2366. Untersuchungsakten in der Strafsache gegen Hubert Henry Lanyon, Sark wegen Verbreitung deutschfeindlicher Nachrichten, Vernehmung Lanyon, 11 April 44.
101 Falla, *The Silent War*, p. 107.
102 John Crossley Hayes (1910–2003), A Sojourn in Guernsey, p. 1, http://www.johncrossleyhayes.co.uk/writings/A_Sojourn_in_Guernsey.php, accessed 14 July 2013.

103 Ibid., p. 68.
104 The graveness of the discovery of a radio in Hayes's house was diminished by the fact that one of the rooms in his own school was used as an official repair-shop for German wireless sets, that it was staffed by local technicians and that Hayes could have easily gained access, if he had wanted; the investigating officers were aware of this, John Crossley Hayes, *A Sojourn in Guernsey*, p. 69.
105 Ibid., pp. 49–50; 69.
106 BA-MA.I/10/Ost Spezial/V4459. Untersuchungsakten in der Strafsache gegen Charles Machon, Cecil Duquemin, Ernest Legg, Joseph Gillingham, Francis Falla, George Collivet, passim.
107 ITS. Digitales Archiv. Hinweiskarte aus der Zentralen Namenkarte, Charles Machon, n.d.
108 Ibid., p. 29.
109 IA. Frank Falla papers. Statement Eveline Le Maitre, Guernsey, October 1964; Guernsey Police records, German convictions of civilians, Vol. 1, 1940–1943, entry no. 188 (Percy Miller).
110 IA. Frank Falla papers, Statement by Norman Dexter, Guernsey, October 1964.
111 IA. Frank Falla papers, Statement Eveline Le Maitre, Guernsey, October 1964; ITS. Digitales Archiv. Hinweiskarte aus der Zentralen Namenkartei, Percy Miller, n.d.
112 Emil Paisnel, convicted of a property offence, on 29 August 1944; Frederick Page on 5 January 1945; George Fox, convicted of a property offence, on 11 March 1945; Clifford Querée, convicted of a property offence, on 1 May 1945. Clifford Cohu, Joseph Tierney and William Marsh perished after their discharge from Naumburg: Cohu on 20 September 1944, Marsh on 12 March 1945 and Tierney in April 1945; Sanders, *The Ultimate Sacrifice*, pp. 38–42.
113 Falla, *The Silent War*, pp. 122–3.
114 IA. Falla papers, loose notes, n.d.
115 IA. Falla papers, Draft article, 'The moment I'll never forget …', by Frank Falla, for inclusion in *The Daily Sketch*, February 1964.
116 Ibid.
117 Falla, *The Silent War*, pp. 134–5.
118 IA. Falla papers, Statement by Ernest Legg, Guernsey, October 1964.
119 Handwritten outline of the experiences of Cecil Duquemin, n.d. (in the possession of Gordon Duquemin); IA. Falla papers, Statement by Cecil Oliver Duquemin, Guernsey, October 1964.
120 ITS. Digitales Archiv. Hinweiskarte aus der Zentralen Namenkartei, Joseph Gillingham, n.d.
121 IA. Frank Falla papers, Statement by Henrietta Gillingham, Guernsey, October 1964.
122 IA. Frank Falla papers, Statement by Frank Falla, Guernsey, October 1964.
123 IA. Frank Falla papers, Statement by Norman Dexter, Guernsey, October 1964 ; Statement by Walter Lainé, Guernsey, October 1964 ; Letter Walter Lainé to War Office, 23 October 1945; ITS. Digitales Archiv. Hinweiskarte aus der Zentralen Namenkarte, Sidney Ashcroft, n.d.
124 That a helping hand was sometimes held over offenders can also be documented by another case, involving three Guernsey vegetable farmers. The case was launched in June 1944 on the initiative of three German soldiers who caught a civilian in the act of listening to a wireless, in a shed, and who signalled their discovery to the German police. The civilian was then charged, with two other civilians who

were not present at the scene. The case clearly pointed to a listening party, as other civilians had escaped the scene on the arrival of the three German soldiers. Two of the defendants received a six-month sentence, to be served in Guernsey prison. Oddly enough, the sentence was counter-signed by Major-General von Schmettow, the highest military authority in the Channel Islands, on 21 June 1944. The third defendant was acquitted on the grounds that the only person he had shared the news with was his wife. In addition, the two convicted men were promptly released in November, when they asked for a remission, BA-MA.I/10/Ost Spezial/V4718. Verfahren gegen Gosselin, Hannis und Burgess, Guernsey, wegen Nichtablieferung von Rundfunkgeräten und Verbreitung deutschfeindlicher Nachrichten, June 1944.

125 William Bell, *Guernsey Occupied but Never Conquered*, Exeter, The Studio Publishing Services, 2002, p. 273.
126 JAS.L/C/144. Diary of the Reverend Ord, entry of 3 January 1943.
127 Falla, *The Silent War*, p. 102.
128 IA. Falla papers, loose notes, n.d.
129 Falla, *The Silent War*, p. 97.
130 IA.FK 11–07. Inselkommandant Alderney, pass provided to Peter Doyle, 30 December 1941.
131 Falla, *The Silent War*, p. 143.
132 Guernsey Greffe, entry of 25 February 1944, concerning Doyle's infringement of the pricing and licensing regulation on 10 February 1944, at a second-hand clothes shop he rented in Saint Peter Port; entry of 17 March 1944, concerning the breaking of the curfew on 16 March 1944.
133 IWM.Documents.13409.Dening 9. Intelligence report on collaboration and occupation, Guernsey, 20 May 1945.
134 BA-MA.I/10/Ost Spezial. Wehrmachtsgerichtsbarkeit, Verfahren gegen Landeseinwohner in den besetzten Gebieten, 1944–45. These files are what remain of German judicial procedures against inhabitants in the occupied territories, including the Channel Islands.
135 D/Z/H9/2. Civil Affairs Unit: Analysis of the case files of the three German Courts; the Geheimefeldpolizei, Hafenüberwachungsstelle and Feldgendarmerie, 10 July 1945.
136 These German files cover 50 per cent of all individuals arrested in connection with radio offences in Guernsey and Sark (32 of 64).
137 Based on an extraction of BA-MA.I/10/Ost Spezial. Wehrmachtsgerichtsbarkeit, Verfahren gegen Landeseinwohner in den besetzten Gebieten, 1944–45.
138 Many of those targeted by denunciations were actually in German employ.
139 Ibid.
140 Falla, *The Silent War*, p. 97.
141 'Man who gave his life for news. G.U.N.S. operator, betrayed, died in Germany', The Star, 17 May 1945.
142 Interview between author and George Sty, 1 November 1997.
143 JAS.R05/B/1. Interview with Father Rey, n.d.
144 Claude Cahun, *Écrits*, ed. François Leperlier, Paris, Jean-Michel Place, 2002, p. 701.
145 Falla, *The Silent War*, p. 97.
146 Sanders, *The British Channel Islands under German Occupation*, p. 122.
147 Interview between author and Bob Le Sueur, 30 June 1997.
148 Interview between author and George Sty, 1 November 1997.
149 178 (of 856) in Jersey and 64 (of 453) in Guernsey.

150 10 out of 29: Clifford Cohu, Arthur Dimmery, Joseph Gillingham, Charles Machon, Percy Miller, John Whitley Nicolle, Frederick William Page, Clarence Claude Painter, Peter Edward Painter, Joseph Tierney.
151 Hensle, *Rundfunkverbrechen*, p. 97, passim.
152 Percy Miller, Frederick William Page, Clarence Claude Painter, Peter Edward Painter.

4

Humanitarian Resistance: Help to Jews and OT Workers

Louise Willmot

Writing to his wife just after the Liberation, Jersey's anti-Nazi activist Noel McKinstry acknowledged that the Germans had been, 'relatively to other places, very kind to us'.[1] His judgement has since been shared by historians of the Occupation. In pursuit of the policy of 'correct relations', the occupiers adopted a cautious and pragmatic approach to their administration of the Channel Islands which had major benefits for the inhabitants: the Germans avoided imposing the death penalty on British offenders between 1940 and 1945, for example, and the Gestapo never gained a foothold in the islands.[2] The troops themselves were also considered, in most cases, to have behaved well. Even before 1945, descriptions of their conduct as 'correct', 'well behaved', and sometimes even gentlemanly, were common.[3] There were, however, significant exceptions to this general account of civilized behaviour. Two specific groups, the islands' Jewish residents and the thousands of *Organisation Todt* (OT) workers imported to construct the German fortifications, were subjected to persecution and ill-treatment based on the Nazis' racialized assessments of their human value. This chapter examines the response of the islands' inhabitants to these policies and assesses the attempts made by local people to aid the victims. The number of Channel Island helpers was considerably greater than was once supposed, and among them were people whose courage bears comparison with that of rescuers anywhere in occupied Europe.

Islanders' responses to the persecution of the Jews

When the Occupation began, most Jewish residents had already left for the mainland.[4] Those who remained were subjected to the same discriminatory legislation as Jews elsewhere. The First Order Relating to Measures against the Jews in October 1940 required all inhabitants with more than two Jewish grandparents to register themselves as Jewish, a definition which was extended the following year to cover half-Jews. Subsequent Orders required the identification of 'Jewish Undertakings' and their sale to non-Jews, banned Jews from almost all forms of economic activity and subjected them to special curfew. The Eighth Order, registered in Guernsey although not in Jersey in June 1942, would have required Jews to wear the Yellow Star had it been enforced.[5] Under the terms of the First Order, 12 Jews in Jersey and 4 in Guernsey had registered; another, Marianne Grunfeld, did not do so but was later added to the Guernsey list. Their fate has been uncovered largely by the efforts of the Jersey historian, Freddie Cohen. Three foreign-born Jewish women – Grunfeld, Therese Steiner and Auguste Spitz – were deported from Guernsey to France in April 1942, and then dispatched in July to their deaths in Auschwitz. In addition, five Jews with British citizenship were sent to internment camps in Germany in February 1943 along with army officers, political offenders and other 'undesirables'.[6] The five survived the war not because of any action on their behalf by the island authorities, but because they had British passports and were probably regarded as suitable candidates for an exchange.[7] Had the Germans chosen to include them in the 'Final Solution', they would have perished.

The island governments offered little opposition to the anti-Jewish measures even though these were presented to Jersey's Superior Council and Guernsey's Controlling Committee for their assent. The first seven Orders were registered in the Royal Courts in both islands. In Guernsey the only protest was from Jurat Sir Abraham Lainé, who refused to approve the registration of the First Order in a stand that was later recognized by Ambrose Sherwill to have been courageous and correct.[8] Lainé's objection was not repeated, leading the historian David Fraser to question the value of a single act of defiance 'followed by years of silence, acquiescence and approbation in the face of increasing evil'.[9] It is worth pointing out, however, that his protests against various German measures earned him a reputation as the least acquiescent member of the Controlling Committee.[10] In the last months of the Occupation, it was also Lainé who provided official materials for an escape party taking documents to England about conditions in the island.[11]

The only other official protest against the anti-Jewish measures came in Jersey in June 1942, when Alexander Coutanche and his Attorney General Duret Aubin went to the Chief Administrator of Feldkommandantur 515, Dr Casper, and objected to the Eighth Order requiring Jews to wear the Yellow Star. Sanders suggests that Coutanche and Aubin acted both on moral principle and in the conviction that the measure would reflect badly on the Council when it was already being criticized for compliance with other German demands.[12] In any event, the measure was not registered in Jersey and was registered but not enforced in Guernsey, and the Jews in the Channel Islands never wore the Yellow Star. This example of successful and courageous opposition inevitably raises uncomfortable questions about the failure of the island authorities to object to the other Orders or to the deportations of Jews. In 2000 they were bitterly criticized by David Fraser, who claimed that the authorities not only failed to resist persecution, but actually collaborated 'wholeheartedly' with the Germans. Their conduct, he argued, was explained by three factors: first, a 'gross and immoral utilitarian calculation' that it was worth sacrificing a few Jews to gain credit that could later be used to defend the rest of the population; second, a blind respect for legal process even when this was directed towards immoral ends; and third, 'an indigenous and widespread anti-Semitism' that made them regard Jewish lives and property as simply less important.[13]

Tellingly, Fraser contrasted the abandonment of the Jews with the efforts made by island officials to defend the interests of Freemasonry.[14]

The assessment of Paul Sanders and Freddie Cohen is less harsh. Although criticizing the failure of the island authorities to oppose the Orders and the over-zealous application of the regulations by the Jersey Aliens Officer, they doubt that this conduct was a direct result of anti-Semitism. For Sanders, the fate of the Jews was affected by their small numbers and, in most cases, relative lack of wealth and status.[15] Richer and more prominent Jews, he notes, did avoid the worst consequences of Nazi policies: for example, Marianne Blampied – wife of the celebrated artist Edmund Blampied – was not deported with other Jews in February 1943 even though she had registered as Jewish. Nevertheless, a deeply questionable 'utilitarian calculation' about numbers certainly played a part, encouraged by a careless assumption that virtually all the Jews had been evacuated in June 1940.[16]

We cannot know whether the other Orders would have been delayed or abandoned if others had followed Lainé's lead or Coutanche and Aubin had made their stand earlier. But even if the Germans had insisted on imposing them, the island governments could have chosen not to register the Orders in the Royal Courts. It was not just the Orders themselves, but their official seal of approval, that shocked critical observers.[17] Such a stand might also have prevented local officials – the Jersey Aliens Officer, the Guernsey Inspector of Police and their subordinates – from taking part in the registrations and the deportation of foreign-born Jewish women from Guernsey.[18]

Once the Orders requiring them to register were in place, Jewish residents had to decide whether to comply.[19] It was a dilemma that was faced by Jews across occupied Western Europe and was always problematic: individuals and families now had to weigh up the possibility of punishment for non-registration against the potential, and unknown, consequences of compliance. In Jersey, the deliberations of Ruby Still demonstrate the problem they faced. Mrs Still initially intended not to register – she was married to a Gentile and was not an observant Jew – but she feared she would be caught and punished, and registered in the hope that the Germans would take no further action.[20] She was interned in Germany with her husband in 1943, but survived the war. Avoiding registration did not always bring safety, since both Mary Erica Richardson in Jersey and Marianne Grunfeld in Guernsey were subsequently identified as Jewish anyway. Nevertheless, it offered the best chance for Jews to escape persecution, as the case of the Netherlands reveals: almost all the 140,000 Jews there were registered and 75 per cent were murdered, by far the highest mortality rate in Western Europe.[21] In the Channel Islands, the registration rate was lower: there were more than 30 Jews there during the Occupation, over twice the number who registered. In Jersey they included two London-born half-sisters who had married local men and lived as Methodists, as well as a Jewish carpenter who confided his identity to friends, while in Guernsey three sisters apparently survived the Occupation unharmed in the main town of St Peter Port.[22] Non-registration was an act of conscious defiance that can be regarded as a form of Jewish resistance.[23] It also depended on the tacit support of friends and neighbours, who knew the truth but kept silent.[24] In the Channel Islands such cooperation was generally forthcoming: Freddie Cohen has found only two cases of denunciation, a relatively small number compared with the rest of Nazi-dominated Europe.[25]

Jews with business interests in the islands faced losing their property under the terms of the Second Order of November 1940, which required law firms to declare which of the businesses they administered were owned by Jewish clients, and to inform the authorities if they even suspected clients to be Jewish. The aim was 'Aryanization' – forced sale of businesses to non-Jews – in a local version of the policy adopted elsewhere. On 18 December 1940 five 'Jewish Undertakings' were reported to the Bailiff, and several firms provided details of clients whom they believed might be Jews.[26] Three of the 'Jewish Undertakings' – Louis and Cie, Messrs Krichefski and Son and Madame Peretz – were owned by evacuated Jews and were earmarked for sale to non-Jews by their legal administrators.[27]

David Fraser has condemned as an 'abject moral failure' the decision of the law firms to provide information on Jewish firms and send details of clients who they merely suspected might be Jewish.[28] Yet this initial compliance did not mean that they were ready to cooperate in dispossessing their Jewish clients. The Jewish businesses marked for 'Aryanization' were handled by two firms, Le Cornu and Le Masurier, Giffard and Poch. As Fraser recognizes, these firms now protected the interests of their clients by arranging fake 'sales' which actually transferred the three businesses to their existing employees. The subterfuge depended on the cooperation of these non-Jewish workers: John Beaton of Krichefski's, Miss White of Peretz and Miss Hawkins of Louis and Cie, all of whom demonstrated a strong personal loyalty to their employers. In 1945 the businesses – or in one case its assets – were returned to their rightful owners.[29]

Although acknowledging that the Jersey lawyers had subverted Nazi intentions, Fraser suggests that their conduct was prompted by respect for property rights rather than a desire to protect the Jews.[30] It is a highly controversial assertion, and at least in the case of Advocate Harold Giffard the evidence suggests otherwise. A partner at Le Masurier, Giffard and Poch, Giffard had already served a two-month sentence in November 1940 for 'insulting' the Germans,[31] an incident that probably persuaded them to select him as a hostage in June 1942 after the distribution of the 'Bulletin No. 1 of the British Patriots'.[32] In the last months of the Occupation, he represented his clients Suzanne Malherbe and Lucy Schwob in their appeal against execution for inciting the troops to mutiny.[33] After the Liberation, Schwob – whose father was Jewish – acknowledged the help he had given them: as well as his kindness after their arrest, he had put himself at risk by smuggling documents into prison on their behalf.[34] 'Mr G', she wrote, was 'a loyalist lawyer' – and nothing in his treatment of her smacks remotely of anti-Semitism.[35]

Apart from the subterfuges of the law firms, only the intervention of private individuals could now help the registered Jews of the Channel Islands. But the number of Jews was so small that very few residents had Jewish friends or acquaintances; many thought that all the Jewish residents had evacuated in June 1940. Even the anti-Jewish Orders were thought to have a largely symbolic significance.[36] Outside the Controlling Committee and Superior Council, only one Channel Islander is known to have made a direct protest against them on grounds of principle. Shortly after the registration of the Third Order in June 1941, Major Marie Ozanne of the Salvation Army in Guernsey delivered a letter to German headquarters condemning the persecution of the Jews and reminding the Germans that Jesus, 'the only one by whom we can inherit eternal life and enter Heaven', was a Jew.[37] Direct protest of this kind was exceptionally rare everywhere in Europe, and in the Channel Islands Ozanne's case was unique.

The most vulnerable of the Channel Islands Jews were Marianne Grunfeld, Therese Steiner and August Spitz in Guernsey, all of whom were foreign-born and were left unprotected once the island authorities decided to cooperate with the Germans in implementing the Orders. Marianne Grunfeld had left her native Poland to study horticulture and had moved to Jersey to work for the farmer Edward Ogier, a former member of the States. When she received her deportation order, Ogier asked for a letter of introduction from John Leale, President of the Controlling Committee, and appealed on Grunfeld's behalf to the *Feldkommandantur*. To his 'rage and sorrow', the appeal was rejected and Grunfeld was deported to France in April 1942.[38] There was sympathy, too, for Steiner and Spitz, Austrian Jews who worked at the Emergency Hospital during the Occupation.[39] Their colleagues were shocked by the decision to deport them, and the minutes of the Hospital Committee recorded its regret at losing them, as their work had been 'of the highest order'.[40]

The response was characterized above all, however, by bewilderment and a sense of helplessness: a suitcase given for the journey, promises to keep possessions safe and company on the walk to the harbour.[41] Recalling a discussion with Steiner after she received her deportation order, the Methodist minister Douglas Ord observed that she had been afraid and that he had tried to comfort her, 'but what can one say or do?'[42] Once they had received notification of deportation, only the decision to go into hiding could have saved Grunfeld, Steiner and Spitz. In April 1942, however, this does not seem to have been considered, either by them or by their friends. This is hardly surprising, since when they left Guernsey the mass deportation of Jews from Western Europe had yet to begin. It was not until July, three months later, that the first major round-up of 'stateless' Jews took place in France. Steiner, Grunfeld and Spitz were all caught up in it.[43]

Later, however, there were two remarkable cases of rescue in the Channel Islands. The first and best-known was by Albert Bedane. Born in 1893, Bedane had been brought to Jersey from France as a baby and was a naturalized British citizen who had served in the Dorset and Hampshire Regiments during the First World War. A successful local athlete, by 1939 he had built up a thriving physiotherapy practice at his home in St Helier's Roseville Street.[44] Among Bedane's acquaintances was a 54-year Jewish woman, Mary Erica Richardson, who lived nearby with her invalid husband. Mrs Richardson, who was of Dutch origin, had done what she could to avoid identification as a Jew: she had not registered under the terms of the First Order and had given a false maiden on the form for her identity card. Nevertheless, on 25 June 1943, after her Jewish origins had been discovered, she was interviewed at the *Feldkommandantur* and told that she would be sent to a pleasant camp where she would 'be well looked after'.[45]

Mrs Richardson was taken home to collect her possessions, but her husband distracted the escort long enough for her to slip out of the house and make her way to the home of Albert Bedane (Figure 4.1).[46] He hid her for almost two years, first in the cellar and later in an upper room, until she returned home to care for her husband

Figure 4.1 Albert Bedane, who sheltered Mary Erica Richardson. Copyright and courtesy Jersey Heritage collections

at the end of the Occupation.[47] By then Bedane was in contact with Noel McKinstry and with the loose network that aided Soviet fugitives from the OT. He gave refuge to several of these men, giving them food provided by local farmers in payment for treatment at his clinic.[48] For two weeks in November 1944, he also treated and hid an escaped political prisoner, Francis Le Sueur. Later, contemplating why Bedane had taken the risk, Le Sueur confirmed that he was known to be 'very anti-Nazi in his views' and liable to respond to appeals for help.[49]

Bedane was remarkably modest about his activities. Once he had decided to defy the Germans, he said later, he thought he would 'rather be killed for a sheep than a lamb', though he admitted to having 'a few nightmares'.[50] This was an understatement: after the Liberation Bedane went to England to be treated for a stress-related illness brought on by his activities.[51] Although both Mrs Richardson and Francis Le Sueur acknowledged his help after the Liberation, it was not until 30 years after his death that Bedane's achievement was fully recognized. In 2000, thanks to the research of Freddie Cohen, Bedane was awarded Israel's highest Holocaust honour, Righteous among the Nations, by the commission of the Yad Vashem Holocaust Memorial in Jerusalem.[52]

The second rescue involved the young Rumanian national Hedwig Bercu, who had arrived in Jersey in November 1938 to work as a maid for a local family. After their evacuation in June 1940 she remained in Jersey, trapped by the terms of the Aliens Act, and worked as a typist for the transport section of the *Organization Todt* (OT).[53] According to her friend Robert Le Sueur, Bercu felt unable to refuse the job because she was vulnerable: she had been registered as Jewish under the terms of the First Order even though there were serious doubts about her heritage.[54] Remarkably, she was left alone by the Germans until autumn 1943, when she was implicated in the theft of petrol coupons at work. Having broken regulations by handing over dockets to local doctors, she was betrayed by a lorry driver who had demanded some for himself and then been caught.⁵⁵ Bercu had reason to fear that being registered as Jewish would now have serious consequences. On 22 November 1943 the Germans placed a notice in the *Evening* Post, complete with photograph, asking for information about her whereabouts and threatening punishment for anyone who helped her. The appeal, which promised to treat information with the 'strictest confidence', was an open invitation to denunciation.⁵⁶

Bercu, however, was already in hiding. On 4 November she had left a 'suicide note' and clothing on the beach at West Park and sought refuge with a friend, a Czechoslovakian housemaid named Bozena Kotyzova. Shortly afterwards she made her way to the home of Dorothea Weber in St Helier's West Park Avenue.⁵⁷ Mrs Weber, who was 30 years old in 1943, was born Dorothea Le Brocq but had married an Austrian-born baker before the war.⁵⁸ She was therefore technically a German citizen, and in 1942 the *Feldkommandantur* had ordered her to provide a certificate from the island authorities to confirm that she had no Jewish parents or grandparents. Since – like Bercu – Dorothea Weber was illegitimate, the authorities had not provided the necessary evidence.⁵⁹ The Germans did not pursue the matter further, but Mrs Weber had good reason to understand how vulnerable Bercu's registration as a Jew made her. She hid her friend at home for 18 months, until the Liberation: apart from occasional gifts of food brought by a German soldier who had befriended Bercu at work, they survived on Weber's rations and occasional night-time forays to the beach to scavenge for food.⁶⁰ Dorothea Weber was, according to Freddie Cohen, 'a real Jersey heroine':⁶¹ more than most, she knew the risks she faced, but still chose to shelter her friend.

Responses to the forced and slave labourers of the Organization Todt

There were so few Jews in the islands that relatively few Channel Islanders had personal contacts with them. Nevertheless, for some inhabitants the anti-Jewish legislation had a galvanizing effect. For the French artists Lucy Schwob and Suzanne Malherbe, it was another proof of Nazi cruelty and an incentive to wage their sustained campaign to persuade German soldiers to lay down their weapons.⁶² For some non-Jews, it was an early sign that the Occupation would be less benign than they had hoped, and that the local administration would be unable to protect vulnerable residents.⁶³ It took time for these sentiments to harden into a commitment to take direct action. When it did, the beneficiaries were not members of the tiny Jewish community, but workers for the OT who had been brought to the islands to build the fortifications.

The order to turn the Channel Islands into an 'impregnable fortress' came directly from Hitler in October 1941. Although he intended to turn St Peter Port into a U-boat base and develop the islands as a holiday destination for German workers, Hitler's immediate objective was to prevent the British from from re-taking the islands.⁶⁴ Despite the sensible reservations of his military commanders in the West, who considered it a waste of resources, work on the fortifications began almost immediately.⁶⁵ Over the following two years, the Germans constructed a series of strong-points, command posts and anti-tank walls along the islands' beaches and coasts. By December 1944, the Channel Islands were better defended than the nearby French coastline and had consumed almost ten per cent of the resources spent on the Atlantic Wall.[66] The hard labour on the fortifications was done by workers from the OT, the army of construction workers established by the engineer Fritz Todt.[67] No fewer than 16,000 of these men were brought to the Channel Islands: in late 1942 there were 6,700 in Guernsey, 5,500 in Jersey and 2,000 in Alderney along with their guards.[68] The numbers fell rapidly after April 1943, so that fewer than 3,000 workers were left in Guernsey towards the end of that year, for example, and under 500 by July 1944.[69]

Approximately 7,500 of the men in Jersey and Guernsey – about 60 per cent – were recruited in Western Europe. Although a few hundred of them were volunteers with proper OT contracts, most were forced labourers. They included a large contingent of Spanish Republicans – some 1,500 in Jersey and hundreds more in Guernsey – who had been interned in France and then handed over to the OT by the Vichy regime.[70] A similar fate befell over 1,000 North Africans, mainly unemployed Algerian dockworkers and smaller numbers of French-Algerian prisoners of war, most of whom were sent to Guernsey.[71] The remaining men from Western Europe – well over 4,000 in the two islands – were French, with smaller contingents from Belgium, the Netherlands and Luxembourg. Although officially designated as volunteers, they had been pressed into work by various means or simply rounded up off the streets. Their rations were rarely provided in full.[72]

The true slave labourers, however, were East European. At the height of the construction programme there were more than 4,000 of them in the islands, and in Jersey they dominated the OT workforce.[73] There were small numbers of Poles and Czechs, but most were from the Soviet Union and included Red Army prisoners-of-war as well as older men and boys from the Ukraine and Western Russia. Unlike the West Europeans, they were kept behind barbed wire in rudimentary camps, each housing several hundred workers; in Jersey there were 11, mainly in the north and west of the island. Until late 1943, thanks to widespread corruption and rake-offs in the OT supply chain, the East Europeans rarely received the rations to which they were entitled. They survived on a staple diet of turnip soup and bread, occasionally supplemented with meat, which was totally inadequate to sustain men working 12-hour days in quarries and on building sites. Thanks to the systematization of Nazi criteria of racial value within the OT, the East Europeans were by far the worst fed and worst treated of the workers.[74] Beatings for minor infringements of regulations were severe, and medical treatment was rudimentary at best.[75] No precise mortality figures are available, but it is likely that several hundred OT workers died as a result of ill-treatment, accidents and sickness – at least 108 in Guernsey and perhaps three times as many in Jersey.[76]

In Guernsey the first contingents of French OT workers in November 1941 were greeted with curiosity and sympathy. According to the diarist Peggy Brock:[77]

> Some are only 12–14 years old and they cry bitterly if anyone is kind to them … They burst into tears and say they wish they could let their parents know where they are. Some were whisked off as they were working in their gardens and others as they came out of a cinema and were not told where they were coming to. It is a ghastly affair.

Apart from makeshift camps at Les Vauxbelets and Saumarez Park,[78] OT workers in Guernsey were packed into houses that had been abandoned by evacuees or confiscated from their owners, especially in the Hauteville-Cornet Street district of St Peter Port.[79] In the early days their unfitness for hard physical labour and their obvious hunger aroused widespread pity.[80] During these weeks, spontaneous acts of kindness and gifts of food and clothing were, according to Douglas Ord, relatively common.[81]

Some of this sympathy was short-lived. The sufferings of OT workers in Guernsey were not always fully understood, since all but the small number of Russians were given days off and were supposed to receive pay and reasonable rations.[82] They were sometimes blamed for the squalid conditions in which they were forced to live, especially in St Peter Port, where toilets broke down and raw sewage spilled into the streets.[83] Revulsion was increasingly accompanied by fear. The conduct of older and tougher arrivals, including released convicts and unemployed dockworkers from the Mediterranean coast, aroused alarm and resentment.[84] It was fuelled by an upsurge in crime, often caused by OT workers who broke into houses looking for food and stole farmers' crops.[85] For the Guernsey police, the presence of OT workers was a law and order issue; much of their work in 1942 and 1943 involved investigating thefts and handing workers over to the OT for punishment.[86] Already in November 1941 K. M. Bachmann was noting of OT workers that 'our people are more afraid of them than of the Germans', and her anxiety was reflected in other contemporary accounts.[87] Diarists referred to the OT workers as 'beastly foreigners',[88] 'dreadful foreign labour people',[89] 'the scum of Europe',[90] and 'more repulsive' than the Germans.[91]

Even so, many Guernsey residents recognized that OT workers were desperate. In August 1942, after meeting a Spanish worker who came to the door to beg, Douglas Ord noted that it was 'the old story – forced to work or starve, irregular or inadequate pay, and only enough food to keep body and soul together'.[92] The diarist Adèle Lainé, whose family gave food to a young Dutchman in February 1942, reported that OT workers were fed only on soup and that 'even if they were well paid, there was nothing for them to buy'.[93] All transactions between OT workers and local farmers were forbidden: even potatoes were strictly rationed, their sale or exchange was forbidden and the police were under instructions to arrest OT workers who bartered for food.[94] The ban on helping OT workers was reinforced by *Feldkommandant* Knackfuss on 9 November 1942, when residents were forbidden to give food to OT workers 'on compassionate grounds' because – he claimed – they already had enough to eat.[95] Subsequently, local people who broke the regulations were liable to six weeks' imprisonment or a fine of £3,000.[96]

Fear of the OT workers, German prohibitions and food shortages all combined to limit the help offered in Guernsey.[97] Nevertheless, contemporary diaries as well as memoirs and post-war interviews provide plentiful evidence that hundreds gave food and clothing, at least occasionally, to OT workers they met.[98] Ord noted in January 1942 that 'local people have tried to help, as best they can, by giving such food and clothing as they might, and braving the threats of Knackfuss for so doing'.[99] Even islanders who feared OT workers could be moved to pity. Despite her own alarm at the 'rabble of humanity with which the island is now overrun', the young mother K. M. Bachmann still gave food to 'innocent victims of forced labour' – at least until so many turned up on the doorstep that she had to turn them away.[100] Her ambivalent response to the OT workers was not uncommon.[101]

Smaller numbers went out of their way to help more often. The nurse Beryl Ozanne later recalled that her uncle, a grower whose property bordered a camp, regularly put root vegetables under the hedge for the workers to find.[102] In some cases Guernsey residents forged genuine friendships with OT workers who were desperate to escape the cramped and insanitary conditions of OT houses or camps.[103] Marion Tostevin's parents, for example, befriended two French boys and regularly gave them food and a bed for the night, and the Ozannes, devout Quakers in Vale, gave hospitality and companionship to Dutch, Belgian and French OT workers for two years.[104] Occasionally the motive was financial rather than humanitarian, as in the case of one Guernseywoman who was fined for renting a room to an Algerian OT worker, but most OT workers lacked the money to pay for decent accommodation and relied on the generosity and decency of their helpers.[105] A few islanders took OT fugitives into their homes and hid them permanently, a decision that involved significant risk.[106] The case of the Mahy family of L'Islet, who befriended a French-Algerian and hid him in their home for 11 months despite food shortages and German searches, was rare but not unique.[107] On other occasions, too, sheltering involved months or even years of secrecy: Guillaume Trubuil, a Guernsey shoemaker, sheltered another OT worker for almost two years until his arrest,[108] while the French consul, Lambert, hid a fellow-countryman in his home for over than 12 months.[109] Douglas Ord, who had contacts throughout the island, reported several more cases in his diary, including one that was brought to an end by denunciation.[110]

Sheltering was never as extensive in Guernsey as it was to become in Jersey, at least in part because there were relatively few Russian slave labourers there. The West Europeans who made up the majority of the Guernsey workforce were often exhausted and hungry, but they were not penned behind barbed wire or beaten and starved like the East Europeans. With few exceptions, they coped by asking local people for food – and sometimes a bed for the night – and avoided serious punishment by returning to work next day. Only in the Vale district in the north-west of the island did residents witness systematic ill-treatment of OT workers on the same scale as in Jersey. Here, at the OT prison 'Paradis', beatings were frequent, occasionally fatal, and inflicted for the most minor offences.[111] People living nearby witnessed the attacks at first hand. One resident, Lilian Ogier Collas, confided her distress to Marie Ozanne, whose family in Vale had been befriending and feeding OT workers for several months.[112] Ozanne, who had already protested to the Germans about the closing of Salvation Army halls and the persecution of the Jews, now wrote to the *Feldkommandant* to demand better treatment of OT workers and an end to the Germans' 'reign of terror'.[113] Not even her arrest in September 1942 silenced her.[114] It is the only known case of direct protest against their treatment in Guernsey.

In Jersey, on the other hand, residents were confronted with the realities of brutal ill-treatment as soon as the first large contingents of Soviet OT workers arrived in St Helier in August 1942. Edward Le Quesne's account was typical:[115]

> A large number were mere boys of from fourteen to sixteen years old. Others were men of seventy and over and hardly any were men who looked anything like

soldiers. Few had boots or shoes, some had no coats ... All looked half-starved and were in the charge of fat-bellied OT guards armed with rubber truncheons and whips. These poor wretches were marched from Town to St Ouen and laggers were whipped and beaten by their guards. Women cried to see the pitiful sight ...

The shock to island opinion was profound.[116] Over the following months, it was common for residents – including children – to witness OT workers being beaten with fists, sticks or spades close to construction sites and on the roads leading to their camps.[117] Although some of the violence was the result of casual sadism, it was also inflicted systematically, on the orders of the OT *Bauleiter*, in order to force more work out of the Russians.[118] Bill Sarre, a farmer in St Lawrence, commented in 1945 that this treatment was 'so common that no particular incident stands out'.[119]

There were some early protests against the brutality. They included a spontaneous demonstration by customers at Brown's Café in St Brelades at the end of August 1942. According to Constance Brown, who ran the café with her mother, the regulars were used to seeing OT workers working on anti-tank defences there, and the Spanish Republicans were sometimes allowed to visit the café. The Russians, though, were never allowed to rest and were apparently starving. When her customers saw one of these men being beaten, they had shouted abuse at the guards and called on them to stop. The Germans took the incident seriously enough for *Feldkommandant* Knackfuss to visit the café next day and threaten to shut it down if the protests continued; in future, customers were forbidden to approach the sea wall or make contact with the Russians.[120] Whether the locals took the matter any further is not clear. Izett Croad reported that local residents had sent a petition of protest to the *Feldkommandantur* and were warned that the bay at St Brelade's would be closed if they persisted, but this may have been a garbled version of the Brown's Café incident.[121] At an official level the Medical Officer of Health, Noel McKinstry, protested to his German counterpart, while Alexander Coutanche attempted to raise the issue with the authorities. It is not likely that their appeals had any effect: though the condition of Soviet OT workers improved after the autumn of 1943, this was apparently triggered by reports from OT doctors after outbreaks of typhus in Guernsey.[122]

Just as in Guernsey, however, initial sympathy for the plight of OT workers was not always sustained. The Russians could not survive on their rations. Increasingly, they resorted to begging from house to house and then to theft, taking vegetables from allotments and gardens along their routes to work and breaking out of their camps at night to steal from farms, shops and houses. By December 1942 an epidemic of robberies, clustered around OT camps in the west, prompted Mary Deslandes to write of a 'reign of terror' in country districts.[123] Violent incidents, though infrequent, were not unknown.[124] In the worst of them, a well-liked 62-year-old shopkeeper in St Peter, Ernest Le Gresley, was stabbed to death and his sister badly beaten by OT workers during a robbery in November 1942, and two OT workers were killed by a local farmer in St Ouen on 23 March 1943.[125] After this incident, the Germans called on islanders to cooperate in handing these Russian 'allies of the English government' over to the authorities.[126]

Clumsy propaganda appeals of this kind had less effect than the German decision to punish residents who helped the Russians. On 21 September 1942, only a month after the arrival of the first large contingents, Jersey farmers were warned not to give or sell food to the Russians because it would only 'encourage' them, and on 9 November – as in Guernsey – residents were forbidden to give food on compassionate grounds.[127] Although the standard punishment was six weeks in prison, a harsh deterrent sentence had already been imposed on the Jersey dentist Edward Ross and his wife Annie ('Nan'), whose home was ransacked in September 1942 by members of the *Feldpolizei* accompanied by the local police.[128] Their crime had been to take food to OT camps and to feed workers at home,[129] although the searchers also discovered an illegal radio which was added to the charges. Edward and Nan Ross were sentenced to six months' imprisonment for 'consorting without authority with prisoners of war' and distributing radio news, and sent to France to serve their sentences.[130] They were then interned in the Vosges until their liberation by American troops in September 1944.[131]

Fear of punishment by the Germans, and alarm at thefts by the Russians, inevitably limited the extent of help by Jersey residents. Few, however, went as far as the St Brelades farmer who claimed in 1945 that he had never seen any Russians ill-treated and that they got better rations than he did.[132] Most blamed the Germans for the situation: diary accounts and post-war testimonies emphasize the OT workers' appalling plight, their cold and exhaustion and, especially, their desperate hunger.[133] Mary Deslandes noted in March 1943 that the thieves were undoubtedly a menace to the community, but 'those poor devils are starving'.[134] Pity led significant numbers to disobey German orders by handing over food. Such help was usually spontaneous and hurried – a bowl of soup or a plate of potatoes at the door, or apples thrown over a camp fence – and, in the words of 10-year-old Louisa Foott in 1945, done 'when the OT were not watching'.[135] Less frequently, acts of kindness were more calculated, as locals waited by the road to hand over warm clothes or bags of potatoes as work parties passed by.[136] After the Liberation, islanders did not exaggerate the significance of these gestures or glorify them as resistance, but described them as occasional acts of kindness; in this form, they occur with striking frequency in both wartime diaries and post-war accounts. According to the French artist Lucy Schwob in St Brelade's, the people there 'resisted on this point and it seemed that everyone, at least around us, gave when the opportunity presented itself'.[137]

More rarely, what began as spontaneous acts of kindness turned into a sustained campaign. When the Russians arrived, the owner of Midbay Stores in St Brelade's, Frank Hamon, supplemented their rations with tomatoes, apples and root vegetables from his store and allotment. Even after it became illegal he continued to do it, filling the Russians' sacks with food and with scraps of bread given by neighbours. Hamon managed to persuade the OT guards to 'turn a blind eye', and it was only when he gave food to two men who had escaped from their camp that he was arrested for 'helping the enemy'.[138] More typical was the case of the Le Ruez family in St Peter, who initially fed two OT workers in September 1942 when they came to lay railway track near their farm.[139] Within days, Russians had begun arriving at their door in large numbers to be fed on potatoes and root vegetables.[140] Despite a real fear of arrest, the family fed and befriended Russian workers for more than 12 months, dealing with occasional thefts of their crops by chasing the offenders away rather than reporting them to the Germans.[141]

Long-term sheltering by individuals and groups

By April 1943, Nan Le Ruez knew of several families who had begun to hide escaped Russians in their homes. It was, she thought, much more dangerous than simply feeding them, and those who did it 'risked their lives' to help.[142] She was right: at least in theory, the Order for the Protection of the Occupying Authority of 18 December 1942 stipulated the death penalty or imprisonment with hard labour for those who helped enemy nationals 'in their intention of concealing themselves from the German authorities'. In what was virtually a demand for denunciation, it also obliged members of the local administration to inform the Germans whenever their orders were disobeyed.[143] The call was reinforced by notices in the local newspaper urging islanders to report fugitives to the authorities, which inevitably meant betraying their helpers.[144] The local police, already charged with investigating thefts by OT workers, were ordered to assist in hunting down the men and arresting those who sheltered them.[145] In one such search conducted by the Germans, 'Basil Martin' – Wasily Lukitch – a young Russian who had been hiding in St Martin – was shot and killed.[146]

By January 1943, 25 fugitives were at large in Jersey.[147] One of them – George Koslov – knew of 17 in May 1945, and a month later the *Evening Post* reported the departure of 'about 30' to the Soviet Union.[148] They had been hidden in barns and farm outbuildings, spare rooms and attics in every island parish and in St Helier itself. Some were sheltered by a single household – Michael Jerovna by the Le Calvez family in St John, for example, and Mischa Ivanov by the Irelands in Trinity – helped only by a few friends and neighbours who supplied extra food and clothes.[149] The majority of the men, however, depended on extended chains of helpers to keep them safe. Perhaps the most helpful way of analysing these group rescues is to compare them with studies of the aid given to Jews in Nazi-occupied Europe, and especially with the emphasis by Gross on the importance of 'social and organizational networks, authoritative leadership and resources' in such rescues.[150] This comparison reveals that in the Channel Islands, the groups were much looser and less formal than Gross suggests. The only one even to resemble an organized network was run by Leslie Huelin and Norman Le Brocq of the Jersey Communist Party (JCP).[151] Supported by sympathizers unconnected with the party, this found homes for several Russians and supplied them with identity cards given by contacts in the town hall, complete with an official stamp and photograph, and with ration cards provided by an employee of the Food Office, Bernard Bree.[152] The network was completed by the Medical Officer of Health, Noel McKinstry, who took men to safe houses by car and ambulance, by Spanish Republican workers with access to the camps, and by an OT worker with good command of English, Mikhail Krokhin, who helped maintain contacts between them.[153]

Other collective rescues were even less structured and had no recognizable leaders. Typical of them was the group that protected Peter Botatenko, who survived for two years in hiding after his escape from St George's camp in St Ouen in May 1943. During this period he stayed in 11 different homes, moving on when his hosts were threatened by German searches or the activities of informers. During these crises his current hosts found him a new home by contacting friends and family on his behalf. Despite the lack of a formal aid structure, by May 1945 Botatenko had

Figure 4.2 Robert Le Sueur, a young Jerseyman who found safe houses for Russian fugitives. Copyright and courtesy Jersey Heritage collections

acquired an identity card, received medical treatment from a local doctor, Mortimer Evans, and been befriended by Noel McKinstry.[154] Similarly, the rescue of Fyodor Burriy was arranged without advance planning and in response to an emergency: the denunciation and arrest of Louisa Gould, in whose home in St Ouen he had lived for 18 months. Her insurance agent Robert Le Sueur (Figure 4.2), who had met Burriy during his business visits to the house, now hid Burriy in his office and the homes of acquaintances for several weeks, before arranging a permanent refuge with two conscientious objectors, Mike Frowd and René Franoux, in St Helier. Burriy stayed there for almost 18 months, supported by their friends and neighbours and given extra food by the man who had taken him in when he first escaped from camp, the tenant farmer René Le Mottée.[155]

Although these operations were informal, most developed some of the elements of an organized rescue: safe houses where fugitives could be sheltered in an emergency,[156] intermediaries who arranged places of refuge and took the Russians to their hosts;[157] ration cards and official identity cards belonging to sympathizers who then claimed to have 'lost' them, with photographs taken by A. J. Laurens of the firm Scotts.[158] According to William Gladden, his own group in St Martin also had a telephone warning system, enabling him to 'pass the word on' to helpers in nearby parishes when a German search was under way.[159]

By 1944 there were tenuous links between the different groups. The fugitives themselves exchanged information and began marking the houses of sympathetic islanders as a signal to others:[160] when Gwenda Sarre and Bill Sarre sheltered three Russians at their farm in St Lawrence, the last two had known before they arrived that they would find food and shelter there.[161] Another link between the groups was provided by two Russian-born sisters, Augusta Metcalfe and Claudia Dimitrieva, whose flat in St Helier became a permanent refuge for one Russian, and a regular meeting place and information exchange for others.[162] Moving between various sets of helpers, too, was Noel McKinstry, a widely trusted source of aid.

When fugitives stayed with their hosts for several months, genuine friendships developed.[163] According to Phyllis Le Breton, whose family sheltered Gavril Denisov, known as 'Tom':[164]

> In the evenings he would sit with me in the kitchen, learning English. He would say, 'What means this? What means that?' At night he slept in our old car in the garage which we locked up permanently, but there was a secret door. We trusted this man. He was the sort of man we could trust. The children loved him and when he could understand some English he used to read them fairy stories.

In the most moving of all tributes paid by fugitives to their helpers, Fyodor Burriy acknowledged that, during his stay with Louisa Gould, she had treated him 'like a son'.[165] In some cases, friendships made during the Occupation were maintained long afterwards. Of all rescues, long-term sheltering was the most dangerous because it greatly increased the chances of denunciation by neighbours or discovery in German searches. There were, Phyllis Le Breton acknowledged, 'a lot of close shaves'.[166]

Rescuers and fugitives tried to reduce the danger by maintaining secrecy and sharing information with as few people as possible. In the JCP network the tactic was effective: Norman Le Brocq, a main organizer, did not even know the identity of many of its supporters until the Liberation.[167] Failure to maintain secrecy, on the other hand, could lead to tragedy. By May 1944 Fyodor Burriy's presence in St Ouen was well-known in the community, and the consequences were catastrophic. Mrs Gould was betrayed by neighbours and arrested, along with her helpers, in May 1944. Found guilty of harbouring a fugitive and of radio offences, she was deported to the continent with her brother and her friend Berthe Pitolet.[168] By good fortune, the others – including her sister Ivy Forster (Figure 4.3), who had also sheltered a Russian – survived the war, but Louisa Gould perished in Ravensbrück women's concentration camp in February 1945.[169] For Robert Le Sueur, who had warned Mrs Gould of the risks she was running, discretion was one of the essential qualities he sought when searching for potential rescuers to ask for help.[170]

A few of the Channel Islands rescuers volunteered to help without being asked. Among them, was the St Martin Air-Raid Protection service warden William Gladden who contacted 'the local underground front, which dealt with the Russians' in 1944 to tell them that he and his wife were willing to shelter a fugitive.[171] He was an exception: most Channel Islands rescuers – like most rescuers of Jews in occupied Europe – began by responding to direct requests, either from intermediaries or from the fugitives who came to their door.[172] According to Norman Le Brocq, he had approached only people he regarded as patriotic and trustworthy, and he was proud that he had hardly ever been refused.[173] Robert Le Sueur's requests for help were also carefully considered: he contacted people he thought would be both sympathetic and discreet, but who also 'had room' at home.[174]

As Le Sueur recognized, potential rescuers needed the resources that enabled them to help, as well as a willingness to do so. Both motivational and situational factors

Figure 4.3 Ivy Forster, who sheltered a Russian fugitive, George Koslov, in the family home. Copyright and courtesy Jersey Heritage collections

thus played a vital role, just as they did in the rescue of Jews. In the densely populated Channel Islands, rescuers needed property with space – elsewhere, cellars or farms – where they could hide the Russians or, in the cases of Albert Bedane and Dorothea Weber, their Jewish acquaintances. As a result, they tended to be more settled – and older – than resisters who conducted minor sabotage operations or tried to escape.[175] Of more than 60 Jersey residents known to have sheltered fugitives, all but 6 were over 30 and most over 40. In 1944, for example, William Gladden and his wife Jane were in their sixties, Louisa Gould and Noel McKinstry in their fifties, Augusta Metcalfe, Claudia Dimitrieva, Albert Bedane and Edward George Osborne – a farmer who served a five-month sentence for harbouring a Russian in 1944[176] – in their forties, and Bill and Gwenda Sarre, Dorothea Weber and Ivy Forster in their thirties.[177]

Younger residents could not usually hide fugitives because they were still living at home with their parents. The conscientious objectors Mike Frowd and René Franoux, who shared a flat in St Helier, were among the few exceptions.[178] When younger Channel Islanders were involved in rescue, it was as intermediaries and organizers or, as in the case of Stella Perkins and Mike Le Cornu, through the activities of their own parents. Robert Le Sueur, who was in his early twenties when the OT workers arrived, later summarized his own situation: unable to offer shelter because there were other people as well as his parents in the house, he took on the task of asking acquaintances for help and guiding the fugitives between safe houses.[179] Apart from their age profile, however, rescuers had little else in common. They were as likely to be women as men – the only form of sustained resistance where this was the case[180] – and they came from a variety of social backgrounds. Albert Bedane ran a successful business, but Renée Le Mottée was a tenant farmer and Stanley Le Cornu a postman. What united them, apart from their resources, was a readiness to respond.

This willingness was rarely based on existing ties of friendship with the fugitives. Among European rescuers of Jews, it has been estimated that perhaps 40 per cent intervened on behalf of friends, neighbours or work colleagues, and this was also true of Albert Bedane and Dorothea Weber in Jersey.[181] The situation among those who sheltered OT workers in Jersey was very different. Apart from Louisa Gould, few had even met the fugitives before agreeing to take them in. Nor did they have a strong sense of cultural or national affinity with the OT workers, of the kind that played a part in many rescues of Jews elsewhere.[182] In the Channel Islands this was significant only in the cases of the French consul, Lambert, who sheltered a fellow countryman in Guernsey, and of the Russian-born sisters Augusta Metcalfe and Claudia Dimitrieva in Jersey.[183] Almost all the others gave refuge to strangers with whom they did not even share a language. In their case the motives for altruism are more complex.[184]

An important part in rescue activities was played by individuals and groups who were already involved in resistance: for them, as for many rescuers of Jews in Europe, hostility to the occupiers came first.[185] Among them were members of the JCP and other individuals who, though politically on the left, were not Communists: they included Noel McKinstry, whose hostility to Nazism was based on liberal principles,[186] moderate reformers such as Robert Le Sueur, a founder member of the Jersey Democratic Movement, and the French artists Lucy Schwob and Suzanne Malherbe, who had been anti-fascists in Paris during the 1930s and had been distributing illegal notes and leaflets since the early months of the Occupation.[187] Other helpers had patriotic rather than anti-Nazi motives. In St Martin, for example, they included Oscar Pallot and William Gladden, who had already been gathering intelligence to smuggle to the Allies. Gladden had considered it his 'duty as an Englishman' to oppose the Germans, and agreed to shelter a fugitive in 1944 as an act of patriotic defiance.[188] Similarly, René Le Mottée, who hid several OT workers on his farm, had already served a short prison sentence for taking railway sleepers from the OT track nearby.[189] He refused to shake hands with German soldiers who were at war with his country, and tucked a Union flag into his daughter's coat pocket to give her courage when she was questioned about an OT fugitive the family had been hiding.[190]

The majority of Channel Island helpers, however, had not been involved in resistance before. Some had even opposed it: in Jersey, Nan Le Ruez had criticized sabotage and illegal leafleting because of the danger of reprisals. 'It is no use going against the Germans', she wrote in June 1942, 'unless it is a question of conscience'.[191] Only three months later, she and her family were befriending and feeding Russian OT workers at their farm in St Peter. For people such as these, a variety of motives can be detected. For Le Ruez, as for the Le Bretons in Jersey and the Ozannes in Guernsey, compassion was underpinned by Christian conviction. When she heard that a local family had hidden a Russian and taught him English from *The Pilgrim's Progress* and the Bible, Le Ruez hoped that other fugitives would also be converted 'through the influence of those people who are risking their own lives for them'.[192] For other helpers, the impulse to action was personal rather than religious. In the case of Louisa Gould, the death of her son in action was the catalyst that made her want to protect 'another mother's son'.[193] For Austrian-born Maria Woodhall, who hid two Russians in the flat she shared with her husband above the German soldiers' home in the Mayfair Hotel, the reasons were both personal and political: her own father had been arrested by the Nazis after the *Anschluss* in March 1938.[194]

Motives for helping could be affected by social circumstances as well as political or religious attitudes. In the case of rescuers of Jews in Europe, Perry London and Nechama Tec have suggested that individuals who had experience of being excluded or marginalized were particularly likely to empathize with the plight of the persecuted.[195] Among the Channel Island helpers, this applied most obviously to those who had links with Jews: to Dorothea Weber, who had been unable to provide proof of 'Aryan' ancestry, to the half-Jewish Lucy Schwob and her partner Suzanne Malherbe, and to the Jersey artist Edmund Blampied, whose wife was Jewish. The conscientious objectors in the island, too, had been ostracized, though this time at the hands of the local community rather than the Germans.[196] Brought to the island in 1940 to work on local farms, about 90 of them remained after the evacuations that June and the deportations of September 1942. A few married local girls and 12 became Methodist lay preachers, but the group was not integrated into Jersey society, and its members were viewed as 'damn wasters' and 'Hitler's fifth columnists' by a significant proportion of the population.[197] First-hand experience of social ostracism may help to explain why several conscientious objectors helped OT workers. One of them, Fred Sowerbutts, was arrested and taken to the *Feldkommandantur*, where he explained that his faith had commanded him to feed the hungry and give refuge to the homeless. Instead of putting Sowerbutts on trial, his unknown interrogator imposed a small fine and sent him home. As his fellow conscientious objector Wilf Butterworth recalled, sometimes 'even the Germans responded decently to the example of moral courage'.[198]

The conscientious objectors, however, were an exception. Most helpers had no personal experience of persecution or social marginality and were fully integrated into Channel Island society. In their case, what Lawrence Baron has called 'the dynamics of decency' – the reasons why some residents risked their lives to help victims of persecution when others stood aside – remain mysterious, although rescuers appear to have possessed those crucial features of character and temperament that have been identified in rescuers of Jews: integrity, empathy and a sense of obligation towards individuals in distress.[199] In the Channel Islands, as everywhere in Nazi-dominated Europe, rescuers and long-term helpers were a small minority of the wartime population. Nevertheless, their numbers were far from negligible. In Jersey, where the plight of the Russians was urgent, the evidence indicates that over 100 people offered their homes as refuges or acted as intermediaries, and that several hundred more provided extra food, clothing and friendship to the fugitives.[200] In Guernsey the need was less and the numbers smaller, but here too there were several cases of long-term rescue. All of them took place in small communities that were traditionally wary of outsiders and where maintaining secrecy for prolonged periods was difficult.

In these conditions, the safety of fugitives and rescuers often depended on the willingness of local communities not to betray them. The Germans came to suspect that, in some Jersey parishes, a conspiracy of silence was operating. In August 1944, the *Platzkommandant*, Major Heider, wrote twice to the Bailiff to demand greater efforts from the local police and the parishes in tracking down escaped Russians and a local political prisoner, Bernard Turpin.²⁰¹ He reminded Coutanche that, under the terms of a notice issued in December 1942, he was entitled to impose collective punishments on parishes for concealing strangers; furthermore, he had already told the Constables as much in March 1944 'in the case of Basil Martin in St Martin'.²⁰² The implication was that people in the parish had known the whereabouts of 'Basil Martin' – the OT fugitive Wasily Lukitch – but had chosen to protect him. It was true: the Russian had felt safe enough to come out of hiding and watch matches played by the local football team. Heider was also right to suspect at least some of the police of being reluctant hunters; one of them, Bert Chardine, was among those who had helped Lukitch, and his parents had hidden another fugitive at their home in Gorey.²⁰³

When ordered to put notices about missing Russians in the *Evening Post*, the editor Arthur Harrison told the head of the civil affairs branch of the military administration, Baron von Aufsess, that islanders were likely to ignore appeals to hand over the fugitives because they knew how severely the men would be punished.²⁰⁴ The protective screen around Lukitch and other Russians suggests that Harrison was right, at least in the last 18 months of the Occupation.²⁰⁵ Even so, fugitives and their helpers always remained in danger of denunciation by informants. Of those mentioned in this chapter alone, Louisa Gould and Fred Sowerbutts were both arrested after being denounced, and Peter Botatenko was threatened with denunciation at least three times during his two years of freedom. Although there were relatively few informers – the decision to maintain silence was more much common than the impulse to betray – they inflicted damage out of all proportion to their numbers. The risk they posed was widely recognized, and it was increased by additional searches conducted by German troops or local police acting on their orders. The response of Albert Bedane and Dorothea Weber, of the Sarres in Jersey and the Mahys in Guernsey and of dozens of others like them, is all the more remarkable because of it.

Notes

1. SJ.GO Box 10/36. Letter from R. Noel McKinstry to Mrs Janet McKinstry, Oxford, 13 May 1945.
2. On the Germans' approach see Paul Sanders, *The British Channel Islands under German Occupation, 1940–1945*, Jersey, Jersey Heritage Trust and Société Jersiaise, 2005, pp. 186–9. At the end of the war a woman was sentenced to death for sheltering a deserter, but reprieved: Edward Le Quesne, *The Occupation of Jersey Day by Day. The Personal Diary of Deputy Edward Le Quesne*, with a foreword and explanatory notes by Michael Ginns, Jersey, La Haule, 1999, 23 April 1945, also p. 288 n. 24; JHT.1995/00045/1. Lucy Schwob (Claude Cahun), account of imprisonment, undated.
3. Of many contemporary comments see TNA.HO.144/22176. A. F. Butterworth, Boots the Chemist, Report of Business during the German Occupation to the end of 1944, Guernsey, 7 May 1945; PL.LF940.53 LAI. Adèle Lainé, 'The German Occupation of Guernsey, 1940–1945', p. 18; JAS.L/C/77/A/1. Izett Croad, Occupation Diary, 8 December 1939 ['correct']; 'Diary of Mary Deslandes', 3 September 1941, in Basil de Carteret, Mary Deslandes and Mary Robin, *Island Trilogy. Memories of Jersey and the Occupation by Mary Robin, Basil de Carteret and Mary Deslandes*, Jersey, Redberry

Press, undated, p. 39; Nan Le Ruez, *Jersey Occupation Diary: Her Story of the German Occupation, 1940–45*, Jersey, Seaflower Books, 1994, 14 January 1942; PL.LF940.53 BRO. Mrs Peggy Brock, The Second Diary of the Occupation, October 1940–January 1942, 13 July 1941 ['well behaved'].

4 Background information from Frederick Cohen, *The Jews in the Channel Islands during the German Occupation 1940–1945*, Jersey, Jersey Heritage Trust in association with the Institute of Contemporary History and Wiener Library, 2000, pp. 13–16.

5 Cohen, *The Jews in the Channel Islands during the German Occupation*, pp. 18–42; Sanders, *The British Channel Islands under German Occupation*, pp. 132–3; David Fraser, *The Jews of the Channel Islands and the Rule of Law, 1940–1945*, Brighton and Portland, Sussex Academic Press, 2000, pp. 2–88.

6 IA.FK 12–14. Transport lists for deportations to Lager Laufen and Compiégne. The five were Elda Brouard, Elisabet Duquemin, Ruby Still, John Max Finkelstein and Esther Pauline Lloyd.

7 See Sanders, *The British Channel Islands under German Occupation*, p. 133.

8 Ambrose Sherwill, *A Fair and Honest Book: The Memoirs of Sir Ambrose Sherwill*, Lulu.com, 2006, p. 233.

9 Fraser, *The Jews of the Channel Islands and the Rule of Law*, p. 105.

10 Peter King, *The Channel Islands War 1940–1945*, London, Robert Hale, 1991, p. 57, notes his complaints against reductions in food rations in May 1942, and against German agricultural demands in November 1941, p. 110.

11 IWM.Documents.5727 96/32/1. Dr Alastair Rose, Impressions of the Occupation of Guernsey, Written by Dr. Alastair Rose between 1944 & 1945.

12 Sanders, *The British Channel Islands under German Occupation*, pp. 132–3, n. 100.

13 Fraser, *The Jews of the Channel Islands and the Rule of Law*, p. 2.

14 Ibid., pp. 217–20.

15 Sanders, *The British Channel Islands under German Occupation*, p. 142.

16 For Coutanche's assumption, see ibid., p. 77. Also Sherwill, *A Fair and Honest Book*, p. 233.

17 For example interview with Robert Le Sueur, 27 June 2000; IWM.Sound Archive. Interview 10101. Norman Le Brocq, 1987.

18 Described by Fraser, *The Jews of the Channel Islands and the Rule of Law*, pp. 89–95.

19 Cohen, *The Jews in the Channel Islands during the German Occupation*, p. 19; Leslie Sinel, *The German Occupation of Jersey: The Wartime Diary of Leslie Sinel*, Jersey, Villette Publishing, 1995, 21 October 1940.

20 Described by her step-daughter Peggy Boléat, *A Quiet Place*, Jersey, Villette Publishing Ltd., 1993, p. 36.

21 Bob Moore, *Victims and Survivors: The Nazi Persecution of the Jews in the Netherlands*, London and New York, Arnold, 1997, pp. 64–6.

22 Cohen, *The Jews in the Channel Islands during the German Occupation*, p. 72; Sanders, *The British Channel Islands under German Occupation*, p. 133, n. 103.

23 On Jewish resistance, see for example James Glass, *Jewish Resistance during the Holocaust: Moral Uses of Violence and Will*, Basingstoke, Palgrave Macmillan, 2004.

24 See Martin Gilbert, *The Righteous: The Unsung Heroes of the Holocaust*, London, Black Swan, 2003, esp. pp. 493–4, the case of Lea Kalin.

25 Cohen, *The Jews in the Channel Islands during the German Occupation*, pp. 22, 83; also Sanders, *The British Channel Islands under German Occupation*, p. 137.

26 Fraser, *The Jews of the Channel Islands and the Rule of Law*, p. 9.

27 Cohen, *The Jews in the Channel Islands during the German Occupation*, pp. 24–6.

28 Fraser, *The Jews of the Channel Islands and the Rule of Law*, p. 4.
29 See Cohen, *The Jews in the Channel Islands during the German Occupation*, pp. 28–9, reporting Beaton's letter to the Krichefski family after the war and Advocate Le Cornu's praise for Miss Hawkins.
30 Fraser, *The Jews of the Channel Islands and the Rule of Law*, pp. 111–12.
31 JAS.D/Z/H6/1. Sentences and Prosecutions by the Field Command and Troop Courts, 1940; JAS.D/AG/B7/1. 'Names of political prisoners August 1940' prison log book: 8 Harold Walker Giffard. Fraser, *The Jews of the Channel Islands and the Rule of Law*, p. 114, recognizes this.
32 JAS.M/28/2. Ralph Mollet, Occupation Diary, Volume 2, 1 February 1941–6 June 1943, 20 June 1942. Mollet was secretary to the Bailiff; also Sinel, 20 and 22 June 1942.
33 JAS.B/A/W50/83. Le Masurier, Giffard and Poch, Solicitors, to Bailiff Alexander Coutanche, 4 December 1944; JAS.B/A/W50/183. Bailiff Alexander Coutanche to Platzkommandant, 22 November 1944.
34 Claude Cahun, *Écrits*, ed. François Leperlier, Paris, Jean-Michel Place, 2002, p. 754.
35 Ibid., p. 742.
36 JAS.L/C/77/A/1–8. Izett Croad, Occupation Diary, 23 October 1940; PL.LF940.53 ORD. Reverend R. Douglas Ord, Occupation Diary, 19 June 1941; Winifred Harvey, *The Battle of Newlands: The Wartime Diaries of Winifred Harvey*, Guernsey, Rosemary Booth, 1995, 20–27 October 1940.
37 SAIHC.Personality Files: Marie Ozanne. Letter from Major Marie Ozanne to the Feldkommandant, Guernsey, 26 June 1941.
38 PL.LF940.53 ORD. Reverend R. Douglas Ord, Occupation Diary', 18 April 1942.
39 Description of Steiner by Douglas Ord: PL.LF940.53 ORD. Reverend R. Douglas Ord, Occupation Diary', 1 March 1943. On Steiner and Spitz see the memoirs of a former nurse, Beryl S. Ozanne, *A Peep behind the Screens: 1940–1945*, Guernsey, Guernsey Press Co. Ltd., 1994, pp. 68–9; also Peter Birchenall and Mary Birchenall, *Operation Nurse: Nursing in Guernsey 1940–1945*, West Sussex, Woodfield Publishing, 2001, p. 162. See also Madeleine Bunting, *The Model Occupation: The Channel Islands under German Rule, 1940–1945*, London, Pimlico, 2004, pp. 107–11; Hazel Knowles-Smith, *The Changing Face of the Channel Islands Occupation: Record, Memory and Myth*, Basingstoke, Palgrave Macmillan, 2007, pp. 154–8.
40 Birchenall and Birchenall, *Operation Nurse*, pp. 143, 163.
41 Cohen, *The Jews in the Channel Islands during the German Occupation*, p. 53; Birchenall and Birchenall, *Operation Nurse*, pp. 143, 163.
42 PL.LF940.53 ORD. Reverend R. Douglas Ord, Occupation Diary, 1 March 1943, recalling their meeting the year before.
43 For details see Cohen, *The Jews in the Channel Islands during the German Occupation*, pp. 53–5. For the deportation of Jews in Western Europe, see Michael R. Marrus and Robert O. Paxton, 'The Nazis and the Jews in Occupied Europe', *Journal of Modern History*, Vol. 54, 1982, 687–714.
44 JAS.D/S/A/4/A817. Registration card of Albert Bedane; Len Stevens, 'The Jersey Pimpernel', *Magnet Magazine*, 17 January 1973, p. 3.
45 Information from Cohen, *The Jews in the Channel Islands during the German Occupation*, p. 75; also SJ.GO Box 14/3. Frederick Cohen, notes on Mary Erica Richardson, 1997.
46 Interview with Patrick Sowden, who witnessed the incident as a child, 12 August 2010; see also Cohen, *The Jews in the Channel Islands during the German Occupation*, pp. 76–7.

47 Information from 'The Secret Cellar that Saved Many Lives: Jeane Milne Meets Albert Bedane', *Jersey Evening Post*, 1 June 1970; also *Jersey Evening Post*, 1 June 1999, p. 3.
48 SJ.GO Box 14/3. Frederick Cohen, notes on Mary Erica Richardson, 1997.
49 Francis Le Sueur, *Shadow of the Swastika. Could It All Happen Again?*, Guernsey, Guernsey Press Co. Ltd., 1992, pp. 90–1; party of escapers praised him in November 1944: Sanders, *The British Channel Islands under German Occupation*, p. 131, n. 95.
50 *Jersey Evening Post*, 1 June 1970, p. 3; 1 June 1999, p. 5; *Magnet Magazine*, 17 January 1973, p. 3.
51 *Jersey Evening Post*, 1 June 1970, p. 3.
52 *Jersey Evening Post*, 24 December 1999, 5 January 2000.
53 Cohen, *The Jews in the Channel Islands during the German Occupation*, pp. 68–9; *Jersey Evening Post*, 21 February 1995, p. 9, 26 June 1997, p. 8.
54 Robert Le Sueur, 'The Hedy I Knew', *Jersey Evening Post*, 21 February 1995. She had apparently been registered because her step-father was Jewish and she had arrived as Hedwig Goldenberg-Bercu.
55 Bunting, *The Model Occupation*, p. 343; Cohen, *The Jews in the Channel Islands during the German Occupation*, p. 69.
56 *Jersey Evening Post*, 22, 23 November 1943, p. 1. See also Cohen, *The Jews in the Channel Islands during the German Occupation*, p. 69.
57 Cohen, *The Jews in the Channel Islands during the German Occupation*, p. 69.
58 JAS.D/S/A/25/25. Registration card of Dorothea Weber.
59 See Fraser, *The Jews of the Channel Islands and the Rule of Law*, pp. 41–4.
60 She was on a list of 'escaped prisoners' produced by the Platzkommandant on 15 August 1944: Cohen, *The Jews in the Channel Islands during the German Occupation*, p. 70.
61 *Jersey Evening Post*, 26 June 1997, pp. 8–9.
62 For their story, see the chapter on women.
63 See for example the later comments by Norman Le Brocq, Robert Le Sueur and Joe Mière: Documents.5750 Misc 189/2 (2826). Norman Le Brocq, transcript of interview; IWM.Sound Archive.Interview 10715. Robert Winter Le Sueur, 1989; interview with Robert Le Sueur, 27 June 2000; interview with Joe Mière, 23 August 2000.
64 Adolf Hitler, *Hitler's Table Talk: Hitler's Conversations Recorded by Martin Bormann*, ed. Hugh Trevor-Roper, Oxford and New York, Oxford University Press, 1998, p. 584.
65 George Forty, *Channel Islands at War: A German Perspective*, Shepperton, Ian Allan, 1999, p. 157.
66 Charles Cruickshank, *The German Occupation of the Channel Islands: The Official History of the Occupation Years*, Guernsey, Guernsey Press Co. Ltd., by arrangement with the Trustees of the Imperial War Museum and Oxford University Press, 1975, pp. 179–205; Sanders, *The Ultimate Sacrifice. The Jersey Islanders who Died in German Prisons and Concentration Camps 1940–1945*, Jersey, Jersey Heritage Trust, 2004, p. 111; Louise Willmot, 'The Goodness of Strangers: Help to Escaped Russian Slave Labourers in Occupied Jersey 1942–1945', *Contemporary European History*, Vol. 11 (2), 2002, 211–27.
67 Rolf-Dieter Müller, 'Todt Organisation', in I. C. B. Dear and M. R. D. Foot, *The Oxford Companion to the Second World War*, Oxford and New York, Oxford University Press, 1995, p. 1114.

68 TNA.WO.311/12. Statements and reports of atrocities committed in the Channel Islands. Statement of Mrs Maria Brock, wife of Belgian OT worker Henri Brock and herself employed in the OT administration in the Islands. Also Sanders, *The British Channel Islands under German Occupation*, p. 222.
69 TNA.WO.311/12. Statements and reports on atrocities committed in the Channel Islands. Report on Organisation Todt, Guernsey, May–June 1945.
70 TNA.WO.311/12. Statements and reports of atrocities committed in the Channel Islands. Statement of Mrs Maria Brock. Also Jane Delmer, *Jersey Evening Post*, 25 May 2001, p. 9.
71 For North African workers in Guernsey see IA.FK 29–05. 18/6a Dienstverpflichtungen nichtortsansässiger Arbeitskräfte 20 April 1943–12 October 1943; *Guernsey Evening Press*, 25 May 1945, p. 2.
72 See the testimony of the Dutch OT worker Gilbert van Grieken: IWM.Sound Archive.Interview 12538. Gilbert van Grieken, 1992. Further evidence is found in the diaries of Channel Islanders: IA.AQ 1018/68. Ella Frampton, Occupation Diary 1940–1945, 22 July 1941; PL.LF940.53 BRO. Mrs Peggy Brock, The Second Diary of the Occupation, October 1940–January 1942, 30 November 1941; PL.LF940.53 LAI. Adèle Lainé, 'The German Occupation of Guernsey, 1940–1945', November 1941; PL.LF940.53 ORD. Reverend R. Douglas Ord, Occupation Diary, 24 November 1941. Also Ronald Mauger, 'Slaves and the Organisation Todt in Guernsey', *Channel Islands Occupation Review*, Vol. 8, 1969, 10–14. Mauger had been a driver for the OT.
73 TNA.WO.311/12. Statements and reports of atrocities committed in the Channel Islands. Statement of Mrs Maria Brock.
74 The Soviet OT workers included Ukrainians and others as well as ethnic Russians. The OT workers and their helpers both used the term 'Russian', however.
75 For conditions see Bunting, *The Model Occupation*, pp. 155–7; SJ.GO Box 10/33. Norman Le Brocq, transcript of talk to Channel Islands Occupation Society, 4 April 1988; John Lewis, *A Doctor's Occupation: The Dramatic True Story of Life in Nazi-Occupied Jersey*, Jersey, Channel Island Publishing, 1982, pp. 152–4.
76 For Guernsey see Michael Ginns, 'Foreign Workers' Burials in Guernsey: A Reappraisal', *Channel Islands Occupation Review*, Vol. 25, 1997, 73–4. On the difficulty of providing precise figures for Jersey, see Willmot, 'The Goodness of Strangers', p. 214.
77 PL.LF940.53 BRO. Mrs Peggy Brock, The Second Diary of the Occupation, October 1940–January 1942, 30 November 1941.
78 TNA.WO.311/12. Statements and reports of atrocities committed in the Channel Islands. Report on Organisation Todt, Guernsey, May–June 1945. See also IWM. Sound Archive.Interview 17517. Marion Elise Tostevin, 1997; IWM.Sound Archive. Interview 17521. Molly Joan Bihet, 1997.
79 IWM.Documents.5750 Misc 189/2. Albert Peter Lamy, Chief Officer Guernsey Police 1942–1965, 'Policing during the Occupation 1940–1945, Talk to Officers of the Force, 1965', p. 5; IWM.Sound Archive.Interview 17521. Molly Joan Bihet, 1997; Harvey, p. 127, March 1941; PL.LF940.53 ROB. Ambrose C. Robin, Occupation Diaries 17 June 1940–18 May 1945, 29 November 1941, 17 February 1942; IA.AQ 0380/03–01. Herbert Williams, Diary of Events, etc. during the Occupation of Guernsey, from 30 June 1940 to 6 July 1945', 20 March 1942; Mauger, 13.
80 PL.LF940.53 LAI. Adèle Lainé, 'The German Occupation of Guernsey, 1940–1945', c. November 1941; IA.AQ 0368/01–11. Violet Carey, Occupation Diaries 1940–1945,

27 November 1941; PL.LF940.53 ROB. Ambrose C. Robin, Occupation Diaries 17 June 1940–18 May 1945, 29 November 1941.
81 PL.LF940.53 ORD. Reverend R. Douglas Ord, Occupation Diary, 21 January 1942; for examples see IA.AQ 0092/12. Gertie Corbin, Diary of the Occupation Years, January 1942; IA.AQ 0368/01–11. Violet Carey, Occupation Diaries 1940–1945, 27 November 1941.
82 PL.LF940.53 ORD. Reverend R. Douglas Ord, Occupation Diary, 1 June 1944; PL.LF940.53 ROB. Ambrose C. Robin, Occupation Diaries 17 June 1940–18 May 1945, 4 October 1942. Most of the 108 men buried in Foulon cemetery, were French, with 15 Belgians and 15 North Africans. Only three were Russian, and one Polish: Ginns, 'Foreign Workers' Burials in Guernsey: A Reappraisal', 73–4.
83 See for example IA.AQ 1018/68. Ella Frampton, Occupation Diary 1940–1945, 23 October 1942; PL.LF940.53 ROB. Ambrose C. Robin, Occupation Diaries 17 June 1940–18 May 1945, 11 February 1942; PL.LF940.53 LAI. Adèle Lainé, 'The German Occupation of Guernsey, 1940–1945', pp. 126–7, Easter 1942; IA.AQ 0380/03–01. Herbert Williams, Diary of Events, etc. during the Occupation of Guernsey, from 30 June 1940 to 6 July 1945, pp. 82–3.
84 PL.LF940.53 BRO. Mrs Peggy Brock, The Second Diary of the Occupation, October 1940–January 1942, 23 November 1941; PL.LF940.53 ROB. Ambrose C. Robin, Occupation Diaries 17 June 1940–18 May 1945, 31 July 1942.
85 For the increase in thefts, see the police files: IA.PC 209–21. 14 April 1941 to 22 June 1941: there were 27 recorded cases of breaking and entering and 41 of larceny; compare with IA.PC 195–05. Police Occurrence Book, 3 September 1942 to 10 October 1942, with 103 cases of breaking and entering and 201 of larceny in five weeks. Not all were by OT workers.
86 IWM.Documents.5750 Misc 189/2. Albert Peter Lamy, Chief Officer Guernsey Police 1942–1965, 'Policing during the Occupation 1940–1945, Talk to Officers of the Force, 1965', pp. 5–7.
87 Bachmann, 22 November 1941. Also PL.LF940.53 ROB. Ambrose C. Robin, Occupation Diaries 17 June 1940–18 May 1945, 11 November 1941.
88 IA.AQ 0368/01–11. Violet Carey, Occupation Diaries 1940–1945, 11 October 1942.
89 IA.AQ 1018/68. Ella Frampton, Occupation Diary 1940–1945, 21 February 1942.
90 IA.AQ 0380/03–01. Herbert Williams, Diary of Events, etc. during the Occupation of Guernsey, from 30 June 1940 to 6 July 1945, pp. 82–3, c. March 1943.
91 PL.LF940.53 LAI. Adèle Lainé, 'The German Occupation of Guernsey, 1940–1945', p. 127, c. Easter 1942.
92 PL.LF940.53 ORD. Reverend R. Douglas Ord, Occupation Diary, 30 August 1942.
93 PL.LF940.53 LAI. Adèle Lainé, 'The German Occupation of Guernsey, 1940–1945', c. February 1942.
94 *The Press*, 27 July 1944, p. 1, Festungskommandant, 21 July 1944, repeating the order. IA.PC 195–03. Police Occurrence Book, 13 June 1942 to 21 July 1942; IA.PC 195–04. Police Occurrence Book, 21 July 1942 to 2 September 1942: arrest of OT workers for stealing or bartering potatoes.
95 *Guernsey Evening Press*, 16 November 1942, p. 3; PL.LF940.53 ORD. Reverend R. Douglas Ord, Occupation Diary, 16 November 1942, calling the order a 'downright lie'.
96 King, *The Channel Islands War 1940–1945*, p. 137.
97 On hunger as a reason not to give, see Bachmann, 16 June 1942.

98 PL.LF940.53 LAI. Adèle Lainé, 'The German Occupation of Guernsey, 1940-1945', February 1942; J. C. Sauvary, *Diary of the German Occupation of Guernsey 1940-1945*, Guernsey, Guernsey Press Co. Ltd., [Self Publishing Association] 1995 (revised edn) [1990], 13 August 1942; PL.LF940.53 ORD. Reverend R. Douglas Ord, Occupation Diary, 30 August 1942.
99 PL.LF940.53 ORD. Reverend R. Douglas Ord, Occupation Diary, 31 January 1942. See IA.AQ 0092/12. Gertie Corbin, Diary of the Occupation Years, March 1943.
100 Bachmann, 16 June 1942.
101 See for example IA.AQ 0368/01-11. Violet Carey, Occupation Diaries 1940-1945, 11 July 1942, 11 October 1942.
102 Ozanne, *A Peep behind the Screens*, p. 58.
103 IA.AQ 0368/01-11. Violet Carey, Occupation Diaries 1940-1945, 20 April 1942.
104 IWM.Sound Archive.Interview 17517. Marion Elise Tostevin, 1997; Marie Ozanne, Diary, 1942 passim, held by and used by kind permission of the Ozanne family; letter from Marie Ozanne to Yves De La Mare, 1 March 1942, used with the kind permission of Pearl De La Mare.
105 IA FK 04-09. Ordnungsstrafverfahren against a Guernseywoman who was fined for renting a room to an Algerian.
106 See for example the case of Elise Hubbard, punished in October 1943 for illegally sheltering an OT worker: IA.FK 04-09. FK 515 Nebenstelle Guernsey: Ordungsstrafliste begun 1 July 1943.
107 'At Liberty: French-Algerian Who Hid at L'Islet. Kindness of Mr and Mrs N. W. Mahy', *Guernsey Evening Press*, 25 May 1945, p. 2.
108 TNA.WO.311/12. Statements and reports of atrocities committed in the Channel Islands. Report on Organisation Todt, Guernsey, May-June 1945. See also Sanders, *The British Channel Islands under German Occupation*, p. 108.
109 Alan Wood and Mary Wood, *Islands in Danger: The Story of the German Occupation of the Channel Islands, 1940-1945*, Sevenoaks, First Four Square, 1965, pp. 160-1.
110 PL.LF940.53 ORD. Reverend R. Douglas Ord, Occupation Diary, 16 July 1943, 25 July 1943.
111 Extract from Lilian Ogier Collas, Diary, 3 September 1942, with permission of Collas family. Violet Carey also noted comments by her friend Mrs de Putron: IA.AQ 0368/01-11. Violet Carey, Occupation Diaries 1940-1945, 20 March 1942.
112 Interview with her son Richard Collas, 8 July 2010.
113 IWM.Documents.13409. Private Papers of Captain J. R. Dening: Dening 9: The Channel Islands Under German Occupation 1945. Resistance: Marie Ozanne. Copy of letter from Ozanne to Feldkommandant, Guernsey, 30 August 1942; see also her letter to Feldkommandant, Guernsey, 9 October 1942.
114 For Ozanne's story, see the chapter on women.
115 Le Quesne, 13 August 1942.
116 For similar comments see JAS.L/C/77/A/1-8. Izett Croad, Occupation Diary, 15 August 1942; de Carteret et al., 'Diary of Mary Deslandes', 15 August 1942; Le Ruez, 13 August 1942. For post war accounts see Joe Mière in Roy McLoughlin, *Living with the Enemy*, Jersey, Starlight Publishing, 1995, pp. 69-70; also the diarist Mrs De Gruchy and the bus driver Roy Luce in Sanders, *The British Channel Islands under German Occupation*, p. 223.
117 TNA.WO.311/11. Testimonies of OT drivers John Pinel, 10 July 1945, and Peter Le Vannais, 9 July 1945; Sanders, *The British Channel Islands under German Occupation*, pp. 224-7.

118 Sanders, *The British Channel Islands under German Occupation*, pp. 217, 224.
119 TNA.WO.311/11. Testimony of William Francis Sarre, 2 July 1945. Among many descriptions of brutality, see Sanders, *The British Channel Islands under German Occupation*, pp. 222-7; Bunting, *The Model Occupation*, pp. 148-50.
120 TNA.WO.311/11. Testimony of Constance Brown, 2 July 1945; also in Sanders, *The British Channel Islands under German Occupation*, p. 229.
121 JAS.L/C/77/A/1-8. Izett Croad, Occupation Diary, 15 August 1942, 30 August 1942.
122 Sanders, *The British Channel Islands under German Occupation*, p. 226. For improvements in conditions, see for example Le Ruez, 5 October 1943; TNA. WO.311/11. Testimony of William Francis Sarre, 2 July 1945; TNA.WO.311/11. Testimony of Frank Victor Hamon, 2 July 1945.
123 de Carteret et al., 'Diary of Mary Deslandes', 1 December 1942. On the robberies, see Sanders, *The British Channel Islands under German Occupation*, pp. 225-6; IWM. Documents.11646. G. Attenborough, Diary, 29 July 1943; IWM.Documents.9775 P324. Mrs I. M. Bullen, Diary, 6-12 December 1942; JAS.L/C/77/A/1-8. Izett Croad, Occupation Diary, 1 December 1942. See also SJ.GO Box 10/42. Letter from Muriel Smith of Greve d'Azette to Auntie Madge, May 1945, including 'I was more scared of the Russians than any German'.
124 See for example Sinel, 24 March 1943 on a farmer attacking a robber with a pitchfork; also TNA.WO.311/11. Testimony of Francis Coutanche, 3 July 1945, on an incident in which a farmer attacked Russians for stealing.
125 On the death of Le Gresley, see Le Ruez, 1 December 1942, 4 December 1942; Sinel, 1 December 1942, 3 December 1942; *Evening Post*, 31 March 1943, p. 1. On the death of the OT workers, Sinel, 24, 25 March 1943; de Carteret et al., 'Diary of Mary Deslandes', 30 March 1943; Le Ruez, 24 March 1943.
126 *Evening Post*, 31 March 1943, p. 1.
127 JAS.B/A/W50/65. FK 515 Feldkommandant Knackfuss to Bailiff Alexander Coutanche, 21 September 1942; Willmot, 'The Goodness of Strangers', p. 215.
128 JAS.B/A/W50/66/2. Police Report, 10 September 1942.
129 Ibid.; Lewis, *A Doctor's Occupation*, pp. 87-8.
130 JAS.D/Z/H6/4. Sentences and Prosecutions by the Field Command and Troop Courts, 33 and 34: Edward and Annie Ross; also JWT.Research Files Box 5. Letter from Annie Ross to German authorities, 25 August 1943.
131 *Evening Post*, 18 July 1945, p. 1.
132 TNA.WO.311/11. Testimony of Louis Clarke, June/July 1945. On reasons for not feeding OT workers, see, for example, TNA.WO.311/11. Testimony of Louis Saout, June/July 1945; TNA.WO.311/11. Testimony of Elias John Le Bailly, 5 July 1945; JAS.L/C/03/A/10. Mabel Ahier, 'Jersey in Wartime during the German Occupation'; also comments by slave labourers in Bunting, *The Model Occupation*, pp. 150-1; IWM.Sound Archive.Interview 11099. Louisa Alexandra Cavey, 1990, who was too afraid of the Germans; also testimony of former fugitive Peter Botatenko, *Evening Post*, 19 May 1945, p. 4, on the difficulty of getting food.
133 JAS.L/C/77/A/1-8. Izett Croad, Occupation Diary, 15 August 1942; Le Quesne, 14 September 1942; TNA.WO.311/11. Testimony of Louisa Foott, June/July 1945; TNA.WO.311/11. Testimony of Francis Coutanche, 3 July 1945; TNA.WO.311/11. Testimony of Constance Brown, 2 July 1945.
134 de Carteret et al., 'Diary of Mary Deslandes', 30 March 1943. See also Leslie Sinel's comment that 'they are more to be pitied than blamed', Sinel, 30 November 1942.

135 TNA.WO.311/11. Testimony of Louisa Foott, June/July 1945; see also TNA. WO.311/11. Testimony of Thomas Gorin, 29 June 1945.
136 Testimony of Vasily Marempolski, in Knowles-Smith, *The Changing Face of the Channel Islands Occupation*, p. 216; also Bunting, *The Model Occupation*, pp. 155–6, with OT worker describing a local girl who gave him a jacket.
137 'Lettre á Gaston Ferdière, 1946', in Cahun, *Écrits*, p. 695.
138 TNA.WO.311/11. Testimony of Frank Victor Hamon, 2 July 1945.
139 Le Ruez, 13 September 1942; JAS.M/45/A1/1. Joyce Le Ruez, 'Memories of the German Occupation of Jersey, 1940–1945', p. 6.
140 Le Ruez, 29 September 1942.
141 Ibid., 16 November 1942, 8 October 1942. For other cases of regular feeding see, for example, Leo Harris, *A Boy Remembers*, Jersey, Channel Island Publishing, 2000, p. 90 describing his parents; IWM.Sound Archive.Interview 10716. Maurice Edwarde Green, 1989; TNA.WO.311/11. Testimony of Francis Killer, 29 June 1945.
142 Le Ruez, 14 October 1943, also 6 April 1943, 8 October 1943, 5 July 1944.
143 Noted in Guernsey by Ord: PL.LF940.53 ORD. Reverend R. Douglas Ord, Occupation Diary, 23 February 1943. See also Sanders, *The British Channel Islands under German Occupation*, pp. 63, 76, 129.
144 *Evening Post*, 31 March 1943, p. 1; also IWM.Documents.11646. G. Attenborough, Diary, 19 December 1942; de Carteret et al., 'Diary of Mary Deslandes', 8 November 1942; JAS.B/A/W50/48. FK 515 Dr Casper, OKVR to Bailiff, 25 February 1942.
145 See, for example, JAS.B/A/W50/126/6. FK 515 to Bailiff, 28 November 1943 on the need for the police to find fugitives 'hidden in the Island'; also JAS.B/A/W50/124/3. Police Report 5 December 1943, reporting arrest of fugitives. Also JAS.B/A/ W50/66/2. Police Report, 10 September 1942: search of No. 23 David Place.
146 *Evening Post*, 30 December 1964.
147 JAS.L/F/54/C/D/12. Duret Aubin to J. du Val, Constable of St Peter on missing OT workers, 7–8 January 1943.
148 *Evening Post*, 19 June 1945, p. 4; 13 June 1945, p. 1.
149 *Evening Post*, 19 June 1945, p. 4. Jerovna was recaptured but survived in prison; *Evening Post*, 13 June 1945, p. 1. See, for example, the case of the Sarres of Millbrook, who relied on 'a few good friends', interview with Gwenda Sarre, 24 August 2000.
150 Michael L. Gross, *Ethics and Activism: The Theory and Practice of Political Morality*, Cambridge, Cambridge University Press, 1997, p. 133.
151 SJ.GO Box 10/33. Norman Le Brocq, transcript of talk to Channel Islands Occupation Society, 4 April 1988.
152 Letter from Fyodor Burriy to *Jersey Evening Post*, 11 August 1992, p. 14; *Jersey Evening Post*, 9 March 1995, p. 3; Mike Frowd, 'A Russian in Hiding – "Bill" Fyodor Burriy', *Channel Islands Occupation Review*, Vol. 27, 1999, 59–70, here 64.
153 SJ.GO Box 10/33. Norman Le Brocq, transcript of talk to Channel Islands Occupation Society, 4 April 1988.
154 Peter Botatenko in *Evening Post*, 19 May 1945, p. 4; also the son of one set of helpers, Dennis Le Flem: JAS.L/C/185/A/16/1. Dennis Le Flem, 'The Occupation of Jersey Channel Islands by the Germans 1940–1945'.
155 Frowd, *Channel Islands Occupation Review*, 64. On temporary refuges, see Burriy in *Jersey Evening Post*, 11 August 1992, p. 14, including Dorothy Huelin, the Desvergez family and Stuart Williams.

156 Letter from Fyodor 'Bill' Burriy to the editor, *Evening Post*, 10 May 1945, p. 2, letter dated 9 May 1945.
157 Robert Le Sueur, letter to author, 28 July 2000; JWT.Research Files Box 6. Mike Le Cornu, 'Distant Memories 1939–1945', pp. 7–9.
158 Letter from Michael Krokhin to the editor, *Evening Post*, 12 June 1945, p. 1; letter from 'Bill' Burriy, *Evening Post*, 10 May 1945, p. 2; Frowd, *Channel Islands Occupation Review*, 64; *Jersey Evening Post*, 11 August 1992, p. 14: the student Oscar Le Breuilly, who 'lost' his for Burriy.
159 William Gladden, account in *Evening Post*, 12 June 1945, p. 5.
160 JWT.Research Files Box 6. Mike Le Cornu, 'Distant Memories 1939–1945', p. 9 on the marking of houses; on moving from house to house see JHT. Slave Worker Testimonies, Phyllis Le Breton; also McLoughlin, *Living with the Enemy*, p. 71.
161 Interview with Gwenda Sarre, 24 August 2000.
162 Interview with Stella Perkins, the daughter of Augusta Dimitrieva-Metcalfe, 28 June 2000; also Vasily Marempolski: JWT.Research Files Box 8. Vasily Marempolski, 'Recollections of a Jersey Prisoner', p. 9.
163 See, for example, JAS.L/C/185/A/1–5. Letters from Peter Botatenko to the Le Flem family between October 1944 and June 1946.
164 JHT. Slave Worker Testimonies; also McLoughlin, *Living with the Enemy*, p. 71.
165 Here see Willmot, 'The Goodness of Strangers', p. 227; Sanders, *The Ultimate Sacrifice*, p. 66.
166 JHT. Slave Worker Testimonies; also McLoughlin, *Living with the Enemy*, p. 71; also interview with Stella Perkins, 28 June 2000, and with Robert Le Sueur, 27 June 2000.
167 SJ.GO Box 10/33. Norman Le Brocq, transcript of talk to Channel Islands Occupation Society, 4 April 1988.
168 Here see Sanders, *The Ultimate Sacrifice*, pp. 69–75.
169 For more details see the chapter on women.
170 Letter from Robert Le Sueur to author, 2 July 1999.
171 *Evening Post*, 12 June 1945, p. 5.
172 On the importance of requests for help in the rescue of Jews, see Federico Varese and Meir Yaish, 'The Importance of Being Asked: The Rescue of Jews in Nazi Europe', *Rationality and Society*, Vol. 12, 2000, 307–34.
173 Norman Le Brocq, quoted in Willmot, 'The Goodness of Strangers', p. 217.
174 Letter from Robert Le Sueur to author, 2 July 1999.
175 Varese and Yaish, 'The Importance of Being Asked', p. 320.
176 D/Z/H6/7. Sentences and Prosecutions by the Field Command and Troop Courts. Trial 87: Edward George Osborne: Duret Aubin, 6 June 1944, Strafverfügung, 25 May 1944.
177 Ages checked with reference to registration cards in JAS.D/S/A/ files.
178 See also the experience of the young Arthur and Yolande Hutchings' in hiding 'Peter': SJ.GO Box 10/32. Letter from Mrs Emma Huchet of St Lawrence to Mrs Dean, 6 June 1945.
179 Interview with Robert Le Sueur, 27 June 2000.
180 See the chapter on women.
181 See the debates in Lawrence Baron, 'The Dynamics of Decency: Dutch Rescuers of Jews during the Holocaust', in M. Marrus (ed.), *The Nazi Holocaust*, Vol. 5 (2), Westport, CT, Meckler, 1989, pp. 608–26, here p. 615.

182 Samuel P. Oliner, 'The Unsung Heroes in Nazi-occupied Europe: The Antidote for Evil', *Nationalities Papers*, Vol. 12 (1), 1984, 129–36.
183 Interview with Stella Perkins, the daughter of Dimitrieva-Metcalfe, 28 June 2000.
184 Willmot, 'The Goodness of Strangers', p. 222.
185 Here see Eva Fogelman, *Conscience and Courage: Rescuers of Jews during the Holocaust*, New York, Anchor, 1994, pp. 41, 52, 54.
186 Letter from his colleague and friend L. J. 'Tim' Simon to author, 25 August 1999.
187 For details of their resistance, see the chapter on women.
188 William Gladden, account in *Evening Post*, 12 June 1945, p. 5; *Evening Post*, 30 December 1964, p. 6.
189 JAS.D/Z/H6/4. Sentences and Prosecutions by the Field Command and Troop Courts. Trial 4: René Le Mottée, sentenced to three weeks' imprisonment in December 1942.
190 Interview with Terry Le Mottée, 10 August 2010. After the Liberation a German soldier returned to the far, and the two men shook hands.
191 Le Ruez, 20 June 1942.
192 Ibid., 5 July 1944.
193 Frowd, *Channel Islands Occupation Review*, esp. 61. Frowd sheltered 'Bill' Burriy after the arrest of Mrs Gould. See also Sanders, *The Ultimate Sacrifice*, pp. 66–8.
194 Letter from Robert Le Sueur to author, 9 August 2002; also JAS.L/D/25/L/39. Robert Le Sueur, 'Foreign Workers of the OT', talk to Channel Islands Occupation Society.
195 Nechama Tec, 'Righteous Christians in Poland', *International Social Science Review*, Vol. 58 (1), 1983, 15–17; Perry London, 'The Rescuers: Motivational Hypotheses about Christians Who Saved Jews from the Nazis', in L. Berkowitz and J. Macaulay, *Altruism and Helping Behaviour: Social Psychological Studies of Some Antecedents and Consequences*, New York, Academic Press, 1970, pp. 241–50. This 'social marginalization' could involve being a member of a minority religious denomination or ethnic group, for example.
196 For their story, by one of those involved, see W. G. A. Gardner, 'The Story of a Group of British War-resisters Who Fell into Enemy Hands in the German-occupied Channel Islands in World War 2', unpublished manuscript, 1991, unpaginated, copy held at Société Jersiaise.
197 The 'damn wasters' comment is in Le Quesne, 12 January 1941; on the tendency of many to see the COs as 'fifth columnists', see Le Ruez, 12 January 1941. For further evidence of hostility see *Evening Post* letters page, 19 May 1945.
198 JWT.Research Files Box 10. Conscientious objectors file: 'A Few Memories – By Wilf Butterworth'.
199 Here see Samuel. P. and Pearl. M. Oliner, *The Altruistic Personality*, New York, The Free Press, 1988, esp. p. 317; also Federico Varese and Meir Yaish, 'Resolute Heroes: The Rescue of Jews during the Nazi Occupation of Europe', *European Journal of Sociology*, Vol. 46 (1), 2005, 153–68, here p. 159.
200 See for example Mike Frowd's estimate that about 20 people knew of Burriy's hiding place, Frowd, *Channel Islands Occupation Review*, 65; also William Gladden, *Evening Post*, 12 June 1945, p. 5.
201 JAS.B/A/W50/165/4. Platzkommandant Major Heider to Bailiff Coutanche, 16 August 1944, on the search for Russians in St John and St Mary; JAS.B/A/W50/165/3. FK 515 Platkommandant Major Heider to Bailiff of Jersey, 15 August 1944.

202 JAS.B/A/W50/165/3. FK 515 Platkommandant Major Heider to Bailiff of Jersey, 15 August 1944.
203 Albert ('Bert') Chardine in *Jersey Evening Post*, 19 July 1990, p. 5.
204 TNA.WO.311/12. Statement of Arthur Guiton Harrison, 29 June 1945; see also Sanders, *The British Channel Islands under German Occupation*, p. 228.
205 On the importance of such 'screens' for protecting victims of persecution, see Jacques Semelin, *Unarmed against Hitler: Civilian Resistance in Europe, 1939–1943*, Westport, CT and London, Praeger, 1993, pp. 141–53.

5

Defiance and Deportations

Gilly Carr

This chapter explores the range of defiance against both the Germans and their orders at the time of the deportation of Channel Islanders to German and French civilian internment camps in September 1942 and February 1943. It argues that after realizing that the deportation order could not be overturned, the civilian authorities decided which battles were worth fighting in order to modify the order. These decisions favoured specific groups and left others to their own fate.

I divide this defiant behaviour into three consecutive periods: before, during and after the deportations. The first took place in Jersey, Guernsey and Sark in the short space of time before people were removed; the second took place on the day of deportation, on board buses, boats or trains, and at the harbours of St Helier, St Peter Port and Sark. The third was enacted in many different ways in the camps themselves, where the defiance which took place in these times and places mirrored or replicated acts which can be observed throughout the whole period of occupation in the Channel Islands.

Introduction to the deportations

The turning point of the Occupation came in the middle of 1942. Over a period of four months, radios were confiscated; hundreds of slave workers arrived in Jersey in a state which shocked all who saw them; and the deportation order was announced.[1] This third consecutive blow to the local population ensured that 'nothing was ever the same again'.[2] It also meant that German actions were increasingly stirring at least a segment of the local population into a state of protest.

The year before, Britain had, along with her Russian allies, invaded pro-German Iran for its oil supplies and deported and interned German nationals working there. Hitler was intent on punitive reprisals and his attention became focused upon Channel Islanders, who were effectively a captive pool of British citizens at his mercy. The Feldkommandant demanded and received various census lists, between September and November 1941, of island men, women and children who were born in the United

Kingdom.³ The German Foreign Ministry tried to use islanders as a barter for the Germans in Iran, threatening to deport and intern them, but Hitler was not content with a like-for-like exchange. He wanted the deportations to be a more punitive measure and demanded a ten-to-one ratio, internment in the Pripet Marshes in what is today southern Belarus/northern Ukraine, and the redistribution of deportees' property among the indigenous islanders.⁴ As 500 Germans had been interned, this meant the potential deportation of 5,000 islanders. It appears that the German Foreign Ministry and the *Wehrmacht* were not entirely happy with this proposal, and a state of confusion and misunderstandings began to develop which lasted for a year. During this time, many communications were taking place across Europe about internment camps and security for the islanders, and the benefits and disbenefits of the proposed deportations.⁵ In September 1942, the Swiss government got involved in the suggestion of a prisoner exchange, which brought the matter to Hitler, who then discovered that the islanders were still in the Channel Islands. The deportation order was re-issued with immediate effect,⁶ although this time the Pripet Marshes were no longer on his agenda. While the re-distribution of deportees' property was not ordered, the homes of many were looted after their departure; not only were other islanders in a state of need, but it was not known when or even if the deportees might return. In total, around 2,200 were sent away.

There were two waves of deportations ordered by the occupiers, and each targeted different groups of people. That of September 1942 was aimed at English-born (as opposed to indigenous Channel Islander) men who were aged between 16 and 70 years old, together with their families. This order also caught those who had been accidentally trapped in the Channel Islands because of the outbreak of war (e.g. holidaying families, honeymooning couples, or those on business). Also served deportation orders were Channel Island men who happened, by chance or accident, to have been born in the United Kingdom. In many if not most cases the men in question, if married, were married to Channel Island women. The deportation order thus did not affect just the English-born, even though it was this group that Hitler wanted to target as they were perceived as most likely to cause trouble or to engage in.⁷

The deportation order was published in the *Jersey Evening Post* and *Guernsey Star* on 15 September. On 16, 18 and 29 September, three batches of deportees left Jersey. They left Guernsey and Sark on 26 September, and Guernsey again on 27 September. People had very little time to prepare for departure. Pets, jobs, houses, savings and possessions had to be disposed of or placed into the hands of friends, with no promise of return within the foreseeable future. Islanders sincerely hoped that they might be rescued by the Royal Navy once on board the boats that were to take them to St Malo. However, their observation of the forced and slave labourers from other occupied countries that the Germans had brought to the Channel Islands were probably enough to disabuse them of any false illusions. This did not stop them from pretending to their children that they were going on an exciting adventure. As those former internees still alive today were mostly children or teenagers at the time of their deportation, the vast majority do not recall anxiety, tears or distress from their parents at this time, even though their final destination was unknown and their safety was not guaranteed.⁸

These memories of emotional self-control are a testimony to the deportees' stoicism during the deportations.

The second wave of deportations, in February 1943, was much smaller and targeted a different group of people, although some of those who had received exemptions first time round found themselves once more on the list. The categories chosen for deportation this time included British Jews (some of whom had acquired British nationality through marriage); British ex-officers; Freemasons; and those who the Germans considered 'undesirable'. The undesirables were so-called because either they had offended against the German military regime and spent time in prison, or else were seen as politically suspect or considered to be work-shy. A number of people from Sark were also on the 1943 deportation list as a reprisal for the British commando raid, Operation Basalt, the previous October. Some people fell into a number of the target groups, such as Bertram Bartlett, for example, who was English-born, had been a WWI officer in the Army, and was also a Freemason. He had gained exemption for himself and his family (but not his brother and sister-in-law) in September 1942, but he, his wife and son were deported in February 1943.[9] While exact numbers of those deported is not known due to the multiple copies of deportation and transport lists, and the later births, deaths and repatriations in the camps, not to mention the transfer of people from one camp to another, it has been calculated that 266 were deported in February 1943.[10]

Pre-deportation protest and defiance

Examples of pre-deportation protest, defiance and circumvention of orders came from four quarters: the islands' authorities in local government; the islands' doctors; islanders who were not being deported; and from the deportees themselves. The earliest cases of protest came from those in local government, and archival records suggest that this was more aggressive in Jersey than in Guernsey. The news of the deportations caused severe panic and shock despite the speculation caused by the requests in September and November 1941, in Jersey and Guernsey respectively, for lists of people living in the islands but born outside them.

Insight into the action taken by the islands' authorities comes from two main sources: the diaries of those who were privy to such information, sometimes by dint of being close friends, colleagues, or related to those involved; and archival records which record minutes of meetings and letters sent and unsent.

Diarist Violet Carey was a well-connected upper-middle-class Guernsey woman, and was married to James Carey, a Jurat of the Royal Court.[11] On 16 September 1942, the day after the deportation order was announced, James brought back the news that the Bailiff was 'fighting hard to keep the men in key positions' and that the Germans and the Controlling Committee had met, and that 'John Leale told them exactly what he thought of them and what the world thought of them. He could not have spoken more strongly or plainly.' We can only take Violet's word for this, because whatever Leale said went un-minuted, or at least does not survive in the archives of the Controlling Committee's minutes.

In his speech to the States of 23 May 1945, Jurat John Leale, President of the Controlling Committee in Guernsey, outlined the problems presented to the Committee by the deportations:

> We had to decide whether we should cut ourselves completely adrift on the grounds that the thing was unclean or take the point of view that if the deportations were due to take place there was nothing we could do to prevent them. If we accepted the latter as our standpoint, we could work to ensure that everything was conducted in an orderly fashion; we could try to get the maximum number of exemptions; we could organise so that everything that was humanly possible was done to lighten the burden of those who had to go. We chose the latter alternative. I don't think we should have gained anything except a little notoriety by the former. We had to try to be realists.[12]

The veracity of this position is backed up by Louis Guillemette, the Bailiff's secretary, who in his diary noted that:

> The Bailiff expressed our concern (that is a very mild word) and asked whether anything could be done to alter the order. Dr Brosch held out no hope at all even though he realised that many of those who would be taken away had lived in the Bailiwick for the major part of their lives. We asked whether the maximum age could be reduced and he said there was no hope at all of this. It is very probable that, in the changed atmosphere after the war, it will be thought that a most unheroic attitude was taken by the administration of the Island in consenting to take any part in the preparation for the evacuation of part of our community but we know that the Feldkommandantur have not the staff to deal with the matter in the way which will make for the alleviation of suffering and that by keeping in close contact with them we will not let any opportunity pass to save our people.[13]

To return to Leale's post-Occupation speech, he noted that 'unfortunately in the early days we did not keep records of all that was said or done. We confined our protests to those of a verbal nature.'[14] This appears to have been the case at the time of the 1942 deportations, as both Guillemette and silent minutes of the Controlling Committee note.

Perhaps the preference for oral protest coupled with a reluctance to commit true feelings to paper is the reason behind the letter of protest written by Victor Carey to the Feldcommandantur on 15 September 1942 – a letter that was struck through in black ink with the word 'cancelled', and presumably never sent:

> Sir. I am in receipt of your letter of 15 September 1942 informing me of British subjects who have to be evacuated immediately to Germany, and I must inform you that I am shocked and extremely disturbed at the content of the letter which, unless there are exemptions made, will have a most disastrous effect and cause great hardship on the administration of the Island, as a proportion of those persons

in charge of the various essential undertakings such as gas and electricity would be affected by the Order. This also applies to the medical profession as well as to the various religious denominations in the Island. I am, Sir, yours faithfully, (signed) Victor G. Carey, Bailiff.[15]

One can only assume that the Bailiff, like Leale, resorted to verbal protests only. Instead, the archival record indicates that on the same day, Carey wrote letters asking for exemption of Colonel Brousson (one of his confidential secretaries) and Mr H. Carey Brock, the Receiver General.[16] By the following day, Victor Carey wrote to Sybil Hathaway, Dame of Sark, enclosing forms for people to fill in. He remarked that while he was afraid that the Seigneur, Robert Hathaway, would have to fill in a form, 'it is understood that all those people in official and key positions will not be affected by the Order'. Carey already sounded confident that he had sufficiently persuaded the Germans on this score. He added 'We have done our best to get the Order modified but without success.'[17]

On 18 September, Violet Carey recorded in her diary that she went to see the Bailiff. She was informed that the German administration had made a list of men in key positions for exemption; the Bailiff was seemingly still sure on this matter. Because many indigenous Guernsey people born in the United Kingdom were also to be deported, Carey told Violet that he was with the Germans for two hours, explaining that 'real Guernsey people are born all over the world'. It seems that the Germans also agreed to make a list of 'genuine Guernsey people for exemption'. Victor also told her that he had tried to reduce the deportation age limit from 70 to 60, but without luck, as the orders came from Berlin.[18]

Two hundred and ninety-three letters asking for exemption from deportation exist in a file in Guernsey's archives.[19] They make interesting reading and shed a little light on German attitudes to different categories of requests. The haste with which letters were written, reflected in the random scraps of paper or backs of envelopes chosen for the request, appears to have had no effect on the outcome. The status of the applicant wasn't always a sure way of predicting who would gain exemption, as a cowman and a grower were both exempted, although those who could produce food for the island were probably in a relatively safe position. Working for the Organisation Todt or for the Germans in some other capacity was not sufficient, and having an important person pleading for you was also no guarantee of reprieve. While a person's birth in the United Kingdom to Guernsey parents made a difference (as the Bailiff suggested to Violet Carey), so too did sycophancy, although there were few examples of this.

In summary, it would seem, therefore, that in Guernsey, the President of the Controlling Committee and the Bailiff had both made verbal protests against the deportation Order, had some success in winning reprieves for people in key positions, and that overall the Committee had decided to accept the Order with the aim of softening its impact. Unfortunately, this meant involving the Guernsey police, who accompanied the German soldiers as they served notices on islanders to be deported.[20]

In Jersey, the reaction of the local government was, at first glance, almost identical: they debated whether to resign or act as a buffer. In Bailiff Alexander Coutanche memoirs, he wrote that:

> On 15 September, there came from Germany an order for the deportation of 1,200 of those British subjects who, while still living in the Island, had not been born in it ... I did everything in my power to prevent its execution but to no avail. Colonel Knackfuss, who was Feldcommandant at the time, showed me the order itself and stated that it was signed by Hitler, for which I had to take his word. However, from my experience of Knackfuss, I do not believe that he would have told a deliberate lie on the matter. When the Superior Council met to consider the situation, their first feelings were that we ought to resign and refuse to carry out the public administration of the Island any longer. However, calmer feelings eventually prevailed and we finally decided, and in this I feel quite sure that we were right, that we could do far better by continuing to act as some kind of buffer between the Jersey people and the Germans.[21]

In a step further than Guernsey, the Superior Council also passed a Resolution on 21 September 1942, which declared that the intention of the Germans to deport 'certain classes of British subjects constitutes a breach of paragraph 8 of the ultimatum of 1 July 1940 ... whereby the Islanders were called upon to surrender'. The ultimatum had guaranteed 'in case of peaceful surrender the lives, property and liberty of peaceful inhabitants'.[22] As this was also signed by the Bailiff and translated into German, it seems likely that the occupiers were given a copy of the Resolution as a protest.

It appears that Alexander Coutanche was more aware than his counterpart in Guernsey of the importance of leaving a paper trail to record his thoughts and actions for posterity. Preserved in the archives are 11 sheets of Coutanche's hurried handwriting, complete with multiple insertions, crossings out and events related out of sequence, indicative of a hastily written document made in a period of high stress. The first set of notes date to 16 September 1942 and are not always entirely legible. Countanche gives us a clear indication of the events of the previous 24 hours. He also tells us what happened behind closed doors, during which he had a private interview with Colonel Knackfuss, the Feldkommandant. Coutanche records that he told Knackfuss that he was 'shocked at, and protested against, the proposed measure'. On learning that he could not stop or delay the deportations as the order came from the Führer, Coutanche announced that he and his government were entitled to resign. Knackfuss replied that it was in the interests of the people of Jersey that the government continued in office. Coutanche noted that he could not consent to the Constables being asked to select the people for deportation, and that it must be done by the German military authorities and the 'Constables' role must be limited to showing cause why the persons selected should *not* be evacuated. Colonel Knackfuss agreed to this and authorised me so to inform the Constables.' Coutanche also noted that 'several Constables then objected to serving the notices', and that he obtained by the Feldkommandant 'the promise that the Evacuation Orders would be served by members of the German Armed Forces – the Constables only being required to supply a 'guide' for finding the addresses.'[23]

On 22 September, he added to the notes to record that the Superior Council decided not to protest against the discrimination in the deportations in favour of Jersey people in case it encouraged the occupiers 'to take a larger number of persons than they at present contemplate'.[24]

As in Guernsey, it seems that those in high places understandably attempted to use their position to gain exemptions for friends, family and colleagues. Deputy Edward Le Quesne, a member of the Superior Council, noted in his diary entry for 16 and 18 September that he was able to 'save many of my staff, and also my son in law, my daughter and my little grandson', for which many people criticized him. On 26 September, he records that he was able to exempt, in all, his family members and 'some seventy others'. On 29 September he noted that he had had 'the good fortune to save all Jerseymen from going'.[25] It seems that self-interest and kinship ties may have been Le Quesne's primary motive for requesting exemptions. Those who were prepared to write letters or argue on behalf of others may have been sticking their heads above the parapet, but were mostly protecting their family, friends and colleagues. Observing Le Quesne and others like him in the most favourable light, we might argue that every person removed from the list might (for all that was known at the time) have been a life saved. Even those members of the Superior Council or Controlling Committee who learned that the deportees were to be sent to civilian internment camps were not to know what conditions were like at those camps, or whether islanders would be forced into labour for the Third Reich, or whether they would ever return. On the other hand, we might observe that after realizing that the order would not be rescinded, the island authorities were keen only to take a stand for what might be perceived as their own people, whether we define these as relations, colleagues or the wider community of indigenous islanders.

A number of islanders showed less self-interest and considerable courage in offering to be deported in place of others. While we do not know who all of those people were, some of the names have been recorded in diaries, although it is likely that many more volunteers existed. Deputy Edward Le Quesne noted, on 22 September, that he offered to be sent in place of a 'key man', but was turned down because he was born in Jersey.[26] In Guernsey, a number of clergymen offered themselves up in place of others. On 19 September, the Reverend Ord in Guernsey wrote that he and his wife offered to take the place of Mr and Mrs Dunk, who were with the Baptist church,[27] but presumably either the Dunks or the Germans refused this offer, as the Ords stayed behind. Eventually the Dunks were not deported; their place was taken by the Reverend Donald Stuart and his wife. Two more ministers, the Reverends Arthur Jackson and Frederick Flint, volunteered to leave the island so that the deportees would have representatives from the Methodist church to look after their spiritual needs.[28] On 30 September, the Reverend Ord noted that four Anglican ministers had gone to Germany but that one of those who remained behind volunteered to take the place of an older colleague, but was disallowed by the Germans.[29]

In Guernsey, Marie Ozanne, a Major in the Salvation Army, wrote to the Germans from her prison cell on 17 September 1942, offering herself for deportation even though she was Guernsey born.[30] She was turned down. Three days later, Violet Carey noted in her diary that the Rector of Torteval and his wife, the Greenhows, had volunteered to go in place of an older clergyman and a maternity nurse; two days later Violet notes that they were turned down.[31] During the second wave of deportations in February 1943, parishioners signed petitions to get clergymen exempted given that so many of them had been taken away the previous September. The Reverend Ord in Guernsey recorded in his diary on 8 February 1943 that both Anglicans and Methodists had successfully signed a petition to get the rector of the Parish of St Sampson, Edward Frossard, exempted.[32] Despite a similar petition for the Reverend Grotius James from the Vale Parish in Guernsey, which received 541 signatures, he was deported.[33] Edward Frossard took over his duties, meaning that he had four churches in his care during the Occupation. He was later to be appointed Dean of the island from 1947 to 1967.

Apart from petitions and letters written on behalf of themselves or others, there was yet another way that islanders could evade deportation, and that was to be judged medically unfit. There was more time to organize such things in Guernsey, as the first two groups in Jersey to be deported left very soon after the announcement of the deportation Order. Dr Lewis in Jersey described in his memoirs how he was able to visit some people at home, but could not get round to them all, and, early in the morning, had to go down to the weighbridge in the harbour to catch some of the deportees to inspect them.[34] Leslie Green was one of the lucky ones who was able to see a doctor in Jersey. Although Dr Gow, his local GP, had lied about his age, and written a note stating that he was suspected of having TB and was awaiting an X-ray, neither ruse worked, and he was deported.[35]

In Guernsey the doctors were so inundated with requests for certificates that they immediately formed an *ad hoc* medical board, which met on 18 September (the date of departure of the second group from Jersey). The board comprised all the medical men on the island and was presided over by Dr Symons. Dr Albert Ogier noted in his diary that they met at 10 a.m. at Lukis House, and worked until 8 p.m. that night, examining about 240 people between them. However, those examined were seen again by a German medical board the following day and many had their applications rejected.[36]

On 30 September, three days after the second group of deportees left Guernsey, Ambrose Robin remarked in his diary that some of the local doctors were being blamed for not recommending more people for exemption to the German medical board.

> I told Dr Sutcliffe this afternoon and he assured me that all the local medicals had worked like Trojans from 10 to 12 hours per day on evacuation cases alone last week. More than 65% of their cases left with a certificate as unfit for the journey, etc. The German doctors kicked up a shindy and told the local men that their recommendations had to be cut down to 2%.[37]

The Bailiff's secretary, Louis Guillemette, echoed Dr Sutcliffe's sentiments, noting that 'we have fought tooth and nail for sick people and for people whose absence would upset the life of our little community'.[38]

Thus, in the hours and days following the announcement of the deportation order, various leaders of the community and local government did what they could to help people avoid deportation. Men such as Coutanche, Carey, Leale and Le Quesne verbally protested and spoke their minds to the Germans about the order. In Jersey, such protests were also made in written form. These men did what they could to modify the order and made choices about who to save. As a consequence, many indigenous islanders and some key people were able to escape deportation, although we might observe that the modifications fought for did not principally include non-indigenous islanders. A number of clergymen offered to go in the place of people on the deportation lists and some were accepted; later on, at the time of the second deportation, parishioners campaigned to keep their few remaining parish priests in the island, and this met with varied success. Doctors, too, did what they could to exempt their patients; in some cases they were prepared to lie about their health and ages. Because not all islanders knew what was being done to keep as many people behind as possible, many of these leaders in the community were blamed for not being more successful and for putting their own friends and family first.

In February 1943 the islands' authorities were more selective about those they tried to save from deportation. Rather than trying to protect people who had previous convictions against their name, the authorities in Guernsey handed over lists of people previously sent to prison and released.[39] The Germans were also able to compile lists of the 'politically unreliable', the 'work-shy', those who were Jewish, a number of clergymen, those from Sark deemed to be eligible for deportation, and former British officers, all based on information already collected by the civil authorities at the request of the Germans.[40] The resulting transport lists show that many people in all of these categories were eventually deported, although only around 50 per cent of the listed officers were sent away.[41]

By order of the German High Command, high-ranking Freemasons were originally included within this list,[42] although the deportation lists in Guernsey do not include any specific record of Freemasons; the lists extant in Jersey are ambiguous and do not list the reason for anyone's deportation.[43] We can probably conclude that the order to deport Freemasons was not carried out. Although the precise reasons are unknown, Sanders suggests that they were protected as members of the islands' elites,[44] although Perrin takes the line that senior military commanders might have had Masonic connections or sympathies.[45] What we do know is that some Freemasons were deported in 1943, but not because of their Masonic status; they were deported because they also happened to fit into one of the other categories, such as that of British officer.[46]

Sanders[47] has argued that the civilian authorities in the Channel Islands operated utilitarian doctrines such as 'differential treatment', whereby certain groups were treated differently by the civilian authorities in both islands if they felt that the issue in question was or was not worth spoiling good relations with the Germans for. Groups were either protected or dropped depending on their social status and position within the community. While the 'in-groups' at the time of the 1943 deportations included British officers and Freemasons, the 'out-groups' included British Jews and those who had committed offences against the occupying authorities. As Sanders adds, 'practically no instances are known where they [those who committed offences] benefitted from intervention on the part of the island authorities. The very existence of offenders was an embarrassment to the island authorities, whose bargaining depended on presenting islanders as calm and in no way disposed to opposition.'[48]

Thus while doctors and the clergy were prepared to fight 'tooth and nail' to do what they could within the powers of their own profession to gain exemptions for as many of the community as possible, the civilian authorities were prepared only to make vigorous efforts for their own kin and indigenous islanders in 1942, and Freemasons and officers in 1943. Their efforts in these areas ranged from moderately to very successful. Those who were considered either an embarrassment (those who had committed offences) or who were too small in number to be worth risking good relations with the Germans, were abandoned to their fate.[49]

Protest and defiance on the days of the deportations

The forms of protest and defiance that took place on the days of the deportations themselves were very different to those which took place before. They can broadly be divided into three forms: symbolic resistance (principally through the use of patriotic insignia and colours); the singing of patriotic songs as a form of protest; and refusing to turn up at the harbour (or turning up too late) in defiance of German orders. The evidence for this latter form of defiance is mostly anecdotal, and the author has heard such anecdotes only in Jersey. However, the papers of Mrs G. Attenborough from Jersey suggested that 'The wise owls keep out of the way and show up when the compliment is filled up for the first sheet: quite a few have worked this dodge and have been lucky.'[50]

By September 1942 it was becoming increasingly dangerous to dress in patriotic colours, as discussed elsewhere in this volume. However, as the deportees were in any case being sent away, they must have felt immune to greater punishment at this time. The Reverend Ord in Guernsey wrote in his diary that at the docks there were 'plenty of union jacks and jokes and smiles'.[51] Violet Carey remarked that 'a woman in St Martin's leaned out of a window in a house on the route and waved a Union Jack until the buses were out of sight.'[52] Such patriotic behaviour was repeated in Jersey, where Izett Croad remarked that she heard about a young woman at the pier 'dressed in navy blue and white and with a big red, white and blue bow at her throat'.[53] Mr L'Amy, also in Jersey, observed in his diary that he saw a small Union Jack sticking out of one deportee's hat band;[54] Arthur Kent noted that 'everyone wore a rosette or ribbons and the older men their medals of other wars', adding a few pages later that, as he watched the scene through his office window,

> ... almost everybody, for the first time since the occupation, took the opportunity of wearing red, white and blue favours. Many ex-servicemen among the deportees proudly wore their war medals. I saw hats and parasols in the national colours. I saw families from the country drive up in farmers' vans, the horses gaily bedecked with ribbons.[55]

Not dissimilar scenes were also reputed to have taken place during the second wave of deportations in 1943. Ambrose Robin noted in his diary that he heard that Captain Jack Falla boarded the boat 'looking like a tramp', but then discarded his coat to reveal 'his uniform of the last war with all medals and everything spick and span'.[56] As this wave of deportations targeted ex-officers, it seems that Jack Falla was defiant in the way that he knew best; in a way that was highly appropriate to an old soldier.

The defiant singing of patriotic songs is a well-known and well-documented event of the deportations in Jersey;[57] almost all diarists and memoirists comment upon this event with variations as to the specific order of events, the number of people involved and the precise movements of the German soldiers. What is less well known is that such patriotic singing also happened in Guernsey and in Sark, but without the subsequent scuffle with soldiers, arrests and further deportations, principally because it was the deportees doing the singing rather than the islanders left behind. I have already noted the feeling of cautious immunity that seems to have been felt by the deportees, which may have boosted their courage and, to their minds, given them licence to defy their deporters. Because of the lesser impact of the singing in Guernsey and the fewer people who recorded it, it is easier to relate here first, and to extend it to the patriotic singing that took place at a pre-deportation party attended by a number of young people.

Violet Carey tells us that Frank Stroobant, who owned the 'Home from Home' café, held a party on Tuesday 22 September, during which all sang 'God Save the King' as loudly as they could as they left.[58] Frank himself recalled that, the night before he was deported, people got together and 'we had a terrific binge, and it was amazing the amount of alcohol that was provided. And at the very last moment, long after curfew had been declared, we opened all the windows and we sang all the truly national songs, expecting there would be a German reaction, but there wasn't and it went on quite peacefully.'[59] It seems unlikely that the Germans would fail to hear such a raucous party in an otherwise quiet town. One can only assume that they decided to turn a blind eye to such an event, perhaps out of compassion for those to be deported.

On the days of the deportations themselves, it seems that the Guernsey and Sark deportees sang as lustily as their counterparts in Jersey. On 21 September, both the Reverend Ord and Violet Carey made an entry in their diaries. Ord commented on the 'bearing of the people', remarking that they 'gave a splendid example and we are proud of the breed. Having cut their ties and faced what has to be they were quiet and brave and even smiling' as they assembled for deportation.[60] Violet, who was told by a friend who had seen people leave, was able to report that 'they were wonderful and were singing 'There'll always be an England' as they went off'.[61] A week later, Ambrose Robin recorded that the second group of deportees had left the harbour singing the popular WWI song, 'The Long, Long Trail' and other patriotic songs.[62] Elizabeth Doig also recorded on the same day that the deportees had sung hymns as the vessels had left the harbour.[63] The Reverend Edward Frossard also added his testimony to the others, remarking that 'those who were going showed great courage and fortitude. As the ships left they sang 'Rule Britannia' and the National Anthem and 'There will always be an England'.[64]

A number of Sarkees were targeted for deportation in February 1943. Norah, daughter of diarist Julia Tremayne, went down to the harbour to wave them off and so was able to report to her mother what had happened. 'Before we all said goodbye to our friends they agreed that as they left the harbour they would burst into song', and Norah said that the tunnel echoed with 'Pack up Your Troubles' and 'There'll Always Be an

England'. Someone thought it would not be too wise to sing 'Rule Britannia'.[65] Even the feeling of temporary immunity seemingly had its limits.

In St Helier, patriotic singing took place on 16, 18 and 29 September, and echoed back and forth between those watching on Pier Road, South Hill and Mount Bingham, from where there was a good view of the harbour and of those on board the boats. Islanders had not been able to watch from the piers, as these had been barred to them since the start of the Occupation.[66] The deportees and those watching spurred each other on using call-and-response, such as 'Are we downhearted?' 'No!' and 'One, two, three, four, who the hell are we for?', 'Churchill!', 'England!', 'Jersey!', etc.[67] Sinel described the events as 'the biggest patriotic demonstrations since the Occupation'.[68] However, on 29 September, the situation became ugly. Larger crowds were involved this time, which Joe Mière (who was involved) estimated in various documents as both a 'thousand plus' and 'five thousand plus',[69] compared to his estimations for the deportations of 16 September, which he put at 'nearly 200'.[70] Izett Croad estimated a crowd of 500 at the demonstration of 18 September.[71] Given that no head count was taken, the actual numbers remain unknown.

Sinel recorded that one young boy

> ... unloosed a beautiful right hook and laid out a German officer; others played football with a German's helmet, and many spectators, whether voluntary or not, added volume to the epithets being hurled at the German soldiers who attempted to interfere, the latter eventually chasing the boys with their bayonets and revolvers ... Fourteen boys ... were arrested and taken by the Germans to their section of the prison in Gloucester Street ...'[72]

Others involved in demonstration were hurt in what became, in the accounts of some, an out-of-control riot; Frank Keiller was hit in the back and on the neck with a rifle butt, and bayoneted in the buttock.[73] The Germans managed to arrest only a small number of the fleeing demonstrators in the subsequent mêlée.

All of those demonstrators arrested[74] were given sentences of either one or two months,[75] except 33-year-old Flavian Emile Barbier, who was deemed to be the ringleader by virtue of being the eldest of those arrested (the rest were mostly teenagers). He was given a sentence of three years in prison by decree of German military tribunal on 12 October 1942.[76] Of the other 18 young men arrested, only four were made to serve their sentences, the others being given suspended sentences conditional on good behaviour. However in February 1943 a different four men from the original group of 18, each of whom had been given a one-month suspended sentence, were sent to Laufen in the deportations during which 'undesirables' were targeted. These four were chosen because they were the eldest in the group and were no longer at school, unlike the others.[77]

Willmot argues that the deportations had a 'profound psychological impact' upon the population; they had been given proof that obedience to German orders was not enough to guarantee their safety. The result was a 'permanent hardening of attitudes' which, for some, persuaded them to take 'more direct action' against the occupiers.[78] While the Germans imagined that the removal of the English-born and those who had served time in prison would reduce the 'troublesome elements' in the population, the very action of their removal instead spawned greater anti-German feeling.

Resistance in the camps

After passing through the transit camps of Dorsten (in 1942) and Compiègne (in 1943), the islanders were spread, for the most part, between four main camps in southern Germany. These were Laufen for single men, a camp shared with American internees; Liebenau for single women, a mixed nationality camp; Wurzach for Jersey families and Biberach for Guernsey and Sark families. While Laufen, Liebenau and Wurzach camps were all former *schlossen* or castles, Biberach was a barrack-style prisoner-of-war (POW) camp.

The first couple of months in all of these camps were marked by shock, sadness, fear and hunger, as the internees began to clean up the buildings in which they found themselves, appointed a camp captain and organized themselves into a variety of different camp roles, jobs and fatigues to keep themselves occupied. In December 1942, Red Cross parcels began to arrive. Having existed on meagre rations provided by the German guards, which were slowly causing malnutrition, spreading discontent and even caused a couple of riots,[79] the parcels were extremely welcome. Former internee Michael Ginns from Jersey later described how the internees felt the tension and depression lift off the camp.[80]

The arrival of the Red Cross parcels was a boon to the internees in more ways than one. Having arrived in the camps with only what they could carry, which for the most part included a few spare clothes and the meal dishes and blankets stipulated in the deportation order, most internees were materially very impoverished. Some had received as little as two hours' notice of their deportation; others had been given a few days or a couple of weeks. In the panic that ensued, few had thought to bring with them things to help them pass the time, although some brought writing paper. Enterprising internees made room in their cases for other objects. Artist Eric Sirett from Guernsey, interned in Biberach with his wife Ruth, wrote that he managed to stow away his watercolours, paintbrushes and sketch pads, while Ruth packed her hairdressing kit.[81]

As well as food, the Red Cross parcels provided the internees with brown packing paper, parcel string, tins, cardboard and strips of coloured cellophane which were used as packing material. All of these items could be recycled into innumerable different objects for creative internees. A letter written to Lionel Levitt from his wife in Liebenau camp records the value of these raw materials to internees:

> You would be really amused if you could see us opening our Red Cross parcels. First comes the string which is never cut but carefully untied, split, knitted, plaited or interwoven for bags, soles of shoes, straps for luggage, serviette rings, egg cups ... then comes the packing used for filling cushions or hay boxes for keeping things warm. Most tins come in handy as cooking utensils or flower pots and the boxes themselves are used for waste paper baskets, brackets, shoe boxes, and of

course to store all manner of treasures in! Even the labels on the tins are carefully taken off and used to decorate trays etc... .[82]

This letter provides just a very small insight into the possibilities of recycling within an internment camp. As argued elsewhere,[83] internees were able to express safely their emotions through their creative outputs, which became a repository for all feelings that would have otherwise been disruptive to camp harmony and communal living if given free reign. Similarly, through creative expression, they were able to voice their dissatisfaction with interned life, with the food, the guards and with the German regime as a whole in a non-confrontational manner.

The defiant stances, complaints and critiques of daily life for people in internment camps, which were rarely acted upon for fear of repercussions, were made tangible and enacted through the creative process. Through the objects and artwork that they made, Channel Islanders were able to maintain their cultural identity in the camps. This involved an espousal of patriotic beliefs and a defiant attitude towards the guards, the war and the specific conditions of internment.

Material produced in camp can often express a continuation of identity and previous way of life before incarceration, as Casella[84] and Dusselier[85] have argued for the interned Japanese Americans during WWII. Dusselier[86] has also discussed how identity expressed through food could be an effective realm of resistant political activity in camp. Archer[87] has shown how the maintenance of aspects of pre-internment identities could be an important survival technique for Western civilians interned by the Japanese. Expressions of identity, ethnicity and culture were often resistant in intent and manifestation as a way of keeping up morale. They were also a way of keeping faith with those who might one day bring about liberation, or a way of making sure that their identity and spirit was not crushed by their jailors.

Discussions of resistance and defiance are not unproblematic. What constitutes 'resistance' and what kind was possible among civilian internees? Extreme responses to internment were probably atypical; gentler words such as 'defiance' or perhaps 'co-operation', 'accommodation', or 'compromise' are probably more useful in understanding the reality of everyday life for most, especially as people or reactions would have fluctuated through time and in response to unexpected opportunities or to certain events in the war and in the camp. Various forms of resistance in the camps are recorded in diaries and memoirs by Channel Islanders, and not all of these were depicted in artwork. For example, we know that secret radios were made in both Laufen[88] and Wurzach.[89] Encoded postcards and letters were also exchanged between islanders and those in the camps.[90] There were also individuals in the camps who were well known for defying German orders. Among such people we might include Robert Hathaway, Seigneur of Sark, who was sent to Laufen. We are told that, for more than two years, he 'refused persistently to obey German orders', 'did his damnest to make himself unpopular with the Germans', and 'occupied himself most of the time by deliberately breaking camp rules'.[91]

Interestingly, but perhaps not unexpectedly, many of the acts of protest and defiance that were being carried out in the Channel Islands were also continued in the internment camps.

In their hand-made objects and artwork we can observe four overlapping areas of creativity: the expression of British or Channel Island identity, which included the use of patriotic symbols (such as colours, crests and flags); support of the British royal family; support of Allied forces and their ultimate victory (often expressed through the V-sign campaign); and protest against conditions in the camp (including overcrowding, inadequate food and unpopular guards). This is not to say that more open aggression towards guards and camp authorities did not take place (indeed it did, albeit very rarely), but riots and demonstrations were clearly confrontational acts, and by their very nature were expressed vocally and physically rather than manifested creatively.

Their identity as Channel Islanders and British citizens was of foremost importance to the internees, and they valued it highly as an integral part of their patriotism. While their experiences as occupied and deported people increased their enmity towards their German guards, these feelings were exaggerated for some (such as former First World War soldiers, political prisoners and British Jews), or more muted in others (such as among the conscientious objectors and the few Irish who were among the deported), although this generalizes the situation to a certain extent. It should also be noted that, after the first three months during which they were guarded by the *Wehrmacht*, the army was replaced by the *Schutzpolizei* (civilian police) who were often old men. Some of them had been well-treated as POWs in the United Kingdom during the First World War, and so were inclined to treat the Channel Islanders well. In fact, such was the 'understanding' between the internees and the guards at the camps of Biberach and Wurzach, that higher authorities demanded that the two sets of guards were exchanged with each other to put a stop to such a 'friendly' state of affairs.[92]

While the display of Union Jacks, patriotic colours and the national anthem was forbidden in the occupied Channel Islands, there is plentiful evidence for their use in the camps. While the many German orders governing camp life do not appear to have survived, former internees agree that these things were not strictly allowed in the camp, but ways around the orders were found. Former internee Michael Ginns suggests that, as long as the guards were slipped a tablet of Red Cross soap or some cigarettes, they were happy to turn a blind eye to some of the activities that took place.[93]

Use of the Union Jack and patriotic colours are visible on sketches and paintings of barrack rooms, where it seems that internees indulged in a form of patriotic interior design. Examples include a photo of a room in Schloss Wurzach, where a British flag was pinned up behind the door;[94] a sketch by Harold Hepburn of a corner of room 56 in the same camp, showing a small horseshoe painted red, white and blue hanging up in front of a shelf;[95] and a pen and ink sketch of people playing cards at Wurzach, with a Union Jack pinned to the wall above a bed, alongside other pictures.[96] The same activities were clearly going on at other camps. An embroidery of room 15, barrack 6 at Biberach, made by Edna Dorrian, clearly shows a small Union Jack above the door.[97] Joan Coles also recalled that her father had a small map on his bedroom wall which showed the movement of Allied troops across France and Germany[98] – a most satisfying piece of defiant interior design!

The Union Jack and patriotic colours appeared in many different forms of internee creativity, including the theatre. In Biberach, 'Café Continental' was performed and black and white photos still circulate among former internees of the cast and the stage set.⁹⁹ One former internee who worked with the men responsible for making the stage set remembers that it was painted red, white and blue.¹⁰⁰ While such an obvious use of patriotic colours would not have passed unnoticed, it may not have been seen as either deliberately subversive or particularly dangerous by the guards.

Patriotic colours are especially frequent in greetings cards and autograph books, but in forms which had a restricted audience. Many pictures of flags are shown in association with other images, such as bulldogs (symbolic of Winston Churchill),¹⁰¹ poems and sketches describing the route taken to the camps through war-torn Europe,¹⁰² signatures of those in the camp, and even ships that would one day aid in repatriation.¹⁰³ While watercolours depicting the Union Jack are also not uncommon, we cannot assume that these were all put on public display in barrack rooms. Many of these were private gifts from one internee to another and were presumably secreted away in suitcases and the like. The exchange of such patriotic gifts, whether private or public, would have been meaningful to other internees as exhortations to keep the faith with King and country and to help boost bravery and morale.

Such patriotic gifts which created bonds between internees would also have aided the building of fellow-feeling in the communal society which existed in the camp. It was further enhanced by the gifting of small objects which could be carried or worn on the body by men and women, such as handkerchiefs and badges.

Women within a barrack room would often embroider a handkerchief for the birthday of another woman in the room or for their husbands. Those made in Biberach typically had the Union Jack in the centre or top of the handkerchief and the names of those in the room were embroidered in a hierarchical form either around a central flag or in a row (according to seniority) beneath the flag, with the barrack leader at the top.¹⁰⁴ Similar examples made for men sometimes gave the names of the camp or barrack football team; these listed the captain and the camp sports committee in a prominent position. Such handkerchiefs can be seen as a microcosm of camp society, and could have carried the message that within the hierarchy, all were united under the flag.

Union Jack badges were popular among the patriotic islanders and were made in all of the camps out of wool, string, glass beads, tin, wood, paper or whatever came to hand. Like the flags on the embroidered handkerchiefs, all were made to a common design, namely, that on the Colman's English mustard jar, which was often included in British Red Cross parcels (Figure 5.1).¹⁰⁵ Internees cut out the little flag and used it as a template for their badges or embroideries. While some gave it cardboard backing and attached a safety pin, others used a variety of other materials. Thomas Webber, interned in Wurzach, painted his on the oval tin lid of the mustard jar itself. He, like others, wore the badges inside the lapels of their jackets, but wore them openly when the guards were not around.¹⁰⁶ Parents were also able to provide their children with these badges, or patriotically painted buttons on clothes, to make a statement about their loyalty.¹⁰⁷ Similar badges were also worn during football matches in Laufen (when they were worn in games against the American internees).¹⁰⁸

The main symbol of Channel Island identity was the crest. There are two noteworthy examples of its use in the camp. The first is on a camp-issue mug, engraved by Byll Balcombe in Biberach.¹⁰⁹ The second is on the costume of a young woman, dressed as Miss Guernsey, at the August Bank holiday fancy dress cavalcade held in Biberach

Figure 5.1 Union Jack from a Colman's mustard tin (courtesy of family of Mr and Mrs A.T. Green. Photo: Gilly Carr)

camp in 1943.[110] The camp commandant, Herr Mayer, filmed this occasion (perhaps as propaganda). The black-and-white film[111] shows the camp inmates in high spirits, parading in a range of exotic costumes. Many diarists recorded the event, mentioning how the costumes were made from recycled Red Cross parcels, old clothes from the Red Cross, bed boards and mattress covers. At a later date, stills were made from the film and these now exist as photographs in the archives of some former internees and collectors.

Many other patriotic characters were present in the cavalcade: St George and the dragon, Britannia, John Bull, Uncle Sam and, poignantly, the figure of Justice – something most internees would have felt was lacking in their interned lives (Figure 5.2). The choice of these characters made a light-hearted yet powerful and highly visible statement to others; one that was not censored by the guards. The internees obviously took the opportunity that the cavalcade provided to make powerful visual statements to each other.

The personification of allied countries, images of their flags, and sketches of allied war machinery such as planes, ships and tanks,[112] were all ways in which internees could show their support of their armed forces. For example, Wurzach internee Harold Hepburn used the motif of three RAF spitfire planes in the corner of all of his greetings

Figure 5.2 Photo from the August Bank Holiday fancy dress cavalcade in Biberach, 1943 (courtesy of Damien Horn/the Channel Islands Military Museum Collection)

cards.[113] Sketches of the RAF symbol, i.e. the crowned and winged roundel with the letters 'RAF' in the centre, were also reproduced in artwork.[114] One internee even crocheted herself a badge in the form of the red, white and blue motif that RAF planes had under their wings, so that she could express her support and solidarity with the pilots when they flew over the camp.[115]

Although the internees in the camps could not fight alongside the allies, there were other ways in which they could form a different sort of army: the 'V-army', who were encouraged by 'Colonel Britton' of the BBC (alias Douglas Ritchie), who spoke on the European service to encourage those of occupied Europe to chalk or paint up the letter V for victory in public places wherever they could in order to make the Germans feel that they were surrounded by a hostile resistance army. The campaign was extremely popular all over Europe and the Channel Islands, as discussed elsewhere in this volume, and was continued in the camps.

It did not take the same form in the camps as it had in the islands; instead Vs were more circumspect, private and hidden. Many examples exist, but a few will suffice here to illustrate the range. Some people brought their V-sign badges with them from Guernsey; these were fashioned from coins (usually shillings), where the letter V was scored and cut under the King's head, which itself was snipped out and filed, and was then turned into a badge that people wore beneath lapels and flashed to friends in the street.[116] Other items made in the camps include a camp-issue mug, engraved with a large letter V in Biberach by Byll Balcombe, presumably so he could drink a toast to victory (Figure 5.3).[117]

Figure 5.3 V-mug made by Byll Balcombe in Biberach camp, in private ownership. Photo copyright Gilly Carr, courtesy of Christine Bailey

In Wurzach, Nora Hadgetts embroidered a tablecloth decorated with colourful Vs around the edge, with national symbols of a rose, a thistle, a harp and a shamrock in the four corners. In the centre was the letter V with a crown on top, victory laurels beneath and the initials 'GR' (George Rex) below the laurel.[118] Through the use of symbols, this humble table cloth was able to combine within it an expression of cultural identity, support for the King, the United Kingdom, and an allied victory. One final example will suffice to show the ability of ordinary, everyday items to make a powerful statement. In Wurzach (as in other camps), Red Cross parcel string was saved up, plaited and stitched to make rope-soled summer canvas shoes. One surviving shoe shows a plaited V stitched onto the sole, which would have enabled the wearer, if they had gone out in the rain, to make victorious footprints around rooms of the schloss.[119] Thus, the 'V-army' continued its work in the camps as it had back in the Channel Islands.

Just as the islanders supported the allies in their own small but intense way, their support for the British royal family was just as strong. While the national anthem, 'God Save the King', was not allowed to be sung in camp, internees found other ways to express their patriotic feelings. Popular ways to end an evening in Biberach, at a camp dance or in the camp theatre, was to sing other patriotic songs such as 'Land of Hope and Glory', 'Jerusalem' and the Guernsey national anthem, 'Sarnia Cherie'.[120]

A beautiful tapestry, begun in Sark, largely completed in Biberach camp and embroidered on potato sacking by Margaret Beaumont, depicts a colourful, flowered garden full of wildlife. Above the foliage is embroidered the poem '*The garden is gay in ye month of May, the fire is the flower of ye winter's day. God Save the King! We humbly pray.*'[121] Such an item might be seen as rather daring, but one of the few former Biberach internees alive today who was an adult rather than a child in the camp, has remarked that the Germans didn't examine what internees made. It seems that they were not particularly interested (perhaps because such items were deemed to be unthreatening because they were 'women's work'). Such an item as the tapestry 'would not have been queried'.[122]

Support for the royal family and the reinforcement and maintenance of cultural identity was also expressed through food, especially on special occasions. A few illustrated and decorated menus survive from communal camp Christmas and New Year dinners, and it is clear from these that not only was the traditional seasonal British meal replicated as closely as possible, cobbled together from Red Cross parcel contents, but that patriotic sentiments were expressed during these occasions. This happened through an after-dinner toast to the King, according to the Christmas menu from Wurzach,[123] and through the colour scheme and V-sign motif of the New Year menu decoration at Biberach.[124]

Portrait artist Arscott Dickinson, one of a minority of Jerseymen in Biberach, produced a series of at least 66 caricatures of camp personalities. At least five of these were humorous images of German camp guards.[125] When referring to the guards today, former internees from all camps refer to them by insulting nicknames based on their physical characteristics. Both of these were creative methods of belittling and undermining the authority of the guards in front of other internees. Such actions would also have reassured nervous camp children. Given that most internees alive today were children in the camps, it is telling that most of them knew the guards only by their nicknames.

The young of Wurzach camp lost their fear of the Germans to such an extent that, during the Christmas pantomime of 'Snow White and the Seven Dwarfs', they sang an alternative version of 'Whistle while you work' that made fun of Hitler and Goering. Although there were German guards in the audience, internee Michael Ginns thinks that those on stage got away with it, either because the guards didn't hear them, or because they didn't understand the British colloquial terms that were used in the song.[126]

Food was often a source of conflict, and the two recorded riots in Channel Islander camps occurred over bread and turnip rations in Laufen and the transit camp of Dorsten respectively.[127] The meagre food rations given to each internee before the Red Cross parcels arrived in the camps in December 1942 were the subject of much complaint that was expressed eloquently in diaries, artwork and poetry.

The thin, watery soup, sometimes-rotten potatoes, often-mouldy black, dry rye bread[128] and fish that was sometimes maggoty[129] was commented upon with grim humour, as were the after-effects on the body. Jersey artist Harold Hepburn who, like most deported Jerseymen, spent time in Biberach before being moved to Wurzach in the late autumn of 1942, produced a watercolour of the (outdoor) soup queue, complete with watchtowers and barbed wire in the background.[130] This theme was echoed in another of his paintings from the same period. Titled 'The night patrol or 3 o'clock in the morning', it showed men queuing for the camp toilets – the effect of a bout of gastroenteritis which hit the camp.[131]

In a third painting from the series he produced during this period, Hepburn drew his barrack room with its inmates asleep. On the table, in mute protest, stood the day's rations: a jug of the much-loathed mint tea, a bowl of thin soup, a small hunk of bread and a tiny cube of cheese or butter. Hepburn was not the only one who expressed his dissatisfaction through creative outlets. Mr Fish, another Wurzach internee, drew and labelled the four different types of watery soup given as rations: 'Blue Danube' (made with red cabbage), 'Black Forest' (which had bits of husk and foliage often found floating in it), 'White Wings' (which contained a single leaf of white cabbage) and 'Golden Glory' (swede soup).[132] These nicknames were also used in Biberach, as Eric Sirett recorded. Although he was an artist himself, he restricted his complaints about the food to verse: '*I think / no other cheese / can stink / like these*' and '*The German bread / that we are fed / on tastes like sawdust / mildew-ed*'.[133] If these sentiments had been expressed to a guard, Sirett might have found himself on even smaller rations. Scribbled on a piece of paper instead, Sirett's desire to protest was satiated in a form which drew no adverse repercussions.

Conclusion

This chapter has documented the range of protest, defiance and resistance that took place in the Channel Islands during the deportations in 1942 and 1943 to civilian internment camps. It provides stark examples of the range of ways in which powerless people can express their true feelings in a situation which they were powerless to prevent or overturn. Interestingly, it highlights the ability of these same people to *modify* the situation, although choices had to be made about which battles to fight. Once the choice was made, those in positions of authority were ultimately relatively successful in their endeavours.

Ordinary people, too, were sometimes able to ameliorate the situation in which they found themselves. Through non-compliance, a small minority seemingly escaped deportation altogether. Through vocal and public protest, islanders who stayed behind were able to show their support to those who were sent away, even though it led to further deportations for some of their number. In the camps themselves, through their creative energies, the internees were able to make a new (albeit temporary) life for themselves. Complaints and protests to the guards were rarely a viable option to elicit change. Instead, internees were able to protest among themselves, to use humour to cheer themselves up, and to decorate their barrack rooms and clothes in ways which made meaningful and emotionally cathartic political statements.

Creativity provided them with a crucial emotional outlet; it enabled them to safely vent their spleens. It also allowed them to continue with the many strands of pre-deportation resistance that had been conducted in the islands to date, through the use of patriotic colours and songs, the V-sign campaign, and the insult of guards – behind their backs. This creativity was critical to the mental health of individuals and the camp as a whole, and it empowered the camp community to face, endure and survive the system of oppression enacted through the enemy-controlled civilian internment camp. Even at their most vulnerable, Channel Islanders were not entirely without power to improve their situation by increments, and they chose and exploited such opportunities to the full.

Notes

1. Louise Willmot, '"Nothing was ever the same again": Public Attitudes in the Occupied Channel Islands, 1942', *The Local Historian: Journal of the British Association for Local History*, Vol. 35 (1), 2005, 9–20.
2. Ibid.
3. Roger E. Harris, *Islanders Deported (Part I)*, Ilford, Essex, Channel Islands Specialists Society Publishing, 1979, p. 3.
4. Ibid.
5. Ibid., pp. 4–5.
6. Ibid., p. 7.
7. Ibid., p. 5.
8. The author has worked with this group of deportees from 2006 onwards and has carried out interviews with around 50 former deportees from Guernsey, Sark and Jersey.
9. Jonathan Bartlett, pers. comm., 2007.
10. Folio 1 of file on Compiègne by Tom Remfrey, given to author.
11. Violet Carey, *Guernsey under Occupation. The Second World War Diaries of Violet Carey*, ed. A. Evans, Chichester, Phillimore, 2009, pp. xxvi–xxvii.
12. John Leale, *Report of Five Years of German Occupation*, Guernsey, Guernsey Press, 1945, p. 3.
13. Louis Guillemette, Diary, pp. 68–69, in private ownership.
14. Leale, *Report of Five Years of German Occupation*, p. 4.
15. IA.CC 09–05. Letter from Victor Carey to Feldkommandantur 515, 15 September 1942.
16. Ibid.
17. Ibid.
18. Carey, *Guernsey under Occupation*, p. 99.
19. IA.FK 12–07. Deportation exemption request letters.
20. For example Ralph Durand, *Guernsey under German Rule*, London, The Guernsey Society, 1946, p. 86.
21. Alexander Coutanche, *The Memoirs of Lord Coutanche: A Jerseyman Looks Back*, ed. H. R. S. Pocock, Chichester, Sussex, Phillimore and Co. Ltd., 1975, pp. 29–30.
22. JAS.B/A/W80/1. Resolution of the Superior Council of the States of Jersey, signed by Alexander Coutanche, 21 September 1942.
23. Ibid.
24. Ibid.
25. Edward Le Quesne, *The Occupation of Jersey Day by Day*. The Personal Diary of Deputy Edward Le Quesne, with a foreword and explanatory notes by Michael Ginns, Jersey, La Haule, 1999, pp. 156–7.
26. Ibid., p. 156.
27. PL.LF940.53 ORD. Reverend R. Douglas Ord, Occupation Diary, 19 September 1942.
28. 'Pulpit References', *Guernsey Evening Press*, 21 September 1942.
29. PL.LF940.53 ORD. Reverend R. Douglas Ord, Occupation Diary, 30 September 1942.

30 IA.FK 12-07. Letter from Marie Ozanne to Feldkommandant, written while in prison, 17 September 1942.
31 IA.AQ 0368/01–11. Violet Carey, Occupation Diaries 1940–1945.
32 PL.LF940.53 ORD. Reverend R. Douglas Ord, Occupation Diary, 8 February 1943; IA.FK 12-12. Petition signed by 322 people from St Sampson to gain exemption for the Reverend Edward Frossard.
33 IA.FK 13-01. Petition signed by 541 people from the Vale parish asking for exemption for the Reverend Grotius James and his wife, dated 10 February 1943.
34 John Lewis, *A Doctor's Occupation: The Dramatic True Story of Life in Nazi-Occupied Jersey*, Jersey, Channel Island Publishing, 1982, p. 177.
35 SJ.OCC 942 GRE. Leslie Green, 'My War Years', p. 18.
36 PL.LF940.53 BIS. Albert Ogier Bisson, 'The Diary of Dr Albert Ogier Bisson in Guernsey during the German Occupation of the Channel Islands in the Second World War, 1940–1945', 24 September 1942.
37 PL.LF940.53 ROB. Ambrose C. Robin, Occupation Diaries 17 June 1940–18 May 1945, 30 September 1942.
38 Louis Guillemette, Diary, p. 71, in private ownership.
39 IA.FK 04-09 and IA.FK 13-02. Names of persons convicted by German courts up to the end of 1942.
40 For example IA.FK 12-12. 1943 deportation lists; see also Frederick Cohen, *The Jews in the Channel Islands during the German Occupation 1940–1945,* Jersey, Jersey Heritage Trust in association with the Institute of Contemporary History and Wiener Library, 2000, pp. 56–9; David Fraser, *The Jews of the Channel Islands and the Rule of Law, 1940–1945*, Brighton and Portland, Sussex Academic Press, 2000, p. 159.
41 IA.FK 12-14. 1943 transport lists.
42 Charles Cruickshank, *The German Occupation of the Channel Islands: The Official History of the Occupation Years,* London, Sutton Publishing, 2004, p. 232.
43 JAS.D/Z/K4/6. 1943 transport lists.
44 Paul Sanders, *The British Channel Islands under German Occupation, 1940–1945*, Jersey, Jersey Heritage Trust and Société Jersiaise, 2005, p. 141.
45 Dennis Perrin, *The German Occupation and Jersey Freemasonry 1940–1945*, Jersey, privately published, 1995.
46 For example Bertram Bartlett, deported with his wife and son in February 1943, was a Freemason; he was also born in the United Kingdom and was also a former WWI officer (Jonathan Bartlett pers. comm.) The deportation lists make clear that he was deported because of his status as a former officer.
47 Sanders, *The British Channel Islands under German Occupation*, pp. 75–7, 141–2; Paul Sanders, 'Managing under Duress: Ethical Leadership, Social Capital, and the Civilian Administration of the British Channel Islands during the Nazi Occupation, 1940–1945', *Journal of Business Ethics*, Vol. 93, 2010, 113–29.
48 Sanders, *The British Channel Islands under German Occupation*, p. 142.
49 Frank Falla, *The Silent War: The Inside Story of the Channel Islands under the Nazi Jackboot,* Guernsey, Burbridge Ltd., 1994, p. 156.
50 IWM.Documents.11646 02/17/1. Mr and Mrs G. Attenborough, 'The Great Deportation 15/9/42', p. 4; see also Leo Harris, *A Boy Remembers,* Jersey, Channel Island Publishing, 2004, p. 97 which documents the case of the Wilkinson family.
51 PL.LF940.53 ORD. Reverend R. Douglas Ord, Occupation Diary, 25 September 1942.
52 IA.AQ 0368/01–11. Violet Carey, Occupation Diaries 1940–1945, 29 September 1942.
53 JAS.L/C/77/A/1–8. Izett Croad, Occupation Diary, 20 September 1942.

54 SJ.*OCC 942 L'AM. J. H. L'Amy, 'The German Occupation of Jersey', undated but written in 1945/46, p. 28.
55 JWT.2004/134/13-16. Arthur Kent, Draft of Occupation Memoirs, 1983; JWT.2004/131/17-73. Arthur Kent, *Diary*, 1945.
56 PL.LF940.53 ROB. Ambrose C. Robin, Occupation Diaries 17 June 1940–18 May 1945, 17 February 1943.
57 For example JAS.C/C/L/C7/2. Joe Mière, testimony on the demonstrations about the 1942 deportations; IWM.Documents.5750 Misc 189/1-2 (2826). Madeleine Bunting papers, interview with Joe Berry, Tape 4482 (transcript); Frank Keiller, *Prison without Bars: Living in Jersey under the German Occupation 1940-1945*, Bradford on Avon, Seaflower Books, 2000, pp. 76–9; JAS.L/C/77/A/1-8. Izett Croad, Occupation Diary, 17, 18, 29 and 30 September 1942; IWM.Documents.9775 P324. Mrs I. M. Bullen, Diary, 18 September 1942; SJ.GO Box 2/13. Nurse Linda Pallot, No. 2 Division, 'Report of the Deportation of English People from Jersey to Germany, September 29 1942'; SJ.OCC 942 GRE. Leslie Green, 'My War Years', p. 18; SJ.*OCC 942 L'AM. J. H. L'Amy, 'The German Occupation of Jersey', undated but written in 1945/46, p. 28; IWM.Documents.1806 91/5/1. Canon E. L. Frossard, Dean of Guernsey 1945–1968, 'The German Occupation of Guernsey', 1969, p. 398.
58 IA.AQ 0368/01-11. Violet Carey, Occupation Diaries 1940–1945, 23 September 1942.
59 IWM.Sound Archive.Interview 12076/Tape 4419. Frank Edward Stroobant, 1991; the same tale is related in Stroobant's book *One Man's War*, Guernsey, Burbridge Ltd, 1997 [1967].
60 PL.LF940.53 ORD. Reverend R. Douglas Ord, Occupation Diary, 21 September 1942.
61 IA.AQ 0368/01-11. Violet Carey, Occupation Diaries 1940–1945, 23 September 1942, 21 September 1942.
62 PL.LF940.53 ROB. Ambrose C. Robin, Occupation Diaries 17 June 1940–18 May 1945, 28 September 1942.
63 PL.LF940.53 DOI. Elizabeth Doig, Diary, 28 September 1942.
64 IWM.Documents.1806 91/5/1. Canon E. L. Frossard, Dean of Guernsey 1945–1968, 'The German Occupation of Guernsey', 1969, p. 399.
65 Julia Tremayne, *War on Sark: The Secret Letters of Julia Tremayne*, Exeter, Webb and Bower, 1981, 12 February 1943.
66 JWT.2004/131/18-73. Arthur Kent, *Diary*, 1945.
67 Alan Wood and Mary Wood, *Islands in Danger: The Story of the German Occupation of the Channel Islands, 1940–1945*, New York, Macmillan, 1955, p. 137.
68 Leslie Sinel, *The German Occupation of Jersey: A Complete Diary of Events from June 1940-June 1945*, Jersey, The Evening Post, 1945, 16, 18 and 29 September 1942.
69 JAS.C/C/L/C7/2. Joe Mière Collection; Joe Mière, *Never to be Forgotten*, Jersey, Channel Island Publishing, 2004, p. 58.
70 Mière, *Never to be Forgotten*, p. 54; JWT. Joe Mière Collection.
71 JAS.L/C/77/A/1-8. Izett Croad, Occupation Diary, 17 September 1942.
72 Sinel, *The German Occupation of Jersey*, 29 September 1942.
73 Keiller, *Prison without Bars*, p. 78.
74 JAS.D/Z/H6. Law Officers' Department. The archives relating to the sentences and prosecutions by the Field Command and Troop Courts in Jersey list 19 people arrested over this incident.
75 JAS.D/Z/H6/4. Troop court sentence files.

76 Ibid. Barbier was sent to France on 22 January 1943 and later transferred to Nieder-Roden concentration camp (Arolsen International Tracing Service Archive, Hinweiskarte aus der Zentralen Namenkartei, Emile Flavien, n.d., ITS Digitales Archiv). He survived the war.
77 JAS.D/AG/B7/1. 'Names of Political Prisoners August 1940' prison log book. The four men deported were Maurice Hill, Arthur Le Borgne, Raymond Hannaford and Eldon Gibaut.
78 Willmot, '"Nothing was ever the same again"', 9-20.
79 Two riots have been documented and both were concerned with food. The first occurred in Dorsten and took place because the turnip tops that were being served were very sandy and had not been properly washed (Eric Sirett archive, courtesy of Peter Sirret); the second took place in Laufen and was caused by a shortage of bread (Michael Ginns, pers. comm., 2008).
80 JWT.2007/1022. Interview with Michael Ginns, 2007.
81 Eric Sirett archive, courtesy of Peter Sirett.
82 Letter from Kate Levitt to her husband Lionel, undated. My thanks to Peter Levitt for letting me quote from this.
83 Gillian Carr, 'Material Culture and the Emotions of Internment', in A. Myers and G. Moshenska (eds), *Archaeologies of Internment, One World Archaeology (WAC)*, New York, Springer, 2011, pp. 129-45.
84 Eleanor C. Casella, *The Archaeology of Institutional Confinement*, Gainesville, University Press of Florida, 2007, pp. 136-42.
85 Jane E. Dusselier, *Artifacts of Loss: Crafting Survival in Japanese American Concentration Camps*, New Brunswick, Rutgers University Press, 2008.
86 Jane E. Dusselier, 'Does Food Make Place? Food Protests in Japanese American Concentration Camps', *Food and Foodways*, Vol. 10, 2002, 137-65.
87 Bernice Archer, *The Internment of Western Civilians under the Japanese 1941-1945*, Hong Kong, Hong Kong University Press, 2008.
88 Stroobant, *One Man's War*, pp. 101-13.
89 IWM.Sound Archive.Tape 4383. Interview with Joan Coles.
90 PL.LF940.53 ORD. Reverend R. Douglas Ord, Occupation Diary, 29 April 1943.
91 Michael Marshall, *Hitler Invaded Sark*, St Peter Port, Guernsey, Paramount-Lithoprint, 1963, pp. 37-8 & fn.
92 Interview with Michael Ginns, 6 April 2008.
93 Ibid.
94 JAS.L/C/01/B/A/23. Photograph of room in Wurzach internment camp.
95 JAS.L/D/25/E3/A/10. Sketch by Harold Hepburn.
96 JAS.L/C/01/B/A/9. Pen and ink sketch done in Wurzach.
97 GOMG. Edna Dorrian, embroidery of room 15, barrack 6 in Biberach camp.
98 IWM.Sound Archive.Tape 4383. Interview with Joan Coles.
99 JAS.L/D/25/E1/1. Photograph of stage set for Café Continental in Biberach camp theatre.
100 Interview with Yvonne Osborn, 30 December 2009.
101 The author is grateful to Sheila Legg and Mary Cornish in Jersey for showing her such images from their own family collections.
102 JAS.L/C/46/B/11. Series of paintings by Preston John Doughty.
103 The author is grateful to Godfrey Le Cappelain for showing her his collection of artwork from Wurzach and Laufen.

104 The author is grateful to Richard Heaume, David Barrett and David Skillet for showing her their examples.
105 Interview with Sylvia Diamond, 24 May 2008; interview with Barry Webber, 14 August 2010.
106 Interview with Barry Webber, 14 August 2010.
107 Interview with Ursula Dingle, 8 April 2010.
108 GOMG. Richard Heaume private collection.
109 My thanks to Christine Bailey for showing me this item.
110 Thanks to collector Damien Horn for showing me this photograph.
111 GOMG. Richard Heaume private collection.
112 For example JAS.L/D/25/E1/2. Album of paintings and objects made in Wurzach.
113 Ibid.
114 My thanks to Godfrey Le Cappelain and Barry Webber for showing me examples of this in their personal collections.
115 My thanks to John Goodwin for showing me this item from his parents' archive.
116 Gillian Carr and Richard Heaume, 'Silent Resistance in Guernsey: The V-sign Badges of Alf Williams and Roy Machon', *Channel Islands Occupation Review*, Vol. 32, 2004, 51–5.
117 My thanks to Christine Bailey for showing me this item.
118 JM.SJM.1992.224. Tablecloth made by Nora Hadgetts.
119 JAS.L/D/25/E1/4. Box containing objects made in Wurzach.
120 Interview with Yvonne Osborn, 30 December 2009.
121 My thanks to Heather Duggan for letting me see this beautiful item.
122 Interview with Yvonne Osborn, 30 December 2009.
123 RCA.Acc0054_2. Christmas menu, Wurzach.
124 La Vallette Military Museum, Guernsey.
125 JAS.L/C/177/A1. Caricatures by Arscott Dickinson.
126 Interview with Michael Ginns, 6 April 2008.
127 Eric Sirett archive, courtesy of Peter Sirett; Michael Ginns archive.
128 For example IA.AQ 0299/22 (1–16). Edna Dorrian, *Diary*, 29 April, 1 May and 4 May 1943.
129 For example ibid., 5 January and 29 December 1943.
130 JAS.L/D/25/E1. Painting by Harold Hepburn.
131 JAS.B/A/L30/22. Painting by Harold Hepburn.
132 I am grateful to the Jersey branch of the Channel Islands Occupation Society for allowing me to study the Fish collection.
133 Eric Sirett archive, courtesy of Peter Sirett.

6

Institutional Resistance: Political Groups, Clergy and Doctors

Louise Willmot

In his ground-breaking survey of civilian resistance in occupied Europe, *Unarmed against Hitler*, Jacques Semelin argues that specific political, social and professional associations played a vital part in the development of opposition to German rule.[1] Surviving party political structures and trade unions, the churches and professional associations of teachers and doctors – all were capable of becoming a focus for resistance and taking collective public action to defend basic freedoms. At its most effective, such action amounted to a genuine 'institutional resistance'.[2] This chapter investigates the prospects for such a mobilization in the Channel Islands, and outlines the factors that limited the development of political and institutional resistance there. With the island governments committed to establishing 'correct relations' with the occupiers and in the absence of a university – so important for the development of intellectual resistance elsewhere – the only real opportunity for collective action lay with underground political groups, the churches and the medical profession. Where collective action was lacking, moreover, clergymen and doctors had to decide whether, and how, to resist alone.

Constitutional and political traditions in the islands

There was less prospect of effective political resistance in the Channel Islands than anywhere else in Western Europe. In their recent history there are few precedents for sustained political opposition; any popular unrest that had developed in the eighteenth and nineteenth centuries was spontaneous and short-lived.[3] The islands were also lacking in strong democratic traditions. Although they had long-established representative institutions, the Assembly of the States in Jersey and the States of Deliberation in Guernsey, their constitutional structures remained archaic and hierarchical even after the First World War, when radicalized ex-servicemen had campaigned for the democratization of the franchise.[4] Reforms were introduced in both islands in 1918–20, but they fell short of full democracy. In 1939 a substantial proportion of States representatives were still parish Rectors appointed by the Crown, or unpaid Jurats who were elected for life either by the ratepayers or by an electoral college. The electoral system effectively disenfranchised many poorer and younger residents and sustained the dominance of a wealthy and interconnected elite. Shortly before the Occupation, streamlined emergency cabinets were established but these, the Superior Council in Jersey and the Controlling Committee in Guernsey, were drawn from the same restricted class.[5] Even more problematic for the development of organized resistance was the absence of political parties. In both islands, candidates for election stood as individuals and not on the basis of any agreed programme. Guernsey had no tradition of party politics at all, and although a small Labour Party branch had been established in Jersey during the 1920s, it did not survive.[6] A Communist Party was formed there in 1938, but it had only a handful of members and most of these were evacuated in 1940.[7]

Trade union membership in the islands, moreover, had declined significantly after the 1926 General Strike and was slow to revive. Only the Transport and General Workers' Union (T&GWU) had any significant presence there. By September 1938, after the appointment of a London-based official, Edward Hyman, with a brief to reconstruct the union, it had approximately 3,000 members – about 17 per cent of the registered workforce in Jersey – and had gained representation on various States committees.[8] In June 1940, however, with invasion imminent, Hyman was recalled to England. Following his departure, and despite some protests, the T&GWU District Committee suspended union business indefinitely even before trade unions were officially banned by the Germans on 4 November.[9] In the absence of union leadership or commitment to clandestine activity, there was no real prospect of strikes or collective action to oppose German policies. The contrast with the situation in the occupied countries of Western Europe, with their long traditions of dissent, multi-party politics and powerful trade unions, was stark. All these states had party and union networks that provided the basis for the development of illegal resistance once the shock of defeat had abated. In the Channel Islands no such structures existed. For a political resistance to emerge, its protagonists had to start virtually from scratch.

The Jersey Democratic Movement

It was in Jersey, where there had at least been minimal party political activity, that a form of political resistance developed. Initially, however, it was inspired less by the conduct of the Germans than by a conviction that their eventual defeat – of which islanders appeared remarkably confident – would provide the ideal opportunity for much-needed political reform. Within a year of the start of the Occupation, pro-reformers such as Robert Le Sueur, who was barely out of his teens when he became involved, began to seek out fellow islanders who shared his hopes for democratic renewal.[10] Reformist sentiments were further fuelled by unease at the conduct of the Superior Council, especially the registration of the Orders against the Jews and the rumours of corruption among wealthy islanders and States officials.[11] The first signs of resentment came in March 1941, when slogans attacking rich hoarders were daubed on walls in St Helier and notes attacking corruption were pushed through letter boxes there.[12] Of course, hostility to the occupiers played a part – the attack on hoarders was accompanied by the mild 'Down with Hitler and his riff-raff!'[13] – but it was the desire for democratic change that first brought individuals together.

At the end of 1941 several reading and discussion groups were meeting secretly in bookshops and private homes in Jersey.[14] Some operated under the cover of supposedly apolitical book clubs and the Jersey Scientific Society, while others, among them a People's Progressive Party, were avowedly political.[15] Not all the participants in these discussion groups were left wing – they included Peter Crill, son of the Constable of St Clement – but the tone of the meetings was reformist and critical of the island authorities.[16] Though the numbers involved were small, rumours of illegal political activity evidently reached the Germans: in November 1941 Attorney General Duret Aubin was ordered to investigate Communist activity, but replied that 'no trace whatsoever' had been found.[17] On the basis of personal contacts between the small groups, the Jersey Democratic Movement (JDM) was founded early in 1942.[18] Initially it had only a dozen members, including three Methodist lay preachers, at least two Communists, and several moderate constitutional reformers.[19]

Over the next year the JDM recruited members in all the island parishes and developed a distinctive programme of reform. It demanded a referendum to decide whether the islands should become English counties after the war; if they chose to maintain their independence, then the constitution should be changed to introduce universal suffrage and the payment of salaries to deputies, which would ensure that ordinary islanders could stand for office and limit domination of the States by the elite. The JDM's social and economic proposals included a graduated income tax, the nationalization of utilities, a 44-hour week, a housing programme, free education and extended health insurance.[20] Already it had the basis for a campaigning strategy in post-war elections.

The Jersey Communist Party and its activities

A few of its members, however, were not content with making plans for a democratic future and came to regard the JDM as little more than a 'talking-shop'.[21] As elsewhere in Western Europe, it was the growing harshness of German rule that provided the catalyst for direct action. Relations between Channel Islanders and the German authorities deteriorated significantly in 1942 after the confiscation of radios in June, the arrival of thousands of *Organisation Todt* (OT) workers in August and the deportation of 2,000 British-born islanders in September.[22] The consequence was a permanent change in the atmosphere, and in behaviour. Although most residents never went further than keeping a radio and listening to the BBC news, a handful of left-wing JDM members resolved to engage in active resistance to the Occupation.[23] In their case, anger at occupation policies was reinforced by a new optimism after the German defeat at Stalingrad early in 1943.[24] Their response was to found the Jersey Communist Party (JCP) that winter.

Figure 6.1 Norman Le Brocq, one of the founders of the Jersey Communist Party. Copyright and courtesy Jersey Heritage collections

The JCP was inspired by two men, Norman Le Brocq and Leslie Huelin. Born in Jersey in 1908, Huelin had worked as a trade union activist and party organizer in Australia during the 1930s. He had returned to Europe to join the International Brigades, but arrived too late to fight and was working in Jersey to fund his passage home when the Occupation began. A committed Marxist with a library of theoretical texts, Huelin exerted a strong influence over the younger members of the JCP.[25] Norman Le Brocq (Figure 6.1), by contrast, was still a teenager on the outbreak of war. The son of a florist, he had been a scholarship boy at the island's Victoria College and was politicized there during the Spanish Civil War: apart from one or two supporters of the Republic, his wealthy fellow-pupils had, he thought, been 'Franco men to a lad'.[26] Le Brocq later described his own wartime political convictions as a 'confused' form of Marxism, though he was also a Methodist lay preacher for a time. During the Occupation he worked for the Fuel Supply Committee, where he was further alienated by what he regarded as preferential treatment for influential islanders.[27]

Initially the JCP had only 7 members, and even in 1945 had only 18. Like other opposition group in the islands, it recruited on the basis of personal recommendations – in the case of the young Warren Hobbs, a tap on the shoulder in the street – and its members were united more by a desire for action than by any Communist orthodoxy.[28] Apart from Huelin, most were young, usually in their twenties, when they joined. It took time for them to mount effective opposition to the Germans, and the JCP's early activities were unproductive: members sketched German fortifications in the hope of helping Allied troops after a landing, but lacked the military knowledge to interpret their findings.[29] Apart from a brief revival in intelligence-gathering after D-Day, the JCP quickly abandoned its 'amateurish' attempts at espionage.[30]

Instead, early in 1943, it began to focus on propaganda and humanitarian work, initially aimed at the recently arrived OT labourers. The breakthrough came when the Germans, fearful of typhus after outbreaks in Guernsey, established sanitary and delousing teams of Spanish Republican OT workers with medical training. In Jersey the men were allowed to move freely between the OT camps and hospital, where they met Ernest Perrée, a JCP member working as a hospital porter, and through him other members of the party.[31] The JCP agreed to produce leaflets for OT workers in the form of typed BBC news digests copied on a flat-bed duplicator, which the Spaniards took into OT camps in an effort to boost morale. Apart from one brief interruption in 1944, these continued to appear until the Liberation, and versions in Spanish and Russian were smuggled into all 11 OT camps by the delousing teams.[32]

In 1943 the JCP also began to give humanitarian aid to Soviet OT workers who had escaped from the camps. Le Brocq and Huelin organized a loose network to feed and shelter them; Le Brocq estimated that, by the end of the war, the group had helped 17 fugitives to remain at liberty.[33] The JCP was far too small to have carried out these activities alone. Instead it relied on the help of ordinary residents who were not party members, but who agreed to shelter fugitives in their homes, or give food and clothing, or provide ration or and identity cards for the Russians.[34] Even the party's propaganda activities were dependent on outside help: sympathizers in the town hall smuggled out paper from the States stores for its leaflets, and the JDM member Robert Le Sueur translated leaflets into Spanish for the camps although he was never a member of the JCP.[35] Personal contacts enabled the party to have more influence on events than its numbers would have suggested possible.

Late in 1943 the JCP extended its propaganda to appeal directly to islanders, producing monthly leaflets for the Communist Party and a 'Workers' Review' for the T&GWU. It also attempted to circumvent the ban on trade unions. In August 1944, Huelin called a meeting to challenge the suspension of union activities and establish a Provisional Organising Committee (POC) of the T&GWU to campaign for the industrial demands of the JDM.[36] The POC gained some influence: its representatives advised a new works committee at the Electricity Company over the introduction of a shorter working week, and in 1945 it negotiated with the States' Labour Department for a reduction in working hours in response to the food crisis. Within the Labour Department, POC representatives – especially Huelin – were regarded as troublemakers intent on disrupting relationships between workers' representatives and the Council.[37]

The most widely read leaflet, however, was produced for the JDM and appeared every three months in print runs of 300–400.[38] The leaflets criticized the Superior Council directly, mixing the demand for constitutional and social reform with 'atrocity stories' of corruption and collaboration by States officials and wealthy islanders, 'that little clique who have held office and power for so many years'.[39] They attacked the legitimacy of the Superior Council by arguing not only that the constitution needed reform, but that the administration had failed to protect the interests of the inhabitants during the Occupation or to ensure that sacrifices were equally shared.[40] Not surprisingly, members of the Superior Council reacted to the accusations with outrage.[41]

After the war Dr Wilhelm Casper, the chief German civil administrator in the islands until November 1943, claimed that the Germans had been aware of the JDM and JCP but chose not to make arrests, because any political crackdown would have resulted in the unwelcome arrival of the SS.[42] His assertion is not entirely convincing. Although the military authorities undoubtedly wanted to keep the SS at bay, they are unlikely to have spared the JCP deliberately, especially at a time when islanders faced arrest simply for possessing radios or reading illegal leaflets. Whatever the reason, the failure to round up JDM and JCP members had serious consequences. Although by October 1944 it was clear that there would be no Allied invasion of the islands, JCP members had reason to hope that the Occupation might be brought to a swift end by an uprising by disaffected German soldiers. Rumours of an anti-Nazi cell in the garrison were confirmed when one of its members, Paul Mülbach, contacted a JCP sympathizer at the German-run soap and tannery works in St Helier.[43] The son of a Koblenz socialist and trade unionist who had died in Dachau, Mülbach had failed in his previous efforts to link up with 'English patriots', but found a welcome reception in the JCP.[44] His objective was to incite a mutiny by German soldiers, several of whom had formed a soldiers' committee inspired by the 'Free Germany' movement. The JCP would play no part in any rebellion – its members had no weapons anyway – but agreed to help the preparations by producing propaganda for distribution among the garrison.

Between October 1944 and May 1945, the JCP produced at least six leaflets for Mülbach's group, all emphasizing the inevitability of German defeat and attacking the Nazis' willingness to sacrifice women and children in a desperate bid to save themselves.[45] They urged the troops to rebel against their officers and fight for 'a future regulated to a certain extent by ourselves'.[46] After their uncertain beginnings, JCP members had learned the skills of small-scale clandestine operation. Le Brocq and his fiancée Rosalie Le Riche borrowed a typewriter to ensure that Mülbach's leaflets were recognizably different to those produced for the JDM and T&GWU, and they used a St Helier bookshop run by a local sympathizer, Paul Casimir, as a 'drop' where Mülbach's handwritten drafts could be collected and the leaflets returned to him.[47] Even when ink supplies in Jersey ran out, the Oxford University chemistry student Wally Le Quesne manufactured enough substitute to keep production going.[48] After Mülbach deserted from the army and went into hiding early in 1945, JCP contacts provided him with a safe house, food and civilian clothes.[49]

The JCP was not involved in the Germans' sabotage operations, which included an arson attack that destroyed a transport repair shop in February 1945.[50] Although its details remain obscure, the most dramatic incident occurred on 7 March, when an explosion and fire at German naval headquarters in the Palace Hotel killed several men.[51] Meanwhile, plans for outright mutiny had hardened after the appointment in February 1945 of a new Military Commander, Vice-Admiral Hüffmeier, who boasted that the garrison would hold out even if German troops surrendered on the continent.[52] For the JCP, an attempt by anti-Nazi soldiers to seize power and surrender to the Allies, eliminating the threat of a prolonged siege or a bloody invasion, seemed well worth supporting.[53] In preparation for the mutiny, which was to take place on 1 May, the JCP produced a final leaflet urging soldiers to arrest 'criminal Nazi officers', but otherwise its role was to be limited to escorting local children safely home from school when the fighting began. At the last moment, however, Huelin hatched a plot to seize control of the Superior Council during the chaos and to 'hang the Bailiff' and his colleagues as traitors.[54] This hare-brained scheme, which horrified his own associates, was never put into practice:[55] with JCP members already in position on 1 May, the mutiny was postponed, apparently as a result of political disputes among the German conspirators.[56] Before the mutineers had time to reorganize, the war in Europe had ended and the garrison surrendered. Paul Mülbach gave himself up to British troops and eventually became a privileged prisoner-of-war (PoW) helping to deal with the repatriation of German soldiers.[57]

The Jersey Democratic Movement after the Liberation

During the Occupation the JCP had offered the only organized political opposition to the Germans, and the JDM the only clear proposals for political and social reform. Their influence over political affairs in the post-war period, however, was limited. In trade union matters Huelin quickly lost control, despite his efforts to present the POC as the legitimate representative of trade unionism in the islands.[58] Its claims were challenged in June 1945 by the reconstituted T&GWU committee, which was promptly recognized by the States and local employers.[59] Amid considerable acrimony, the POC was disbanded and Edward Hyman returned to lead the T&GWU.[60] In political affairs, on the other hand, the JDM seemed likely to have a lasting impact. According to Norman Le Brocq, it now had 'a couple of hundred' members and the support of several thousand sympathizers in the island.[61] Its propaganda campaigns had brought its ideas to a wide audience: its leaflets were brought to Britain by parties of escapers after D-Day,[62] and its proposals were debated by political prisoners in Gloucester Street in October 1944.[63] After the Liberation JDM leaders set about transforming the movement into a campaigning political organization, holding mass meetings and calling for change along the lines proposed in its programme.[64] The JDM fielded a full slate of candidates at the States election of December 1945, and a poll indicated strong support for the reforms it advocated.[65]

By then constitutional change was inevitable in both islands, even though Guernsey had produced no movement to compare with the JDM. In his official history of the Occupation, Charles Cruickshank argues that reform would have come even without the German invasion, but that the disruption of mass evacuation and the patchy wartime record of the island administrations helped to hasten its arrival.[66] A wartime Channel Islands Study Group composed of 20 prominent islanders based in Britain had advocated greater democracy, economic development and social reform, and its reports seemed likely to provide the basis for change. Already, in the aftermath of the Liberation, the States in Guernsey had agreed to consider an increase in direct representation there. Nevertheless, it was not clear how radical these developments would be, and an election triumph for the JDM would have been the catalyst for far-reaching reform in both islands.

Its hopes of victory were dashed by the formation of a Jersey Progressive Party (JPP) in October 1945. Linked to some members of the States and to influential business groups, the party was a direct response to the threat posed by the JDM. One of its instigators was the editor of the *Evening Post*, Arthur Harrison, whose paper backed its campaign by accusing the JDM of 'irresponsible behaviour' during the Occupation and of supporting 'narrow aims and class interests' rather than the welfare of all citizens.[67] JDM prospects were probably also damaged by its own campaign tactics, which continued to allege corruption and collaboration on the part of States officials. These muddied the waters of the campaign by conflating proposals for democracy and social reform with an attack on the legitimacy of the wartime Superior Council, and undoubtedly alienated some voters. In the event it was soundly beaten by the JPP at the polls. None of its candidates was elected, although the JDM received 39 per cent of the vote in urban constituencies.[68]

Its defeat did not mean total failure: the JPP had won only by adopting several JDM proposals and presenting itself as a moderate force between the radicalism of the Movement and the reactionary stance of the prewar States.[69] Even so, the constitutional changes that were introduced before 1950 fell short of full democracy in both Jersey and Guernsey. Although directly elected representatives subsequently formed a majority in the States, an element of indirect election was retained. Furthermore, the procedure for registering voters remained more complex and difficult for poor residents than for ratepayers, which continued to distort the electoral system and protect the influence of the traditional and business elites.[70] It was some years before these anomalies were addressed. Eventually, however, the once-radical demands of the JDM became part of Jersey's political mainstream, and several former JDM members were elected to the States. Among them was Norman Le Brocq, who was first elected in 1966, still as a Communist but with a personal support that transcended political divisions. On his death 30 years later, it was the *Evening Post* that led the tributes to his humanity and integrity.[71]

The response of the Channel Islands clergy

Political resisters in the JDM and JCP were forced to operate in secret, relying on their illegal leaflet campaigns and their personal contacts. Amid the uncertainties of occupation, however, islanders naturally sought guidance from trusted *public* figures. Some guidance, of course, was offered by the island governments, but during the Occupation this was limited in scope. Committed to cooperating with the occupiers in the interests of the inhabitants, the Superior Council and Controlling Committee made no public criticism of the Germans and, when they did oppose specific initiatives, did so behind the scenes.[72] Their approach, based on the conviction that a substantial degree of cooperation was essential in order to prevent the Germans from taking direct control of the government, severely restricted the extent of their opposition to any policy.[73] The only other group in the islands with a public voice was the clergy, which, as elsewhere, had a long tradition of commenting on social and political issues from the pulpit. To do so during the Occupation, however, entailed significant risk.

In his study of Methodism during the Occupation, David Chapman accepts that ministers of all denominations were 'no more outspoken than civilian leaders'.[74] More scathingly, Madeleine Bunting has condemned the failure of the churches to speak out against the ill-treatment of slave labourers and the islands' Jews.[75] The most unflattering contrast is with Scandinavia: in Denmark, where the churches played their part in the rescue of the country's Jews in 1943,[76] and in Norway, where the leaders of the Lutheran Church broke off their ties with the state after the appointment of a Norwegian Nazi administration early in 1942.[77] There was no comparable stand in the Channel Islands.

The lack of a collective response to German policies can be explained, in part, by the fact that religious life was more diverse and fragmented than in Norway, where 96 per cent of the population were Lutherans and the churches spoke with one voice on issues of public concern.[78] In the Channel Islands there was no dominant church: Anglicanism and Methodism were strongest, but there were also several Roman Catholic churches and small Baptist, Reformed and Pentecostalist congregations. All were accustomed to operating independently, and the Anglican churches looked to the See of Winchester for leadership. No united response to German policies was likely in these circumstances. Second, all the churches experienced a personnel crisis after the evacuations of June 1940, later intensified by the deportation of British-born islanders. In Guernsey, for example, three of the 18 Church of England clergymen left for the mainland in June 1940, and six more were deported in September 1942 or February 1943.[79] Among the Methodists, the problem was exacerbated by its itinerant system: in 1939, four of the 16 Methodist ministers in the islands were new arrivals who had yet to build close ties with their congregations.[80] As the Jersey minister Clement Mylne acknowledged, the Methodist circuits would have collapsed altogether but for their lay preachers.[81] These disruptions to church leadership further undermined the prospects for a strong response to German policies.

Initially the Germans adopted a conciliatory approach to the churches. On 8 July 1940 they declared that freedom of worship would be maintained and that clergymen would be permitted to say prayers for the Royal Family and the Empire, although they must not use their services 'for any propaganda or utterances against the honour or interests of the German Government or Forces'.[82] Only one organization – the Salvation Army – faced a direct challenge. Just days after the positive declaration of July 1940, the *Feldkommandant* refused to allow the Army to continue its open-air meetings.[83] Six months later, on 19 January 1941, the organization was banned altogether: no further religious services were allowed and the wearing of uniform was forbidden.[84] In Guernsey, Commandant Joseph Griffiths of L'Islet Corps pleaded for the Army to be permitted to continue its work, but without success.

Thereafter, senior Salvationists reluctantly accepted the ban and, under Griffiths's leadership, concentrated on maintaining the morale of members through home visits, prayer meetings and Bible fellowships.[85] The Methodist churches, in particular, offered their support and cooperation. Their congregations shared prayer meetings with Salvationists and hid Army banners in their premises, while the children of Salvationists were christened in Methodist churches but had their names added to cradle rolls in Army citadels.[86] These strategies allowed the Salvation Army to survive the Occupation with its membership intact: L'Islet Corps in Guernsey, for example, held an open-air meeting, complete with banners and the Salvation Army band, on Liberation day in May 1945.[87] The non-confrontational approach taken by Griffiths and his colleagues was widely accepted by Salvationists. Only one officer, Major Marie

Ozanne, acting officer-in-charge of St Sampson's Corps in Guernsey, protested against German policy. She appeared in full uniform outside the local hall on the first day on the ban, continued to hold illegal open-air meetings and, for more than 18 months, preached and read from the Bible in St Peter Port.[88] In letters to the *Feldkommandant* and in interviews with the local and German police, Ozanne condemned the closure of Army halls and pleaded for 'freedom to worship God in the way in which He calls us, and also for freedom to follow the dictates of conscience'.[89] It was the first of several challenges to the occupiers that were to end in her death.[90]

The other churches faced no such threat to their existence. Nevertheless, the warning that services must not be used for 'anti-German activity' was serious: clergymen quickly became aware that their services were being observed – at least intermittently – by members of the *Geheime Feldpolizei*.[91] On 1 August 1940, less than a month after the German proclamation, Guernsey's Methodist ministers were warned that they would lose their privileges if they continued to criticize the Germans in their sermons.[92] According to Clement Mylne in Jersey, the prevailing atmosphere among the clergy was one of 'uncertainty, anxiety and fear', and some were clearly cowed into silence.[93] In Guernsey, the Methodist Douglas Ord was appalled by the weakness of one (unnamed) colleague, who was so afraid of offending the Germans that he refused to deliver any sermon at all and read a psalm to his congregation instead.[94] These fears were intensified by the apparent targeting of clergymen for arrest or deportation.[95] Mylne, for example, was sentenced to two years' imprisonment, later reduced to a year, in February 1943 for possession of an illegal radio.[96] He was sure that the charges had been invented – his radio was broken and he had handed in the one that worked – and was told by sympathetic German officers that he had been singled out as 'an enemy of the Reich'.[97] Other clergymen, so their parishioners believed, were included in the deportations of September 1942 or February 1943 as punishment for publicly criticizing the Germans.[98]

In these circumstances, the islands' clergy faced a dilemma in advising their congregations how to deal with German troops. Some urged that contacts be kept to a minimum: the Anglican rector of St Martin's in Jersey, for example, advised his parishioners to answer politely when asked a direct question, but otherwise to have nothing to do with the occupiers.[99] A few – and only a few – took the opposite approach of toadying to the Germans in the hope of gaining favour and, especially, gaining exemption from the deportations in September 1942.[100] But there were also honourable reasons for ministers' reluctance to 'cold shoulder' the occupiers. Christian belief in a universal church persuaded many to invite German soldiers to their services, especially at Easter and Christmas, even though the troops had services and clergy of their own.[101] In a few cases these contacts led to lasting friendships between clergymen and soldiers 'who became friends though they were supposed to be enemies', and whose families kept in touch long after the war was over.[102] The danger, of course, was that Christian solidarity with individual Germans might involve silence in the face of injustice.

The most revealing demonstration of the dilemma is provided by Douglas Ord, whose Occupation diary chronicles his struggles to reconcile his patriotism with his faith. An Englishman who had studied in Leipzig and been a PoW in Germany during the First World War, Ord saw it as his duty to welcome German soldiers to his church. He never fell into the trap of identifying all Germans as Nazis, and greatly admired officers who shared his philosophy and outlook, particularly members of the Confessing Church.[103] Though desperate for Allied victory, he wanted to avoid a 'destructive atmosphere of revenge' once the war was won. Those guilty of terrible crimes must be punished, but the German people must be reintegrated into the 'comity of nations' so that future conflicts could be avoided.[104] On a day-to-day basis, however, Ord was careful to limit his contacts with the occupiers. Although he was an unofficial intermediary in dealings between the church authorities and the military administration, he refused to act as an official translator. His sympathies lay with non-Nazi Germans and, especially, with their victims: he was disgusted by the anti-Jewish Orders and appalled by the treatment of OT workers, to whom he offered encouragement and – thanks to his wife – occasionally food.[105]

Ord was convinced that his congregation came to church to seek guidance as well as to worship. During the first two years of Occupation this was not easy to find. With even Scouts' and Brigades' meetings banned, church activities were restricted to religious services, Sunday Schools and the playing of recordings of sacred music. According to Clement Mylne, clergymen struggled to find 'the way between the extremes – of doing *nothing* except church services, or of doing as near as possible to peace-time scope'.[106] Their sermons had traditionally offered the way for them to guide their congregations but, after the initial flurry in July and August 1940, very few clergymen were prepared to criticize the Germans openly before 1943. Ord's warning against 'rumour-mongering' after the confiscation of radios, combined with his assurance that 'victory for right over wrong' was certain, was rare enough to be recorded by a parishioner, Ambrose Robin, in his diary.[107] Ord was not, however, completely alone. Also in Guernsey, the Anglican Hartley-Jackson, vicar of St Stephen's, had given critical sermons and apparently refused to allow the playing of Beethoven in his church. This, in the opinion of Violet Carey, was the reason he was deported in September 1942. She also thought that her own vicar, the Reverend Finey, was lucky to escape the same fate: he had told his congregation that Channel Islanders were 'in the hands of the cruellest enemy in the world', and condemned local girls who went out with German soldiers.[108]

As relations between the occupiers and local people deteriorated in 1942, more ministers in the islands – and, it seems, especially in Guernsey – spoke out.[109] The Methodist Henry Foss was deported along with army officers and political 'undesirables' in February 1943, apparently after sermons in which he criticized the conduct of German officers.[110] Douglas Ord now took great care with his own sermons which, he recognized, 'have had a bad press for years now'.[111] He hoped to boost the morale of his congregation by referring to the Allied cause, but to do it so obliquely that the Germans could not object. His congregation was evidently attuned to his allusions: a quotation from Hebrews – 'We of Italy salute you!' – to acknowledge the invasion of Italy, for example, or a sermon that began 'The hour has come!' to celebrate D-Day.[112] Their instant response, he wrote after one service, was rich reward 'for the purgatorial efforts in my study'.[113] In November 1943 Ord also attempted an oblique criticism of anti-semitism. After arguing with the censor over the inclusion of a piece by the Jewish composer Mendelssohn in a Sunday concert, he told his congregation that they would shortly be hearing the work of a great master, but 'I am not permitted to tell you who wrote it'.[114] He was delighted that his audience understood the message and by the large turn-out for the concert.[115] Ord was careful, though, not to give way to triumphalism or jingoism. Shortly after D-Day, in a sermon on Conscience and Patriotism, he reminded his parishioners that their faith demanded 'love even for our enemies, and that all our enemies are not Germans'. Patriotism, he noted in his diary, was not enough.[116]

Few ministers were as subtle as this. As the tide of war turned, and especially after D-Day, more of them used their services to pray openly for victory. Violet Carey, once deeply critical of her own vicar, the Reverend Finey of Forest parish church, had changed her mind completely by late June 1944. He had become very bold, and had hung the white ensign openly in his church after D-Day to celebrate Allied success.[117] On 25 June, Carey noted:[118]

> Mr Finey gave us a beautiful service. All of us who thought him a coward and a rabbit must certainly eat our words in lumps. The prayers he says, prayers for our deliverance, protection for the King's forces on sea and land, victory for our Sovereign. In his sermon he could not have been more outspoken.

Another local clergyman, MacCartney, had prayed for a just and lasting peace, and indeed 'for everybody except Stalin!'[119] Ord, by now, had begun to ignore German restrictions altogether and to give political talks at his church – including one on the prospects for democratic government in Russia.[120]

All the ministers who spoke out publicly faced the possibility of arrest and, at least until August 1944, of deportation. The decision to do so undoubtedly took courage. Nevertheless, very few clergymen engaged in more active resistance. Among the exceptions was the Jesuit priest Father Charles Rey. The son of a French colonial official, Rey had studied in Jersey as a young man and, after a career as a missionary and scientist in South Africa, had returned to run a meteorological station in the island. Following the confiscation of radios in June 1942, he used pieces of African crystal from the Jesuit College geological museum to make tiny crystal sets that could be fitted into telephones, matchboxes or even watches.[121] According to the early historians of the Occupation, Alan Wood and Mary Seaton Wood, Rey made over 60 of these sets before May 1945, although the claim that he tried to jam German radio transmissions as well cannot be confirmed. Although he was evidently regarded with suspicion by the occupiers, he was never arrested.[122]

Also involved in the dissemination of news was Clifford Cohu, who was born in 1883 in Guernsey and had settled in Jersey in 1937 on his return from India, where he had served as canon of Allahabad.[123] In wartime he was appointed acting rector of St Saviour's church and chaplain of the General Hospital, where he was known for his kindness, good humour and outspoken patriotism.[124] Cohu was rare among the clergy in making no attempt to veil his opinions. He first came to the attention of the authorities as early as October 1940, when members of his own congregation told the Constable of St Helier that he had been preaching against the Germans.[125] Despite this early warning, he did not change his approach. In March 1941, for example, he encouraged his congregation to sing the National Anthem; the Bailiff's secretary Ralph

Mollet, who was there, reported that they 'sang the roof off'. Warned that he was 'sailing close to the wind', Cohu said only that he was not afraid.[126] Subsequently, after the confiscation of radios, he spread the BBC news in the Jersey Hospital and maternity unit, and on the streets while riding his bicycle, to which he added a large bell to attract the attention of passers-by.[127]

Cohu's conduct was so indiscreet that his eventual arrest was almost inevitable. In March 1943 he was taken into custody with 18 of his parishioners, who had hidden a radio and created a rudimentary network for spreading the news.[128] The crime, as observers noted at the time, was relatively minor, and other residents had escaped serious punishment for similar offences.[129] A decision seems to have been taken to make an example of the defendants: the trial was well publicized, and, according to Edward Le Quesne of the Superior Council, the police had to be mobilized to clear crowds out of Royal Square after the verdict.[130] Cohu's wife was convinced that he had been 'singled out as a minister of the church' for his punitive 18-month sentence, but it is not clear that this was the case, since two other members of the group received even longer prison terms.[131] Cohu was deported, first to France and later, in December 1943, to prisons and work camps in Germany. Until July 1944 he was able to send letters to his wife, in the last of which, according to their friend Nan Le Ruez, he confided that 'he did not think he could bear it much longer'.[132] Although Cohu's sentence was suspended at the end of August 1944, he was sent to Zöschen 'work-education camp' near Naumburg instead of an internment camp. There, already emaciated and weak, he was beaten and abused until his death seven days later.[133]

Among those who knew Cohu, the medical student Frank Killer remembered him as kindly, but 'over-trusting and rather naive', while the young curate Kenneth Preston later judged that his behaviour had been foolish and dangerous.[134] Still, Cohu's terrible fate – for a crime that consisted of little more than trying to cheer people up – offers a salutary warning against unthinking condemnation of the Channel Islands clergy for not denouncing the occupiers from their pulpits. Even private protests to the Germans had serious consequences, as the case of Marie Ozanne in Guernsey amply demonstrates. Already known to the authorities for defying the ban on the Salvation Army, Major Ozanne also tried to defend the victims of Nazi persecution. In June 1941, shortly after the registration of the Third Order against the Jews, she wrote to the *Feldkommandant* to protest.[135] Later, she and her family fed and befriended West European OT workers at their home in Vale until, appalled by their ill-treatment, she wrote to German headquarters in August and September 1942 to demand better conditions for them. Ozanne did not mince her words: she was, she told him, in 'revolt against the rule of terror and oppression that you exercise wherever you go'.[136] Her faith, on the other hand, had taught her 'to love everybody, whether they are Germans, Dutch, French, or British', and she hoped for reconciliation between Britain and Germany after the war.[137] Ozanne's protests led to her arrest in September 1942, and she was released from prison only after contracting the illness that eventually killed her. Hers was a remarkable example of Christian conscience in action, rare everywhere in Nazi-occupied Europe. In the Channel Islands, her case was unique.

As the cases of Cohu and Ozanne reveal, religious leaders in the Channel Islands were so exposed that their failure to speak out individually against persecution is hardly surprising. Discreet acts of decency and courage, on the other hand, were not unknown. OT workers were welcomed at several churches; at least two Russian fugitives in Jersey attended services regularly and were protected by the silence of their ministers and congregations.[138] Another, George Koslov, counted the Dean of Jersey among his own acquaintances.[139] Despite these individual acts of kindness, however, Madeleine Bunting is surely correct to ask why there was no *collective* response to the persecution of the Jews and the ill-treatment of OT workers. As we have seen, the prospects for such a response were already limited by the fragmentation of religious life in the islands and the absence of a dominant church. This explanation, however, does not tell the whole story. Although the Dutch churches were equally fragmented, six Protestant denominations still issued a joint protest there against the 'Aryan declaration' requiring civil servants to declare their Jewish ancestry in October 1940.[140]

The failure of Channel Islands clergy to make a response to the anti-Jewish Orders can be attributed to three factors. The first was fear of arrest: there were so few clergy that the occupiers could easily have cracked down on any protest. Second, the clergy apparently shared the mistaken belief that the members of the small Jewish community were already 'safely in England' and that the legislation would have no practical impact. Douglas Ord certainly thought so in 1940, until he met Therese Steiner.[141] Finally, there were no mass round-ups of Jews in the islands to compare with those that spurred protests from religious leaders elsewhere in Europe. Only 16 Jews were registered in the islands, of whom 8 were deported during the Occupation.[142] By the time OT labourers arrived in large numbers in 1942, the clergy's cautious response to the Occupation was well established, and not even the open brutality inflicted on these workers changed it. Instead, ministers tended to their congregations as best they could, and made the compromises necessary to keep their churches open. After the war, Clement Mylne argued that the churches had helped the population to come through the Occupation 'with unbroken spirit', and that the Germans had missed the chance to intimidate Channel Islanders by closing them down.[143] It is true that some congregations undoubtedly valued their ministers enough to submit petitions asking for them to be exempted from deportation in 1942.[144] Nevertheless, Mylne's optimistic assessment inevitably leaves some questions unanswered.

The response of the Channel Islands doctors

Channel Islands doctors, with the exception of those in public health posts, were under less scrutiny than the clergy and had more freedom of action. After the evacuations of June 1940, only seven GPs were left to provide medical care for 23,000 inhabitants of Guernsey, and only 17 to care for 43,000 people in Jersey, where several took on additional duties to support their eight colleagues at the General Hospital.[145] Their efforts on behalf of the residents were remarkable. Hospital wards and shift patterns were reorganized, special units established to deal with outbreaks of infectious disease, and blood transfusion services maintained.[146] Auxiliary medical students and nurses were recruited and trained, and shortages of drugs and equipment managed by the manufacture of local substitutes.[147] Preventive medicine was prioritized, for example in the form of vaccination programmes to combat outbreaks of diphtheria.[148] Doctors regularly worked 12-hour days, and in Guernsey the nurses worked a 7-day week with one day's leave a month.[149] Tragedies were inevitable, above all the high incidence of TB and the deaths of insulin-dependent diabetics, but – under extraordinary pressure – the medical professionals did much to maintain the health of the population.

Direct dealings with the German authorities were the responsibility of the public health officials – Jersey's Medical Officer of Health Noel McKinstry, Guernsey's Medical Officer of Health, Rowan Revell, and its Medical Services Officer A. N. Symons. Conflicts with the occupiers, over food supplies and the danger of disease, were inevitable. However, this opposition does not fit any simplistic resistance/collaboration paradigm, since the officials worked with the German authorities where necessary and made their challenges on a case-by-case basis. Thus, for example, Revell's annual medical reports criticized the Germans' failure to provide proper sanitary and delousing facilities for foreign labourers and their own troops, which increased the risk of epidemics. Basic delousing procedures for all arrivals would offer a 'practically certain safeguard' against disease, and it was 'very extraordinary' that these had not been carried out.[150] Outbreaks of diphtheria and typhus proved that Revell's judgement had been correct, as he noted in his next annual report.[151]

In 1942, Revell's colleague A. N. Symons orchestrated an attempt to put pressure on the occupiers over the food supply. That April, the diarist Violet Carey had noted a rumour that her own GP, Dick Gibson, had been evicted from his house 'for saying people were dying from "Occupational Malnutrition"'.[152] Two months later, a retired Royal Air Force (RAF) officer named Randall complained to the Controlling Committee that the Germans had confiscated his land, which ought to be used to grow food because islanders were dying of malnutrition.[153] Challenged for evidence to support his assertion, Randall sent five death certificates citing malnutrition as a contributory cause of death, accompanied by a statement from Symons and signed by all Guernsey's doctors confirming that the allegation was 'substantially true'.[154] The Germans believed that the affair had been 'inspired by higher authority' – Symons – and contemplated putting him on trial, as well as searching doctors' homes for hoarded food and distributing it to 'English workers working for the Wehrmacht'.[155] Cooler heads prevailed: the search was restricted to the homes of Randall and Symons and nothing was confiscated.[156] Having decided that a court case against Symons would be 'problematic', the authorities contented themselves with insisting that the deaths were caused by old age rather than malnutrition and that food shortages were 'a result of the blockade imposed by England'. The Bailiff was told to appeal to garden owners to grow more crops.[157] Symons was clearly regarded as a troublemaker, and he seems to have earned his reputation.[158] He was dismissed late in 1944 after an 'unsuitable' response to proposals to cut off the water supply which was, according to his clerk Ken Lewis, only the last of several 'very cheeky letters' to the Germans.[159] Within weeks Symons had been reinstated, even though he was 70 years old, apparently because his expertise in the field of public health was indispensable.

Jersey's Medical Officer of Health, Noel McKinstry, clashed even more frequently with the Occupation authorities, and particularly with the senior German Army Medical Officer, Dr Bleckwenn. McKinstry made several complaints about inadequate child nutrition and the need for better supplies, but his interpretation of his remit was significantly wider than his colleagues'. He made an official protest against the siting of a German battery next to Overdale Hospital, which he regarded as a contravention of the rules of warfare, and complained to Bleckwenn about the ill-treatment of OT workers in Jersey.[160] McKinstry also tried to improve conditions for political prisoners in Gloucester Street prison, calling in 1942 and 1944 for better sanitation and health care and regular inspections by prison visitors. He regarded the behaviour of the local prison authorities as too passive: instead of waiting for the Germans to approve their suggestions, they should have taken the initiative themselves until ordered to stop.[161] Again in February 1945 he protested against overcrowding and 'conditions contrary to humanity and common sense' in the prison.[162] When the prison authorities defended their conduct, he indicated that he wanted to force the release of minor offenders and 'to strengthen your hand in making representations to the Germans about the gross overcrowding that undoubtedly prevails'.[163] McKinstry's activities made him thoroughly unpopular with the Germans and at one stage they wanted him sacked.[164] He remained in post because, though 'an absolute pain' to the authorities, he – like Symons – was irreplaceable.[165]

Despite the efforts of the public health officials, their protests had little effect. Although Revell's annual medical reports and Symons's recommendations were admired for their 'courageous frankness',[166] sanitary arrangements for the German garrison and its workforce remained inadequate to the end. McKinstry's protests were also usually ignored: the gun battery at Overdale was established anyway, the prison remained insanitary and overcrowded until the Liberation, and conditions for OT workers improved only after internal OT inspections in the wake of outbreaks of disease. Nevertheless, on one vital subject, public health officials did manage to sabotage German policy, when they opposed the transfer of mentally ill patients to the continent for reasons of 'population policy'.[167] In Guernsey, Symons circumvented the demand in November 1941, first protesting on the grounds of the Hague Convention and then agreeing to reopen the town asylum so that the Germans could requisition Vauquiedor mental hospital without deporting the patients. In Jersey, however, it took concerted protests by McKinstry and Coutanche to prevent their removal. In January 1942, after *Feldkommandant* Knackfuss had decided to transfer 450 patients from St Saviour hospital, McKinstry alerted the Superior Council and Coutanche sent a strong letter of protest that led to the abandonment of the plan.

The project was revived early in 1944 with a request for a list of mental hospital patients and 'cripples' in Jersey, who were to be removed to the continent and, apparently, sent to 'concentration camps'. Further protests from McKinstry and Coutanche, supported by the Medical Superintendent of St Saviour, resulted in the 'deferral' of the scheme. The patients remained safely in the islands until the Liberation.[168] Given the Nazis' treatment of mentally ill and disabled people elsewhere, which resulted in the murder of tens of thousands by gassing, lethal injection and sheer neglect, the significance of these protests should not be under-estimated.[169] Although there is no evidence of a specific plan to kill the Channel Islands patients, McKinstry's German counterpart Bleckwenn had remarked that the occupiers had 'a better way' of dealing with such people, and had told the surgeon Averell Darling that they would not survive if they were deported.¹⁷⁰ The response of Coutanche and the medical professionals probably saved many lives.

These protests, even the last, were made as part of the professional duties of the public health officials and in open discussion with the occupiers. However, a similar concern for the welfare of the inhabitants also led some Channel Islands doctors into illegal resistance. In Guernsey in November 1944, the GP Alastair Rose contributed material to a report on food shortages and health that was due to be smuggled off the island by an escape party.¹⁷¹ Rose had already refused to act as an anaesthetist at the Victoria Hospital when it was taken over by the Germans, and had broken regulations after the radio ban, at least to the extent of supplying a set of earphones to friends so that they could listen to the news on their crystal set.¹⁷² But he was not a natural rebel: he was initially reluctant to help what might be 'a foolish attempt to escape by irresponsible people', and agreed to take part only when he discovered that the plan had been approved by members of the Controlling Committee. Rose gathered his documents and broke the curfew to take them to Frederick Noyon, who delivered the material safely to the British government.¹⁷³ Otherwise, there is no evidence that Guernsey's doctors engaged in illegal resistance, although – as Gilly Carr demonstrates elsewhere in this book – they bent the rules to breaking point in order to exempt people from deportation in September 1942.

Illegal activities by doctors were much more common in Jersey, where the humanitarian need was greater. After September 1942, there were always at least a dozen escaped Soviet OT workers who needed shelter and, in some cases, medical treatment. In the last months of the war their numbers were boosted by the escape of several young political prisoners from Gloucester Street prison, some of whom were injured in the attempt. At least a third of the doctors in the island helped these fugitives, either occasionally or as part of a loose network.¹⁷⁴ They had more opportunity to engage in clandestine activities than most other islanders: they could make house calls without arousing suspicion; they had the use of cars and ambulances which they could use to transport fugitives; and they carried special passes allowing them to enter prohibited zones near the beaches.¹⁷⁵

Probably the most important factor was that the doctors were trusted by those who asked them for help. During the Occupation, social cohesion – defined by Semelin as the strength of the ties binding individuals to each other and to the values of their society – came under great strain, as it did everywhere in German-occupied Europe.¹⁷⁶ Bonds of trust and solidarity were eroded by the conduct of a small minority who denounced their neighbours, either out of spite or for the rewards on offer, for withholding radios, sheltering OT workers, or making anti-German remarks.¹⁷⁷ The diarist Izett Croad noted the corrosive effect on community cohesion: 'one begins to doubt everybody', she wrote after a number of denunciations in February 1943, 'or almost everybody'.¹⁷⁸ Later, Joyce Le Ruez was blunt about the impact: 'We got to trust nobody except our families and close friends'.¹⁷⁹

Despite this depletion of social cohesion, relationships between doctors and their clients apparently survived almost unscathed. The Sarres of St Lawrence still trusted their GP, Mortimer-Evans, to treat the escaped OT worker they were hiding,¹⁸⁰ just as the political prisoner Donald Bell turned to his own doctor, Mattas, after he was injured during his escape from prison in February 1945.[181] Sometimes trust was reinforced by friendship: after his own escape from prison that month, Frank Killer was treated by the hospital doctor Raymond Osmont and the physiotherapist John Le Sueur, with whom he had worked as an unofficial medical student at the hospital. Subsequently, he turned to his family GP, Mortimer Evans, for help.[182] Personal relationships also underpinned the decision by Osmont and the resident medical officer, Averell Darling, to falsify the medical records of Ivy Forster, a subterfuge that kept her in hospital and saved her from deportation to a concentration camp alongside her sister Louisa Gould for the crime of harbouring an escaped OT worker. Osmont had been at school with Gould's son, recently killed in the Royal Naval Volunteer Reserve (RNVR), and felt a personal obligation to help.[183] The lie was subsequently supported by the hospital surgeon, Arthur Halliwell.[184]

Jersey doctors were linked by ties of trust not just to their patients, but to each other. Theirs was a small and tightly knit group, and they drew one another into illegal activities. By the summer of 1942 they were sharing the BBC news they heard on illegal sets,[185] and later they cooperated to help OT workers or prison escapers. John Lewis, who ran a GP practice and ran the maternity hospital during the Occupation, befriended OT workers and helped transport them across the island; Harold Blampied, who shared a house with Noel McKinstry, helped him to hide an OT worker there for several weeks; the surgeon Claude Avarne befriended the OT fugitive George Koslov and played chess with him.[186] At the heart of illegal activity by doctors in Jersey, however, were two remarkable individuals: Arthur Halliwell and Noel McKinstry.

Halliwell, who was English-born, was in his early forties when the Occupation began. Having evacuated his wife and young children to England, he chose to remain as consultant surgeon at Jersey General Hospital rather than 'abandon' his patients, for whom he worked long hours and with considerable skill throughout the Occupation.[187] A Surgeon-Lieutenant in the Royal Navy during the First World War, Halliwell was patriotic, dedicated and intense, and his personal example did much to ensure that relationships between local and German medical staff at the General Hospital remained coldly formal (Figure 6.2).[188] Professional and correct in his dealings with German doctors and patients, he was distressed when his offer to operate on the German wounded was rejected after the evacuation of St Malo in August 1944.[189] Outside his professional duties, however, he had 'no time for the enemy'.[190] Halliwell refused to shake the hands of German colleagues in case they interpreted it as a gesture of friendship, and was angered by occasional romantic attachments between Irish nurses and German officers at the hospital – a reaction he later thought had been 'foolish'.[191] His influence on younger colleagues, especially Averell Darling, who befriended an OT fugitive at his church, was strong and lasting.[192]

Halliwell was drawn into illegal resistance by a combination of patriotism and humanitarianism. From 1943 he worked with Noel McKinstry to transport and shelter escaped Soviet OT workers, and hid one of them in his home for several weeks.[193] Subsequently, in November 1944, he helped a group of young men – one of whom, John Floyd, was a family friend – to escape to France by taking their outboard motor to the beach in his car and using his pass to enter the militarized zone.[194] Halliwell became a vital element in the loose network that aided political prisoners as well as OT workers: in the last few weeks of the Occupation, he hid Donald Bell at his home after his escape from prison. Bell later acknowledged the kindness and 'selfless generosity' of his host.[195] Halliwell was also dependable and discreet, two qualities which qualified him for clandestine activity.[196]

Even more involved in illegal resistance was Halliwell's colleague, the Ulsterman Noel McKinstry (Figure 6.3). Like Halliwell a veteran of the Royal Navy, McKinstry had been Deputy Commissioner of Public Health in Shanghai before settling in Jersey

Figure 6.2 Arthur Halliwell, consultant surgeon at Jersey General Hospital. Copyright and courtesy Jersey Heritage collections

Figure 6.3 Noel McKinstry, Medical Officer of Health in Jersey. Copyright and courtesy Jersey Heritage collections

in 1929 and building up a GP practice there. During the 1930s he had acted as medical inspector of schools and was appointed Medical Officer of Health in 1939.[197] In his official role, as we have seen, McKinstry worked with the Germans where necessary, while challenging policies he regarded as 'contrary to humanity and common sense'. Privately, however, he was involved in every significant form of resistance to the Occupation. According to his clerk 'Tim' Simon, McKinstry did not hate the Germans, but was disgusted by the Nazi regime.[198] Though not a Communist or a member of the JCP, he attended a left-leaning discussion group which met secretly at a St Helier bookshop during the Occupation.[199]

McKinstry's official role left him vulnerable to German pressure, but also enabled him to engage in more effective resistance than many of his fellow islanders. As a result of his work as a GP and in schools in the 1930s, he was already a public figure, widely respected and known to be hostile to Nazism. During the Occupation his role as Medical Officer of Health brought him into contact with a wide range of Jersey residents – civil servants and Air-Raid Protection service (ARP) wardens as well as doctors and medical students – and enabled him to act as an unofficial link between various resistance groups. His most sustained illegal activity was to provide help to OT workers who had escaped from the island camps. McKinstry was a reliable supporter of the loose network run by the JCP, and he also worked with Arthur Halliwell to protect fugitive OT workers and political prisoners. He took these men to 'safe houses' by car and ambulance, and provided them with ration and identity cards supplied to him by contacts.[200] With his colleague Harold Blampied, McKinstry sheltered a Russian in his own home for several months. Finally, after the SS Vega began to supply the island with Red Cross parcels in December 1944, he manipulated the population statistics to obtain extra parcels for the Russians.[201]

Helping OT workers was only one aspect of McKinstry's activities. From 1942 he was in touch with the intelligence-gathering group led by Jersey's ARP Controller William Crawford-Morrison. When Crawford-Morrison concocted a plan to smuggle a miniaturized plan of the German fortifications to the Allies, it was McKinstry who provided faked X-ray evidence of tuberculosis and a letter recommending that he be sent to a Swiss sanatorium for treatment.[202] After the plan failed, McKinstry stayed in contact with the intelligence-gathering network: he provided the petrol for a party of escapers taking military information for the Allies in February 1945, and hid the ARP group's radio transmitter in an office at the Les Vaux TB isolation annexe shortly before the Liberation.[203] Even escapers unconnected to the ARP network, such as the young Canadian-born Belza Turner, had apparently heard of him: in September 1944, before attempting her escape, she contacted an (unnamed) doctor in St Helier – almost certainly McKinstry – for military information to take to the Allies.[204] By the end of the war, he was in touch with virtually every resistance group in the island and an indispensable link between them.

The illegal activities of the Jersey doctors were so extensive that it is reasonable to ask whether their conduct can be described as a form of 'institutional resistance'. According to Semelin's definition, which deals with collective action on a mass basis and with a public dimension, it cannot. First of all, there were so few doctors in the islands that there could be no possibility of *mass* action. Second, they made no *public* or *collective* attempt to mobilize opposition to Occupation policy of the kind undertaken by Dutch doctors, who undermined German attempts to force them into a Nazified Chamber of Physicians in 1941 by sending open letters and making peaceful protests.[205] Yet it is hardly reasonable to judge the Channel Islands' doctors for not responding to a challenge they never faced; the German administration in the islands never tried to Nazify the profession there, so no collective public response was called for. They should be judged instead by their response to the challenges confronting them and the options open to them. On this basis, the record of the Jersey doctors is impressive. A much larger proportion of them engaged in clandestine activity than was true of the general population, while Halliwell and, especially, McKinstry were key figures of Channel Island resistance.

As this chapter has demonstrated, the prospects for institutional resistance were limited in the islands by the absence of party organizations, the weakness of trade unionism and the small number of clergy and medical professionals. The clergy took no collective action, partly because they were under surveillance, and opposition to German policies was offered – if at all – on an individual basis. For their part, doctors in the islands never faced any challenges that called for a collective public response, but in Jersey a significant proportion co-operated in secret to help shelter fugitives and would-be escapers from the island. The most extensive collective action in the islands, however, was political and clandestine, and was undertaken by the JDM and JCP. By the end of the war the JDM had recruited several hundred members and produced plans for constitutional reform, but its members did not offer active resistance to the Germans. This was the preserve of the JCP and of those non-members who agreed to help it. They engaged in various propaganda and humanitarian activities designed to undermine German morale, help victims of persecution and increase support for democratic change after the Liberation. Although the party had fewer than 20 members even in 1945, its capacity for organized action was considerably greater than its numbers would suggest: using their personal contacts, JCP members persuaded many more islanders to supply documents, food and safe houses for OT fugitives and supplies for propaganda leaflets. In this small community, these contacts helped to compensate for the absence of formal resistance structures.

Notes

1 Jacques Semelin, *Unarmed against Hitler: Civilian Resistance in Europe, 1939–1943*, Westport, CT and London, Praeger, 1993, p. 186.
2 Ibid., p. 28.
3 Paul Sanders, *The Ultimate Sacrifice. The Jersey Islanders who Died in German Prisons and Concentration Camps 1940–1945*, Jersey, Jersey Heritage Trust, 2004, p. 132.
4 See, for example, Roy G. Le Hérissier, *The Development of the Government of Jersey, 1771–1972*, Jersey, The States of Jersey, 1973, pp. 88–9; also Richard Hocart, *An Island Assembly. The Development of the States of Guernsey, 1700–1949*, Guernsey, Guernsey Museum and Art Gallery, 1988, pp. 94–6.

5   Reginald F. C. Maugham, *Jersey under the* Jackboot, London, W. H. Allen, 1946, pp. 71–4; Charles Cruickshank, *The German Occupation of the Channel Islands: The Official History of the Occupation Years*, Guernsey, Guernsey Press Co. Ltd., by arrangement with the Trustees of the Imperial War Museum and Oxford University Press, 1975, pp. 179–205; Peter King, *The Channel Islands War 1940–1945*, London, Robert Hale, 1991, pp. 52–4.
6   Norman Le Brocq, *Jersey Looks Forward*, London, The Communist Party, 1947, p. 82.
7   IWM.Sound Archive.Interview 10101. Norman Le Brocq, 1987.
8   This was Norman Le Brocq's estimate, *Jersey Looks Forward*, pp. 79, 81.
9   Leslie Sinel, *The German Occupation of Jersey: The Wartime Diary of Leslie Sinel*, Jersey, Villette Publishing, 1995, 4 November 1940.
10 Interview with Robert Le Sueur, 27 June 2000.
11 IWM.Sound Archive.Interview 10101. Norman Le Brocq, 1987; Interview with Robert Le Sueur, 27 June 2000.
12 JAS.B/A/W50/16/2. Mr A. Le Seeleur, Gt Union St, Jersey, to Bailiff Coutanche, 31 March 1941; Sinel, *The German Occupation of Jersey*, p. 41, 20 March 1941; Basil de Carteret, Mary Deslandes and Mary Robin, *Island Trilogy. Memories of Jersey and the Occupation by Mary Robin, Basil de Carteret and Mary Deslandes*, Jersey, Redberry Press, undated, 'Diary of Mary Deslandes', 16–23 March 1941.
13 Sinel, *The German Occupation of Jersey*, 20 March 1941.
14 JWT.Research Files Box 10. Warren Hobbs, interview with Chris Addy, 8 July 2004. Norman Le Brocq, 'Clandestine Activities. Norman Le Brocq's Story', *Channel Islands Occupation Review*, Vol. 27, 1999, 39–53 (transcript of talk given, 4 April 1988); Francis L. M. Corbet, 'Leslie Huelin', in Francis L. M. Corbet (ed.), *A Bibliographical Dictionary, Volume 2*, Guernsey, Guernsey Press Co. Ltd., 1998, p. 114.
15 Le Brocq, *Jersey Looks Forward*, p. 84.
16 IWM.Sound Archive.Interview 11096. Peter Leslie Crill, 1990.
17 JAS.B/A/W50/30. Attorney General Duret Aubin to Demmler, FK 515, 8 November 1941.
18 IWM.Sound Archive.Interview 10101. Norman Le Brocq, 1987; interview with Robert Le Sueur, 27 June 2000.
19 Founder members included the teacher Lionel Robson, the baker Harold Baal, Steven Venables, Robert Le Sueur and the Communists Leslie Huelin and Norman Le Brocq: Interview with Robert Le Sueur, 27 June 2000; IWM.Sound Archive.Interview 10101. Norman Le Brocq, 1987.
20 Le Brocq, *Jersey Looks Forward*, pp. 85–6.
21 SJ.GO Box 10/33. Norman Le Brocq, transcript of talk to Channel Islands Occupation Society, 4 April 1988.
22 See the author, '"Nothing was ever the same again": Public Attitudes in the Occupied Channel Islands, 1942', *The Local Historian: Journal of the British Association for Local History*, Vol. 35 (1), 2005, 9–20.
23 SJ.GO Box 10/33. Norman Le Brocq, transcript of talk to Channel Islands Occupation Society, 4 April 1988; IWM.Sound Archive.Interview 10101. Norman Le Brocq, 1987.
24 Documents.5750 Misc 189/2 (2826). Norman Le Brocq, transcript of interview, p. 17. For attitudes elsewhere, see Dick van Galen Last, 'The Netherlands', in Bob Moore (ed.), *Resistance in Western Europe*, Oxford and New York, Berg, 2000, pp. 189–221, here p. 212; also Peter Lagrou, 'Belgium', in the same volume, pp. 27–64, here p. 33.
25 Corbet, 'Leslie Huelin', p. 114; IWM.Sound Archive.Interview 10101. Norman Le Brocq, 1987. Among the young members were Les Portlock, Warren Hobbs, Wally Le

Quesne and Ernest Perrée; JAS.D/S/A/4/A6155. Registration card of Leslie Francis Huelin. See also JWT.Research Files Box 10. Warren Hobbs, interview with Chris Addy, 8 July 2004.
26   IWM.Sound Archive.Interview 10101. Norman Le Brocq, 1987.
27   Ibid.
28   JWT.Research Files Box 10. Warren Hobbs, interview with Chris Addy, 8 July 2004. Also Le Brocq, who recruited him, 'Clandestine Activities', 40.
29   Le Brocq, 'Clandestine Activities', 40.
30   Le Brocq, *Jersey Looks Forward*, p. 88.
31   Paul Sanders, *The British Channel Islands under German Occupation, 1940–1945*, Jersey, Jersey Heritage Trust and Société Jersiaise, 2005, pp. 226–7; SJ.GO Box 10/33. Norman Le Brocq, transcript of talk to Channel Islands Occupation Society, 4 April 1988; IWM.Sound Archive.Interview 10101. Norman Le Brocq, 1987.
32   SJ.GO Box 10/33. Norman Le Brocq, transcript of talk to Channel Islands Occupation Society, 4 April 1988; Le Brocq, 'Clandestine Activities', 45. JWT.Research Files Box 10. Warren Hobbs, interview with Chris Addy, 8 July 2004.
33   SJ.GO Box 10/33. Norman Le Brocq, transcript of talk to Channel Islands Occupation Society, 4 April 1988; interview with Stella Perkins, whose future husband Len fed them from his Co-op bread round.
34   Le Brocq, 'Clandestine Activities', 42–5.
35   Ibid.
36   Le Brocq, *Jersey Looks Forward*, p. 91.
37   Edward Le Quesne, *The Occupation of Jersey Day by Day. The Personal Diary of Deputy Edward Le Quesne*, with a foreword and explanatory notes by Michael Ginns, Jersey, La Haule, 1999, 13 January 1945, 10 February 1945.
38   Madeleine Bunting, *The Model Occupation: The Channel Islands under German Rule, 1940–1945*, London, Pimlico, 2004, p. 213; Le Quesne, *The Occupation of Jersey Day by Day*, 21 January 1944, 2 and 3 November 1944.
39   JAS.L/D/25/A/10. Jersey Democratic Movement leaflet: 'Make Liberation Day a day of protest'.
40   On legitimacy see Martin Conway and Peter Romijn, *The War for Legitimacy in Politics and Culture 1936–1946*, Oxford and New York, Berg, 2008, pp. 2–3.
41   See, for example, Le Quesne, referring to the allegations as 'scurrilous', 21 January 1944, and 'libellous', 21 April 1944, also 2 and 3 November 1944.
42   Letter from Michael Ginns to author, 9 June 1999.
43   JWT.Research Files Box 10. Warren Hobbs, interview with Chris Addy, 8 July 2004; Sam Russell, *Spotlight on the Channel Islands*, London, Daily Worker, 1945, p. 12; Le Brocq, *Jersey Looks Forward*, p. 89.
44   JAS.L/F/62/A/2. Paul Mülbach to Les Huelin, May 1945.
45   JWT.Research Files Box 10. Warren Hobbs, interview with Chris Addy, 8 July 2004.
46   See, for example, JAS.L/D/25/A/10. Leaflet of 27 February 1945; JAS.L/F/62/A/10. Undated typed leaflet, probably from April 1945; also JAS.L/F/62/A/1. Leaflet by Paul Mülbach, undated.
47   IWM.Sound Archive.Interview 10102. Rosalie Le Brocq, 1987; Le Brocq, 'Clandestine Activities', p. 46.
48   JWT.Research Files Box 10. Warren Hobbs, interview with Chris Addy, 8 July 2004.
49   IWM.Sound Archive.Interview 10102. Rosalie Le Brocq, 1987; Bunting, *The Model Occupation*, p. 214.
50   IWM.Sound Archive.Interview 10101. Norman Le Brocq, 1987.

51 Sinel, 7 March 1945, noted that 'the Germans suspect sabotage'. See Robert Le Sueur, 'Some Notes on a Planned Mutiny of the German Armed Forces in Jersey on 1st May 1945, and on the German Deserter, Paul Mülbach', *Channel Islands Occupation Review*, Vol. 29, 2001, 44–52, here 47; JWT.Research Files Box 10. Michael Ginns, interview with Chris Addy, 2009.
52 On Hüffmeier see Alexander Coutanche, *The Memoirs of Lord Coutanche: A Jerseyman Looks Back*, ed. H. R. S. Pocock, Chichester, Sussex, Phillimore and Co. Ltd., 1975, p. 43; *Evening Post*, 3 March 1945, p. 1; Sinel, 28 February 1945.
53 This was the view of Robert Le Sueur, who agreed to take part: Le Sueur, 'Some Notes on a Planned Mutiny of the German Armed Forces in Jersey on 1st May 1945', 48.
54 JWT.Research Files Box 10. Warren Hobbs, interview with Chris Addy, 8 July 2004; Le Sueur, 'Some Notes on a Planned Mutiny of the German Armed Forces in Jersey on 1st May 1945', 47–8.
55 See, for example, JWT.Research Files Box 10. Warren Hobbs, interview with Chris Addy, 8 July 2004. Robert Le Sueur – a JDM member who had agreed to keep watch – later admitted to a sense of paralysis: he was appalled by the plans, but felt bound by loyalty not to betray the mutiny: Le Sueur, 'Some Notes on a Planned Mutiny of the German Armed Forces in Jersey on 1st May 1945', 47–8.
56 IWM.Sound Archive.Interview 10101. Norman Le Brocq, 1987; JWT.Research Files Box 10. Warren Hobbs, interview with Chris Addy, 8 July 2004; Le Sueur, 'Some Notes on a Planned Mutiny of the German Armed Forces in Jersey on 1st May 1945', 49–50. Norman Le Brocq thought there had been disputes between socialist and anti-socialist officers: *Jersey Looks Forward*, p. 90.
57 Le Sueur, 'Some Notes on a Planned Mutiny of the German Armed Forces in Jersey on 1st May 1945', 51.
58 Letter from Les Huelin, Acting secretary, Provisional Organising Committee, to the editor, *Evening Post*, 25 May 1945, p. 1. See also 'Workers Fill the Town Hall. Channel Islands Representative of T&GWU Outlines Uunion's Aims', article in *Evening Post*, 23 July 1945.
59 *Evening Post*, 14 June 1945, p. 1.
60 Le Brocq, *Jersey Looks Forward*, pp. 92–4; *Evening Post*, 14 June 1945, p. 1: T&GWU official statement that 'the body of men styling themselves the POC' had no authority to use the union name.
61 IWM.Sound Archive.Interview 10101. Norman Le Brocq, 1987; *Evening Post*, 17 October 1945, p. 1. Also Le Hérissier, *The Development of the Government of Jersey, 1771–1972*, p. 120.
62 See, for example, TNA.HO.144/22237 MI19 (RPS)/2510. 'Statement issued by the JDM and brought over by informants, November 1944'; TNA.WO.208/3741 MI 19 (RPS)/2438. Interrogation of escapers who left Jersey on 20 September 1944, 2 October 1944.
63 Le Quesne, 19 October 1944.
64 Its 12-point programme outlined in 'JDM Meeting at Town Hall', *Evening Post*, 20 October 1941; see also Le Hérissier, *The Development of the Government of Jersey, 1771–1972*, p. 120.
65 See *Evening Post*, 12 October 1945, p. 1; 17 October 1945, p. 1.
66 Cruickshank, *The German Occupation of the Channel Islands*, p. 320.
67 *Evening Post*, editorial, 4 August 1945, p. 1; 31 October 1941, p. 1.
68 Le Hérissier, *The Development of the Government of Jersey, 1771–1972*, p. 123: it received under 22 per cent of the rural vote.

69 Coutanche, *The Memoirs of Lord Coutanche*, pp. 117–19; *Evening Post*, 7 November 1945; also Le Hérissier, *The Development of the Government of Jersey, 1771–1972*, p. 120.
70 John Uttley, *The Story of the Channel Islands*, London, Faber and Faber, 1966, p. 215; Le Hérissier, *The Development of the Government of Jersey, 1771–1972*, p. 139.
71 'Death of a Democrat', *Jersey Evening Post*, 27 November 1996, p. 1, also p. 5.
72 See the chapter on administrative resistance elsewhere in this volume.
73 Paul Sanders, 'Managing under Duress: Ethical Leadership, Social Capital, and the Civilian Administration of the British Channel Islands during the Nazi Occupation, 1940–1945', *Journal of Business Ethics*, Vol. 93, 2010, 113–29, here 115.
74 David M. Chapman, *Chapel and Swastika: Methodism in the Channel Islands during the German Occupation*, Jersey, ELSP, 2009, p. 4. See also Sanders, *The British Channel Islands under German Occupation*, p. 118.
75 Bunting, *The Model Occupation*, p. 332.
76 Semelin, *Unarmed against Hitler*, pp. 151–4. On the rescue of the Danish Jews, see M. B. Jensen and S. L. B. Jensen (eds), *Denmark and the Holocaust*, Copenhagen, Institute for International Studies, Department for Holocaust and Genocide Studies, 2003.
77 Semelin, *Unarmed against Hitler*, p. 67.
78 Ibid., p. 66.
79 IWM.Documents.1806 91/5/1. Canon E. L. Frossard, Dean of Guernsey 1945–1968, 'The German Occupation of Guernsey', 1969, p. 392.
80 Chapman, *Chapel and Swastika*, pp. 25–6.
81 JAS.L/C/20/D/8. Reverend Clement Mylne, Under the Crooked Cross. Jersey 1940–1945: Church Life.
82 Orders of the Commandant of the German Forces, 8 July 1940, in Sinel, 9 July 1940; PL.LF940.53 ORD. Reverend R. Douglas Ord, Occupation Diary, 1 August 1940.
83 Chapman, *Chapel and Swastika*, p. 43.
84 K. M. Bachmann, *The Prey of an Eagle: A Personal Record of Family Life Written throughout the German Occupation of Guernsey 1940–45*, Guernsey, Guernsey Press Co. Ltd., 1972, 30 January 1941; PL.LF940.53 ORD. Reverend R. Douglas Ord, Occupation Diary, 21 January 1941; de Carteret et al., 'Diary of Mary Deslandes', 2–9 February 1941.
85 Michael Thierry, 'An Army Oppressed', chapter 10: Marie Ozanne, manuscript on the Salvation Army under Occupation, undated, unpaginated, by kind permission of Michael Thierry.
86 Marie Ozanne, acting officer-in-charge of the St Sampson's Citadel in Guernsey, Diary, 12 March 1942, 10 May 1942, 19 July 1942, 11 August 1942, Diary held by and used by kind permission of the Ozanne family. On the hiding of Salvation Army banners, letter from Alec Podger to author, 23 July 2010.
87 Letter from Guernsey Salvation Army member Colin Bond, Salvationist, 1 May 1999, p. 7.
88 GOMG. William John 'Bill' Bougourd, 'The Marie Ozanne Story', undated; Richard Heaume, 'Marie Ozanne', *Channel Islands Occupation Review*, Vol. 23, 1995, 79–81.
89 SAIHC.Personality Files: Marie Ozanne. Letter from Major Marie Ozanne to the Feldkommandant, Guernsey, 22 June 1941.
90 Major Ozanne's activities are described in the chapter on women and resistance.
91 Chapman, *Chapel and Swastika*, p. 85; PL.LF940.53 ORD. Reverend R. Douglas Ord, Occupation Diary, 15 September 1940. See also JAS.L/C/20/D/8. Reverend Clement Mylne, Under the Crooked Cross. Jersey 1940–1945: Church Life.

92 Chapman, *Chapel and Swastika*, p. 43. See also PL.LF940.53 ORD. Reverend R. Douglas Ord, Occupation Diary, 1 August 1940.
93 JAS.L/C/20/D/8. Reverend Clement Mylne, Under the Crooked Cross. Jersey 1940–1945: Church Life.
94 Chapman, *Chapel and Swastika*, p. 42.
95 JAS.L/C/77/A/1-8. Izett Croad, Occupation Diary, 27 February 1943; Sinel, 26 February 1943; Le Quesne, 25 February 1943.
96 JAS.L/C/77/A/1-8. Izett Croad, Occupation Diary, 4 February 1943; JAS.D/AG/B7/1. 'Names of Political Prisoners August 1940' prison log book: 252–4: Clement Noble Mylne, Winifred Nellie Mylne, Vivienne Mylne.
97 JAS.L/C/20/D/5/1. Reverend Clement Mylne, 'A Travesty of Justice', galley for The Methodist Recorder.
98 IA.AQ 0368/01–11. Violet Carey, Occupation Diaries 1940–1945, 29 September 1942, on Hartley-Jackson; Chapman, *Chapel and Swastika*, p. 187, on Henry Foss.
99 Sanders, *The British Channel Islands under German Occupation*, p. 161.
100 See, for example, Chapman, *Chapel and Swastika*, p. 185.
101 Ibid., pp. 83–5.
102 SJ.GO Box 10/37. Joachim Morlingerhaus, Zündenscheid, to the Lieutenant Governor, St Helier, 15 August 1997, describing the friendship between his father and the later Dean of Jersey, Kenneth Preston.
103 PL.LF940.53 ORD. Reverend R. Douglas Ord, Occupation Diary, 4 March 1942, 21 August 1942; Sanders, *The British Channel Islands under German Occupation*, p. 60. On the Confessing Church and German Protestantism, see Shelley Baranowski, *The Confessing Church, Conservative Elites and the Nazi State*, Lewiston, The Edwin Mellen Press, 1986.
104 PL.LF940.53 ORD. Reverend R. Douglas Ord, Occupation Diary, 25 August 1944.
105 See, for example, ibid., 30 August 1942, 18 May 1943.
106 JAS.L/C/20/D/8. Reverend Clement Mylne, Under the Crooked Cross. Jersey 1940–1945: Church Life.
107 PL.LF940.53 ROB. Ambrose C. Robin, Occupation Diaries 17 June 1940–18 May 1945, 21 June 1942.
108 IA.AQ 0368/01–11. Violet Carey, Occupation Diaries 1940–1945, 29 September 1942.
109 See also a reference to a 'courageous sermon' by the vicar of St Marks in Jersey, Reverend Killer: JAS.L/C/03/A/10. Mabel Ahier, 'Jersey in Wartime during the German Occupation', 20 September 1942.
110 Chapman, *Chapel and Swastika*, p. 187.
111 PL.LF940.53 ORD. Reverend R. Douglas Ord, Occupation Diary, 12 September 1943.
112 Ibid., 12 September 1943, 11 June 1944.
113 Ibid., 12 September 1943. See also references to the Dambusters raid and D-Day, 23 May 1943, 11 June 1944.
114 Ibid., 27 September 1943, 4 November 1943.
115 Ibid., 4 November 1943.
116 Ibid., 30 July 1944.
117 IA.AQ 0368/01–11. Violet Carey, Occupation Diaries 1940–1945, 11 June 1944.
118 Ibid., 25 June 1944.
119 Ibid., 12 June 1941.
120 IA.AQ 1212/098. Kenneth G. Lewis, Diary of Events 1940–1945, 21 August 1944.

121 Sanders, *The British Channel Islands under German Occupation*, pp. 118-19; Alan Wood and Mary Wood, *Islands in Danger: The Fantastic Story of the German Occupation of the Channel Islands, 1940-1945*, Sevenoaks, First Four Square, 1965, p. 235.
122 Sanders, *The British Channel Islands under German Occupation*, p. 118 n.; Wood and Wood, *Islands in Danger*, p. 235.
123 Sanders, *The British Channel Islands under German Occupation*, p. 115; *Evening Post*, 29 September 1945.
124 TNA.WO.311/105. Letter from Mrs H. H. Cohu, Five Oaks, Jersey, for consideration of War Crimes Commission, 10 December 1945; Nan Le Ruez, *Jersey Occupation Diary: Her Story of the German Occupation, 1940-45*, Jersey, Seaflower Books, 1994, 4 August 1944; SJ.OCC 942 GRE. Leslie Green, 'My War Years', unpublished manuscript, not dated.
125 Sanders, *The Ultimate Sacrifice*, p. 22.
126 JAS.M/28/2. Ralph Mollet, Occupation Diary, Volume 2, 1 February 1941–6 June 1943, 23 March 1941. See also Sanders, *The British Channel Islands under German Occupation*, p. 115.
127 See the comments by a patient, Peggy Boléat, *A Quiet Place*, Jersey, Villette Publishing Ltd., 1993, pp. 54, 110; also SJ.OCC 942 GRE. Leslie Green, 'My War Years'; Frank Keiller, *Prison without Bars: Living in Jersey under the German Occupation 1940-1945*, Bradford on Avon, Seaflower Books, 2000, p. 89; Barry Turner, *Outpost of Occupation: How the Channel Islands Survived Nazi Rule 1940-1945*, London, Aurum Press Ltd., 2010, pp. 158-9.
128 See the chapter elsewhere in this book.
129 Sanders, *The British Channel Islands under German Occupation*, p. 115; SJ.*OCC 942 L'AM. J. H. L'Amy, 'The German Occupation of Jersey', undated but written in 1945/46, p. 24.
130 See Le Quesne, 9 April 1943; see also Sinel, 9 April 1943; Sanders, *The British Channel Islands under German Occupation*, p. 115.
131 TNA.WO.311/105. Letter from Mrs H. H. Cohu, Five Oaks, Jersey, for consideration of War Crimes Commission, 10 December 1945; Sanders, *The British Channel Islands under German Occupation*, pp. 115-16; Sanders, *The Ultimate Sacrifice*, p. 24.
132 Le Ruez, 4 August 1944.
133 The most detailed description of Cohu's fate is Sanders, *The Ultimate Sacrifice*, pp. 21-7; also Sanders, *The British Channel Islands under German Occupation*, pp. 115-17. See also TNA.WO.311/105. G. C. Allchin, Foreign Office, to Treasury Solicitor's Office, 27 March 1946 enclosing letter of Przemysl Polacek, Brno, 25 October 1945.
134 Keiller, *Prison without Bars*, p. 88; Michael Halliwell, *Operating under Occupation: The Life and Work of Arthur Clare Halliwell FRCS, Consultant Surgeon at the Jersey General Hospital during the German Occupation 1940-1945*, Jersey, Channel Islands Occupation Society, 2005, p. 108.
135 SAIHC.Personality Files: Marie Ozanne. Letter from Major Marie Ozanne to the Feldkommandant, Guernsey, 26 June 1941. Ozanne's case in described in detail in the chapter on women.
136 IWM.Documents.13409. Private Papers of Captain J. R. Dening: Dening 9: The Channel Islands Under German Occupation 1945. Resistance: Marie Ozanne. Letter from Ozanne to Feldkommandant, Guernsey, 6 September 1942.

137 Ibid. Letter from Ozanne to Feldkommandant, Guernsey, 6 September 1942, also letter to Feldkommandant, 30 August 1942.
138 See, for example, SJ.GO Box 10/30. Anne Perchaud, 'Childhood Memories', transcript of talk to Channel Islands Occupation Society, 1995, p. 7, on the Russian at St Martin's parish church; also Dr Averell Darling on 'Tom'at the Gospel Hall of the Plymouth Brethren, interview with Geraldine des Forges, 1995 Occupation Project by Val Sherman Garnier for Jersey Health Promotion.
139 Testimony of Koslov in Halliwell, *Operating under Occupation*, p. 79.
140 van Galen Last, 'The Netherlands', p. 195.
141 PL.LF940.53 ORD. Reverend R. Douglas Ord, Occupation Diary, 24 November 1940. Steiner who was subsequently deported to her death.
142 For more details see the chapter on humanitarian resistance in this volume.
143 JAS.L/C/20/D/8. Reverend Clement Mylne, Under the Crooked Cross. Jersey 1940–1945: Church Life.
144 See the chapter on deportations in this volume.
145 For Guernsey see the testimony of IWM.Documents.5727 96/32/1. Dr Alastair Rose, 'Impressions of the Occupation of Guernsey, Written by Dr. Alastair Rose between 1944 & 1945'; on Jersey see Halliwell, *Operating under Occupation*, pp. 23–4 and IWM.Sound Archive.Interview 10878. Raymond Leonard Osmont, 1989.
146 JWT.Research Files Box 10. Ken Podger, interview with Chris Addy, 26 November 2003. Mr Podger worked for the States Pathology Laboratory during the Occupation; Louise Willmot, 'Noel McKinstry', *Channel Islands Occupation Review*, Vol. 31, 2003, 25–30; Val Garnier, *Medical History of the Jersey Hospitals and Nursing Homes during the Occupation, 1940–1945*, London, Channel Islands Occupation Birth Cohort Study, University of London, 2002, p. 15.
147 John Lewis, *A Doctor's Occupation: The Dramatic True Story of Life in Nazi-Occupied Jersey*, London, New English Library, 1983, pp. 49, 61; IWM.Documents.5727 96/32/1. Dr Alastair Rose, 'Impressions of the Occupation of Guernsey, Written by Dr. Alastair Rose between 1944 and 1945'; Halliwell, *Operating under Occupation*, pp. 19–24.
148 Ibid., p. 84: 7,000 children and 600 adults were vaccinated.
149 Peter Birchenall and Mary Birchenall, *Operation Nurse: Nursing in Guernsey 1940–1945*, West Sussex, Woodfield Publishing, 2001; Halliwell, *Operating under Occupation*, p. 49; Lewis, *A Doctor's Occupation*, pp. 124–5; Keiller, *Prison without Bars*, p. 61.
150 See, for example, IA. Annual Report of Medical Officer of Health 1941, 7 February 1942.
151 IA. Annual Report of Medical Officer of Health 1942, 18 May 1943.
152 IA.AQ 0368/01–11. Violet Carey, Occupation Diaries 1940–1945, 20 April 1942.
153 IA.FK 06-02. Group Captain C. R. J. Randall, St Martin's, to President of Controlling Committee, 16 June 1942.
154 IA.FK 06-02. A. N. Symonds, Health Services Officer, to FK 515 Nebenstelle Guernsey, 23 June 1942.
155 IA.FK 06-02. Dr Bosch, Kriegsverwaltungsrat Nebenstelle Guernsey to FK 515 Jersey, 6 July 1942.
156 Cruickshank, *The German Occupation of the Channel Islands*, pp. 136–8.
157 IA.FK 06-02. FK 515 Military Administration Guernsey to John Leale, President of the Controlling Committee, 18 June 1942. The appeal was published in *The Star*, 30 June 1942.

158 V. V. Cortvriend, *Isolated Island*, Guernsey, Guernsey Star and Gazette, 1945, p. 305.
159 IA.AQ 1212/098. Kenneth G. Lewis, Diary of Events 1940–1945, 5 December 1944; also Cortvriend, *Isolated Island*, p. 305.
160 Letter from L. J. 'Tim' Simon to author, 25 August 1999; also JAS. Noel McKinstry, Medical Officer of Health Annual Report for 1945, September 1946, p. 16.
161 Sanders, *The British Channel Islands under German Occupation*, p. 76.
162 JAS.B/A/W81/19. McKinstry, Halliwell and Blampied, Inspection of Prisons, 26 February 1945.
163 JAS.B/A/W81/9. Medical Officer of Health to C. S. Le Gros, President, Jersey Prison Board, 18 April 1945.
164 Letter from L. J. 'Tim' Simon to author, 25 August 1999.
165 JWT.Research Files Box 10. Ken Podger, interview with Chris Addy, 26 November 2003. Mr Podger worked for McKinstry at the States Pathology Laboratory.
166 This from the diary of Douglas Ord, who had a copy of the Report, 10 June 1942: PL.LF940.53 ORD. Reverend R. Douglas Ord, Occupation Diary. Also Cortvriend, *Isolated Island*, p. 305.
167 Sanders, *The British Channel Islands under German Occupation*, p. 123.
168 Halliwell, *Operating under Occupation*, p. 111; Hazel Knowles-Smith, *The Changing Face of the Channel Islands Occupation: Record, Memory and Myth*, Basingstoke, Palgrave Macmillan, 2007, p. 149.
169 On the murders of the disabled, see recently Patricia Heberer, 'The Nazi "euthanasia" Programme', in Jonathan Friedman (ed.), *The Routledge History of the Holocaust*, London and New York, Routledge, 2010, pp. 137–47.
170 Dr Averell Darling, in interview with Geraldine des Forges, 1995. 1995 Occupation Project by Val Sherman Garnier for Jersey Health Promotion.
171 IWM.Documents.5727 96/32/1. Dr Alastair Rose, 'Impressions of the Occupation of Guernsey, Written by Dr. Alastair Rose between 1944 & 1945', pp. 28, 30; Cortvriend, *Isolated Island*, p. 298.
172 IWM.Sound Archive.Interview 12532.Reel 4. Mabel Vera Green, 1992.
173 IWM.Documents.5727 96/32/1. Dr Alastair Rose, 'Impressions of the Occupation of Guernsey, Written by Dr. Alastair Rose between 1944 & 1945'.
174 Letter from George Koslov to Michael Halliwell, Halliwell, *Operating under Occupation*, p. 79.
175 See, for example, John Lewis, interview with Geraldine des Forges, 1995 Occupation Project by Val Sherman Garnier for Jersey Health Promotion; Halliwell, *Operating under Occupation*, p. 116.
176 Semelin, *Unarmed against Hitler*, p. 65.
177 SJ.*OCC 942 L'AM. J. H. L'Amy, The German Occupation of Jersey, undated but written in 1945/46, p. 25.
178 JAS.L/C/77/A/1-8. Izett Croad, Occupation Diary, 8 February 1943; similar comments made by Robert Le Sueur, interview 4 August 2010.
179 JAS.M/45/A1/1. Joyce Le Ruez, Memories of the German Occupation of Jersey, 1940–1945, p. 4.
180 TNA.WO.311/11. Testimony of William Francis Sarre, 2 July 1945; account of Peter Botatenko in *Evening Post*, 19 May 1945, p. 4; interview with Gwenda Sarre, 24 August 2000.
181 Halliwell, *Operating under Occupation*, p. 20.
182 IWM.Sound Archive.Interview 10878. Raymond Leonard Osmont, 1989; Keiller, *Prison without Bars*, p. 149. Both were hurt dropping over the perimeter wall.

183 IWM.Sound Archive.Interview 10878. Raymond Leonard Osmont, 1989.
184 JAS.D/Z/H6/7/491. Correspondence relating to the treatment of Ivy Forster: Harmsen, Kriegsgerichtsrat, to Duret Aubin, 1 August 1944.
185 Claude Avarne was arrested for having a set: de Carteret et al., 'Diary of Mary Deslandes', 29 February 1944; McKinstry and Harold Blampied shared a set: SJ GO10/36. Letter from R. Noel McKinstry to Mrs Janet McKinstry, Oxford, 13 May 1945; Lewis, *A Doctor's Occupation*, p. 40; Halliwell, *Operating under Occupation*, p. 65.
186 Lewis, *A Doctor's Occupation*, p. 158.
187 Halliwell, *Operating under Occupation*, p. 19.
188 See, for example, interview with Mary Le Sueur by Geraldine des Forges, 1995 Occupation Project by Val Sherman Garnier for Jersey Health Promotion; Keiller, *Prison without Bars*, p. 67.
189 Halliwell, *Operating under Occupation*, p. 173.
190 IWM.Sound Archive.Interview 10878. Raymond Leonard Osmont, 1989; also Dr Averell Darling, quoted in Halliwell, *Operating under Occupation*, p. 38.
191 Halliwell, *Operating under Occupation*, pp. 50-1.
192 Interview with Dr Averell Darling by Geraldine des Forges, 1995 Occupation Project by Val Sherman Garnier for Jersey Health Promotion. The fugitive was 'Tom', who was sheltered by the Le Breton family in St Mary.
193 Koslov's reminiscences in Halliwell, *Operating under Occupation*, pp. 78-9.
194 Ibid., p. 116.
195 Letter from Donald Bell to Michael Halliwell, reproduced in ibid., p. 129.
196 The memory of Kenneth Preston, then a newly appointed curate, to Michael Halliwell, ibid., p. 81.
197 Averell Darling, 'McKinstry, Robert Noel', in Francis L. M. Corbet (ed.), *A Bibliographical Dictionary, Volume 2*, pp. 288-90; *Evening Post*, obituary, 6 March 1961.
198 Letter from L. J. 'Tim' Simon to author, 25 August 1999.
199 Letter from Robert Le Sueur to author, 2 July 1999.
200 Keiller, *Prison without Bars*, p. 152; Bell, in Halliwell, *Operating under Occupation*, p. 129; Francis Le Sueur, *Shadow of the Swastika. Could It All Happen again?*, Guernsey, Guernsey Press Co. Ltd., 1992, pp. 86-94.
201 William Gladden, in *Evening Post*, 12 June 1945, p. 5; Wood and Wood, *Islands in Danger*, p. 160; Willmot, 'Noel McKinstry', 28.
202 Wood and Wood, *Islands in Danger*, p. 165.
203 William Gladden, account in *Evening Post*, 12 June 1945, p. 5; SJ.GO Box 10/37. Victoria Livingstone, 'So Many Brick Walls, Driving under the Nazis: A True Story of the German Occupation of Jersey', p. 14. Livingstone was a licensed driver for medical staff.
204 Roy Thomas, *Lest We Forget: Escapes and Attempted Escapes from Jersey during the German Occupation 1940-1945*, Jersey, La Haule, 1992, p. 24.
205 Semelin, *Unarmed against Hitler*, pp. 70-2.

7

Women and Resistance

Louise Willmot

For decades after the Second World War, women were the 'forgotten people' of the European Resistance.¹ In wartime their domestic responsibilities, especially caring for children and the elderly, had made them much less likely than men to go 'underground', while gendered roles within resistance organizations ensured that female resisters were secretaries, carers and liaison agents rather than saboteurs or partisans.² After the Liberation, restored national governments concentrated on honouring the senior figures in resistance organizations and their armed fighters, almost all of whom were men.³ Although understandable in the contemporary context of restoring national pride after defeat and occupation, this focus meant that women's contribution to the Resistance was overlooked. The same neglect also characterized early histories of these movements. Since the 1970s this omission has been remedied, especially in France, by studies of the extent and nature of women's participation.⁴ This chapter attempts a similar analysis in the Channel Islands, and shows the extent to which women's contribution was shaped by their social, economic and political position in island life. When women did defy the Germans, they did so overwhelmingly in a domestic setting. Except for their defiance of the radio ban and in giving humanitarian aid to OT workers, they were a minority of those who engaged in active opposition to the Occupation. Nevertheless, among them were some of the most courageous of Channel Island resisters.

Women in the arrest and court records during the Occupation

During the Occupation, the conduct of women in the islands was subjected to close scrutiny. Most of it focused on the 'Jerrybags', the women and girls who formed romantic and sexual relationships with German soldiers and who, as elsewhere in Western Europe, were considered guilty of a particularly contemptible form of collaboration.⁵ In some popular histories of the Occupation, too, they are accorded a degree of attention their numbers do not warrant.⁶ Yet there had also been cases of defiance by island women which were much remarked on before 1945. Two incidents which were remembered in the early histories of the Occupation involved Guernseywomen: Winifred Green, a waitress at the Royal Hotel, who served six months in France after shouting 'To hell with Hitler!' when ordered to give the Nazi salute in return for a rice pudding, and Ruby Langlois, who was imprisoned for 14 days early in the Occupation for denouncing the Germans as 'blackguards'.[7]

Other incidents, equally well known at the time, have since been largely forgotten. In September 1940, Klara Crawford-Morrison, the 54-year-old wife of Jersey's Air-Raid Protection service (ARP) Controller, was arrested for thumbing her nose at German soldiers who insulted her in the street. When interviewed by the Kommandant, Mrs Crawford-Morrison, who spoke fluent German, allegedly told him 'exactly what she thought of the Nazis as a whole and himself in particular',[8] and received a two-week sentence for insulting the German army.[9] A similar incident occurred in December 1943, when a 22-year-old Jersey riding teacher, Nanetta Butterworth, threw a shovelful of manure at German soldiers and, because of her history of 'anti-German demonstration', was sentenced to six months.[10] A few other women, too, were arrested for various 'insults' to the occupying forces.[11] Their actions were recorded by diarists either with satisfaction or, at least, without the disapproval reserved for sabotage and escape attempts, which were condemned as irresponsible. Instead the women's tales grew in the telling: Mrs Crawford-Morrison's nose-thumbing turned into 'a knockout blow', and Butterworth's scattering of dung into a deluge.[12] Such stories acquired a symbolic significance as a brave response by vulnerable women to disrespectful behaviour.

Even minor acts of defiance were risky, because German responses were unpredictable. Whereas Winifred Green was arrested for refusing to give the Hitler salute, a similar response by the Jersey hospital radiographer, Miss Lowry, went unpunished – but one of her colleagues, the nurse Agatha Bott, went to prison for a month in 1943 after abusing an Irish colleague for associating with German soldiers.[13] Although sentences were usually short, one incident ended in tragedy when June Sinclair, a Londoner working in a Jersey hotel, was arrested for slapping a German soldier who had molested her. She was deported and died in Ravensbrück concentration camp in 1943, aged only 23.[14] Sinclair was probably a victim of the practice identified by Charles Cruickshank and Paul Sanders, whereby mainland-born offenders received longer sentences than islanders and were more likely to be sent to the continent to serve them.[15] Incidents such as this inevitably caused unease. Reporting rumours of an arrest in Guernsey in December 1941, the diarist Mary Deslandes felt that it was 'not safe to open one's mouth in the streets'.[16]

Despite the attention they received, arrests of women for such incidents were rare. There were only 14 cases of women 'insulting' the Germans in the two islands and only 17 of anti-German demonstration or 'manifestations', compared with 94 involving men.[17] In fact, the arrest and court records reveal that women were significantly less likely to be arrested and sentenced for all political offences against the occupiers. Of the 447 arrests in Guernsey by the Germans, only 67 (15 per cent) were of women, and in Jersey only 128 of the 857 people tried for these offences were female (also 15 per cent).[18] Of course, the records tell only part of the story, since most people who defied or resisted the Germans were never caught. It is also probable that women were less likely than men to be arrested for offences committed by both, either because male family members took the blame on their behalf or because the Germans chose to punish men.[19] The records are often tantalizingly incomplete. Two Guernseywomen, the housemaid Marjorie Gill and the nurserymaid Leona Le Blond, received long prison sentences for inciting treachery in 1941, but the exact nature of their of their offence is unclear and the charges may have been trumped up.[20] Nevertheless, testimony from diaries, memoirs and oral records confirms that some forms of resistance – and especially *organized* activity – were undertaken almost exclusively by men. Where women were involved, moreover, it was usually in background roles. The explanation lies, above all, in their social and economic position in the islands.

The impact of economic, social and political factors on women's activities

Before the Second World War, women played a more restricted role in economic and political life than their counterparts on the mainland. Fewer were in paid employment: in 1931 only 31 per cent had jobs outside the home in Jersey and under 27 per cent in Guernsey, compared to 34 per cent in England and Wales. Of those in work, by far the largest category were in domestic or other 'personal' services such as cooks.[21] The pattern was maintained during the Occupation. In Guernsey, for example, a 1941 survey showed that there were almost 11,000 women over the age of 14 in the island, 7,376 or 67 per cent of whom were housewives not employed outside the home. The category included such different groups as economically inactive members of the islands' wealthy elites, and farmers' wives whose labour went unrecorded in the statistics. Another 1,078 (10 per cent) were domestic servants, and 98 were cooks or cleaners. Almost 80 per cent of all adult women in occupied Guernsey, therefore, were either housewives or employed in domestic services. Of the rest, by far the largest category consisted of shop workers and clerks or secretaries, who accounted for 7 per cent of adult women between them.[22] Few were employed in industry and almost none in professional or managerial roles. This concentration in the domestic sphere did much to limit women's involvement in *organized* illegal activity since, in the absence of political networks or universities, much of the organized resistance in the islands developed in the workplace, in paid or voluntary jobs dominated by men.

Women's role in the political life of the islands was similarly limited. Although Jersey and Guernsey had granted women the vote after the First World War, they were not encouraged to be politically active. In Guernsey the first States Deputy was elected in 1924, but no others had followed her.[23] In Jersey, women were permitted to stand for election after 1924, but the measure had been 'fiercely resisted by the diehards' and no women were elected to the States before the outbreak of war.[24] Such attitudes proved tenacious even in the reformist atmosphere of 1945–50, when the Guernsey States' proposals for widening the pool of candidates for election were specifically designed to open the route to office for 'young men'.[25] Before 1939 women were not encouraged to take an active part in the political life of the islands, and few of them did so.

This situation helps to explain why they played only a minor role in the political organizations that emerged during the Occupation. None were among the founder members of the Jersey Democratic Movement (JDM), although a significant number joined subsequently and four were on its ten-strong executive committee in July 1945.[26] For its part, the small Jersey Communist Party (JCP) never had any women members before the Liberation. The only woman known to have been associated with it was Rosalie Le Riche, the fiancée of Norman Le Brocq, who typed leaflets for the party and helped the German deserter Paul Mülbach in 1944/45. She was never a member of the JCP and became involved through her loyalty to Le Brocq.[27] In a European context, there was nothing unusual about her participation, or the form it took. As Hanna Diamond and Paula Schwartz have demonstrated in the case of France, it was common for women to be drawn into anti-German activities through family and personal ties, especially in support of their husbands, and to be concentrated mainly in secretarial and caring roles.[28]

Lucy Schwob and Suzanne Malherbe

Elsewhere in Europe, the women most likely to become involved in resistance activities on their own initiative, rather than through family members, were those who had already been politically active before the Occupation in the trade unions and the Communist Party.[29] In the Channel Islands, where there were no political parties and women's involvement in trade unions was minimal, the most active political resistance by women came not from locals but from two Frenchwomen, Lucy Schwob and Suzanne Malherbe, who had settled there shortly before the war. Schwob was born in Nantes in 1894 to a Catholic mother and a liberal Jewish father, the editor of the city's newspaper.[30] Educated in England and the Sorbonne, she had adopted the pseudonym of Claude Cahun and established a reputation as an avant garde artist, chiefly for her photographs and photo-collages dominated by the themes of masks, mirrors and shifting gender identity. Her artistic collaborator on several of these projects was her life partner Suzanne Malherbe, a gifted graphic designer and illustrator who worked under the name Marcel Moore.[31] The two women were also step-sisters from 1913, on the re-marriage of Schwob's father to Malherbe's mother. It was the most significant relationship of both their lives.

Spurred on by the rise of fascism, the two women joined the Communist-inspired *Associations des Écrivains et Artistes Revolutionnaires* (AEAR) in 1932, convinced that the Communists were 'the only ones to oppose Hitlerian racism and maintain certain values, among them liberty of expression'.[32] They were swiftly disillusioned: only two years later they left the AEAR, rejecting the Communists' argument that artists must restrict the style and content of their output in the interests of revolutionary change.[33] Subsequently, they found a more congenial political and artistic environment in the Surrealist movement. Along with André Breton and Georges Bataille they were founder members of the group *Contre Attaque*, which campaigned against fascism and for the Republican cause during the Spanish Civil War.[34] This political engagement ended in 1937 when Schwob and Malherbe settled at St Brelade's Bay in Jersey, apparently after a deterioration in Schwob's health.³⁵ When the Germans came, nevertheless, their anti-Nazi credentials were well established.

In June 1940 the couple deliberately chose not to evacuate, despite the risks posed by their record of anti-fascism and Schwob's Jewish heritage.³⁶ Against the horrors of Nazi racism and brute force, she commented later, Comintern theories of 'revolutionary defeatism' were inadequate. Instead, artists had a duty to make a stand.³⁷ Their opposition to Nazism drew them into active resistance earlier than other residents in the islands, though Malherbe acknowledged that they 'started in a small way in 1940' and developed only gradually.³⁸ Their aim was to liberate Jersey without bloodshed by persuading German soldiers to lay down their arms.³⁹ Their first activities, however, were so obscure that they were scarcely recognizable as resistance at all: the German phrase 'Ohne Ende' ('without end', short for 'horror without end') scribbled on cigarette packets and dropped on footpaths for German soldiers to find, along with a photocollage of Oscar Wilde and Lord Alfred Douglas superimposed on a photograph of German soldiers. It made sense to adopt a cautious and oblique approach in 1940, but the two women were also gloriously eccentric.⁴⁰

In 1942, however, they launched a 'news service of our own for the benefit of the German troops'. It was based on BBC bulletins, supplemented with political commentary by Lucy Schwob and translated into fluent German by Suzanne Malherbe.⁴¹ The typed leaflets purported to be the work of an anti-Nazi German soldier ('the nameless soldier') who, by winter 1941/42, had become 'the nameless soldier and his comrades'.⁴² They distributed their bulletins several times a week for two years, initially in St Brelade's and later in St Helier, putting them in cigarette packets and matchboxes, leaving them in shops and cafes, pushing them through the windows of empty military vehicles, and stuffing them in post-boxes.⁴³ After September 1942 they also sent material directly to *Feldkommandant* Knackfuss, whom they held responsible for the deportation of British-born residents to Germany.⁴⁴ By now they had devised verse templates that could be adapted to take account of military and political developments – the Allied landings in Italy and France, Soviet advances on the eastern front, and the Allied bombing of Germany. The leaflets contrasted the sufferings of German soldiers and civilians with the privileges of the Nazi elite, emphasized the brutality of the regime and the strength of the Allies, and urged the troops not to fight.⁴⁵ 'Idiot, that you may die so that the Führer can live a little longer' was the message in one, while another asked soldiers to work for 'freedom, peace and Fatherland'.⁴⁶ By the time they were caught, Schwob and Malherbe had distributed several hundred versions of these leaflets.⁴⁷ In 1943 they also smuggled them – sometimes translated into haphazard Czech with the aid of the *International Surrealist Bulletin* – into a local OT camp to boost morale.⁴⁸

Schwob and Malherbe grew increasingly bold. They put black crosses with the inscription 'For you the war is over' on German soldiers' graves in St Brelade's, and placed a placard – 'Hitler is greater than Jesus. Jesus died for men, but men are dying for Hitler' – above the church altar.⁴⁹ They also fed OT workers in St Brelade's and, in 1944, befriended an escaped Soviet OT worker, Peter Botatenko, offering him occasional shelter in their home.⁵⁰ The relationship with Botetanko was one of the few

Figure 7.1 Sketch made by Suzanne Malherbe in prison, showing the view through the cell keyhole. Copyright and courtesy Wendy Tipping

indications that they had any links with other Jersey resisters: he was brought to them by a young friend, the postman's son Mike Le Cornu, when his parents could no longer shelter the Russian.[51] Otherwise, however, they operated alone.

Despite their efforts to avoid discovery – Schwob did not register as Jewish and both women reverted to their birth names – their eventual capture was always likely once the Germans focused their attention on the leaflets and placards in St Brelade's. On 25 July 1944, after they had been distributing leaflets in St Helier, their bus was stopped on the journey home and their bags were searched.[52] According to Edward Le Quesne, a fellow-passenger, all the travellers were 'cross-questioned', but only those without identity cards were singled out for a police visit.[53] It is not clear, therefore, whether Schwob and Malherbe had been targeted or caught in a random raid. Whatever the truth of it, that night the *Feldpolizei* searched their home and found a suitcase full of leaflets, a typewriter, a radio and a First World War revolver. They were defiant – 'Too late: Germany has lost the war'[54] – but Schwob and Malherbe expected to be tortured and had prepared accordingly. At St Helier's Gloucester Street prison, they took poison that they had hidden in medicine bottles. Although they survived this and later suicide attempts, Schwob never fully recovered.[55]

Tried by a military tribunal in November 1944, the two were sentenced to death for inciting the troops through propaganda – deemed to be a 'spiritual weapon' more dangerous than a gun – and to six years' penal servitude for illegal possession of a radio, arms and a camera.[56] They took pride in their resistance, asking what their judges would have wanted their own womenfolk to do and refusing to appeal for clemency. As a result they faced the prospect of a firing-squad, although – especially with the war near its end – the military authorities had no wish to execute them.[57] The threat of execution was lifted on 20 February 1945, following appeals by the French consul and by Alexander Coutanche, who argued that it would cause considerable distress in the island.[58] Schwob and Malherbe were released on 8 May, the day before the Liberation, among the last of the political prisoners to be set free.[59] Though anti-Nazi they were never anti-German, and had befriended several German soldiers who were imprisoned with them for desertion and other offences. Two of these men were executed in the days before the surrender, but Schwob and Malherbe subsequently made representations to British officers on behalf of another, an anti-Nazi named Kurt. At the same time, they acknowledged the decent treatment they had received at the hands of their guards.[60]

In prison their spirits had been sustained by their fellow political prisoners, mostly young locals who were serving sentences for spreading the BBC news, escape attempts or sabotage. These prisoners told Schwob and Malherbe the latest BBC news and, according to Malherbe, 'did everything to keep our morale up' with songs, jokes and gifts.[61] Schwob, too, praised 'their impulsive confidence in me, their marvellous gaiety'.[62] The Frenchwomen respected the courage and patriotism of their companions. At a time when many Channel Islanders regarded sabotage and escape bids as futile gestures that might lead to reprisals, Schwob and Malherbe saw them as genuine acts of resistance by young islanders with no other means of offering it. As outsiders, moreover, they were well placed to offer a critical assessment of the extent and limitations of local resistance.

After the Liberation, in letters and essays for friends based on her prison notes, Schwob attributed the lack of militant resistance in the islands to the 'semi-feudal' nature of the constitution and to a hierarchical social structure in which the different classes lived largely separate lives. These social divisions had persisted even among the political prisoners. Although many belonged to what she called 'that indeterminate class which takes the place of the proletariat in Jersey', they also included privileged young men from the local fee-paying schools.[63] Each of these groups, she thought, had 'a class or clan sentiment' which made them unwilling to mix or even to consider creating a united resistance organization after the war.[64] Where resistance had emerged in the islands, she attributed it to a characteristic and 'ferocious' individualism. As an example she cited her elderly neighbour, Ethel Armstrong, whose ingrained prejudices did not prevent her from befriending Schwob and Malherbe (on the grounds that her own anti-Semitism was 'not like the Germans', and in any case she had decided that Schwob was not really Jewish), or from feeding OT workers near her home. After the two women were arrested, Mrs Armstrong had also visited the *Feldkommandantur* to protest and to tell the *Feldpolizei* officer what she thought of 'his nincompoop of a Führer'.[65]

Figure 7.2 Lucy Schwob (Claude Cahun) – self portrait (with Nazi badge between her teeth), 1945. Copyright and courtesy Jersey Heritage collections

Although Schwob's insights help to explain some of the limits of Channel Island resistance, they were distorted by the circumstances in which she and Malherbe lived. Isolated from all but a few of their neighbours by their background and sexuality – and to an extent by their own choice – they underestimated the strength of the personal connections between residents which helped to compensate for the absence of an organized resistance movement. The clearest example of this is the experience of Peter Botatenko, the OT fugitive they had helped. Before he came to them, Botatenko had stayed in ten other private homes, received food and clothing from many more islanders, and been given an identity card and medical treatment. [66] For the sake of security he did not tell them about his experiences, and Schwob and Malherbe were unaware of the chain of helpers that had kept him safe. Schwob's assessment of Channel Island resistance is valuable, but less than the whole story.

Symbolic resistance and defiance of the radio ban

Their anti-fascist history made Schwob and Malherbe unique in the islands during the Occupation: theirs was the only case of long term, politically motivated resistance activity by women there.⁶⁷ Most other women – like most men – contented themselves with symbolic resistance: they attended the funerals of Allied servicemen or the protests against the deportations; they displayed the national colours of red, white and blue on their clothes, window dressings, or flower arrangements; in a few cases they took part in the V-sign campaign of 1941. For both sexes, however, the most common form of illegal defiance was the refusal to accept the radio ban after June 1942: families hid sets together, listened to the news together, and occasionally were arrested together.⁶⁸ However, the police and court records are of limited use in revealing the widespread defiance of the ban by either men or women. In Guernsey only one woman was ever arrested for a radio offence and in Jersey only 34, compared with 207 men in the two islands combined.⁶⁹ Everything we know about radio offences suggests that the discrepancy is artificial, since the only aspect of activity not to involve women was apparently the manufacture of crystal sets. The preponderance of men in the arrest and prison records was probably the result of German decisions to focus on them, and of attempts by men to protect their womenfolk.

This was certainly true in the case of Henrietta Gillingham, who was involved in the creation of the Guernsey Underground News Service (GUNS). She and her husband Joe Gillingham hid a radio under the window sill of their home and, with Hennrietta's brother Ernest Legg, noted the main points of the BBC bulletins and made carbon copies for friends. Henrietta was also part of the distribution network and, after the birth of her daughter, carried leaflets in the baby's pram. When GUNS was betrayed, her husband and brother lied to protect her: Legg took responsibility for writing down the news and was deported with the other members of GUNS. Although he survived the war, Joe Gillingham and the linotype operator Charles Machon both died in captivity. They had saved Henrietta's life, but her role in GUNS was largely forgotten.⁷⁰ A courageous and resourceful woman, she later protected her nephew during a German search by smuggling a gun out of his house in her apron.⁷¹ Other women, such as Madeline Simms, the wife of a printer at the *Star* who gave copies to States officials at work, also played a part in the informal distribution of news-sheets.⁷²

Most news, however, was spread by word-of-mouth among friends and neighbours – at home, at the shops, at work and in church. The involvement of Vivienne Mylne was typical of many of the women involved, in everything except the harsh sentence she received. A 20-year-old teacher and the daughter of the Methodist minister Clement Mylne, Vivienne was arrested with her parents in February 1943 and charged with possession of an illegal radio and a camera and, in her case, with distributing the news. Although Clement Mylne complained later that the charges had been trumped up, it is clear that the family had listened to the news and that Vivienne had been passing it on: Izett Croad wrote that she was 'one of my main sources of supply of news, though I don't think she knew it'.⁷³ At the trial, the accusation that Vivienne had been distributing news-sheets was dropped, but she was still sentenced to three years' imprisonment, reduced to ten months to be served in France.⁷⁴ She was punished for refusing to incriminate her friends, though she probably did not help her cause when, asked if she had discussed Germany's defeat at Stalingrad with them, she admitted that she had, but if that was a crime then the Germans might as well round up another 20,000 people too.⁷⁵

'Military' resistance and escape

In some forms of resistance, however, women played little part. Effective intelligence-gathering was the work of army veterans in the ARP and of young men and teenage boys. Women and girls, without the knowledge of military hardware – or, in many cases, any interest in it – appear hardly to have been involved at all: for example, only one woman was involved in the 17 trials in Jersey for taking illegal photographs or for possession of a camera.[76] Similarly, minor sabotage and military larceny were almost always carried out by young men. Some women did turn road signs, scrawl graffiti on the homes of collaborators, or act as lookouts during robberies by teenage boys as well, but they were only a tiny minority of those involved.[77] Of the 55 trials in Jersey for military larceny, only 6 were of women, most of whom had been caught hiding weapons in their homes in the last months of the war.[78]

Attempts to escape from the islands, too, were usually made by young men. The exception was in Guernsey between 1 July and 6 September 1940, when 18 women and girls were among the 62 people who left to re-join family members who had evacuated in June.[79] In Jersey, on the other hand, only 16 of the 152 people known to have attempted escape were women. The proportion was even smaller after September 1944, when the Allied advance in France opened up the coastline to young men hoping to join the armed forces. Only seven out of 106 would-be escapers from Jersey in these months were women, all in their early twenties. They included the 22-year-old Barbara Hutchings, who was part of a successful escape from Rozel to Carteret in October 1944 with three friends,[80] and Rose Perrin and Rosanna Touzel, whose party of four reached Bricqueville that same month. Another young woman, Madeleine Bisson, drowned with her husband and two friends when their boat drifted onto rocks at Saline Bay in November. The waters were so heavily mined that the Germans were unable, or unwilling, to attempt a rescue.[81]

The most daring escape bid by a woman involved Belza Turner, a 21-year-old shop-worker. Alongside family and friends, she had engaged in small-scale sabotage early in the Occupation and had already served a prison sentence in September 1943 for 'disseminating information hostile to Germany' by passing on the news.[82] On 16 September 1944, in one of the earliest escape attempts after D-Day, Turner left St Helier in a small dinghy with a Dutch friend, Siebe Kosta, carrying details of the German fortifications provided by a local doctor.[83] After more than three days at sea, the couple were washed ashore at La Corbière and captured. Turner was sentenced to six months in prison for the escape and attempting to 'stir trouble' among the workers, presumably from the OT.[84] She served her six-month sentence alongside Lucy Schwob and Suzanne Malherbe, who praised her for her courage and 'outspoken patriotism'.[85]

Women were actually more involved in escapes than the statistics suggest, but mostly in supporting the attempts rather than trying to leave themselves. As early as August 1943, a 40-year-old Guernseywoman, Mabel Legg, was arrested for 'aiding the enemy' after the flight of a fishing boat to England.[86] After D-Day the involvement of women is easier to detect, especially in the case of failed escapes that resulted in arrest. In December 1944, for example, the teenager Una Sheail was sentenced to three months' imprisonment for helping to plan an escape,[87] and that same month Evelyn

Janvrin and Muriel Costard were among those implicated – by information from a 'confidential' source – for planning the departure of another party with intelligence for the Allies.[88] Initially sentenced to five months' imprisonment, Janvrin was regarded as a ringleader and threatened with 'indefinite' detention for refusing to betray other suspects.[89] These and other cases suggest that in the last months of the Occupation, planning escape from the island was often a family affair.[90]

The most striking example of women's involvement in escapes, however, concerns the 'Fauvic embarkation point', the site in south-east Jersey from which over 50 people left for France after D-Day. The role played by Wilfred 'Bill' Bertram and his cousin Thomas, who helped escape parties from their farms by the beach, has been widely recognized. However, the women of the extended family also played their part by giving escapers food and drink and helping to launch the boats. In May 1945 Emily Bertram recalled that they had been glad to help, and that 'after each party had gone we always took care to obliterate any trace of boat keels or footprints and got rid of any empty tins which had been left by the parties as they had a meal before they left'.[91] Although their contribution was remembered in Alan Wood and Mary Seaton Wood's popular history of the Occupation in 1955, it has since been neglected.[92] Even so, the numbers of women involved in escape, petty sabotage and military larceny were very small – perhaps no more than 50 in the two islands combined. Most illegal defiance of the Germans by women had a domestic setting.[93]

Aid to OT workers: The forgotten role of women

In terms of its impact on human lives, the most significant illegal activity by women during the Occupation was to help OT workers. In its most basic form, this simply meant giving food or clothes to these men, either by the roadside or when they came to the door to beg. Diaries, memoirs and oral histories of the Occupation contain many references to such acts of kindness, especially by women. Douglas Ord's experience of finding his wife feeding a Spanish Republican OT worker in Guernsey, or Peter Gray's story of his mother giving potatoes, 'which was all that we had', to a Russian at her door in Jersey, or Clarissa Poignard's description of her mother taking a young Russian to a nearby house after a beating, where a woman treated his injuries and gave him a drink, were typical.[94] In this spontaneous form, it was the only illegal defiance of the Germans to involve more women than men. Writers seeking to explain the prominence of women in humanitarian rescue of Jews in occupied Europe have pointed to their capacity for empathy, fostered by their upbringing and socialization.[95] This may or may not have been the case with OT workers in the Channel Islands as well. But a more practical explanation, also adapted from these analyses, is situational: when they knocked at the door to ask for food, OT workers usually encountered a woman, because women were more likely to be at home. They were, quite simply, more 'available' to help.[96]

The choice of whether and how much to give was not straightforward. Giving food to OT workers was punishable by prison sentences. Moreover, fear of the Germans was compounded by fear of the workers themselves, whose desperation led them to commit a spate of robberies in both islands in 1942/43.[97] Perhaps even more important, however, was the food shortage, which meant that even small gestures of kindness came at a price. Many Channel Island families, especially those from poorer backgrounds, increasingly went hungry. Bread, meat, sugar, butter, milk, fats, potatoes and tea were all rationed, in amounts that were cut significantly over the course of the Occupation: the bread ration from 4.5lb per adult per week in 1941 to 1lb in 1945, the meat ration from 12 oz to 1 oz, and the potato ration from 7lb to 5lb. After the Liberation, Jersey's Medical Officer of Health calculated that the average daily calorie intake for a working class adult had fallen to 1,700 a day,[98] and in Guernsey the situation was worse. People coped by making the most of non-rationed vegetables, by eking out their supplies and by an exhausting search for substitute products – pea pod and bramble leaf teas, dandelion coffee, seaweed jelly, sugar beet syrup and so on and interminably on.[99] Channel Islanders never starved, but significant weight loss was common and, especially towards the end, hunger more or less constant.[100] The burden of using rations wisely and foraging for food, as Madeleine Bunting has emphasized, fell mainly on the women.[101] Sharing food with OT workers had implications for whole families.

Nevertheless, the evidence suggests that though they remained a minority, hundreds of islanders – many of them women – helped OT workers. On one occasion, in Jersey, the giving of aid was orchestrated. Vasily Marempolski, a Ukrainian who was brought to the island as a boy of 15, recalled his working-party in St Ouen being met by a group of women who came forward to hand them bags of fruits and vegetables. The organizers were Louisa Gould and her sister Ivy Forster.[102] Within three months of the Soviets' arrival in Jersey, both women had also begun hiding fugitives in their homes. Mrs Gould, who was 48 when the Occupation began and ran a grocery store at Millais, was a widow who had lost one of her two sons, an anti-aircraft officer in the Royal Naval Volunteer Reserve, killed in action in 1941.[103] She was introduced to Fyodor ('Bill') Burriy by a local tenant farmer, René Le Mottée, who had hidden Burriy on his farm after his escape from Brinkworth Camp in September 1942. Le Mottée and his wife, who had five children, later gave refuge to two other fugitives at the farm, but were forced to move Burriy late in 1942 when the Germans searched the district following thefts of railway sleepers from the OT track nearby. At the same time, Ivy Forster and her husband gave shelter to another Russian, George Koslov, in the attic of their home in St Helier. According to Mrs Gould's insurance agent Robert Le Sueur, the family was solidly patriotic, but it was the wish to help 'another mother's son' that persuaded Louisa Gould to intervene.

Koslov and Burriy stayed with their rescuers for 18 months. Their testimony and that of their surviving helpers reveal the ordinary human kindness involved: a handkerchief given to Burry by Mrs Gould's friend Berthe Pitolet, a French-born housekeeper, which was presented in evidence against her;[104] the birthday card Burriy drew for Gould's maid, Alice Gavey;[105] the Christmas party held for them by another friend, the schoolteacher Dora Hacquoil; evenings listening to the news on a radio that Louisa Gould kept hidden under the floorboards in her home.[106] Unlike her sister, Mrs Gould seems not to have understood the risks she ran. She told customers the BBC news despite the danger of informers, and she took insufficient precautions to hide Burriy's presence in St Ouen.[107] In May 1944 she was betrayed by neighbours. However,

Figure 7.3 Louisa Gould, whose decision to shelter Fyodor Burriy was to cost her life. Copyright and courtesy Jersey Heritage collections

the letter had been wrongly addressed and was opened by the vice-principal of Victoria College, Pat Tatam, who had time to warn the household before the Germans came. Burriy escaped and survived in hiding until the end of the war, assisted, among others, by René Le Mottée.[108] Mrs Gould had not managed to destroy all traces of his presence, and the Germans also found a camera and the hidden radio. It was enough evidence to arrest Louisa Gould, Ivy Forster and their brother Harold Le Druillenec as well as Pitolet, Gavey and Hacquoil.

At the subsequent trial, Mrs Gould was sentenced to two years' imprisonment for failing to surrender a radio, prohibited reception of radio broadcasts and 'aiding and abetting breach of the working peace and unauthorized removal' (sheltering an OT fugitive). Harold Le Druillenec – the only man on trial – was singled out for harsh treatment: though there was no evidence linking him to Burriy, he was sentenced to six months' imprisonment for radio offences alone. The other women received prison terms of up to six months for radio offences and 'abetting'.[109] The most fortunate was Dora Hacquoil, who was sentenced to only two months because Louisa Gould testified – falsely – that she had never listened to the news. As a result, Hacquoil avoided deportation with Mrs Gould, Le Druillenec and Berthe Pitolet on 30 June 1944. 'How grateful I am to Lou', she wrote to her mother in May 1945, 'but for her statement I should have suffered the same fate … Where Lou is no one knows, she has not yet reached England.'[110] A year later, news of Louisa Gould's fate reached Jersey, brought by two Frenchwomen she had befriended in prison: she had perished in a makeshift gas chamber at Ravensbrück in February 1945.[111] Only good fortune prevented greater loss of life. Of those deported with Louisa, Harold Le Druillenec was close to death in Belsen when British forces liberated the camp in April 1945, while Berthe Pitolet avoided Mrs Gould's fate by escaping from Rennes prison, where the two women were being held, during the Allied bombardment of the city. Back in Jersey, Ivy Forster was not deported because local doctors invented medical evidence to 'prove' that she was too ill to serve a prison term.[112]

Gould's was the great tragedy of humanitarian rescue in the islands and her name, along with those of Albert Bedane and Dorothea Weber, who hid Jewish acquaintances in their homes, has rightly been honoured in recent years.[113] Otherwise, however, the role of women in sheltering victims of persecution has been neglected. In part this was the result of a general under-estimation of the extent of humanitarian aid to OT workers by men as well as women. In 1966, when the Soviet government sought to honour Jersey people who had taken part, only 20 came forward. Some rescuers were no longer alive, but others either shunned the publicity or were reluctant to be associated with awards given by the Soviet Union.[114] Despite their own protests, the recipients came to be regarded as the sum total of the island's helpers, when in reality they had been a relatively small proportion. Of the 20, moreover, only four were women: Louisa Gould, Ivy Forster and the Russian-born sisters Augusta Metcalfe and Claudia Dimitrieva, who had befriended a dozen of their fellow-countrymen and hidden one in their home in St Helier for six months.[115] In all but the most famous cases, the award was made to a single head of household – which meant, in almost every case, to a man.[116] Even in 1945, the same process had been at work when the OT workers came forward to praise their rescuers. With the exception of Ivy Forster, they thanked families by naming male heads of household; only women who lived alone, or with other women, were mentioned.[117] The real circumstances of long-term rescue were already being obscured.

What this meant is illustrated by the case of Bill and Gwenda Sarre, who sheltered OT workers at the family farm in St Lawrence. It was Gwenda Sarre, at home with two small children, who opened the door to a young Russian OT worker called Wasily, burned his lice-ridden clothes and washed and fed him; it was Bill Sarre who went to the local OT camp to see the ill-treatment of OT workers for himself, and it was the two together who decided shelter Wasily and two other Russian fugitives who came to their door. In February 1945 they also hid a political prisoner, Frank Killer, after his escape from Gloucester Street.[118] Theirs was a remarkable story of rescue, carried out even though German soldiers were billeted across the field from their home. As the head of household, though, it was Bill Sarre alone whose name was mentioned by the OT fugitive Peter Botatenko in 1945 and who was awarded a gold watch by the Soviet government more than 20 years later. The Sarres' story is typical: though it was never the intention of those involved, the extent of women's part in humanitarian aid was gradually 'hidden from history'.[119]

'A question of conscience': Marie Ozanne

One of the women who fed and befriended OT workers in Guernsey was Major Marie Ozanne of the Salvation Army. Her case, however, was unique in the Channel Islands because her opposition to the Germans was not clandestine but open, made in direct challenge to their rule rather than in secret opposition to it. The third of four children born to the Salvationist tomato-grower Daniel Ozanne and his French wife, Ozanne was 34 years old in June 1940.[120] Intelligent and idealistic, she had been encouraged by her teachers to apply to university but had chosen instead to join the Salvation Army. Ozanne had risen to the rank of Major during her service in France, where she was spiritual director of the Army's *Palais de la Femme* for disadvantaged women in Paris, and in Belgium. According to Commissioner Alfred Benwell, Chief Secretary in France during her service there, she had already gained a 'widespread reputation for saintliness'.[121] In March 1940 Ozanne returned to Guernsey on leave, apparently after becoming mentally and physically exhausted, and was caught by the German invasion.[122] However, her health recovered enough for her to take an active role in the life of the community. Ozanne was appointed temporary officer-in-charge of the St Sampson's Corps of the Army, speaking at services, organizing prayer meetings and women's groups, and engaging in charitable work.[123] She also continued to learn French and German and supplemented the family income by tutoring the children of friends in Vale.[124]

Marie Ozanne first came to the attention of the authorities early in 1941, when the Salvation Army was banned in the Channel Islands. Its citadels were closed and the wearing of uniform was forbidden.[125] The Army's senior officers accepted the situation reluctantly, opting to maintain links with members through home visits, private prayer meetings and cooperation with local Methodist churches. Ozanne, however, refused to comply with the ban. On 19 January she went to St Sampson's Citadel to make a silent protest, and continued to organize small open-air meetings on the grounds that 'the Gospel must not be suppressed'.[126] Warned that these activities would end in the arrest of her supporters, she made her subsequent protests alone, continuing to wear uniform and reading the Bible each week in St Peter Port.[127] In April 1941 Ozanne went directly to the *Feldkommandantur* to demand the reopening of Salvation Army halls, and was sent for the first of several interviews with the chief of the Guernsey police, William Sculpher. She was, he reported, 'very obstinate' on the uniform issue and maintained that her response was 'a question of conscience'. He was, however, hopeful that she would listen to reason, since she had removed her Salvation Army bonnet before she left his office.[128] Rather than ending her protests, Ozanne intensified them, visiting the *Feldkommandantur* and writing to demand 'freedom to worship God in the way in which he calls us, and also for freedom to follow the dictates of conscience'.[129] On 23 July 1941, she notified the Germans that she intended to re-open the St Sampson's citadel.[130] Only then did the *Feldpolizei* arrest her and hand her over to the local police; her uniform was confiscated and her parents were advised to seek medical advice about her mental state.[131] At this stage, both the Germans and the local police tried to deal with her by asserting that she was 'not responsible for her actions' and attempting to intimidate her into silence.[132]

If the ban on the Salvation Army had been the only subject of her protests, Ozanne's actions would have been regarded as a brave but limited attempt to defend the right of the Salvation Army to continue its work. On 26 June 1941, however, nine days after the Third Order against the Jews was registered in Guernsey's Royal Courts, she had written to the *Feldkommandantur* to condemn the persecution of the Jews. They were, she told the Commandant, God's chosen people and Jesus himself, 'the only one by whom we can inherit eternal life and enter heaven', was a Jew. She ended by quoting

Figure 7.4 Marie Ozanne in Salvation Army uniform. Copyright and courtesy the Ozanne family

Romans 2.11 in a direct challenge to Nazi anti-Semitism: 'And with God there is no respect of persons, but in every nation he that feareth Him and worketh righteousness is accepted of Him'.¹³³ It was the only known protest against the treatment of the Jews by a religious figure in the islands and was apparently an act of principle, since very few Jews lived in Guernsey and there is no indication that Ozanne knew any of them.

On the other hand, she was soon aware of the plight of OT workers and was moved to offer them practical help. In November 1941 she and her family began to feed and support Dutch, Belgian and French OT workers who had arrived in Guernsey to build the fortifications.¹³⁴ They were strangers there, she wrote to a friend, 'and we are glad to befriend them'.¹³⁵ Ozanne was increasingly distressed by the ill-treatment of these workers, especially at the OT prison, 'Paradis', close to the family home in the Vale parish. She heard first-hand accounts of beating there from family friends whose children she tutored, and whose home was next to the prison grounds.¹³⁶ Two days after witnessing an incident herself, Ozanne wrote to the *Feldkommandantur* to protest, and to warn that German rule could not survive because it was 'a reign of terror, both physically and morally'.¹³⁷ Christ, 'who came to teach us that the nations are brothers', would call the Germans to account for their treatment of other peoples.¹³⁸

As she had anticipated, these letters led to her arrest on 3 September 1942.¹³⁹ The Germans initially sent Ozanne for medical examination, apparently in the hope that she would be judged unfit to stand trial, but she was found to be fully responsible for her actions and sent to prison to await court martial.¹⁴⁰ She continued to write to the *Kommandant*, refusing to retract 'a single word' of her revolt against 'the rule of hatred and oppression that you exercise wherever you go'.¹⁴¹ Ozanne also condemned the arbitrary decision to deport British-born islanders that month, and offered to accompany them to Germany.[142] After six weeks in prison, she was released without warning on 16 October 1942, and eight days later the Court suspended its proceedings against her.[143] The decision was probably triggered by signs that her health was deteriorating. After attempting to resume her charitable work, she was taken to hospital on 2 November and diagnosed with a stomach abscess. In the absence of antibiotics, the condition could not be treated effectively. Ozanne endured her agonizing illness with courage and grace, but grew steadily weaker. On 23 February 1943, she wrote some of her favourite lines from the Bible in her diary: 'Let not your heart be troubled'.[144] Two days later, at just 37 years of age, she was dead.

It was widely believed at the time – and has been accepted by historians since – that Ozanne's death was the result of ill-treatment in prison.[145] There is no evidence for this, and Ozanne herself never claimed it. She was allowed food parcels, books and extra clothing by her German guards, was transferred to a better room and allowed time in the fresh air, and was given a typewriter which she used to send more letters to the *Kommandant*.[146] Rumours of beatings or poisoning apparently spread only because she collapsed with stomach problems soon after her release, and because sympathetic German soldiers brought her food before she was overwhelmed by septicaemia.[147] Ozanne was already frail, and her stay in prison simply coincided with the development of the abscess that killed her. In fact, both the Germans and the local police were hesitant in their dealings with her – largely, it seems, because she was a woman. Compared with the harsh punishment meted out to the clerics Clifford Cohu and Clement Mylne in Jersey, she was treated leniently – repeatedly warned about her conduct, moved on by the local police when preaching and ignored by German soldiers in the town. Sculpher even made an unsuccessful request for an exemption from the uniform ban in her case.[148] Ozanne was arrested only when she challenged the occupiers directly, by threatening to re-open Salvation Army halls and by condemning the brutality of German rule.

The protection given by her gender, however, came at the cost of a systematic belittling of her protests. After her first arrest in July 1941, the Germans had sent her home on the grounds that she was not responsible for her actions, and Sculpher's explanation for them had included a nervous breakdown and symptoms that recurred 'monthly'. He had also advised her parents (she was 36!) to consult doctors about her mental state; though she was not 'mentally deranged' at present, he did not rule out the possibility in future.[149] Suggestions of hysteria and mental illness re-emerged after her arrest in September 1942, when the Germans sent her for examination by their own doctors, only to have them confirm that she was responsible for her actions. The eventual suspension of proceedings against her was justified by an interpretation of the medical evidence that effectively undermined it: the Court ruled that, though sane, Ozanne was driven by a desire for martyrdom and by religious fantasies – the proof was, apparently, that when interrogated by the *Feldpolizei*, she had begun to pray.[150] In future, the Germans would deal with the 'querulousness' of her petitioning by ignoring it.[151] All these explanations were a travesty of the truth. Ozanne was neither hysterical nor a religious maniac, and she was certainly not driven by the vagaries of her menstrual cycle. Her letters of protest, far from being 'querulous', were brief and direct.

Marie Ozanne was compelled by duty to bear witness to her faith. It was a demanding path for a shy and sensitive woman who found public speaking excruciatingly difficult, and who feared arrest for her own sake as well as that of her family.[152] She made her protests without bitterness or hatred of the occupiers, whose gestures of kindness she recognized and for whose welfare she prayed.[153] Her opposition to the occupiers was dictated by her religious convictions: she hoped not only to defend freedom of conscience and protect victims of persecution, but also to change the hearts and minds of the Germans and achieve their 'salvation'.[154] Although her stance was idealistic and even naïve, her judgment of the worst aspects of Nazi Occupation policy was unerring. It is for this clear moral vision, and the courage with which she followed her conscience, that she deserves to be recognized. In 1947 Ozanne was posthumously awarded the Order of the Founder by the Salvation Army in recognition of her 'self-sacrificing concern for men's freedom to serve God and for the saving of others'.[155]

Interpretations of women's conduct

Ozanne's story, like others in this chapter, offers a corrective to histories of the occupied Channel Islands which, if they consider women at all, view their experiences primarily through the prism of collaboration and concentrate on the behaviour of the 'Jerrybags'.[156] Accusations of widespread 'horizontal collaboration' emerged in the British press in the weeks after Liberation and have since proved depressingly tenacious. They have been revived since 1990 by Madeleine Bunting's *The Model Occupation* and Tim Binding's novel *Island Madness*.[157] No historian of the Occupation can ignore the issue. Of course, some women did have relationships with German soldiers, just as they did everywhere in German-occupied Europe, and for similar reasons. In the Channel Islands outright prostitution accounted for a relatively small number of those involved, since the Germans had their own brothels staffed by women brought in from France. Much more common were pragmatic relationships, influenced by women's hope of obtaining extra food for themselves and their families and remaining – in the words of Lucy Schwob – 'among the well-nourished'.[158]

Not all the motives were mercenary, however. The most important factor was probably the most obvious: the shortage of local men aged between 18 and 30, the age group to which most 'horizontal collaborators' belonged (at least in France and, the anecdotal evidence suggests, in the islands too).[159] Recruitment to the armed forces and the evacuations of June had resulted in a surplus of more than 1,000 women aged between 18 and 30 in the two islands combined.[160] Not all of the relationships these women made were with Germans: more than 20 Spanish Republican OT workers stayed in Jersey after the war to marry local women,[161] for example, while in Guernsey Douglas Ord noted the frequency of liaisons between local girls and foreign workers.[162] Nevertheless, relationships with German soldiers were more frequent, and some were genuine love matches.[163]

Even during the war there were wild allegations about the number of women involved. The diarist Bert Williams commented in 1943 that hundreds of German babies had already been born in Guernsey 'and many more to come',[164] and even the island's Bailiff, Victor Carey, alleged at the Liberation that 'a large number of young women and a few of the older ones' had been involved.[165] Parties of escapers from Jersey after D-Day were sometimes bitter about the 'Jerrybags', of whom there were said to be 'a great many' in relation to the size of the island population.[166] In the months before the Liberation, anonymous threats were made to cut off offenders' hair, and groups of 'Underground Barbers' or 'Patriotic Leagues' wrote to women warning that their turn was coming.[167] Although Channel Island women did not suffer the same fate as 'horizontal collaborators' elsewhere in Europe, where they were singled out in large numbers for beating and head-shaving by vengeful crowds, in Jersey at least it was a close-run thing.[168] On 10 May 1945 British troops from the Liberation force joined local men to protect a woman who had been chased and beaten near the harbour in St Helier.[169]

Nevertheless, calmer observers condemned the exaggerated claims about numbers. That same month Noel McKinstry wrote to his wife to ridicule British press reports and insist that the Jerrybags were 'not really a large percentage' of the population,[170] while the ARP warden Major L'Amy thought they had been 'a brazen crew, albeit a small one'.[171] Even the angry young escapers modified their views: one, for example, abandoned his claim that over half of Jersey girls had liaisons with German soldiers and later assessed the real figure at around three per cent.[172] The number of illegitimate babies born to such relationships was nowhere near the 800 or 900 claimed by the press, which Jersey's Attorney General castigated for giving a 'ridiculously false impression'.[173] The Germans themselves thought that their soldiers had fathered between 60 and 80 illegitimate children in the islands, and by August 1945 the British security services had revised their own estimates – it is not clear how – to 180 (out of 320 illegitimate births in the wartime islands).[174] Paul Sanders has emphasized that most flirtations never went beyond the platonic stage anyway, and that most of those that did were stories of 'human flesh and blood' rather than calculated collaboration.[175] Still, it is worth emphasizing that the great majority of Channel Islands women never had relationships with German soldiers. Probably even more than their menfolk, they were mindful of need to avoid what McKinstry called 'the eternal chatter about whether this or that person was too friendly with the German, or had acted unpatriotically'.[176] Some avoided all but essential contacts with German soldiers to avoid any chance that innocent gestures – a conversation, or even a handshake – might be misinterpreted.[177]

Above all, however, the issue of 'horizontal collaboration' demonstrates that simplistic resistance/collaboration paradigms do not adequately explain conditions in the islands as a whole, or even the conduct of the 'Jerrybags' themselves. There were, undoubtedly, a few cases where these women became confirmed collaborators who passed on information about their fellow islanders to the Germans.[178] On the other hand, there is no evidence that they were a major source of denunciations for wireless offences or the sheltering of OT fugitives, and not even their detractors claimed that they were. For most, having a relationship with a German marked the beginning and the end of their collaboration. For a minority, the reality was more complex still. Shortly after the Liberation, McKinstry wrote to his wife to distinguish between informers and economic collaborators, who deserved punishment, and the 'Jerrybags'. Most of the latter, he thought, were drawn from the less privileged sections of society who had 'never received much', and should be treated leniently.[179] Some had actually behaved 'very oddly', a point he illustrated by referring to a local laundry that had been taken over by the German army. Its workforce contained a number of notorious 'Jerrybags', but when they were ordered to work for the Germans they refused, even after a fine, and were sent to prison. It was strange, he told his wife, 'but nevertheless it is true'.[180]

Despite her own focus on 'horizontal collaboration', Madeleine Bunting had hinted briefly at this complexity of behaviours when recounting the story of Dolly Joanknecht, a Guernseywomen who fell in love with – and later married – a German. As a teenager she had played 'patriotic pranks' on soldiers, spitting in their soup and stealing their clothes on the beach. Later she had served a prison term in France for black-marketeering, which she saw as an act of resistance because the goods had been meant for the German troops. It was on the boat home after serving her sentence that she met the soldier who later became her husband.[181] Another woman who faced abuse as a 'Jerrybag' after the Liberation was Colleen Querée, one of a handful of women to attempt escape from the islands after D-Day. In July 1944, the 23-year-old Querée used a borrowed French passport to deceive the harbour police and board the SS *Minotaur*, which was due to depart for France carrying several hundred foreign workers. Like dozens of young men in the island, she hoped to make contact with Allied troops there and eventually reach England.[182] The ship was attacked by British torpedo boats in the Channel, and Querée was lucky to escape with her life. Denounced to the Germans by a French worker after she reached shore, she spent three weeks in Rennes prison before being sent back to Jersey, where she was kept under surveillance until the end of the war. Querée told her story to the *Evening Post* in July 1945, when 'horizontal collaboration' was still a live issue; it took courage for her to point out that she was now being vilified as a 'Jerrybag'.[183] For these women at least, the terms 'resister' and 'collaborator' do not adequately describe a more complicated reality.

Most women in the islands – like most men – were neither active resisters nor any kind of collaborators. In most cases they adapted reluctantly to the Occupation, longed for liberation and coped with everyday hardships as best they could. Women's displays of patriotic sentiment were largely passive, taking the form of displays of national colours and occasional attendance at public gatherings, such as the funerals of British servicemen and the demonstrations of September 1942. Defiance of the radio ban was the only form of illegal activity to involve a large proportion of the female (as well as the male) population. Women played little part in most organized and long-term forms of resistance such as intelligence-gathering through the ARP, the news-sheets of GUNS and the activities of the JCP, a fact which reflected their position in prewar island society and economic life. Where they were involved, it was usually in background roles which were largely forgotten when the war was over. Here there are clear similarities with the experience of resisters elsewhere. The only long-term political opposition to Nazism by women in the islands was provided by Lucy Schwob and Suzanne Malherbe, whose views had been shaped in the very different political culture of interwar France. On the other hand, hundreds of women – and in Jersey perhaps thousands – gave food to OT workers, and much smaller numbers took in fugitives from the camps, sometimes alone but more often as part of a family unit. Humanitarian aid was the only form of resistance to the Germans in which women played a part equal to that of men, and in terms of occasional and spontaneous help exceeded it. It is no accident that the most remarkable cases of resistance by island-born women – by Louisa Gould, Ivy Forster, Dorothea Weber, Marie Ozanne – all involved assistance to victims of persecution. In these small islands, the courage displayed by these and other women deserves greater recognition than it has received.

Notes

1 François Bédarida, 'World War II and Social Change in France', in Arthur Marwick (ed.), *Total War and Social Change*, Basingstoke and London, Macmillan, 1988, pp. 79–94, here p. 90.
2 For those rare women involved in partisan operations and for the prevalence of gendered roles, see Paula Schwartz, 'Partisans and Gender Politics in Vichy France', *French Historical Studies*, Vol. 16 (1), 1989, 126–51; Paula Schwartz, 'Redefining Resistance: Women's Activism in Wartime France', in Margaret Randolph Higonnet, Jane Jenson, Sonya Michel and Margaret Collins Weitz (eds), *Behind the Lines: Gender and the Two World Wars*, New Haven and London, Yale University Press, 1987, pp. 141–53; Hanna Diamond, *Women and the Second World War in France 1939–1948: Choices and Constraints*, Harlow, Pearson Education, 1999, pp. 100–1.
3 For example, of the 1,059 people awarded the Compagnon de la Libération, the highest French honour for resisters, only 6 were women: Schwartz, 'Redefining Resistance', p. 144.
4 See also Vera Laska, *Women in the Resistance and in the Holocaust: The Voice of Eyewitnesses*, New York, Praeger, 1983; Margaret L. Rossiter, *Women in the Resistance*, New York, Praeger, 1985; Margaret Collins Weitz, *Sisters in the Resistance: How Women Fought to Free France, 1940–1945*, New York, John Wiley and Sons, 1995.
5 For 'horizontal collaboration' see Claire Duchen, 'Crime and Punishment in Liberated France: The Case of the Femmes Tondues', in C. Duchen and I. Bandauer-Schoffmann (eds), *When the War was Over: War and Peace in Europe 1940–1956*, London, Leicester University Press, 2000, pp. 233–50; Claire Duchen, 'Opening Pandora's Box: The Case of les femmes tondues', in M. Cornick and C. Crossley (eds), *Problems in French History*, Basingstoke, Palgrave, 2000, pp. 213–32; Fabrice Vergili, *Shorn Women: Gender and Punishment in Liberation France*, Oxford, Berg, 2002. On contempt for the 'Jerrybags' see, for example, IA.AQ 0380/03-01. Herbert Williams, Diary of Events, etc. during the Occupation of Guernsey, from 30 June 1940 to 6 July 1945, 12 June 1943; IWM.Documents.13409. Private Papers of Captain J. R. Dening: Dening 9: The Channel Islands under German Occupation, 1945; IA.AQ 0025/08. Arthur Mahy, Memorandum of meeting held at Royal Court House, Guernsey, 14 May 1945; Basil de Carteret, Mary Deslandes and Mary Robin, *Island Trilogy. Memories of Jersey and the Occupation by Mary Robin, Basil de Carteret and Mary Deslandes*, Jersey, Redberry Press, undated, 'Diary of Mary Deslandes', 12 July 1944, 25 September 1944.
6 Madeleine Bunting, *The Model Occupation: The Channel Islands under German Rule, 1940–1945*, London, Pimlico, 2004, pp. 54–74; Peter King, *The Channel Islands War 1940–1945*, London, Robert Hale, 1991, pp. 76–81.
7 Alan Wood and Mary Wood, *Islands in Danger: The Story of the German Occupation of the Channel Islands, 1940–1945*, Sevenoaks, First Four Square, 1965, pp. 145–9.

8   de Carteret et al., 'Diary of Mary Deslandes', 15–22 September 1940. See also JAS.L/C/77/A/1. Izett Croad, *Occupation Diary*, 24 September 1940.
9   JAS.D/Z/H6/1. 5 Maria-Luisa Klara Crawford-Morrison: Occupation – Sentences and Prosecutions by the Field Command and Troop Courts.
10 JAS.D/Z/H6/7. Sentences and Prosecutions of Field Command and Troop Courts, December 1943–December 1944; JAS.D/AG/B7/1. 'Names of Political Prisoners August 1940' prison log book: 428 Nanetta Butterworth.
11 See for example de Carteret et al., 'Diary of Mary Deslandes', 6 December 1941, describing the arrest of a young Jerseywoman for 'gross impertinence' at Wrentham Hall. Also JAS.M/28/2. Ralph Mollet, Occupation Diary, Volume 2, 1 February 1941–6 June 1943, 4 September 1941, reporting the sentencing of a Guernseywoman 'for smacking a German soldier in the face'. For other examples see JAS.D/Z/H6/5. Sentences and Prosecutions by the Field Command and Troop Courts: Janine Josette Falle, born April 1919, sentenced to four months on 20 January 1943 for 'insulting the German forces'; JAS.D/Z/H6/6. Sentences and Prosecutions by the Field Command and Troop Courts: Yvonne Le Chevalier, kitchenmaid, born April 1926, sentenced for 'insulting the German forces of Occupation' and discharged on 12 January 1944.
12 See also de Carteret et al., 'Diary of Mary Deslandes', Christmas 1943; Leslie Sinel, *The German Occupation of Jersey: The Wartime Diary of Leslie Sinel*, Jersey, Villette Publishing, 1995, 20 December 1943; Nan Le Ruez, *Jersey Occupation Diary: Her Story of the German Occupation, 1940–45*, Jersey, Seaflower Books, 1994, 7 September 1944. The Germans doubled her three-month sentence when she appealed against it.
13 Miss Lowry's case is described in Michael Halliwell, *Operating under Occupation: The Life and Work of Arthur Clare Halliwell FRCS, Consultant Surgeon at the Jersey General Hospital during the German Occupation 1940*–1945, Jersey, Channel Islands Occupation Society, 2005, p. 23. JAS.D/Z/H6/5. Sentences and Prosecutions by the Field Command and Troop Courts: 314. Agatha Bott, born 3 July 1895, sentenced on 27 September 1943.
14 Paul Sanders, *The Ultimate Sacrifice. The Jersey Islanders who Died in German Prisons and Concentration Camps 1940–1945*, Jersey, Jersey Heritage Trust, 2004, p. 97.
15 Ibid., p. 118; Charles Cruickshank, *The German Occupation of the Channel Islands: The Official History of the Occupation Years*, Guernsey, Guernsey Press Co. Ltd., by arrangement with the Trustees of the Imperial War Museum and Oxford University Press, 1975, pp. 339–40.
16 de Carteret et al., 'Diary of Mary Deslandes', 6 December 1941.
17 The figures are for arrests in Guernsey and trials in Jersey.
18 GPHQ. Guernsey Police records, German convictions of civilians, 2 vols, 1940–1945; JAS.D/AG/B7/1. 'Names of Political Prisoners August 1940' prison log book, covering 18 August 1940 to 27 July 1944; JAS.D/AG/B1/4. Prisoners Register, 22 August 1931–8 September 1948. The statistics are compiled from both registers. Guernsey Police records, German convictions of civilians, 2 vols, 1940–1945.
19 See the arrest of the farmer Edward George Osborne for harbouring a fugitive from the OT, although he shared the farm with his wife: D/Z/H6/7. Sentences and Prosecutions by the Field Command and Troop Courts. Trial 87: Edward George Osborne. See also BA.MA/I/10/Ost Spezial/V4713. Wehrmachtgerichtsbarkeit. Akte Osborne. Case No. C17637.
20 JAS.D/AG/B7/1. 'Names of Political Prisoners August 1940' prison log book: 19 and 21; JAS.D/Z/H6/2. Sentences and Prosecutions by the Field Command and Troop Courts: Marjorie Gill, born November 1924, sentenced to seven months for

'inciting to treachery', 18 April 1941; see also Bunting, *The Model Occupation*, p. 199. Marjorie Gill protested later that they had been wrongly accused after shining a torch at night.
21 Above information from *Census 1931. Jersey, Guernsey and Adjacent Islands*, London, HMSO, 1933, pp. xv–xviii.
22 IA.CC 01-05. Census of Guernsey Population 1940–45. Census July 1940.
23 Richard Hocart, *An Island Assembly. The Development of the States of Guernsey, 1700–1949*, Guernsey, Guernsey Museum and Art Gallery, 1988, p. 95.
24 Marguerite Syvret and Joan Stevens, *Balleine's History of Jersey*, Chichester, Phillimore, 1981, p. 253.
25 'Guernsey States Reform', *Evening Post*, 4 October 1945, p. 1.
26 *Evening Post*, 14 July 1945, p. 13.
27 IWM.Sound Archive.Interview 10102. Rosalie Le Brocq, 1987; Le Brocq, 'Clandestine Activities', pp. 46–7.
28 Diamond, *Women and the Second World War in France 1939–1948*, pp. 112–14; Schwartz, 'Redefining Resistance', esp. pp. 147–8.
29 Diamond, *Women and the Second World War in France 1939–1948*, pp. 112–14.
30 François Leperlier, *Claude Cahun: L'Écart et la Métamorphose*, Paris, Jean Michel Place, 1992, pp. 19–40.
31 Abigail Solomon-Godeau, 'The Equivocal "I": Claude Cahun as Lesbian Subject', in Shelley Rice (ed.), *Inverted Odysseys: Claude Cahun, Maya Deren, Cindy Sherman*, New York, MIT Press, 1999, pp. 111–25, here p. 111.
32 See, for example, Claire Follain, 'Constructing a Profile of Resistance – Lucy Schwob and Suzanne Malherbe as Paradigmatic Résistantes', BA Contemporary History with French dissertation, University of Sussex, 1997, p. 5.
33 Schwob's response was Les Paris sont Ouvert, (published as Claude Cahun), Paris, José Corti, 1934).
34 On Breton see Mark Pollizotti, *Revolution of the Mind: The Life of André Breton*, London, Bloomsbury, 1995. An example of the group's campaigning is JHT.1995/00045/95. Paper against fascism and Gil Robles signed by Breton, Cahun and other Surrealists, 20 July 1936.
35 JAS.D/S/A/24/1434. Registration card of Lucy Schwob.
36 Claire Follain, 'Lucy Schwob and Suzanne Malherbe – Résistantes', in L. Downie (ed.), *Don't Kiss Me: The Art of Claude Cahun and Marcel Moore*, London, Tate Publishing, in association with the Jersey Heritage Trust, 2006, pp. 83–95, here p. 84.
37 Her collected writings were published as Claude Cahun, *Écrits*, ed. François Leperlier, Paris, Jean-Michel Place, 2002. Here see 'Le Muet dans la Mêlée', ibid., p. 648.
38 In an interview after the war in *Evening Post*, 30 June 1945, p. 4. See also Follain, 'Lucy Schwob and Suzanne Malherbe', p. 83.
39 'Confidences au miroir', ibid., p. 584.
40 'Lettre á Gaston Ferdière', 1946', in Cahun, *Écrits*, pp. 679–81.
41 Interview in *Evening Post*, 30 June 1945.
42 'Lettre á Gaston Ferdière', in Cahun, *Écrits*, p. 693. See also Sanders, *The British Channel Islands under German Occupation*, p. 120.
43 'Lettre á Gaston Ferdière, in Cahun, *Écrits*, p. 692.
44 'Lettre á Paul Levy, 1950', ibid., pp. 737–8; also 'Confidences au miroir', ibid., p. 607.
45 For examples of these leaflets see JHT.1995/00045/53/1–7, 15, 25, 32, 36–7, 83. See also Sanders, *The British Channel Islands under German Occupation*, p. 120.
46 JHT.1995/00045/53/20, 35. Leaflets.

47 'Lettre á Gaston Ferdière', in Cahun, *Écrits*, p. 693. Similarly, at the funeral of Leutnant Zepernick, adjutant to the Inselkommandant von Schmettow. Also Follain, 'Lucy Schwob and Suzanne Malherbe', p. 86.
48 'Lettre á Gaston Ferdière', in Cahun, *Écrits*, pp. 698–9.
49 'Lettre á Paul Levy, 1950', ibid., pp. 720–3; 'Le Muet dans la Melée', ibid., p. 647; 'Lettre á Gaston Ferdière', ibid., p. 684. See also their message at the funeral of Leutnant Zeprnick, adjutant to Inselkommandant von Schmettow, Sanders, *The British Channel Islands under German Occupation*, pp. 119–20.
50 Interview with Joe Mière, who was imprisoned with them, 23 August 2000; Peter Botatenko in *Jersey Evening Post*, 26 March 1992, p. 6.
51 JWT.Research Files Box 6. Mike Le Cornu, 'Distant Memories 1939–1945', pp. 7–8.
52 Edward Le Quesne, *The Occupation of Jersey Day by Day. The Personal Diary of Deputy Edward Le Quesne*, with a foreword and explanatory notes by Michael Ginns, Jersey, La Haule, 1999, 26–27 July 1944.
53 Ibid., 26–27 July 1944.
54 Recalled in 'Le Muet dans la Melée', in Cahun, *Écrits*, p. 631.
55 Described in 'Lettre á Paul Levy, 1950', ibid., pp. 714–16, 724–6. Both attempted suicide again in prison: see the testimony of fellow prisoner Belza Turner, letter from Belza Greene (née Turner) to Joe Mière, 3 November 2003, Joe Mière Archive, Mière family.
56 Follain, 'Constructing a Profile of Resistance', p. 15; Follain, 'Lucy Schwob and Suzanne Malherbe', pp. 87–8.
57 See the diary of Hans Max von Aufsess, The von Aufsess Occupation Diary, ed. and trans. K. J. Nowlan, Chichester, Phillimore, 1985, 28 October 1944.
58 JAS.B/A/W50/183. Bailiff Alexander Coutanche to Platzkommandant, 22 November 1944. Also Sanders, *The British Channel Islands under German Occupation*, p. 122.
59 Follain, 'Constructing a Profile of Resistance', p. 22.
60 JHT.1995/00045/3. Lucy Schwob (Claude Cahun), handwritten account, undated; 'Lettre á Paul Levy', in Cahun, *Écrits*, p. 739.
61 *Evening Post*, 30 June 1945. See also 'La Muet dans la Melée', in Cahun, *Écrits*, pp. 632–3.
62 JHT.1995/00045/1/58. Lucy Schwob (Claude Cahun), diary written after having been imprisoned and sentenced to death for inciting the German soldiers to rebellion, undated; see also *Evening Post*, 30 June 1945; 'Lettre á Paul Levy, 1950', in Cahun, *Écrits*, pp. 721–2.
63 'Lettre á Gaston Ferdière', in Cahun, *Écrits*, p. 633.
64 'Le Muet dans la Melée', ibid., pp. 632–3.
65 'Lettre á Gaston Ferdière', ibid., p. 696.
66 For Botatenko's story see *Evening Post*, 19 May 1945, p. 4.
67 Claire Follain, 'A Study of the Specificities of Resistance during the German Occupation of Jersey, 1940–1945', MA Contemporary History dissertation, University of Sussex, 1999, pp. 45–6.
68 A sample of these cases: JAS.D/Z/H6/6. Sentences and Prosecutions by the Field Command and Troop Courts: May Evelyn Griffiths-Tizard, vegetable dealer, sentenced with others to two months for listening to the radio; Edith May Kirwan, household help, sentenced to three months in prison in October 1943 with family members for listening to the radio in company and spreading hostile information; JAS.D/Z/H6/7. Sentences and Prosecutions by the Field Command and Troop

Courts: Gwendoline Bull, born June 1912, sentenced to two months in July 1944 for 'continued prohibited reception of wireless stations in company with other persons'.
69 Material from JAS.D/Z/H6/1-8. Sentences and Prosecutions by the Field Command and Troop Courts; GPHQ. Guernsey Police records, German convictions of civilians, 2 vols, 1940-1945.
70 Information from Jean and Allen Harris, 16 June 2013. Mrs Harris is the daughter of Joe and Henrietta Gillingham. Henrietta does not appear in the descriptions of GUNS by Wood and Wood; King; Bunting; Barry Turner, *Outpost of Occupation: How the Channel Islands Survived Nazi Rule 1940-1945*, London, Aurum Press Ltd., 2010; Peter Tabb, *A Peculiar Occupation: New Perspectives on Hitler's Channel Islands*, Hersham, Ian Allan, 2005; or Knowles-Smith, *The Changing Face of the Channel Islands Occupation: Record, Memory and Myth*, Basingstoke, Palgrave Macmillan, 2007.
71 Information from Jean and Allen Harris, 18 June 2013.
72 William M. Bell, *Guernsey Occupied but Never Conquered*, Exeter, The Studio Publishing Services, 2002, p. 275; he also records that Matron Finch at the Emergency Hospital distributed GASP.
73 JAS.L/C/77/A/1-8. Izett Croad, Occupation Diary, 4 February 1943.
74 JAS.L/C/20/D/5/1. Reverend Clement Mylne, 'A Travesty of Justice', galley for The Methodist Recorder; JAS.D/Z/H6/5. Sentences and Prosecutions by the Field Command and Troop Courts: Vivienne Mylne, born October 1922, sentenced in March 1943.
75 JAS.L/C/20/D/5/1. Reverend Clement Mylne, 'A Travesty of Justice', galley for The Methodist Recorder; JAS.L/C/20/D/2. Vivienne Mylne, Cell 428, a fictionalized account of her trial and imprisonment.
76 JAS.D/Z/H6. Trials in German Field and Troop Courts.
77 See, for example, IWM.Sound Archive.Interview 10105. Stella Alexandra Perkins, 1987; interview with Stella Perkins, 28 June 2000; also Bunting, *The Model Occupation*, p. 259; letter from Belza Greene (née Turner) to Joe Mière, 3 November 2003, Joe Mière Archive, Mière family; also Joe Mière, *Never to Be Forgotten*, Jersey, Channel Island Publishing, 2004, p. 65, on his sister Marguerite acting as a look out, and p. 54, demonstrating against the deportations.
78 JAS.D/Z/H6. Trials in German Field and Troop Courts.
79 King, *The Channel Islands War 1940-1945*, pp. 100-1.
80 *Jersey Evening Post*, 28 May 1977, p. 3.
81 Roy Thomas, *Lest We Forget: Escapes and Attempted Escapes from Jersey during the German Occupation 1940-1945*, Jersey, La Haule, 1992, pp. 89-93.
82 JAS.D/Z/H6/6. Sentences and Prosecutions by the Field Command and Troop Courts, June 1943-May 1944; Thomas, *Lest We Forget*, pp. 22-3; also letter from Belza Greene (née Turner) to Joe Mière, 3 November 2003, Joe Mière Archive, Mière family.
83 Thomas, *Lest We Forget*, p. 24.
84 JAS.D/Z/H6/8. Sentences and Prosecutions by the Field Command and Troop Courts: Belza Anthea Turner, sentenced to six months in October 1944 for 'attempted flight'; also JAS.BA/W50/170. Platzkommandant Heider to Constable of Grouville, 22 September 1944.
85 JHT.1995/00045/7. Lucy Schwob (Claude Cahun), handwritten prison notes, undated.

86 IA.FK 01–11. FK 515, Nebenstelle Guernsey to FK 515, Jersey, 17 August 1943: Notification of the arrest of Mabel Lilian Legg, born April 1903, for 'aiding the enemy'.
87 JAS.D/Z/H6/9. Sentences and Prosecutions by the Field Command and Troop Courts: Una Sheail. Two other young women were freed without serving a sentence.
88 JAS.D/Z/H6/9. Sentences and Prosecutions by the Field Command and Troop Courts: Evelyn Janvrin, born April 1919, sentenced to five months in December 1944 for attempting to escape and disseminating anti-German news.
89 JHT.1995/00045/7. Lucy Schwob (Claude Cahun), handwritten prison note, undated. Janvrin was released in May 1945.
90 See also JAS.D/Z/H6/9. Sentences and Prosecutions by the Field Command and Troop Courts; also Elise Floyd, head of the physiotherapy department at the General Hospital in Jersey, who helped her brother and his friends escape in October 1944: Halliwell, *Operating under Occupation*, pp. 116–17.
91 *Evening Post* 26 May 1945, p. 6; also Thomas, *Lest We Forget*, pp. 123–4.
92 See for example King, *The Channel Islands War 1940–1945*, p. 100 and Turner, *Outpost of Occupation*, pp. 273–4, who do not mention the Bertram women. There is a brief reference in Knowles-Smith, *The Changing Face of the Channel Islands Occupation*, p. 203. In 1955 Wood and Wood had mentioned them in *Islands in Danger*, p. 236.
93 See Follain, 'A Study of the Specificities of Resistance during the German Occupation of Jersey', p. 42.
94 PL.LF940.53 ORD. Reverend R. Douglas Ord, Occupation Diary, 30 August 1942; Peter Gray, 'Island of Beauty, Island of Secrets', unpublished manuscript, p. 13, used by kind permission of Mr Peter Gray; TNA.WO.311/11. Testimony of Clarissa Poignard, 9 July 1945; IA.AQ 0092/12. Gertie Corbin, Diary of the Occupation Years, January 1942; IA.AQ 0368/01–11. Violet Carey, Occupation Diaries 1940–1945, incidents 16 December 1941, 27 November 1941; TNA.WO.311/11. Testimony of Francis Killer, 29 June 1945; interview with Gwenda Sarre, 24 August 2000.
95 Varese and Yaish have shown that women were more likely than men to offer help to Jews: Federico Varese and Meir Yaish, 'The Importance of Being Asked: The Rescue of Jews in Nazi Europe', *Rationality and Society*, Vol. 12, 2000, 307–34, esp. 320.
96 Ibid., 320.
97 See chapter on humanitarian aid in this volume.
98 Cruickshank, *The German Occupation of the Channel Islands*, pp. 135–6; Bunting, *The Model Occupation*, pp. 121–2.
99 Sanders, *The British Channel Islands under German Occupation*, pp. 8–9; Bunting, *The Model Occupation*, pp. 122–4.
100 For references to weight loss, see Noel McKinstry on himself and his colleague Harold Blampied: SJ.GO Box 10/36. Letter from R. Noel McKinstry to Mrs Janet McKinstry, Oxford, 13 May 1945, p. 5; on the Bailiff's weight loss in Guernsey, IA.FK 06–02. A. N. Symonds, Health Services Officer, to FK 515 Nebenstelle Guernsey, 23 June 1942; on the weight loss of the Dean of Jersey: Sanders, *The British Channel Islands under German Occupation*, p. 31. See also JAS.B/A/W49/14/20. 'Survey of the Effects of the Occupation in the Health of the People of Jersey', undated.
101 Bunting, *The Model Occupation*, p. 123.
102 Cited in Knowles-Smith, *The Changing Face of the Channel Islands Occupation*, p. 216.

103 Sanders, *The Ultimate Sacrifice*, p. 65.
104 Letter from Dora Hacquoil to her mother, 20 May 1945, by kind permission of Pauline Hacquoil.
105 JAS.L/D/25/F3/10. Material relating to the Gould case.
106 Letter from Dora Hacquoil to her mother, 20 May 1945, by kind permission of Pauline Hacquoil. Also Sanders, *The Ultimate Sacrifice*, pp. 69–70.
107 Here see Sanders, *The Ultimate Sacrifice*, p. 68.
108 Ibid., pp. 68–9.
109 JAS.D/Z/H6/7/104. Attorney General to C. J. Cuming, Constable of St Helier, 25 October 1944.
110 Letter from Dora Hacquoil to her mother, 20 May 1945, by kind permission of Pauline Hacquoil.
111 Sanders, *The Ultimate Sacrifice*, pp. 72, 78–9.
112 JAS.D/Z/H6/7/104. Gould trial; also Sanders, *The Ultimate Sacrifice*, pp. 70–1. The correspondence diagnoses 'chronic kidney disease'.
113 For Bedane and Weber see the chapter on humanitarian resistance.
114 See Louise Willmot, 'The Goodness of Strangers: Help to Escaped Russian Slave Labourers in Occupied Jersey 1942–1945', *Contemporary European History*, Vol. 11 (2), 2002, 211–27, here p. 225, on efforts by Norman Le Brocq to persuade people to come forward.
115 Interview with Stella Perkins, the daughter of Augusta Dimitrieva-Metcalfe, 28 June 2000.
116 Interview with Robert Le Sueur, 27 June 2000. In two cases only, this obscured the contribution of men, Arthur Forster and Mike Frowd, who shared a flat with an older conscientious objector, René Franoux.
117 See for example *Evening Post*, 19 May 1945, p. 4, Peter Botatenko's story; 'The Story of George', 19 June 1945, p. 4.
118 Interview with Gwenda Sarre, 24 August 2000; TNA.WO.311/11. Testimony of William Francis Sarre, 2 July 1945.
119 Taken from Sheila Rowbotham's *Hidden from History: 300 Years of Women's Oppression and the Fight Against It*, London, Pluto Press, 1973.
120 *Guernsey Evening Press*, 8 December 1947, p. 1; IA.ID 248. Deceased files: Ozanne, Marie.
121 SAIHC. Personality Files: Marie Ozanne. Letter from Alfred Benwell to General Albert Orsborn, 22 October 1946.
122 Michael Thierry, 'An Army Oppressed', unpaginated manuscript, chapter 10, with thanks to Mr Thierry; Marie Ozanne, *Diary*, 28 March 1942, held by and used by kind permission of the Ozanne family.
123 Bell, *Guernsey Occupied but Never Conquered*, p. 229; see, for example, notices on the *Guernsey Evening Press*, 21 July 1940, p. 1; 17 August 1940, p. 3; 21 September 1940, p. 3; 26 October 1940, p. 3; 16 November 1940, p. 3; Marie Ozanne, Diary, passim, Ozanne family.
124 Letter from William I. Ozanne to Richard Heaume, 5 November 2002, copy used by kind permission of William Ozanne. The family kept a copy.
125 PL.LF940.53 ORD. Reverend R. Douglas Ord, Occupation Diary, 21 April 1941. See also David Chapman, *Chapel and Swastika: Methodism in the Channel Islands during the German Occupation*, Jersey, ELSP, 2009, p. 43.
126 GOMG. William John 'Bill' Bougourd, 'The Marie Ozanne Story', undated. Mr Bougourd, who was afraid for Ozanne and the others, tried to break up the

meeting. The incident was first described by Richard Heaume, 'Marie Ozanne', *Channel Islands Occupation Review*, Vol. 23, 1995, 79–81.

127   This concern for others can be seen in her letter to the Feldkommandant, Guernsey, of 22 June 1941, emphasizing that her parents had no knowledge of her actions: SAIHC.Personality Files: Marie Ozanne.

128   IA.BF 014-17. Inspector W. R. Sculpher to G. P. J. Ridgway, Law Officer, 10 April 1941.

129   SAIHC.Personality Files: Marie Ozanne. Letter from Major Marie Ozanne to the Feldkommandant, Guernsey, 22 June 1941; see also letter from Major Marie Ozanne to the Feldkommandant, Guernsey, 14 July 1941.

130   SAIHC.Personality Files: Marie Ozanne. Letter from Major Marie Ozanne to the Feldkommandant, Guernsey, 23 July 1941.

131   IA.PC 194-04. Police Occurrence Book, June 1941 – August 1941: 194 Inspector W. Sculpher, 26 July 1941, Illegal uniform wearing.

132   IWM.Documents.13409. Private Papers of Captain J. R. Dening. Dening 9: The Channel Islands under German Occupation, 1945. Resistance: Marie Ozanne. Note on Ozanne for the files of the Nebenstellem Guernsey, FK 515 (translation).

133   SAIHC.Personality Files: Marie Ozanne. Letter from Major Marie Ozanne to the Feldkommandant, Guernsey, 26 June 1941.

134   Marie Ozanne, Diary, 1942 passim, Ozanne family.

135   Letter from Marie Ozanne to Yves De La Mare, 1 March 1942: letter kindly provided by Pearl De La Mare.

136   Extracts from the private diary of Lilian Ogier Collas, 17 October 1942, 26 December 1942, kindly made available by Victor Collas, October 2000. Interview with her son Richard Collas, one of Ozanne's tutees, 8 July 2010. See also Heaume, 'Marie Ozanne', 81.

137   SAIHC.Personality Files: Marie Ozanne. Letter from Major Marie Ozanne to the Feldkommandant, Guernsey, undated, but clearly the letter she described sending in her Diary on 30 August 1942.

138   IWM.Documents.13409. Private Papers of Captain J. R. Dening. Dening 9: The Channel Islands under German Occupation, 1945. Resistance: Marie Ozanne.

139   IA.PC 195-5. Police Occurrence Book, 3 September 1942 to 10 October 1942, incidents 3, 32: Sgt G. Dyson, 3 September 1943. Sgt Dyson was instructed to accompany the German police; Marie Ozanne, Diary, 30 August 1942, 31 August 1942, 1 September 1942, Ozanne family.

140   IWM.Documents.13409. Private Papers of Captain J. R. Dening. Dening 9: The Channel Islands Under German Occupation, 1945. Resistance: Marie Ozanne; Marie Ozanne, Diary, 5 September 1942, Ozanne family.

141   IWM.Documents.13409. Private Papers of Captain J. R. Dening. Dening 9: The Channel Islands Under German Occupation, 1945. Resistance: Marie Ozanne. Ozanne's letter to Feldkommandant, Guernsey, 6 September 1942; Sanders, *The British Channel Islands under German Occupation*, pp. 118–19.

142   IWM.Documents.13409. Private Papers of Captain J. R. Dening. Dening 9: The Channel Islands Under German Occupation, 1945. Resistance: Marie Ozanne. Ozanne's letters to Feldkommandant, Guernsey, 16 September and 21 September 1942.

143   IWM.Documents.13409. Private Papers of Captain J. R. Dening. Dening 9: The Channel Islands Under German Occupation, 1945. Resistance: Marie Ozanne. Report of Court of FK 515 on the suspension of proceedings against Marie Ozanne,

signed by Knackfuss and Dr Seger, President of the Court, 24 October 1942. For her health, see her Diary, 12–16 October 1942.
144 Ibid., 23 February 1943, Ozanne family.
145 See, for example, the comment in IWM.Documents.13409. Private Papers of Captain J. R. Dening. Dening 9: The Channel Islands under German Occupation, 1945. Resistance: Marie Ozanne. See also comments by this author, 'The Channel Islands', in B. Moore (ed.), *Resistance in Western Europe*, Oxford and New York, Berg, 2000, pp. 65–92, here p. 75; also Sanders, *The British Channel Islands under German Occupation*, p. 119; Bunting, *The Model Occupation*, p. 324, claims she was tortured.
146 Marie Ozanne, Diary, 11, 24 and 28 September 1942, Ozanne family.
147 See for example *Evening Post*, 8 December 1947, p. 2; letter from William I. Ozanne to Richard Heaume, 5 November 2002, recalling his grandmother's remarks about Ozanne being 'full of poison': copy used by kind permission of William Ozanne.
148 IA BF 14–17. Inspector W. R. Sculpher to G. J. P. Ridgway, Law Officer, 10 April 1941.
149 IA.PC 194–04. Police Occurrence Book: 194 Inspector W. Sculpher, 26 July 1941, Illegal uniform wearing.
150 IWM.Documents.13409. Private Papers of Captain J. R. Dening. Dening 9: The Channel Islands Under German Occupation, 1945. Resistance: Marie Ozanne. Nebenstelle Guernsey to FK 515, Report by Medical Officer, September 1942.
151 IWM.Documents.13409. Private Papers of Captain J. R. Dening. Dening 9: The Channel Islands Under German Occupation, 1945. Resistance: Marie Ozanne. Report of Court of FK 515 on the suspension of proceedings against Marie Ozanne, signed by Knackfuss and Dr Seger, President of the Court, 24 October 1942.
152 Marie Ozanne, Diary, 12 January 1942, 28 February 1942, 10 April 1942, 27 September 1942, 6 October 1942, 7 October 1942, 13 January 1943, Ozanne family.
153 See Marie Ozanne, Diary, 14 September 1942, 24 September 1942, 25 September 1942, 28 September 1942, 9 October 1942, Ozanne family. Also IWM.Documents.13409. Private Papers of Captain J. R. Dening. Dening 9: The Channel Islands Under German Occupation, 1945. Resistance: Marie Ozanne. Letter from Ozanne to Feldkommandant, Guernsey, 6 September 1942.
154 Marie Ozanne, Diary, 25 September 1942, Ozanne family.
155 SAIHC.Personality Files: Marie Ozanne. Citation; also *The War Cry*, 6 December 1947, p. 3; *Guernsey Evening Press*, 8 December 1947, pp. 1–2.
156 See for example King, *The Channel Islands War 1940–1945*, pp. 76–82.
157 See Bunting, *The Model Occupation*, pp. 55–73; Tim Binding, *Island Madness*, London, Picador, 1998.
158 'Lettre á Gaston Ferdière', in Cahun, *Écrits*, p. 669. See also Sanders, *The British Channel Islands under German Occupation*, pp. 170–1.
159 According to Diamond, *Women and the Second World War in France 1939–1948*, p. 85, in France over 90 per cent of them were under 30.
160 IA CC 01–05. Census of Guernsey Population 1940–45. Census July 1940; JAS.B/A/W91/10. Jersey Census, 10 August 1940: there were 4,118 men and 5,220 young women in that age-group.
161 *Jersey Evening Post*, 24 May 2001, p. 9.
162 PL.LF940.53 ORD. Reverend R. Douglas Ord, Occupation Diary, 29 July 1943.
163 Bunting, *The Model Occupation*, pp. 70–1.
164 IA.AQ 0380/03–01. Herbert Williams, Diary of Events, etc during the Occupation of Guernsey, from 30 June 1940 to 6 July 1945, 12 June 1943.

165 IA.AQ 0025/08. Arthur Mahy, Memorandum of meeting held at Royal Court House, Guernsey, 14 May 1945. Present were the Bailiff, John Leale, Home Secretary Herbert Morrison and members of the Controlling Committee.
166 IWM.Documents.13409. Private Papers of Captain J. R. Dening. Dening 9: The Channel Islands under German Occupation, 1945.
167 de Carteret et al., 'Diary of Mary Deslandes', 12 July 1944, 25 September 1944, 29 October 1944; IA.AQ 1212/098. Kenneth G. Lewis, Diary of Events 1940–1945, 5 September 1943; Le Quesne, 28 July 1944.
168 According to Fabrice Vergili, 20,000 French women suffered this fate: for a detailed survey see Vergili.
169 Incident described in *Evening Post*, 11 May 1945, p. 1. Bunting, *The Model Occupation*, pp. 257–60, apparently overestimates the number.
170 SJ.GO Box 10/36. Letter from R. Noel McKinstry to Mrs Janet McKinstry, 18 May 1945.
171 SJ.*OCC 942 L'AM. J. H. L'Amy, The German Occupation of Jersey, undated but written in 1945/46, p. 26.
172 See Jenny Chamier Grove, 'Engineering an Escape', *Channel Islands Occupation Review*, Vol. 33, 2005, 23–34.
173 For contemporary estimates see TNA.HO.45/22399. Duret Aubin to J. B. Howard, 7 July 1945; TNA.HO.45/22399. Home Office Report: Illegitimate Children Born in the Channel Islands during the Occupation.
174 Sanders, *The British Channel Islands under German Occupation*, pp. 168–9.
175 Ibid., p. 172.
176 SJ.GO Box 10/36. Letter from R. Noel McKinstry to Mrs Janet McKinstry, 18 May 1945, p. 4.
177 Interview with Gwenda Sarre, 24 August 2000; interview with Robert Le Sueur, 4 August 2010.
178 For cases where it happened, see IA. Frank Falla Archive. Statement of Mr and Mrs John Alfred Ingrouille of Milette Bay, Vale, given to Frank Falla, October 1964. Also the testimony of Peter Botatenko, *Evening Post*, 19 May 1945, p. 4.
179 SJ.GO Box 10/36. Letter from R. Noel McKinstry to Mrs Janet McKinstry, 18 May 1945, p. 4.
180 SJ.GO Box 10/36. Letter from R. Noel McKinstry to Mrs Janet McKinstry, 10 June 1945, p. 2. See brief reference in Louise Willmot, 'Noel McKinstry', *Channel Islands Occupation Review*, Vol. 31, 2003, 25–30, 28.
181 Bunting, *The Model Occupation*, pp. 144–5, 195.
182 'A Jersey Girl's Story', *Evening Post*, 9 July 1945, p. 5; JAS.L/C/24/C/8. 'The Colleen Querée Story', 9 July 1945.
183 JAS.L/C/24/C/8. 'The Colleen Querée Story'. There had been a spate of letters to the editor of the *Evening Post* on the subject of Jerrybags: 19 May 1945, p. 1; 22 May 1945, p. 1; 26 May 1945, p. 3; 27 May 1945, p. 1; 29 May 1945, p. 1.

8

Sabotage, Intelligence-gathering and Escape

Louise Willmot

There was no possibility of partisan or maquis-style activity in the occupied Channel Islands. Several factors – their geography and wartime demographics, the number of German troops, the lack of weapons or help from outside, the certainty of reprisals – combined to rule it out. The inhabitants knew it, even the teenagers and young men who were often dismissed by fellow islanders as irresponsible hotheads, and there were no assassination attempts on German soldiers during the Occupation. Nevertheless, efforts to damage the German war effort and contribute to Allied victory still took place, and took three main forms. The first involved low-level sabotage and the theft of weapons and equipment by teenagers and young adults. A second, more organized, form was the gathering of information on German military installations, often carried out by adolescents but also by army veterans in the Jersey Air Raid Protection Service. Finally, and especially after D-Day, dozens of young residents risked their lives to escape from the islands by boat, often in the hope of joining the armed forces, but also to take intelligence to the Allies.

Conditions limiting military-related activities

The British government never encouraged resistance in the islands, and had demilitarized them before the Occupation even began. In June 1940, on the grounds that the islands had no strategic value and that available troops were needed to defend the mainland, it ordered the disbanding of the local militias and the evacuation of two battalions of British troops.[1] Subsequent British and Allied strategy assumed that the Channel Islands would be liberated by Allied victory on the continent rather than by invasion or fighting in the islands themselves. In these circumstances, even sabotage appeared pointless: there were no factories producing goods for the German war effort and no major transport hubs – the only railway was the light gauge track built by the occupiers in 1942/43 to transport construction materials for the fortifications. Consequently, the War Cabinet never sought to contact potential resisters, and excluded them from BBC broadcasts designed to encourage resistance in other occupied territories. Although

Special Operations Executive (SOE) dispatched its agents across Europe 'to co-ordinate all action, by way of subversion and sabotage, against the enemy overseas',[2] none was sent to the Channel Islands.

The only military activities authorized by the British government took the form of minor intelligence-gathering commando operations by Channel Islanders serving in the armed forces. Charles Cruickshank has described these in his official history of the Occupation, and only one case is mentioned here to shed light on Channel Islanders' attitudes towards military operations.[3] In September 1940, Second Lieutenants Hubert Nicolle and James Symes were landed on Guernsey to gather information about food, fuel and medical supplies there. When bad weather prevented their rendezvous with the rescue boat, the men went into hiding for over six weeks, protected by their families, friends and casual acquaintances. They slept in their own homes, in empty houses and occasionally – with the help of the groundsman – in the sports pavilion of the local school.[4] Their position became untenable when the Germans began searching for potential British agents and military personnel in the island. On the understanding that they would be treated as prisoners-of-war (PoWs) and that their helpers would not be punished, Nicolle and Symes acquired British army uniforms and presented themselves to the authorities on 21 October 1940.

Despite these reassurances, the men were court-martialled and found guilty of espionage, and their helpers were convicted of high treason and deported to Cherche-Midi prison in Paris. Guernsey's Attorney-General Ambrose Sherwill, who had known of their presence but failed to report them, was also sent to France. Islanders were shocked by the verdicts, which the Methodist minister Douglas Ord regarded as an attempt to deter the population and 'keep us silent mice in the future'.[5] It took an intervention by the new *Inselkommandant*, Major-General von Schmettow, to find a solution: although the guilty verdicts stood, Nicolle and Symes were after all treated as PoWs and their helpers released. By then the episode had claimed the life of Louis Symes, the father of James, who died in Cherche-Midi.[6] Even before this incident, Sherwill had been opposed to military action by British forces.[7] After his release, he was angry that islanders had been damaged by operations that could achieve no useful purpose and were bound to lead to reprisals. Nor was he alone in believing that the landing should never have taken place.[8] Throughout the Occupation, most islanders considered that military operations by the British army were undesirable, and by local residents impossible, because of the danger of bloodshed and reprisals. Islanders were, in the words of the escaper Peter Crill, 'sitting ducks'.[9]

The assessment was realistic. Jersey and Guernsey are small and flat – Jersey is 12 miles by 7 at its greatest breadth and Guernsey covers only 24 square miles – and surrounded by dangerous seas.[10] They offer few places to hide and, in the words of resistance historian M. R. D. Foot, 'nowhere to run away'.[11] Furthermore, the occupiers were soon to transform the islands into the most heavily occupied and fortified region in Western Europe. By May 1943 there were 13,000 German troops in Guernsey and another 10,000 in Jersey: every fifth person in Jersey, and in Guernsey every third, wore German uniform (the ratio in Norway was 1:10, and in France approximately 1:100).[12] Billeted in requisitioned hotels and private dwellings, the troops were a constant presence in every island community, and they controlled the islands to an extent that was never possible elsewhere in occupied Europe.[13] Local people could not conceivably have fought them. The only weapons not in German hands were shotguns owned by local farmers, old souvenir pistols from the First World War that were kept hidden, and equipment pilfered from German stores. The Jersey resister Norman Le Brocq was right to insist, years later, that the islands simply could not be compared with occupied France: unlike the French, Channel Islanders had no mountains to hide in and no guns to fight with.[14]

Le Brocq might also have noted that they lacked men of fighting age as well. Most men of military age had left for England in 1939 or the evacuations of June 1940: out of a total population of 67,000 people still in the islands that July, fewer than 5,000 were young men between the ages of 17 and 30.[15] For those who remained, furthermore, there was not the same incentive to go 'underground', or escape, as in France, Belgium and the Netherlands. In 1942/43 the Germans introduced forced labour service in these countries in order to provide a supply of foreign workers for hard-pressed German factories. Its introduction acted as 'the catalyst for a mass movement towards illegality', by persuading several hundred thousand men and women to go into hiding in order to evade the draft.[16] Although only a minority of these *réfractaires* joined organized resistance groups, mass disobedience became the norm rather than the exception in much of occupied Europe by late 1943.[17] In the Channel Islands, by contrast, the Germans never introduced forced labour service and young residents had no reason to 'go missing' to avoid conscription.

Of the inhabitants left in the islands after the evacuations, only a handful saw active service during the war. One was Denis Vibert, whose exploits are described later in this chapter. Another was Jack Soyer, a wood merchant in his early forties who had been sentenced to a year's imprisonment in August 1943 for withholding a radio and passing on the news.[18] Transferred to Fresnes prison in France to serve his sentence, Soyer escaped early in 1944 and made his way to Bréhat on Normandy's Granville-Coutances highway. He fought with a French Resistance unit there in June and July before being killed in action during the liberation of the town. Known by his comrades as 'L'Anglais', Soyer was buried in Bréhat on 1 August 1944.[19] His case was remarkable and exceptional. For those who remained in the islands, the issue was whether active resistance to the Germans was even possible at all.

Most of the military-related incidents that did occur were in Jersey rather than Guernsey. A major reason for the imbalance was wartime demography: most escapes and acts of sabotage were carried out by young men between the ages of 17 and 25 years, and by 1944 there were almost twice as many of them in Jersey (2,400 compared with roughly 1,250 in Guernsey).[20] Two-fifths of Guernsey residents and four-fifths of the children had been evacuated in June 1940; communities were fractured, many schools closed and friendship groups disrupted.[21] In Jersey, by contrast, where fewer than 7,000 of the 50,000-strong population had left, schools remained open and youth groups and 'gangs' remained intact.[22] Such groups played a major part in small-scale sabotage and escape attempts, especially in St Helier, where a third of young men were concentrated. The other reason for the imbalance was geographical: after August 1944, Jersey's proximity to the French coast encouraged young islanders to risk the crossing to France, and allowed for the development of an 'escape culture' that was absent in Guernsey.

Minor acts of sabotage and the theft of weapons and equipment

Most small-scale sabotage was the work of teenagers who had been too young to join the armed forces in 1939/40. As the Occupation dragged on they became increasingly frustrated, and dissatisfied with the cautious methods adopted by some older islanders to show hostility to the occupiers. These passive behaviours, adopted everywhere in German-occupied Western Europe, are described by the Swiss historian Philippe Burrin as 'erecting a wall' between Germans and local people: however decent individual members of the occupying forces might be, they must never forget that they were unwelcome and that friendly relationships with them were impossible.[23] Channel Islanders left cinemas when German newsreels were shown, refused to shake hands with soldiers they met, and ignored attempts at conversation.[24] Still more tried to go about their business 'as if the Germans were not there'.[25] According to the French artist Lucy Schwob, around a fifth of local people had cold-shouldered the Germans in this way.[26]

Rebellious adolescents, however, wanted to express their hostility more actively. Even in July 1940, audience members at Jersey's Forum cinema had greeted the German newsreels with catcalls and footage of Hitler with choruses of 'Run, rabbit, run!' and were warned by the Bailiff that the discourtesy had to stop.[27] Deliberate infringements of curfew regulations, and exaggerated saluting of everyone in uniform (including the postman), were relatively common even in the early months of the Occupation.[28] This was cheek, not resistance – but for some of those involved, the step to small-scale sabotage and military thefts was a small one. There were many such incidents, beginning relatively early in the Occupation. Youths broke into the German field post office in December 1941 and stole items of Christmas mail;[29] they defaced or turned German signposts;[30] they damaged bicycles belonging to German soldiers, smeared tar on car seats or painted 'RAF' on the sides;[31] they pushed nails into the tyres of military vehicles, and sand, stones or metal into their gear boxes and engines;[32] and they siphoned off petrol for their own unregistered vehicles, and later as fuel for escape by boat.[33] Most knew well enough that these incidents had no real military significance. As two Guernseymen acknowledged after their escape from Alderney in April 1944, they were 'local and individual pin-pricks', intended to annoy the occupiers rather than do them serious damage.[34]

More significant acts of sabotage were rare, largely because of the shortage of suitable targets or explosives with which to attack them. In these circumstances, German telephone cables were the most obvious targets. The first incidents of cable-cutting occurred near Mouilpied Tower in Guernsey in March 1941 and had spread to Jersey by May.[35] Subsequently they occurred at irregular intervals throughout the Occupation.[36] From autumn 1942, the other main sabotage target was the light railway constructed by the *Organisation Todt* (OT): its wooden sleepers were dug up, and occasional attempts were made to derail it by putting stones on the track or throwing the points.[37] Older islanders were rarely involved in these incidents, although they included the First World War veteran Ludovic Bertrand, who sabotaged telephone cable close to his home in Guernsey.[38] Younger members of the Guernsey police also claimed responsibility for various acts of cable-cutting and low-level sabotage, usually during their night-time patrols, before they were caught breaking into German and local stores and disgraced.[39] Further acts of sabotage were committed by OT workers. In May 1943, for example, Douglas Ord reported that a French contingent had managed to destroy an underground cable they were laying by dropping acid on it.[40] Otherwise, the most effective way for OT workers to damage the Germans was by adopting the traditional strategy of the powerless – by dragging their feet and working badly, but without attracting attention and punishment. Violet Carey recorded an incident in April 1942, when a French youth explained his own approach: 'We go slow, Madame, very slow.'[41] There were undoubtedly many such cases.

Nevertheless, the Germans rightly suspected that most small-scale sabotage was the work of local juveniles.[42] After several attacks on signposts in Jersey in May 1941, head teachers were instructed to warn their pupils against 'stupid and wicked acts of sabotage', and Alexander Coutanche insisted that the Germans would impose collective punishments if 'senseless acts on the part of irresponsible persons' continued.[43] In the event, punishments were relatively mild: curfews in the affected areas were tightened and groups of local men forced to stand guard over cables at night.[44] After an initial flurry of concern, the military authorities downplayed the importance of the incidents and, in Jersey, sometimes blamed the damage on stray cows or German soldiers.[45] They were apparently reassured by the response of the inhabitants. After the first cases in Guernsey, *Feldkommandant* Schumacher advised the military administration in France not to impose collective reprisals, since local people did not support sabotage and had even reported the damage to the authorities.[46] A few days later, the military administration emphasized that 'the population shows no inclination at all for sabotage acts and indeed appears resolutely opposed to them'.[47] The assessment was almost certainly correct. Although the Guernsey diarist Adèle Lainé thought that the cables were strewn about so carelessly that the Germans 'deserved to have them cut',[48] other observers condemned minor sabotage activities as selfish, futile and liable to provoke reprisals.[49]

In stark contrast to this leniency, the Germans cracked down hard on anything that even hinted at potential armed resistance. Any doubts on this score were dispelled by the death penalty imposed on the young Frenchman François Scornet in February 1941. With 15 companions, he had sailed from Brittany hoping to join the Free French, but the party landed in Guernsey believing they had reached the Isle of Wight. They were tried in Jersey, convicted of treason according to Vichy law, and Scornet was executed.[50] The incident was deeply shocking to islanders and, as the occupiers must have intended, acted as a further deterrent to resistance.[51]

Although the occupiers never imposed the death penalty on islanders for military-related activities, even uttering vague threats against the Germans could have fatal consequences. Even before Scornet's execution, the 20-year old Guernseyman John Ingrouille had been arrested at Vale Mill, where he worked as a cook for the occupiers. He was denounced by a local woman and her teenage daughter who, his parents claimed, were 'not only working for the Germans, but cohabiting with them'.[52] Originally suspected only of pilfering cutlery, Ingrouille was found guilty of treason and espionage at his trial in Jersey and was sent to Berlin, where he was accused of 'organising armed resistance' by several hundred men.[53] His denouncers were brought to Germany to give evidence against him although, as the Germans must have known, the allegation was ludicrous. It was either, as his parents believed, a 'figment of the evil imaginations' of his denouncers, or the result of a casual remark that they reported to the authorities out of spite. Despite an appeal by Victor Carey, Ingrouille was sentenced to five years' hard labour for his 'crime'.[54] Although he survived Brandenburg prison and was located in a Displaced Persons Camp in May 1945, he died on 13 June 1945 before he could be brought home.[55]

Islanders accused of stealing military equipment, especially weapons, were also harshly treated. Between 1943 and 1945, dozens of young men in Jersey were involved in such incidents, usually hoping – so they explained after the Liberation – to 'do something' if the Allies invaded.[56] Elsewhere in occupied Europe, being caught in possession of weapons that could be used against the Germans often resulted in the death penalty, but in the Channel Islands FK 515 remained eager not to pass death sentences on islanders. Here, the 'Night and Fog' (NN) decree of 7 December 1941 offered a convenient alternative, since it allowed suspect individuals to be taken to Germany for trial by special courts if there were political reasons not to execute them on the spot.[57] The NN decree was apparently used against the English-born businessman Clarence Painter and his 19-year-old son, Peter, late in 1943. Peter Painter had recently left Victoria College, where he had been a member of the Officer Training Corps (OTC). He had defied German regulations by running a scout group after the ban on associations and uniforms in October 1940, and by breaking into his local parish hall to steal radios after the ban on sets in June 1942 (Figure 8.1).[58] Painter had enrolled in the Nautical and Marine Engineering College established by George Sowden in 1941, probably in the hope of learning the skills to enable him to escape.[59] He had also made a map of the German fortifications and, with his friends, had taken photographs of German aircraft.[60]

On 11 November 1943, acting on information from an unknown source, the *Feldpolizei* searched the Painters' home. The family had kept an illegal radio and passed on the news to friends, 'as well as allowing some to listen when there was something of importance',[61] and it may have been this that provoked the search.[62] The Germans found the radio, a camera and photographs though not, according to Painter's mother, any incriminating maps. Fatally, however, they also found a souvenir Mauser pistol from the First World War which Peter Painter had hidden, and it was this discovery that opened up the possibility of deportation under the terms of the NN decree.[63] Although the young man admitted his responsibility, Clarence Painter was arrested with his son, presumably because of his service in the army and Royal Flying Corps during the First World War. On 21 December, the two men were deported without warning, first to Natzweiler and then to a forced labour camp in Silesia. In November 1944 Peter Painter died of bronchial pneumonia in Gross-Rosen, a satellite camp of Sachsenhausen. His father survived until February 1945, when the remaining camp inmates were evacuated westwards. After three days' travel in goods wagons without food or proper clothing, Clarence Painter also perished.[64]

The case of James Houillebeq was equally tragic. Houillebeq, who was 17 years old and had only recently left school, had joined a group of friends hoping to prepare

Figure 8.1 Peter Painter. Copyright and courtesy Jersey Heritage collections

for an Allied invasion and had hidden a stolen Schmeisser pistol and ammunition in his home. These were discovered in a house search in May 1944. The entire family was arrested, though all except James were released some weeks later.[65] According to Edward Le Quesne of the Superior Council, the Germans considered the case 'the most serious' they had faced during the Occupation, which does much to explain why Houillebeq was deported four months later in August 1944.[66] The lack of a trial in Jersey, or of evidence about his fate, makes it likely that he, too, was a victim of the NN decree. Deporting him saved the military authorities from the unpalatable prospect of imposing a death sentence in the islands for possession of firearms, and handed responsibility for his fate to the German prison and concentration camp system. Houillebeq was taken to Neuengamme camp near Hamburg, where he died early in 1945.[67]

Other young islanders escaped this fate only because they were caught after August 1944 and could not be deported: the low death-rate among political offenders in the Channel Islands was, at least in part, the fortunate consequence of geography and the Allied advance in France.[68] Among these offenders was Richard Weithley, who had witnessed the scuffles between local youths and German troops during the deportations of September 1942. He and his school-friends admired those involved in the 'rebellion' and wanted to emulate them.[69] Over several months in 1943 and 1944 they raided German military stores in St Helier, managing to steal a crate of grenades, a revolver and ammunition. Although they timed the raids to avoid German patrols, they were helped by lax security: the stores were easy to break into, the patrols predicable, and the thefts went unreported for months. The young men were arrested late in 1944 after weapons and ammunition were found at their homes.[70] One of them, Donald Bell, escaped from prison in February 1945 and took refuge in the home of the surgeon Arthur Halliwell until the Liberation, but Weithley broke an ankle in the attempt and remained in custody with his friend Francis Harris.[71] Theirs was one of several small groups which combined thefts of German weapons and equipment with small-scale sabotage and intelligence-gathering.[72] In the last year of the war, these groups engaged in a persistent campaign of military thefts, minor sabotage and anti-German demonstrations. When the 19-year-old hairdresser Joe Mière and his friends received 18-month sentences in March 1945 for 'continual' anti-German activities, the verdict was an accurate description of their conduct.[73] In St Helier at least, such behaviour was so common that the teenager Bernard Hassall was told by his teacher that he had virtually no class left.[74]

None of the weapons and ammunition stolen in raids on German stores was ever put to use. The closest any local group came to violence was in November 1944, when the intended targets were not Germans but local residents. In the last months of war, resentment against collaborators had intensified: in Jersey, teenagers daubed swastikas on the homes of suspects, and in both islands threatening letters – from a Guernsey Underground Barbers and a Jersey Patriotic League – were sent to alleged informers and 'Jerrybags'.[75] British Intelligence interviews with young escapers also revealed that feelings against collaborators were running high.[76] It was in this atmosphere that Peter Gray, then only 17 years old and working as an electrician, decided with his friends to 'do something about informers' by bombing a hairdressing salon in Helier owned by a man who was notoriously pro-German.[77] According to his co-conspirator Arnold Bennett, they were attempting 'to exterminate a well-known Quisling'.[78] The group managed to steal a stock of German explosives, but were denounced and arrested before the attack could be launched. Although Gray escaped with a 14-month sentence because of his youth, the older men – the 19-year-olds Arnold Bennett and Bernard Carratu – were sentenced to six years with hard labour. All had a history of anti-German activity: as well as planning murder and conspiracy to cause an explosion, their offences included military larceny, the manufacture of radios and the production of anti-German leaflets.[79]

In a European context there was nothing unusual in the desire to punish collaborators: resistance groups on the continent targeted hundreds of informers and pro-Nazis for assassination in order to punish the guilty and deter others from following their example. Where the victims were proven and high-profile collaborators, especially the leaders of fascist and anti-Semitic organizations, such attacks had a claim to be regarded as legitimate acts of resistance.[80] In the Channel Islands, however, no such collaborationist organizations existed. The only conceivable targets there were 'Jerrybags', alleged informers and individuals identified as being somehow 'over-friendly' towards the Germans. There is no evidence that islanders regarded summary justice against them as even remotely legitimate; in the last months of war, even the tarring of suspects' homes was dismissed as the work of 'hooligans' rather than patriots.[81] If the bomb plot had succeeded, it would undoubtedly have horrified most islanders. At the Liberation, the dangers of vigilantism were demonstrated when at least one woman – a well-known 'Jerrybag' – was cornered and beaten in St Helier before being rescued by local men and British troops.[82] Later, Joe Mière was contemptuous of the attackers, none of whom, he thought, 'had done anything in the war to resist the Germans'.[83] The following day the Bailiff and the *Evening Post* condemned 'mob rule', which undoubtedly helped to calm the atmosphere and prevent further attacks.[84] Subsequently, the debate about the punishment of informers, economic collaborators and 'Jerrybags' was confined to the letters pages of the local newspaper – where it was notable for its restraint – and to a petition presented to the States by a group of 'Jersey Loyalists'.[85]

Intelligence-gathering

Sabotage and military larceny, as we have seen, were almost exclusively the work of teenagers and young men. Older islanders were hardly involved at all, and some army veterans in Jersey refused outright to lead or advise the youths involved.[86] Intelligence-gathering, however, was a different matter: because it was secret, there would be no danger of reprisals against the population, and there was more chance that it would actually be useful if the Allies invaded the islands.[87] As a result, a more diverse group of islanders engaged in it. Initially they included members of the fledgling Jersey Communist Party, but its members soon abandoned their 'amateurish' efforts in favour of propaganda and humanitarian activities.[88] More numerous were teenage boys, who collected information in the hope of handing it over to British troops or smuggling it off the island by boat.[89] Later, Frank Killer recalled how he and his friends had mapped out German fortifications, memorizing the details of strong-points and gun emplacements to record later so they would leave no incriminating evidence if they were stopped and searched.[90] None, however, had the specialist military knowledge to help them assess what they had seen.

As the Ogier case in 1943 revealed, the German military authorities treated intelligence-gathering as an offence comparable to the possession of weapons. In February, the *Feldpolizei* arrested the Jersey lawyer Leonce Ogier and his son Richard after a search of their home that was probably instigated by an informant. Richard Ogier, who was 22 years old and had been a student at Cambridge, had aroused suspicion by regular cycling tours across the island past military installations.[91] The Germans found an illegal camera and a map marked with German fortifications in the house, and the Ogiers were deported for interrogation by a military court in Paris. Richard Ogier was charged with espionage, but did not stand trial because he was clearly unwell.[92] He was dispatched to a Paris hospital for treatment and, diagnosed with Parkinson's disease, remained there until the Liberation.[93] His father was sentenced to six months' imprisonment for 'harbouring' a spy, but the court was evidently unconvinced by the evidence and he was pardoned and sent home in May. The warmth of his reception probably convinced the occupiers that Leonce Ogier was a troublemaker, because he was summarily deported to Biberach internment camp six weeks later. He collapsed almost immediately with an advanced intestinal cancer, and died on 1 August 1943.[94] Ogier was well respected in Jersey, and the circumstances of his arrest and trial had turned him into a local hero. According to the diarist Leslie Sinel, 'every section of the island community' was represented at his memorial service.[95]

Intelligence-gathering operations by young men such as Richard Ogier and Peter Painter, however brave, were inevitably amateurish. By far the most effective operation

Figure 8.2 William Gladden, who gathered intelligence as well as sheltering a Russian OT fugitive. Copyright and courtesy Jersey Heritage collections

in the islands was organized by army veterans in their fifties and sixties associated with the Jersey Air-Raid Protection service (ARP). The group was led from ARP headquarters in St Helier by its Controller, Major William Crawford-Morrison, the States Surveyor Major J. H. L'Amy, and two brothers, J. C. M. and R. H. Manley. The men had important advantages over other would-be spies; as former army officers they understood what they saw, and they were permitted to travel freely across the island by car as part of their duties. According to L'Amy, they initially collected information as an 'absorbing hobby', and only began to pool and organize it in 1942.[96] Subsequently, the St Helier group worked with the ARP's Chief Warden in St Martin, the retired builder William Gladden, who had gathered details on the fortifications between Trinity and Gorey (Figure 8.2).[97] The plan, according to L'Amy, was to make 'a complete survey of the enemy fortifications throughout the island and then to tabulate this information systematically, and in such a way that it would occupy the minimum of space in transmission when the time and opportunity presented itself.'[98]

During 1942 the ARP 'spies' recruited a group of helpers, including ARP wardens and messengers who crossed the island on cycles or motorcycles and memorized the details of the fortifications. They were aided, too, by men recruited from outside the organization. Some already worked for the Germans as drivers while others – including Frederick Cook, gardener for *Feldkommandant* Knackfuss – were 'placed' in the hope of discovering useful information.[99] Although the group was small, it was larger than was once thought; Gladden, for example, estimated that his group had included around 20 men.[100] Crawford-Morrison's team produced a detailed schedule of German fortifications, searchlight positions, bunkers and underground ammunition stores, which they mapped onto a sheet of paper compatible with a standard Ordnance Survey map.[101] The intelligence was useless, however, unless it could be smuggled off the island to the Allies. Here the ARP network had one further advantage over younger and less influential members of the community, in the form of their contacts across the island. Among these was Stanley Green, the manager of West's cinema, who photographed the plans and produced a miniaturized negative barely larger than a postage stamp.[102] Subsequently, the Medical Officer of Health, Noel McKinstry, provided Crawford-Morrison with faked X-ray evidence of tuberculosis and a letter recommending treatment in a Swiss sanatorium. Crawford-Morrison was refused permission to leave, but in February 1943 he was included in the deportation of army officers, political 'undesirables' and British Jews to Germany. He took with him the miniaturized information, hidden in his hat, and entrusted it to a deportee who was due to be repatriated to England on medical grounds. The information reached British Intelligence as the network had planned.[103]

The ARP, however, was already under suspicion. Crawford-Morrison had already served a short prison sentence in September 1940 and was regarded as a trouble-maker.[104] Assertive in his dealings with the Germans, he became so unpopular that, according to L'Amy, the deputy *Feldkommandant*, Demmler, threatened to shoot him during a row about the role of the ARP.[105] In April 1942 the organization was subjected to petty regulations limiting members' right to wear badges and put signs on buildings, and in May 1943 its responsibilities were transferred to the Constables in their parishes.[106] Even so, aided by Gladden and his 'St Martin's Underground Movement', the group continued to gather information after the deportation of Crawford-Morrison, and especially after D-Day.[107] On 22 February 1945, its latest documents and photographs, sealed into copper tubes so that they could be thrown overboard in an emergency, were handed to five young escapers. They left for France in a boat built by Gladden and passed the information to British Intelligence in London.[108]

In the last weeks of the war, leading figures in the ARP network formed the Jersey Loyalists, a group dominated by ex-servicemen, to demand a special court to try the worst collaborators after the Liberation.[109] They had not, however, abandoned intelligence-gathering. In February 1945, when the new *Feldkommandant*, Vice-Admiral Hüffmeier, threatened to hold out even if German troops on the continent surrendered, L'Amy and his colleagues decided to establish contact with London by using a radio transmitter provided by the chief engineer at the General Post Office. At McKinstry's suggestion, they hid the transmitter at Les Vaux isolation hospital (where the Germans were unlikely to risk infection by searching), but were unable to get the cipher to England when bad weather prevented the departure of another escape party late in April.[110] Two weeks later, German troops surrendered.

Escape from the Channel Islands

ARP members could not know that the intelligence they provided would never be used, and by their own lights they achieved considerable success. In attempting to smuggle information to the Allies by boat, moreover, they came into contact with parties of escapers whose age and background were very different to their own. The number of escapes was so large, in fact, that it can be regarded as a form of defiance or resistance in its own right. Thanks largely to research by Richard Mayne and Joe Mière, the number of people known to have attempted escape stands at 228, 152 from Jersey and 76 from Guernsey, though even this tally does not include every failed attempt.[111] Escapes can be divided into three periods: between July and September 1940, when most of Guernsey's escapers and smaller numbers from Jersey left for England; between October 1940 and June 1944, when only a few people attempted the dangerous crossing; and between August 1944 and April 1945, when the Allied advance in Europe opened up the French coastline to escapers from Jersey. Escapes always involved risk: the islands are surrounded by small satellite islets and rocky outcrops, and have fierce tidal currents that make navigation hazardous even in good weather. Those who left during the Occupation, often in small open boats, were in real danger of drowning.

Of Guernsey's 76 escapers, 63 crossed to England in the first three months of Occupation, and no fewer than 50 had left within a week of the Germans' arrival. During this period, 38 people made the longer and more difficult crossing from Jersey. Early escapes were the least dangerous: most were in bigger boats, and took place before the Germans had mined the coastlines or established prohibited zones. They also had more limited objectives. Early escapers usually left in family groups – the departures from Guernsey in the first week included 19 women and a child – often hoping to re-join relatives who had left in the June evacuations.[112] Clifford Falla, who took 26 people to England in his 42' cabin cruiser on 1 July, remarked that he could have filled the boat twice over with volunteers.[113] Shock at the reality of occupation, and regret at not having left before, accounted for the rest, although Jersey's escapers included an Englishwoman who had returned at the eleventh hour to rescue her dog.[114] These early departures were acts of defiance and desperation rather than resistance.

After the escape of a party of eight from Guernsey in September 1940, the occupiers imposed restrictions to stem the tide. Fishing was permitted only from designated harbours, in registered and marked boats and in the hours of daylight, while harbour police could demand to accompany the vessels without prior warning. Unregistered boats were taken to designated harbours and had their oars and engines removed to put them out of use.[115] In November, the Germans also created military zones in coastal areas, protected by strict curfews and regular patrols. In one well-publicized incident, a Jerseyman – Henry Turpin – was shot and killed in the St Ouen zone in February 1941 when he failed to stop under challenge.[116] In December 1940, the Germans also began laying anti-personnel and anti-tank mines along the foreshores and in the waters close to harbours and landing sites. By April 1944 over 100,000 of them had been laid, and even though they were intended primarily as a defence against invasion, they also made escapes hazardous.[117]

Subsequently, the number of escapes fell dramatically. Between late September 1940 and August 1944, fewer than 30 people made the attempt to reach England.[118] When they did, it was usually for family reasons, as before: the 38-year-old tomato grower Jack Hubert, for example, left Guernsey in a party of seven in August 1943 to join his wife and child in England, while the organizer of his escape, the sea pilot William Corbet, was desperate to take his sick wife to safety there.[119] Some escapers took information about German patrols and fortifications with them, but this was not – for most – the main reason for leaving.[120] However, the situation was beginning to change: the period also saw the first departures by younger islanders who were intent on resistance. The most remarkable was by a 22-year-old Jerseyman, Denis Vibert, who made his second escape bid in September 1941 when he set out from St Aubin's Bay in an 8' dinghy. After one of his engines failed and the other was washed overboard by heavy waves, Vibert rowed for three days without food before being picked up by the destroyer HMS Brocklesby off Portland.[121] Described by the Bishop of Winchester as 'very modest and sensible, a gentleman',[122] Vibert had patriotic motives: he had been frustrated by the Occupation, hated the Germans, and wanted to join the armed forces. After giving MI6 a sober assessment of conditions in the islands, he joined the Royal Air Force and served in Coastal Command.

According to Leslie Sinel, Vibert's escape was the 'main topic' of island conversation, and it inspired others to emulate him.[123] But while Vibert had a reasonable knowledge of seamanship learned during training as a merchant navy cadet, other would-be escapers had no such skills.[124] Peter Hassall was only 15 years old when he heard what Vibert had done. Like his school-friend Dennis Audrain, he was ashamed by what he saw as the islanders' 'pacific' response to the Occupation and shocked by showings of the anti-Semitic film *Jud Süss* at the local cinema. The two youths, who had already defaced signposts and made a map of the fortifications, now decided to attempt the crossing to England. Hassall also had personal reasons for wanting to escape, in his 'frustration and shame' over his mother's black-market activities and relationship with German soldiers.[125] The boys recruited their friend Maurice Gould, an 18-year-old apprentice mechanic and blacksmith, to join them. They also made basic preparations, water-proofing their 12' dinghy with oakum and linseed oil, and asking for help with navigation.[126] But they ignored warnings that they should not go: from PC Albert Chardine, who gave petrol but told them they would be foolish to attempt the crossing, and from the master mariner George Sowden, who advised them about navigation but insisted that they would be killed if they went ahead. They had received good advice from honourable men, Hassall acknowledged later, but had been 'too arrogant and pumped up to pay any heed'.[127] Audrain could not even swim.

The three youths set off on the night of 3 May 1942 from La Motte, on the southeast point of Jersey, where the rocks and tides were so dangerous that the Germans had not laid mines or established regular patrols. Less than 400 yards from the shore, the boat took on so much water that it began to sink. Audrain and Hassall, who had taken off their lifejackets to row, had no time to put them back before they were thrown into the sea. For the rest of his life Peter Hassall was haunted by his unsuccessful efforts to save his friend from drowning, and of his own frantic struggle to stop himself being dragged under by the dying boy. When Hassall and Gould returned to shore, they were caught by the German Water Police and *Feldgendarmerie* and beaten. Subsequently, under the provisions of the 'Night and Fog' decree, they were deported to Fresnes prison and then to Germany. Although Hassall survived the war, Maurice Gould, who had contracted tuberculosis, died in Wittlich prison in October 1943.[128]

Collective punishments – restrictions on fishing, boats and access to the beaches – were regularly imposed after escape bids during this period.[129] Islanders were inconvenienced, fishermen found it harder to earn a living, and seafood supplies were reduced at a time when rations were already being cut. As a result, there was little sympathy for escapers: Mary Deslandes, who thought that Denis Vibert ought to 'get a VC for his nerve', was an exception.[130] Few went as far as the Guernseyman Herbert Williams, who wrote after the Corbet-Hubert escape that the party 'should be shot' for the trouble they caused,[131] but news of escapes was frequently received with trepidation or disapproval in both islands.[132] Jack Hubert was probably right to suspect that many of his fellow islanders would see his escape in August 1943 as thoroughly selfish.[133] Violet Carey, reporting the atmosphere in St Peter Port afterwards, noted that locals were 'very angry with those men for going'.[134]

The mood in Jersey changed significantly after D-Day, and particularly from September 1944, when the Allied advance in France opened up a short escape route from Jersey to the coast less than ten miles away. However, the route from Guernsey was significantly longer and more dangerous, and only two boats made the crossing during this period. One of these, by two fishermen – the Le Page brothers – and a French worker named Golivet, took military information provided by Golivet and the French consul, Lambert.[135] The other was made with the specific purpose of alerting the British government to food shortages and deteriorating conditions in Guernsey: on 3 November 1944, the pilot Frederick Noyon and the fisherman William Enticott left St Sampson's with papers secretly provided by Controlling Committee officials, including Abraham Lainé, and by the local GP Alastair Rose.[136] Although the escape was a sign of growing dissatisfaction with the passivity of Bailiff Victor Carey, it did not greatly add to British knowledge of conditions.

By contrast, 106 people (among them seven women) are known to have left Jersey for France after D-Day, 97 of them between August and November 1944. Even more would have done so but for a shortage of petrol and suitable boats. The escapers included several French and Dutch workers and two American PoWs.[137] The most ingenious attempt was by Dennis Le Cuirot, who was only 17 when he reached France in July 1944. Le Cuirot, who had been placed on probation for demonstrating against the deportations two years before, had simply carried his suitcase aboard the SS *Minotaur* when it docked in Jersey en route to France. The *Minotaur* was carrying hundreds of French workers home from Alderney, and Le Cuirot had discovered that the workers' papers were not properly checked as they boarded the ship. During the crossing the vessel was attacked by British motor torpedo boats and many lives were lost, but Le Cuirot reached Granville safely. Although Le Cuirot was arrested, he escaped from custody with two French companions and made his way to St Lo, where he made contacted with the American forces and, briefly, acted as an unofficial interpreter. He reached England safely August 1944.[138] A young Jerseywoman, Colleen Querée, had boarded the same ship; she also survived the sinking, only to be betrayed by a fellow passenger in St Malo and brought back to Jersey.[139]

Other Jersey escapers left in small boats, as Vibert had done. In the final months of the war, their exploits were more warmly received than before, probably because of the absence of serious reprisals and the growing conviction that the war was in its final stages. The new mood was reflected in the German decision to close down a local sports club, the Jersey School of Physical Culture, in November 1944 after 40 of its members had gathered to discuss the chances of escape.[140] Escapers' prospects of success were improved because the Germans were increasingly careless, failing to identify popular embarkation sites or to patrol them properly.[141] At least 50 escapers left from a single location – Fauvic beach, in the south-east corner of Jersey – and smaller numbers from Pontac and Rozel.[142] Even so, escape remained difficult and dangerous. Frank Killer, who made an unsuccessful attempt in September 1944, later outlined the problems to be overcome:[143]

> The first and perhaps the most difficult was to find a seaworthy boat ... You had to find a safe place to work on your boat, to caulk it and make it waterproof, and if possible to paint it a dull colour. You needed a reliable engine and a good supply of petrol. You had to find a gap in the German defences at a point where you could get the craft into deep water and navigate it between the rocks and other hazards to the open sea. You needed some form of transport to get the boat to the shore and helpers to lift it over the seawall, or to carry it over the sand or between the rocks to where she would float. You had to do all this in complete silence, and with a constant watch for patrols.

Successful escapes required proper planning and took time to organize.

The biggest problem was to find a suitable boat. They were obtained in various ways: borrowed or bought from farmers who had disobeyed German orders and hidden their dinghies;[144] smuggled from store, where they had been taken in August 1942;[145] stolen from harbours, where they had been left by locals or the Germans;[146] or, in the case of the English builder William Gladden, built from scratch for an escape party taking military intelligence to the Allies in February 1945.[147] Many of the boats were not seaworthy. They had to be hidden for caulking and repair and fitted with outboard motors that had been borrowed, bought or stolen.[148] Petrol, which was strictly rationed and unavailable to most islanders, had to be siphoned from German vehicles or, more commonly, provided by sympathizers with access to supplies.[149] Finally, the boats had to be transferred to suitable sites along the coast in horse-drawn drays,[150] or carried on trolleys (with or without a horse to pull them),[151] or loaded into borrowed furniture vans.[152] Even then, escapers often needed help to get their boats over sea walls and across the beaches to the sea.

A few escape parties succeeded even though their boats were unsuitable. One party of eight teenagers left Pontac in September 1944 in two patched-up canoes and a 14' beach-float. Remarkably, two of the boats reached France safely, and the young men in the third – Killer, Hugh Le Cloche and Peter Curwood – managed to swim ashore when their boat sank. But escape bids that were hastily organized and relied on flimsy boats were likely to fail. When the Caen University graduate Francis Le Sueur left in September 1944 with Garnet Briard and George Whithy, they went on beach-floats that had been caulked with masking-tape and fitted with inflated car inner tubes for buoyancy. Not surprisingly, all three boats became waterlogged, and the men were lucky to survive when the currents swept them to the north of the island at Ronez, where they were caught by a German patrol.[153] Other would-be escapers were less fortunate: in October and November 1944 seven people lost their lives in failed attempts. They included a young married couple, Ronald and Madeleine Bisson, who drowned with their companions André Gorvel and Roy Luciennes when their boat drifted onto rocks at Saline Bay and capsized.[154] Two brothers, John and Bernard Larbalastier, who ran a pharmaceutical business in St Helier, suffered the same fate when they sailed from Fauvic, although their companion Peter Noel was captured and imprisoned.[155] The party had ignored warnings by a local farmer that the weather and seas were too rough for the attempt.[156]

In October 1944 another party of four left Grouville Bay to attempt the crossing to France. The youths involved were young – Michael Neil was only 17 years old – and had little experience of the sea, though they had asked for advice about tides and navigation. Neil had collected information about German fortifications with escape in mind, but joined the Grouville party only at the last moment and barely knew his companions. They had sailed only a few hundred yards, past mines and barbed wire, when their boat began to fill with water and they were forced to turn back. Although they reached the beach at Anne Port Bay safely, they were spotted by a German patrol, which opened fire when the boys did not respond to a call for surrender. As they huddled behind the boat, Douglas Le Marchand, a 19-year old who had organized the escape, was hit and killed. Many years later, Michael Neil acknowledged that the attempt had little chance; it was doomed, he thought, by 'little preparation and a leaky boat'.[157] On the other hand, escapes which had been carefully planned, and included men with more experience, now had reasonable prospects of reaching France.[158]

The history of these attempts reveals much about the nature of resistance in the islands. Most escapes were by small groups of friends, many of whom were already involved in illegal activities. Almost all of them received extra advice and support, especially from family members and old school-friends who provided petrol and helped transport their boats to the beaches.[159] Also vital, however, was the help given by individuals whom escapers knew only slightly, or by reputation alone, but regarded as patriotic and trustworthy. The Medical Officer of Health, Noel McKinstry, provided the petrol for at least one attempt and information about German fortifications for more; the garage owner Ted Le Gros tuned several engines at his Pontac garage;[160] experienced sailors, including the States pilots Peter Guiton and Silver Le Riche and the fisherman Sydney Le Clerq, gave advice – and warnings – to various escape parties.[161]

Among these helpers was the master mariner George Sowden (Figure 8.3). Born in Liverpool in 1883, Sowden had been appointed to skipper the freighter SS *Normand*, which carried essential commodities between Granville and France, in October 1940.[162] Four months later he refused to carry German ammunition on the *Normand* and, after being confined on board the vessel for several days, was dismissed. Sowden's principled stand was much admired: Peter Hassall commented that he and Audrain had seen it as 'the first act of meaningful resistance on the island', and it was probably this that led him to ask Sowden for advice about navigation and tides before his escape bid.[163] Shortly afterwards, Sowden was involved in disputes with the Germans over their proposals to site an anti-aircraft gun on his property, or to requisition part of it for their own use. In May 1941 he was sentenced to two months in prison for 'insulting' the armed forces: he had refused them access to his flats and accused the Nazis of murdering children in Poland.[164] After his release, he earned a living by opening a Nautical and Marine Engineering College to provide courses in navigation, seamanship and nautical astronomy for local youths. They included Denis Vibert, Frank Killer and

Figure 8.3 The master mariner George Sowden. Copyright and courtesy Jersey Heritage collections

several more would-be escapers, and Sowden also gave expert advice about tides and navigation to a number of escape parties.[165] Guided by a strong sense of patriotism and honour, Sowden never encouraged escapers to risk their lives and warned strongly against ill-prepared attempts, but tried to give them the best chance of success if they went ahead.[166]

The most prolific helpers, however, were the Bertram families at Fauvic beach. Fauvic was the most favourable of Jersey's embarkation points: although the beach was swept by light from Fort Henry, German patrols were infrequent and predictable and there were relatively few mines. Even so, boats still had to be hidden to wait for favourable tides and calm weather before being carried across rough ground, down steep steps in the sea wall and across the rocky beach.[167] The necessary shelter was provided by 'Bill' Bertram, a First World War veteran and States Deputy for Grouville, and by his brother Thomas and his family, at their farms by the beach. According to Roy Thomas, at least eight escape parties – over 50 would-be escapers – left Fauvic with the help of the Bertrams and their friends and neighbours, who stored boats in their outbuildings and provided escape parties with food and drinks before helping them launch their boats.[168] The Bertrams played a vital part in the escape story, and their willingness to offer help was well known among potential escapers.

Motives and conclusions

In Charles Cruickshank's official history of the Occupation, escapers' motives were considered briefly and without great sympathy. Although some had left to join the forces, he thought that others had 'simply wanted to escape from the harsh life in the occupied islands, on the assumption that life in Britain was less disagreeable'. Nor had they been deterred by the trouble they caused for those left behind.[169] This judgement requires some amendment. Especially after D-Day and with one or two notable exceptions, such as the Guernseyman who admitted to MI6 that he was a 'loafer' who was fed up with the Occupation,[170] escapers had patriotic motives. Peter Crill, son of the Constable of St Clement, who left with six friends on 11 November 1944, commented later that they had wanted to join the armed forces and 'have a go at the Germans'; another, Basil Le Brun, recalled that he had been 'itching to get into the action'.[171] MI6 did not doubt their enthusiasm and commitment. Its report on the Charles Bondis-Douglas Davey group of five, who made their escape in September 1944, judged them to be 'excellent types, keen and loyal, who have attempted to form a small "maquis" on Jersey'. The assessment could equally have been made of other parties.[172] Almost all the escapers after D-Day were aged between 18 and 25; they were the same age – and had much the same motives – as the young men who, in France, formed the core of the *maquis* (Figure 8.4).[173]

Even more negative assessments have been made, at the time and since, of the young people who engaged in sabotage and military larceny. Joe Mière's remark to Madeleine Bunting that, if he had been young today and behaved that way, 'they'd call me a delinquent', was a hostage to fortune.[174] It allowed Bunting to argue that the unique circumstances of occupation had allowed acts of 'childish mischievousness and teenage delinquency' to be interpreted as patriotic resistance, when in reality they were nothing of the kind.[175] In a few cases, the accusation contains an element of truth: one or two young men who robbed the Germans after June 1940 had already been robbing their fellow islanders before it, and one or two more stole indiscriminately from locals as well as Germans. Nevertheless, they were the exception rather than the rule.[176] It is also true that many of the young men who engaged in small-scale sabotage and stole military equipment, or made escape bids, rather enjoyed the excitement. They freely admitted it later. Bernard Cavey, who escaped in September 1944 after various anti-German escapades, summarized the approach as 'taking great delight in annoying the German Occupation Forces, and taking the resultant "roughing up", when one did not get away with it, with defiant pride'.[177]

Even so, the case of Bernard Turpin demonstrates that the behaviour of these young men should not be dismissed as mere hooliganism. Turpin, an 18-year-old mechanic, had served a short prison sentence in May 1943 for stealing petrol from the occupiers, which he had done both to annoy the Germans and to keep his unregistered motorcycle on the road.[178] In August 1944, however, he was sent to prison again, this time on an issue of principle, for refusing to handle German guns and ammunition at work because it was a task of military significance.[179] Turpin escaped from Gloucester Street shortly afterwards, tearing ligaments in his legs when he dropped from the prison wall, and was hidden first by an old school-friend and then, for several months, under the floorboards of the family home.[180]

It is also a mistake to dismiss small-scale sabotage and military thefts as if they were less worthy forms of resistance than intelligence-gathering and escape. In fact, there was considerable overlap between the groups involved: many of the young men who risked their lives in escape bids after September 1944 had already stolen military

Sabotage, Intelligence-gathering and Escape   231

Figure 8.4 Patriotic watercolour painted in Gloucester Street by the political prisoner Dennis McLinton, showing 'Britannia' escaping from Jersey. Copyright and courtesy Jersey Heritage Collections. Copyright and courtesy Wendy Tipping

equipment, or engaged in sabotage and intelligence-gathering, or scuffled with German soldiers during demonstrations against the deportations of September 1942. Saboteurs and escapers alike came from all social groups in the island. Jersey's two private schools, De La Salle Catholic college and, especially, Victoria College, which had an active Officer Training Corps and a tradition of supplying officers for the armed forces, were well represented: 20 of the young Jerseymen who attempted escape after D-Day, for example, had attended Victoria College.[181] One former pupil at the school, Frank Killer, recalled his own, and his family's, acceptance of 'all the tenets of the English public schoolboy', including an uncritical patriotism and commitment to empire.[182]

Other young resisters, however, were less privileged. According to Lucy Schwob, most were not members of the island elites but came 'from that class which takes the place of the proletariat in Jersey'.[183] The prison diaries, letters and mementos they left behind suggest that they, too, were motivated by patriotic and anti-German sentiment as well as by a desire for adventure.[184] Of course, the islands' escapers and saboteurs never faced the dangers that confronted members of the resistance movements in occupied Europe: they were members of no formal organizations, did not go 'underground', and never engaged in armed rebellion. It is also fair to assume that there would have been fewer of them if the Germans had imposed death penalties on Channel Islanders for possessing guns or attempting sabotage. Nevertheless, they deserve to be judged according to the conditions they faced and the limited choices available to them. For the young Channel Islanders who engaged in them, these were acts of genuine resistance when few others were possible.

As this chapter has demonstrated, there was no Channel Islands *maquis*, because conditions made the existence of one impossible. The activities that did take place were sporadic and unorganized, usually undertaken by small groups of former schoolfriends or, in the case of intelligence-gathering, by older men in the ARP network. Only a minority of Channel Islanders ever took part in them, but the numbers – in Jersey at least – were not insignificant. Here, the evidence suggests that more than 200 young men under the age of 25 – at a rough estimate, between 10 and 15 per cent of the age-group – took part in escape attempts, small-scale sabotage, intelligence-gathering or military larceny in 1943–5. Their actions had no effect on the course of the Occupation, and were greeted with alarm and often hostility by other inhabitants. Yet while historians are entirely correct to conclude that there was no organized resistance 'movement' in the Channel Islands, we ought at least to note that some of those involved thought that there *had* been one, and that they were part of it.[185] The spies and escapers, at least, had been able to rely on trusted contacts to help them gather information and smuggle it out. Although they had relied mostly on their family and friends, they had also been helped by contacts who were not close friends or even members of the same social circle. It was these links that enabled the ARP group to smuggle military information out of Jersey in 1943 and 1945, and provided escapers with enough knowledge of the tides and currents to give them a chance of surviving the journey. Men such as William Gladden, Noel McKinstry, William Crawford-Morrison and Bill Bertram played an indispensable role in linking the disparate groups and allowing some limited cooperation between them.

Notes

1 Charles Cruickshank, *The German Occupation of the Channel Islands: The Official History of the Occupation Years*, Guernsey, Guernsey Press Co. Ltd., by arrangement with the Trustees of the Imperial War Museum and Oxford University Press, 1975, pp. 28–32.
2 Quoted in Michael R. D. Foot, *Resistance: An Analysis of European Resistance to Nazism 1940–1945* London, Eyre Methuen, 1976, p. 137.

3   Cruickshank, *The German Occupation of the Channel Islands*, pp. 80–102, 231–58.
4   PL.LF940.53 BRO. Mrs Peggy Brock, The Second Diary of the Occupation, October 1940–January 1942, 4 November 1940; PL.LF940.53 LAI. Adèle Lainé, 'The German Occupation of Guernsey, 1940–1945', p. 20: November-December 1940.
5   PL.LF940.53 ORD. Reverend R. Douglas Ord, Occupation Diary, 24 December 1940.
6   Alan Wood and Mary Wood, *Islands in Danger: The Story of the German Occupation of the Channel Islands, 1940–1945*, Sevenoaks, First Four Square, 1965, p. 95. Officially he had committed suicide, but the family believed the Nazis killed him. See IA. Frank Falla Archive. Testimony of Rachel Symes.
7   In July 1940 he had drafted a letter to the British authorities asking that none be attempted. It was not sent. IA.AQ 1212/098. Kenneth. G. Lewis, Diary of Events 1940–1945, 19–20 October 1940; Charles Cruickshank, *The German Occupation of the Channel Islands*, p. 89.
8   PL.LF940.53 BRO. Mrs Peggy Brock, The Second Diary of the Occupation, October 1940–January 1942, 4 November 1940, 13 November 1940.
9   IWM.Sound Archive.Interview 11096. Peter Leslie Crill, 1990.
10 Cruickshank, *The German Occupation of the Channel Islands*, p. 2.
11 Foot, *Resistance*, p. 270.
12 Madeleine Bunting, *The Model Occupation: The Channel Islands under German Rule, 1940–1945*, London, Pimlico, 2004, p. 50; George Forty, Channel Islands at War: A German Perspective, Shepperton, Ian Allan, 1999, pp. 157–82. See Cruickshank, *The German Occupation of the Channel Islands*, pp. 193–4.
13 On Islanders feeling swamped, see PL.LF940.53 BRO. Mrs Peggy Brock, 'The Second Diary of the Occupation', October 1940–January 1942, 31 March 1941, 4 August 1941; K. M. Bachmann. *The Prey of an Eagle: A Personal Record of Family Life Written throughout the German Occupation of Guernsey 1940–45*, Guernsey, Guernsey Press Co. Ltd., 1972, 13 August 1941; IA.AQ 1018/68. Ella Frampton, Occupation Diary 1940–1945, 28 April 1941.
14 Documents.5750 Misc 189/2 (2826). Norman Le Brocq, transcript of interview, p. 17. See Louise Willmot, 'The Channel Islands', in B. Moore (ed.), *Resistance in Western Europe*, Oxford and New York, Berg, 2000, pp. 65–92, here p. 69.
15 IA.CC 01–05. Census of Guernsey Population 1940–45; JAS.B/A/W91/10. Jersey Census, 10 August 1940.
16 Bob Moore, 'Comparing Resistance and Resistance Movements', in B. Moore (ed.), *Resistance in Western Europe*, Oxford and New York, Berg, 2000, pp. 249–64, here p. 255.
17 For example Julian Jackson, *France: The Dark Years 1940–1944*, Oxford and New York, Oxford University Press, 2003, pp. 480–2, 503; Alan S. Milward, 'The Economic and Strategic Effectiveness of Resistance', in S. Hawes and R. White (eds), *Resistance in Europe, 1939–1945*, London, Allen Lane, 1975, pp. 186–203, here pp. 197–8.
18 JAS.D/Z/H6/3. Sentences and Prosecutions by the Field Command and Troop Courts: John Soyer.
19 'Fate of Jerseyman in France: Escapes from German Gaol, Dies Fighting with Maquis', *Evening Post*, 11 August 1945, p. 1. Information from the Justice of the peace for Granville, Poullain; *Daily Mail*, 2 July 1952, p. 2.
20 IA.CC 01–05. Census of Guernsey Population 1940–45: male population over 14 years of age, February 1944; extrapolation from JAS.B/A/W91/10. *Jersey Census*, 10 August 1940.

21 See Paul Sanders, 'Managing under Duress: Ethical Leadership, Social Capital, and the Civilian Administration of the British Channel Islands during the Nazi Occupation, 1940–1945', *Journal of Business Ethics*, Vol. 93, 2010, 113–29, here 120.
22 See Peter D. Hassall, 'Night and Fog Prisoners', on the Victoria College Gang, the Beeches Gang, the Havre-des-Pas Gang, the Pier Road Gang, etc. Manuscript published online. http://www.jerseyheritage.org/templates/jerseyheritage/occupation_memorial/pdfs/hassallbookcomplete.pdf, 1997, accessed 1 August 2013.
23 Philippe Burrin, *France under the Germans*, New York, New Press, 1996, pp. 192–3.
24 See for example Nan Le Ruez, *Jersey Occupation Diary: Her Story of the German Occupation, 1940–45*, Jersey, Seaflower Books, 1994, 14 January 1942; in Guernsey see PL.LF940.53 BRO. Mrs Peggy Brock, The Second Diary of the Occupation, October 1940–January 1942, 15 May 1941, describing the locals as 'utterly cold and contemptuous'. In Jersey, JAS.L/C/77/A/1. Izett Croad, Occupation Diary, 16 June 1941 on refusing to shake hands, and 22 December 1940 on the determination to 'treat the Germans with contempt and take no notice of them'. On the refusal to shake hands see also Michael Halliwell, *Operating under Occupation: The Life and Work of Arthur Clare Halliwell FRCS, Consultant Surgeon at the Jersey General Hospital during the German Occupation 1940–1945*, Jersey, Channel Islands Occupation Society, 2005, p. 50; interview with Terry Le Mottée, 10 August 2010 on René Le Mottée's refusal on principle to shake hands with German soldiers until the Liberation; also interview with Terry Sowden, Patrick Sowden and Ros Rice, 12 August 2010 on George Sowden.
25 As in the case of PC Albert Chardine, who also aided escapers: SJ.OCC 942 CHA. Albert Alfred Chardine, reminiscences taped by his daughter Colette Chardine and transcribed, 1995, here p. 7. The order to salute is found in JAS.B/A/W50/1. Order for policemen and traffic control men to salute German officers and military officials, 19 September 1940. JAS.B/A/W50/56. Complaints from the Feldkommandantur against police officers in general and specific officers in particular for failing to salute. They included Arthur Clifford, PCs De la Gaye and Rasil, and Samuel Leslie. See also JAS.B/A/W50/180. Prosecution and sentence against PC McDonald, 30 October 1944.
26 Claude Cahun, *Écrits*, ed. François Leperlier, Paris, Jean-Michel Place, 2002; here 'Le Muet dans la Mêlée', p. 634.
27 SJ.GO Box 10/27. Mrs Dorothy Monckton, Diary, 29 July 1940; also IWM. Documents.2986. R. E. H. Fletcher, Diary.
28 See for example Documents.5750 Misc 189/2 (2826). Dixie Landick, transcript of interview; IWM.Sound Archive.Interview 10716. Maurice Edwarde Green, 1989.
29 *Daily Mail*, 21 December 2012, p. 5.
30 For example IWM.Sound Archive.Interview 10683. Joseph Arthur Mière, 1989; JAS.B/A/W50/133. FK 515 Knackfuss to Heider, 8 February 1944.
31 TNA.HO.144/22834 Part 2. Further interrogation of informants, p. 6.
32 JAS.B/A/W50/21. FK 515 Colonel Schumacher to Bailiff, 20 May 1941; JAS.B/A/W50/25. Report of sand put into a German lorry, 26–28 July 1941; Bunting, *The Model Occupation*, pp. 200–1, on Mike Le Cornu.
33 Interview with Bernard Turpin, 14 August 2010. See also JWT.Research Files Box 10.
34 TNA.HO.144/22834 Part 2. Further interrogation of informants, p. 6.
35 IA.FK 01–11. Militärische Führung (Ic) (f1): Inselkommandant Guernsey to B.d.b.K. Feldkommandantur 515, 18 March 1941; JAS.B/A/W50/57. Sabotage to telephone cable at Five Oaks, 26 May 1942; Leslie Sinel, *The German Occupation of Jersey: The*

Wartime Diary of Leslie Sinel, Jersey, Villette Publishing, 1995, 19 June 1942; IA.FK 01-11. FK 515 Nebenstelle Guernsey: Feldgendarmerie Tgb. Nr.252/41 to Nebenstelle 515 re cutting of telephone cables in Channel Islands Hotel; IA.FK 01-11. Island Police, Guernsey to President of Controlling Committee, 2 October 1941, on cable-cutting at Torteval; JAS.B/A/W50/64. FK 515 Feldkommandant von Aufsess to Bailiff, 21 September 1942. See also Hassall, 'Night and Fog Prisoners', p. 31.

36   See the diary entry by Ralph Mollet, the Bailiff's secretary, on the land line of the France cable being cut: JAS.M/28/2. Ralph Mollet, Occupation Diary, Volume 2, 1 February 1941-6 June 1943, 26 May 1942.

37   JAS.D/Z/H6/4. Sentences and Prosecutions by the Field Command and Troop Courts. Trial 4: René Le Mottée, 22 December 1942; JAS.D/AG/B7/1. 'Names of Political Prisoners August 1940' prison log book: 230 René Le Mottée. Interview with Terry Le Mottée, 10 August 2010. Sinel, 25, 28 August 1942; for another incident, see Richard Weithley, *So It Was: One Man's Story of the German Occupation from Boyhood to Manhood*, Jersey, Starlight Publishing, 2001, p. 46 on Donald Bell's derailing the train near Red Houses, and Bell himself in Halliwell, *Operating under Occupation*, p. 120; for another incident see IWM.Sound Archive.Interview 10716. Maurice Edwarde Green, 1989.

38   Paul Sanders, *The British Channel Islands under German Occupation, 1940-1945*, Jersey, Jersey Heritage Trust and Société Jersiaise, 2005, pp. 112-13. See also Ludovic E. Bertrand, *A Record of the Work of the Guernsey Secret Press*, Guernsey, Guernsey Star and Gazette, 1945, pp. 15-17.

39   Here see William M. Bell, *I Beg to Report: Policing in Guernsey during the German Occupation*, Guernsey, Guernsey Press Company Ltd., 1995, pp. 133-5. Bailey claimed that he and PC Frank Tuck had cut the cables; they were among the officers arrested for stealing from civilian stores in 1942 and may have hoped to restore their reputation.

40   PL.LF940.53 ORD. Reverend R. Douglas Ord, Occupation Diary, 29 May 1943.

41   IA.AQ 0368/01-11. Violet Carey, Occupation Diaries 1940-1945, 20 April 1942. On low productivity as an effective form of resistance, see Milward, "The Economic and Strategic Effectiveness of Resistance", pp. 186-203.

42   IA.FK 01-11. FK Nebenstelle Guernsey to President of Controlling Committee, 25 November 1941; IA.FK 01-11. Steinberger to Nebenstelle FK 515, Guernsey, 17 November 1941.

43   JAS.B/A/W50/21. FK 515 Colonel Schumacher to Bailiff, 20 May 1941; JAS.B/A/W50/21. Attorney General Duret Aubin to Parish Constables, 21 May 1941.

44   PL.LF940.53 LAI. Adèle Lainé, 'The German Occupation of Guernsey, 1940-1945', p. 29, 15 March 1941; JAS.M/28/2. Ralph Mollet, Occupation Diary, Volume 2, 1 February 1941-6 June 1943, 26 May 1942; JAS.B/A/W50/64. FK 515 Feldkommandant von Aufsess to Bailiff, 21 September 1942.

45   See for example IA.FK 01-11. FK 515 Nebenstelle Guernsey Feldgendarmerie Tgb.Nr. 252/41 to Nebenstelle 515, 25 July 1941.

46   IA.FK 01-11. FK 515 Schumacher to Bezirkschef A Abt Ic Kommandostab, St Germain, 30 April 1941.

47   IA.FK 01-11. FK 515 Nebenstelle Guernsey to Inselkommandantur Guernsey, 9 May 1941.

48   PL.LF940.53 LAI. Adèle Lainé, 'The German Occupation of Guernsey, 1940-1945', 15 March 1941. The Germans thought that their cables provided sabotage opportunities: IA.FK 01-11. FK 515 Nebenstelle Guernsey to Inselkommandantur Guernsey, 9 May 1941.

49 Thus IA.AQ 1212/098. KennethG. Lewis, 'Diary of Events 1940–1945', 23–24 April 1941; Interview with Robert Le Sueur, 27 June 2000; Nan Le Ruez, 20 June 1942.
50 SJ.GO Box 3/1. Father Maré, 'The Execution of François Scornet. Eyewitness Account'; also Peter Tabb, *A Peculiar Occupation: New Perspectives on Hitler's Channel Islands*, Hersham, Ian Allan, 2005, p. 94.
51 See for example Basil de Carteret, Mary Deslandes and Mary Robin, *Island Trilogy. Memories of Jersey and the Occupation by Mary Robin, Basil de Carteret and Mary Deslandes*, Jersey, Redberry Press, undated, 'Diary of Mary Deslandes', 16–23 February 1941; Le Ruez, 23 March 1941; Sinel, 23 March 1941.
52 IA. Frank Falla Archive. Statement of Mr and Mrs John Alfred Ingrouille of Milette Bay, Vale, given to Frank Falla, October 1964. Also statement of Alice M. Hubert, who knew the family, taken by Lt. W. G. Barber: Joe Mière Archive, held by and used by the kind permission of the Mière family.
53 See JAS.D/AG/B7/1. 'Names of Political Prisoners August 1940' prison log book: 13 John Henry Ingrouille; JAS.L/C/24/C/16. John Henry Ingrouille, information collected by Joe Mière; see also Bunting, *The Model Occupation*, p. 141, with a diary entry by Ingrouille's father.
54 Bunting, *The Model Occupation*, pp. 141–2.
55 IA. Frank Falla Archive. Statement of Mr and Mrs John Alfred Ingrouille of Milette Bay, Vale, given to Frank Falla, October 1964.
56 On the emotions see for example interview with Bernard Turpin, 14 August 2010; IWM.Sound Archive.Interview 10683. Joseph Arthur Mière, 1989; *Jersey Evening Post*, 15 March 1986, p. 24: memories of Dougie Baton and Michael 'Roy' Grove; also Peter Gray, 'Island of Beauty, Island of Secrets', unpublished manuscript, pp. 38–9, used by kind permission of Mr Peter Gray. For further examples of military larceny see JAS.D/Z/H6. Sentences and Prosecutions by the Field Command and Troop Courts: Case 321. Troop Court to Duret Aubin, 2 October 1943: Ronald Harris and Maxwell Weeks, sentenced to six weeks for 'joint military larceny' and damage to military equipment; also JAS.D/Z/H6/8. Duret Aubin to Cuming, 9 July 1943 on three Irishmen sentenced to two to three months for military larceny 'in company with others'. See also Frank Killer and his group of about a dozen young men, in Frank Keiller, *Prison without Bars: Living in Jersey under the German Occupation 1940–1945*, Bradford on Avon, Seaflower Books, 2000, p. 112; also JWT.Research Files Box 7. Letter from Bernard Cavey to Joe Mière, undated.
57 Sanders, *The British Channel Islands under German Occupation*, pp. 59, 63–4. Under its terms almost 7,000 people were arrested, some 5,000 of them in France.
58 IWM.Sound Archive.Interview 11096. Peter Leslie Crill, 1990. Crill stole the radios with Painter.
59 Interview with Terry Sowden, Patrick Sowden and Ros Rice, 12 August 2010; Paul Sanders, *The Ultimate Sacrifice. The Jersey Islanders who Died in German Prisons and Concentration Camps 1940–1945*, Jersey, Jersey Heritage Trust, 2004, p. 54.
60 Sanders, *The Ultimate Sacrifice*, p. 54; the friends were Roy Mourant and Victor Huelin.
61 TNA.WO.311/11. Testimony of Mrs D. M. Painter, June 1945 to the British Military Authority in Jersey, June 1945; Sanders, *The Ultimate Sacrifice*, p. 54.
62 TNA.KV.4/87. British Intelligence Reports, 1945.
63 TNA.WO.311/11. Testimony of Mrs D. M. Painter, June 1945 to the British Military Authority in Jersey, June 1945.

64 The most detailed account is by Sanders, *The Ultimate Sacrifice*, pp. 53–63. The Painters' fate was described by a Frenchman, Roger Hardy, who was with them in prison. *Evening Post*, 2 June 1945, p. 1.
65 Keiller, *Prison without Bars*, pp. 111–12. After becoming a doctor, he wisely changed his name from Killer.
66 Edward Le Quesne, *The Occupation of Jersey Day by Day. The Personal Diary of Deputy Edward Le Quesne*, with a foreword and explanatory notes by Michael Ginns, Jersey, La Haule, 1999, 4 May 1944.
67 Sanders, *The Ultimate Sacrifice*, pp. 63–4.
68 See for example JAS.D/Z/H6/9. Sentences and Prosecutions by the Field Command and Troop Courts: Arnold Bennett; Veronica Bichard; Bernard Carratu; Fred Cauvain; Allan Costard; Charles Gruchy; Basil Le Breton; Patrick McGarry; Claude Saunders; Victor Webb; Dennis Williams; Keiller, *Prison without Bars*, pp. 111–12.
69 Weithley, *So It Was*, p. 43.
70 Ibid., pp. 65–70; also Leo Harris, *A Boy Remembers*, Jersey, Channel Island Publishing, 2000, pp. 129–41.
71 See Donald Bell, in Halliwell, *Operating under Occupation*, p. 120; Weithley, *So It Was*, p. 120–39.
72 See for example the teenagers Ronald Harris and Maxwell Weeks, sentenced to six weeks on 30 September 1943: JAS.D/Z/H6/6. Truppenkriegsgericht to Duret Aubin, 2 October 1943; JAS.D/Z/H6/8. Sentences and Prosecutions by the Field Command and Troop Courts: John Philip Richardson, aged 21, sentenced to six weeks for 'military larceny' on 31 August 1944. The case of Michael 'Roy' Grove and his friends Ron and Gordon Newton, Gordon Vautier, Tom Renouf, Derek Hatch is described in the *Jersey Evening Post*, 4 January 1996.
73 JAS.D/Z/H6/9. Sentences and Prosecutions by the Field Command and Troop Courts: Joe Mière, Frank Le Pennec and David Dawson, sentenced for 'continual anti-German activities'.
74 Bunting, *The Model Occupation*, p. 200.
75 See for example IA.AQ 1212/098. Kenneth G. Lewis, 'Diary of Events 1940–1945', 5 September 1943; de Carteret et al., 'Diary of Mary Deslandes', 25 September 1944, 29 October 1944; Le Quesne, 28 July 1944; Bunting, *The Model Occupation*, p. 259, interviewed Stella Perkins, who had been involved.
76 See for example TNA.WO.208/3741 MI 19 (RPS)/2438. Interrogation of escapers who left Jersey on 20 September 1944, 2 October 1944; also Jenny Chamier Grove, 'Engineering an Escape', *Channel Islands Occupation Review*, Vol. 33, 2005, 23–34, here 31, 33 on comments by two escape parties.
77 Gray, 'Island of Beauty, Island of Secrets', see esp. pp. 38–40, used by kind permission of Mr Peter Gray.
78 JWT.Research Files Box 3. Arnold Bennett, handwritten prison note in the possession of Lucy Schwob.
79 Gray, 'Island of Beauty, Island of Secrets', pp. 51–3, used by kind permission of Mr Peter Gray; JAS.D/Z/H6/9. Duret Aubin to Cuming, record of sentences passed by the Gericht des Festungskommandants, 15 February 1945. The plotters included Peter Gray, Arnold Bennett, Bernard Carratu and Claude Saunders.
80 Henri Michel, *The Shadow War: Resistance in Europe 1939–1945*, London, The History Book Club, 1972, p. 219; also Moore, 'Comparing Resistance and Resistance Movements', p. 258; Peter Lagrou, 'Belgium', in B. Moore (ed.), *Resistance in Western Europe*, Oxford and New York, Berg, 2000, pp. 27–64, esp. p. 45.

81 The descriptions of Le Quesne, 27 October 1944; de Carteret et al., *Diary of Mary Deslandes*, 29 October 1944.
82 Described in 'Mob Law: Last Night's Regrettable Scenes', *Evening Post*, 11 May 1945, p. 1.
83 Bunting, *The Model Occupation*, p. 259.
84 'Mob Law: Last Night's Regrettable Scenes', *Evening Post*, 11 May 1945, p. 1: also Bailiff's appeal to Islanders not to take the law into their own hands.
85 *Evening Post*, 30 August 1945, p. 2.
86 TNA.WO.208/3741 MI 19 (RPS)/2438. Interrogation of escapers who left Jersey on 20 September 1944, 2 October 1944; also Keiller, *Prison without Bars*, p. 112.
87 See for example the material brought over by young escapers after D-Day, for example TNA.HO.144/22237 MI 19 (RPS)/2468, 21 October 1944: Report Jersey German Battle HQ, etc.
88 SJ.GO Box 10/33. Norman Le Brocq, transcript of talk to Channel Islands Occupation Society, 4 April 1988.
89 See for example Weithley, *So It Was*, p. 92; Keiller, *Prison without Bars*, pp. 111–13; Peter Gray, 'Island of Beauty, Island of Secrets', pp. 38–9, used by kind permission of Mr Peter Gray. Also Ron Smith, who photographed German aircraft, *Jersey Evening Post*, 24 November 1994, p. 14.
90 Keiller, *Prison without Bars*, pp. 111–13. See also Weithley, *So It Was*, p. 92.
91 Sanders, *The Ultimate Sacrifice*, p. 85; also commented on by Izett Croad: JAS.L/C/77/A/1. Izett Croad, Occupation Diary, 11 February 1943.
92 JAS.L/C/77/A/1. Izett Croad, Occupation Diary, 11 February 1943; de Carteret et al., 'Diary of Mary Deslandes', 6 June 1943.
93 JWT.Research Files Box 3. Ogier Family File. Letter from Richard's brother Kenneth Ogier to Joe Mière, 3 May 1987.
94 For more details see Sanders, *The Ultimate Sacrifice*, pp. 86–9.
95 Sinel, 30 August 1943; Sanders, *The Ultimate Sacrifice*, pp. 87–8.
96 SJ.*OCC 942 L'AM. J. H. L'Amy, The German Occupation of Jersey: 'Underground Movements', undated but written in 1945/46, p. 1.
97 William Gladden, account in *Evening Post*, 12 June 1945, p. 5.
98 SJ.*OCC 942 L'AM. J. H. L'Amy, The German Occupation of Jersey, undated but written in 1945/46, p. 2.
99 William Gladden, account in *Evening Post*, 12 June 1945, p. 5; SJ.*OCC 942 L'AM. J. H. L'Amy, The German Occupation of Jersey, undated but written in 1945/46, p. 4. See also Wood and Wood, *Islands in Danger*, pp. 164–5.
100 William Gladden, account in *Evening Post*, 12 June 1945, p. 5.
101 SJ.*OCC 942 L'AM. J. H. L'Amy, The German Occupation of Jersey, undated but written in 1945/46, p. 4. See also Hazel Knowles-Smith, *The Changing Face of the Channel Islands Occupation: Record, Memory and Myth*, Basingstoke, Palgrave Macmillan, 2007, pp. 196–7.
102 SJ.*OCC 942 L'AM. J. H. L'Amy, The German Occupation of Jersey, undated but written in 1945/46, p. 4; Wood and Wood, *Islands in Danger*, p. 165; Green was later imprisoned for failing to surrender his camera and radio: JAS.D/Z/H6/7. Sentences and Prosecutions by the Field Command and Troop Courts. Trial 48: Stanley George Green.
103 Wood and Wood, *Islands in Danger*, p. 165.
104 JAS.D/Z/H6/1. Court of FK 515 to Attorney General Duret Aubin, 26 September 1940. He had visited his wife illegally after her arrest in September 1940 for 'insulting the German army'.

105	SJ.*OCC 942 L'AM. J. H. L'Amy, The German Occupation of Jersey, undated but written in 1945/46, p. 4.
106	Audrey Falle, Slaves of the Third Reich: Jersey 1940–1945, no place of publication or publisher given, 1994, 29 April 1942; Sinel, 29 April 1942, 15 May 1943; Le Quesne, 17 May 1943.
107	William Gladden, account in Evening Post, 12 June 1945, p. 5; SJ.*OCC 942 L'AM. J. H. L'Amy, 'The German Occupation of Jersey', undated but written in 1945/46, p. 4.
108	William Gladden, account in Evening Post, 12 June 1945, p. 5: the group consisted of Luxon, Havard and the Le Gallais brothers.
109	'Deal With Quislings', Evening Post, 18 June 1945. They presented a petition to the States, but it was not acted upon.
110	SJ.*OCC 942 L'AM. J. H. L'Amy, The German Occupation of Jersey, undated but written in 1945/46, p. 20.
111	Knowles-Smith, p. 202; Sanders, *The British Channel Islands under German Occupation*, p. 110. For example Terry Sowden, the teenage son of the master mariner George Sowden, made several unsuccessful attempts.
112	See for example Daily Mail, 27 September 1940, p. 3 on the escape of eight Guernseymen including the 47-year old signalman Frederick Hockey and his three sons. Hockey's wife had already evacuated; also The Methodist Recorder, 10 October 1941, p. 3, on the comment by Wildred Duquemin, who escaped with Clifford Falla, who was rejoining his wife and daughters in England; also *Evening Post*, 12 July 1945, p. 3, on the escape by F. W. Burnett-Craigie, who had returned to Jersey on business and left to rejoin his wife and daughter in London.
113	The Methodist Recorder, 10 October 1940, p. 3.
114	JWT.Research Files Box 7. Mrs Doris Miles, Chichester, to Joe Mière, 27 May 1985, on the story of her mother May Clayton-Green.
115	Peter King, *The Channel Islands War 1940–1945*, London, Robert Hale, 1991, p. 99.
116	Sinel, 1 February 1941; JAS.M/28/2. Ralph Mollet, Occupation Diary, Volume 2, 1 February 1941–6 June 1943, 2 February 1941; JAS.L/C/77/A/1–8. Izett Croad, Occupation Diary, 3 February 1941; Le Quesne, 4 February 1941.
117	See for example Barry Turner, *Outpost of Occupation: How the Channel Islands Survived Nazi Rule 1940–1945*, London, Aurum Press Ltd., 2010, p. 138; Tabb, *A Peculiar Occupation*, pp. 112–13.
118	Not all the details can be verified: for instance, a couple named Kleinstein, said to have drowned in an escape attempt in March 1941.
119	TNA.HO.144/22834 Part 1 MI 19 (RPS)/1742. Interrogation of escapers from Guernsey, 23 August 1943, also with cutting from News of the World, 9 April 1944; IA.AQ 0368/01–11. Violet Carey, Occupation Diaries 1940–1945, 16 August 1943; also William Corbet's story, 'Guernsey Fisherman Escapes from German Occupied Island, 1943', contributed by Guernsey Museum, http://www.bbc.co.uk/history/ww2peopleswar/stories/78/a7749778.shtml, accessed 29 July 2013. See also IA FK 01–11. FK 515, Nebenstelle Guernsey to FK 515, Jersey, 18 August 1943.
120	TNA.HO.144/22834 Part 1 MI 19 (RPS)/1742. Interrogation of escapers from Guernsey, 23 August 1943.
121	JWT.Research Files Box 7. Letter from Frederick Troughton to Joe Mière, 10 February 1984: Troughton was aboard HMS Brocklesby; also *Daily Mirror*, 5 November 1941; TNA.HO.144/22831 Part 2: Cyril Winton, Bishop of Winchester, to Prime Minister, 25 November 1941. Also King, *The Channel Islands War 1940–1945*, p. 101.

122 TNA.HO.144/22831 Part 2. Cyril Winton, Bishop of Winchester, to Prime Minister, 25 November 1941; see also Bunting, *The Model Occupation*, p. 202. Also described in Wood and Wood, *Islands in Danger*, p. 137; King, *The Channel Islands War 1940–1945*, p. 101.
123 Sinel, 30 September 1941; see also IWM.Documents.2986. R. E. H. Fletcher, Diary, p. 122, October 1941; Le Ruez, 10 November 1941.
124 TNA.HO.144/22831 Part 2. Cyril Winton, Bishop of Winchester, to Prime Minister, 25 November 1941; Sanders, *The British Channel Islands under German Occupation*, pp. 27–8; Sanders, *The Ultimate Sacrifice*, p. 27; Hassall, 'Night and Fog Prisoners', pp. 41–2. He and his friends had 'little, or no, knowledge of navigation'.
125 Hassall, 'Night and Fog Prisoners', pp. 29–31.
126 Sanders, *The Ultimate Sacrifice*, p. 24.
127 Hassall, 'Night and Fog Prisoners', p. 42.
128 Gould's death is described by Hassall, 'Night and Fog Prisoners', pp. 164–5; see a detailed account in Sanders, *The Ultimate Sacrifice*, pp. 35–6.
129 See for example JAS.B/A/W50/55. Notice by Major-General Graf von Schmettow, 8 May 1942, after Audrain's death, threatening 'severe measures as a result of which the whole population will suffer'; Sinel, 9 May 1942; PL.LF940.53 LAI. Adèle Lainé, 'The German Occupation of Guernsey, 1940–1945', 17 August 1943, 23 August 1943.
130 de Carteret et al., 'Diary of Mary Deslandes', 26 October 1944.
131 IA.AQ 0380/03-01. Herbert Williams, Diary of Events, etc during the Occupation of Guernsey, from 30 June 1940 to 6 July 1945, here 15 August 1943.
132 Also see IWM.Documents.2986. R. E. H. Fletcher, Diary, October 1941, p. 122; Le Ruez, 10 November 1941; Le Quesne, 4 May 1942. Further comments in IA.AQ 0380/03-01. Herbert Williams, Diary of Events, etc during the Occupation of Guernsey, from 30 June 1940 to 6 July 1945, 12 June 1942, 1 July 1942.
133 TNA.HO.144/22834 Part 1. Jack Hubert, Private and Confidential: Guernsey, August 1943.
134 IA.AQ 0368/01-11. Violet Carey, Occupation Diaries 1940–1945, 19 August 1943.
135 The escape is outlined in Wood and Wood, *Islands in Danger*, pp. 264–6.
136 IWM.Documents.5727 96/32/1. Dr Alastair Rose, Impressions of the Occupation of Guernsey, written by Dr. Alastair Rose between 1944 & 1945, pp. 30–2; V. V. Cortvriend, *Isolated Island*, Guernsey, Guernsey Star and Gazette, 1945, p. 298.
137 Roy Thomas, *Lest We Forget: Escapes and Attempted Escapes from Jersey during the German Occupation 1940–1945*, Jersey, La Haule, 1992, pp. 101–17.
138 *Evening Post*, 16 June 1945, p. 6; JAS.L/C/24/C/9. 'The Dennis Le Cuirot Story'.
139 JAS.L/C/24/C/8. 'The Colleen Querée Story'; *Evening Post*, 9 July 1945, p. 3.
140 JAS.B/A/W30/13/176. Platzkommandant, Major Heider, to Bailiff Coutanche, 28 November 1944.
141 TNA.HO.144/22237 MI 19 (RPS)/2510. Further interrogation of three Jersey escapers, 27 November 1944; see also Sanders, *The British Channel Islands under German Occupation*, p. 178.
142 Thomas, *Lest We Forget*, p. 123.
143 Keiller, *Prison without Bars*, p. 49; see also Turner, *Outpost of Occupation*, pp. 193–4.
144 TNA.HO.144/22237 MI 19 (RPS)/2468. Interrogation of men leaving 9 October 1944, 21 October 1944; according to Thomas, *Lest We Forget*, p. 3, Denis Vibert bought his boat.
145 Peter Crill, 'The Story of an Escape from Jersey', *Société Jersiaise Bulletin*, Vol. 24, 1985–1988, 107–12, here 107.

146 Thomas, *Lest We Forget*, p. 24, on the attempt by Belza Turner and the Dutchman Siebe Kosta; another stolen boat was the failed attempt by Costard, McLinton and Webb in October 1944: Sinel, 21 October 1944.
147 See Gladden's account in *Evening Post*, 12 June 1945, p. 5; also story of the escape on p. 1 of the same issue: 'How Brave Men Dared and Fooled Germans'; also SJ.*OCC 942 L'AM. J. H. L'Amy, 'The German Occupation of Jersey', undated but written in 1945/46, pp. 17–18.
148 Hassall, 'Night and Fog Prisoners', p. 38.
149 SJ.OCC 942 CHA. Albert Alfred Chardine, reminiscences taped by his daughter Colette Chardine and transcribed, 1995, pp. 9–10; Hassall, 'Night and Fog Prisoners', pp. 40–1.
150 Thomas, *Lest We Forget*, pp. 70–1. PC Chardine provided the petrol for Hassall's escape bid.
151 Letter from René Havard to Joe Mière, 27 September 1987, Joe Mière Archive, Mière family.
152 Thomas, *Lest We Forget*, pp. 70–1; letter from René Havard to Joe Mière, 27 September 1987, Joe Mière Archive, Mière family; Crill, The Story of an Escape from Jersey', 107.
153 Thomas, *Lest We Forget*, p. 16.
154 Sinel, 14 November 1944, 17 November 1944; Thomas, *Lest We Forget*, p. 89.
155 Thomas, *Lest We Forget*, pp. 95–6.
156 Sinel, 29 November 1944; Thomas, *Lest We Forget*, pp. 95–6.
157 Interview with Michael Neil, 13 August 2012.
158 Dennis Vibert had been a merchant navy cadet; Harry Macfarlane was an engineer in the merchant navy; Peter Crill had his own dinghy.
159 See for example letter 'Escapees' thanks', from Kenneth Jesty and Basil Machon, *Evening Post*, 6 June 1945, p. 1; also *Evening Post*, 26 May 1945, p. 1; Halliwell, *Operating under Occupation*, pp. 116–17; Keiller, *Prison without Bars*, p. 115.
160 Thomas, *Lest We Forget*, p. 124.
161 See for example ibid., p. 56, on the help given by Guiton to the Macfarlane, Huelin and Woods party; Francis Le Sueur, *Shadow of the Swastika. Could It All Happen Again?*, Guernsey, Guernsey Press Co. Ltd., 1992, p. 49, on Bob La Cloche; and interview with Michael Neil, 13 August 2010, on Silver Le Riche. On the involvement of Syd Le Clerq in a number of escapes from Fauvic, see *Evening Post*, 26 May 1945, p. 6.
162 *Evening Post*, 28 October 1941, p. 1.
163 Hassall, 'Night and Fog Prisoners', p. 26.
164 JAS.D/Z/H6/2. Sentences and Prosecutions by the Field Command and Troop Courts: George Sowden; 'Occupation Experiences of Captain George Henry Sowden', used by kind permission of the Sowden family.
165 JAS.B/A/W31/3/5. George Sowden to Bailiff Coutanche, 5 September 1941; *Evening Post*, 18 October 1941. He gave information, among others, to Denis Vibert, Eric Hamon and Peter Hassall. Interview with Terry Sowden, Patrick Sowden and Ros Rice, 12 August 2010; also Thomas, *Lest We Forget*, p. 52; Keiller, *Prison without Bars*, pp. 48–9.
166 Interview with Terry Sowden, Patrick Sowden and Ros Rice, 12 August 2010; Hassall, 'Night and Fog Prisoners', pp. 41–2. He would not shake hands with German soldiers, but felt honour-bound to intervene with the British authorities on behalf of a German officer who had helped his daughter after an accident.

167 *Evening Post*, 26 May 1945, p. 6; King, *The Channel Islands War 1940–1945*, p. 100; Le Sueur, *Shadow of the Swastika*, p. 92.
168 Thomas, *Lest We Forget*, pp. 123–6; for details of some of the escapes see *Evening Post*, 26 May 1945, p. 1.
169 Cruickshank, *The German Occupation of the Channel Islands*, pp. 157–8.
170 TNA.HO.144/22834 Part 1 MI 19 (RPS)/2122. On an escape from Alderney on 8 April, 12 April 1944.
171 Comment made by Crill in IWM.Sound Archive.Interview 11096. Peter Leslie Crill, 1990; see also Crill, The Story of an Escape from Jersey', 107–12; Thomas, *Lest We Forget*, p. 45. Many joined the force, including Roy Mourant, John Floyd, David Blandin, Basil Le Brun, Douglas Davey, Bernard Cavey, Eddie Le Corre, Victor Huelin, Robert Woods, Alex Renouf, Kenneth Parris, Michael Price, George Le Couteur, René Havard, Peter Desvergez. *Evening Post*, 18 May 1945, p. 1; 31 May 1945, p. 1; 22 June 1945, pp. 3, 4; Thomas, passim. Also William Gladden, account in the *Evening Post*, 12 June 1945, p. 5; Thomas, *Lest We Forget*, pp. 118–20.
172 TNA.WO.208/3741 MI 19 (RPS)/2438. Interrogation of escapers who left Jersey on 20 September 1944, 2 October 1944.
173 Of 67 locals who attempted escape from Jersey after D-Day and whose birthdates have been confirmed, 59 were 25 years of age or younger: Jersey Identification Cards, JAS.D/S/A/ files. On the average age of maquisards, see Ian Ousby, *Occupation: The Ordeal of France*, London, Pimlico, 1999, pp. 256–7.
174 Bunting, *The Model Occupation*, p. 200.
175 Ibid., p. 199.
176 For example the case of Frank Le Villio, in Sanders, *The Ultimate Sacrifice*, pp. 83–5. Brought up without parental guidance, Le Villio was deported to Neuengamme and then Bergen-Belsen. He died in 1946. Also the case of Tony Faramus, described in his autobiography, *Journey into Darkness*, London, Grafton, 1990.
177 JWT.Research Files Box 7. Letter from Bernard Cavey to Joe Mière, undated.
178 JAS.D/Z/H6/6. Sentences and Prosecutions by the Field Command and Troop Courts: Bernard James Turpin, sentenced to a week in prison for attempted larceny; interview with Bernard Turpin, 14 August 2010.
179 JAS.D/Z/H6/7. Sentences and Prosecutions by the Field Command and Troop Courts: Bernard Turpin, born 8 September 1925, sentenced for 'disturbing the working peace', disobedience and insulting the occupying forces. 'Disturbing the working peace' was used for a variety of misdemeanours, including refusal to work for the Germans or encouraging others to refuse.
180 Interview with Bernard Turpin, 14 August 2010.
181 Victoria College Register, 1930–1956, information provided by Tony Bellows.
182 Keiller, *Prison without Bars*, p. 13. See also similar comments by Hassall, 'Night and Fog Prisoners', pp. 8, 12. Hassall had recently left De La Salle.
183 Cahun, *Écrits*, p. 633.
184 See also Schwob's memories of their patriotism, ibid., pp. 721–2, 743–4.
185 The phrase was used, for example, by William Gladden, account in *Evening Post*, 12 June 1945, p. 5; SJ.*OCC 942 L'AM. John H. L'Amy, The German Occupation of Jersey, undated but written in 1945/46: L'Amy spoke of the 'St Martin's Underground Movement' and of 'underground movements' in general. Also Gray, 'Island of Beauty, Island of Secrets', p. 40, used by kind permission of Mr Peter Gray.

9

The Peculiarities of Being under the Swastika and the Crown: Officials and Their Resistance

Paul Sanders

The Nazi Occupation in the Second World War is acknowledged as a defining juncture and an important identity-building experience throughout contemporary Europe. Civilian disobedience, defiance and resistance is what 'saves' European societies from an otherwise chequered record of collaboration on the part of their economic, political, cultural and religious elites. Opposition to Nazism took pride of place as a legitimizing device and as a focus of reconciliation in the post-war world. Although historians have questioned the exclusive claims of the resistance paradigm, the latter remains an indelible part of the collective consciousness and public discourse.

Among the previously occupied territories, one bucks the trend: the British Channel Islands. Here collective identity construction still relies on the notion of 'orderly and correct relations' with the occupier, while talk of 'resistance' earns raised eye-brows. The general attitude to those resisters who existed in the islands remains ambiguous. This stance is justified through the allegedly benign character of the Occupation. Opposition – thus the argument – was not only unnecessary; it was also foolish or irresponsible, as it exposed the wider population to the risk of reprisals. Accordingly, it could only have been the handiwork of a delusional minority. Recent studies on the persecution of Jewish islanders and on atrocities against forced workers or islanders on the 'wrong' side of occupation law have put this argument into perspective.[1] In an absolute sense the Channel Islands Occupation was anything but benign. What is it then that prevents genuine acts of heroism from receiving the recognition they deserve, almost seven decades after the end of the Second World War?

In order to get to the bottom of this question, it is of paramount importance to take a good look at the islands' elites. Over the past two decades, the wartime activities of Channel Islands officials and other members of the local elites have generally been interpreted as a more or less nuanced form of collaboration. Some will remark that it is odd for a chapter on administrative resistance, in a book on resistance, to begin with a discussion of collaboration. Others might say that 'administrative resistance' is an oxymoron, and therefore not worth the historian's trouble. Both these assertions are incorrect. First of all, the neat categorical separation of resistance and collaboration is artificial. If one needed a categorical term to frame the reality of administering in occupied Europe, then 'dilemma' would be the more appropriate one. Secondly, the local administrations of the Channel Islands were not monoliths, but accommodated various personalities who could be more or less resistance-minded (and vice-versa as regards collaboration). Considering this dynamic, the act of 'filing' a social group into a neat category is inequitable. Its lop-sidedness emerges in clearer profile when we consider that both positions (resistance and collaboration) were legitimate up to a certain point, and that the precise breaking points where legitimacy was lost or won are difficult to define. Matters of life and death such as the ones we have to grapple with here complexify moral quandaries and cloud perception (this is not intended as an excuse; serious errors and abuses were committed).

The overall ambition of this chapter then is to deconstruct the black-and-white dichotomy that has dominated historiography. For this we will take some cues from Primo Levi's *The Drowned and the Saved*.[2] Although Levi was chiefly concerned with cases of 'collaboration' in the extreme context of the Jewish ghettoes and the camps, his reflections also apply elsewhere. Levi takes particular aim at 'a certain hagiographic and rhetorical stylisation', which one can detect in the heroic narratives of the immediate post-war era. These narratives could not deal with the ambiguity of the period. They approached their subject with a tendency to operate neat distinctions between good and evil, but, at the same time, glossed over the fact that 'the harsher the oppression, the more widespread among the oppressed [...] the willingness to collaborate'. In Levi's analysis heroic bias in approaching collaboration was a falsehood, as the Nazi system tried to bind complicities by compromising its victims and burdening them with guilt:[3]

> (A)n infernal order such as National Socialism [...] exercises a frightful power of corruption, against which it is difficult to guard oneself. It degrades its victims and makes them similar to itself, because it needs both great and small complicities.[4]

In a chapter titled 'The grey zone', Levi spoke of the *impotentia judicandi*, the imprudence 'to hasten to issue a moral judgment'. Levi himself was prepared to absolve all individuals 'whose concurrence in the guilt was minimal and for whom coercion was of the highest degree', for, in his view, responsibility lay with the system. Circumstances were extenuating.[5] In the light of Levi's remarks on the 'grey zone', we will ask whether a leader who gets his community through hard times should be admired (rather than despised), even if this requires him to 'dirty his hands'.

The rationale for a collaboration narrative

A collaboration narrative of the Channel Islands Occupation is most unequivocally formulated in *The Model Occupation*, a book published by the *Guardian* journalist Madeleine Bunting in 1995. Whereas the post-war consensus had argued that neither resistance nor collaboration had been necessary, due to the mediation of islands officials and German respect for 'correct relations', Bunting's thesis was that of voluntary, deliberate collaboration and fraternization. Rather than there having been 'no need' for resistance, Bunting held that islanders could (i.e. should) have resisted more, but chose not to do so.[6] Among the new evidence presented by Bunting was a particularly damaging file detailing 'measures against the Jews'. Significantly, this paperwork was not of German, but of island provenience. In this, as in other areas, islanders collaborated with the occupier.[7]

One important interpretive act in assessing collaboration is to check for margins, i.e. the limited sphere in which action was possible. 'Margins' as a measuring device tally with 'fair share' principles, according to which responsibility is proportionate to one's ability to leverage and influence outcomes.[8] Across occupied Europe margins were subject to variable geometries. They were particularly wide in the framework of the power-sharing agreements established in indirect occupation regimes, where national governments continued to function and were able to instruct officials. In these types of regimes German interference was limited to security and policy initiatives and formal oversight of the local administration, rather than the routine issuing of direct orders to administrators in occupied lands. In parallel, the German authorities could avail themselves of the rights of the occupying power, bypass national governments and issue their own orders to the local administration, but this had a specific political cost, as it could cause an upset with the respective national government. This description fits the case of France and Denmark, but also the microstates of the occupied Channel Islands.

What does a discussion of margins in the context of the Channel Islands Occupation amount to? In the early days of the Occupation the Germans offered guarantees that no harm would befall the lives and property of Channel Islanders, if they abstained from acts of hostility. However, the understanding that the mutual relationship could be based on 'correctness' was not grounded in the reality of the Nazi regime or wartime emergency. After a brief 'honeymoon', the situation eroded in a way as to significantly diminish the leverage of the local authorities, in particular in Guernsey. Although a trigger was not necessary to bring out the genuine face of Nazi rule, the fact that the British military started sending raiding parties to Guernsey, almost immediately after the German arrival, did not help things. These repeat 'visits' were conducted in a very amateurish manner and they raised German suspicion that islanders were scheming behind their backs. When one of these missions failed to repatriate two agents, native Guernseymen Hubert Nicolle and James Symes, the latter were hidden by the population for six weeks. Having received German assurances that no reprisal action would be taken, they surrendered in mid-October 1940. The German side then reneged on its promise, arresting and incarcerating over a dozen civilians connected to the two officers – among them Ambrose Sherwill, the Attorney General of Guernsey. If the affair came to a relatively lenient conclusion in December, then it created a debt towards the Germans that islanders would have to repay. It also bolstered the position of those islanders who felt that in the future an even more activist stance in cooperating with the Germans was necessary in order to avoid friction. Thus was created a 'marketplace' for tactical bargaining.[9] The blackmail potential of the situation was compounded by the islands' dependence on German assistance for shipping essential supplies from France.

It would certainly be wrong to insist that granting tactical concessions is always a bad strategy for small communities. The Channel Islands' administrations did not have the depth and resources to fight a steady course of institutional resistance. Their principal hope lay in taking advantage of the German willingness to engage. One direct result of tactical bargaining was the registering of German orders into the laws of the islands, something the islanders were under no obligation to do, but went ahead with when they felt that the issue in question was not worth spoiling relations for. Sometimes, however, utilitarian 'greater good' reasoning could overshoot the mark. It is particularly objectionable where it involves selectivity in the application of the rules of the game. We can see such selectivity at work in the authorities' interventions on behalf of certain 'in-groups', which owed more to social differentiation or community fault-lines than to duress.[10]

A good illustration of the application of greater good ethics in the context of the Occupation is the case of Frederick Page, a Jerseyman reported to the Germans for a 'wireless offence' in spring 1943. Significantly, the information leading to Page's arrest did not originate from a denunciation, but was surrendered by the island police. Tried by a German court, Page was deported to Germany, where he died in 1945.[11] As so often, the local police chanced upon this information while investigating a different case. When they followed it up, they discovered three wireless sets at the home of a James Davey, two of which were the property of Frederick Page.[12] The police now faced a dilemma: since the passing of a specific German order in late 1942 they, as all officials, were obliged to surrender all information bearing a relation to infractions of German regulations. Submitting such a report, however, would lead to the prosecution of a fellow islander. The alternative was for the police to do nothing and run the risk of being themselves denounced; a risk that was high, as the original tip-off had come from the population and the discovery of the wirelesses was public knowledge. The officer in charge, Centenier Garden, then made an informal approach to the Attorney General, Charles Duret Aubin, who later testified[13] that Garden 'was gravely disturbed in his own mind as to what action he should take'.[14] Duret Aubin advised that he could not 'give him an order one way or the other in a matter into which considerations of conscience entered so strongly', and that Garden 'must decide with his own conscience where his duty lay'. He added, however, that if he did receive a formal police report he would have 'no alternative but to forward it' to the Germans. When Garden put the matter to his colleagues their unanimous opinion was that their duty was to the community rather than to the individual, and that he should report.[15] The Attorney General received Garden's report on 2 June 1943, which he then forwarded to the Germans.

Moral philosophy takes the line that an agent forced to make a decision in the face of a dilemma which has arisen in a manner beyond his control, can claim diminished moral responsibility.[16] This axiom does not hold, however, when a dilemma is partially or entirely self-made. The question here is whether 'sacrificing' groups or individuals to safeguard the 'greater good' could have been avoided through better foresight. If there was nothing the authorities could do to prevent the June 1942 wireless confiscation, obliging them to assist in the prosecution and punishment of 'radio crimes', acts that constituted no offence under the laws of the islands, went a step too far. Considering that the authorities of Jersey had protested against the wireless confiscation, it would have been only logical for them to decline all support in the prosecution of radio offenders. This, however, they did not consider.

The pitfalls of the collaboration narrative

Distasteful as crude bargaining, the inability to foresee consequences and a lack of steadfastness are in retrospect, Channel Islands collaboration was tame stuff compared to what was going on in other parts of Europe. Most of this 'collaboration' was more a result of the routine operation of government than of any particular willingness to support the Nazi occupier. Clearly, Channel Islanders never 'collaborated' in the common sense of the term. Although the authorities were embroiled in the prosecution of radio offenders from 1942, they never tried to persuade their fellow islanders that what they were hearing on British radio was propaganda.[17]

The other problem with 'collaboration' is definitional, as the term relates to many different phenomena. If in some cases collaboration operated on the level of the state, in others it was limited to the police, economic, ideological, administrative or private spheres. Also several types of collaboration existed: heart-and-soul collaboration, shield philosophy, conditional collaboration, tactical collaboration, submission on the grounds of superior force and wait-and-see collaboration (*attentisme*).[18] Seen through this prism, collaboration in the Channel Islands was largely the result of 'submission on the grounds of superior force'.

An even more valid objection against emphasizing 'collaboration' is that the latter is only one part of a much wider story. Relying on a collaboration narrative does no more justice to the genuine complexity of the period than relying on a narrative of resistance. The problem with these claims is that they miss out entirely on what is probably the *key* feature of the entire period, the 'grey zone'. And it is this 'grey zone' that complicates the task of assessing the behaviour of Europeans in the face of the Nazi challenge. It explains how some wartime officials could literally get away with aiding and abetting murder, while others who did nothing more controversial than letting their civic sense prevail, paid a much higher price. Because binary opposites eradicate the 'grey zone', current historiography prefers neither of the two 'totalist' narratives ('resistance' or 'collaboration'). In his monograph on Vichy France Julian Jackson belies any neat categorizations, by enumerating the strange hybrid behaviours he encountered while studying the wartime French. Rather than clear-cut archetypes, what Jackson found were anti-Semitic resistance fighters, philo-Semitic Vichy officials or Pétaino-resisters.[19]

These fundamental issues underpin some of the dead ends in Bunting's *Model Occupation*. Focusing on collaboration entailed selectiveness in the treatment of the available material. This first *faux pas* was compounded by a second, the heavy interpretive bias that was slanted onto unreliable sources. Contrary to what the book suggested, the 'real' collaboration of islanders was not the pivotal focus of interest.

What the book was *really* interested in was the hypothetical collaboration of mainland Britons with Nazi Germany. A second criticism must concern the book's insufficient regard to the historiographical state-of-the-art. One example of this was its advocacy of the anachronistic model of active or armed resistance as the most 'worthy' form of resistance, a misconception further compounded by the author's inability to put the various forms of passive resistance into the appropriate context.[20] Also, beginning with the mid-1990s, most historians started to dismiss the previous soul-searching about collaboration in favour of a pragmatic assumption that a certain measure of *it* was probably inevitable.[21] The general reorientation led to a more differentiated and nuanced portrayal of Channel Islanders: as accommodators and survivors, in their majority; and as victims themselves at times.[22]

Finally, the moral absolutism of the collaboration emphasis fits uneasily with the anachronism of judging the past by today's standards of political correctness. The thing that emerges, of course, is that rationalizing human behaviour in a situation of high complexity through the means of a moralistic measuring stick is an interpretive dead-end. What is needed is a systemic, objective (or 'a-moral') variable. This quest has diverted much attention towards the idea that social actors and entities alike act in conformity with a political, legal and constitutional 'regime' whose rules and norms they respect. Nobody can be condemned for being a conformist and not going against the grain, however desirable dissidence may be in some circumstances. As regards, for example, resistance, individuals can only be reasonably expected to engage in such unusual, anti-systemic behaviour, if the legitimacy of the rule or regime to which they are subject has been answered in the unequivocally negative. Rather than approaching the subject through the relativistic (and, ultimately, unanswerable) prism of individual or collective culpability, legitimacy helps in understanding how officials, citizens and others could realistically be expected to behave.[23]

Environment and institutions: The unique context of the Channel Islands Occupation

Having investigated the pitfalls of the collaboration narrative, the sections that follow will demonstrate how the frameworks of environmental conditioning and legitimacy can widen our understanding of resistance and collaboration during the Channel Islands Occupation.

One of the most important specifics of the Channel Islands Occupation was that there was zero scope for armed or military resistance. An MI5 report, written in 1945, stated that the islanders enjoyed 'none of the advantages of space or comparative freedom of action which have nourished the resistance movement on the mainland. It is difficult to be obstructive with impunity within parochial limits'.[24] This view was adopted by later writers, such as the British resistance scholar M. R. D. Foot. If it was impossible to comb France in its entirety, then the same was imminently possible in these islands, where, proportionately, there were more Germans per square mile of islands than in Germany herself.

Secondly, in order to become a force to be reckoned with, resistance in Europe required Allied support. The necessary condition for such a build-up was a political or military objective (or both) that was worth such a risk. In the Channel Islands no such objective existed. They had no strategic, merely prestige, value, and they were too heavily fortified to warrant any build-up of resistance.[25] Pursuing any kind of political objective in the islands would have been an equally serious mistake.[26]

While the context was extremely unfavourable to armed or military resistance, the potential for non-violent civilian resistance in the islands was higher. The first of the favourable contingencies was the fact that establishing a strong German foothold in the islands was impeded by a window of opportunity that was too short. The dashing of German hopes of a speedy victory over Britain in 1940 plus persistent British resistance convinced many Channel Islanders that the motherland's cause was far from lost. As a result, rare were those who seriously contemplated Germany winning the war.[27] Islanders had their prewar norms to fall back onto; norms that were nourished by the continued reception and spreading of British radio news. 'Winning hearts and minds', one of the objectives of German occupation policy, therefore never got off the ground. And even the little that German propaganda efforts may have achieved in the islands was quickly undone by the maltreatment of the foreign forced and slave labourers brought to the islands for fortification work from 1942. After witnessing an atrocity in February 1943 Edward Le Quesne, a prominent Jerseyman and member of the Superior Council, commented in his diary:

> Some of us had imagined that the tales we heard of similar atrocities in Russia were simply for propaganda purposes [...] Even those who have sympathised with Jerry can hardly do so after witnessing this or similar scenes.[28]

Another important contingency was Hitler's wish that islanders be treated with more consideration than the inhabitants of other occupied territories.[29] Thus within the East–West gradient of the Nazi Empire, the islands found themselves at the benign end. This unique status is visible in the fact that, although there were such condemnations, no death sentence was executed against an islander in any of the islands. Some of this no doubt owed to the realization that any wrongdoing had the potential to backfire against Germans in Allied-controlled areas.[30] One good example of such scruples was the successful blocking, by the German Foreign Office, of military calls to remove the bulk of the civilian population from the islands. And, for reasons that have remained unelucidated, the execution of a 1941 order by Hitler himself, earmarking certain categories of islanders for deportation to German internment camps, was delayed for almost one year.[31] The second explanation of why islanders were treated differently is cultural. John Leale, the second president of the Guernsey Controlling Committee, confirmed that the Germans were not indifferent about what islanders thought of them,[32] and that the German attitude could have ripened into something 'warmer', had Channel Islanders wished for it.[33]

Finally, island society was also more cohesive, and therefore better armoured to withstand an onslaught of this magnitude, as their institutions remained intact. One of the results of this disposition was that Channel Islanders showed none of the signs of defeatism or political blame games common in occupied Europe at this time.[34] As we have seen, the administration of these territories continued along prewar lines. Their robustness was such that they would also be the *only* collaborating administrations in the whole of occupied Europe that remained in office in the post-war era. Two repositories that avoided the kind of ideological drift that was characteristic of other occupied nations were constitutional continuity and the link with the British Crown. With the state of war between Britain and Germany continuing, islanders still had an outside power they could refer to, and whose legitimacy remained intact. Contrary to, say, France, the occupation of the islands was not the result of an armistice with wide political implications, but of a reversible withdrawal on purely military grounds. And although British prestige took a severe beating in June 1940, it remained intact. Islanders could avail themselves of precisely this prestige in order to garner leverage. Leale himself used this screen to try to shame individual Germans into sticking to their promises, a tactic that he writes 'did not always work'.[35] Holding on to the relationship with the Crown was not only dictated by sentiment and tradition, but also by plain self-interest. Both the native elite and the general public sensed that the fortification of the islands was a forewarning of the German desire to retain the islands as war booty, even in the event of a compromise peace.[36] As islanders witnessed daily, German rule equalled loss of status and rights, and reduced them to foreigners in their own land. An Allied victory was the only conceivable way to re-establish the islands' autonomy.

The Janus face of legitimacy

If cohesion was good, why did this not translate into more spectacular outpourings of institutional or administrative resistance? This question puts into perspective the flip-side of the solidity of the islands' institutions. On the one hand, they protected against drift, but, on the other, they diffused a conformism which neutralized opposition. Conformism is deeply inscribed in island culture. The Germans themselves noticed this feature, commenting, for example, that there had never been any need for the Sark prison in its 50 years of existence.[37] During the Occupation social conformism was reinforced by the authorities' decision to avoid anything susceptible to provoke the occupier. The bedrock of this conformist occupation government was the 'permanency' of the law, and this in turn was influenced by the idea of the continuity of the legal-constitutional order. The conviction that the 'law was the law', no matter what the consequences, took legal positivism to dizzying heights. 'Rule worship' found its most potent expression in the islands' authorities' over-reliance on the legal foundation of the Occupation, the Hague Convention. Of the latter John Leale stated that it best safeguarded islanders' 'rights and interests as British people'.[38] This quasi-religious faith was not quite deserved: the Convention represented a lukewarm international minimum standard of rules of engagement, on whose agenda protection of civilians did not figure very highly.[39] As a consequence, a large amount of legal space requiring definition remained void, enabling an occupier to bestow upon the Hague rules the interpretation that best suited him. While the Convention required civilians to abstain from hostile acts against the occupying authority, it also placed upon the occupier an obligation of proportionality. However, the punishment that minor manifestations of popular discontent could elicit was anything but proportional. Likewise the Hague rules placed a burden on the occupier not to punish the community for the acts of individuals. Again this provision was routinely dispensed with, through an invocation of 'military necessity' or 'necessity of war'.[40] Finally, sticking to the Hague rules could undermine the civilian leadership, as it could look like assisting the enemy.[41] As the Nicolle-Symes affair demonstrates, it could also give a false feeling of security.

There was another problem with taking an inelastic stance with regard to the application of the law in this particular situation: neither did it take into account the volatility of the environment, nor the fact that the islands' authorities were dealing with an occupier who had no interest in an equitable rule of law. In their attempt to maintain the formal aspects of law and order, the islands' authorities often no longer asked whether their fiction still conformed to a certain idea of Britishness. Over time, however, it became apparent that German rule eclipsed characteristic attributes of Britishness within the islands' polities, such as the right to a fair trial. Other 'crimes and misdemeanours' punished under the occupation regime, such as not registering as a Jew or listening to one's radio, bore no link to justice at all, this was Nazi law. All this widened the perceived gap between law and justice, and sapped the authorities' legitimacy. The emergence of such a legitimacy deficit mirrored developments elsewhere.

The German occupiers lost any legitimacy they may have had to begin with relatively quickly. What remained of legitimacy was vested – to a greater or lesser extent – in the collaborating governments or rump administrations who continued to work under the indirect or direct instructions of the occupying authorities; or simply in the exiled governments (example: Norway), most of which operated out of London. Often, however, the association of collaborating governments and elites with the German occupier entailed a rapid loss of legitimacy – if they had had any to begin with – and the meteoric rise of movements of opposition who now contested the legitimacy vacuum. In the islands, the battle for legitimacy was less vociferous than in other parts of Europe, but no less real for that. A substantial minority within the islands' communities drew different conclusions from the experience of catering to German whims, which they felt provoked islanders into spirals of pre-emptive obedience, and demanded a sterner attitude on the part of the islands' authorities. They differed from the official appreciation of what constituted correct, due and proper behaviour, and judged the general line pusillanimously. This new constituency faced off a larger majority who were unfavourably disposed to anything likely to irritate the Germans, and amenable to giving in to their demands. The public opinion shift and legitimacy watershed of the second half of 1942 turned the tables on this majority. In the wake of the wireless confiscation, the arrival of the forced workers and the deportations of civilians to internment camps an increasing number of people became, in principle, more favourably disposed to opposition.[42] The legitimacy of the islands' authorities was now vested in the ability to navigate a median course between the Scylla of compliance and the Charybdis of patriotism calling for 'something to be done'. To this calling they rose extremely hesitatingly, if at all, and this created a legitimacy gap. That so much faith continued to be placed in formal rules is a direct result of the maintenance of the political fiction of the continuity of British law – and of a good working constitutional order – and that despite Nazi overlordship. The islands' unwritten constitutions magnified this effect. The argument was summarized by William H. Arnold, the Guernsey Procureur, in 1952.[43] Arnold saw no reason to question the notion that the enemy had adhered to the Hague Convention. The backbone of his reasoning rested on the fact that the occupier had attempted no formal annexation of the islands' institutions. And because island courts did not cease to be the King's Courts, their wartime rulings were no less valid than their peacetime rulings. On this matter the legal position taken in Jersey was identical:

> During the whole of the Occupation the substantive law applied in the administration of criminal and civil justice by the Insular Courts [sic] was the law as it was before the Occupation. Legislative measures taken by the Occupying Authority [sic] effected no change in the civil and criminal law of the Island [sic] and in the result, therefore, the Judgments of the Insular Courts [sic] pronounced during the Occupation were, upon Liberation, accepted as valid and binding.[44]

This line of argument continues to this very day. It leaves entirely unanswered whether the King's Courts were still able to uphold the King's Law, free from the political pressure of the occupying power. The opposite case was outlined by the *Feldkommandantur* in 1942. Arguing that the Crown was no longer able to exercise her prerogative, the executive powers of the Guernsey authorities during the Occupation derived from the occupying power.[45] The Privy Council followed this argument in a ruling of 1952, confirming that the Crown's sovereign rights over the islands were suspended during the Occupation.[46] Nevertheless, the legal 'Absurdistan' of the post-war period led to a situation where it became possible to argue the maintenance of British law and order during the Occupation; and, at the same time, its exact opposite. The British government became an unwitting accomplice in this scheme, for the continued administration of the islands could be presented as a consequence of the 'advice' given to the islanders in June 1940. If the question of legitimacy was so convoluted, then it was because the UK government had given the islands' authorities *carte blanche*.

A tale of two islands

We will now turn to how the authorities in both islands filled the room for manoeuvre granted by their respective environments and how they interpreted the legitimacy issue. The question is worth asking because of the conspicuous differences that emerged in the leadership style in both islands. One of these differences was the paternalistic, sometimes even patronizing rhetoric and tone that characterized official communications with the general population in Guernsey. Another was the passing into Guernsey legislation of an Order requiring Jews to wear a six-pointed yellow star, in June 1942. It has to be said that this order was also submitted to the civilian authorities of Jersey, where it was rejected.[47] Finally, the little active resistance there was in the islands generally had a harder time gaining a foothold in Guernsey than in Jersey.

Table 9.1 Billeting of German soldiers (1942)[48]

	Jersey	Guernsey
Private properties	6,503	10,800
Hotels and boarding houses	4,285	1,240

The first, environmental factor one must consider in order to account for difference between both islands was Guernsey's more pronounced strategic position. This exposed the island more fully to the vagaries of the conflict. Throughout the Occupation the island's strategic value would attract attention from both sides. As a result Guernsey was more heavily fortified than Jersey. The island also played host to the German military staff headquarters, a fact that 'militarized' relations with the civilian population. Between mid-1941 and late 1943 the island had to accommodate a constant stream of soldiers and foreign labourers that often outnumbered the 25,000 civilian residents.[49] The smaller size of the Guernsey tourism industry (compared to Jersey) meant that fewer hotel rooms were available for military use and that more civilian dwellings had to be requisitioned (Table 9.1).

Not all the soldiers arriving in Guernsey could find quarters in the vacant dwellings of islanders who had evacuated in 1940, and were therefore billeted within private properties that were still occupied. An even worse scenario was eviction. Many of these took place in 1941–2, and they were synonymous with outright plunder.[50] Guernsey was also disadvantaged from an economic point of view, as the challenge of converting the island economy to self-sufficiency was less smooth than in Jersey. Other environmental factors impacting on Guernsey were its centralized police system, and the fact that this came under tight German supervision in 1942. On the whole Guernsey officials had less negotiation margin than their Jersey counterparts, as they could not call on the German civil affairs unit, headquartered in Jersey, to act as an intermediary.

Environmental and institutional factors do not explain all. Guernsey's more unfavourable environment was a necessary, but not a sufficient condition in explaining how the island travelled somewhat further down the slippery slope of collaboration than her sister island.[51] Equally important was the erosion of social capital. This began to take shape during that fateful week in June 1940, when 40 per cent of the civilian population of Guernsey evacuated to England. Overwhelmed by the swift and sudden fall of France, the British government had wavered for a long time as to what was to be done about the population of the Channel Islands. When they finally suggested evacuation, on 19 June 1940, panic ensued, as the orders that reached people were worded in a way as to suggest that evacuation was mandatory. In Jersey the Bailiff, Alexander Coutanche, then decided to make a public declaration, stating that he (and his wife) would not leave the island, which calmed the waves: out of the 23,000 Jersey residents initially registered for evacuation (total population: 50,000), only 6,600 would eventually leave, and the population structure of the island was to retain its prewar character. Meanwhile, in Guernsey, the authorities failed to make a similar show of sangfroid. Relying on conflicting advice, they first encouraged islanders to remain, only to change track sometime later. None of this could have reassured islanders,

17,000 of whom (total population: 42,000) left the island.[52] Although positive from a public health point of view, the compulsory evacuation of four-fifths of the Guernsey child population was also demoralizing, as it tore families apart. Many of those who stayed behind were old and vulnerable, or too weak or too poor to leave, and it is questionable how much faith they had in their decision.[53] Guernsey's viability as a community was further compromised by a leap in mortality rates, especially during the winter of 1941–2.[54]

The next *faux-pas* of the collective leadership of Guernsey lay in the adoption of a tough line of zero tolerance for 'troublemakers', coupled with a soft line ('correct relations') with regard to the German occupier. The new social contract in occupied Guernsey was formulated a few days before the arrival of the German occupying force, when John Leale, a leading member of the Guernsey Controlling Committee, declared:

> Should the Germans decide to occupy this Island, we must accept the position. There must be no thought of any kind of resistance, we can only expect that the more dire punishment will be meted. I say this, the man who even contemplates resistance should the Germans come is the most dangerous man in the Island [*sic*] and its most bitter enemy. The military have gone. We are civilians.[55]

In view of the need to stabilize the situation and garner popular support for the arduous tasks ahead it is subject to dispute whether stigmatization ('most bitter enemy') was what enlightened leadership commanded.[56] Nevertheless, one of the first acts of the new political line was for members of the island police force to call on potential dissenters, and ask them to 'tone down' for the duration.[57] Once the Germans were in occupation of the island, Sherwill sought to foster relations with Major Lanz, the first German island commandant and his aides. Sherwill's grand strategy was to combine 'correct relations' with the principle of mutual abidance by standards of international law. A first outline of his vision appeared in the local press, some days into the Occupation, when he stated that relations with the Germans were not merely 'correct […], they are cordial and friendly'.[58] This was without counting in the volatile environment, for the political line advocated by the island administration immediately went into choppy waters.

On the night of 14–15 July 1940, a small-scale British operation codenamed 'Ambassador' took place in Guernsey. About 40 men took part in the landing, erecting a barricade, cutting telephone cables and then withdrawing to the vessels that had ferried them across the Channel. Four British servicemen had to be left behind as they could not swim, but no reprisal measures were taken against the civilian population, as it was clear from the start that the incident was not an inside job.[59] A less alert administrator would have perhaps contented himself with the idea that this was a storm in a teacup, but Sherwill, who had served in the military, must have sensed that this was not an isolated incident. The next time around a similar situation might lead to violence and civilian deaths, exactly the kind of scenario he saw as his duty to avoid. Sherwill therefore tried to counter, by reassuring the Germans and briefing the island police to report (to him) the presence of all strangers in the island.[60] In a letter of 18 July to the Home Office – a letter the Germans never delivered – he explained his apprehension, writing that the raid seemed 'senseless', and that it had exposed islanders to great risk.[61] Nevertheless, only a fortnight after this first shock, on 28 July, Sherwill received a knock on his door that must have made his heart stop. Two men, Philip Martel and Desmond Mulholland, introduced themselves as members of HM forces. Having landed in civilian clothes over a fortnight earlier, on 10 July, to gather information and prepare for the commando raid, they had since become stranded in the island, and they now wanted Sherwill to arrange their surrender. Sherwill's first reflex was to obtain uniforms, to spare the two men from being treated as spies and shot and, only then, to contact the Germans.[62] Thanks to his efforts they were indeed treated as prisoners-of-war (PoWs), but it was the last time he would be so lucky, as he himself was now embroiled in the business of espionage. Having already tried to solve his dilemma as a senior administrator responsible for the safety of islanders through internal surveillance, Sherwill now stepped up his efforts to create further 'goodwill'. These efforts included his famous 7 August speech, at the first States meeting in the presence of Lanz; with its specific reference to making the Occupation a 'model to the world', the two pillars of which were to be the 'tolerance […], courtesy and correctness' of the German military, and the 'dignity […] and exemplary behaviour' of the civilian population.[63] Other gestures were more controversial and heavy-handed.[64] However, one should give Sherwill the benefit of the doubt and assume that the thought of other British agents at large in the island was affecting his calculus.

The wait for the final blow was not a long one. Sherwill's strategy of reciprocity was buried in the wake of the Nicolle-Symes affair. Nicolle and Symes had landed on 4 September 1940 and had missed their rendezvous, thus becoming stranded in the island for six weeks. In his memoirs Sherwill wrote that he was informed about their presence in the island through Nicolle's father, who was the secretary of the Controlling Committee.[65] By that time they were probably already contemplating surrender. The question that remained to be answered was whether the Germans could be trusted to treat them as PoWs, and not as spies. Sherwill's input had been instrumental in 'misleading' the Germans into accepting the surrender of Mulholland and Martel in July. He knew, however, that it was impossible to pull off the same feat twice, especially as Nicolle was the son of a States cadre. The details of supplying the two men with uniforms and arranging their surrender were therefore left to others. Sherwill had only one way in which he could weigh in on the outcome – his close relations with the German *Kommandant*. The evidence of the continued presence of British military personnel in the island became hard to ignore when the Germans arrested a third British officer, Captain Parker, landed in Guernsey to liaise with Nicolle and Symes. Major Bandelow, Lanz's successor in Guernsey, may have sensed that Sherwill knew something, but what he suggested seemed like a golden opportunity out of the dilemma. The idea was for Sherwill and Bandelow to publish a correspondence in the local press which included an amnesty deadline to all British military personnel, and their helpers, in exchange for their orderly surrender. For the first time, however, the offer was accompanied by a direct threat, transmitted orally to Sherwill by Bandelow's aide, that 20 hostages might be shot, if the orders of the occupying authority continued to be defied.[66] Without giving the game away, Sherwill accepted the offer to publicize the amnesty deadline.

Having meanwhile been fitted with uniforms, Nicolle and Symes surrendered before the expiry of the deadline, on 21 October 1940. However, the German side then reneged on Bandelow's promise, setting in motion an official investigation, on a charge of espionage against 13 people connected to the case, including Sherwill.[67] All were arrested and transported to Paris for interrogation. Sherwill's knowledge of the two men's presence in the island had placed him in a 'damned if you do, damned if you don't' situation. Not revealing what he knew to the Germans went counter to the policy of mutual trust and cordial relations that he was trying to build; on the other hand, saving the two officers and keeping their helpers out of trouble was a patriotic duty. The hardened German interrogators in Paris called Sherwill's bluff, claiming that he had given the German authorities the impression that he was 'their man', and accusing him of betrayal. Being a British civil servant, Sherwill had no choice other than to act the way he did. At the same time, and this is where the crux of the problem lies, the Convention leaves a huge gap as to provisions for dealing with conflicts of interest between opposing loyalties. There were no such provisions and the issue of loyalty is another 'grey area'. Article 45 of the Hague Convention of 1899 acknowledges that an occupier may not pressure the population of an occupied territory into swearing an oath of loyalty, i.e. they remain the subjects of their sovereign and have patriotic duties to their country; but at the same time the commentary says that the population owes the occupier the same obedience – short of acknowledging sovereignty or engaging in military action on his behalf – as its own government. The occupying power also has the right to dismiss disloyal civil servants and in certain particular serious cases, where damage occurs to the occupier, may treat such behaviour as treason.[68] Sherwill refuted the allegation that he had duped the Germans, but he also realized that he had committed an error in not having made it unmistakably clear to the Germans, from the very beginning, that in case of conflict of interest his loyalty to his country would always trump his loyalty to the occupying force. As he would write later, when the interest of one's country or the safety of one's countrymen is at stake, one must, if necessary, 'lie and lie'.[69] This was a more or less exact rendition of Machiavelli's critical insight that in politics as in war 'normal' standards of morality are often not appropriate.

What caused Sherwill's downfall? Increasing leverage through relationships with German commanders had clear limitations. For one thing, relations that became too 'cordial' did not make the most of British prestige. The policy also offered no protection against loyalty problems, as happened in 1940. Tying oneself to a standard as ambivalent as 'correct behaviour' was also a miscalculation, as it placed the burden of proof on the occupied and set German expectations too high. According to British post-war investigators '(m)any islanders felt that a stronger line would not, as the States have argued, have ended in disaster and drastic reprisals, but would have increased the German respect for the people'.[70] The same islanders prepared to invoke the might of Britain were often proven right by subsequent events. In fact, the situation in the Channel Islands was not unlike a hostage situation. This status was made more than clear by the Germans in late 1944, when they declared that they would let islanders starve to death rather than surrender their islands' fortresses. What kind of relation with the hostage-taker best serves the interests of the hostage? Certainly no hostage would want to come across as hostile or uncooperative to the hostage-taker. There is also a lot to be said about establishing rapport and creating empathy; 'transference' makes it less likely for the hostage-taker to harm a hostage. However, there is also a grey area, where compliance is inappropriate: for one thing, you do not make unnecessary overtures or volunteer information that could be used against you or others.[71] You also do not compromise your integrity, as this could lead to a very unhealthy denouement.

The other reason why it was wise to watch one's back carefully when cultivating relations with German commanders was that they constituted an unknown variable. Some inflated their power and influence in order to get the locals to comply, while at the same time advancing their own careers. On an individual basis, many were frequently shuffled about and a great number were anything but good faith negotiators in their dealings with locals in occupied territories. Sherwill appears somewhat indiscriminate in his generally positive appreciation of the Germans he had business with, of whom he writes that there were 'some swine but many less than I would have expected'.[72] One can contrast his attitude with that of the Revered Douglas Ord, a Methodist minister in Guernsey, whose understanding of what needed to be done was very similar to Sherwill's. What distinguished him, however, was that he only cultivated relations with those Germans whose anti-Nazi credentials were impeccable.[73] The business of government under enemy occupation held a great many more pitfalls in store than the dangerous, but straightforward military engagement Sherwill himself had experienced as an officer in the trenches; to all practical intents this situation rendered his own notions of chivalry redundant, if not pernicious. A similar verdict applies to his absolute trust in rules-based legal frameworks governing relations between the civilian authorities and the German occupier.

After the case was dropped, in December 1940, the group, save Symes's father – who died in his prison cell in dubious circumstances[74] – returned to the island. Nicolle and Symes were sent to a PoW camp. Sherwill, who had lost the Germans' trust, had been replaced as President of the Controlling Committee by John Leale. The latter's interpretation of the system the Germans represented was perhaps more accurate than that of his predecessor, but this was of little assistance in unravelling what had become an extremely delicate situation: the lenient way in which the Nicolle-Symes affair had concluded had, in fact, created a debt towards the occupier which islanders now had to repay. The Germans immediately took advantage of this new situation and raised the stakes. Throughout 1941 they continued to harass the local population with threats of reprisals, mostly in connection with cable sabotages.[75] Under the weight of the circumstances, Leale increased the hard-line rhetoric of 'no resistance' by one notch. Painful as his intercessions were to the patriotically minded, he still managed to resist overstepping the invisible moral line.[76] The Rubicon was finally crossed by Victor Carey, the Bailiff, who submitted to German hectoring, in July 1941. He did this by offering a £25 reward, in the local newspaper, for anyone willing to volunteer information on a V sign, over which the Germans had cooked up their customary brouhaha.[77] The effect was devastating, as to all practical intents the island's chief representative was exhorting denunciation, with all that this entailed in terms of erosion of trust. One month later Carey published another misguided notice reminding the population that the sheltering of escaped PoWs or 'enemy forces' carried the death penalty. On this occasion the problem was semantic, the 'enemy forces' referred to in the notice being not the Germans, but the British. The common explanation is that this was a technical gaffe, produced by a Bailiff rubber-stamping a document placed before him by the Germans without further editing. But there are also less generous explanations for the Bailiff's 'oversight', such as a determination to avoid any friction with the Germans by submitting on all issues of minor importance in his understanding.[78]

Resistance of administrators versus administrative resistance

Due to the general stance adopted by the islands' authorities, campaigns of sustained administrative or institutional resistance of the type described in Jacques Semelin's ground-breaking work[79] are nowhere to be found in the Channel Islands. This makes individual acts of *Resistenz* by Channel Islands officials stand out all the more.

Resistenz is a concept coined by the influential 'Bavaria Project' on resistance and persecution, which ran from 1973 to 1983. In German the term itself denotes 'resistance' or 'immunity', as employed in physics and medicine. In its application to the historical context of Nazi Germany the concept was to account for those manifestations in the lower strata of society that were thought to have provided a bulwark against the totalist claims of Nazism. The focus was on non-conformism and partial opposition, rather than ideological motives and system-changing goals. *Resistenz* departed from the notion that questions of morality never stand on their own, as in a vacuum, but are context-driven. This means that resistance as a human and a moral activity can never be entirely free from interests or human bias. If one disregards context, one creates a meta-political ideal of conscience and morality that is separated from reality; it puts demands on people that are unreasonable. This approach filled a gap in the historiography which had tended to focus on fundamental opposition (or resistance), regardless of the effect this may have had.[80] As Ian Kershaw writes:

> The *Resistenz* concept [...] made possible a deepened understanding of the social base of conflict with the regime, and a more nuanced explanation of the spheres of underlying consensus with aspects of Nazi rule.[81]

In terms of measuring a society's capacity to withstand a totalitarian regime, *Resistenz* was the more adequate answer than other, more activist forms of resistance.[82] Its societal outlook allows a worthy glimpse at spheres of conflict and cooperation between rulers and ruled. It shows 'how they (the ruled, n.b.) compromised with the regime but also where they drew the line'.[83] Although the context of an occupied society is different, the ambiguous mix of conformism and non-conformism that characterizes *Resistenz* strikes a familiar chord. As Martin Broszat wrote, its fine lens raises the human and historical profile of conformists who became resistance-minded after having undergone painful learning experiences. A number of Channel Islands' officials provide illustration of precisely such conflicting tendencies: first, the wartime Bailiff of Jersey, Alexander Moncrief Coutanche. The key characteristic of Coutanche's approach to conflict management was to use the prestige of his office for special pleading. Unlike his Guernsey counterpart, Victor Carey, he only intervened in a limited number of duress cases as a last resort. He described his approach of 'restraint and influence' as follows in a post-war memo:

> I almost invariably found it better to hold myself in readiness to make a final appeal to the Germans for mercy when all other means had failed. Constant intervention by me at an early stage would, it always appeared to me, have weakened my ultimate influence for good.[84]

Coutanche intervened as a matter of principle in the event of death sentences against islanders. Two French artists residing in Jersey, Suzanne Malherbe and Lucie Schwob were sentenced to death in late 1944 for resistance activities. The same penalty was imposed on Alice Thaureux, the local girlfriend of a German deserter, in April 1945. In both cases Coutanche pointed to the island's legal traditions, arguing that no death sentence against women had been executed for time immemorial and that this was likely to upset the local population, and in both cases he was successful.[85] Coutanche's ability to plead was also manifest during the September 1942 deportations when he pushed for exemptions.[86] He also put the plight of the forced workers on the table in his talks with von Schmettow. And in spring 1945 he approached the Red Cross for permission to include forced workers in the distribution of food parcels.[87] Coutanche did not limit his activities to special pleading alone. An example of 'thought resistance' emerges from an exchange between himself and Professor Karl-Heinz Pfeffer, a senior associate in a Nazi think-tank. In 1941 Pfeffer was sent to the islands on a fact-finding mission. This included an informal discussion with the Bailiff, which had, at first, focused on a discussion of the constitution of Jersey, but then digressed into the topic of Jewish ritual slaughter. How the conversation got there is unclear, but Coutanche sought to use the prewar exemption for kosher butchers, through a special Jersey law introduced in 1937, to demonstrate the flexibility of the island constitution:

> As a decent Christian, I instantly came to an agreement with this respectable Jew and allowed an exception, of which little practical use was made. You can see how a respectable Christian can intercourse with a respectable Jew.[88]

In fact, what Coutanche was telling Pfeffer – a high-profile ideological warrior with several anti-Semitic publications to his name – was that living with Jews was possible.[89] Coutanche's moral courage emerged again in 1942, when he blocked the passing into Jersey law of a German order that would have required Jews to wear the six-pointed yellow star inscribed 'Jew'.[90]

Although Coutanche was remarkable, his occupation record was not without ambiguity, which is consistent with *Resistenz*. During the 1942 deportations he claims to have been tempted to resign. These deportations to internment camps affected many women, children, and harmless retirees in their sixties and seventies. They were illegal, for, other than in the case of men of military age, internment is not sanctioned in international law. That Coutanche was uneasy about the appropriateness of continuing in office can be inferred from the following statement describing his reaction to the deportation order:

> I said that in view of what was proposed I and any member of the island government who wished to do so would be entitled to resign and that I must have time to consider whether that step were not the proper one to be adopted by me and the members of the government and to be urged upon the Constables.[91]

Ultimately, the Feldkommandantur officials prevailed with their 'buffer argument', peddling the idea that it was in the interest of the people of Jersey that their government stay in office. They also made it clear that the deportation order came straight from Hitler and that it could not be aborted or modified. After some time for thought, Coutanche and his government resigned themselves to the inevitable. What is more problematic is the fact that the little sanction the island authorities had announced in response to this illegal measure was not followed through. In December 1942, when the Germans asked for lists of unemployed men, the administration obliged, despite a pledge made in September that they would no longer supply lists of islanders for 'statistical purposes'.[92]

Coutanche's other lapse was his lack of authority in restraining bureaucratic zealots who were still functioning on prewar 'scripts'. But, in any case, this was a delicate task. It clashed head-on with the problem of legitimacy as well as with the fact that the multiple sources of authority by which a junior administrator could feel bound during the Occupation automatically weakened that of his island boss. In the absence of the customary checks and balances it was easy for managers or officials to lose sight of the common good and play a role similar to that of Lieutenant-Colonel Nicholson, the principal character in *The Bridge on the River Kwai*.[93]

The negative test case for this type of failure in Jersey was the Aliens Officer, Clifford Orange, who supervised, among other tasks, the registration of the Jewish population. In doing so he applied over-inclusive criteria, registering people as Jews who should not have been registered, even according to the legal provisos.[94] Other officials could have been called to task for not realizing the responsibility (and leverage) that British prestige conferred, and for showing poor judgement in the mutual forms they adopted with the Germans.[95] Over-cautious rather than over-zealous is how one might characterize the disposition of Coutanche's right hand, the Attorney General, Duret Aubin. The tendency to avoid 'upsetting' the Germans is also evident in another case. In March 1944 the governor of the Jersey prison received a letter from Dr Noel McKinstry, the Public Health officer, urging him that, in view of the degrading health standards, two political prisoners should be put on TB rations. However, as these prisoners were, technically speaking, German prisoners the governor stalled. Wavering over whether he should consider the recommendation of the medical officer at all, he first wrote to the *Feldkommandantur* for permission to put the men on TB rations. The Germans then deferred the matter to the Attorney General who 'passed the chip' back to the prison governor, asking him for his 'opinion'.[96]

McKinstry's case is the reason why it would be fallacious to limit the spin-offs of Coutanche's leadership to Clifford Orange. In terms of 'en-couraging' others,

Coutanche also groomed follower effects in the opposite direction.[97] Another senior Jersey politician who could be described as 'resistance-minded' was deputy Edward Le Quesne. He relates two cases of clashes with the Attorney General in his published diaries. One in September 1943, when he undercut a 'news embargo' designed to prevent a 'sympathetic demonstration' at the funeral of American airmen found at Bonne Nuit Bay; a second in January 1944, when Le Quesne entered a successful protest against the fact that the paid police in St Helier, who came under the Attorney General's authority, were assisting the Germans in finding the addresses of shorthand typists.[98] The list of resistance-minded officials might also include the General Post Office workers who steamed open letters of denunciation and warned persons in danger.[99] Similar practices are also known to have occurred under the offices of Head Postmaster H. C. Chapell in Guernsey.[100] Frank Falla also credited Albert Lamy, the acting chief inspector of the Guernsey police after 1942, with having destroyed informers' letters, 'lost vital anonymous communications' or having given locals, on whom the GFP had set their sights, a word of warning to remove their sets.[101]

McKinstry's resistance credentials are particularly solid, though. One key event in this respect was Coutanche's endorsement of the latter's opposition to a German plan to 'evacuate' the Jersey Mental Hospital, in spring 1942.[102] Sensing the 'slippery slope', Coutanche resisted any suggestion of even a removal to a different location in the island, urging the *Feldkommandantur* to consider 'the disastrous consequences which must inevitably follow the removal of so large a number of persons of unsound mind from the only place in the island suitable for their detention'. His refusal to contemplate a removal from the island was even more categorical. Accentuated by uncharacteristically unequivocal and sharp language, he insisted that this was

> [a] step which most assuredly would lead to the death of many of them and the suffering of most grievous discomfort by the remainder. In addition, the shock to the feelings of the relatives and to the inhabitants of the island generally would, it is feared, produce the most serious consequences.[103]

The quote leaves little doubt that Coutanche had some idea of the fate of the mentally impaired in Hitler's Germany. Considering that they were the first victims of the Holocaust, having resisted in this manner was, indeed, significant.

Ambrose Sherwill, the Attorney General and first President of the Controlling Committee in Guernsey, cut a rather similar figure to Coutanche. He showed his colours during the repeat 'visits' of the British military in summer 1940, despite his own misgivings over their utility. The manner in which he saved four British officers from being shot as spies was a supreme act of chivalry, specifically acknowledged as such in Home Office correspondence in 1944.[104] On the other hand, Sherwill was handicapped by a number of issues, none of which Coutanche had to contend with. When the Germans invaded, Sherwill was to all practical intents the 'top man' in the island. The only other contender, Jurat Leale, had turned down the opportunity to become President of the Controlling Committee in June 1940. The additional workload came on top of Sherwill's official duties as Attorney General, as well as the executive business that he conducted on behalf of the Bailiff.[105] This brought with it two major disadvantages: he was overburdened by this accumulation of work, while lacking the undivided authority and prestige of the Bailiff. The arrangement between himself and the Bailiff meant that he could not avail himself of the same degree of teamwork as Coutanche who worked in tandem with Duret Aubin. This tandem saw Duret Aubin do most of the low-level pleading, while Coutanche played the role of the 'big gun', ready to be wheeled out *in extremis*. This 'game' contained an element of political showmanship aimed at leveraging influence with those high-ranking German officials whose foreign policy sensitivities or Anglophilia could be exploited. Sybil Hathaway, the Dame of Sark, played a very similar 'game'.[106] Already during evacuation week her firm authority avoided scenes of panic as seen in the other islands. The other advantage the Dame used to great effect was her knowledge of Germany and the Germans, whose language she spoke fluently, and her noble extraction, which enabled her to see eye-to-eye with her German peers, of whom there were a considerable number in the islands.

Similar things must have been intended for Guernsey, but failed because the Bailiff resisted encroachments onto his prerogative; at the same time he lacked the charisma and energy of a Coutanche or Hathaway.[107] Guernsey therefore never managed to speak with one voice. This increased internal contradictions and played into the hands of those Germans who saw greater utility in the 'iron fist' than in the 'velvet glove'. It could also not fail to have an impact on those members of the Guernsey political class disposed to risking a more confrontational stance on occasion, such as Sir Abraham Lainé,[108] the Vice-president of the Controlling Committee, or Dr A. N. Symons, the chief Medical Officer.[109]

Finally, character was not entirely without relevance either. One of the first histories of the Channel Islands, written in the 1950s, credited Sherwill with a touch of political naivety to which 'exceptionally brave men are often prone'.[110] What stand out in particular are his extravagant gestures, which could verge on eccentricity. This penchant emerged on several occasions. As we have seen, in July 1940, Sherwill lobbied the Germans to drop a letter of his, addressed to the Home Office, in England. In this letter Sherwill had intended to do three things: stress the correct demeanour of the occupying troops, plead with the British government so that they may refrain from future landing attempts in Guernsey, but then also, oddly, to ask for the return to German-occupied Guernsey of a vessel suitable for transporting supplies from France.[111] Naturally, nothing came of this well-intended if quixotic initiative, but this did not stop Sherwill in his efforts to communicate across the lines. A short time later he seized the opportunity to record a speech for Radio Bremen containing the ominous reference that he had no pistol pointing to his head while he was speaking. This was intended to reassure Channel Islands evacuees about the well-being of their compatriots under Occupation, but back-fired as a German propaganda coup.[112] Four years later, in the wake of the Normandy landings, when Sherwill was already interned at Laufen, he tried to get yet another awkward letter across the lines, to the Home Office in London. The purpose of this letter was to give a voice to the apprehension of Channel Islanders about the possibility of an impending British attack, as well as the effects of a prolonged siege:

> In so small an area troops and civilians are inextricably mixed up [...] My wife, who is in the midst of one such situation says the officer in charge is very courteous

and considerate and the troops are very kind to the children. By the way, lest you should be tempted to misunderstand, I haven't succumbed to propaganda. Please, however, may the situation of the Channel Islanders be given special consideration by His Majesty's Government [...] I hope the flying bomb is not inconveniencing you unduly.[113]

Surprisingly, this letter did get through to the Home Office, who had no reason to doubt Sherwill's good intentions. What they could not be so certain about, however, was whether Sherwill wasn't being used, by the Germans, for an attempt to open up back channels of communication to the Western Allies, of which there were many at this stage in the war.[114]

These comments are by no means intended as criticism of Sherwill, for the latter was in good company regarding his penchant for the grand gesture. In fact, he shared this disposition with no other than the British Prime Minister, Winston S. Churchill. However, the big difference between Churchill and Sherwill was that the PM was surrounded by advisers who could talk him out of his more harebrained schemes,[115] whereas Sherwill was on his own.

Can good government ever be resistance?

If the legitimacy issue did not favour the outright resistance of officials, were there any affinities between good government and *Resistenz*? Generally regarded as a pure ex-post-facto legitimation device conceived by post-war apologists of collaboration, 'good government' has been dismissed by the literature on resistance. This dismissal raises an important question: are there no aspects of routine administrative action which did *not* play into the hands of the Germans? Was all this activity hopelessly compromised? Is it irrelevant, for example, that the islands, whose future looked extremely bleak in 1940, managed to pull through comparatively well? And could this positive result have something to do with the civilian administration of the islands?

Good government is a particularly commendable and necessary thing in times of crisis. One of the exceptions in the catalogue of crises would be occupation by enemy forces. Most occupiers will identify ways of inducing an occupied society to continue to function under their rule, which is often not identical with the interest of the occupied themselves. Business as usual (good government) in this case may even be counterproductive from the point of view of national interest. International law has made provision for this eventuality, stipulating that there are certain limits to enforcing obedience to an occupation regime. If a particular country continues to be at war with a belligerent occupying part of its territory, the occupier cannot oblige the population of this territory to work against the interests of their own country, as this is akin to committing treason. This leaves any collaborating administration in a delicate position.

If good government is potentially counterproductive, is 'bad government' or perhaps no government at all preferable? On the face of it the case for bad government is an alluring one: the sophistication of modern societies disposing of vast state apparatuses facilitates their ready exploitation and control by an occupying force.[116] Disorder and anarchy, on the other hand, deny the enemy this access and facilitate opposition. This train of thought, however, leaves the rights of non-combatants out of the equation. Considering the routine use of reprisals by the Germans, any deterioration in the governance of a territory affected civilians directly and drove their chances of survival down. This feature appears in particularly stark profile in partisan warfare zones, where civilians faced certain death if they stayed put in their villages and towns, where they could be decimated by German reprisals (or by partisans, for their real or imaginary collaboration); or almost certain death if they took to the hills or forests and joined the partisans.

Even for members of groups specifically targeted by Nazi persecution it was by no means a foregone conclusion that state collapse or disorder increased their chances of survival. As the example of Denmark shows, a sophisticated and functioning industrial society was, indeed, capable of rescuing its Jewish population. The high level of institutional and organizational differentiation of modern industrial societies did not work in a linear manner, merely propping up the Nazi enterprise of exploitation and submission. This sophistication could also benefit centrifugal forces. The point of view has recently been bolstered by Ethan Hollander's ongoing study of victimization rates during the Holocaust. According to Hollander these rates are persistently higher in countries under direct German rule than in those countries run by collaborating administrations, which points in the direction of officials influencing the process.[117] It may well be then that historians, by averting their eyes for too long, have been focusing on the 'wrong' phenomenon in terms of explaining survival rates: armed and, later, civil society resistance, rather than the *Resistenz* of officials. The weakness of the civilian resistance paradigm emerges in a comparison of the implementation of the Holocaust in countries where the civilian resistance factor was very prominent, such as the Netherlands and Norway, with countries such as Denmark and France where civilian resistance had a harder time crystallizing (because of the legitimacy surrounding collaborating governments).[118] The paradox is that Jewish survival rates in Denmark and France were significantly higher than in the Netherlands and in Norway, which counters the Paxtonian assertion that collaboration always made things worse.[119] It also turns on its head the wider notion that state collaboration was the ultimate stage of evil, as it supposedly smoothed the Nazification of a territory. The traditional learned opinion for the higher survival rates in France and in Denmark has been to attribute this success to civil society actors (e.g. the 'Righteous among the nations'), the pressure of public opinion on collaborating governments and the level of organization and salvage acumen of the persecuted themselves. Any inputs that collaborating governments or officials may have had in making this happen have been more or less eclipsed, in particular as regards the French case. This argument no longer convinces. Although the three traditional factors of explanation were a part of the equation, the survival of quarter of a million people in France and the massive rescue operation undertaken in Denmark in October 1943 are things that could not succeed without the active support or, at least, connivance of large numbers of officials at every level of government.[120]

A final element militating against the blanket endorsement of 'bad government' as a resistance strategy lies in the nihilistic tendencies of the Nazi creed. The principal drivers of Nazism were conquest, exploitation and destruction. Solving problems through violence was deeply ingrained in this psyche, it was part of the system, a feature that would ultimately turn against the German *folk* itself. Disorder only amplified these nihilistic and destructive tendencies.

The evidence is rather thin then as concerns the claim that intentional bad government is necessarily a good thing. As concerns most parts of occupied Europe, some form of good government was, to all practical intents, the preferable option. This makes particularly good sense for Western Europe, where the Nazis' prime interest was economic exploitation, and not destruction. Any best practice of administration under duress then is more likely to be framed in terms of resourcefulness or resilience rather than outright resistance. And instances of good government that avoided the setting in motion of cycles of violence were a form of *Resistenz*. The principal constraint in terms of defining what acceptable behaviour may have been in the case of the authorities of the Channel Islands is to solve the contradiction that 'good government' not only benefited the occupied, but also the Nazi occupier. An assessment therefore needs to register whether and to what extent the authorities minimized the windfalls of good government to the Nazis, as well as to what extent they safeguarded British interests. A benchmark for optimal desirable outcomes could be formulated around the following axes: the action of the authorities had to be consistent with limiting collaboration to the minimum, and it had to cater to the legitimate disposition of those patriotic citizens who felt uneasy about collaboration, allowing them limited forms of disapproval. At the same time it also had to avoid 'hasty sacrifices' of the collective safety, well-being and survival of the population. A framework for dealing with this type of quandary exists in 'fair share' principles, which are used in human rights and management ethics. The principal idea is that of a correlation between an actor's leverage over outcomes on the one hand, and the moral obligation to use any such leverage for positive impact ('fair share') on the other. This 'fairness factor' is applied to relationship, effectiveness and capacity; i.e. the closer a relationship, the stronger the duty to intervene or protect; the greater the capacity to withstand retaliation, the greater the obligation to influence a situation; the greater the chance of making a real impact, the greater the obligation not to remain inactive.[121] A corollary of this is the duty to build coalitions for collective action, wherever this is possible.

Generally, the situation of civilians in occupied Europe went from bad to worse as the war progressed. This is not what could be said of the Channel Islands, for the authorities of these islands did not serve, primarily, the purposes of the occupier. Starting from a macroeconomic position in June 1940 that was hopeless, their administrative resilience reigned supreme in areas of existential interest such as economic conversion and control, and public policy, finance, purchasing and health provision.[122] As a UK Treasury report remarked in 1945, the economic effort undertaken in the islands disclosed 'reserves of administrative capacity', in the face of which 'it was difficult not to remain impressed'.[123] Without such astute management, the population of the islands may well have starved as early as 1943. If Channel Islanders survived the Occupation in relatively acceptable shape, then this outcome was owed to their own resourcefulness and ingenuity, to the action of the civilian authorities, and to the benevolence of certain Germans empathetic to their concerns.

Conclusion

Referring back to Primo Levi's 'grey zone', the issue of official behaviour during the Channel Islands Occupation cannot be a matter of moral absolutes, or be argued, conclusively, one way or another. The hypothesis that resistance was always the most appropriate and desirable response to Nazi rule is about as valid as the critical counterclaim that collaboration was unavoidable. Neither of these two, in fact, has the power to close the debate. The solution then can only lie in adopting a 'golden mean'. Where officials in occupied Europe had margins, this was situated between a moderate good government strategy and a moral obligation to resist, if important and non-negotiable principles were at stake. At the same time, the lives of the innocent could not be needlessly sacrificed or endangered.

From the point of view of the 'fairness factors' of relationship, effectiveness and capacity, in the aggregate, no major fault can be ascribed to the authorities of the Channel Islands: the authorities' capacity to withstand retaliation, and the effectiveness in doing so, was limited at the best of times. It would be difficult to claim that the obligation to intervene or protect those closest to them, their fellow islanders, was grossly or routinely neglected, although there were exceptions where the bargaining becomes discomforting. The only thing that could be criticized in earnest is that they did not always maximize the prestige and leverage that British power still commanded. One might object that Guernsey's ability to contest the Germans ended very early, in October 1940, when Sherwill's 'game' was up. This, however, changes little about the fact that Sherwill had set German expectations too high to begin with. His later claim that some Germans (such as Dr Maas) were a god-send[124] should not lead us to the assumption that keeping more distance would have necessarily led to worse outcomes. Naturally, Britishness could not be relied on as a fail-safe insurance policy; it depended on the situation. However, even the worst off, the Channel Islands prisoners languishing in German jails, had tales to tell that sometimes being British could make a difference. As Frank Falla would write later, '(t)hough not immune from occasional "beatings-up", the fact was that we British were treated by the majority of the Nazi guards with a certain amount of respect and this became more noticeable as the days and months moved into 1945.'[125]

The other sore point concerns the duty to build coalitions that moral action calls for. Here, as well, the authorities did not maximize the potential. To illustrate the point we will begin with the exception, the final phase of the Occupation, from late August 1944, when the islands were cut off from France. In September 1944 the German occupier rejected any suggestions of an early surrender, and by late October starvation stared both islanders and Germans in the face. To this was added the potential for wide-spread bloodshed, as the Germans were, seemingly, determined to go through with a last stand. This period witnessed the authorities of the Channel Islands not only becoming more outspoken in their demands towards the occupier, but also coordinating collective action. An important event falling into this period was the unprecedented Red Cross relief operation that started to gain traction from December 1944. The chances of this operation succeeding were slim to begin with. Although, initially, many British government officials seem to have welcomed such a plan, the consensus quickly shifted when the idea was slammed by Churchill on 2 September 1944 ('let them starve!'). He feared that relief would merely reinforce the defensive capacity of the German garrison and that very little would, in fact, reach the starving islanders. An important element in changing the tide was the intelligence on the food situation that reached individual British officials from those most concerned by any relief, islanders themselves. By late 1944 this intelligence was trickling in rather steadily, via escapees leaving the islands by boat. Edward Le Quesne in Jersey distinguished himself as the first Channel Islands official to have taken such an initiative to communicate directly, in a letter addressed to Ernest Bevin. The latter then circulated it to his colleagues, ahead of a decisive Cabinet meeting that overruled Churchill and authorized the principle of a Red Cross relief mission.[126] Although the Germans were informed of this decision on 7 November, through the Swiss, this was not immediately evident to the Bailiffs, who sent over more clandestine envoys with letters in the days that followed.[127] The general enbolding of the islands authorities also diffused down the ranks. One typical example of this is contained in a report written by a Jersey policeman, Albert Chardine, in February 1945. In this report to his superiors Chardine outlined the reasons why he refused to patrol the vicinity of the local prison, from where many escapes were taking place:

> I beg to report that at the above stated time I was instructed by P.Sgt. Griffin to patrol Gloucester St & Newgate St. re. Political Prisoners [sic] attempting to escape from prison. On receiving the instructions I refused to carry them out because I don't think it is the duty of a civilian policeman, and I have friends who have been put in prison by the Germans for very little reason, and I would not like them to know that I was outside waiting to catch them if they tried to escape; and as you know I, and several other policemen have been in prison for the Germans, and I am sure if any of us were in their [sic] today we would not like to know that our own workmates were waiting to try and stop us from escaping.[128]

Such open defiance from an official would have been inconceivable outside the acute crisis of the siege period. For the four years preceding the siege, however, the picture was less rosy. The impression one gains is that the authorities often overlooked that, for small communities under duress, the highest form of political intelligence revolved around 'pulling ranks'. The importance of social trust is owed to the fact that, under stress conditions, fear can tip societies in a self-destructive direction. Crisis leaders have a particular responsibility to build trust and avoid any regression to a Hobbesian 'state of nature'. Leadership is the 'cement' for negotiating positive outcomes, and this task required mediating between the two constituencies in the islands: the timorous majority, who were unfavourably disposed to anything likely to irritate the Germans (and amenable to 'caving in' to their demands); and the typically substantial minority who felt that islanders emerged relatively unscathed from the Occupation not because they respected international law, but because they were members of an enemy nation whom the Germans considered their equals. As we have seen already, in terms of earning German respect, this soft power (might) often trumped right. The second group also felt that a firmer stance was advisable, as it neutralized the temptation to pre-empt German demands through anticipatory obedience. The very real danger of this scenario was that it would reinforce mutual surveillance, turn denunciation into a public virtue and create a self-policing environment.

This minority could not be overlooked, as it enjoyed significant support. This can be attested through the massive popular movement of defiance, in both islands, that followed the wireless requisition in 1942. The logistical, moral and material assistance provided to escaped forced and slave labourers, an effort that was particularly strong in Jersey, speaks a very similar language. To arbitrate between the two constituencies, leaders therefore had to build a new consensus. This was more essential than reliance on legal provisions, top-down command, paternalism or disciplinary measures. Not that the task of striking a new balance was an easy one. Officials were right in taking a dim view of incidents which could lead to spirals of violence. They could not afford to stir up sentiment that may have encouraged irresponsible hotheads. It was equally sound to give the impression that German law was to be obeyed. On the other hand, they could not be strangers to cunning and they needed a lot of imagination. Leaders had to discreetly point the way; they had to leave no ambiguity about the mainspring of their authority, the Crown; and they had to take good care of not manoeuvring themselves into inextricable corners. Any good government under occupation required the recognition of *Realpolitik* and Machiavellian power play, but also could not turn a blind eye to considerations of justice. The basic idea was that of the famous 'double game'.

If we compare social contracts, we will find that the opportunistic Jersey version ('live and let live') was more in line with the leadership style outlined in the preceding paragraph. Resistance was never encouraged, but the Jersey leaders were not pro-active in rooting out designs that countered occupation government. While they took a dim view of anything susceptible to provoke the occupier, they granted space to their fellow islanders to decide for themselves. The signal given to the people was that those who got into trouble with the Germans should not rely on any assistance; but the overall orientation was to neither encourage nor discourage passive resistance. This took into account the growing despondence among certain people, who might revert to desperate means, if they were not given a lid to let off steam. The Page case, mentioned earlier, offers perfect illustration of the attitude prevailing in Jersey. Notwithstanding the misgivings over the Attorney General's ambiguous role, doesn't the fact that a resistance-minded policeman[129] would confide in the Attorney General, on a problem of conscience related to his official duties, tell an astounding story about the level of social trust that still existed in Jersey in mid-1943? If, under occupation law, Duret Aubin had to signal *all* anti-German occurrences, wouldn't this have included his conversation with Garden? And didn't he indicate that he would only forward the case to the German authorities if he received a *written* report? Contrast this with the statement of a Guernseyman who escaped to England in August 1943 and according to whom the authorities 'would not even close their eyes to instances of passive resistance'.[130]

The respective stance with regard to resistance, dissidence or disobedience is what made the *real* difference between the two islands; and the pro-active discouragement of opposition in Guernsey is what made ethical leadership performance there less optimal than in Jersey.

Notes

1 Frederick Cohen, *The Jews in the Channel Islands during the German Occupation 1940-1945*, Jersey Heritage Trust in association with the Institute of Contemporary History and Wiener Library London, 2000; Paul Sanders, *The Ultimate Sacrifice. The Jersey Islanders who Died in German Prisons and Concentration Camps 1940-1945*, Jersey, Jersey Heritage Trust, 2004.
2 Primo Levi, *The Drowned and the Saved*, London, Abacus, 1989.
3 Ibid., p. 28.
4 Ibid., p. 49.
5 Ibid., pp. 43, 28-9, 49.
6 The allegations of collaboration were not entirely new, see Solomon Steckoll's *The Alderney Death Camp* (1982) and Peter King's *The Channel Islands War* (1991).
7 Paul Sanders, *The British Channel Islands under German Occupation 1940-1945*, Jersey, Jersey Heritage Trust, 2005, pp. 57-98.
8 Michael Santoro, *Profits and Principles: Global Capitalism and Human Rights in China*, Ithaca, Cornell University Press, 2000, pp. 143-58.
9 Sanders, *Channel Islands under German Occupation*, passim.
10 Ibid., pp. 75-6.
11 Sanders, *The Ultimate Sacrifice*, p. 39.
12 JAS.D/Z/H5/335. Centenier Garden to the Attorney General of Jersey, 2 June 1943.
13 JAS.D/Z/H5/448. Memorandum, Attorney General of Jersey, 4 August 1945.
14 A subsequent escapee report stated that Garden was favourably disposed towards resistance, see TNA.HO.144/22237. MI19. Report no. 2510. Jersey Siege Conditions. Interrogation of three escapees from Jersey, November 1944.
15 JAS.D/Z/H5/448. Memorandum, Attorney General of Jersey, 4 August 1945.
16 Hugo Slim, 'Doing the Right Thing. Relief Agencies, Moral Dilemmas and Moral Responsibility in Political Emergencies and War', Working paper, Nordiska Afrikainstitutet, Uppsala, 1997, 7.
17 Sanders, *Channel Islands under German Occupation*, pp. 110-12, 160-3.
18 Peter Davies, *Dangerous Liaisons*, Harlow, Pearson, 2004, pp. 23-8.
19 Julian Jackson, *France: The Dark Years 1940-1945*, Oxford, Oxford University Press, 2001, p. 4.
20 Pathbreaking in this respect, Martin Broszat and Elke Fröhlich, *Alltag und Widerstand: Bayern im Nationalsozialismus*, München, Piper, 1987; Jacques Semelin, *Unarmed against Hitler. Civilian Resistance in Europe 1939-1943*, Westport and London, Praeger, 1993.
21 Philippe Burrin, *France under the Germans: Collaboration and Compromise*, New York, New Press, 1998; Julian Jackson, *France: The Dark Years*; Paul Sanders, *Histoire du Marché Noir 1940-1946*, Paris, Perrin, 2001; Robert Gildea, *Marianne in Chains: In Search of the German Occupation 1940-45*, London, Macmillan, 2002; Richard Vinen, *The Unfree French: Life under the Occupation*, New Haven, Yale University Press, 2007.
22 Sanders, *The Ultimate Sacrifice*; Sanders, *Channel Islands under German Occupation*; Barry Turner, *Outpost of Occupation: How the Channel Islands Survived Nazi Rule 1940-45*, London, Aurum, 2010.
23 Harm Schröter, 'Thesen und Desiderata zur ökonomischen Besatzungsherrschaft', in Joachim Lund (ed.), *Working for the New Order. European Business under German*

Domination 1939–1945, University Press of Southern Denmark and Copenhagen Business School Press, 2006, pp. 43–4.
24 IWM.Documents.13409.Dening 4. Report on German morale and factors likely to hasten or postpone capitulation, by Capt Dening, 10 I(b), September 1944.
25 TNA.WO.32/13750. Charles Markbreiter (HO) to Brigadier French, 4 April 1944.
26 Sanders, *Channel Islands under German Occupation*, pp. 100–5.
27 IWM.Misc 189/2 (2826). Interview with Michael Ginns, n.d.
28 Edward Le Quesne, *The Occupation of Jersey Day by Day*, Jersey, La Haule, 1999, entry of 20 February 1943, p. 182.
29 British intelligence investigators cited a Colonel Vierbahn, of Army HQ in St Lô, who visited the islands with Colonel Schmundt, a member of Hitler's general staff (Führerhauptquartier), in November 1941. According to Vierbahn, Hitler 'wished to deal with the Channel Islands population with the utmost tact and leniency', and that the islands should be differentiated from Northern France (the original sources has, unfortunately, been lost), IWM.Documents.13409.Dening 9. Force 135, I (b). *History of the GFP in the Channel Islands*, 1945.
30 The members of a 1943 escape party from Guernsey thought that in the current situation 'Jerry will do some very serious thinking before carrying out any too severe reprisals against British subjects', TNA.HO.144/22834. Memo, J. T. D. Hubert, 23 August 1943.
31 The measure was in retaliation against the internment of German nationals, following the British occupation of Iran in 1941.
32 TNA.HO.144/22179. John Leale to Sir Francis Newsam (HO). Memorandum 'On Germans', 15 June 1945.
33 TNA.HO.45/22424. Report of the President of the Controlling Committee on the activities of the Committee during the German Occupation, 23 May 1945.
34 Sanders, *Channel Islands under German Occupation*, pp. 57–80.
35 TNA.HO.45/22424. Report of the President of the Controlling Committee on the activities of the Committee during the German Occupation, 23 May 1945; TNA. HO.144/22179. John Leale to Sir Francis Newsam (HO). Memorandum 'On Germans', 15 June 1945.
36 See the entry for 22 June 1942, in Adolf Hitler, *Hitler's Table Talk, 1941–1944: His Private Conversation*, ed. H. Trevor-Roper, New York, Enigma Books, 2000.
37 See the final report of the first German Kommandant of Guernsey, IWM. Documents.13409.Dening 4. Report by Major Lanz, 216 ID, the first German Commandant, 1940.
38 TNA.HO.45/22424. Report of the President of the Controlling Committee on the activities of the Committee during the German Occupation, 23 May 1945.
39 Christopher Greenwood, 'International Humanitarian Law (Laws of War)', in Fritz Karlshoven (ed.), *The Centennial of the First International Peace Conference – Reports and Conclusions*, The Hague, Martinus Nijhoff Publishers, 2000, pp. 252–4.
40 TNA.HO.45/22424. Report of the President of the Controlling Committee on the activities of the Committee during the German Occupation, 23 May 1945.
41 Sanders, *Channel Islands under German Occupation*, pp. 69–70, 92.
42 Louise Willmot, '"Nothing Was Ever the Same Again": Public Attitudes in the Occupied Channel Islands June-December 1942', *The Local Historian: Journal of the British Association for Local History*, Vol. 35 (1), 2005, 9–20.
43 TNA.HO.284/6. W. H. Arnold, Attorney General of Guernsey to Sir Leslie Brass (HO), 27 May 1952.

44 Charles Duret Aubin, 'Enemy Legislation and Judgments in Jersey', *The Journal of Comparative Legislation and International Law*, Vol. 31, 1949, 2.
45 IA.FK 05–11. Feldkommandantur 515 to the Bailiff of Guernsey. Re. Amtsbezeichnung, 3 January 1942, the Feldkommandantur tried to push the same point in Jersey, urging that criminal prosecutions should be instituted in the name of the Attorney General without reference to His Majesty, but it was ignored, Charles Duret Aubin, 'Enemy Legislation and Judgments in Jersey', 3.
46 TNA.HO.284/6. W. H. Arnold, Attorney General of Guernsey to Sir Leslie Brass (HO), 28 May 1952.
47 Cohen, *The Jews in the Channel Islands during the German Occupation*, p. 41.
48 JAS.D/AU/V1/3. FK St Helier, Vermerk, 5 March 1942.
49 TNA.T.161/1196. Population distribution in the Channel Islands, n.d.; AN.AJ40/547. FK 515, Verwaltungsüberblick über die Kanalinseln, June 1943.
50 Sanders, *Channel Islands under German Occupation*, pp. 164–5.
51 Paul Sanders, '"Managing under Duress": Ethical Leadership, Social Capital and the Civilian Administration of the British Channel Islands during the Nazi Occupation, 1940–1945', *Journal of Business Ethics*, Vol. 93 (1), 2010, 113–29.
52 Charles Cruickshank, *The German Occupation of the Channel Islands*, London, Oxford University Press for the Trustees of the Imperial War Museum, 1975, pp. 41–5; Sanders, *Channel Islands under German Occupation*, p. xx.
53 Guernsey school-teacher John Crossley Hayes referred to the syndrome suffered by Guernsey islanders during the Occupation as 'Robinsonism', John Crossley Hayes (1910–2003), *A Sojourn in Guernsey*, p. 67, http://www.johncrossleyhayes.co.uk/writings/A_Sojourn_in_Guernsey.php, accessed 14 July 2013.
54 Sanders, *Channel Islands under German Occupation*, p. 152.
55 IWM. Documents.13409.Dening 9. Force 135, I(b). Report 'Resistance during the Occupation', n.d.
56 One source clearly hints that the majority of the population was aware that hot-headed resistance was not what the situation required, s. IWM. Documents.13409. Dening 4. *Sabotage and Betrayal*, Unknown author (Guernsey), n.d.
57 TNA.HO.144/22237. MI19. Report no. 2507 'Guernsey Side Lights on Island Affairs', 20 November 1944; 'Excerpts from private letter of Guernsey Commission Agent brought over by informant 2503/2503A', n.d.
58 IWM.Documents.13409.Dening 4. *Sabotage and Betrayal*, Unknown author (Guernsey), n.d.
59 Cruickshank, *The German Occupation of the Channel Islands*, pp. 85–8.
60 Ibid., pp. 88–9.
61 Ambrose Sherwill, *A Fair and Honest Book*, Lulu.com, 2007, p. 259.
62 Cruickshank, *The German Occupation of the Channel Islands*, pp. 90–1.
63 'Report Delivered to States of Guernsey by A.J. Sherwill, 7 August 1940', reprinted in Sherwill, *A Fair and Honest Book*, p. 272.
64 See the case of the manager at Le Riche's, IWM.Documents.13409.Dening 4. *Sabotage and Betrayal*, Unknown author (Guernsey), n.d.; Sherwill, *A Fair and Honest Book*, pp. 139–42; also IWM.Documents.13409.Dening 4. *Sabotage and Betrayal*. Typescript of letter to the public by Sherwill, 28 September 1940.
65 Sherwill, *A Fair and Honest Book*, p. 146.
66 Ibid., p. 147; in his post-war report John Leale referred to the Nicolle-Symes affair as 'as near to an atrocity' as the island ever came, TNA.HO.45/22424. Report of the President of the Controlling Committee of the States of Guernsey on the activities

of the Committee during the five years of German occupation, 23 May 1945; also William Bell, *The Commando Who Came Home to Spy*, Guernsey, 1998, p. 29.
67 How this came about is unknown, but Bandelow's absence from the island at the moment of their arrest is likely to have had some bearing.
68 IA.G 01-07. Typescript, 'Extract from the Commentary of the Manual of Military Law, issued by the War Office, 1929 Edition', n.d.
69 Sherwill, *A Fair and Honest Book*, p. 92.
70 The passage also read: 'The I(b) Reports state that without hesitation it can be said that the feeling of the people in Jersey and Guernsey is against the States for the policy adopted during the occupation', s. TNA.KV.4/78. Consolidated report 'The I(b) Reports on the Channel Islands', by Major J. R. Stopford, 8 August 1945, 6. The passage was also adopted for the final report, entitled 'The Channel Islands under German Occupation', and submitted to the Home Secretary on 17 August 1945, see TNA.HO.45/22399.
71 Frank Bolz Jr, Kenneth J. Dudonis and David P. Schulz, *The Counterintelligence Handbook. Tactics, Procedures and Techniques,* Boca Raton, London, New York, Washington DC, CRC Press, 2002.
72 Sherwill, *A Fair and Honest Book*, p. 91, for further illustration, pp. 244-6.
73 Sanders, *Channel Islands under German Occupation*, p. 160.
74 IA. Frank Falla papers. Statement by Rachel Symes, Guernsey, 10 November 1964.
75 IA.FK 01-11. Feldkommandatur 515 (Knackfuss) to the Bailiff of Guernsey, and to Nebenstelle Guernsey. Re. Plakatierung einer Proklamation, 5 April 1941.
76 After a cable sabotage in March 1941, for example, Leale stated that anyone who had wished to do so could have left the island the year before; he concluded, that those who stayed had accepted the position and would 'act as good citizens', 'Extract from Jurat Leale's speech in the States', Guernsey Star, 22 March 1941.
77 Similar to the arrangement in Jersey, the 'big gun' (the Bailiff) was supposed to have been held in reserve and 'brought to bear on the Germans when some more than usually difficult or unpleasant matter was under discussion'. This, however, was not consistent with Carey's general disposition, which, according to Sherwill, was to 'worry himself sick', Sherwill, *A Fair and Honest Book*, p. 185.
78 TNA.HO.45/22399. Lord Justice du Parq, Note on complaints against Channel Islands administration, 14 June 1945.
79 Semelin, *Unarmed against Hitler*, passim.
80 Ian Kershaw, *The Nazi Dictatorship: Problems and Perspectives of Interpretation*, London, Arnold, 2000, pp. 183-217 (specifically pp. 192-4).
81 Ibid., pp. 194-5.
82 Martin Broszat and Elke Fröhlich, *Alltag und Widerstand: Bayern im Nationalsozialismus*, München, Piper, 1987, pp. 52; 61.
83 Kershaw, *The Nazi Dictatorship*, p. 204.
84 TNA.HO.45/22399. Memorandum, Alexander Coutanche to Sir Donald Somervell, 3 July 1945.
85 JAS.B/A/W50/201. Bailiff Coutanche to Platzkommandant, 25 April 1945.
86 JAS.B/A/L/33/1. In the matter of German war crimes and in the matter of Alexander Moncrief Coutanche, Statement under oath, 12 June 1945.
87 Sanders, *Channel Islands under German Occupation*, p. 124.
88 IA.FK 05-06. Professor Pfeffer, 'Bericht über Studienreise nach den britischen Kanalinseln', 1941.

89 With Pfeffer relating Coutanche's remarks in an official report, there is no reason to doubt their authenticity. The text passage itself is situated within a wider critical argument highlighting the 'lukewarm' attitude of islanders towards Nazi Germany. To use a colloquial expression: Pfeffer found islanders' liberal attitude to Jews 'pathetic'.
90 By contrast, the same order passed in Guernsey, on 30 June 1942, Cohen, *The Jews in the Channel Islands during the German Occupation*, p. 41.
91 TNA.WO.311/13. In the Matter of War Crimes, Statement by A. Coutanche, Bailiff, 12 June 1945.
92 TNA.WO.311/13. In the Matter of War Crimes, Statement by Clifford Orange, Aliens Officer, 12 May 1945; JAS.D.Z.H5/248. Duret Aubin to the 12 Constables of Jersey, 29 December 1943.
93 *The Bridge on the River Kwai* (1957) is an Oscar-winning motion picture, directed by David Lean. In order to restore discipline and morale among his battered and abused co-prisoners in a Japanese labour camp, Nicholson galvanizes the men into focusing on a common goal, the building of a railway bridge. Nicholson is of the opinion that the men can only survive if they 'stick together', rather than expending their energy on escape or sabotage, which he considers futile and dangerous. In exchange for meeting the construction target, the Japanese commander in charge of the camp abandons his policy of prisoner abuse and Nicholson is given a free hand. Nicholson restores the captives' self-respect and earns the reluctant respect of his Japanese guards, but he also becomes increasingly oblivious to the fact that, by providing the enemy with a strategically important asset, he is working into their hands. In cognitive psychology Nicholson's behaviour would be referred to as escalation of commitment or goal perseverance. The final sequence sees him trying to rescue the bridge from an Allied demolition team sent into the jungle to destroy it, before finally realizing the treasonous consequences of his action. The denouement of the inner conflict is provided by Nicholson's death in the ensuing combat and his accidental (or deliberate?) fall, which triggers the explosive device and destroys the bridge.
94 Cohen, *The Jews in the Channel Islands during the German Occupation*, p. 68.
95 Francis Falla, *The Silent War. The Inside Story of the Channel Islands under the Jackboot*, Guernsey, Leslie Frewin Ltd, 1967, p. 156.
96 JAS. B/A/W81/3. R N McKinstry, Medical Officer of Health to A M Coutanche, Bailiff, 11 March 1944.
97 The MI 19 debriefings of Channel Islands escapees include a list of 'reliable personalities' in Jersey: Centenier Garden, the policeman involved in the Page case, Major Manley, the acting head of the ARP, and Alfred Sarre, the Guernsey representative in Jersey. Other officials mentioned were food controller Alfred Le Gresley, his assistant, Mr Mourant, and Jurat Dorey, the President of the Department of Finance, TNA.HO.144/22237. MI19. Report no. 2510(S), 'Jersey Reliable Personalities. Further interrogation of three Jersey escapees', 27 November 1944.
98 Le Quesne, *The Occupation of Jersey*, entries of 24 September 1943 and 12 January 1944.
99 Leslie Sinel, *The German Occupation of Jersey: The Wartime Diary of Leslie Sinel*, Jersey, Villette Publishing, 1995, entry of 26 February 1943.
100 William Bell, *Guernsey Occupied but Never Conquered*, Exeter, The Studio Publishing Services, 2002, p. 273.
101 Falla, *The Silent War*, p. 98.

102 That the Germans were intent on going ahead with the evacuation is detailed in their correspondence of January 1942, s. BA-MA.RH26/319/8. KTB 319. I.D., Anlage 179., FK 515 to 319 I.D., 23 January 1942. When a German doctor requested a feasibility report, McKinstry alerted the Jersey Superior Council, on 25 February 1942, s. JAS.B/A/W66/3. McKinstry to the President of Department of Public Health, 25 February 1942. Coutanche's reaction followed three days later.
103 JAS.B/A/W66/3. Bailiff Coutanche to FK, 28 February 1942.
104 TNA.TS.26/89. J A R Pimlott (HO) to J M Martin CVC, 18 September 1944.
105 IWM. Documents.13409.Dening 4. 'Report by Major Lanz, 216 ID, the First German Commandant', 1940.
106 James Marr, *The History of Guernsey. The Bailliwick's Story*, Guernsey, The Guernsey Press, 2001, p. 320.
107 In 1944 Max von Aufsess referred to the Guernsey statesmen as 'weaker characters' and to the Guernsey government as less 'politically sound and stable' than Jersey's. Letter to Major-General von Schmettow, 14 September 1944, reprinted in his diary, Max Freiherr von Aufsess, The von Aufsess Occupation Diary, Chichester, Phillimore, 1985, p. 24. Further evidence can be obtained through the internal staff evaluations conducted by the German military administration, AN.AJ40/543. Description des fonctionnaires. Filing cards for Victor Gosselin Carey, Bailiff of Guernsey and Alexander Moncrieff Coutanche, Bailiff of Jersey, n.d.
108 Sherwill, *A Fair and Honest Book*, p. 234.
109 William Bell, *I Beg to Report. Policing in Guernsey during the German Occupation*, Guernsey, Guernsey Press, 1995, pp. 131; 151; 240.
110 Alan Wood and Mary Wood, *Islands in Danger. The Story of the German Occupation of the Channel Islands*, New York, Macmillan, 1955, p. 42.
111 Sherwill, *A Fair and Honest Book*, pp. 259–61.
112 Cruickshank, *The German Occupation of the Channel Islands*, pp. 78–9.
113 TNA.HO.144/22834. Sherwill, Ilag VII, Lager Laufen, to Sir Alexander Maxwell, 6 July 1944.
114 TNA.HO.144/22834. Brigadier French (WO) to Markbreiter (HO), 12 August 1944.
115 Andrew Roberts, *Hitler and Churchill. Secrets of Leadership*, London, Weidenfeld & Nicolson, 2003, passim.
116 The thesis of Peter Liberman's *Does Conquest Pay? The Exploitation of Occupied Industrial Societies*, Princeton, Princeton University Press, 1996.
117 Ethan Hollander, 'Swords or Shields? Implementing and Subverting the Final Solution in German-occupied Europe', Working paper, Department of Political Science, Wabash College, 2011, http://papers.ssrn.com/sol3/papers.cfm?abstract_id=1906430, accessed 6 September 2013.
118 See the fourth chapter, on legitimacy, in Semelin's *Unarmed against Hitler*; also Jørgen Kieler, *Dänischer Widerstand gegen den Nationalsozialismus. Ein Zeitzeuge berichtet über die Geschichte der dänischen Widerstandsbewegung 1940–1945*, Hannover, Offizin, 2008
119 See the final chapter ('Was Vichy a Lesser Evil?') in Robert Paxton's paradigmatic and highly influential Vichy France. *Old Guard and New Order*, New York, Columbia University Press [New York, Knopf], 2001 [1972 1st ed.], pp. 357–73.
120 Alain Michel, Vichy et la Shoah. Enquête sur le paradoxe français, Paris, CLD, 2012.
121 Santoro, *Profits and Principles*, pp. 143–58.
122 Sanders, *Channel Islands under German Occupation*, pp. 1–45, 95–7; 147–55.
123 TNA.WO.32/13750. Treasury document 'The Islands Budgets', 1945–6.

124 Sherwill, *A Fair and Honest Book*, p. 244.
125 Frank Falla, *The Silent War*, p. 119.
126 Turner, *Outpost of Occupation*, pp. 197–201.
127 TNA.HO.45/22399. Memorandum, Alec Coutanche to Sir Donald Somervell, 3 July 1945.
128 JAS.M/03/2. Photocopy of a Police Report written by Police Constable Albert Chardine relating to the patrolling of Gloucester Street and Newgate Street, St Helier, 15 February 1945.
129 Garden is mentioned as such in the intelligence debrief of three Jersey escapees, TNA.HO.144/22237. MI19. Report no. 2510(S), 'Jersey Reliable Personalities. Further interrogation of three Jersey escapees', 27 November 1944.
130 TNA.HO.144/22834. Memo, J. T. D. Hubert, 23 August 1943.

10

Economic Resistance and Sabotage*

Paul Sanders

The problems of defining economic resistance are legion. Dutch economic historian Hein Klemann once gave the fictional example of a toy manufacturer in the occupied territories exporting to Germany, and thus freeing capacity for war production, to show that 'economic collaboration' is relatively meaningless as a definitional category. The problems one confronts when attempting to define economic resistance are very much of the same order. In most accounts of resistance, economic resistance involves something like 'going slow', not working with the Germans or denying them access to goods and service. The latter two themselves were often already rather unrealistic: short of going out of business altogether, not working with the occupier was difficult or impossible, as the latter was often the only solvent client left. Can or should businesses be obligated to patriotically self-destruct?

This is not all. Add to this first conundrum the opacity of economic dissidence, which, by its nature, involves behaviour that, by peacetime standards, is illegal, criminal or both – theft, pilfering, receiving stolen goods, black-marketeering or sabotage – and you get an idea of the scope of the problem. Similar to administrative resistance, this type of activity was inextricably tied up with the legitimacy issue: stealing or robbing could only ever be a virtue, if it was done with a patriotic motive or result. Normally a felony, such activity could be sanctioned as a method of economic warfare between competing powers.

The objective of this particular chapter is to first probe the double meaning of economic resistance. This exercise passes via a recognition and discussion of the ambiguity of common law offences during the Occupation. Students of the period should get used to the idea that islanders were not duped by the formal exigency placed upon them to adhere to standard rules. The Occupation entailed the pauperization of a large section of the population of the Channel Islands. And the worsening material conditions led many law-abiding people who, under normal circumstances, would not have strayed from the straight and narrow, to engage in activities that could have the look of property offences. The first range of cases discussed in the section that follows will be the obvious 'clean' categories, followed by the less straightforward cases. As a key exemplar of this second category, we will provide a detailed study of the still controversial case of the purported sabotage undertaken by members of the Guernsey police force, in 1941–2. Criteria will be proposed to enable a more adequate portrayal of these activities, for example why, on reflection, the action of the Guernsey policemen can qualify as economic resistance.

Probing the double meaning

The example of sabotage is a good case in point for probing the double meaning of economic resistance. How are we to distinguish whether an act of sabotage was driven by politics, vandalism or anti-social behaviour?

The exploits of French railway workers are among the most celebrated episodes of sabotage in the Second World War. René Clement's heavily stylized film *The Battle of the Rails* (1945) depicts the important role this resistance played in the success of Overlord; to the point that the 'good work' undertaken by *Résistance-Fer*, the network responsible for railway sabotage, was cited by General de Gaulle after the war. Yet railway sabotage was not the norm of behaviour for railway-men in occupied France. On the whole, more railway-men continued to do their job than sabotage or delay their trains. Resistance-minded French railway-men had good reasons for limiting their sabotage to the endgame in 1944. For one thing, the German reprisal policy made the human and moral cost of any such action prohibitively high.[1] Sabotage was unsustainable as a method for longer campaigns of attrition. Only in very exceptional cases, such as in June 1944, could railway sabotage seriously dent the fighting capacity of Nazi Germany. In other circumstances the damage was minimal or quickly repaired. Elsewhere the story was little different. The overriding characteristic of sabotage then is its ambiguity, and not its scope or impact, which was limited at best. The genuine importance of sabotage lay not so much in the irreparable damage it did to the Germans than in its symbolic or political value. In the end the greatest saboteurs of all were often the Germans themselves; for the repressive nature of the Nazi regime incited many Europeans to see to it that the occupiers benefited as little as possible from the fruits of their labour. And, on balance, this economic dissidence (or non-compliance) did more damage than outright sabotage.

Besides sabotage, another good example for gauging the ambiguity of the notion of 'economic resistance' is the black market. In many cases there simply is no way of telling whether someone engaging in black-marketeering during the Occupation was following patriotic instincts or simply trying to line his or her own pockets. It was only natural for black market operators to have sought to legitimize their actions by claiming that diverting goods into illegal channels equalled depriving the Germans. In reality, however, things were less forgiving, for the Germans controlled black market demand through their superior purchasing power.[2] An indication of this is their massive importation of occupation currency into the islands. On the other hand, the black market was an important factor in the survival of the civilian population of the Channel Islands. What one needs to understand is that the black market was Janus-faced: while much of it was indeed German-controlled, sometimes it also worked in favour of the occupied. Albert Lamy, acting chief officer of the Guernsey police force from June 1942, described the necessary distinction as follows:

> There was one type of Black Market [sic] in which we took no interest at all. This consisted of goods illicitly imported by the Germans and sold by them. As this had no adverse effect on the population as a whole we were not interested. But on the other side locally produced foodstuffs, namely meat, butter, eggs, root vegetables etc. came in for stringent attention.[3]

This supply-side focus was a pragmatic and reasonable approach. A truly comprehensive control effort was out of the question, unless one wanted to introduce draconian punishment. At the same time it was impossible to stop German smuggling, which contributed to the haemorrhage of cash reserves and other stable value items still in the island. But these illegal trades in gold, antiques or real estate had no effect on those areas that mattered most for survival. Rather than controlling what was uncontrollable, the effort focused on what one could control, i.e. black market supply draining island-produced or island-financed resources. Despite the many diversionary loopholes in the distribution system, it was also fundamentally sound to act before products were brought to market, in the farms, greenhouses and fields at the bottom of the supply chain.

The minuscule windfalls that the Channel Islands' economies could provide to the German war effort compound the problem of ambiguity. Economic resistance presupposes economic value; yet the islands were close to valueless in macroeconomic terms. As to opportunities for meaningful sabotage, the most obvious and alluring choice were the military installations. However, attacking these would have been suicidal. Paradoxically, the greatest economic contribution the Channel Islands made to the Allied war effort was an unintended consequence of the German fortification programme: keeping the German fortresses up and running was a formidable drain on the Nazi economy and prevented these resources from being deployed to other frontlines.

Where Channel Islanders had a better chance of 'scoring' directly was in the battle of the wits. Another alternative was passive economic resistance. This could extend to ignoring orders, not filling in forms and stopping in its tracks the requisitioning of motor cars, tyres, refrigerators and other items on which the occupier had set his eyes. One Guernsey resident stored such items in a secret cache, admitting, nevertheless, that this was easier for people living in isolated houses in the country than for those in more crowded locations.[4] A variation on this theme was to make life awkward for the Germans. One line of business at the forefront of this was the Channel Islands banks. This was cast into relief when the Germans attempted to introduce a 'clearing system' between the islands and occupied France, in 1942. One specific challenge for the banks was that the clearing system smoothed the transfer of foreign funds, allowing the relatively unchecked conversion of francs into sterling, and the placement of such funds in Channel Islands' banks. In February 1943 Barclays in St Helier made it clear to the German banking commissar in Paris that it was unwilling to be party to money laundering. Barclays also pointed to the smuggling of occupation currency into Jersey, suggesting that the island's authorities should be given the chance to rid themselves of this excess liquidity through purchases in France. In 1942 the banks also attempted to 'defend' customers whose nationality they had been called upon to disclose. This German move aimed at identifying the holdings of evacuees and others residing in 'enemy territory', and it could be a preliminary to sequestration. The banks countered, replying that they did not enquire about nationality when opening accounts, only respectability. They were then told to group customer balances under headings such as 'believed to be British', 'believed to be French' etc. Tongue-in-cheek defiance of this sort is also known from other financial companies in Jersey, which replaced terms such as 'enemy property' with 'holdings of shares in the names of persons out of the island' in their correspondence. When one company finally coughed up a list containing a few names, it concluded with a mischievous 'All the above shareholders are of British Nationality. There are no enemy holders of shares in Jersey.' The secretary of the company then put 'BRITISH' [sic] behind her signature.[5] Significantly, no company called upon to declare 'enemy property' in the islands responded to question number seven: 'Are any shareholders Jewish?'[6]

The cause célèbre of the 1942 Guernsey police trial

Conceding ambiguity may not seem like much, but it is a step forward from previous wartime and post-war narratives, which simply condemned all illegal economic activity outright, regardless of the fact that some of it may have been a form of protest, defiance or resistance. A variation on this theme is that of 'patriotic theft'. If one needed a case to cast into relief not only this idea, but also the important grey zones between 'law' and 'resistance', then there could be no better than the two trials against 18 policemen in Guernsey (i.e. over half the entire force), in spring 1942. The men were investigated for their participation in the pilfering of a number of German and islander-owned depots between autumn 1941 and spring 1942. The raids on the German depots were the object of a military trial conducted in the court of Feldkommandantur 515 in April 1942. Convicted on criminal grounds, the men received varying sentences of up to four-and-a-half years' hard labour. Once they completed their trial, the Germans handed over the case to the Royal Court of Guernsey for prosecution of the raids on the islander-owned stores, alleged to have been committed by ten of these men: Kingston Bailey, William Burton, Charles Friend, Jack Harper, Alfred Howlett, William Quin, Frederick Short, Percival Smith, Frank Tuck and Frank Whare. On acknowledging receipt of the German case files, something curious happened; for the deputy solicitor general, Advocate Martel, indicated to Dr Biel, the German judge advocate, that the prosecution in the civilian trial would not be able to rely on the statements made previously to the German police:

> You say that these statements constitute confessions but I would remind you that if they are denied it will not be possible to use them in view of the fact that your officers before whom they were made would not be available to give evidence before our Court.[7]

The scenario outlined by Martel owed to the precedent of a similar Royal court trial, in early 1941. In this trial, dealing with pillaging by a Guernsey work party in Alderney, the case had collapsed when the Germans had refused to let members of the occupying force take the witness stand. The case was then taken into German jurisdiction. What prompted Martel's reply was the fact that the defendants had let it be known that they would deny their earlier 'confessions', claiming that these had been extracted in an unlawful manner. And as to making any incriminating statements, they were intent on pleading 'not guilty'. Biel's reply to Martel followed on 8 May 1942. It read that if the accused denied their prior confessions to the German investigators, the Germans would do as in the 1941 Alderney plunder affair and take over this civilian case.[8] This drove the civilian authorities into a corner, leaving them with no option other than to go ahead with the trial on the basis of the available evidence; unless, of course, they were prepared to risk an early collapse of the trial. The latter, however, was a very unpalatable prospect, as it would have led to a clash, followed by a thorough pounding of the island authorities from the German-controlled press. The authorities therefore tried to get the defendants back into line. This they achieved by drawing their attention to Biel's letter and by intimating that they could be sent back to the German court for a second trial. The blow was softened by Martel suggesting 'that it would all count for nothing after the War and would be washed out'.[9] Most of the men then reconsidered their attitude and reversed track, confirming their prior 'confessions'. The majority also switched their pleas back to 'guilty'.

The impact of Biel's letter, in terms of initiating counter-retractions and contradictions, is visible throughout the trial. Despite these, the letter was not submitted as evidence. The court also chose to ignore the numerous distress signals given by the accused. Bailiff Carey, the presiding judge, simply brushed aside concerns with comments that he was not interested in 'the letter' that was being referred to. The contradictions were particularly conspicuous in the charge against Bill Burton, Charles Friend, Fred Short and Bill Quin, concerning an alleged theft of eight bottles of alcoholic beverages from Waterloo House, a store belonging to a company by the name of Bucktrout's. Questioned about his involvement, during the civilian procedure, Short said that he 'made that statement voluntarily and pleaded guilty after [he] had read the contents of a letter', followed by an immediate contradiction, 'I know in my own mind I have never entered this store for any illegal purpose.'[10] The depositions of the other three indicted were similarly garbled. Concerning different alleged thefts, Alfred Howlett changed track a total of four times over the course of the two trials. During his interrogation by the Germans on 17 March 1942, he first declared: 'Asked as to whether I have at any time participated in the burglary of the above stores, I declare: that it is a lie, I have never been involved in a theft of any form.' However, when he was shown Percy Smith's 'confession' of 11 March 1942, which incriminated him directly, he retracted, stating: 'After having had read to me the imputing deposition [...] I admit that I have lied just now. I am now prepared to tell the truth.' Howlett then 'admitted' that he had entered the stores in question, together with Smith.[11] Two months later, on 10 May, when the civilian authorities asked him to confirm the validity of his statement to the Germans he repudiated this, declaring: 'I have read the statement I am alleged to have made and wish to plead not guilty.' Six days later, presumably under the influence of Biel's letter, he changed track once more, now admitting again that he had entered the store in question, that 'it was the only time' and that he would not have done this had he known it was a civilian store. The presiding judge would have none of this, however, and chose to interpret his U-turns as nothing more than a sign of the untrustworthiness of 'this man Howlett [who] doesn't seem to know the first thing about the truth'[12] – a man who, by the way, had served on the Guernsey police force for over 20 years.[13]

One might be forgiven for thinking that not admitting Biel's letter as evidence was the main procedural shortcoming of the trial. However, an even bigger role was played by the *nature* of the German 'confessions' which the Royal Court entered into evidence. Only a small part of this material was the result of legitimate police techniques, such as house searches, standard interrogations or forensics. Most of it, in fact, was the result of third-degree interrogations by the German police, employing various means of abuse, threats and trickery. Many of the men were pressured into signing statements on the understanding that their colleagues had made statements incriminating them. They were later to find out that this was pure fabrication. A taste of what these methods entailed can be gleaned from the experience of one of the defendants in the German trial, Archibald Tardif:

> I was shown signed statements by other men and was eventually told that if I did not sign I would be shot, so I eventually signed. All these statements were typed in German. After I had signed my alleged statement, it was returned to the typewriter and additions made.[14]

There is very little variation in the accounts of Tardif's co-defendants, except that his experience was not the worst. The routine use of such methods by the German police is corroborated by third parties. One of these was the long-time chief of the island police force, Albert Lamy. Commenting on the arrest and interrogation, in 1943, of Jean Binet, 'one of the finest cat burglars you could wish to find', he wrote:

> I was the unfortunate witness of the German Third Degree methods at this time. Binet had been taken to prison and three German Police Officers came to interrogate him. They came armed with a rubber hose about half an inch – very flexible, and in turn the three of them got at him. By the time they had finished he was just a crying wreck. Another of their methods was to leave a man in the cells all night with lights on, a couple of nights later the lights would be left off and they would come along in the early hours of the morning, wake him up and question him. Of course it was quite obvious that waking under these conditions it was easy to extract a statement, just the kind of statement they wanted. Often statements were taken from accomplices incriminating another, the statement would then be prepared, brought along to the accused, told to read it, that it was true and he had to sign it. These standards were often signed just for the sake of peace and quietness; the prison sentence being the lesser of two evils.[15]

Another witness to German police methods was Ambrose Sherwill, who served as the men's defence counsel in the German trial. His take was a peculiar one, and diverged from Lamy's opinion: deploring the use of force, he also believed that the policemen's statements would have been no different had the method been any other:

> I received a message through the German Feldgendarmerie that the accused wished me to represent them at their trial. I then obtained permission to visit them and saw them all in the absence of any German.
>
> A number of them had been beaten up to secure admissions of guilt but it was clear that, however much I deplored the method of obtaining such admissions, those admissions were in accordance with the truth.[16]

On this issue, modern criminology would weigh rather more in favour of Lamy. The issue of 'false confessions' has received considerable media exposure in recent years, following a number of exonerations on the basis of DNA analysis. The point driven home by the current debate is that police interrogations leading to false confessions are very commonplace, even in strong rule of law regimes.[17] Naturally, the situation is all the more alarming where rule of law is non-existent and third degree methods are the norm. To make matters worse, the heading of 'false confessions' as a frame for the Guernsey police trials misses the point. The problem here is not one of defendants adapting their stories to what an interrogator 'wants to hear'. The issue is one of phantasmagoric statements drafted by German policemen being submitted to the accused for signature, in a language they could not read. It was only in the German courtroom that many of the signatories found out about the accusations their confessions contained. The unreliability of the 'evidence' gathered by the Germans emerged in the post-war discussion surrounding the alleged theft of spirits and wine from the premises of Bucktrout Company Limited. The following passage appears in the post-war petition requesting the Privy Council to grant the men 'leave to appeal':

> Although, as stated, Your Petitioners had taken food from the Germans and had distributed it to civilians and others on the Island [sic], the Germans were not aware of the exact extent of this and appeared to have acted solely on suspicion. Thus the charges as formulated were, to a large extent, speculation by the Germans. For example, the eight bottles or thereabouts of spirits and wine included in the charges against William Quin, Charles Albert Friend and Frederick Winzer Short and the twelve bottles or thereabouts of spirits and wine in the charge against Frank William Whare were alleged to have been taken from the premises of 'Bucktrout Company Limited', yet one Alec Adams, the foreman of this Company [sic], gave evidence that no liquor at all was in fact missing.[18]

What was stated to be missing, was not, in fact, actually missing. The way in which the German material was assembled even raises the question whether the policemen weren't framed from the very beginning. This was already suggested in the men's post-war Privy Council petition:

> Your petitioners believe that it was the suspicion that they were engaged in (a) general campaign rather than the specific charges made later which was the cause of their arrest by the Germans.[19]

The view is also shared by Bill Bell, a local historian in Guernsey and the only post-war author to have taken a serious interest in the case. He writes:

> It quickly became clear, by the speed of the German reaction, that the operation to catch PCs Tuck and Bailey (the prelude to the wave of arrests in March 1942, n.b.) had been carefully planned well in advance and the removal of Inspector Sculpher was one of their prime aims.[20]

Although there is some indication that OT stock management was patchy, the thefts, which stretched over several months, could not have gone unnoticed. And it did not require much imagination to come up with ideas for who was responsible for the raids, which were occurring at night-time. Any investigator would have invariably focused his sights on the two groups of islanders who had the right to be out after curfew: the police and the island doctors.[21] The fact that nobody was ever apprehended and that no suspicious goings-on were ever reported would have pointed the finger at the police, all the more as the force was known for its anti-German sentiment. Since the beginning of the Occupation, the occupiers had reprimanded several members of the force for their 'failure to salute' and similar disciplinary lapses.[22]

It is an interesting thought experiment to consider what would have happened if all the accused had adopted more spirited defence tactics. The circumstantial evidence being weak, it is questionable whether the accusations would have stood up. Two of the accused, Bill Burton and Jack Harper, went against the grain and decided to stick to their initial pleas of 'not guilty' in the civilian trial.[23] While the first was acquitted, the second had 3 months added to the 12-month sentence called for by the prosecution. The difference between both was that Harper had signed a German 'confession' incriminating colleagues, whereas Burton had not. This meant that in the civilian trial Burton 'was not embarrassed by having to maintain it' against his co-defendants.[24] Burton later stated that Biel's letter had left him unimpressed, and that he was not afraid about his case going back to the Germans. This was in keeping with the general disposition of this old soldier who, having fought in the trenches during the Great War, had, presumably, seen worse in his life.[25] Harper's 'non-cooperation', on the other hand, was seen as an aggravating factor. The impression was certainly influenced by the Germans having named him the ringleader and having awarded him the stiffest sentence of all, four years' hard labour. His conviction was, in the main, based on the incriminating German 'confessions' other men had made about him. The same applied to the other sentences, which ranged between 3 and 16 months' hard labour, and which were to be served concurrently with the German sentences.

Falling out with the bosses

The official line on this event for over 70 years has been that the island bosses acted as they always did, as paternalistic fathers holding out their hands over their 'fallen sons'. After the war the Guernsey Police Committee tried to attribute the responsibility for the demoralization of the force to the police supervisor, Inspector Sculpher, but the real issues transcended Sculpher's leadership. Contrary to the prevailing myth, the policemen and their hierarchy had been divided by an ever widening ocean of incomprehension since even before the Occupation. Following the outbreak of war in September 1939 many in the island police force – which contained several ex-servicemen – had wished to enlist in the armed forces. While it is unclear whether pressure was exerted to compel the men to remain at their posts,[26] the fact is that by the time the Germans invaded, none had joined up. Once the trap shut many of the men began to realize their predicament, and regretted their decision. Policing their fellow islanders in the interest of a policy of frictionless collaboration with the enemy was not something they had bargained for. Resentment against officials for putting them in this situation mounted. Torn between two antagonistic, but equally legitimate positions – the duty to do something for King and Country, on the one hand, and the call to ensure that the Occupation stayed frictionless, on the other – the police force became confused as to where their duty lay. Short described the situation they faced in the following terms:

> The Police Force [...] was in a difficult position, because we had to convince the Germans that we were working for them, at the same time as we were [...] doing our best not to help them.[27]

Such a situation is commonly termed a dilemma or a 'catch-22', after the title of Joseph Heller's bestselling novel.

In order to come out of this situation without 'fouling one's nest', the authorities had to recognize the profound implications of this immensely difficult and unprecedented situation for all public officials; they had to use their discretion to the full; their subordinates needed guidance in order to tackle the worst ethical pitfalls; and it was imperative to maintain social trust. An indication of how this challenge could be negotiated is given by the Frederick Page case, detailed in the chapter on administrative resistance, which involved an exchange between the Attorney General of Jersey, Duret Aubin, and a member of the local police, Centenier Garden, in 1943. Even this far into the occupation, trust between the police and their superior authority in the sister island still existed to an extent that a policeman could make an informal approach to his hierarchical superior on an extremely sensitive matter, without fear of reprimand or worse. It points in the direction of the Jersey authorities having understood the double-binds in which the occupation placed all officials. Enforcing blind obedience could not be relied upon in this situation; what was needed were additional informal arbitrages. The police in both islands were in a particularly acute predicament because they were the best-informed collective group of islanders. We know that it was no secret to the police in Guernsey that often two measures were being applied. They had first-hand knowledge of the black market trades in the island; and they also knew who was working the system to his or her advantage, and how.[28] At the same time they experienced the deprivation suffered by islanders without the right connections to get them through these difficult times. The period during which the raids on the German depots occurred, autumn 1941 to spring 1942, coincided with the pinnacle of civilian suffering in occupied Guernsey.[29] It was the period that prompted the medical officer of the island to write 'that a large part of the population were on diets having calorific values below the subsistence level'. As a result 'older people were unable to withstand the privations [...] the death returns for these months bear witness to this'.[30] According to

Kingston Bailey, 'those who could not afford to buy on the flourishing "Black Market" [...] were already in a state of semi-starvation'.[31] Men in this kind of exposed position need to be led in a particular manner; invoking strict obedience to authority can no longer suffice. This is where the crux of the problem lies, for this cluster of men had no guidance on how to behave in the political vacuum that was the occupation, and in particular how to navigate the 'Syclla und Charybdis' of legitimacy. The inability of their leaders to explain why they could not afford to tackle the Germans head-on led to a void in communication. Like other islanders the policemen did not understand why the island elite wanted to get close to the Germans. A memo drafted by Frank Tuck in 1950 leaves no doubt that the police had wanted to do anything *but* open the doors to German officers and salute them.[32] Bailey confirmed this, saying that, as a branch of executive government, the police became practically useless: 'I turned a blind eye on almost everything, completely ignoring our Police duties and averting my attention, as far as possible, to the Germans'.[33] From there, things went adrift, and an inclination to take 'things' into their own hands began to emerge. Soon enough the police were not only at the forefront of anti-German sentiment, but also of anti-German action.

Bailey placed the commencement of these resistance activities in March 1941, with the cutting of German telephone wires, the putting of sand in German cars and similar pinpricks. He and Tuck took delight in flashing torches at German positions on dark nights, prompting the Germans into search efforts or in moving German vehicles to other positions when parked.[34] Other members of the force reverted to more drastic means, such as the 'roughing up' of individual Germans roaming the streets of St Peter Port in advanced stages of inebriation.[35] The embryonic movement was then galvanized into further action by the radio broadcasts of Douglas Ritchie (alias 'Colonel Britton'), a BBC radio agitator exhorting populations across occupied Europe to engage in 'gentle disruptive activities' against the occupier. Britton's missives fell onto exceptionally fertile ground among the men of the Guernsey police force:

> We [...] felt that he was talking to us and inciting us to action. After all, he was talking to us in English, and we were the only part of the realm occupied. Why would he speak in English to the French, the Poles, the Dutch, or the Belgians?[36]

The culmination of the effort in 1941 was the plastering of 'V signs all over the Island [sic] in places where they would be most seen by the Germans'.[37] Later that year the policemen shifted their target to German food stocks in the island, which they raided on regular intervals. A child of desperation, these were the deeds of people who could no longer contain their anger and resentment. As much as he understood where the policemen were coming from, fellow Guernseyman Wilfred Renouf found their action naïve,[38] compared to his own more covert forms of Švejkism.[39]

The political dimension

The force's political unreliability had been no secret to Prince Eugen zu Öttingen-Wallerstein, the head of the Guernsey *Nebenstelle* branch of the *Feldkommandantur* at the time of the two trials. Öttingen had held Inspector Sculpher personally responsible for this state of affairs and was interested in bringing the force under his own direct command. This denotes a first political dimension,i.e. the German intention to destroy an anti-German force. The second political dimension of the affair was the considerable pressure that was brought to bear on the Royal Court. This contrasts with the official version that the authorities were autonomous in their action, and that they were driven by the desire to spare the men from worse. It has been argued that the two 'worse scenarios' that were successfully avoided by the authorities of Guernsey were either the lengthening of the policemen's sentences (which is what a second German trial would have amounted to); or convictions on the grounds of sabotage.

Neither of these two exculpatory charges holds up to scrutiny. Considering the coercive methods at their disposal, it is inconceivable that the Germans could not have mounted and sustained a charge of sabotage in their first trial, had they wanted to. If the Germans did not press such charges, then this was because they chose not to do so. All indication to the contrary was bluff to pressurize defendants into making statements or to put the island authorities on the back foot. The reason for the German lack of interest in a sabotage trial was its political undesirability. Convictions on a charge of sabotage could have led to death sentences, a scenario that was out of the question, as this was in direct contradiction to Hitler's wish that Channel Islanders be treated with a greater degree of consideration than people in neighbouring France.[40] This tied the administration's hands. The second reason why a sabotage charge was undesirable is related to the first. The policemen had gained widespread notoriety in the island, and not necessarily in a negative sense. This public status provided cover against being treated as saboteurs. Contrary to the assumption of islanders' docility, there is no reason to believe that they did not resent the plenty to which Germans had access, while they went without. Equally, no reason exists to believe that the raids on German stores were not viewed with sympathy.[41] In 1945 Frank Whare even suggested that the police might have 'worked' with the local population, by covering food thefts committed by civilians:

> After the occupation I continued to serve the police force functioning under German supervision which, after a short time, became very irksome and distasteful to many of us, and German orders were ignored whenever possible, consequently duty and discipline grew rather slack.
>
> Finally, early in 1942, when the population got hungry, pilfering of German food stores commenced, often with our knowledge, which, instead of preventing, we encouraged, sometimes even assisting, and receiving food for ourselves and families.[42]

The Achilles heel of the policemen's invocation of 'sabotage' always was the notion that they did not limit their activities to the Germans, but also 'helped themselves' to civilian supplies. The Germans realized this weak point in the defence only too well, and diverted public opinion from the policemen's raiding of German stores to their raiding of islander-owned stores. The overall political objective of the trials was to destroy the reputation of the policemen. Their action had to appear as petty thieving, and the defendants themselves as craven pilferers and common law criminals, rather than latter-day Robin Hoods. Without these additional civilian charges the German proceedings against the policemen may have very well turned into a propaganda debacle. A criminal storyline was thus created that has survived for over 70 years.

That civilian charges could be formulated against the policemen was also welcome from two other points of view. First of all, de-focusing from sabotage allowed the Germans to save face. As Bailey would write later, the fact that the local police had been able to con the Germans for many months made them 'look very silly indeed'.[43] Secondly, the case deflected public attention from the impunity with which members of the occupation force were comporting themselves in the island, and which the local police authorities had had the temerity to report to their German counterparts. In a diabolical twist, in the spring 1942 German investigation into at least one such German looting may have been pinned onto the local police.[44] These new elements take much of the wind out of the established narrative that the local authorities 'saved' the men from a sabotage charge. The argument that the civilian trial prevented a lengthening of the sentences – the military and civilian sentences were served concurrently – is equally hollow. A potent counterargument is whether the men themselves would have considered their loss of reputation (which is what the second trial achieved) a price worth paying for the shortening of a hypothetical combined sentence (had they been sent back to the Germans for a second trial). Their post-war correspondence, as well as their dogged efforts to gain rehabilitation, does not confirm such a view. The way in which the authorities blocked any rehabilitation initiatives after the war makes the hypothetical longer sentence scenario appear as the decidedly lesser evil. The second counterargument is that 'shortening the men's sentences', as a motive, pales in comparison to the much stronger political concern of safeguarding the autonomy of the Royal Court from German encroachment. An ancillary benefit of a civilian trial, from the German perspective, was that it leveraged pressure on the island authorities to 'show their colours'. Rather than islanders playing or duping Germans, it was the other way around. And the moment the game started was when Biel sent his infamous letter to Martel. We can see the pressure mounting in the Royal Court's resignation to accepting evidence which Martel himself had considered doubtful in his first correspondence with Biel. If the second trial went ahead, then it was because the political price of obstruction was considered too high. Once more it is worth referring back to the 1941 Alderney plunder case trial. German propaganda had exploited its collapse as 'proof' of the Royal Court's lukewarm attitude and unwillingness to prosecute offenders. One of the more specific criticisms was that island justice was slow and ineffective. This challenge went straight to the heart of islanders' natural interest in the independence of their institutions. If these were to be more than a lifeless chimera, future German encroachment would have to be resisted. From this institutional point of view the situation in spring 1942 was even more dangerous than the previous year; for the island authorities now also had to save face in a deeply embarrassing situation, which had shown the backbone of their executive to be entirely out of control. A refusal or delay of prosecution would have handed the Germans the perfect propaganda weapon to demonstrate how deep the 'rot' ran in the island polity, and alienated public opinion.

Deportation

The convicted policemen were deported from Guernsey in June 1942. About half of the men, including those with the heaviest sentences, were sent to Germany, some in 1942, others in 1943.[45] All of the men – save Smith – survived, albeit with more or less severe effects on their physical and mental health. The probable reason for the high survival rate was that the policemen were more familiar with the carceral environment, that they had more time to adapt than others and that they could count on their *esprit de corps*. This belies the post-war image of the convicted policemen as hooligans in uniform.

The movements of the prisoners through the Third Reich's prison and camp system were complex and the fate of the men was by no means identical. Thomas Gaudion, for example, was able to join his family at Biberach internment camp in July 1944;[46] Quin ended his war at an unidentified labour camp in the Alps;[47] Bailey, on the other hand, was taken to the SS concentration camp at Dachau once his prison sentence ended, on 23 November 1944.[48] Two trails seem to dominate: one leading from the hard labour prison in Rheinbach, in the Rhineland, to Bernau prison; and another leading from the prisons of Augsburg, to Kaisheim and then to Landsberg, all in Bavaria. Four prisoners, Harper, Friend, Tuck and Smith, were sent on this second trail. Smith died (or was 'murdered', as Friend and Tuck put it[49]) relatively early into his detention, in April 1943. At this time all four detainees were toiling on railway installations at Neuoffingen, a brutal satellite labour camp of Augsburg prison.[50] In a post-war letter Frank Tuck confided that the guards 'killed Smith before the German family [...] bribed the guards to lay off'.[51] This is a reference to the fact that the three Channel Islanders found themselves within a larger group of French political prisoners who had established contact with German civilians; the latter then interceded on their behalf. Foremost among these good Samaritans were Anna Stadler and her sister-in-law Anni Sailer, both of whom received the *légion d'honneur* in 1958. The two women persuaded the guards to 'farm out' the prisoners to their family business, where, instead of toiling, they were fed and nursed back to health.[52] Although the Neuoffingen work detail was transferred elsewhere in May 1944, this breathing space probably increased the prisoners' chances of survival.[53]

Seeking post-war rehabilitation

In view of not only the questionable evidentiary basis of the civilian trial, but also the men's suffering (which bore little relation to the purported crime), one could be forgiven for assuming that it could not have taken very much, indeed, to 'clear up' the matter once the global conflict had come to an end. That hopes of post-war rehabilitation were not misplaced can be inferred from the denouement of a rather similar case, involving the deputy president of the Essential Commodities Committee and Guernsey States flour controller, Frederick Hill-Cottingham. The latter had stolen 660 lb of flour from a local store in December 1943 and was fined £200, in a case tried in the Royal Court in January 1944. On Liberation, Hill-Cottingham was granted a Royal Pardon, on the grounds of procedural irregularities.[54] When the returning policemen tried to do something similar, the political character of the case raised its face again. Their first move was to approach an official enquiry set up in Guernsey, in late 1945, to investigate the events of spring 1942. This enquiry was chaired by a C. W. Bickmore, a civil servant in the Colonial Office, and its task was to sound out whether Inspector Sculpher should be reinstated at the helm of the island police force. This issue had become acute following Sculpher's return to duty from internment in Germany. At first providing a negative assessment of Sculpher's role during the 1942 crisis and advising that he be dismissed, the commission later had to do a U-turn, when Sculpher enlisted the support of the Home Office. The latter criticized Bickmore's handling of the matter and suggested 'that the Island authorities might wish to review the position'.[55] Sculpher's dismissal was then withdrawn, but none of this had any impact on the treatment of his former subordinates, who were shunned by the enquiry.

The former policemen then tried a different route, petitioning the Privy Council in 1951. This petition was drafted under the legal guidance of Geoffrey Bing MP QC, and the solicitors Sydney Silverman MP and Eric Goldrein, on behalf of eight of the ten defendants in the 1942 Royal Court trial (Figures 10.1 and 10.2).[56]

While, originally, it had been planned to involve the defendants in both the German and the civilian trials in this approach, it quickly became apparent that the Privy Council could only provide a ruling on the case brought before the Royal Court, but that it had no jurisdiction over the German court ruling. The petition argued that the 'confessions' used in the civilian court had been obtained in an irregular manner, and that they should have been dismissed. In both trials the defendants had been unable to argue their genuine motives, which they claimed was 'sabotage'. The showing of Biel's 'letter' increased the duress, as it prevented them from pleading 'not guilty'. Specifically, the petition raised the following four questions:

1. whether any real or proper trial took place;
2. whether the evidence upon which the convictions were obtained was admissible;
3. whether the pleas and the evidence tendered at the trial were affected by Biel's letter;
4. whether convictions obtained during the occupation as a result of proceedings instigated by the enemy authorities should be upheld if it could be shown that such convictions were in respect of acts aimed at HM enemies, and as part of a campaign of opposition advocated by HM government.[57]

The petition passed its first hurdle on 7 November 1951, when it was granted 'special leave to appeal'.[58] Expectations that this would pave the way to the rehabilitation of the policemen were understandably high. This made the final rejection of the plea, rendered almost four years later, all the more disappointing.

This ultimate failure is bewildering. It led Bill Bell to argue that British common law was not equipped to deal with the unprecedented legal problems raised by enemy occupation.[59] According to Bell, the fault lay with the absence of a proper appeals process in Guernsey, which pushed the policemen into the Privy Council system. However, as last resort jurisdictions elsewhere, the Privy Council was not habilitated

Economic Resistance and Sabotage 291

Figure 10.1 The legal team of the eight policemen who took their case to the Privy Council on a flying visit to Guernsey, February 1952. From left to right (foreground): Eric Goldrein, Sydney Silverman MP and Geoffrey Bing MP QC, courtesy of Eric Goldrein

to examine issues of evidence; its purview was limited to the detection of procedural irregularities. Geoffrey Bing was aware of this gap, and the perhaps more realistic option would have been to ask for a Royal Pardon, as Hill-Cottingham had done. On the other hand, going down this route would have amounted to an implicit admission of guilt, something the defendants were probably unwilling to do. The other consideration was that if they asked for a Royal Pardon, and this was refused, the route to further initiatives would be barred. The formal limitations of the Privy Council purview shine through in the reasons for the dismissal of the petition. Whether the policemen's action may have been sabotage was a question of interpretation, and therefore not something the judges would pronounce themselves on. They showed equally little interest in the political context or the validity of the 'confessions', which should have been a matter for the Royal Court or an appropriate appellate court to investigate. The only genuine criticism allowed was a procedural issue, the failure of the prosecution in its duty to produce Biel's letter to the Court:

> (T)heir Lordships are [...] of the opinion that in the case of those appellants who contended that their confessions had been induced by the production of the letter from the German authorities and who did not subsequently admit before the Royal Court that they had committed the thefts the convictions must be quashed.[60]

Figure 10.2 Frank Tuck and Eric Goldrein at the time of the Privy Council appeal, ca. 1951–2, courtesy of Eric Goldrein

Only on one charge, that against Burton, Friend, Short, Quin concerning an alleged break-in at Bucktrout's and a theft of eight bottles of alcoholic beverages, did the judges concede that the letter had led to a false conviction. And this conviction alone they advised to be quashed. Still, this move had no incidence on the overall outcome, as the defendants in this case had been convicted on other charges.

The problems of purview go a long way towards explaining the failure of the attempt. But, considering the amount of discretion at the judges' disposal, it is hard to resist a complementary political reading. That the Guernsey authorities had raised concern 'about the position that may arise with regards to the appellants should their appeal be successful' is stated in Home Office correspondence in 1952.[61] As far as the British government is concerned, one might note that their supposedly apolitical view of the Channel Islands occupation is another myth. The considerable interdepartmental squabbling over what was to be done about allegations of collaboration, in summer 1945, speaks a very different language. A majority in British government circles, led by the Home Office, had then recommended the rapid 'clearing' of the islands' authorities, an endeavour crowned by the award of knighthoods and other honours to islands leaders, in January 1946.[62] Ten years on, how desirable would a Privy Council revision of the wartime ruling of an island court, presided by no other than the Bailiff of Guernsey himself, have been? Chances are that this would have reopened the can of worms which the British political establishment had done so much to close earlier. When it came to the crunch, Whitehall did not get involved in the internal affairs of the islands in 1945; and neither, one might venture, did the Privy Council, a decade later. No further attempts to rehabilitate the men were made for some time. Three decades later, Short, Friend and Tuck are understood to have made a last attempt to obtain a Royal Pardon. The three petitioners, then in old age, were the last of the surviving convicted policemen. Short's application was rejected and nothing further is known about the attempts of the other two, except that their criminal convictions stand to this very day. In the end, the only vindication the men ever received was in the form of compensation from the West German government, the legal successor of their former enemy, in the mid-1960s. Rehabilitation in the eyes of their own country, however, this was not. Nor could it ever be.

One of the policemen's strongest supporters throughout these years was the Guernsey journalist, Frank Falla. Falla's tireless efforts were instrumental in advising their applications and securing them compensation from the West Germans. Falla had a keen eye for the centrality of the 1942 police trial, which he singled out as one of the two most significant events of the entire Occupation, together with the 1940 Nicolle Symes affair. In his recently discovered private papers we can see Falla deploring that these two events were 'belittled into meagreness' by the Germans; and also that public opinion in Guernsey lacked any real perspective on them.[63] Falla had shown his sympathies earlier, in April 1942, when he published a piece on the military trial in the Guernsey press, without running it past the German censor (he was fined for this). In 1951, Falla supported the Privy Council bid with evidence supporting the policemen's resistance credentials, describing them as an integral part of the Guernsey 'underground'.[64] It is all the more surprising then that the same Falla drew a veil of silence over the convicted policemen in his book detailing his experiences in occupied Guernsey, *The Silent War* (1967). Although the bulk of the book is autobiographical and focuses heavily on the GUNS episode, other resisters do get a mention, in a separate chapter at the end.[65] Although we know that Falla considered the 1942 police trials extremely significant, there is not a single reference to any policeman in the entire book, with the notable exception of Albert Lamy, Sculpher's interim successor at the helm of the island police force, from 1942 to 1945. This omission runs counter to the fact that the policemen convicted in 1942 were the earliest adopters of the V sign campaign, in 1941, and that Falla cites this episode in *The Silent War* (but without mentioning the policemen's inputs). Was this a lapse of attention? Hardly. Falla is more likely to have come up against the grey zones in the policemen's actions, and to have found them a tad too ambiguous for his own more straight-laced understanding of resistance. These difficulties in assessing the case remain with us today.

An assessment

Although many, now and then, believe that the raiding of German stores, under occupation, was misguided, the legitimacy of such action can be argued both ways. As we have seen in an earlier chapter, where the duties of officials are concerned, a conflict of interest exists between loyalty to King and Country and the necessary loyalty to the occupying authority. As far as the evidence goes, the policemen were not instructed in an appropriate manner on how they were to behave or, where such efforts were undertaken, these were unpersuasive. The policemen therefore could give to the issue of legitimacy the interpretation they wanted.

As to the evidence that the action against German stores was sabotage, we need to consider that the Privy Council testimonials of the policemen corroborate on this point, despite geographic distribution and time laps: Jack Harper had been residing in the United States for some time when he swore his affidavit in 1950. Yet the information he gave was very similar to the version of events as presented by Frank Tuck, who, by then, was residing in Liverpool. These two statements again tally with the earliest version of the sabotage effort we know of, a letter sent by Frank Whare to British officials in Guernsey, in summer 1945, at a time when the men had not even thought that it would become necessary to coordinate a common rehabilitation effort.[66]

The issue is more complex as regards the raids on the civilian stores, where the justification is obviously lesser. The ambiguity that surrounds this part of the story is expressed in the reaction of an unnamed Home Office official to Frank Tuck's memo, in 1950:

> It is difficult to assess the truth of some of Mr. Tuck's statements, & even harder to weigh the merits of his actions during the occupation. On reading through his story one feels a certain amount of sympathy with him from time to time. It must have been impossible immediately after the Germans came to decide by what standards one should live.[67]

The people at the Home Office dealing with the Privy Council application were not the only ones who experienced difficulties in assessing the case. How polarized opinion could be on one and the same group of people was demonstrated by British intelligence operatives who arrived in Guernsey in May 1945, to investigate allegations of collaboration. Had the occupier considered the Guernsey police anti-German, then, ironically, the intelligence corps described the force as a bastion of collaboration in a report to London in summer 1945.[68] They interpreted the 1942 affair as an attempt, by the policemen, to get in on the supply side of the black market with stolen goods, a move discounting 'any patriotic motive'. Furthermore the police were criticized for having interrogated civilians (in some cases, even children) at the time of the V sign campaign and on other such occasions. Had the author of the report realized that many of the cable cuttings and V signs the policemen were ordered to investigate in 1941 were their own 'work', his take on the 'harmonious' relations between them and the Germans would have been very different. It was certainly extremely unfortunate that at the time this report was distributed none of the men concerned were available to present their own version, for they would have described their situation more as one of being stuck 'between a rock and a hard place'. This intelligence analysis (which is anything but particularly intelligent) begs the question of why the Germans disposed with over half of the force in 1942, if they had so much reason to rejoice in their collaboration? Another problem with this report is that it uses no chronology. The occupation is treated, a-historically, as one continuous period that did not experience fluctuations. This is flawed. Following the terrible bloodletting of spring 1942, the rump Guernsey police force that survived would have, naturally, been a more docile organization. The report is coloured by what the police force became later and omits the first two years of the occupation, when it had a very different orientation. It is in itself a rather typical manifestation of the core ideological bias that has distorted the vision of mainland observers on island resistance.

If the conclusions of this report – that the force was pro-German, docile and greedy – must strike one as ludicrous, how likely is it that the effort of the Guernsey policemen was something altogether different? In 1996 French director Jacques Audiard introduced cinema-goers to his anti-hero Albert Dehousse (played by Matthieu Kassowitz) in his film *A Self-Made Hero*. Dehousse is the archetype of the bystander from the French province who spent the Occupation loafing about. As the conflict draws to an end, Dehousse is intent on making the most of the unique opportunities and invents himself an artificial resistance pedigree. Relying on the fact that resisters kept their real identities hidden, he tricks his way into the inner circle of a former resistance network. The *manœuvre* catapults the protagonist up the ranks of post-war France. Towards the end of the film he is nominated to a prestigious post in the French zone of occupation in Germany, in recognition of his service in the Resistance that never was. How likely is it that the effort undertaken by the Guernsey police force was a mix of such fake resistance and opportunism?

The charge is best disproved by the relatively naïve modus operandi, which stands in clear contrast to Dehousse's scheming. The path chosen was not the path of corrupt policeman intent on using their privileged position to cash in on a crisis situation. There were safer and betters ways of maximizing that profit potential. Then there is the testimony of the men themselves. Bill Burton, the father figure to whom most of the younger members of the force looked up to, said that three quarters of what the policemen stole came straight from German stores. This is borne out by the figures used in the two trials, which would indicate that the majority of items were stolen from German depots.[69] The inference then is that the effort was, in the main, directed against the Germans. Some of the policemen explained that they had access to information on all registered islander-owned stores; that they only targeted stores that were not on their list; and that they never willingly targeted civilian stores. This, however, is not where one should let the argument end. The real point of interest is whether or not it was justifiable to enter into possession of goods located on the premises of local companies, but earmarked for German consumption. Bill Burton is affirmative about their having been no difference:

> I, in common with other Police officers entered German stores in order to take foodstuffs and to distribute it amongst people in need. About 75% or 80% of the stuff we took was from German Stores. The remainder was taken from people who were dealing directly with the Germans and distributing it on their behalf. Colonel Britton, in his broadcasts, made no differentiation between civil or military stores.[70]

This stance is confirmed by Frank Tuck who admitted that they targeted the stores of islanders which they *knew* were commandeered by the Germans.[71] They also knew which local traders were working the black market or collaborating with the Germans.

Quizzed at the civilian trial, about his theft of six pounds of butter from the States Dairy, Bailey responded that a lively black market trade had developed there, at the expense of rations provided to the general public, and that he and Tuck sought to remedy the situation.[72] As to 'interpreting the rules', they had witnessed sufficient German thieving to know that the rules disfavoured islanders. Some of the stolen food and drink the policemen kept for themselves, whereas other was hidden away or distributed among relatives, friends and other trustworthy people. Older people, many of whom were on the brink of starvation, also benefited.[73] This was to have unforeseen consequences; for when islanders were asked in 1951 to volunteer information for the Privy Council enquiry, only very few came forward with testimony in favour of the policemen. While many potential witnesses were cowed into submission by the powerful propaganda that had surrounded the trial, many of the elderly had passed away.[74] One of the exceptions was Joseph Bretel, a tomato grower at St Martins, who stated under oath that he received food from Tuck 'on several occasions' and that he had needed it 'badly'. No questions had been asked, although Bretel understood that the food was 'obviously not picked up in the road'. He explained:

> I couldn't have cared less. I know that was the attitude of people generally in those black days. Even though it appears that some are afraid for some reason to admit it now, such is not the case with me.[75]

Not all of the men's efforts were as conscious of the public interest. What raises an eyebrow are the thefts of alcoholic beverages, the reality of which seem fairly well established. Some of this alcohol they used for their own inebriation, while more seems to have ended up in the cavern of a local pub. The men's explanations on this matter, such as the need for stress relief, feel rather contrived. This taint is the reason why it is hard to be unreservedly sympathetic about the effort. Still, we must ask what justification, if any, there could be for this action? The Privy Council petition did not fail to point out that

> all spirits and wine on the Island [*sic*] were commandeered by the Germans for the use of their own Forces [*sic*] but were left on civilian premises until they required them.[76]

Further justification for considering alcohol a legitimate target could be derived from the fact that spirits were banned from civilian consumption.[77] The policemen might then have been forgiven for assuming that any spirits they came across in civilian depots were, ultimately, destined to go to the Germans. A duty to withhold drink from the Germans could also be based on the recommendations of 'Colonel Britton':

> One thing that the Germans like very much is food. And they like drink. And they prefer your food and drink to their own. You should make sure that the food and drink are suitable to people who are uninvited guests. Many of you do this already I know. I had one letter from a café proprietor who said he could never restrain his chef from spitting on food ordered by German guests. And why should

I restrain him (wrote the Café proprietor) I do it myself when he has a night off. I had another letter from the owner of a beer hall in one of the occupied countries. This man said he always kept a bottle of dirty liquid under the counter to pour into the German beer. I don't think it does them any harm (he wrote). They don't seem to notice it. But it makes me feel better. Well, I shouldn't care to be a German soldier buying beer from a man like this.[78]

One also needs to ask just how safe the 'facts of the case' are. The general source problems, in terms of reliability and completeness of record, have already been noted. The most fitting expression of this is the fact that an entire charge, concerning a 'theft' of alcoholic beverages from Bucktrout's, was disallowed in the Privy Council ruling. If we base ourselves on the surviving judicial material, we find the following:

- No charges concerning alcohol thefts could either be formulated (or maintained) against four of the ten indicted: Tuck, Bailey, Howlett and Short.
- Of the remaining six men, only two, Quin and Smith, committed a truly significant theft of alcohol (86 bottles of port, found on the premises of a local pub during the 1942 investigation), in a raid on a store occupied by R.W. Randall Ltd.
- Three others, Burton, Whare and Friend, were involved in two minor alcohol raids.
- Harper was charged with having received a total of nine bottles of alcohol from these two minor raids.[79]

If we compare this record to what is known about the general effort,[80] then the only conclusion can be that the alcohol thefts are a minute by-product of an effort that, primarily, targeted foodstuffs in German stores.[81] The German propaganda efforts undertaken in connection with this case over-emphasized the alcohol thefts, as this made the action of the policemen appear in a particularly negative light.

As a general conclusion we claim that the conflicting evidence allows no definitive statements, other than that a significant amount of the action of the policemen was likely to have been motivated by higher motives such as an intention to harm the German war effort or to relieve vulnerable members of the island community. Although the effort clashed head-on with the legitimate principle of orderly occupation, it could be justified on moral grounds. Nowhere is there any indication that the policemen's effort was primarily driven by the desire to appropriate food and drink for themselves and their families. A better explanation of why things went astray is contained in Bailey's later remarks on the effort's lack of centralization, where 'it was impossible to know what each man was doing'.[82] This tallies with the general experience of the logistics of grassroots protest or resistance movements, from which a certain degree of anarchy and arbitrariness can never be entirely eradicated.

The argument of a miscarriage of justice is even more compelling with regard to the conduct of the Royal Court trial and the inadmissibility of the evidence it used to convict. That it has been possible to argue the exact opposite, namely that this Gestapo evidence was valid, strikes this author as a glaring injustice. The argument that the Bailiff's reprimand of the policemen in the 1942 verdict was mere 'posturing', designed to save the men from worse or to placate the Germans, does not hold up to scrutiny. No official attempt was made after the war to investigate the circumstances of the ruling. Ideally, there should have been an interest in determining the exact quantities purported to have been taken from any civilian stores. A proper enquiry would have also examined in which quantities the stolen food and drink found their way into civilian hands. Finally, a comparison of the quantities taken from the Germans to those taken from islander-owned stores would have been in order. None of this was ever attempted. The reason for the post-war inaction lies in the contention that 'the law was the law', even under German occupation. If we look at the formal side of things, there is nothing to detract from the impression that the Royal Court proceedings of 1942 were anything other but the orderly and fair prosecution of a property crime under British common law. The particular colouring of the goings-on as having been done 'by the book' became the doxa of the post-war era. It appears as early as 1946, in a correspondence ostensibly addressed to the Home Office by C. W. Bickmore, the chairman of the post-war enquiry looking into the reinstatement of Inspector Sculpher:

> It would be possible to take high ground and say that all trials before the German Military Court were a nullity; in which case presumably the same would apply to the trials before Allied Military Courts now being held abroad. On any lower ground this German military trial was not open to criticism; it was extensively reported in the local press, and Mr. Sherwill, the defending counsel, admitted in court that the sentences were such as he might have asked for himself.
>
> As regards the trial before the Royal Court it is true that a perfectly proper letter from the German legal authorities to H. M. Controller came into the hands of the Police, and through them was brought to the notice of the accused persons, thus giving them room to allege that their pleas of guilty (in this second trial) were extracted from them under duress, but in fact their premises entered were States or civilian property; a defence which was patently worthless.
>
> Public opinion in Guernsey is not at all disposed to accept the contention that it was a meritorious action on the part of their Police to commit depredations on German Army property; in any event the thefts went far beyond that. The Island Police Committee decided after the Royal Court trial to dismiss all the persons convicted; and they seem to have extended this decision to cover convictions before the German Court. The recent committee of enquiry appointed by the Bailiff came to the conclusion that this decision was right.[83]

A critique of this passage will note the relativistic comparison of Nazi trials and post-war trials in Allied-occupied areas. Even more serious, however, is that Bickmore decontextualizes the case: the fact that the civilian trial was occurring under the watchful eye of the occupier and was overshadowed by an extremely powerful political and military contingency is eclipsed. Bickmore offers no indication as to the fact that the press was German-controlled. He is dismissive about the way in which the 'confessions' were obtained and about a possible sabotage motive. Commending the German police work he tells his readers that '(t)he investigations by the Feldgendarmerie (assisted by the Gehenne Feldpolizei) [sic] were very thorough', as well as 'it is very unlikely that they left out any guilty persons'.[84] It was this 'thoroughness' that deluded him into claiming that the case evidence had given no reason for concern. Bickmore's source about the 'correctness' of the goings-on is an 'appeal to authority', i.e. Ambrose Sherwill's sole opinion that the punishment was fair. This is followed up by a false contention, namely that the condemnation of the policemen by the general population was supposedly outright. His final remarks about 'German property' betray a somewhat pedantic peace-time bias and omit that, under occupation, German property was often the result of pillage and could therefore in many cases be considered fair game.

As on other occasions, the fiction of an intact legal and constitutional order was maintained with regard to the case against the policemen. Revising a court ruling or even admitting that a 'mistake' had been committed was therefore out of the question. Any suggestion otherwise was in contradiction with the court's self-image, which saw itself as having upheld British justice (and remained the King's Court) throughout. The idea that the court may have operated in – or been influenced by – a political context was as unprecedented as it was inadmissible.

That the political colouring of the 1942 civilian trial against the Guernsey policemen escaped the post-war consensus of the 1950s is one thing. But that the myth of 'due justice done' should endure indefinitely is a different matter. Unwittingly, Bickmore's post-war discourse on the justification for the dismissal of *all* the policemen involved in the affair goes to the heart of the matter. Ten of the eighteen men tried by the German court also went before the civilian court, for crimes purported to have been committed against the law of the island. This leaves one with the other eight, convicted in the German court alone. One finds the names of five of these men on an official list submitted to the consideration of the Guernsey authorities in 1945.[85] This list featured all States servants who had been deported and who might be entitled to payments. It was decided that all permanent and salaried staff should receive half pay for the period of their internment on the Continent, *except* the policemen, and irrespectively of whether their convictions were pronounced in the German court or in the Royal Court of Guernsey.[86] In terms of official sanction, the fate of the men convicted by the German court alone was identical to that of the group convicted in both courts. It is unknown whether the five surviving former policemen convicted in the German court alone took steps to be reinstated after the war, but it is unlikely.[87] The fact is that they all later worked in civilian jobs.[88]

Why, one must ask, were they treated in the same way as the group sentenced in both courts? Why were they not rehabilitated after the war if they had committed no offence against the law of the island? This question answers itself. In Guernsey, offences against the occupying authority were viewed with the same dim eye as offences against the law of the island. The idea was brought to the point in September 1945, when the Guernsey Police Committee decided 'that no police officer who has been convicted by either the British or German court for receiving or stealing can be reinstated in the Force [sic]'.[89] It is interesting to compare this absolutist stance with the post-war view taken in Jersey, where the standard adopted was that

> (n)o question arose after Liberation regarding the validity of German convictions, whether of a political or of a non-political character, the German Commandant

having released from German custody, some thirty-six hours before Liberation, all civilian prisoners serving German sentences.[90]

The difference in stance betrays the subtle difference that existed in the two islands in terms of defining legitimacy: economic offenders in Guernsey who had only run into trouble with the Germans were put in the 'same boat' as those who had run into trouble with the Germans *and* with the island authorities. This denotes an attempt to legitimize German law-making, for which there was no equivalent in Jersey. Economic crimes profile this reality in particularly sharp contrast, as they go to the very heart of the legitimacy question. No other category of 'crime' during the Occupation evoked quite the same passion as this one, and for no other was the assessment more convoluted. This was linked to the nature of the 'crime', which concerned those commodities essential to basic well-being. It is a fairly well-established fact that securing their daily food procurement monopolized the attention of civilians throughout occupied Europe. At the same time, the border between war profiteering and economic collaboration, on the one hand, and denying resources to the occupier, on the other, was always going to be wafer-thin.

Conclusion

Out of a total of 453 recorded offences against the occupying authorities in Guernsey, 239 (52.9 per cent) had an economic character. The parallel figure for Jersey is 284 (out of 856, i.e. 33.2 per cent); these Jersey figures include 55 cases of 'military larceny', involving Channel Islanders working in German employ.[91] The first, rather straightforward conclusion one can draw from this is that economic offences were the most frequent type of offences tried by German courts during the Occupation. Further evidence on the scope and frequency of economic offences (and the risk involved) is provided by a breakdown of the 28 Channel Islanders convicted of offences against the occupying authorities who died in continental prisons and concentration camps. Of these, six men (21.4 per cent) were economic offenders.[92] They were, in fact, the second largest group, behind radio offenders. This implies that offenders in this category had a somewhat better chance of escaping the ultimate fate than radio offenders, who, although overall a smaller group, were more prominent among the casualties.

Distinguishing economic offences as a form of protest, defiance and resistance from those that constituted 'pure' common law offences is a more difficult exercise. The discussion on the Guernsey policemen shows that only a detailed probing of the intentions and motivations of the protagonists can provide a degree of clarity on this issue. It is to the former policemen's credit to have brought their case to bear in the post-war era, thereby creating an ample documentary record, from which the historian can build an informed opinion. Only this allows us to say today that, on balance, the bedrock of the action of the policemen was patriotism. As in grassroots efforts elsewhere, a certain opportunism and self-serving attitude among some of the participants could not be entirely eradicated, though. The leaders of the effort were unaware, unable or unwilling to do this, and the effort therefore got 'out of hand'. At the same time it strikes us as inequitable to over-emphasize this feature.

If the case of the Guernsey policemen has many grey zones, then the level of information available in other cases involving economic offences is even poorer. This situation calls for a proxy. Why, for example, were economic offences more prevalent in Guernsey than in Jersey? The only variable that can explain this difference is the harsher regime, the greater destitution and vulnerability of the population and the more unfavourable supply situation in Guernsey, as compared to Jersey. Rather than judging economic offences by their 'face value', one needs to factor in the disruptive impact of the fortification programme, as well as the generally exploitative agenda of the occupying force. One also needs to relativize: what is the theft of a loaf of bread or a pair of boots against the massive and unprecedented transfer of wealth and labour from entire societies to the German war economy? It does credit to those islanders who committed economic offences that they were not fooled by the formal rules. They had the intelligence to distinguish between 'ordinary theft' and 'patriotic theft' (or other such offences), and acted accordingly: German property, in many cases itself a result of direct and indirect looting, became fair game.

The final remark concerns the selectivity applied in the prosecution of economic crimes, which constituted a method of social control. This topos, already noted in the chapter on radio resistance, emerges in particularly stark contrast with regard to black-marketeering, a practice that, under the material conditions prevailing at the time, was ubiquitous. The prosecution of such 'crimes' could be the welcome pretext to ship 'surplus' people off the islands, turning the administration of law into a tool of population policy.

Notes

* This chapter is dedicated to Eric Goldrein, previously with the Liverpool firm of solicitors Silverman & Livermore and a member of the legal team that took the appeal of eight policemen against their 1942 conviction by the Royal Court of Guernsey to the Privy Council, in 1952.
1 A total of 819 French railway-men were shot on the spot and, of those deported by their fellow railway-men, 1,200 died in the camps, Christian Bachelier, La SNCF sous l'Occupation allemande, 1940–1944, Association pour l'histoire des chemins de fer, http://www.ahicf.com/ww2/rapport/partie6.htm, accessed 28 June 2013.
2 See Paul Sanders, *Histoire du marché noir 1940–1946*, Paris, Perrin, 2001.
3 Albert Peter Lamy, Chief Officer Guernsey Police, 1942–1965, *Policing during the Occupation 1940–1945*, n.d., p. 11.
4 IWM.Documents.13409.Dening 4. Unknown author, 'Sabotage and Betrayal (Guernsey)', n.d.
5 Paul Sanders, *The British Channel Islands under German Occupation 1940–1945*, Jersey, Jersey Heritage Trust, 2005, pp. 21–8.
6 AN.AJ40/990. Declaration of Enemy Property. Channel Islands, April 1942.

7 Letter of the deputy solicitor general to the Tribunal of FK 515. Re. prosecution of policemen, 5 May 1942, In the Privy Council on Appeal from the Royal Court of the Island of Guernsey between William George Quin and others, and Her Majesty the Queen, No. 10, 1952, exhibit 14A, p. 19.
8 Letter of the tribunal of FK 515 to the Deputy Solicitor General. Re. prosecution of policemen, 8 May 1942, In the Privy Council on Appeal from the Royal Court of the Island of Guernsey, No. 10, 1952, exhibit 14B, p. 20.
9 IA.AQ 1214/17. William M. Bell Collection. Affidavit Bailey, 10 February 1951 (copyright in the estate of Kingston Bailey).
10 In the Privy Council on Appeal from the Royal Court of the Island of Guernsey, No. 10, 1952, p. 42.
11 Ibid., exhibit 'R', p. 123.
12 Ibid., exhibit 'Q', p. 122.
13 Ibid., exhibit no. 81, Evidence as to the antecedents of all the accused, pp. 89–90.
14 IA.AQ 1214/17. William M. Bell Collection. Affidavit Tardif, 9 February 1951 (copyright in the estate of Archibald Tardif).
15 Albert Peter Lamy, Chief Officer Guernsey Police, 1942–1965, *Policing during the Occupation 1940–1945*, n.d., p. 15.
16 TNA.HO.284/6. The Bailiff of Guernsey to the Government Secretary, Government Office, Guernsey, 16 September 1950; Major Cotton states that he was 'reliably informed by Dr. R.B. Sutcliffe and others that the accused police officers were ill-treated' while in German custody, TNA.HO.284/6. Major Sidney Cotton, Civil Affairs Unit to Colonel Power, Secretary to H. M. Lieutenant-Governor. Re. Island police Guernsey, 25 September 1945.
17 For illustration of the issue see the website of the Innocence Project, Benjamin N. Cardozo School of Law, Yeshiva University, http://www.innocenceproject.org/fix/False-Confessions.php, accessed 14 November 2012; also Laura Beil, 'The Certainty of Memory Has Its Day in Court', *The New York Times*, 29 November 2011.
18 'Petition for special leave to Appeal to His Majesty in Council', in: In the Privy Council on Appeal from the Royal Court of the Island of Guernsey, No. 10, 1952, exhibit no. 84, p. 103.
19 Ibid.
20 Ibid., p. 141.
21 TNA.HO.284/6. Letter of Mess. Tuck and Bailey to Advocate Randell, 26 July 1950, p. 4.
22 Two letters detailing 'failures to salute', and involving Prince Öttingen, the Controlling Committee and Inspector Sculpher, are in the Guernsey files, IA.FK.4–8. Inspector Sculpher to the President of the Controlling Committee. Re. Police Discipline, 29 September 1941; Nebenstelle Guernsey to the Controlling Committe of the States of Guernsey, 13 October 1941. Öttingen advised the Controlling Committee that lapses in discipline would not be tolerated.
23 William Bell, *I Beg to Report. Policing in Guernsey during the German Occupation*, Guernsey, Guernsey Press, 1995, p. 181.
24 In the Privy Council on Appeal from the Royal Court of the Island of Guernsey, No. 10, 1952, Transcript of proceedings of 4 October 1955, p. 21.
25 IA.AQ 1214/17. William M. Bell Collection. Affidavit Burton, February 1951 (copyright in the estate of William Burton).
26 Harper claimed that Inspector Sculpher prevented him from joining HM forces in 1940, IA.AQ 1214/17. William M. Bell Collection. Affidavit Harper, 10 January

1950 (copyright in the estate of Jack Harper). As to Tuck's description there is some conflict: in the 1942 civilian trial he stated that the men received no straight answer to the question as to whether they had to 'stay' or could 'join', In the Privy Council on Appeal from the Royal Court of the Island of Guernsey, No. 10, 1952, p. 33. In their 1950 memo to Advocate Randell, however, Tuck and Bailey contended that the men were prevented from joining, through a threat of forfeiture of their pension rights, TNA.HO.284/6. Letter of Mess. Tuck and Bailey to Advocate Randell, 26 July 1950; also Bell, *I Beg to Report,* p. 133.
27 IA.AQ 1214/17. William M. Bell Collection. Affidavit Short (date missing, presumably 1951) (copyright in the estate of Frederick Short).
28 IA.AQ 1214/17. William M. Bell Collection. Affidavit Tuck, 28 February 1951 (copyright in the estate of Frank Tuck).
29 The winter of 1941–2 had the highest civilian mortality rate of the entire occupation, Sanders, *British Channel Islands under German Occupation,* pp. 151–5.
30 Extract from the report of the Medical Officer of Health for the Island of Guernsey for 1942 and appendices to report headed 'Infant Mortality and Nutrition', n.d., In the Privy Council on Appeal from the Royal Court of the Island of Guernsey, No. 10, 1952, exhibit no. 83, pp. 99–100.
31 Kingston Bailey, *Dachau,* London, Brown Watson, 1961, p. 16; several such cases appear in the men's post-war affidavits, IA.AQ 1214/17. William M. Bell Collection. Affidavits, passim (various copyright holders).
32 TNA.HO.284/6. Letter of Mess. Tuck and Bailey to Advocate Randell, 26 July 1950.
33 IA. AQ 1214/17. William M. Bell Collection. Affidavit Bailey, 10 February 1951 (copyright in the estate of Kingston Bailey).
34 Bailey, *Dachau,* pp. 15–16; IA.AQ 1214/17. William M. Bell Collection. Affidavit Harper, 10 January 1950 (copyright in the estate of Jack Harper).
35 IA.AQ 1214/17. William M. Bell Collection. Affidavit Burton, February 1951 (copyright in the estate of William Burton); Bell, *I Beg to Report,* pp. 106–8, 133–8.
36 IA.AQ 1214/17. William M. Bell Collection. Affidavit Harper, 10 January 1950 (copyright in the estate of Jack Harper).
37 Bailey, *Dachau,* pp. 15–16.
38 Such a 'double game' approach was perhaps more realistic, German Occupation Museum Guernsey. 12 Misc. Papers. Personal files. W. J. Renouf. Occupation memoir, pp. 62–71; when Renouf was charged with the possession of a radio apparatus in 1944, he claimed that he was a listener and had not engaged in the dissemination of news, which was considered the more serious offence. He also made a point of proving that he was not hostile to Germany and was finally let off with a four-month sentence, BA-MA.I/10/Ost Spezial/V4713. Akte Renouf, December 1944–January 1945.
39 The term relates to the passive resistance (or subversion) of *The Good Soldier Švejk* (1923), the main character of a satirical novel by Czech author Jaroslav Hašek set during the Great War. Similar to Yossarian in Joseph Heller's best-selling novel *Catch-22* (1961), Švejk is in a double bind: he wants to survive the war, but the murderous orders he receives will lead to his almost certain death. Challenging authority head-on is out of the question, so he must develop more underhand ways in order to survive. Contrary to Yossarian, who tries to feign madness, Švejk opts for a form of insubordination that is anywhere between insolence and incompetence.
40 The source of this information is a Colonel Vierbahn, of Army HQ in St Lô, who visited the islands with Colonel Schmundt, a member of Hitler's general staff

(*Führerhauptquartier*), in November 1941, IWM.Documents.13409.Dening 9. Force 135, I (b). History of the GFP in the Channel Islands, 1945.

41 This reading is compounded by the fact that none of the policemen who returned to Guernsey after the war, seem to have suffered from ostracism on the part of fellow islanders, see Gillian Carr's interviews with Margaret Godfrey (née Gaudion), 2011 and Rose Short (née Duquemin), 2010. The same statement applies to the wives and children of the convicted policemen who were deported to Biberach internment camp together with other islanders, in September 1942.

42 TNA.HO.284/6. Letter to unknown official (probably Lieutenant-Governor's office) signed Frank Whare, 8 August 1945.

43 Bailey, *Dachau*, p. 25.

44 IA.AQ 1214/17. William M. Bell Collection. Affidavit Harper, 10 January 1950 (copyright in the estate of Jack Harper).

45 Of the policemen convicted in the two trials, the following nine were imprisoned in Germany: Bailey, Duquemin, Friend, Thomas Gaudion, Harper, Quin, Short, Smith and Tuck, ITS. Digitales Archiv. Hinweiskarten aus der Zentralen Namenkartei, n.d.

46 ITS. Digitales Archiv. Hinweiskarte aus der Zentralen Namenkartei, Thomas Gaudion, n.d.

47 IA. Falla papers. Littler, FO to Frank Falla, 4 March 1966.

48 ITS. Digitales Archiv. Hinweiskarte aus der Zentralen Namenkartei, Kingston Bailey, n.d.

49 Charles Friend, Correspondence, November 1964 (by kind permission of Bob Baker).

50 Two decades after the war Harper wrote in a letter to Frank Falla that during his time at Neuoffingen he was beaten 'every other day', IA. Falla papers. Harper to Frank Falla, 1 February 1965; Tuck described the treatment as 'brutal, premeditated torture', Letter of F. H. Tuck to British Red Cross Society, 12 July 1945 (by kind permission of Bob Baker).

51 IA.AQ 1214/17. William M. Bell Collection. Letter Tuck to Bell, 27 November 1992.

52 Tuck's detailed description of his experience is included in Louis Dutot's *Du Pain entre les Rails. Anna Stadler, une Allemande au Secours des Déportés*, Coutances, OCEP, 1988, pp. 37–40.

53 ITS. Digitales Archiv. Hinweiskarten aus der Zentralen Namenkartei, Jack Harper, Charles Friend, Frank Tuck, n.d.

54 The discrepancy in treatment between Hill-Cottingham and the policemen was noted by J. D. L. Edwards, LLB, in his MA dissertation 'The German occupation of the Bailiwick of Guernsey 1940–1945 – A critical examination of the response of the Guernsey Authorities to an occupation by enemy forces, with particular reference to the criminal justice system, and the extent that social class impacted on that response', University of Liverpool, School of History, 20 September 2002.

55 TNA.HO.284/6. L. S. Brass, Home Office, to D. Neill, Office of the Treasury Sollicitor. Re. Quin & Others and the King, 17 July 1952.

56 Burton, who had been acquitted in the civilian trial and Smith, who had died in 1943, were not party to the petition.

57 'Petition for special leave to Appeal to His Majesty in Council', In the Privy Council on Appeal from the Royal Court of the Island of Guernsey, No. 10, 1952, exhibit no. 84, p. 104.

58 TNA.HO.284/6. W. H. Arnold, Attorney General of Guernsey to Sir Leslie Brass, Home Office, 1 April 1952.

59 Bell, *I Beg to Report*, p. 390.

60 'Privy Council Appeal No. 10 of 1952, William Quin and others v. The Queen, from the Royal Court of the Island of Guernsey, Reasons for the Report of the Lords of the Judicial Committee of the Privy Council', 6 October 1955, Privy Council Decisions, http://www.bailii.org/uk/cases/UKPC/, accessed 15 August 2012.
61 TNA.HO.284/6. Minutes, L. S. Brass to Mr Walker, 31 October 1952.
62 Sanders, *British Channel Islands under German Occupation*, pp. 231–54.
63 IA. Frank Falla papers. Loose notes, n.d.
64 IA.AQ 1214/17. William M. Bell Collection. Affidavit Falla, 17 February 1951 (copyright in the estate of Francis Falla).
65 Frank Falla, *The Silent War. The Inside Story of the Channel Islands under the Nazi Jackboot*, Guernsey, Leslie Frewin, 1967, pp. 156–69.
66 TNA.HO.284/6. Letter to unknown official (probably Lieutenant-Governor's office) signed Frank Whare, 8 August 1945.
67 TNA.HO.284/6. Channel Isles, Guernsey police. The case of Mr F. H. Tuck. Handwritten minutes, 12 August 1950.
68 IWM.Documents.13409.Dening 9. Files of Captain J. R. Denning, Intelligence Corps. Report on the Island Police – Guernsey, 1945.
69 The amounts are documented in TNA.HO.284/6. Final report of the Bickmore enquiry, 23 November 1945; also Bell, *I Beg to Report*, pp. 135–9, 179–81; only some of the civilian charges detailed in the German case files were brought to trial, as already in pre-trial conflicting statements concerning dates and quantities disallowed a certain number of cases from being pursued in the Royal Court, Bell, *I Beg to Report*, p. 181.
70 Quoted in Bell, *I Beg to Report*, p. 135.
71 In the Privy Council on Appeal from the Royal Court of the Island of Guernsey, No. 10, 1952, exhibit 12 (i), p. 14.
72 Ibid., Statement by Kingston George Bailey, p. 35; Bailey, *Dachau*, p. 19.
73 Ibid., pp. 16–17; IA.AQ 1214/17. William M. Bell Collection. Affidavit Harper, 10 January 1950 (copyright in the estate of Jack Harper).
74 According to Bailey, a Mrs Hawke at Les Croutes died after the police stopped supplying her with stolen food, IA.AQ 1214/17. William M. Bell Collection. Affidavit Bailey (copyright in the estate of Kingston Bailey).
75 IA.AQ 1214/17. William M. Bell Collection. Affidavit Bretel, 10 February 1951 (copyright in the estate of Joseph Bretel). Another islander who admitted having received food from the policemen, Charles Roger from St Sampsons, stated that he and his ailing wife received food from Smith. Affidavit Roger, 22 February 1951 (copyright in the estate of Charles Roger). Other names of people who received food were given by Bill Burton, IA.AQ 1214/17. William M. Bell Collection. Affidavit Burton, February 1951 (copyright in the estate of William Burton).
76 TNA.HO.284/6. In the Privy Council on appeal from the Royal Court of the Island of Guernsey, between William George Quin and others, and the King, 7 November 1951, p. 3.
77 Note published in 'La Gazette Officielle', 12 November 1940, signed FK 515 (Brosch), In the Privy Council on Appeal from the Royal Court of the Island of Guernsey, No. 10, 1952, exhibit 4, p. 8.
78 'Hints for Housewives', Broadcast of 'Colonel Britton' to the Occupied Territories, 21 November 1941, In the Privy Council on Appeal from the Royal Court of the Island of Guernsey, No. 10, 1952, exhibit 12 (i), p. 14.

79   The trial in the Royal Court contained a total of 10 charges, of which 4 concerned the theft of alcoholic beverages and one the reception of stolen alcoholic beverages: one theft of 86 bottles of port from a store occupied by R.W. Randall Ltd, involving Smith and Quin; one theft of 20 bottles of spirits from a store occupied by Mr Le Lièvre, involving Burton, Friend and Quin; one theft of 8 bottles of wine and spirits from a store occupied by Bucktrout & Co. Ltd, involving Quin, Friend, Burton and Short (charge disallowed by Privy Council); one theft of 12 bottles of wine and spirits from Bucktrout & Co. Ltd, involving Friend, Whare and Burton; Jack Harper was charged with having received 5 bottles from the raid on the Le Lièvre store and 4 bottles from the raid on the Bucktrout store involving Friend, Whare and Burton, Privy Council Appeal No. 10 of 1952, William Quin and others v. The Queen, from the Royal Court of the Island of Guernsey, Reasons for the Report of the Lords of the Judicial Committee of the Privy Council, 6 October 1955, Privy Council Decisions, http://www.bailii.org/uk/cases/UKPC/, accessed 15 August 2012.
80   Bell, *I Beg to Report*, pp. 135–6, 153–4.
81   Of the 70 raids listed by the Bickmore enquiry, 39 concerned German stores and 31 islander-owned stores; only 4 of these concerned thefts of alcoholic beverages, TNA. HO.284/6. Final report of the Bickmore enquiry, 23 November 1945.
82   Bailey, *Dachau*, 19.
83   TNA.HO.284/6. Letter signed C W Bickmore, 9 January 1946.
84   Ibid.
85   One of the policemen tried in the German Court in 1942, Sergeant Pill, was acquitted; another, PC Bretel, had died during the Occupation, Bell, *I Beg to Report*, pp. 162, 365.
86   Ibid., p. 377.
87   Some of those convicted in both courts had tried to be reinstated; they were given the unmistakable message that 'no men convicted of stealing or receiving could be re-employed on the Force [sic]', Bell, *I Beg to Report*, pp. 366–7. Significantly, no distinction was made between the German convictions and the Royal Court convictions.
88   Bell, *I Beg to Report*, p. 368.
89   TNA.HO.284/6. Major Sidney Cotton, Civil Affairs Unit, to Colonel Power, Secretary to H. M. Lieutenant-Governor. Re. Island police Guernsey, 25 September 1945.
90   Charles Duret Aubin, 'Enemy Legislation and Judgments in Jersey', *The Journal of Comparative Legislation and International Law*, Vol. 31, 1949, 3.
91   D/Z/H6. Law Officers' Department. Sentences and prosecutions by the Field Command and Troop Courts in Jersey; Guernsey Police records, German convictions of civilians, 2 vols, 1940–5.
92   Jersey: George Fox, Frank Le Villio, Clifford Bond Querée, Emile Joseph Paisnel; Guernsey: Herbert Smith, Sidney Ashcroft.

11

Heritage, Memory and Resistance in the Channel Islands

Gilly Carr

There are many parallels that can be drawn between the German Occupation of the Channel Islands and that of continental Western Europe. However, it is readily apparent to the casual visitor to war or occupation museums in both areas that the resultant narratives of the dark years of 1940–5 and the subsequent heritage, in both the Channel Islands and on the continent, differ in important ways. Memorials, war museums and annual ceremonies on the continent have long focused on the narratives of resistance and deportation, emphasizing the suffering, victimhood and martyrdom of the local population, especially those who were sent to prisons and camps for acts of resistance. Such narratives were conspicuously lacking in the Channel Islands until around 1995 in Jersey and until recently in Guernsey. Even today, such narratives of war do not dominate, although they have slowly come to occupy a position on the periphery.

This chapter explores this discrepant phenomenon and the reasons for it. Specifically, it asks how similar experiences have come to result in dissimilar memories, and why people who were imprisoned for acts of resistance in the Channel Islands did not become heroes, as elsewhere in Europe. It also charts what I term here 'political prisoner consciousness'; the changing attitudes towards resisters and political prisoners over time; and the struggle of those who became the self-appointed 'guardians of memory' who fought for recognition of this group. Taking a chronological approach, this chapter focuses on three time periods. It takes as its starting point the Occupation period and the years immediately following it before moving forward to the 1960s. During the middle of this decade, those who had suffered in Nazi prisons and camps fought for compensation from the West German government, and we will explore the central role of Guernseyman Frank Falla in helping Channel Islanders obtain compensation. Finally, we will move forward another 30 years to examine the roles of guardian of memory Joe Mière, and the former Bailiff of Jersey, Sir Philip Bailhache, in supporting and honouring victims of Nazi persecution in that island, and the after-effect of the fiftieth anniversary of Liberation in 1995 in the Channel Islands today.

Political prisoners: An overview

As this chapter concerns, in large part, a group of people who described themselves as political prisoners – who claimed this term and embraced it with pride, most especially in Jersey – it is worth exploring what is meant by and who was included within such a term. Those who were proud to describe themselves as such were those who disobeyed German orders (most often deliberately) to commit acts of resistance (as defined in this volume) as a statement of patriotism. However, this generalizes the variety of acts, intentions and motives of individuals arrested; it also by definition excludes those who committed the same acts but who were not caught.

It is important to stress that political prisoners were rarely from any organized resistance groups who knew each other before their internment. The vast majority of those who committed acts of protest, defiance or resistance in the Channel Islands acted alone, although a very small number did form tiny groups with a handful of members at most. Thus, those who were to claim the status of political prisoners mostly met each other for the first time in prison in Jersey or Guernsey and formed their group membership only at this point.

In his discussion of terminology at the start of *The Ultimate Sacrifice*, Paul Sanders explores the problematic nature of the 'political prisoner' epithet.[1] As German regulations increasingly limited the freedoms of Channel Islanders, so it became increasingly easy to commit an offence through infringement of German orders.[2] To commit an offence was not always a political act and so to label the 'crime' as a 'political' one, and to politicize non-conformist behaviour, is to endorse the occupier's logic. Despite this, many islanders, most especially young Channel Island men, were proud to have spent a period of time in jail during the Occupation; to have defied the Germans and received a prison sentence was, for some, quite literally a badge of honour. As many were proud to call themselves 'political prisoners', and as it became a mode of self-identification for a marginalized group after the war, I use this term throughout this chapter not least as a way of moving the long-marginalized to the centre ground.

In any consideration of political prisoners, one of the most important things to emphasize is that beneath this umbrella term lies a wide variety of people. Not only were the 'crimes' committed by the prisoners very different but, more importantly, the *perception* both of the 'crimes' and those who committed them varied greatly among and between the other islanders, as well as over time. This point cannot be over-emphasized and provides the key to understanding why the memory of political prisoners has been suppressed on the public stage for so long.

It is not sufficient for our understanding of this point simply to label the acts committed as 'patriotic' or not, and to praise or condemn those concerned accordingly; it is difficult to put such a black-or-white gloss on acts of resistance (or even to decide what constitutes resistance and what does not). Generally speaking, the bottom line for many islanders in deciding the value or worthiness of an act was the consideration of whether it benefited the wider community or whether it resulted (or could potentially result) in reprisals. This distinction was not easy to make, as some acts could potentially do both. V-signs, for example, gave many people heart and satisfaction, and was a morale-boosting exercise. Yet in the perception of some, it was a cowardly and selfish act which resulted only in reprisals. Similarly, to escape from the island with the aim of joining the Allied armed forces both benefited the Channel Islands in a broad sense, was a brave and patriotic thing to do, and yet could also result in reprisals.

A number of islanders discussed in their diaries the conflicting views of their friends towards resistance acts, and I use here the example of two diarists to illustrate attitudes towards escaping from the islands in a boat. With reference to a particular episode, Dr Alistair Rose in Guernsey wrote that:

> ... most people were furious when they heard of the escape. 'Aren't they selfish? Now we shall be punished', they said. Personally, I said, 'good luck to them, they are some use where they are and no use here'. I am glad to say that I found a few who shared this view, and were willing to take what punishment we should receive, cheerfully.[3]

Contrasting with this is the attitude of Louis Guillemette, the Bailiff of Guernsey's secretary, who was against such acts. He discussed in detail reactions to an escape from Guernsey in August 1943. He recorded in his diary that opinion was sharply divided on the question of whether or not it was right for people to escape, but recorded that 'more than half' of the population was against it. Those in favour, he noted, thought that everyone had the right to decide on the question for themselves and that it was the duty of those left behind on the island to 'take the punishment without cringing', whereas those against argued that it was selfish and only for 'comfort and personal glory' and quoted the German threats of reprisals.[4] Such conflicting points of view for any number of punishable acts are recorded in many diaries.

On another more dangerous and less equivocal level, we might examine the actions of those young men who, most especially in St Helier, conducted (both pseudo- and overtly) military acts involving forms of armed resistance (as explored elsewhere in this volume). These encompassed mainly stealing weapons and conducting reprisals against perceived collaborators rather than targeting German soldiers per se. These are not so dissimilar to some of the resistance groups in France and other countries who were so lauded after the war. Armed resistance is often perceived to be the most worthy form of resistance as it is seen to have contributed most clearly to the Allied war effort, carried the highest risks and was sometimes perceived to have been carried out by the bravest people who risked the highest penalties if they were caught. Yet in the Channel Islands, the perception was very different and such young men were perceived to be nothing more than 'troublemakers', as we shall see. This lies at the heart of wartime condemnation and post-war marginalization.

Thus, the *perception of the legitimacy* of action of political prisoners – and, indeed, the local civilian government – both in their own eyes and in the eyes of the local population, is key here. As Conway and Romijn put it, legitimacy is a 'dynamic and fluid reality that existed in the critical space between the ruler and the ruled'.[5] They argue that when wartime governments failed to meet the needs of their population, perhaps by failing to protect them from the depredations of the Occupation, they 'lost whatever legitimacy they had formerly possessed'[6] – at least, in this case, in the eyes of political prisoners or those who would commit acts of resistance. Legitimacy, it seems, was in the eye of the beholder.

Additionally, in our analysis of political prisoners and our attempts to understand the difference between perceptions on the continent and in the Channel Islands, we must bear in mind the crucial deciding factor of the island nature of the communities with which we are dealing in this volume. The population of the Channel Islands were arguably, more so than elsewhere in Europe, 'sitting ducks' because of their island status. They were already captive in what many metaphorically perceived to be a 'jail' or 'prison without bars'.[7] The population could not easily escape, move away or go into hiding en masse. Therefore, reprisals were a very real and constant threat,[8] and could affect everyone equally. Reprisals took or could take the form of hostage taking; enforced guard duty in areas where acts classed as sabotage were committed, imprisonment, or deportation. Channel Islanders were indeed fortunate not to face firing squads or armed divisions tasked with committing massacres in the islands. While this is perhaps because Britain was still a fighting force and not occupied territory, it should also be borne in mind that no Channel Islander killed a German soldier as an act of resistance, which may have saved them from more serious reprisals such as those faced by other European countries.

As discussed in the introduction of this volume, the reasons why Channel Islanders did not kill German soldiers are well rehearsed and will be repeated only briefly here. The lack of means to do so; the lack of assistance from London in the form of weapons drops or Special Operations Executive (SOE) operatives; and the suffocatingly high proportion of occupying soldiers to islanders were all limiting factors. We must also take into account the attitude of the local authorities at the start of the Occupation.

Those who chose to commit acts of defiance against the occupiers, either as a deliberate and political act, or as a bit of youthful fun to annoy the Germans, were heavily censured by the local authorities. The States (legislative body) of Guernsey and Jersey had made it very clear that acts such as these against the occupiers were unacceptable. On 7 August 1940, Ambrose Sherwill, President of the Controlling Committee in Guernsey, delivered a speech at the first Occupation meeting of the States, in which he laid out the position to be adopted by the island's government towards their occupiers:

> May this occupation be a model to the world. On the one hand, tolerance on the part of the military authority, and courtesy and correctness on the part of the occupying forces, and on the other, dignity and courtesy and exemplary behaviour on the part of the civilian population.[9]

This 'exemplary behaviour' was to involve obedience to the occupiers and a rejection of any form of resistance; compliance and co-operation was expected instead.[10] Retrospective legislation was brought in by Sherwill at the end of July 1940 and backdated to the start of the occupation, making 'an offence any behaviour by a civilian likely to cause a deterioration in the relations between the occupying forces and the civilian population'.[11] In his memoirs Sherwill revealed that his stance of 'avoiding difficulties between the occupying authorities and the civilian population' was 'not because of any lack of loyalty to my own country but because I was convinced that, during an enemy occupation, this was the only way of securing the greatest possible measure of liberty and normality for the people of the island'.[12]

Such attitudes by the authorities made it very clear to the islanders that defiant or resistant behaviour would be punished by the Royal Court of the islands and not just by a military court. Islanders were even encouraged to inform on each other if they witnessed or suspected resistant behaviour. On 22 March 1941, for example, the *Star* newspaper in Guernsey published a speech made by the Bailiff to the members of the States, prompted by the cutting of a telephone cable near the island's airport. Such action was described as 'grave sabotage' and deemed to be 'stupid and criminal'; the perpetrators risked the death penalty and brought 'the whole island under the grave displeasure of the German authorities'. The Bailiff declared that it was the islanders' 'duty and obligation to co-operate with them [the Germans] in carrying out their Orders and regulations', and also their 'duty' to inform the police with information about the saboteur.

With such strict legislation in place from the beginning of the Occupation, and with attitudes towards resisters dictated from above, those who planned to defy the occupiers were on their own and could not always count on the support of others, and certainly not that of the authorities. Although the Jersey authorities were less vocal in their denunciation of resistance, their position was to prove much the same.

Political prisoner consciousness and the creation of memory

It is not easy to pinpoint with certainty the first time that people referred to those imprisoned by the occupiers for acts of protest, defiance or resistance as 'political prisoners'.[13] It does not appear to have been in (widespread) use in the early days of the Occupation. Rather, it emerges in common parlance in the autumn of 1944 with reference to the young people imprisoned at this time in Jersey's Gloucester Street jail in St Helier. Francis Harris, a former political prisoner during this period, confirmed that the term was 'in universal currency throughout the prison, amongst civilian warders, the Governing Board, and ourselves'.[14] This is not to say that the term was not in use before this date; however, the emergence of a particular consciousness and form of self-identity – the proud claiming of a certain appellation – appears to have been made only at this time.

The autumn of 1944 was a formative – and, indeed, a fortunate – time for political prisoners. After August of that year, those who committed serious offences were no longer able to be deported to prisons and camps on the continent. Following the D-Day landings and the Allied landing in Normandy that June, the continent was now cut off from the Channel Islands as all islanders would have been increasingly aware. This meant that those who got into serious trouble at this time had to remain in the islands. The local prison population of this demographic could only grow and was not the constantly renewed source that it was before, when those deported to continental prisons were replaced by new inmates. As a number of these young people in Jersey jail would quite likely have otherwise ended their lives in concentration camps, they were fortunate to be spared this fate even though the life of a political prisoner in the island was dismal. It included episodes of solitary confinement (or, conversely, overcrowding), dysentery, inadequate bedding, rats, and cold, damp cells (as experienced by Frank Keiller),[15] interspersed with questioning or, for the unlucky and uncooperative, beatings at Silvertide, the HQ of the *Geheime Feldpolizei* in Jersey. As former political prisoner Joe Mière later wrote 'It was like death row in that German prison in Jersey, 1944–1945 … so you could see why we all formed a bond of friendship.'[16]

Numbers were increasing in the local prisons; Keiller describes the jail in St Helier as 'overflowing' in late 1944, commenting that new offenders in early 1945 either had to take their beds in with them or sleep on the floor of their cells.[17] It was a local joke in both Guernsey and Jersey that those who received sentences often had to wait for a cell to become free before they were imprisoned.[18] Diarist Leslie Sinel commented that some sentences were curtailed to allow more to go to jail,[19] and Frank Keiller noted that minor offenders were let out early.[20] It is also inevitable that, with the tide of war clearly changing, some young people were becoming more daring in their actions against the occupiers. Sanders argued that this age group was motivated by patriotism but was sometimes prone to daredevilish and unruly behaviour so typical to teenagers.[21] In any event, the autumn of 1944 was a period when a large number of adolescents, mostly but not entirely male, found themselves imprisoned.

Despite the strict prison rules, regulations and conditions, the political prisoners found a variety of ways in which to communicate with each other in addition to chatting during the hour-long morning exercise in the yard.[22] Michael Neil remembers two boys, Jimmy and Ron, whose job it was to bring the soup and coffee, and who were willing to take notes and put them under other people's cell doors.[23] He also recalled that people on the outside could pass notes through the railings to exercising prisoners when no-one was looking. In his unpublished memoirs, Mr J. H. L'Amy reproduced details of a letter from Lucy Schwob in which she discussed details of her time in prison. She wrote that after her and Suzanne Malherbe's reprieve from a death sentence, they were able to communicate unofficially with other political prisoners, made possible by one of their guards who was 'definitely anti-Nazi'.[24] Other modes of contact were made possible by careless guards, who occasionally (or deliberately) left cell doors open so that a prisoner could walk down their corridor to speak to other prisoners or to slide letters under doors.[25] There was also an unusual indoor and outdoor 'postal system' in operation in the prison, whereby a length of string was passed down to the floor directly below, usually through an air vent in the cell, or by lifting a floor board.[26] Using this method, messages could be passed between floors, as could writing implements (which had sometimes been smuggled into the prison in food parcels[27]) and small gifts such as tobacco (gleaned from the German guards' cigarette butts).[28] This was all deemed to be possible due to the lack of vigilance of the guards.[29] Sometimes string could be slipped out through a window and swung into a neighbouring cell. Because the political prisoners' Block C was overflowing, some of these prisoners were placed in the civilian wing (Block B). In this way messages were able to be smuggled back and forth between the different wings of the prison.[30] Such smuggling was also facilitated by civilian prisoners, who were allowed parcels and visitors, and sometimes received notes for political prisoners. When this happened, they would throw a stone at the window of the prisoner concerned to alert their attention and tell them they had a message. This was transmitted either by tying it to a stone and throwing it for the political prisoner to catch, or else tying it to a length of string lowered by the anticipated recipient.[31]

Paper was sourced in two ways: either by ripping pages out of prayer books[32] or library books (the circulation of the latter of which was also used for secreting messages[33]), or by stealing toilet paper from the guards' toilets, which caused much amusement among the prisoners.[34] Communication did not always need paper, however. A heating pipe (which never seemed to offer any heat) passed just above ground level through every cell. Some prisoners discovered that the cement-and-lime mix around the pipe could be scraped away, leaving a small gap in the wall through which prisoners could speak.[35] This pipe could also be tapped, which would transmit a ringing noise along the line, which was the signal to others that a guard was coming.[36]

By all of these methods, a real camaraderie was built up between prisoners. They cheered each other up by patriotic singing songs;[37] Canadian political prisoner, Belza Turner, imprisoned for trying to escape by boat with Dutchman Siebe Koster, also used to play a guitar in prison, and Siebe would sing along from a different cell.[38] The prisoners soon got to know each other and, through all of the methods of communication outlined earlier, were able to pass around and compile autograph books and 'political prisoner certificates'. A number of these are in existence today, in archives or in the possession of former prisoners or their family members (Figure 11.1).

While some comprise just a long list of names and acts of resistance, or include encouraging quotes, poems or song lyrics, yet others are beautifully and carefully painted in colour by prisoner Dennis McLinton. As he was sentenced at the end of December 1944, this gives us a date after which the certificates were made. While it seems incredible that McLinton would have had paints in prison, the system of illicit smuggling, sometimes aided by the guards and warders,[39] was fully functioning. Francis Harris confirms that the certificates were made during the last months of the war and none were made subsequently. While they certainly had a souvenir status, Harris believes that they had another purpose: 'they formed some sort of "guarantee" that should any inmate disappear, there would be a record of some sort'.[40]

The illustrated autograph books are full of patriotic symbols, V-signs and flags. A number of the pages were illustrated with cartoons showing the sequence of events that led to the arrest and imprisonment of the artist. They depict young men in the act of listening to crystal radio sets, insulting German soldiers, holding a pot of tar and a paintbrush, and even about to blow up the premises of a local hairdresser deemed to be a collaborator. They also show young men before military tribunals and languishing in prison cells. As Francis Harris recalled, 'We all saw ourselves as patriots and were proud that we had done something.'[41] While these drawings were done with pride at patriotic behaviour, they were also made to cheer up the recipient. Most of all, they were ways of creating bonds of camaraderie, friendship and solidarity. By signing their names and listing their 'crimes', they were reaching out to each other with messages of fellow-feeling and sympathy (Figure 11.2). They were all in it together, whatever their eventual fate would be. Not only prisoners were the recipients of such colourful souvenirs: nurse Renee Griffin[42] who often signalled the news from the window of

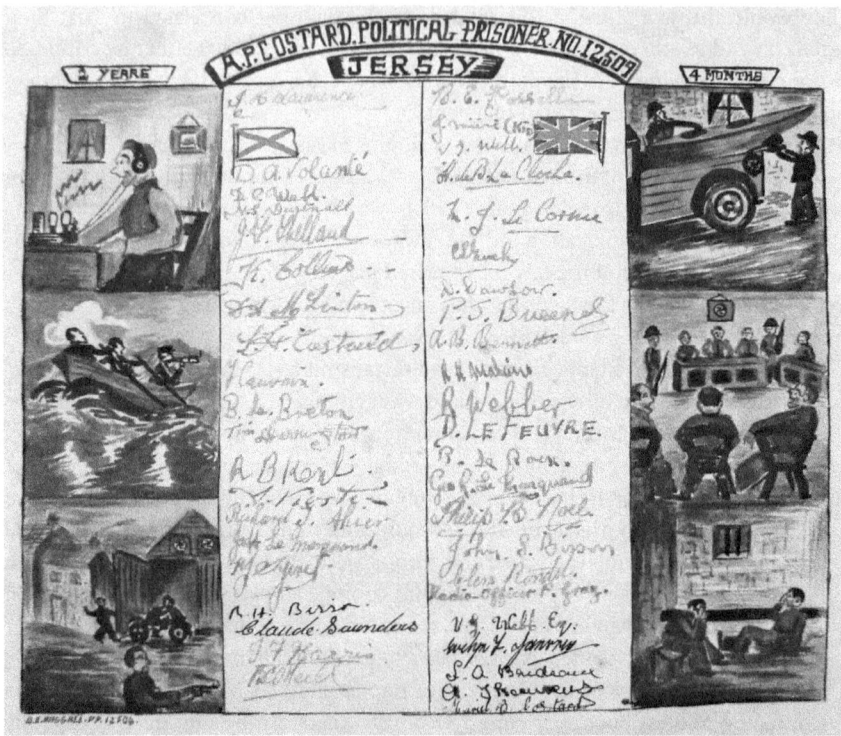

Figure 11.1 Political prisoner certificate (copyright and courtesy Wendy Tipping)

the hospital next to the prison, and a friendly prison guard, were also given their own versions as gifts of thanks for their help and kindness.

It is worth noting that there was also resistance inside prison, in addition to all of the rules broken by smuggling and communication listed above. Three examples will suffice and both were made possible, unsurprisingly, through the smuggling of illicit materials. Francis Le Sueur tells us that many of those in prison still managed to listen to the BBC on a crystal radio set while inside. This is because local French hairdresser, André Aune, who was locked up for supplying crystal radios to the population, managed to bring in the necessary components with him when he was imprisoned.[43] The second example took place in April 1945, in a large wooden hut built in the grounds of the civilian side of the prison in late 1944 to house 22 political prisoners in 3 rooms. Joe Mière tells how he used to keep a silk and cotton Union Jack in the top pocket of his jacket. When he was put in prison, it was confiscated along with his other possessions, but 'strangely enough … (was) sent over to the civilian side of the prison and finally came back to me'.[44] Although he doesn't give any detail about how it was returned to him, we are given the impression that it was through unofficial means. The flag was hung over the back of the door and the words 'political prisoners Jersey 1945' were painted on it. Although the prison governor and a German general carrying out an inspection saw the flag, they inmates were allowed to keep it up, probably because

Figure 11.2 Image from nurse Renee Griffin's autograph book (image reproduced courtesy of the Société Jersiaise)

it was so late in the war. We should not forget the ultimate defiance of prison rules, enacted by those who climbed out of their cell windows and over the outer wall of the prison. A number of political prisoners managed this feat, including Frank Keiller, George Whithy and Peter Curwood.[45]

Thus, as a result of the emerging political prisoner consciousness in the autumn of 1944, which can be tracked by the dates written on certificates and in autograph books, the prisoners began, as a group, to ask for their conditions to improve and to demand their rights. A small example of this can be seen during the short imprisonment of Deputy Edward Le Quesne, convicted of wireless offences. Elected as a spokesperson by other political prisoners in his cell and, later, in the prison, he secured some small but important privileges for his fellow convicts in October 1944.[46] Later he managed to secure the early release of some prisoners similarly convicted for wireless offences.[47]

Perhaps inspired by this group action, the following month the political prisoners signed a petition asking for the right to weekly rather than monthly visits from their families, but this was refused.[48] Three months later, in February 1945, four prisoners, representing the wider community of prisoners, wrote to the Bailiff to complain of 'unjust treatment' in the distribution of Red Cross parcels. Three days later the Bailiff visited them and asked the prison board to sympathetically consider their requests.[49]

On 10 April, the issue of overcrowding of those 'in prison by Order of the German Court' belatedly made its way to the attention of the prison board, the Bailiff and the German authorities.[50] Accompanying the correspondence about this case is a list of the 38 political prisoners in jail at this time, their ages and the reason for their imprisonment.[51] This provides us with an interesting and illuminating snapshot of a cross-section of this group. Although their ages range from 17 to 66 years old, the vast majority were under 25 (26 people or 68 per cent), and 31 (82 per cent) were 35 years old or younger. Eighteen of the prisoners were convicted of attempting to escape or aiding an escape attempt (47 per cent); a further seven had been convicted for radio offences (18 per cent), remembering that a number of this group had been released the previous October due to the action of Edward Le Quesne. Three were imprisoned for sabotage or for being in possession of weapons (8 per cent). The remaining prisoners had been convicted for lying to or insulting the occupying authorities (five), for black market offences (three), or for theft (one).[52]

The analysis of the composition of the political prisoner group is useful in enabling us to understand the situation at liberation, one month later. The political prisoners were let out in two waves, on 7 and 8 May 1945. Joe Mière, one of those imprisoned at the time, later wrote that 'The Bailiff of Jersey came down to the prison at about 6.30 pm on the evening of 7 May 1945 … (and) released 30 of us political prisoners … who were being held on the public side of the prison. He told us not to kick a dog when it was down, in other words, do not make trouble and leave the Germans alone.'[53] Edward Le Quesne, keeping an eye on his old friends, also recorded this fact in his diary, as did Leslie Sinel.[54] We can only guess which 30 political prisoners were released and which remained inside; however, we know that Peter Gray, convicted for being in possession of arms and ammunition, was kept behind, and we can assume that others convicted for similar offences were not released at this time. In his memoirs, Gray wrote that the political prisoners lined up in the prison yard and a States official read out a list of names of those who were to be released. He states that 'around ten' people were not on the list. They were ordered by the same official to return to prison to await prosecution by the Jersey authorities.[55] Gray was later to tell Mière that the Attorney General wanted to make sure that they 'had not broken any Jersey law, or had not damaged civilian property or stolen any civilian goods'.[56] Gray recalls in his memoirs that the remaining prisoners were so angry that they started a riot, 'creating uproar' that night, the next morning and into the afternoon of the next day (presumably 8 May, although Mière strongly argues that it was 9 May; it is likely that prisoners were released on both days), until they were released to the 'great crowds' that were waiting outside the prison gates.[57]

If the local government had been unsure what official position to take on political prisoners after the liberation, correspondence between the Home Office and the Bailiff of Jersey in the summer of 1945 makes the situation very clear. In the context of discussing a possible amnesty of prisoners, Coutanche admitted that 'many 'occupation' crimes were highly detrimental to the common welfare'.[58] In Home Office's subsequent assessment of the situation, their view was:

> strongly against any amnesty in the Channel Islands … the question remains, however, whether there be cases of offenders sentenced during the German

occupation which may deserve review on account of the exceptional circumstances in the islands at that time, and the changed conditions now. Any such cases should be reviewed and submitted to us on their merits ... it would be very undesirable that crimes which were in fact highly detrimental to the common welfare should be condoned in any way.[59]

Ultimately, this was to become both the official and the popular position for decades to come.

Aftermath of liberation

After the joy of liberation, former political prisoners discovered that the general population held mixed feelings towards them. It is important at this juncture to distinguish not just between the types of 'crime' for which they were sentenced, but also the date at which they went to prison. There is a sense from the available evidence that the later group of political prisoners – those in jail from the autumn of 1944 onwards and who developed a sense of political prisoner consciousness and who afterwards coined the term among the general population – were perceived differently from those imprisoned at an earlier date. It seems that these two things (epithet and 'crime') were conflated and that those who claimed the name were branded as 'troublemakers' along with those whose 'crime' was more 'honourable' or 'legitimate' (such as owning a crystal radio set and distributing the news).

On the one hand, we see that towards the end of the war there was a sense of pride among freed political prisoners. Leslie Sinel noted that 'prisoners returning home after a long term are usually feted by their friends and relations, and there has been at least one induction into the 'Order of the Old Glostonians'!'[60] This sense of pride was felt by others who had been in prison, including Dora Hacquoil, who was imprisoned for two months in the summer of 1944 for her role in sheltering a Russian slave worker. Less than a fortnight after liberation, she wrote that 'I was amazed to hear that we [political prisoners] are all heroes!'[61]

On the other hand, Evelyn Janvrin, convicted in December 1944 for trying to escape from the island, and for the furthering and dissemination of anti-German news, received a different response. Her sister had made her a blazer badge embroidered with the words 'political prisoner 12516' and 'victory 1945' (Figure 11.3).[62] An acquaintance, Eric Walker, later wrote that 'a few days after the liberation ... I noticed that Eve suddenly removed the embroidered 'political prisoner' badge ... she had discovered that in post-war Jersey, former political prisoners were not being hailed as heroes.'[63]

In a further complication to this picture, we must consider the situation in Guernsey, which seems to have been quite different. No sense of political prisoner consciousness appears to have emerged in this island's prison towards the end of the war. This is perhaps because the profile of those inside was different. Of the 59 people convicted by the German military court in Guernsey between 1 January and 14 March 1945,[64] 23 people or 39 per cent were convicted of radio offences, 19 people or 32 per cent were convicted of theft, and 9 people or 15 per cent were convicted of receiving

Figure 11.3 Evelyn Janvrin's political prisoner badge, courtesy and copyright Wendy Tipping

stolen goods.[65] These are not crimes which one might naturally associate primarily with patriotism.

Jersey, being closer to France, had more escapees (whose aim was to join the allied armies and fight). Jersey (or rather, St Helier) had a higher number of youths,[66] and it was this age group who tended to form small resistance groups whose aim was to steal weapons in order to fight alongside the allies when they arrived. As these young patriots, as they thought of themselves, formed the majority of the political prisoners in Jersey, the different prison demographic in Guernsey explains the lack of consciousness among this group. As will be discussed later, it was those from Guernsey who spent time in continental prisons and camps who were later to form associations and groups, and also to think of themselves as political prisoners. Coysh, writing a decade after Guernsey's liberation, argued that 'A prison sentence in the Occupation was not ... anything of which to be ashamed and certainly no social stigma was attached to it. Indeed, going to jail could be an honourable experience, as in the case of those who were caught with radio sets, spreading the news or other meritorious practices.'[67]

Again, the issue of honour and merit in regard to resistance acts is highlighted. Those convicted for radio offences were deemed to be 'courageous people, and may their names be honoured for it'. Those who tried to escape and failed received 'both sympathy and admiration'.[68] As already discussed, however, the acts of these same people could also bring reprisals.

The mixed feelings of sympathy, admiration and vilification of political prisoners came despite the knowledge that very few members of the population would have escaped a jail sentence had every infraction of the German decrees been punished.[69]

The over-riding concern and abiding feeling towards political prisoners appears to have been the realization that resistance was impossible 'without disastrous consequences' to both the resister and everyone else,[70] and that sabotage or the possession or use of arms could result in a death sentence. Thus, it seems that this category of political prisoners – those who were not released from Jersey jail on 7 May 1945 – were at least partly 'responsible' for the negative connotations associated with the group as a whole. There were many, however, who believed that all who committed acts of protest, defiance and resistance, and certainly all political prisoners, jeopardized the lives of the whole population through their actions. Given that a large swathe of the population of Guernsey and Jersey indulged in 'figuratively breathing in when they should have been breathing out',[71] this attitude may perhaps be considered slightly hypocritical.

Despite the negative attitudes directed towards political prisoners, it seems that in the immediate post-war years, while the *offenders* may have been vilified, the *offences* were not. This impression can be gleaned not just from the pride and detail with which protest, defiance and resistance are discussed in post-war memoirs and accounts of occupation, but also in the film made in the Channel Islands in 1945, several months after liberation, which gave a potted account of the Occupation for British audiences.[72] This film places unusual emphasis upon resistance, showing that this was the narrative that they initially wanted to construct and how they wanted to be judged by outsiders. The film opens with an escape attempt, moving on to show secret listening to the BBC – a theme which featured heavily throughout the film through scenes showing home-made crystal radio sets and illicit newsletters. Islanders were keen to portray themselves as loyal and patriotic subjects, but while the offences which earned prison sentences were emphasized, those who were sent to prison or who died were mentioned but not dwelt upon. The Churchillian narrative, which emphasized victory over victimhood, was in the process of being adopted. Through the virtue of being British, Channel Islanders were able to share in the victory and the rewards that it bought.

Just as islanders portrayed themselves as loyal British subjects in film, so this was reflected in the first post-war New Year's honours list, in which Occupation Bailiffs Victor Carey and Alexander Coutanche, and also John Leale (President of the Controlling Committee in Guernsey) were knighted. CBEs, MBEs and OBEs were also distributed to other members of the islands' authorities.[73]

There was much bitterness among former political prisoners in Guernsey and Jersey that they had been excluded from post-war honours. As the Woods famously noted, 'it seemed unfortunate that, for the most part, the Honours were given to those in high places and official positions, and included few who had risked their lives doing anything which might offend the enemy.'[74] They found it 'strange' for the Home Office to continue the anti-resistance attitude after the war, although John Leale commented to them that 'it might be difficult for a Government which is a signatory to the Hague Convention to recommend Honours for those who broke the convention.'[75] The lack of honours for people who committed acts of resistance can perhaps be seen in terms of the precarious position of the island authorities, already under heavy criticism during this period. The Home Office may have seen the honours as a way to show ordinary islanders, displaying signs of unrest and demands for reform at this time, that the

United Kingdom was firmly on the side of the authorities. Popular historian Barry Turner suggested that to shower praise on those who committed acts of resistance would have been 'to imply that those who had taken the more conventional route … had failed in their duty'. It appears not to have occurred to anyone that 'failure to acknowledge [those who committed acts of resistance] … would necessarily denigrate their efforts'.[76]

What struck the Woods as 'even more strange' was that no attempt had been made to compile a 'Roll of Honour' of those who had 'died for their courage', and no complete list of islanders existed for those who died in prisons and concentration camps. Such work was not to be tackled for another 40 years, although the figures who I term here 'guardians of memory', both of them former political prisoners, were working behind the scenes to make sure that the sufferings of their friends and fellow prisoners would not be forgotten.

Guardians of memory: 1940s–60s

Although the stories of acts of defiance continued to circulate in the Channel Islands, it seems that as time passed, people acted to put a traumatic past behind them and to rebuild the islands and their lives. Although a number of Occupation museums opened in the first few decades after the war, islanders went through a period of 'voluntary amnesia' whereby a curtain of silence descended regarding the dark years of 1940–5.

Elsewhere I have discussed the successive phases of memory displayed by attitudes towards the legacy and heritage of the Occupation in the Channel Islands.[77] I have classified the period between 1945 and the early 1950s as one of 'mourning and cleansing', as the islands were cleared of the debris of war and islanders mourned their war dead. Between the early 1950s and the mid-1970s deliberate amnesia reigned, until the islands began to indulge in a form of 'Occupation nostalgia', led by the second generation, for whom bunker restoration became a major hobby from 1977 onwards.

During the period of amnesia, two men (Joe Mière in Jersey and Frank Falla in Guernsey), took on the mantle of 'guardians of memory'. The two men were not in contact with each other (though may have known of each other's work) and did not begin to correspond until 1980.[78] Mière began his life's work over 30 years earlier. In 1948 he was demobbed from the army and started his collection of testimonies and photos of his fellow political prisoners 'in a serious way'. He wrote that 'friends and people of the Occupation were very kind to me, always ready to tell me their war history and give me their photographs … they were only too pleased that someone was recording the history of themselves or their family'.[79] In 1976, he became the deputy curator at the German Underground Hospital, a tourist venue in Jersey (Figure 11.4), and he displayed his collection, by then quite large, in the tunnels. He became a curator from 1983 until 1991, when he retired.[80] Even in the face of 'considerable indifference and even some hostility', Mière continued to collect information about those arrested by the Germans.[81]

Like Mière, Frank Falla's work was done alone, although he did not come into his own until the 1960s. After the war, he and his former GUNS (the Guernsey

Figure 11.4 Painting of Joe Mière by Andrew Tift, courtesy and copyright Jersey Heritage and Andrew Tift

Underground News Service) friends, and 'one or two other Guernseymen' who had survived imprisonment on the continent, had a reunion dinner on the last Saturday of April each year to celebrate their liberation from prison. This was an occasion on which, as Falla described it, 'We eat what we like … we drink what we like. We have as many cigarettes as we want. Our toast is 'Absent Friends,' and we think about the chaps who died …'[82] The Frank Falla Archive, rediscovered in 2010 and discussed later, contains photographs from a number of these events in the 1950s and 1960s, and it shows between six and eight regular attendees (Figure 11.5).

It is hard to pin-point precisely when Falla began to see himself as a spokesperson for other former political prisoners from Guernsey. However, as he was a journalist by trade, he used his position to tell his story in local papers in July 1945.[83] In 1946, the new Bailiff of Guernsey, Ambrose Sherwill (who had spent time in Cherche-Midi prison in Paris in 1940), was invited by the *Conseil National de la Resistance* in Brussels to attend a rally of war-time resistance movements from all over Europe.[84] Although he appointed Harold Le Druillenec, a British survivor of Belsen, to represent the Channel Islands, Le Druillenec was in no shape to go.[85] Falla was chosen instead, as a surviving member of GUNS, to be the only British delegate to attend the meeting. It took place in Vielsalm, Belgium, in June 1946, a date chosen to coincide with the anniversary of the D-Day landings. The meeting was held on the site of a former clandestine landing strip for RAF pilots dropping arms and food.[86] It is likely that this was a formative

Figure 11.5 Photo of the twenty-first annual reunion of political prisoners, Guernsey 1966. Back row: Frank Falla, Bill Symes, Gerald Domaille. Front row: Cecil Duquemin, Ernest Legg, Norman Dexter, Walter Lainé. Courtesy of the family of Frank Falla

experience for Falla; he was later to describe it as a 'considerable honour' to have represented Guernsey.[87]

In the ten years that followed, Falla went back to work as a journalist but also began to take an interest in the compensation agreements that were carried out between West Germany and countries which had experienced Nazi occupation. This began to be discussed in the Foreign Office in the 1950s with regard to an agreement with Britain. In 1959, the Home Office contacted the Lieutenant-Governors of Guernsey and Jersey to ask for information about the precise number and categories of people deported from the Bailiwicks during the Occupation, what treatment they received, and how many died.[88] As the Woods had discovered a few years earlier, this information was not readily available although the Lieutenant-Governors were able to give the numbers of those deported to civilian internment camps. While Coutanche was doubtful whether an accurate figure of people sent from Jersey for imprisonment on the continent could be ascertained, Sherwill was able to provide the Home Office with the number of 'certain' and 'probable' deportations (the latter compiled from memory by police officers), and the number of people convicted of offences by German military courts.[89]

With this information, the British government was able to make informed negotiations with the West German government. On 9 June 1964, an agreement for one million pounds of compensation was signed, and the following month, the Foreign Office was able to publish advertisements prominently and extensively across the country and colonies, inviting applications from 'United Kingdom nationals who were victims of Nazi persecution and suffered detention in a concentration camp or comparable institution (NOT in an internment or prisoner of war camp)'. The deadline for registrations was 31 July 1965.[90] Prisoners of War were excluded from the process because their numbers were so vast that the amount of compensation able to be distributed to others would have been negligible and derisory.[91] The notes for guidance for filling in the application form stated that 'hardships suffered in a normal civil prison' did not qualify a person for compensation,[92] which ruled out the political prisoners who had 'only' suffered in island prisons. Although the compensation was for UK nationals, the Foreign Office had factored Channel Islanders into their calculations, estimating that around 2,000 islanders might be eligible.[93]

In order to prove that they were eligible for compensation, applicants had to provide four key pieces of information about their imprisonment, namely: (a) the name of the camp or other place of detention, its situation, its general conditions and regime; (b) the dates of imprisonment and release; prison number; reasons for imprisonment and circumstances in which it arose; (c) the full details of the nature and cause of permanent disability suffered as a result of treatment received during imprisonment; (d) any other information considered useful and relevant. Proof was needed of these four elements, and medical documents had to be submitted. Many applicants had to attend a medical board to have their state of health verified.[94]

Proving that one had indeed been in a camp and had suffered ill health as a result was not always easy to do. Not everyone had received or kept their prison cards. Some of those who had suffered ill health had received head injuries which affected their ability to write a coherent case for compensation. Some had been mentally, psychologically or emotionally so badly affected that they, too, found it difficult to express what had happened to them. The Foreign Office was aware of such potential problems, and officials were urged to be sensitive in accepting 'unofficial and informal paperwork as evidence'.[95]

With this background to the compensation procedure in mind, we turn back to Frank Falla. His archive, filled with newspaper clippings and letters, gives an insight into his correspondence with various MPs and the Foreign Office from approximately 1957 onwards (Figure 11.6). The other half of this correspondence can be found in the Foreign Office files in The National Archives. These sources, coupled with Falla's memoirs, make it clear that he was closely following events regarding the protracted negotiations with the West German government on the subject of compensation for people who had been ill-treated by the Nazis. In his memoirs, he wrote that in around 1957 he learned that the subject was being considered, and watched other countries receive compensation. At last, when Britain also decided to seek compensation, he followed questions on the subject in the House of Commons and devoured articles in newspapers.

> I stood by anticipating a local awakening. Surely some official in the Channel Islands would realise that there were in Jersey and Guernsey people who merited compensation. I waited in vain ... I would have thought Statesmen in the Channel Islands would have stirred themselves and got things organised on an official basis. But not a bit of it. No one raised a finger to help, indeed no one seemed the

slightest bit interested. So I decided to do my best to find out what it was all about, and before long found that I had become a kind of unofficial official.[96]

Between 1957 and 1964, he wrote to various MPs such as Barnett Janner and Airey Neave, and to people in the Foreign Office. His regular letters at quite an early stage in the proceedings caused a Miss K. M. Graham at the Foreign Office to comment in 1962 that Falla 'appears to act as a kind of spokesman for the Channel Islanders in the context of compensation to victims of Nazi persecution'.[97]

As soon as the period of registration for compensation opened, Falla wrote to the Foreign Secretary to offer his services and to explain the different groups of Channel Islanders who might put in claims.[98] Throughout the period of registration, Falla regularly wrote to the Foreign Office, asking for application forms for compensation to distribute them to those he knew would need them. He also passed on the names of those from Guernsey and Jersey who suffered in prisons and camps, helped the Foreign Office track down islanders and clarify identities, and passed on details of suffering and death that he had witnessed in particular prisons, writing that 'in an effort to spare the feelings of the families of these men I have never communicated the full facts to them as I do to you and you will readily appreciate why'.[99]

Drafts of testimonies from a number of people are in Falla's archive, and it is clear that he used his literacy as a journalist and experience as a former prisoner to help others get their memories in order and write their testimonies – especially those who had suffered too greatly physically and mentally to be able to fill in the form. He also helped the next of kin write testimonies on behalf of their deceased relatives. However, Falla could not be sure that all Channel Islanders were discussing their applications with him, nor necessarily receiving their forms solely from him, and so was keen to find out how many had put in claims or been accepted, although the Foreign Office did not share this information.[100]

As a freelance journalist during this period, Falla was keen to draw attention to those who had suffered in Nazi prisons and camps. He wrote articles in local newspapers to inform his fellow islanders when compensation began to arrive, but also to tell his own story about his fight on their behalf. 'Originally it was intended', he wrote, 'that compensation should be paid to UK nations only, but Mr Falla took this matter up with Mr Airey Neave ... and after a great deal of correspondence and negotiation Channel Islanders were allowed to share in the million pounds granted by the Federal German Government for this purpose'.[101] Despite all he was doing, not all other islanders were supportive. An anonymous letter in a local newspaper argued that those deported for offences against the occupying forces should be last in the queue for compensation, as they risked the safety of the whole island population. 'In war time, why should an offender, involving the safety – the lives – of others expect compensation after he or she has suffered imprisonment brought about entirely by his or her actions?'[102] The old ill-feelings towards political prisoners had not been forgotten, even if former political prisoners and their children were grateful to Falla.[103]

Towards the end of the registration period, the Foreign Office grew worried by the small number of applicants and the large numbers that they had to reject, and so extended the period of registration until 31 March 1966.[104] By the end of this date, a

Figure 11.6 Photo of Frank Falla's briefcase, in which his letters, testimonies and newspaper cuttings were kept. Copyright Gilly Carr

total of 868 UK nationals had successfully applied for compensation in respect of the persecution of 745 victims. Separate payouts for disability brought the total number of awards to 1015,[105] with an average payment of £985 4s 1d.[106] Compensation was worked out on a basis of units, whereby a person would be awarded so many units for each month of imprisonment in a concentration camp, and so many for permanent damage to body or health or for death. The total number of victims and their total units could only be known at the end of the period of registration, and it was only then that the monetary value of each unit was worked out.[107] While the number of Channel Islanders who received compensation is unknown (because all of the application forms exist as closed files with the Foreign Office), it is estimated that over 110 applied, of whom almost half received compensation.[108]

It should be noted that the number of those who applied for compensation is far fewer than those who were deported to prisons and camps. While some died before 1965, others decided not to apply because it was too painful to recall bad memories or because they were too proud to accept German 'blood-money'. Yet others were ineligible as their prisons were not deemed to be comparable to concentration camps or because they had emigrated and had changed citizenship. Further, it has proved impossible to track the names of all deported Channel Islanders as some deportations were not recorded in the surviving archives. Some German military tribunals, imprisonments and subsequent removals to the continent happened without notifying the local authorities in the Channel Islands. The author has also heard from some families who testify to the disappearance of family members or to accounts of imprisonment when there is no surviving record to verify the fact. To complicate matters, the prison log for Guernsey is missing, as is the German copy of the military court tribunal records. The copy kept by the local police, who were not kept fully informed by the Germans, has its last entry in February 1945. Jersey's political prisoner prison log lists its last entries of confinement and transport to France at the end of July 1944. In other words, the statistics available are based on incomplete sources.

In the 1960s, long before any archival sources were open and perhaps before some were lost, Frank Falla was instrumental in helping to publicize compensation in the Channel Islands (not just in his own island), in distributing forms to islanders, and in helping islanders successfully claim compensation, even those who had initially been rejected. He thus acted as a guardian of memory for political prisoners who had been interned on the continent and was prepared to fight for their cause, which was also his own. Joe Mière was a guardian of memory first and foremost for Jersey's political prisoners who were imprisoned with him in the island. As a number of Jersey's political prisoners were also deported to the continent, Mière was very interested in collecting their testimonies as well. Between them, these two men deserve to be remembered for their years of work on behalf of Channel Islanders who committed acts of resistance. Neither received any help or thanks from the islands' authorities, and both faced hostility and unpopularity for the work they undertook with courage and tenacity.

The fight for memorialization: The 1990s and beyond

The First World War memorials in Jersey and Guernsey were altered or annotated soon after the Second World War to remember Channel Islanders who fought and died in the armed services between 1940 and 1945. By contrast, the era of memorialization of other groups or aspects of the Occupation did not begin in earnest until 1985, with victims of Nazism beginning to join the large cluster of memorials in St Peter Port and St Helier from 1995 onwards.[109] While Frank Falla died in 1983 and thus could not campaign for memorialization of those who defied the occupiers, Joe Mière was, predictably, the man to take this on in Jersey.

In 1995, when Sir Philip Bailhache became Bailiff of Jersey, he began to be called upon to unveil memorial plaques and make speeches about victims of Nazism. This cause was close to his heart and he became known as the man to ask to undertake this kind of work. During his period of office, he unveiled a number of such memorials, and the change in the Occupation narrative in Jersey today to include such previously marginalized groups is now referred to as the 'Bailhache effect'.

Before Bailhache came into office, Sir Peter Crill, a former Occupation escapee, was the previous Bailiff. To mark his retirement, Crill was asked to unveil a series of memorial plaques to people who had escaped from the island at various places along the south-east coast. Joe Mière contacted the local paper to ask whether political prisoners would also be remembered at some point, writing that 'It seems they are always overlooked or not recognized by the States of Jersey and Guernsey ... Why have no States Members even brought forward a petition on behalf of our 'forgotten people', to place a memorial plaque outside the old prison wall in Gloucester Street?'[110]

It seems that Mière was galvanized by the escapee plaques because, after all, he had been imprisoned with a large number of escapees – or rather, those who had failed to escape and who had become his fellow political prisoners. But the new escapee plaques did not acknowledge these people. In the month following his newspaper article, Mière wrote to the Lieutenant-Governor of Jersey, Sir John Sutton, asking for a memorial plaque to political prisoners. Sutton forwarded the letter to the Bailiff and to the fiftieth Anniversary Occupation and Liberation Committee.[111]

At last, nearly 50 years after the end of the Occupation, it seems that the time was right. Two months after writing to the Lieutenant-Governor, Mière received a letter to say that it was unlikely that any memorial stone could be unveiled on Liberation Day, but that he should think about an alternative occasion.[112] To be denied recognition on one of the most important public holidays in the island would have come as no surprise to Mière, but he chose instead 27 April as a suitable date as it was when the Germans shot one of their own soldiers, who had occupied a prison cell next to Mière, for desertion; their 'last piece of real savagery'.[113] Just as Mière was denied a prominent unveiling date, he was also nearly denied his preferred location for the memorial. While the authorities wanted it to be placed 'in a corner where no-one would have seen it', Mière confided later to a fellow former political prisoner that he had held his ground and so it was placed outside the site of the wartime prison in Gloucester Street,[114] the original building having been demolished in 1973. While Mière undoubtedly would have had an opinion on the memorial text, and may even have submitted his own ideas,[115] like all other plaques erected in a public place, it would have had to go through official channels of approval. The available documents suggest that this occurred at the highest levels.[116]

Mière would undoubtedly have been pleased that the memorial would be unveiled by the new Bailiff, Sir Philip Bailhache, in the presence of the Lieutenant-Governor. However, as the big day approached, he was disturbed and upset by both the lack of publicity surrounding the imminent unveiling and its absence in the programme for liberation celebrations.[117] He was told by the Occupation and Liberation Committee that they did 'not intend the unveiling to be a huge ceremony'.[118] A member of the Committee confirmed to another former political prisoner that in the past there had been 'considerable reluctance by the Government of Jersey to recognise political prisoners at all'.[119] In the event, with just one day to go, a small announcement about the unveiling was placed in the local paper by the Committee.[120] Archival evidence shows that the authorities deliberately decided to give the event very little advance publicity because of the 'perceived sensitivities' surrounding the belief that 'many of the offences [committed by political prisoners] would have been punishable under normal civilian law and indeed could have been described as criminal'.[121] Mière and Falla's interpretation of the situation had been right all along. With regard to the lack of acknowledgement in Guernsey, Falla wrote that:

> It all dated back to the days of the German Occupation when we were naughty lads and stepped out of line with the Germans. We were disowned by the civil authorities at that time; for instance, they didn't even come to our aid by insisting that we as islanders and under International Law had a right to be defended before a Nazi tribunal by our own lawyers. As far as we know they made no tangible effort to find out where we were so that our relatives could be informed. They disowned us blatantly then – and they have never got around to owning us again.[122]

Figure 11.7 Lighthouse Memorial, St Helier, Holocaust Memorial Day. Copyright Gilly Carr

While the authorities in Jersey had at last got around to 'owning' political prisoners again, the memorial is ignored today. As it is on the edge of the commercial district of St Helier and plays no part in any annual commemorative ceremonies, it looks neglected. The lettering is peeling and partially obscured by ivy, making it difficult to read.

In 1996, the Lighthouse Memorial was erected in St Helier and unveiled by Sir Philip Bailhache (Figure 11.7). This memorial commemorates the 'Jersey 21'; those who died in continental prisons and camps after being deported and did not return to the island. The names and deeds of the men and women remembered were recovered thanks to Mière's research. The memorial is the centre of ceremonies on Holocaust Memorial Day each year, and hundreds of islanders gather for the commemorations and speeches, after which the full spectrum of island authorities and community leaders lay wreaths.

Elsewhere on the island, other people who defied the Occupiers are remembered today. Plaques exist on the former houses of Albert Bedane, who sheltered a Jewish woman during the Occupation, and of Louisa Gould, who sheltered a Russian slave worker and who died in Ravensbrück. Gould has also been listed in a special addition to her parish war memorial in St Ouen. The overall impression gained is that Jersey's Occupation narrative has increasingly embraced those who defied German orders, even if the role of those whose acts might have been judged as 'criminal' has never been fully accepted into mainstream memory. Nonetheless, that there were islanders prepared to take up arms against the occupiers, as elsewhere in Europe, is something that allows elements of Channel Islands resistance to be directly compared with acts on the continent, as discussed elsewhere in this volume, and gives lie to those who claim that there was no armed resistance of any sort in the Channel Islands.

In Guernsey there is no memorial to political prisoners. Neither the offences nor the offenders are remembered in memorial form today. There are at least three main reasons for this. First, Falla did not live to see the era of commemoration in the Channel Islands and so was not provoked by the appearance of new memorials, as Joe Mière was, to fight for his own cause. As the sole guardian of memory of this group in Guernsey, there has been no-one else to take up his mantle. The second reason, not unrelated to this, is the lack of a 'Bailhache effect' in Guernsey. No Bailiff, member of local government, or community leader has made it his or her cause to support these particular victims of Nazism. It is possible, however, that the long and prominent career in the island of respected former Bailiff, Sir de Vic Carey, who held office from 1999 to 2005, and who was the grandson of the wartime Bailiff, has indirectly, unintentionally, and through no fault of his own, suppressed activism in this area (the 'Carey effect', as it were). As political prisoners were 'disowned', as Falla put it, and not protected from deportation during the Occupation, anyone who might have wanted to explore the reasons for the lack of protection could have been dissuaded, perhaps by others, out of a desire not to criticize Carey's grandfather. This remains conjectural.

Thirdly, we might also observe the late emergence (compared to Jersey) of memorials to other victims of Nazism in the island. Forced labourers who died in the island were remembered in 1999, Jews in 2001 and deportees in 2010. This may be part of the same related phenomenon, as these groups were also unprotected by local authorities during the Occupation. The late emergence in Guernsey of a narrative which embraces victims of Nazism (the fourth consecutive phase of memory in the Channel Islands; see Carr 2014) is perhaps because the island is still dominated by the previous war narrative: that of 'Occupation nostalgia', which has liberation and the display of the spoils of war as its prime focus. It is also strongly influenced by the Churchillian paradigm, which espouses a narrative of victory and not victimhood.

The 'Carey effect' and the dominance of the 'Occupation nostalgia' narrative together combine to create a sense of unspoken taboo when it comes to discussion of those who committed acts of resistance and their later suffering in prisons and camps across Europe. Three examples will suffice to illustrate this, and all are to be found in the memorial arena.

The apparent unofficial and historical taboo against a memorial to resistance in Guernsey is not evidence that people in this island have no interest in remembering resisters or no desire to see a memorial. The continued lack of a memorial has caused islanders to seek other modes in which to express their desire to remember. Pre-existing memorials have been used to remember this group. Every year, the daughter of Joseph Gillingham, one of the men involved in the GUNS newsletter who did not return after the war, puts a small wooden cross bearing her father's name in front of St Peter Port's war memorial on Armistice Day. Her mother, Henrietta, was told that Joseph's name could not be engraved on the memorial because he had not died while serving in the Armed Forces,[123] but in the absence of an alternative, the family of Joseph Gillingham remember him still (Figure 11.8).

Figure 11.8 Memorial cross to Joseph Gillingham at the Guernsey War Memorial. Copyright Jonathan Bartlett

Other islanders have used the grave of the deceased or their spouse to inscribe their brave acts. For example, the headstone of the grave of Hubert Lanyon in Sark recalls that he was a member of GUNS. At the foot of Henrietta Gillingham's grave is a plaque to her husband that also recalls his membership of GUNS. The neglected grave of Guernseyman John Ingrouille, buried in the Vale parish churchyard, records the fact that he died aged 25 after having been a political prisoner in a concentration camp. A stained glass window was dedicated by his parents to his memory in the church. In the same graveyard, the gleaming white headstone of Marie Ozanne's grave stands out in contrast to the others. Marie was a member of the Salvation Army who preached against German orders and who protested against their acts towards forced labourers and the Jews. She was sent to Guernsey prison and died soon after.

The rarity on a European scale of the nature of Marie Ozanne's resistance encouraged two authors of this volume (GC and LW) to seek local support in 2010 in the form of Marie Ozanne's nephew, William Ozanne, for a blue plaque on her former house in the Vale parish. At the first attempt they were unsuccessful and a local artist and poet was given a plaque instead, despite funding being in place for Marie's plaque. Fortunately the second attempt was successful. However, the final text on the plaque described

Marie somewhat ambiguously as a 'resister against oppression'. Apart from the date of her death in 1943, no reference was made to Nazism or the German Occupation.

The third example concerns the memorial plaque to the deportees, those mostly English-born civilians deported to German internment camps in 1942 and 1943. This memorial was unveiled in 2010 by former Bailiff Sir Geoffrey Rowland, who has been a strong supporter of this group. The post-script to the memorial is particularly revealing for what it withholds from stating. It reads 'Also remembering other islanders who were *for other reasons* deported and died in labour camps and prisons in Europe' [my italics]. The explanation for this dance of avoidance around the subject of resistance is usually given as the role of 'perceived sensitivities'. For too long this has been allowed to stifle proper remembrance of those who committed acts of protest, defiance and resistance.

While local activism has been muted, self-marginalized or self-censoring because of these sensitivities, it has, in the end, taken outside intervention to facilitate recognition of resisters, as the wider project behind this volume has illustrated. In 2010, after the author's search for the children of Frank Falla, his daughter came forward. Not realizing its historic value, she gave Falla's large collection of papers to the author, and these will eventually be placed in the island's official archives. It was immediately clear that these files represented the most important and intact resistance archive ever to emerge from the island. Falla's correspondence with former resisters and the Foreign Office, and his collection of testimonies of suffering contained within the files, are a vital part of a three-piece historical jigsaw. While the other half of the correspondence is available in The National Archives in Kew, the Falla files gave a rare and partial insight into the complete collection of testimonies of Channel Islander sufferings in continental prisons and camps, which currently only exist as closed Foreign Office files. Without the Falla archive, we would not know what still existed to be discovered and its importance for one day writing a forgotten chapter of Channel Island history. As Channel Island men and women rarely spoke to their families about their suffering in prisons and camps on the continent for fear of passing on traumatic memories, many of these stories are lost today.[124] The Frank Falla files provide the key to recovering these testimonies and thus paying tribute to the suffering of islanders.

Conclusion: Remembering resistance today and tomorrow

This chapter has highlighted the changing memory, mediated through objects, diaries, autograph books and heritage, of resistance in the Channel Islands. It has explored the key roles of Joe Mière and Frank Falla acting not only as record keepers and guardians of memory, but also in fighting long and hard for the memory and legitimacy of the actions of former political prisoners. These two men have played a vital role in safeguarding the history of resistance in the Channel Islands, fuelled by indignation over their own wartime experiences.

This chapter has also highlighted the gap that exists between private and public memory; between that which has resided in unpublished diaries, autograph books and graves, and that which has been proclaimed on memorial stones and in public speeches. While the gap has significantly narrowed in Jersey since 1995, its width is more obvious in Guernsey, where acquiescence to 'local sensitivities' are responsible for the continued careful wording and absences in the memorial landscape. Despite this, private Occupation museums in both islands today carefully curate and proudly display the material culture and testimonies of those who committed acts of protest, defiance and resistance.

Those who committed acts which could have resulted in reprisals are still perceived by some to have been 'troublemakers'. This epithet has been applied uncritically to all those who spent time in prison. It is likely that the lack of exploration and scholarship on this topic for the first 50 years after the Occupation, and any subsequent public discussion which this might have been engendered, is one clear reason why old perceptions have not died out. Now that much of the research has been conducted, it is possible that this will act as a catalyst to galvanize new guardians of memory from among family members of political prisoners – or at least will prompt the erection of a resistance memorial in Guernsey. However, until the closed Foreign Office files are open, we will not be closer to acquiring either the full list of Channel Islanders who suffered in camps and prisons on the continent for acts carried out against the occupiers, or the full list of those who did not return. Nor will we have the full complement of testimonies of those islanders who suffered in those camps and penal prisons. Until that day, the full Occupation history of protest, defiance and resistance in the Channel Islands cannot be written.

Notes

1. Paul Sanders, *The Ultimate Sacrifice. The Jersey Islanders who Died in German Prisons and Concentration Camps 1940–1945*, Jersey, Jersey Heritage Trust, 2004, pp. 13–14.
2. Le Sauteur wrote in his diary on 15 February 1943 that 'The resemblance of life under the German Occupation to Alice in Wonderland in its unreality grew all the time, the parallel to the Queen's 'Off with his head' being now 'off to Germany' as a reward for figuratively breathing in when one should be breathing out' (Peter Le Sauteur, *Jersey under the Swastika*, London, Streamline Publications Ltd, 1961, p. 129).
3. IWM.5727 96/32/1. Dr Alastair Rose, 'Impressions of the Occupation of Guernsey, Written by Dr. Alastair Rose between 1944 & 1945', p. 11.
4. Louis Guillemette, Diary, 14–19 August 1943, in private ownership.
5. Martin Conway and Peter Romijn, *The War for Legitimacy in Politics and Culture 1936–1946*, Oxford and New York, Berg, 2008, p. 10.
6. Ibid., p. 16.
7. For example Frank Keiller, *Prison Without Bars: Living in Jersey under the German Occupation 1940–1945*, Bradford on Avon, Seaflower Books, 2000; Horace Wyatt and Edmund Blampied, *Jersey in Jail 1940–1945*, Jersey, La Haule Books Ltd, 1985.
8. For example Le Sauteur, *Jersey under the Swastika*, p. 94.
9. Quoted in Madeleine Bunting, *The Model Occupation: The Channel Islands under German Rule, 1940–1945*, London, BCA/HarperCollins, 1995, p. 77.
10. Ibid., pp. 77, 193.
11. Ambrose Sherwill, *A Fair and Honest Book: The Memoirs of Sir Ambrose Sherwill*, Lulu.com, 2006, p. 140.

12 Ibid., p. 143.
13 While Jersey Archives contain a log book titled 'Names of political prisoners', dated August 1940 (JAS.D/AG/B7/1), this does not in itself indicate any form of political prisoner consciousness among those incarcerated.
14 Letter from Francis Harris to author, 6 September 2010.
15 Keiller, *Prison without Bars*, pp. 127–9.
16 JWT. Joe Mière Collection. Private letter from Joe Mière to a Yale University researcher, 4 November 1995.
17 Keiller, *Prison without Bars*, p. 137.
18 Le Sauteur, *Jersey under the Swastika*, p. 105; Leslie Sinel, *The German Occupation of Jersey: A Complete Diary of Events from June 1940-June 1945*, Jersey, The Evening Post, 1945, 11 January 1945; Keiller, *Prison without Bars*, p. 137.
19 Sinel, *The German Occupation of Jersey*, 31 March 1945.
20 Keiller, *Prison without Bars*, p. 137.
21 Sanders, *The Ultimate Sacrifice*, pp. 101–2.
22 Edward Le Quesne, *The Occupation of Jersey Day by Day. The Personal Diary of Deputy Edward Le Quesne*, Jersey, La Haule Books, 1999, 9 October 1944.
23 Interview with Michael Neil, 14 August 2010.
24 SJ.*OCC 942 L'AM. J. H. L'Amy, 'The German Occupation of Jersey'.
25 JHT.1995/00045/2. Lucy Schwob (Claude Cahun), account of period in prison, pp. 10–11.
26 'Lettre à Paul Levy, inédit, 1950' in Claude Cahun, *Écrits*, ed. François Leperlier, Paris, Jean-Michel Place, 2002, pp. 709–57.
27 Claire Follain, 'Constructing a Profile of Resistance – Lucy Schwob and Suzanne Malherbe as Paradigmatic Résistantes.' Unpublished undergraduate dissertation in Contemporary History with French, University of Sussex, 1997, p. 20.
28 JHT.1995/00045/2. Lucy Schwob (Claude Cahun), account of period in prison, p. 8.
29 Cahun, *Écrits*, p. 737.
30 Follain, 'Constructing a Profile of Resistance …', p. 20.
31 Phone call between Michael Neil and author, 12 August 2010.
32 Joe Mière, *Never to be Forgotten*, Jersey, Channel Island Publishing, 2004, p. 215.
33 Cahun, *Écrits*, p. 721.
34 Ibid., p. 736.
35 For example Francis Le Sueur, *Shadow of the Swastika. Could It All Happen Again?*, Jersey, Starlight Imports Ltd, 1990, p. 70.
36 Letter from Francis Harris to author, 6 September 2010.
37 JHT.1995/00045/2. Lucy Schwob (Claude Cahun), account of period in prison, p. 12; Cahun, *Écrits*, p. 722.
38 Keiller, *Prison without Bars*, p. 141.
39 Mière, *Never to be Forgotten*, p. 211.
40 Letter from Francis Harris to author, 6 October 2010.
41 Letter from Francis Harris to author, 6 September 2010.
42 SJ.GO Box 3/21. Nurse Rene Griffin, *Diary*. Unpublished diaries should not have italicised titles
43 Le Sueur, *Shadow of the Swastika*, p. 63.
44 Mière, *Never to be Forgotten*, p. 230.
45 Keiller, *Prison without Bars*, p. 146 ff.
46 Le Quesne, *The Occupation of Jersey Day by Day*, 13 October 1944.
47 Ibid., 21 and 31 October 1944.

48 JAS.D/Z/H6/6/133. Letter from Duret Aubin to the Viscount (president of Jersey Prison Board) regarding the petition from political prisoners, 10 November 1944.
49 JAS.B/A/W81/5/2. Letter from political prisoners to the Bailiff of Jersey, 9 February 1945.
50 JAS.B/A/W81/11. Letter from the Viscount (president of Jersey Prison Board) to the Bailiff, 10 April 1945.
51 It is likely that this list is not complete as it misses a number of well-known prisoners of this period, including Lucy Schwob and Suzanne Malherbe among others.
52 JAS.B/A/W81/11. List of political prisoners as of 12 April 1945.
53 Letter from Joe Mière to Michael Ginns, undated, Joe Mière Archive, held by and used by the kind permission of the Mière family.
54 Le Quesne, *The Occupation of Jersey Day by Day*, 7 May 1945; Sinel, *The German Occupation of Jersey*, 7 May 1945.
55 Peter Gray, 'Island of Beauty, Island of Secrets', unpublished manuscript, p. 57, used by kind permission of Mr Peter Gray.
56 Letter from Joe Mière to Michael Ginns, undated, Joe Mière Archive, Mière family.
57 Peter Gray, 'Island of Beauty, Island of Secrets', unpublished manuscript, p. 57, used by kind permission of Mr Peter Gray. There is much controversy among political prisoners as to whether the remaining numbers were released on 8 or 9 May. It seems likely that they were released on both days. Leo Harris recalls that his brother, Francis, was released on 9 May, which irked the family as the war was already over. Leo and Francis' father eventually went to the prison with a gun and threatened to use it unless Francis was released immediately – a demand that was met (Leo Harris, *A Boy Remembers*, Jersey, Channel Island Publishing, 2004, p. 159). On the other hand, Lucy Schwob wrote that on 8 May, the prisoners on the military side of the prison were released 'one by one' but that several others had to wait. She wrote that, for several hours, the joyous cries of departure were incessant (Cahun, p. 742). Leslie Sinel also records that young men were seen coming out of prison and carrying their beds on 8 May.
58 JAS.D/Z/H5/456. Letter from Bailiff Alexander Coutanche to J. B. Howard, 21 June 1945.
59 JAS.D/Z/H5/456. Letter from Charles Markbreiter (Home Office) to Duret Aubin, 16 July 1945.
60 Sinel, *The German Occupation of Jersey*, 31 March 1945.
61 Letter written by Dora Hacquoil to her mother, about her two-month stay in prison from 3 July–29 August 1944, 20 May 1945. Letter used by kind permission of Pauline Hacquoil.
62 Tipping Archive. My thanks to the owner for letting me examine this archive.
63 Eric Walker, *Don't Annoy the Enemy*, Guernsey, Guernsey Press Co. Ltd, 1998, p. 39.
64 GPHQ. Guernsey Police records, German convictions of civilians, 2 vols, 1940–5. The last conviction listed in the Guernsey police's list of those tried by the German courts is 14 March 1945; the log book ends at this point. It is likely that there were more prosecutions after this date but no record exists of them.
65 Ibid.
66 Their counterparts in Guernsey had, for the most part, evacuated.
67 Victor Coysh, *Swastika over Guernsey*, Guernsey, Guernsey Press Co. Ltd, 1955, p. 29.
68 R. C. F. Maugham, *Jersey under the Jackboot*, London, W. H. Allen, 1952, pp. 54, 67.
69 Le Sauteur, *Jersey under the Swastika*, p. 69.
70 Ibid., p. 103.

71 Ibid., p. 129.
72 IWM.Film Archive.UKY 727. 'The Channel Islands 1940–1945', 1945.
73 Alan Wood and Mary Wood, *Islands in Danger: The Story of the German Occupation of the Channel Islands, 1940–1945*, New York, Macmillan, 1955, pp. 244–5.
74 Ibid., p. 236.
75 Ibid., p. 237.
76 Barry Turner, *Outpost of Occupation: How the Channel Islands Survived Nazi Rule 1940–1945*, London, Aurum Press Ltd, 2010, p. 273.
77 Gillian Carr, *Legacies of Occupation: Archaeology, Heritage and Memory in the Channel Islands, 1945-Present*, 2014 (Springer, New York).
78 This can be gleaned through their correspondence, which is kept in the Joe Miére Collection at Jersey War Tunnels. The archives show that in 1980, Frank Falla was addressing Joe formally as 'Mr Miére', but by 1981 it was 'Joe' and their letters were more informal in content. Frank Falla died in 1983.
79 JWT.Research Files Box 5. Statement written by Joe Miére.
80 Ibid.
81 Obituary to Joe Miére, *Jersey Evening Post*, 22 June 2006.
82 Wood and Wood, *Islands in Danger*, p. 233.
83 Frank Falla, 'Revelations of Prison Life in Germany', *Guernsey Weekly Press and Advertiser*, 11 July 1945; 'Channel Islanders in Nazi Camp', *Evening Post*, 4 July 1945.
84 IA. Frank Falla Archive. 'Guernsey Joining Celebration of Resistance', cutting from unknown newspaper, 31 May 1946.
85 'Personal Postscript', page 6, taken from unpublished novel by Frank Falla, 'Guernsey Ink in My Veins'. In personal possession of the author.
86 Editorial, 'Maquis Leaders of Six Countries to Meet Again', *Daily Sketch*, 4 June 1946; C. Davis, 'Europe's Underground Hold V-night in Forest Glade', *Daily Sketch*, 7 June 1946.
87 Frank Falla, *The Silent War: The Inside Story of the Channel Islands under the Nazi Jackboot*, Guernsey, Burbridge Ltd. [Leslie Frewin Ltd.], 1994 [1967], p. 151.
88 TNA.FO.371/146013. Letter from the Under-Secretary of State to the Lieutenant-Governors of Guernsey and Jersey, 17 November 1959.
89 TNA.FO.371/146013. Letter from Alexander Coutanche to Home Office, 1 December 1959; letter from Ambrose Sherwill to Home Office, 30 November 1959.
90 TNA.FO.950/740. Circular no. 97, dated 31 July 1964.
91 TNA.FO.950/741 subfile HG11811/22. Minute noted by E. A. S. Brooks, 20 July 1964.
92 IA. Frank Falla Archive. Notes for guidance.
93 TNA.FO.371/183129. Claims Department, 'Memorandum on pledges given to the Germans on numbers during negotiations to compensate British victims of Nazi persecution', February 1965.
94 TNA.FO.950/741 subfile HG11811/22. Compensation for victims of Nazi persecution.
95 TNA.FO.950/741 subfile HG11811/22. Document signed by G. C. Littler, 21 September 1964.
96 Falla, pp. 161–2. Letters written by Frank Falla to other islanders and MPs (now in the Frank Falla Archive, Island Archives, Guernsey) also make clear the extent of the lack of help from the Channel Island governments, even after Falla showed the Bailliff of Guernsey, in May 1964, his correspondence with Airey Neave and the Foreign Office.
97 TNA.FO.950/741 subfile HG11811/22. Note made 23 June 1962.

98   TNA.FO.950/765 subfile HG11811/30. Letter from Frank Falla to Richard Austen Butler, Foreign Secretary, 6 July 1964.
99   TNA.FO 950/765 subfile HG11811/30. Letter from Frank Falla to Mr G. C. Littler, Foreign Office, 13 April 1965.
100   TNA.FO.950/765 subfile HG11811/30. Letters from Frank Falla to Mr G. C. Littler, Foreign Office, 11 November 1964 and 10 June 1965; letter from Mr G. C. Littler to Frank Falla, 28 July 1965.
101   Frank Falla, 'Victims Get Compensation', *Guernsey Star,* 23 August 1965; Frank Falla, 'Germany Pays Compensation to Guernsey Sufferers', *Guernsey Evening Press,* 23 August 1965.
102   Letter titled 'Reparations' from 'Sleeping Dog' to the editor of the *Guernsey Evening Press,* 21 September 1964.
103   The son of Charles Machon (deceased member of GUNS) wrote to Falla on 23 March 1965, saying 'I take my hat off to all of you who suffered and am proud to be called a Guernseyman when there were Guernseymen like you.'
104   TNA.FO.950/766 subfile HG11811/59. UK victims of Nazi persecution.
105   Numbers calculated as follows: imprisonment: 639 victims; disability = 151 victims; death = 225 victims.
106   TNA.FO 950/820 subfile HG11811/55. Report by Claims Department, 'Compensation for United Kingdom victims of Nazi persecution', 21 December 1966.
107   TNA.FO.950/741 subfile HG11811/22. Compensation for victims of Nazi persecution.
108   It is estimated by the author that around 100 Channel Islanders applied for compensation. This number is based on compilations derived from the prison list in Jersey (JAS.D/AG/B7/1) of those sent to prison in France plus lists of names available in the National Archives of those who actually received compensation (TNA.FO.950/767).
109   Gillian Carr, 'Examining the Memorialscape of Occupation and Liberation: A Case Study from the Channel Islands', *International Journal of Heritage Studies,* Vol. 18 (2), 2012b, 174–93.
110   Joe Mière, 'What About the Island's "Forgotten People"?', *Jersey Evening Post,* 25 July 1994.
111   Letter from Sir John Sutton to Joe Mière, 18 August 1994. Joe Mière Archive, Mière family; JWT, Joe Mière Collection. Letter from Sir John Sutton to Joe Mière, 26 August 1994.
112   Letter from 50th Anniversary Occupation and Liberation Committee Secretary to Joe Mière, 24 October 1994. Joe Mière Archive, Mière family.
113   Letter from Senator Jean Le Maistre to former political prisoner Peter Gray, 18 April 1995. Joe Mière Archive, Mière family.
114   Letter from Joe Mière to unnamed individual, 28 January 1999. Joe Mière Archive, Mière family.
115   While there appears to be no record of Mière's preferred text, it is telling that the final memorial text does not contain the words 'political prisoners'.
116   JAS.C/C/L/C9/1. Occupation and Liberation Committee.
117   Letter from Joe Mière to chair of 50th Anniversary Occupation and Liberation Committee, 7 April 1995. Joe Mière Archive, Mière family.
118   Letter from 50th Anniversary Occupation and Liberation Committee to Joe Mière, 11 April 1995. Joe Mière Archive, Mière family.

119 Letter from chair of 50th Anniversary Occupation and Liberation Committee to Peter Gray, 18 April 1995. Joe Mière Archive, Mière family.
120 *Jersey Evening Post*, 26 April 1995, p. 40.
121 JAS.C/C/L/C9/1. Occupation and Liberation Committee.
122 Falla, *The Silent War*, p. 167.
123 IA.BF 026-09. Letter from Bailiff's secretary to Mrs Gillingham, 13 December 1949.
124 There are a few exceptions to this rule, for example Falla; Peter D. Hassall, 'Night and Fog Prisoners', http://www.jerseyheritage.org/templates/jerseyheritage/occupation_memorial/pdfs/hassallbookcomplete.pdf, 1997, accessed 28 February 2013.

12

Conclusion

Gilly Carr, Paul Sanders and Louise Willmot

Introduction

From the very start of this project, a particular local concern was made known to us: how should we judge or rank those who committed acts of protest, defiance and resistance in the Channel Islands? Were those whose actions were of a military nature more 'worthy' than those which were 'only' symbolic? Was one more patriotic or 'honourable' than the other? We debated constructing a hierarchy of resistance. But how was this to be ranked? Were the more dangerous acts to be considered more important than those which were anonymous or less visible? We had problems agreeing on how to define 'dangerous'. Covertly listening to a hidden radio could result ultimately in the death penalty, as could being discovered with a weapon hidden in the wardrobe. Could resistance be judged in terms of bravery? But who was the braver – Marie Ozanne, who wrote (with her name and address at the top of the notepaper) to the Germans to condemn their actions, or Clifford Cohu, who cycled through St Helier, openly spreading the latest news, or the Guernsey policemen who broke into food stores to distribute the food to those in need? Were these people actually foolhardy and not brave at all? Ultimately, we decided that a moral judgement of any kind was not appropriate or workable.

If morality were to be omitted from the equation, perhaps a way could be found to rank resistance acts based on the number who took part? But there was no way in quantifying this. We could only quantify those who were caught, and we could not be sure that this was in any way in proportion to those who were carrying out the acts. In the end, we decided that constructing a hierarchy was an invidious and subjective exercise that would have no benefit to our analysis. Instead, rather than constructing models and trying to make all cases fit, we decided that the best way to understand the particularities of resistance in the Channel Islands was to look for patterning in the data and to let that speak for itself.

As the chapters in this book have demonstrated, the nature of resistance in the Channel Islands was shaped and limited by a number of factors: the geography and topography of the islands, which made both hiding and escape very difficult; the size of the German garrison, which made the islands the most heavily occupied region in Europe; the relative mildness of the Occupation regime, at least until the events of 1942; the demographic composition of the islands after recruitment to the armed forces and the evacuations in June 1940, which resulted in the departure of many younger residents; the lack of weapons, or encouragement of resistance activities on the part of London and Special Operations Executive (SOE); and the clear instructions to the inhabitants, from both the Superior Council and the Controlling Committee, that acts of provocation and resistance were counter-productive and should be avoided at all costs. Active resisters were, as everywhere else in occupied Western Europe, never more than a small minority of the population, even at the end of the war.

In addition, islanders had less margin for effective action than other West Europeans, especially in the sphere of military-related activities. Nevertheless, the claim that they were simply less likely to resist *at all* is highly questionable. They did not succumb to the defeatism or bitter social divisions that were apparent, for example, in other occupied countries, and the numbers who attended patriotic demonstrations and flouted the wireless ban demonstrates the extent of solidarity and social cohesion, despite German efforts to erode it. Resistance activisim, furthermore, was far more common than was once supposed, as the numbers involved in sheltering *Organisation Todt* (OT) workers and attempting to escape both show. The *potential* for resistance, as Paul Sanders has argued elsewhere, does not seem to have been less than in France and other occupied territories,[1] even though the unique geographic, social and political conditions of the islands meant that it never developed the same structured and highly organized forms.

Phases in the development of resistance

For islanders not faced with the dilemmas of office-holding, it was possible, as Henri Michel suggests, to identify phases in the development of opposition and resistance, linked both to the conduct of the occupiers and to the progress of the war.[2] According to this analysis, the period between July 1940 and December 1941 can be regarded as a phase of *minor individual and symbolic resistance*. During it, as elsewhere in occupied Western Europe, acts of opposition to the Germans were extremely rare and took the form of isolated acts of defiance, often in the form of insults to German troops and attempts to escape to England. A combination of factors – shock at the reality of occupation, the reinforcement of the Occupation garrison, relief at the moderation of German rule, the clear instructions from the Superior Council and Controlling Committee to avoid any resistance – all these contributed to the quiescence of the population during this period. However, even during this period, islanders still began to express their unhappiness at German rule through the use of 'buttonhole resistance', such as the wearing of patriotic colours or symbols on and in their clothing. 'Intangible resistance', in the form of anti-German joke telling, also began in this early phase. We can see such actions both as testing the water (to gauge the reaction of both the occupiers and other islanders), and as the beginning of an assertion of identity that was being threatened.

Only in March 1941, almost nine months after the start of the occupation, did the first small acts of sabotage, with a symbolic rather than material significance, appear in both islands. This type of action became amplified in July 1941, when a minority also took part in the 'V-for Victory' campaign that swept Western Europe in response to broadcast appeals by the BBC, and recurred at intervals throughout the Occupation. While islanders were divided in their response to the 'V-signers', the overwhelming attitude of Channel Islanders at this stage towards the Occupation was a grumbling conformity, combined with a confidence in eventual British victory that never appears to have wavered. Elsewhere in Western Europe, the German invasion of the Soviet Union in June 1941 brought a dramatic increase in resistance activities as local Communist parties threw themselves wholeheartedly into the struggle against Nazism. No such 'Communist effect' was perceptible in the Channel Islands, where the lack of traditions of party politics and political opposition hampered the development of organized resistance organizations. In this first phase, political contacts between islanders were restricted to a handful of pro-reformers in Jersey who had begun to discuss the prospects for democratic change once the war was won.

The second period in the development of resistance in the islands occurred between December 1941 and June 1944, and can be described as a *phase of organizational development*. It began with the establishment of the Jersey Democratic Movement (JDM) early in 1942, with the objective of gathering support for political reform, and marked the beginning of a recruitment campaign that, by May 1945, had gathered perhaps 200 supporters across the island. The key period in the development of resistance activities, however, fell between June and October 1942, several months later than in the rest of occupied Western Europe. It was marked by a deterioration in relations between occupiers and occupied that was a direct consequence of three German policies: the confiscation of radios in June, the arrival of large contingents of slave labourers in Jersey in August, and the deportation of 2,200 British-born islanders in September. There is overwhelming evidence, in contemporary diaries as well as post-war recollections, that islanders were profoundly shocked and unsettled by the 'tightening of the screws' of occupation.[3] On a mass basis, they showed the strength of their feelings in the demonstrations of support for the deportees in September 1942, by the mass gatherings for the funerals of British sailors a year later, and by the huge turnout for a local football match in May 1944 when both teams – and the crowd – demonstratively wore patriotic colours. While these mass protests were spontaneous rather than planned or organized, they were arguably carried out in the knowledge that many people would be turning out for the occasion and that there would be safety in numbers. In a way, these three examples can be seen as a flexing of local muscles – again, a way of testing the water to see how far the Germans could be pushed. Only a small minority of people were punished for the first of these protests, which grew violent, and this may have given people courage to protest peacefully through show of numbers and patriotic colours during the second and third gatherings.

The confiscation of radio sets, which was bitterly resented, was the trigger that persuaded a large proportion of the population to disobey regulations as a matter of course, by withholding sets and passing the news to trusted friends and neighbours. In the absence of a forced labour directive of the kind that was introduced in France,

Belgium and the Netherlands, defiance of the wireless ban was the only form of *ongoing* deliberate mass disobedience to German orders during the Occupation. In Guernsey, the confiscation of sets also led to the only organized resistance to develop there, in the shape of the underground news services GUNS and GASP, and these months also saw, on an individual basis, the giving of humanitarian aid to OT workers. Equally noteworthy in terms of organization is the effort undertaken by members of the Guernsey police force, who raided German and civilian food stores and are believed to have distributed some of their 'loot' to islanders in need. This, however, came to a rapid end in spring 1942, when the group was arrested and put on trial. In Jersey the impact of German policies was more profound. By the end of 1942, in addition to spontaneous help to OT workers, a minority of islanders had established small organizations with the aim of opposing the Germans more directly: army veterans in the island's Air-Raid Protection service (ARP) gathered intelligence for the Allies and, at the end of the year, a handful of younger islanders formed the Jersey Communist Party (JCP). On a wholly informal and unstructured basis, small groups of teenagers and young adults also began to band together to plan the theft of guns and military equipment from German stores. These developments were a response to the conduct of the Germans rather than the course of the war, although the young Communists of the JCP were further encouraged by the German defeat at Stalingrad early in 1943.

If the organizational phase came later in the Channel Islands and was more rudimentary than elsewhere, then this had two main reasons: the relative mildness of German occupation policy before 1942, which made the events of that year even more of a shock, and the lack of an institutional or organizational basis – in the form of political parties, functioning trade unions or a university. Would-be resisters had to start from scratch. During 1943, the ARP network continued to operate even after the deportation of its leader Crawford-Morrison in February, but the year was particularly significant for the extension of JCP activities to include the production of propaganda leaflets and the establishment of a loose network of support for escaped Russian slave labourers. Other islanders, unconnected with the Party, also sheltered slave labourers and in some cases made use of personal connections and contacts to establish rudimentary assistance networks. These activities continued, and became better organized, in 1944.

In the case of the Channel Islands it is inappropriate to apply Michel's third and final phase of resistance development – a phase of battle – to the period between May 1944 and June 1945, because the islands were liberated without an Allied landing. For this reason there were also no attacks on German soldiers or major sabotage operations by islanders. For most of those engaged in resistance, therefore, the period between June 1944 and May 1945 was marked by the continuation of their earlier activities rather than by more direct action against the Germans. Nevertheless, for a significant minority of predominantly younger islanders in Jersey, the period can be described as one of *preparation for battle*, the stimulus for which was the successful Allied landing in France in June 1944. In this limited case, the Allied conduct of the war decisively affected the nature of resistance in the islands. In the following months, over 100 young residents made the dangerous crossing to the French coast, usually in the hope of joining the armed forces. In the belief that an invasion of the islands might be imminent, the small ARP network continued to gather intelligence and used its contacts with escapers to smuggle it to London, and many more tiny groups of teenagers and young adults stole guns and ammunition from German stores in the hope of helping Allied troops in the event of invasion. In the final months of the war, JCP members and their contacts supported disaffected members of the garrison in their efforts to stage a mutiny and bring the Occupation to a swift end without the need for invasion. These efforts were brought to an end by the surrender of German forces on the continent on 8 May 1945.

A tale of two islands: Resistance in Guernsey and Jersey

The level of organization displayed by entities such as the ARP, the JDM and the JCP, escapes after July 1944, thefts of military equipment and so forth had no substantial equivalent in Guernsey. The impact of demographics and geography go a long way to explaining why resistance in Jersey was more active and varied than it was in Guernsey. Most escapes after October 1940, and most minor acts of sabotage, were carried out by young men between the ages of 17 and 25: there were almost twice as many of these in Jersey, with a significant proportion based in the capital of St Helier. Many of their activities were based on school and local friendships, left undisrupted by the evacuations of June 1940 which had done so much to fracture community life in Guernsey. Another reason for the imbalance was geographical. After August 1944, Jersey's proximity to the French coast made it feasible for young islanders to risk the shorter crossing to France, and allowed for the development of a form of resistance that was scarcely possible in Guernsey. The greater occurrence of humanitarian rescue in Jersey also has a straightforward explanation: the vast majority of Russian OT workers, by far the worst treated and most likely to escape their captors, were based here. In Guernsey, on the other hand, most OT workers were West European or North African. Although badly treated and sometimes hungry, their labour camps were not as harsh as those in Jersey, and very few of them risked serious punishment by leaving work altogether and seeking refuge with sympathetic islanders. Other factors that precluded the emergence of more activist forms of resistance in Guernsey were the larger German garrison and higher density of fortification; the tougher occupation regime than in Jersey, with less FK interposition; the social capital depletion, first, by the massive draining of the island of young males joining the British forces in 1939–40; second, by the June 1940 evacuation, which fractured kinship and family ties; and, finally, the particular and overtly anti-resistance stance adopted by the civilian authorities in Guernsey, plus Guernsey's economic problems and its more pronounced dependence on imports, especially food (compared to Jersey). One could argue therefore that Guernsey showed the limits of a particular type of militancy common in other parts of occupied Europe, and of which one can see rudimentary traces in Jersey. This explains why other, more subversive forms of purely civilian resistance, such as symbolic resistance and mass protests, but also the news-sheeting, were so huge in Guernsey. This again would explain why, despite an absence of militancy, the number of people sent to gaol was, relative to the size of the populations, broadly similar in the two islands: 1.81 per cent of the population in Guernsey and 1.97 per cent in Jersey.[4]

Who were the resisters?

The experience of the Channel Islands demonstrates with striking clarity the extent to which different resistance activities were carried out by different social groups. Age was, with few exceptions, a key determinant of the type of resistance undertaken. Low-level sabotage, military larceny and – after October 1940 – escape attempts were almost always the work of young men between the ages of 17 and 25, who had grown frustrated by the passivity of Occupation and were all too aware that their counterparts elsewhere were either in the armed forces or – so they had been led to believe by Colonel Britton's broadcasts – in maquis-style groups. The only older islanders to engage in military-related activities were the army veterans in the ARP, who made use of their skills and positions to collect and synthesize information about the fortifications and garrison. In general, older islanders avoided the provocations of low-level sabotage and military larceny. For them, the most common form of defiance was to withhold sets and listen – and sometimes communicate – the BBC news, usually individually or in small groups. This activity seems to have been particularly pronounced in Guernsey, which saw the emergence of regularly published and distributed news-sheets, which had a substantial following. The creators of the most famous of these, GUNS, made use of their skills and contacts in the newspaper business. The most effective resistance by older islanders was not only to provide help to forced and slave labourers, most commonly in the form of spontaneous gifts of food and clothing but also, especially in Jersey, by sheltering fugitives in their homes. Almost all those who offered long-term shelter were over 30, as were the two islanders who saved Jewish residents. As well as having the motivation to help, they – unlike most younger inhabitants – had the basic resources that enabled them to do so, in the form of properties they either rented or owned. Where younger islanders were involved in humanitarian rescue, it was as a result of the activities of their parents or because, unable to provide refuge themselves, they acted as intermediaries and matched fugitives with islanders prepared to help them.

Women played a particularly important, and often neglected, role in helping OT workers, usually by handing out food and clothing at the roadside but also as part of family units who hid fugitives for several months. Otherwise, however, their role in island resistance was relatively limited: they hardly participated in military larceny, petty sabotage or intelligence-gathering, though they were more involved in escape attempts from the island than the bare statistics suggest, largely in supporting roles. Their part in more organized activities was restricted by their limited role in political and economic life. In a situation in which the illegal newssheets of GUNS were mostly produced by men working for the local newspaper, intelligence-gathering was carried out by army veterans in the ARP; and in a situation in which the Jersey doctors took advantage of their skills and positions to oppose German measures, women had little role to play except, occasionally, in background or secretarial tasks. The JCP, too, was composed of predominantly younger men, although the JDM had successfully recruited a significant number of women by 1945. The most prominent women resisters – Lucy Schwob and Suzanne Malherbe, Marie Ozanne, Louisa Gould, Ivy Forster and Dorothea Weber – acted alone or in family units, and not as part of any organized group.

The evidence regarding social class and background is less clear-cut and suggests that resisters came from all social groups in the islands, and from both British- and island-born inhabitants. Radio resistance was one such area where blue-collared and white-collared men rubbed shoulders. The JDM and JCP included students and teachers as well as ordinary workers, and the social profile of young saboteurs and escapers, and of those who aided forced and slave labourers, was also mixed. On the other hand, blue-collared men were more exposed to deprivation and could therefore not always afford to turn down the only type of steady work available, i.e. German work. And this would have put them in the line of certain specific categories of occupation offences, such as military larcency or 'insulting Germans'.

The lack of a resistance movement and the role of individuals

As other historians have argued and this book has confirmed, there was never any united 'resistance movement' in the Channel Islands to compare with those that emerged, for example, in France or Norway. Not only that: resistance was less organized than elsewhere; most opposition to the Occupation was carried out by individuals and small groups operating independently. One factor was the lack of any encouragement for resistance and resistance unity from London and SOE. Even more critical, however, was the absence of the institutional forms that acted as a seedbed for the emergence of organized resistance: well-established political parties, strong self-confident trade unions, a university to foster intellectual resistance, or professional associations with enough members to provide some hope of safety in the event of public dissent at the policies of the Germans or their collaborators. Islanders made up for the absence of full democracy and the efforts of the occupiers to erode social cohesion by retaining a strong sense of their own identity and an unbroken loyalty to Britain. These elements of cohesion were strengthened by a network of personal and professional contacts across the islands. Although the Germans had some success in their efforts to erode ties of trust in the islands by encouraging denunciations and informers, enough of these survived to compensate, at least to some extent, for the lack of organizational structures. The result was a limited measure of cooperation between disparate resistance groupings. In Guernsey, for example, professional or personal contacts led to the creation of GUNS and the development of an unstructured distribution network to ensure its circulation. In Jersey, similarly, personal links enabled would-be escapers to get in touch with men who could give them guidance or intelligence, and allowed the creation of loosely structured networks of safe houses for OT fugitives and escaped political prisoners and provided them food and, where necessary, with medical treatment.

In this situation, especially in Jersey, a key role was played by a relatively small number of men: among the doctors, by Noel McKinstry and Arthur Halliwell, by the ARP warden and boat-builder William Gladden, who also sheltered a Russian fugitive;

by the ARP Controller William Crawford-Morrison. These were men in positions of leadership or influence, but younger and less powerful islanders, such as Leslie Huelin and Norman Le Brocq of the JCP, were also able to make use of personal friendships and contacts in their opposition to the Germans, and to exert an influence well beyond the tiny circle of Jersey Communists. Without the determined and courageous leadership of a small number of individuals, island resistance would have lacked such coherence and direction as it possessed.

No efforts of this kind crystallized in Guernsey, although the level of fortification would have justified such efforts. One of the known exceptions to this rule was the intelligence gathering activity of William Symes. But Symes was 'taken out' by the GFP as early as 1941. He was therefore unable to form an organizational 'memory' that could enable a cohesive group to continue in the same mould in his absence, as seen in the case of Crawford Morrison and the Jersey ARP. The absence of proto-resistance leaders of this calibre in Guernsey brings us once more to the general orientation adopted by the authorities of that island before the arrival of the German forces, which was to avoid all friction with the occupying force. At first applied in a relatively nonchalant and benign manner, and personified by Ambrose Sherwill, the stance solidified into dogma in the wake of the disaster of the Nicolle-Symes affair in late 1940. From this point onwards it became an act of faith in Guernsey that resistance was dangerous and that a more resolute attitude was necessary to stifle any inclination on the part of the population to tackle the occupier in any too confrontational a manner. These efforts never went quite as far in Jersey. In fact, in his chapter on administrative resistance, Paul Sanders describes how the social contract in the two islands varied between a more opportunistic 'live and let live' in Jersey and proactive efforts to discourage resistance in Guernsey. To be sure, resistance in Jersey was never encouraged by the authorities of that island and those who got into trouble with the Germans could not rely on their assistance. But at the same time islanders were granted space to decide for themselves how far they wanted to take their efforts to uphold the legitimacy of British rule.

How many Channel Islanders were sent to prison during the Occupation for resistance acts? And how many were deported to the continent?

As a prelude to calculating how many Channel Islanders were sent to prison and tried for acts of resistance, it is important to emphasize the obvious at the outset. The figure we have for this category is not identical with the total number of resisters, as many of those who committed acts that could qualify as resistance were not caught and left no or little paper trail. It has been estimated, for example that as many as one in three in Jersey retained their wireless sets after they were confiscated. While there is no statistical record to support this estimate, radio resistance, in one form or another, certainly involved hundreds of islanders and was practiced on a level that news of the genuine developments in the war never 'dried up'. Other statistics suggest that proportionately more people were convicted for radio offences in Jersey (21% vs 14%

in Guernsey); this may indicate that more people in Jersey kept their radios, perhaps because of the harder line taken in Guernsey against resistance. And this may have led to a greater demand in Guernsey for underground newsletters such as GASP and GUNS, which had no equivalent in Jersey.

Another problem concerns which offences to include in our 'accountancy' of resistance, and where one draws the line. Did going out without an ID card constitute defiance? How can one we tell whether someone was just forgetful or had other motives? And what about riding a bicycle two abreast when the Germans had forbidden it – did that constitute defiance? What one needs to remember about the context is that many acts that to us seem innocuous, unpatriotic or even anti-social had become criminalized during the occupation, and thus assumed a political connotation. In the end it was the archival sources themselves that suggested which offences needed including, namely whatever the Germans themselves had considered worthy of prosecution by one of their courts.

The next step was to track down the names of people in this category. In Guernsey the police kept a log book of those who had been arrested and tried by the German courts; it contains 453 entries and the first person was convicted on 26 August 1940. We know that this source is not a definitive record for two reasons. First, the last date of conviction was 14 March 1945. Statistically we know that the number of sentences passed steadily increased (broadly speaking) throughout the occupation and it seems unlikely that not a single sentence was passed after this date, although the numbers do drop in both islands at the very end of the Occupation (Graph 12.1). Second, not everybody tried and convicted was listed in the log book, as there were islanders whose offences were considered serious enough to earmark them for inclusion in extra-

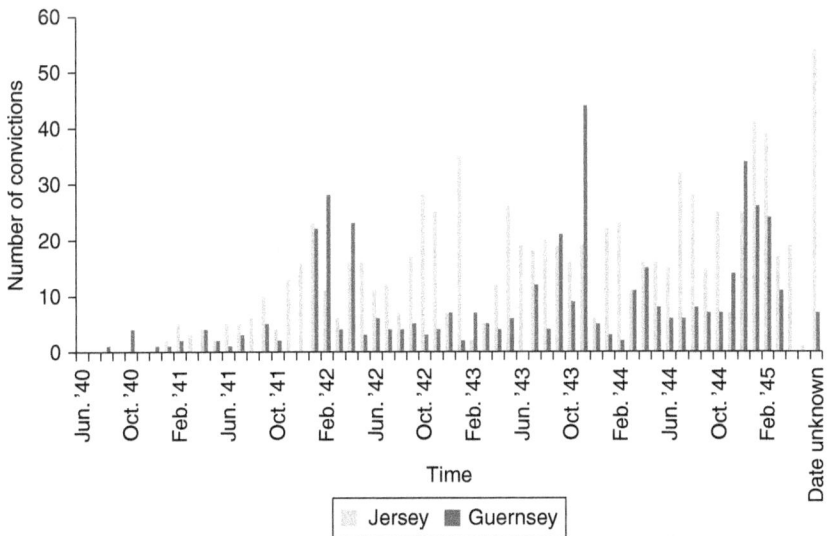

Graph 12.1 Convictions over time in Guernsey and Jersey

judiciary schemes, such as Hitler's Night and Fog (NN) decree. Other disappearances seem to have been at the whim of the occupiers and were not always associated with a particularly serious offence. This has been borne out by two experiences: people who have approached us about family members known to have been deported, but without an entry in the police log; and the absence of traces, in the files, of certain people known to have committed offences (such as the contingent of 16 people sent from Guernsey sent to Cherche-Midi and Caen prisons in the autumn of 1940 for sheltering commandos).

In Jersey, a similar record was kept of the 'names of political prisoners'.[5] To all intents and purposes, the logs in the two islands held similar information. The first entry in Jersey was 18 August 1940 and the last, 27 July 1944; 506 people are listed, but the Jersey log, too, is incomplete and finishes before the end of the war. In addition, a second record of offenders against the occupying authorities exists in Jersey, in the form of loose pages of German notifications relating to 856 sentences and prosecutions by the Field Command and Troop Courts.[6] These can be used to supplement the above list of political prisoners, and they have the advantage of continuing right up until the end of the Occupation. Although the two sources do not seem to be an exact match of names for the period of overlap, there is good reason to assume that the second record, the papers relating to sentences and prosecutions, constitute the more complete list of names. The difficulty of exploiting these two sources resides in the fact that the Jersey log book also contains a small number of Guernsey people who were sent to Jersey to be tried by military court, sometimes as a precursor to deportation to a continental prison. The 856 sentences and prosecutions also contain a number of names that appear more than once, as well as the names of some foreign workers. Departing from this documentary basis, it would take a fine tooth comb to be able to arrive at a definitive number of individuals from Guernsey and Jersey who were tried by a German military court; and even then we would still have to ask ourselves whether we were prepared to count twice those who had been tried for two different crimes. *Without taking out that comb, we estimate that the minimum number probably lies, give or take, in the region of 1,300 people.* We might still be able to add a fudge factor for Guernsey for those who were sentenced after mid-March 1945 by comparing numbers with Jersey,[7] but the final count is probably not far out from this number. We conclude that, out of a combined population in Guernsey and Jersey of around 68,400[8] at the start of the occupation, *around 2 per cent were tried and convicted for offences against the occupying authorities.*

The next issue concerns 'weeding' the political act of resistance or defiance from activities that would have been the subject of a trial even in 'normal times', always keeping in mind the aforementioned criminalization of more or less ordinary behaviour during the Occupation. The trail of records listing Channel Islands offences includes people who were imprisoned for trivial offences, such as infractions against traffic orders, but also more serious charges such as theft, receiving stolen goods, infractions against rationing and economic control orders or trading on the black market. Such people could theoretically be tried by German or by civilian court, but it was the Germans who took them into their jurisdiction. What we are faced with here is the ambiguity of economic offences, showcased in the case of the Guernsey policemen tried and convicted by German and island courts, in 1942. This case shared one key feature with other economic offences: it had the attributes of an ordinary common law case, and it was treated as such by the Royal Court of Guernsey. This interpretation has endured to this very day, but it suffers from a fundamental oversight which needs addressing. No judicial activity can be dissociated from its political, economic and social context, and we should not confuse following the letter of the law – through the maintenance of its formal and procedural trappings – with being in conformity with the spirit of the law.

We may illustrate the problem of factoring in political context through a contemporary example: current-day Russian jurisprudence. Contrary to popular belief this is quite often in conformity with the procedural and formal rules of the game. A 2011 European Court of Human Rights decision, for example, ruled that, despite some formal and procedural irregularities, the two trials conducted against former Russian oligarch and founder of the Yukos oil company Mikhail Khodorkovsky were not politically motivated, And yet, the misgivings over whether a formal democracy such as Putin's Russia will fully adhere to the separation of powers that is a hallmark of fully functioning democracy remain. This is not gratuitous criticism, but can be supported by ample circumstantial evidence and several other court cases that mirror the Yukos experience. The argument of an (at least partial) politicization of Russian law-making and law-breaking is reinforced by the fact that there were (and are) thousands of Russian tax evaders and corporate fraudsters such as Khodorkovsky, but that only certain people are ever targeted by law enforcement and the courts; usually those who have fallen out with the Kremlin, or those whose assets have come within the sights of certain power-brokers. The Russian justice system can therefore be described as highly selective in how it goes about its business. While the rule of law may look sound, there is good reason to assume that it is not free from considerable political influence.

Returning to jurisprudence during the Occupation, we uphold that a correct interpretation needs to factor in the impact that this political and military fact had on a formerly independent judiciary. As we have shown in the case of the 1942 police trial in the Royal Court of Guernsey, there is irrefutable evidence that the political context weighed on the manner in which this civilian trial was conducted. This is even more the case with the German procedures, such as those initiated against the family of the Reverend Mylne in Jersey, or against the men and women involved in the St Saviour's wireless case, also in Jersey. They provide further evidence of the presence of a strong political or propaganda element in the rule of the law during the Occupation.

Context is also important in another way. As Paul Sanders noted in *The Ultimate Sacrifice*, worsening material conditions in the islands led many people who, under normal circumstances, would have not strayed from the straight and narrow path, to engage in activities which, at least formally, constituted property offences. It strikes us as inequitable to not factor in the profoundly disrupting impact of the fortification programme and the generally exploitative agenda of the occupying force. What is the theft of a loaf of bread or a pair of boots against the massive and unprecedented transfer of wealth and labour from entire societies to the German war economy? Many islanders were not fooled by the formal rules that favoured the occupier. They understood the subtle difference between 'ordinary theft' and 'patriotic theft', and acted accordingly: German property, or should one rather say 'loot', became fair game.

On the other hand, some property crimes were no doubt what they seemed to be, just that. If we subtract the number of people imprisoned for these offences, then the total figure of offences reduces to 786,[9] although there is no way of knowing how many of these 'economic crimes' had a political element.

How many people were deported to the continent for their offences against the occupiers? Here we do not discriminate between types of offences. It is our conviction that those who suffered in Nazi prisons or camps should not be ignored because their offence was supposedly less 'honourable' or 'patriotic' than those who committed acts of characterized protest, defiance and resistance. In any case, there is no way of knowing.

Jersey's file of papers listing sentences and prosecutions offers no information on who was to be deported for their offence, and we must therefore rely on Jersey's log book of political prisoners. This informs us that a total of 105 people from Jersey and an additional 12 from Guernsey and 1 from Sark were deported. Those deported had sentences which ranged from as little as six weeks to as much as five years. The last logged date of deportation was 31 July 1944. Arriving at a total figure of Guernsey deportees for offences is more difficult, as the police log of those convicted by military court does not state whether the individuals concerned were deported.

At the same time, the Jersey log which lists the Guernsey prisoners who were tried in Jersey does not reflect the real number of Guernsey prisoners deported to the Continent. This means, that as far as Guernsey goes, we have to start with the known and work backwards. While this is a straightforward exercise for high profile court cases such as the Guernsey policemen discussed in this volume, or the men involved in GUNS, it becomes a next to impossible task for other, lesser-known individuals, especially as the names of some are excluded from the records altogether, such as the 16 deported to Caen and Cherche-Midi prisons for their role in the Nicolle-Symes affair. The only solution, therefore, is to rely on a proxy, the length of prison sentence, which was indicative of deportation, and to reconstruct an approximate figure. For this exercise, we provide two figures: an upper one of *236* for those with sentences of 3 or more months and who were convicted before the end of July 1944, and a lower one of *205* those who received sentences of 6 months or more.[10] However, not too much weight should be attached to these specific figures, as we have no reliable information to indicate how long a sentence had to be before a person was deported, and, secondly, because the Germans themselves did not stick to their own rules in the matter. Further criteria known to have influenced decisions for deportation were the type of crime itself, or whether someone was considered 'anti-German', 'British-born', a 'loafer without useful employment' or simply a 'useless eater'. Compare, for example, the sentences of two islanders mentioned in the chapter on radio resistance, Arthur Dimmery in Jersey and John Crossley Hayes in Guernsey: Dimmery received a short three-and-a-half-month sentence, which should have been served in Jersey, but was deported; and Crossley Hayes received a longer six-month service, for which, as he writes himself, he should have been deported, but was allowed to serve his sentence in Guernsey. The difference that mattered in these two cases was not the respective length of sentence, but the fact that the Germans considered Dimmery a 'British-born useless eater' engaged in anti-German propaganda (the spreading of BBC news) and Crossley Hayes a 'British-born islander with useful employment' and caught in the lesser crime of simple retention of a wireless at his home.[11]

The story does not end there. We also know that the 1943 wave of deportations in retaliation for Operation Basalt targeted those who had been previously convicted. This batch included the previously convicted who had already served a sentence on the Continent, returned home, and who were deported again; one must be vigilant to avoid the risk of double-counting.

The 1943 transport lists in Guernsey helpfully contain a reason for the deportation of each individual; *18* are listed as *vorbestraft* (previously convicted). The previous sentences of these people ranged from 14 days to 12 months. Subtracting those already counted earlier, our lower figure increases to *214* and our upper increases to *241*.[12]

The situation for Jersey is far from simple as the deportation and transport lists do not list the reason for deportation. This means that the names have to be compared to the political prisoner log book which makes the task in hand much slower and more complicated. However, of the 78 people deported from Jersey at this time, 17 had previous convictions, of which 5 had already been deported once,[13] leaving an additional *12* to be added to our list. Therefore, *the minimum number of people deported from the Channel Islands for offences against the occupier is likely to lie between 226 and 253*[14] *– around a fifth of our original estimate of c. 1300 imprisoned islanders. Just over one-tenth of these people died in the prisons or camps to which they were sent.*

There is yet a final chapter. Between 1964 and 1966, British nationals who had been victims of Nazi persecution and sent to concentration camps or comparable institutions received compensation from the British government after it had reached a settlement with West Germany. Those who had been prisoners of war or who had been in a civilian internment camp were not eligible for compensation, although some in this category applied (unsuccessfully) for compensation. We cannot know for sure how many Channel Islanders applied for compensation as these Foreign Office files are still closed. However, a perusal of the list of all of those from the United Kingdom as a total who applied suggests that the number is around 55 from Guernsey and 46 from Jersey (101 in total).[15] The greater number from Guernsey is likely to be due to the 'Frank Falla factor' in that island. This number cannot be verified, as the files of only those aged 100 or over at the present time have been acknowledged/confirmed by the Foreign Office to one of the authors (GC). Even this figure does not represent the total number of islanders who *actually* suffered in a concentration camp or comparable institution. There were those who did not want to apply for compensation, either because they were too proud or because the process brought back traumatic memories. Others didn't want what they might have perceived as German 'blood money'. Yet others had died before 1964, or had become too incapacitated to fill in the form, or had moved country and given up their British citizenship (and with it any rights to claim compensation). Some may even have not bothered applying because they assumed that they were not eligible. We find, for example, that there is no record of any application from people such as Guernseywoman Julia Barry (who was in Ravensbrück concentration camp),[16] or Jerseymen Peter Hassall (author of *Prisoner of Night and Fog*, sent to various prisons and camps including the SS camp Hinzert)[17] or Walter Dauny (imprisoned in Villeneuve St Georges).[18]

In order to reach more accurate numbers, there are certain missing documents which need to be located, such as the Guernsey prison log, which we believe still exists and which is likely to list all of those from the island who were deported. It would also greatly assist if the Foreign Office were to open all of its closed records on British victims of Nazi persecution. This would then allow us to see how many people applied for compensation from the Channel Islands. However, a full list of islanders deported to prisons and camps on the continent could *only* and realistically be possible today by collating evidence from the International Tracing Service (ITS) in Arolsen, and from regional archives in France and Germany.

There is clearly a companion volume that needs to be written which not only resolves the real number of deported islanders, but also details their experiences in continental prisons and camps. While a number of these testimonies are to be found in the Frank Falla files, the others still with the Foreign Office files, one of the authors (GC) has decided that, when the two can be brought together, she will write the second volume. Because of the graphic and sensitive nature of the Falla testimonies, their uncensored and decontextualized publication here would inevitably breach ethical standards and copyright restrictions. Therefore, the second volume will focus both on the testimonies and experience of Channel Islanders in Nazi prisons and camps, and the long-term effects of Nazi persecution on the second- and third generation of Channel Islanders. Such a volume can only be written with care, attention and due consideration of ethical standards in publication; this will involve tracking down the families of around hundred people to seek their permission for reproduction and publication – a task which would have taken too long to be included in this volume.

Conclusion

As we have shown throughout this book, many aspects of protest, defiance and resistance in the Channel Islands find their counterparts in other parts of occupied Europe. At the same time, the precise nature of all acts of resistance was also unique to the Channel Islands. More than anywhere else in Europe, the role of the individual was all-important. In a place where the formation of large or even medium-sized resistance groups was impossible, we see that even small groups were eventually caught, whether for listening to the radio, for disseminating the BBC news via newssheets, or for stealing food from German stores. Only by acting alone, or in very loose networks (such as those who organized the sheltering of escaped Russian slave workers in Jersey), and by maintaining the utmost in discretion, could people hope to remain unmolested. In fact, for almost every type of resistance discussed in this book, islanders were caught, imprisoned and sometimes deported to continental prisons and camps – a destination from which not all returned after the war.

The importance of the role of the individual and of keeping silent about what one was doing has certainly contributed to the long-term public silence and, indeed, ignorance on the subject of war-time resistance in the Channel Islands, both locally and nationally. Because people did not know what everyone else was doing, and because those who committed acts of resistance were seen as troublemakers after the war, most simply kept quiet about what they had done.

The role of the individual matters in small islands, both then and now. It was individual men – Frank Falla and Joe Mière – who played a large part in keeping alive the memory and experiences of resisters until the present day, when memorials could be erected as a way of leaving a permanent reminder in the urban fabric. While this process has been underway in Jersey since 1995, it is only just beginning in Guernsey. We hope that those memorials – and this book – will stand as a testimony to all Channel Islanders who committed acts of protest, defiance and resistance during the Occupation; both those who were caught and those who were not. And, of those who were caught, imprisoned and deported, we particularly dedicate this book to those who did not survive: the Jersey 21 and the Guernsey 8.

Notes

1. Paul Sanders, *The Ultimate Sacrifice. The Jersey Islanders who died in German Prisons and Concentration Camps, 1940–1945*, Jersey, Jersey Heritage Trust, 2nd edition, 2004, pp. 127–8.
2. Henri Michel, *The Shadow War: Resistance in Europe 1939–1945*, London, The History Book Club, 1972, pp. 13–14.
3. Louise Willmot, '"Nothing was ever the same again": Public Attitudes in the Occupied Channel Islands, 1942', *The Local Historian: Journal of the British Society for Local History*, Vol. 35, 2005, 9–20, here p. 17. The phrase came from Norman Le Brocq.
4. 453 people out of a population of 25,000 in Guernsey and 856 out of a population of 43,400 in Jersey.
5. JAS.D/AG/B7/1. 'Names of Political Prisoners August 1940', prison log book, covering 18 August 1940 to 27 July 1944.
6. JAS.D/Z/H6. Sentences and Prosecutions by the German Field and Troop Courts.
7. In Jersey, 33 people were sentenced by the military courts from March 1945 onwards. If we take into account the population ratio between the two islands, this may indicate about 19 people imprisoned in Guernsey during and after March 1945.
8. Charles Cruickshank, *The German Occupation of the Channel Islands: The Official History of the Occupation Years*, Guernsey, Guernsey Press Co./Trustees of the Imperial War Museum, 1975, p. 56.
9. Here we have defined these offences as 'economic crimes' and have included everything from theft to operating on the black market. We have included the following as theft: 'larceny', 'military larceny', 'receiving stolen goods', 'pilfering', 'plundering' and similar offences. The number in Guernsey convicted of these crimes is 239; in Jersey it is 284.

10 The sum of 105 from Jersey, 12 from Guernsey, 1 from Sark, 16 deported for their role in the Nicolle-Symes affair, added to either 102 who had sentences of 3 months and over, and 71 who had sentences of 6 months and over.
11 Sanders notes that in the latter part of the war, those with sentences of 9 months or more were deported to Germany; Sanders, *The Ultimate Sacrifice*, p. 31.
12 An extra 5 have been added to those who would not have been included in the 3 months and over total and an extra 9 have been added to those who would not have been included in the 6 months and over total. The length of sentences of this group comes from the police convictions book in Guernsey.
13 This involved a comparison of file refs. D/AG/B7/1, 'Names of Political Prisoners August 1940' covering 18 August 1940 to 27 July 1944, with transport lists B/A/W80/1.
14 This figure relies upon guesswork with regards to Guernsey, and is based on two assumptions: the first concerning the relationship between length of sentence and deportation; and another concerning the Jersey logbook containing the names of all deportees. The Jersey logbook contains only 59 per cent of all convictions. As 105 people out of 506 in Jersey's logbook were deported (a rate of 20.7 per cent), we might conjecture that if a similar percentage of the 856 convictions from that island were deported, perhaps as many as 178 (rather than 105) people could have been deported in total from that island. Although this method of fudge-factoring is unreliable, it indicates that the minimum range of between 226 and 253 could potentially be increased to between 299 and 326. Given our assumptions and the fudge-factoring involved in the calculations overall, these figures should only be taken as a general indication. On this basis, we believe that it is reasonable to assume that the maximum number of islanders deported is less than 350.
15 This number is based on name recognition by the authors, and a comparison of prison and transport records by GC, with a Foreign Office electronic database of all applicants.
16 Frederick Cohen, *The Jews in the Channel Islands during the German Occupation 1940–1945* Jersey, Jersey Heritage Trust in association with the Institute of Contemporary History and Wiener Library, 2000, p. 22.
17 Sanders, *The Ultimate Sacrifice*, pp. 47–53.
18 Ibid., p. 96.

Bibliography

Key for archival sources listed in chapter endnotes

AN	Archives Nationales de France, Paris
BA	Bundesarchiv, Germany
CAC	Churchill Archives Centre
GG	Guernsey Greffe records
GM	Guernsey Museum and Art Gallery
GOMG	German Occupation Museum, Guernsey
GPHQ	Guernsey Police Headquarters
IA	Island Archives, Guernsey
ITS	International Tracing Service Archive, Arolsen
IWM	Imperial War Museum
JAS	Jersey Archives
JHT	Jersey Heritage Trust
JM	Jersey Museum
JWT	Jersey War Tunnels
MA	Militärarchiv, Freiburg
PL	Priaulx Library, Guernsey
R	Reichsbestände, Berlin
RCA	Red Cross Museum and Archives, London
SAIHC	Salvation Army International Heritage Centre
SJ	Société Jersiaise
TNA	The National Archives, London

Published sources

Archer, B., *The Internment of Western Civilians under the Japanese 1941-1945*, Hong Kong, Hong Kong University Press, 2008.

Aubin, C. D., 'Enemy Legislation and Judgments in Jersey', *The Journal of Comparative Legislation and International Law*, Vol. 31 (3/4), 1949, 8-11.

Aufsess, B. H. M. von, *The von Aufsess Occupation Diary*, ed. and trans. K. J. Nowlan, Chichester, Phillimore, 1985.

Bachelier, C., 'La SNCF sous l'Occupation allemande, 1940-1944', Association pour l'histoire des chemins de fer, http://www.ahicf.com/ww2/rapport/partie6.htm, accessed 28 June 2013.

Bachmann, K. M., *The Prey of an Eagle: A Personal Record of Family Life Written throughout the German Occupation of Guernsey 1940-45*, Guernsey, Guernsey Press Co. Ltd., 1972.

Bailey, K., *Dachau*, London, Brown Watson, 1961.

Bajohr, F., *'Aryanisation' in Hamburg: The Economic Exclusion of the Jews and the Confiscation of their Property in Nazi Germany*, Oxford and New York, Berghahn, 2002.
Baranowski, S., *The Confessing Church, Conservative Elites and the Nazi State*, Lewiston, The Edwin Mellen Press, 1986.
Barnett, V., *For the Soul of the People: Protestant Protest against Hitler*, Oxford, Oxford University Press, 1992.
Baron, L., 'The Dynamics of Decency: Dutch Rescuers of Jews during the Holocaust', in M. Marrus (ed.), *The Nazi Holocaust*, Vol. 5 (2), Westport, CT, Meckler, 1989, pp. 608–26.
Bédarida, F., 'World War II and Social Change in France', in A. Marwick (ed.), *Total War and Social Change*, Basingstoke and London, Macmillan, 1988, pp. 79–94.
Bell, W. M., *I Beg to Report: Policing in Guernsey during the German Occupation*, Guernsey, Guernsey Press Co. Ltd., 1995.
— *The Commando Who Came Home to Spy*, Guernsey, The Guernsey Press, 1998.
— *Guernsey Occupied but Never Conquered*, Exeter, The Studio Publishing Services, 2002.
Bennett, R., *Under the Shadow of the Swastika: The Moral Dilemmas of Resistance and Collaboration in Hitler's Europe*, New York, New York University Press, 1999.
Bertrand, L. E., *A Record of the Work of the Guernsey Secret Press*, Guernsey, Guernsey Star and Gazette, 1945.
Binding, T., *Island Madness*, London, Picador, 1998.
Birchenall, P. and Birchenall, M., *Operation Nurse: Nursing in Guernsey 1940–1945*, West Sussex, Woodfield Publishing, 2001.
Blades, J., *Drum Roll: A Professional Adventure from the Circus to the Concert Hall*, London, Faber and Faber, 1977.
Boléat, P., *A Quiet Place*, Jersey, Villette Publishing Ltd., 1993.
Bolz, F., Dudonis, K. J. and Schulz, D. P., *The Counterintelligence Handbook. Tactics, Procedures and Techniques*, Boca Raton, London, New York, Washington DC, CRC Press, 2002.
Braham, R., *The Politics of Genocide: the Holocaust in Hungary*, New York, Columbia University Press, 1981.
Broszat, M. and Fröhlich, E., *Alltag und Widerstand: Bayern im Nationalsozialismus*, München, Piper, 1987.
Bunting, M., *The Model Occupation: The Channel Islands under German Rule, 1940–1945*, London, Pimlico [London, BCA/HarperCollins], 2004 [1995 1st edn].
Burleigh, M., *Death and Deliverance: 'Euthanasia' in Germany c. 1900–1945*, Cambridge, Cambridge University Press, 1994.
Burrin, P., *France under the Germans: Collaboration and Compromise*, New York, New Press, 1996.
Cahun, C., *Les Paris sont Ouvert*, Paris, José Corti, 1934.
— *Écrits*, ed. François Leperlier, Paris, Jean-Michel Place, 2002.
Carey, V., *Guernsey under Occupation. The Second World War Diaries of Violet Carey*, ed. A. Evans, Chichester, Phillimore, 2009.
Carr, G., 'Material Culture and the Emotions of Internment', in A. Myers and G. Moshenska (eds), *Archaeologies of Internment*, One World Archaeology (WAC), New York, Springer, 2011, pp. 129–45.
— 'Of Coins, Crests and Kings: Symbols of Identity and Resistance in the Occupied Channel Islands', *The Journal of Material Culture*, Vol. 17 (4), 2012a, 327–44.

— 'Examining the Memorialscape of Occupation and Liberation: A Case Study from the Channel Islands', *International Journal of Heritage Studies*, Vol. 18 (2), 2012b, 174–93.
— 'Occupation Heritage, Commemoration and Memory in Guernsey and Jersey', *History and Memory*, Vol. 24 (1), 2012c, 87–117.
— *Legacies of Occupation: Archaeology, Heritage and Memory in the Channel Islands, 1945-Present*, forthcoming (ms. with Springer, New York).
Carr, G. and Heaume, R., 'Silent Resistance in Guernsey: The V-sign Badges of Alf Williams and Roy Machon', *Channel Islands Occupation Review*, Vol. 32, 2004, 51–5.
Casella, E. C., *The Archaeology of Institutional Confinement*, Gainesville, University Press of Florida, 2007.
Census 1931. Jersey, Guernsey and Adjacent Islands, London, HMSO, 1933.
Chamier Grove, J., 'Engineering an Escape', *Channel Islands Occupation Review*, Vol. 33, 2005, 23–34.
Chapman, D. M., *Chapel and Swastika: Methodism in the Channel Islands during the German Occupation*, Jersey, ELSP, 2009.
Churchill, W., *The War Speeches of the Rt. Hon. Winston S. Churchill, Volume 2*, ed. C. Eade, London, Cassell, 1952.
Cohen, F., *The Jews in the Channel Islands during the German Occupation 1940–1945*, Jersey, Jersey Heritage Trust in association with the Institute of Contemporary History and Wiener Library, 2000.
Conway, M. and Romijn, P., *The War for Legitimacy in Politics and Culture 1936–1946*, Oxford and New York, Berg, 2008.
Corbet, F. L. M., 'Leslie Huelin', in F. L. M. Corbet (ed.), *A Bibliographical Dictionary, Volume 2*, Guernsey, Guernsey Press Co. Ltd., 1998, p. 114.
Corbet, W., 'Guernsey Fisherman Escapes from German-occupied Island, 1943', contributed by Guernsey Museum, http://www.bbc.co.uk/history/ww2peopleswar/stories/78/a7749778.shtml, accessed 29 July 2013.
Cortvriend, V. V., *Isolated Island. A History and Personal Reminiscences of the German Occupation of the Island of Guernsey, June 1940–May 1945*, London, Streamline Publications Ltd. [Guernsey, Guernsey Star and Gazette], 1960 [1945].
Coutanche, A., *The Memoirs of Lord Coutanche: A Jerseyman Looks Back*, ed. H. R. S. Pocock, Chichester, Sussex, Phillimore and Co. Ltd., 1975.
Coysh, V., *Swastika over Guernsey*, Guernsey, Guernsey Press Co. Ltd., 1955.
Crill, P., 'The Story of an Escape from Jersey', *Société Jersiaise Bulletin*, Vol. 24, 1985–8, 107–12.
Cruickshank, C., *The German Occupation of the Channel Islands: The Official History of the Occupation Years*, London, Sutton Publishing [Guernsey, Guernsey Press Co. Ltd., by arrangement with the Trustees of the Imperial War Museum and Oxford University Press], 2004 [1975 1st edn].
Darling, A., 'McKinstry, Robert Noel', in F. L. M. Corbet (ed.), *A Bibliographical Dictionary, Volume 2*, Guernsey, Guernsey Press Co. Ltd., 1998, pp. 288–90.
Davies, P., *Dangerous Liaisons*, Harlow, Pearson, 2004.
De Carteret, B., Deslandes, M. and Robin, M., *Island Trilogy. Memories of Jersey and the Occupation by Mary Robin, Basil de Carteret and Mary Deslandes*, Jersey, Redberry Press, undated.
De Jong, L. and Stoppelman, J. W. F., *The Lion Rampant: The Story of Holland's Resistance to the Nazis*, New York, Querido, 1943.
Diamond, H., *Women and the Second World War in France 1939–1948: Choices and Constraints*, Harlow, Pearson Education, 1999.

Doyle, P. and Foster, C., *British Army Cap Badges of the First World War*, Oxford, Shire Publications Ltd., 2010.
Duchen, C., 'Crime and Punishment in Liberated France: The Case of the femmes tondues', in C. Duchen and I. Bandauer-Schoffmann (eds), *When the War was Over: War and Peace in Europe 1940–1956*, London, Leicester University Press, 2000a, pp. 233–50.
— 'Opening Pandora's Box: The Case of les femmes tondues', in M. Cornick and C. Crossley (eds), *Problems in French History*, Basingstoke, Palgrave, 2000b, pp. 213–32.
Durand, R., *Guernsey under German Rule*, London, The Guernsey Society, 1946.
Dusselier, J. E., 'Does Food Make Place? Food Protests in Japanese American Concentration Camps', *Food and Foodways*, Vol. 10, 2002, 137–65.
— *Artifacts of Loss: Crafting Survival in Japanese American Concentration Camps*, New Brunswick, Rutgers University Press, 2008.
Dutot, L., *Du Pain entre les Rails. Anna Stadler, une Allemande au Secours des Déportés*, Coutances, OCEP, 1988.
Edwards, J. D. L., 'The German Occupation of the Bailiwick of Guernsey 1940–1945 – A Critical Examination of the Response of the Guernsey Authorities to an Occupation by Enemy Forces, with Particular Reference to the Criminal Justice System, and the Extent That Social Class Impacted on That Response', MA dissertation, University of Liverpool, School of History, 2002.
Ellison, G., Jeffs, D. and Harvey, J., 'How Did the Occupation Affect the Health of Channel Islanders? A Rationale for the Channel Islands Birth Cohort Study', *The Channel Islands Occupation Review*, Vol. 26, 1998, 39–43.
Eriksson, K. and Simonsen, E. (eds), *Children of World War Two – The Hidden Enemy Legacy*, Oxford and New York, Berg, 2005.
Falla, F., *The Silent War: The Inside Story of the Channel Islands under the Nazi Jackboot*, Guernsey, Burbridge Ltd. [Leslie Frewin Ltd.], 1994 [1967].
Falle, A., *Slaves of the Third Reich: Jersey 1940–1945*, no place of publication or publisher given, 1994.
Faramus, A., *Journey into Darkness*, London, Grafton, 1990.
Ferguson, N., Roberts, A., 'Hitler's England: What If Germany Had Invaded Britain in May 1940', in Niall Ferguson (ed.), *Virtual History: Alternatives and Counterfactuals*, London, Picador, 1997, pp. 281–320.
Fogelman, E., *Conscience and Courage: Rescuers of Jews during the Holocaust*, New York, Anchor, 1994.
Follain, C., 'Constructing a Profile of Resistance – Lucy Schwob and Suzanne Malherbe as Paradigmatic Résistantes', BA Contemporary History with French dissertation, University of Sussex, 1997.
— 'A Study of the Specificities of Resistance during the German Occupation of Jersey, 1940–1945', MA Contemporary History dissertation, University of Sussex, 1999.
— 'Lucy Schwob and Suzanne Malherbe – Résistantes', in L. Downie (ed.), *Don't Kiss Me: The Art of Claude Cahun and Marcel Moore*, London, Tate Publishing, in association with the Jersey Heritage Trust, 2006, pp. 83–95.
Foot, M. R. D., *Resistance: An Analysis of European Resistance to Nazism 1940–1945*, London, Eyre Methuen, 1976.
Forty, G., *Channel Islands at War: A German Perspective*, Shepperton, Ian Allan, 1999.
Fox, J., 'How Far Did Vichy France "sabotage" the Imperatives of Wannsee?', in D. Cesarani (ed.), *The Final Solution: Origins and Implementation*, London and New York, Routledge, 1986, pp. 194–214.

Fraser, D., *The Jews of the Channel Islands and the Rule of Law, 1940–1945*, Brighton and Portland, Sussex Academic Press, 2000.
Frowd, M., 'A Russian in Hiding – "Bill" Fyodor Burriy', *Channel Islands Occupation Review*, Vol. 27, 1999, 59–70.
Galen Last, D. van, 'The Netherlands', in B. Moore (ed.), *Resistance in Western Europe*, Oxford and New York, Berg, 2000, pp. 189–221.
Garnier, V., *Medical History of the Jersey Hospitals and Nursing Homes during the Occupation, 1940–1945*, London, Channel Islands Occupation Birth Cohort Study, University of London, 2002.
Garrett, S. A., 'Political Leadership and the Problem of "Dirty Hands"', *Ethics and International Affairs*, Vol. 8 (1), 1994, 159–75.
Gilbert, M., *The Righteous: The Unsung Heroes of the Holocaust*, London, Black Swan, 2003.
Gildea, R., *Marianne in Chains: In Search of the German Occupation 1940–45*, London, Macmillan, 2002.
Ginns, M., 'Foreign Workers' Burials in Guernsey: A Reappraisal', *Channel Islands Occupation Review*, Vol. 25, 1997, 73–4.
Glass, J., *Jewish Resistance during the Holocaust: Moral Uses of Violence and Will*, Basingstoke, Palgrave Macmillan, 2004.
Greenwood, C., 'International Humanitarian Law (Laws of War)', in F. Karlshoven (ed.), *The Centennial of the First International Peace Conference – Reports and Conclusions*, The Hague, Martinus Nijhoff Publishers, 2000, pp. 161–260.
Grint, K., *Leadership: A Very Short Introduction*, New York, Oxford University Press, 2010.
Gross, M. L., *Ethics and Activism: The Theory and Practice of Political Morality*, Cambridge, Cambridge University Press, 1997.
Guppy, A., *Stone de Croze! The Original Guernseyman, Volume Two*, Guernsey, The Guernsey Press Co. Ltd., 1979.
Halliwell, M., *Operating under Occupation: The Life and Work of Arthur Clare Halliwell FRCS, Consultant Surgeon at the Jersey General Hospital during the German Occupation 1940–1945*, Jersey, Channel Islands Occupation Society, 2005.
Harris, L., *A Boy Remembers*, Jersey, Channel Island Publishing, 2004 [2000].
Harris, R. E., *Islanders Deported (Part I)*, Ilford, Essex, Channel Islands Specialists Society Publishing, 1979.
Harvey, W., *The Battle of Newlands: The Wartime Diaries of Winifred Harvey*, Guernsey, Rosemary Booth, 1995.
Hassall, P. D., 'Night and Fog Prisoners', http://www.jerseyheritage.org/templates/jerseyheritage/occupation_memorial/pdfs/hassallbookcomplete.pdf, 1997, accessed 28 February 2013.
Hayes, J. C., 'A Sojourn in Guernsey', http://www.johncrossleyhayes.co.uk/writings/A_Sojourn_in_Guernsey.php, accessed 14 July 2013.
Heaume, R., 'Marie Ozanne', *Channel Islands Occupation Review*, Vol. 23, 1995, 79–81.
Heberer, P., 'The Nazi "euthanasia" Programme', in J. Friedman (ed.), *The Routledge History of the Holocaust*, London and New York, Routledge, 2010, pp. 137–47.
Hellbeck, J., *Die Stalingrad-Protokolle: Sowjetische Augenzeugen berichten aus der Schlacht*, Frankfurt, Fischer, 2012.
Hensle, M., *Rundfunkverbrechen. Das Hören von 'Feindsendern' im Nationalsozialismus*, Berlin, Metropol, 2003.
Hitler, A., *Hitler's Table Talk: Hitler's Conversations Recorded by Martin Bormann*, ed. H. Trevor-Roper, Oxford and New York, 1998.

Hocart, R., *An Island Assembly. The Development of the States of Guernsey, 1700–1949*, Guernsey, Guernsey Museum and Art Gallery, 1988.
Hockenos, M. D., *A Church Divided: German Protestants Confront the Nazi Past*, Bloomington, Indiana University Press, 1992.
Hollander, E., 'Swords or Shields? Implementing and Subverting the Final Solution in German-occupied Europe', Working paper, Department of Political Science, Wabash College, 2011, http://papers.ssrn.com/sol3/papers.cfm?abstract_id=1906430, accessed 6 September 2013.
In the Privy Council on Appeal from the Royal Court of the Island of Guernsey between William George Quin and Others, and Her Majesty the Queen, No. 10, 1952.
Jackson, J., *France: The Dark Years 1940–1944*, Oxford and New York, Oxford University Press, 2003.
Jensen, M. B. and Jensen, S. L. B. (eds), *Denmark and the Holocaust*, Copenhagen, Institute for International Studies, Department for Holocaust and Genocide Studies, 2003.
Journeaux, D. P., *Raise the White Flag: A Life in Occupied Jersey*, Leatherhead, Ashford, Buchan and Enright, 1995.
Keiller, F., *Prison without Bars: Living in Jersey under the German Occupation 1940–1945*, Bradford on Avon, Seaflower Books, 2000.
Kershaw, I., *The Nazi Dictatorship: Problems and Perspectives of Interpretation*, London, Arnold, 2000.
Keynes, J. M., 'How to Pay for the War', in D. Moggridge (ed.), *The Collected Writings of John Maynard Keynes, Vol. 22, Activities 1939–1945: Internal War Finance*, London, Macmillan, 1978, pp. 40–9.
King, P., *The Channel Islands War 1940–1945*, London, Robert Hale, 1991.
Kirchoff, H., 'Denmark: A Light in the Darkness of the Holocaust? A Reply to Gunnar S. Paulsson', *Journal of Contemporary History*, Vol. 30, 1995, 465–79.
Knowles-Smith, H., *The Changing Face of the Channel Islands Occupation: Record, Memory and Myth*, Basingstoke, Palgrave Macmillan, 2007.
L'Amy, J. H., *The German Occupation of Jersey*, unpublished diary of events, n.d. (in custody of Société Jersiaise).
Lagrou, P., 'Belgium', in B. Moore (ed.), *Resistance in Western Europe*, Oxford and New York, Berg, 2000, pp. 27–64.
Lamy, A. P., Chief Officer Guernsey Police, 1942–1965, *Policing during the Occupation 1940–1945*, n.d.
Laska, V., *Women in the Resistance and in the Holocaust: The Voice of Eyewitnesses*, New York, Praeger, 1983.
Le Brocq, N., *Jersey Looks Forward*, London, The Communist Party, 1947.
— 'Clandestine Activities. Norman Le Brocq's Story', *Channel Islands Occupation Review*, Vol. 27, 1999, 39–53 (transcript of talk given 4 April 1988).
Le Hérissier, R. G., *The Development of the Government of Jersey, 1771–1972*, Jersey, The States of Jersey, 1973.
Le Quesne, E., *The Occupation of Jersey Day by Day. The Personal Diary of Deputy Edward Le Quesne*, with a foreword and explanatory notes by Michael Ginns, Jersey, La Haule, 1999.
Le Ruez, N., *Jersey Occupation Diary: Her Story of the German Occupation, 1940–45*, Bradford-on-Avon, Seaflower Books, [Jersey, Seaflower Books], 2003 [1994].
Le Sauteur, P., *Jersey under the Swastika*, London, Streamline Publications Ltd., 1961.
Le Sueur, F., *Shadow of the Swastika. Could It All Happen Again?*, Guernsey, Guernsey Press Co. Ltd., [Jersey, Starlight Imports Ltd.], 1992 [1990].

Le Sueur, R., 'Some Notes on a Planned Mutiny of the German Armed Forces in Jersey on 1st May 1945, and on the German Deserter, Paul Mülbach', *Channel Islands Occupation Review*, Vol. 29, 2001, 44–52.
Leale, J., *Report of Five Years of German Occupation*, Guernsey, Guernsey Press, 1945.
Leperlier, F., *Claude Cahun: L'Écart et la Métamorphose*, Paris, Jean Michel Place, 1992.
Levi, P., *The Drowned and the Saved*, London, Abacus, 1989.
Lewis, J., *A Doctor's Occupation: The Dramatic True Story of Life in Nazi-occupied Jersey*, London, New English Library [Jersey, Channel Island Publishing], 1983 [1982].
Liberman, P., *Does Conquest Pay? The Exploitation of Occupied Industrial Societies*, Princeton, Princeton University Press, 1996.
London, P., 'The Rescuers: Motivational Hypotheses about Christians Who Saved Jews from the Nazis', in L. Berkowitz and J. Macaulay (eds), *Altruism and Helping Behaviour: Social Psychological Studies of Some Antecedents and Consequences*, New York, Academic Press, 1970, pp. 241–50.
Longmate, N., *How We Lived Then: A History of Everyday Life during the Second World War*, London, Arrow, 1971.
Marr, J., *Guernsey People*, Chichester, Phillimore and Co. Ltd., 1984.
— *The History of Guernsey. The Bailliwick's Story*, Guernsey, The Guernsey Press, 2001.
Marrus, M. and Paxton, R. O., 'The Nazis and the Jews in Occupied Europe', *Journal of Modern History*, Vol. 54, 1982, 687–714.
Marshall, M., *Hitler Invaded Sark*, St Peter Port, Guernsey, Paramount-Lithoprint, 1963.
Mauger, R., 'Slaves and the Organisation Todt in Guernsey', *Channel Islands Occupation Review*, Vol. 8, 1969, 10–14.
Maugham, R. C. F., *Jersey under the Jackboot*, London, W. H. Allen, 1952 [1946 1st edn].
McLoughlin, R., *Living with the Enemy*, Jersey, Starlight Publishing, 1995.
Michel, A., *Vichy et la Shoah. Enquête sur le paradox français*, Paris, CLD, 2012.
Michel, H., *The Shadow War: Resistance in Europe 1939–1945*, London, The History Book Club, 1972.
Mière, J., *Never to be Forgotten*, Jersey, Channel Island Publishing, 2004.
Milward, A. S., 'The Economic and Strategic Effectiveness of Resistance', in S. Hawes and R. White (eds), *Resistance in Europe, 1939–1945*, London, Allen Lane, 1975, pp. 186–203.
Moland, A., 'Norway', in B. Moore (ed.), *Resistance in Western Europe*, Oxford and New York, Berg, 2000, pp. 223–48.
Mollet, R., *Jersey under the Swastika*, London, Hyperion Press Ltd., 1945.
Moore, B., *Victims and Survivors: The Nazi Persecution of the Jews in the Netherlands*, London and New York, Arnold, 1997.
— 'Comparing Resistance and Resistance Movements', in B. Moore (ed.), *Resistance in Western Europe*, Oxford and New York, Berg, 2000, pp. 249–64.
Müller, R.-D., 'Todt Organisation', in I. C. B. Dear and M. R. D. Foot, *The Oxford Companion to the Second World War*, Oxford and New York, Oxford University Press, p. 1114.
Nora, P., 'Between Memory and History: *les lieux de mémoire*', *Representations*, Vol. 26, 1989, 7–25.
— 'From *lieux de mémoire* to Realms of Memory', in D. Kritzman (ed.), *Realms of Memory: Rethinking the French Past. Volume I: Conflicts and Divisions* (English language edition with a foreword by L. D. Kritzman, trans. Arthur Goldhammer), New York, Columbia University Press, 1996, pp. xiv–xxiv.

Oliner, S. P., 'The Unsung Heroes in Nazi-occupied Europe: The Antidote for Evil', *Nationalities Papers*, Vol. 12 (1), 1984, 129–36.
Oliner, S. P. and Oliner, P. M., *The Altruistic Personality*, New York, The Free Press, 1988.
Ousby, I., *Occupation: The Ordeal of France*, London, Pimlico, 1999.
Overy, R., *Why the Allies Won*, London, Pimlico, 1996.
Ozanne, B. S., *A Peep behind the Screens: 1940–1945*, Guernsey, Guernsey Press Co. Ltd., 1994.
Ozanne, R., *Life in Occupied Guernsey: The Diaries of Ruth Ozanne 1940–1945*, ed. W. Parker, Stroud, Amberley, 2011.
Paulsson, G. S., 'The "bridge over the Øresund": The Historiography of the Expulsion of the Jews from Nazi-occupied Denmark', *Journal of Contemporary History*, Vol. 30, 1995, 431–64.
Paxton, R., *Vichy France. Old Guard and New Order*, New York, Knopf, 1972.
Perrin, D., *The German Occupation and Jersey Freemasonry 1940–1945*, Jersey, privately published, 1995.
Pollizotti, M., *Revolution of the Mind: The Life of André Breton*, London, Bloomsbury, 1995.
Privy Council Appeal No. 10 of 1952, William Quin and Others v. The Queen, from the Royal Court of the Island of Guernsey, Reasons for the Report of the Lords of the Judicial Committee of the Privy Council, 6 October 1955, *Privy Council Decisions*, http://www.bailii.org/uk/cases/UKPC/, accessed 15 August 2012.
Rees, L., *Auschwitz: The Nazis and the Final Solution*, London, BBC Books, 2005.
Roberts, A., *Hitler and Churchill. Secrets of Leadership*, London, Weidenfeld & Nicolson, 2003.
Rolo, C. J., *Radio Goes to War*, London, Faber and Faber, 1943.
Rossiter, M. L., *Women in the Resistance*, New York, Praeger, 1985.
Rowbotham, S., *Hidden from History: 300 Years of Women's Oppression and the Fight Against It*, London, Pluto Press, 1973.
Russell, S., *Spotlight on the Channel Islands*, London, Daily Worker, 1945.
Sanders, P., *Histoire du marché noir 1940–1946*, Paris, Perrin, 2001.
— *The Ultimate Sacrifice. The Jersey Islanders who Died in German Prisons and Concentration Camps 1940–1945*, Jersey, Jersey Heritage Trust, 2004 (2nd edn).
— *The British Channel Islands under German Occupation, 1940–1945*, Jersey, Jersey Heritage Trust and Société Jersiaise, 2005.
— 'Managing under Duress: Ethical Leadership, Social Capital, and the Civilian Administration of the British Channel Islands during the Nazi Occupation, 1940–1945', *Journal of Business Ethics*, Vol. 93, 2010, 113–29.
— 'Narratives of Britishness: UK War Memory and Channel Islands Occupation Memory', in J. Matthews and D. Travers (eds), *Islands and Britishness: A Global Perspective*, Newcastle, Cambridge Scholars, 2012, pp. 24–39.
Santoro, M., *Profits and Principles: Global Capitalism and Human Rights in China*, Ithaca, Cornell University Press, 2000.
Saunders, N. J., 'Apprehending Memory: Material Culture and War, 1919–1939', in P. Liddle, J. Bourne and I. Whitehead (eds), *The Great World War 1914–45. Volume 2, The Peoples' Experience*, London, Hammersmith: HarperCollins, 2001, pp. 476–88.
— *Trench Art: Materialities and Memories of War*, Oxford and New York, Berg, 2003.
Sauvary, J. C., *Diary of the German Occupation of Guernsey 1940–1945*, Guernsey, Guernsey Press Co. Ltd., [Self Publishing Association] 1995 (revised edn) [1990 1st edn].

Schröter, S., 'Thesen und Desiderata zur ökonomischen Besatzungsherrschaft', in J. Lund (ed.), *Working for the New Order. European Business under German Domination 1939-1945*, University Press of Southern Denmark and Copenhagen Business School Press, 2006, pp. 29-44.

Schwartz, P., 'Redefining Resistance: Women's Activism in Wartime France', in M. R. Higonnet, J. Jenson, S. Michel and M. C. Weitz (eds), *Behind the Lines: Gender and the Two World Wars*, New Haven and London, Yale University Press, 1987, pp. 141-53.

— 'Partisans and Gender Politics in Vichy France', *French Historical Studies*, Vol. 16 (1), 1989, 126-51.

Scott, J., *Weapons of the Weak: Everyday Forms of Peasant Resistance*, New Haven and London, Yale University Press, 1985.

Semelin, J., *Unarmed against Hitler: Civilian Resistance in Europe, 1939-1943*, Westport, CT and London, Praeger, 1993.

Sherwill, A., *A Fair and Honest Book: The Memoirs of Sir Ambrose Sherwill*, Lulu.com, 2006.

Sijes, B. A., 'Some Observations Concerning the Position of the Jews in Occupied Europe', *Acta Historiae Neerlandicae*, Vol. 9, 1976, 170-92.

Sinel, L., *The German Occupation of Jersey: A Complete Diary of Events from June 1940-June 1945*, Jersey, The Evening Post, 1945; republished as *The German Occupation of Jersey: The Wartime Diary of Leslie Sinel*, Jersey, Villette Publishing, 1995.

Slim, H., 'Doing the Right Thing. Relief Agencies, Moral Dilemmas and Moral Responsibility in Political Emergencies and War', *Working paper*, Nordiska Afrikainstitutet, Uppsala, 1997.

Solomon-Godeau, A., 'The Equivocal "I": Claude Cahun as Lesbian Subject', in S. Rice (ed.), *Inverted Odysseys: Claude Cahun, Maya Deren, Cindy Sherman*, New York, MIT Press, 1999, pp. 111-25.

SPD Preungesheim, '8. Mai 1945, 8. Mai 1985. Preungesheim 40 Jahre danach – erinnern oder vergessen?'

Steckoll, S., *The Alderney Death Camp*, London: Granada Publishing, 1982.

'Stikkerlikvidering – Modstandskampens blodige byrde', *Nationalmuseet*, http://natmus.dk/historisk-viden/danmark/besaettelsestiden-1940-1945/flammen-og-citronen/modstandskampens-blodige-byrde/, accessed 5 August 2013.

Stokker, K., *Folklore Fights the Nazis: Humour in Occupied Norway, 1940-1945*, Madison, University of Wisconsin Press, 1997.

Straede, T., 'Dänemark unter deutscher Besatzung 1940-45: Kollaboration, Widerstand und Erinnerung Zugleich ein Nachwort', in J. Kieler (ed.), *Dänischer Widerstand gegen den Nationalsozialismus. Ein Zeitzeuge berichtet über die Geschichte der dänischen Widerstandsbewegung 1940-1945*, Hannover, Offizin, 2008, pp. 351-67.

Stroobant, F., *One Man's War*, Guernsey, Burbridge Ltd., 1997 [1967].

Syvret, M., *Edmund Blampied: A Biography of the Artist 1886-1966*, London, Robin Garton for Société Jersiaise, 1986.

Syvret, M. and Stevens, J., *Balleine's History of Jersey*, Chichester, Phillimore, 1981.

Tabb, P., *A Peculiar Occupation: New Perspectives on Hitler's Channel Islands*, Hersham, Ian Allan, 2005.

Tangye Lean, E., *Voices in the Darkness: The Story of the European Radio War*, London, Secker and Warburg, 1943.

Tec, N., 'Righteous Christians in Poland', *International Social Science Review*, Vol. 58 (1), 1983, 15-17.

— *When Light Pierced the Darkness: Christian Rescuers of Jews in Nazi-occupied Europe*, Oxford and New York, Oxford University Press, 1986.

Thierry, M., 'An Army Oppressed', manuscript on the Salvation Army under Occupation, undated, unpaginated, by kind permission of Michael Thierry.
Thomas, R., *Lest We Forget: Escapes and Attempted Escapes from Jersey during the German Occupation 1940–1945*, Jersey, La Haule, 1992.
Tremayne, J., *War on Sark: The Secret Letters of Julia Tremayne*, Exeter, Webb and Bower, 1981.
Turner, B., *Outpost of Occupation: How the Channel Islands Survived Nazi Rule 1940–1945*, London, Aurum Press Ltd., 2010.
Uttley, J., *The Story of the Channel Islands*, London, Faber and Faber, 1966.
Varese, F. and Yaish, M., 'The Importance of Being Asked: The Rescue of Jews in Nazi Europe', *Rationality and Society*, Vol. 12, 2000, 307–34.
— 'Resolute Heroes: The Rescue of Jews during the Nazi Occupation of Europe', *European Journal of Sociology*, Vol. 46 (1), 2005, 153–68.
Vergili, F., *Shorn Women: Gender and Punishment in Liberation France*, Oxford, Berg, 2002.
Vinen, R., *The Unfree French: Life under the Occupation*, New Haven, Yale University Press, 2007.
Walker, E., *Don't Annoy the Enemy*, Guernsey, Guernsey Press Co. Ltd., 1998.
Weisberg, R. A., *Vichy Law and the Holocaust in France*, New York, New York University Press, 1996.
Weithley, R., *So It Was: One Man's Story of the German Occupation from Boyhood to Manhood*, Jersey, Starlight Publishing, 2001.
Weitz, M. C., *Sisters in the Resistance: How Women Fought to Free France, 1940–1945*, New York, John Wiley and Sons, 1995.
White, R., 'The Unity and Diversity of European Resistance', in S. Hawes and R. White (eds), *Resistance in Europe, 1939–1945*, London, Allen Lane, 1975, pp. 7–23.
Wievorka, O., 'France', in B. Moore (ed.), *Resistance in Western Europe*, Oxford and New York, Berg, 2000, pp. 125–56.
Willmot, L., 'The Channel Islands', in B. Moore (ed.), *Resistance in Western Europe*, Oxford and New York, Berg, 2000, pp. 65–92.
— 'The Goodness of Strangers: Help to Escaped Russian Slave Labourers in Occupied Jersey 1942–1945', *Contemporary European History*, Vol. 11 (2), 2002, 211–27.
— 'Noel McKinstry', in *Channel Islands Occupation Review*, Vol. 31, 2003, 25–30.
— '"Nothing was ever the same again": Public Attitudes in the Occupied Channel Islands, 1942', *The Local Historian: Journal of the British Association for Local History*, Vol. 35 (1), 2005, 9–20.
Wilson, C., *Jokes: Form, Content, Use and Function*, European Monographs in Social Psychology, no. 16, London, Academic Press, 1979.
Wood, A. and Wood, M. S., *Islands in Danger: The Story of the German Occupation of the Channel Islands, 1940–1945*, Sevenoaks, First Four Square [New York, Macmillan], 1965 [1955 1st edn].
Wyatt, H. and Blampied, E., *Jersey in Jail 1940–1945*, Jersey, La Haule Books Ltd., [Ernest Huelin], 1985 [1945].

Newspapers

Daily Mail
Daily Mirror

Daily Sketch
Evening Post
Guernsey Evening Press
Guernsey Star
Guernsey Weekly Press and Advertiser
Jersey Evening Post
News of the World
The Sunday Island Times

Magazines, etc.

Magnet Magazine
The Methodist Recorder
The War Cry

Index

administrative margins, 245, 266
Air Raid Protection Service (ARP), 172, 184, 192, 201, 202, 222–3, 232, 342–6
Alderney, 16, 84, 104, 216, 226, 281, 288
anti-semitism, 213, 216, 312
Armstrong, Ethel, 189
Arnold, William H., 252
Ashcroft, Sidney, 82, 83
Association des Écrivains et Artistes Revolutionnaires (AEAR), 186
Audiard, Jacques, 295
Audrain, Dennis, 225
Aufsess, Hans Max von, 16, 115
Augsburg, 289
Aune, André, 314
Avarne, Claude, 170

Bachmann, K. M., 105, 106
Bailey, Kingston, xxii, 48, 280, 284, 286, 288, 289, 296, 297
Bandelow, Fritz, 255–6
banking, 279–80
Banneville, Frederick, 83
Barbier, Flavian Emile, 138, 151
Baron, Lawrence, 114
Bataille, Georges, 186
The Battle of the Rails (1945), 278
battle of the wits, 65, 279
Bayonne, 67
BBC, 2, 9, 11, 34, 43–5, 48, 67–8, 72–3, 75–7, 86–7, 144, 155, 157, 165, 170, 187, 189, 191, 194, 213, 286, 314, 319, 341, 344, 351–2
Beaton, John, 100
Bedane, Albert, 101–2, 112–13, 115, 196, 328
Bell, Donald, 169–70, 171, 219
Bell, William, 284, 290
Belsen, 195, 321
Bennett, Arnold, 220
Benwell, Alfred, 197

Bercu, Hedwig, 102–3
Bernau, 289
Bertram, Emily, 193
Bertram, Thomas, 193, 229
Bertram, Wilfred ('Bill'), 193, 229, 232
Bertrand, Ludovic E., 75–6, 83, 216
Bevin, Ernest, 267
Biarritz, 67
Biberach, 31, 55, 67, 139, 141, 142, 144–7, 221, 289
Bickmore, C. W., 290, 298, 299
Binding, Tim, 200
Binet, Jean, 282
Bing, Geoffrey, 290, 291
Bisson, Madeline. 192, 227
Bisson, Ronald, 192, 227
black market, 13, 84–5, 202, 225, 277–9, 285–6, 294–6, 301, 316
Blampied, Edmund, 99
Blampied, Harold, 170, 172
Blampied, Marianne, 99
Bleckwenn, Dr, 167–9
Bochum, 73
Bödeker, Heinrich, 67
Body, Norman, 87
Bondis, Charles, 230
Botatenko, Peter, 109, 115, 187, 190, 196
Bott, Agatha, 184
Bree, Bernard, 109
Bretel, Joseph, 296
Breton, André, 186
Briard, Garnet, 227
The Bridge on the River Kwai, 260
'British Patriots', 71, 100
Brock, Peggy, 54, 104
Broszat, Martin, 12, 258
Brown, Constance, 107
Brown's Café, St Brelade's, 107
Buchenwald, 52, 67
Bunting, Madeleine, 5–6, 160, 166, 194, 200, 202, 230, 244–5, 247

Burrin, Philippe, 216
Burriy, Fyodor ('Bill'), 110–11, 194–5
Burton, William, 280, 281, 284, 292, 295, 297
Butterworth, Nanetta, 184
Butterworth, Wilf, 114
buttonhole resistance, 21, 27–33, 38, 340

cable-cutting, 98–9, 100, 163, 189, 198
Capper, Harry, 87
Carey, James, 26, 54, 129
Carey, Victor, 4, 46–7, 54, 58, 66, 130–1, 134, 201, 218, 226, 257, 259, 281, 319, 329
Carey, Violet, 23–4, 26, 27, 30, 31, 52, 54, 55, 129, 131, 133–4, 136, 137, 163, 164, 167, 217, 226
Carr, Gilly, 4, 10, 169, 329, 330
Carratu, Bernard, 220
cartoons, 35–8
Casimir, Paul, 158
Casper, Wilhelm, 16, 98, 157–8
Castel school, 46, 47
cavalcade, 142–4
Cavey, Bernard, 230
Celle, 75
Channel Islands Study Group, 159
Chapell, H. C., 261
Chapman, David, 160
Chardine, Albert, xxii, 25, 26, 56, 115, 225, 267
Christian X, King, 29
Churchill, Winston, 27, 36, 45, 76, 79, 83, 142, 263, 267, 319, 329
Churchillian paradigm, 319, 329
civilian resistance, 8–9, 19, 68, 153, 249, 264, 343
class/social structure, 3, 22, 153–4, 160, 189–90, 262, 345
clearing, 279
Clement, René, 278
clergy, 34, 73–5, 133–4, 135, 136, 153, 160–6, 173
Cohen, Freddie, 98–9, 102, 103
cohesion, 8–9, 11, 59, 114–15, 169–70, 250, 340, 345
Cohu, Clifford, 72–5, 82, 164–5, 199, 339
'cold-shoulder', 162
collaboration, 2, 4–6, 10–12, 45, 83, 157, 160, 167, 183, 200–2, 220, 243–8, 253, 263–6, 277, 285, 292, 294, 300
Collas, Lilian Ogier, 106
Cologne, 74
Colonel Britton, 44, 45, 48–50, 52, 54, 56, 144, 286, 295, 296, 344
commando raids, 31, 129, 245, 255
compensation scheme (for victims of Nazism), 1, 14, 81, 293, 307, 322–6, 351, 352
Compiègne, 31, 67, 139
conformism, 250, 258
Conscientious Objectors 110, 112, 114, 141
constitutional structure, 153–4, 159–60, 250, 252, 299
Controlling Committee, Guernsey, 15, 45, 46, 47, 98, 100, 101, 129–31, 133, 154, 160, 167, 169, 226, 249, 254–5, 257, 261, 262, 310, 319, 340
Cook, Frederick, 222
Corbet, William, 224, 226
corruption, allegations, 154–5, 157, 160
Costard, Muriel, 193
Coutanche, Alexander, 4, 15, 27, 30, 52, 66, 71, 98, 99, 107, 115, 132, 134, 168–9, 189, 217, 253, 258–62, 316, 317, 319, 322
Coutanche, Henry, 73
Crawford-Morrison, Klara, 184
Crawford-Morrison, William, 172, 184, 222–3, 232, 342, 346
crest, 10, 28, 31, 32, 39, 141, 142
Crill, Peter, 155, 214, 230, 326
Croad, Izett, 22, 25, 28, 53, 107, 136, 138, 169, 191
Croix de Lorraine, 21
Crossley Hayes, John, 79, 88, 350–1
Cruickshank, Charles, 4, 5, 6, 50, 159, 184, 214, 229–30
Curwood, Peter, 227, 315

Dachau, 83, 158, 289
Darling, Averell, 168–9, 170
Davey, Douglas, 230
Davey, Isaac, 73
Davey, James, 73, 246
D-Day, 37, 74, 85, 86, 156, 159, 163, 164, 192, 193, 201, 202, 213, 223, 226, 230, 231, 311, 321

Index 369

de Gaulle, Charles, 21, 278
de Guillebon, Xavier, 53–4, 58
De La Salle College, 231
de Lavelaye, Victor, 44
Denmark, 8, 29, 66, 161, 245, 264
denunciation, 7, 34, 46, 47, 58–9, 100, 103, 106, 109–11, 115, 169, 201, 246, 257, 261, 268, 311, 345
deportation (to civilian internment camps), 4, 6, 10, 11, 12, 16, 21, 24, 31, 54, 58, 73, 114, 127–48, 155, 161, 162, 166, 169, 187, 191, 219, 223, 226, 231, 249, 251, 259, 260, 341, 342, 351
deportation (to Nazi prisons and camps), 53, 98, 99, 101, 164, 170, 195, 218, 289, 310, 322, 325, 329, 348, 350, 351
deportation of leading citizens (threat of), 46–7
de Sausmarez, Cecil, 59 n14
Deslandes, Mary, 107, 108, 184, 226
detector (crystal set), 76, 85–8, 164, 169, 191, 313–14, 317, 319
Dexter, Norman, 80, 82, 83, 322
Diamond, Hanna, 186
differential treatment, 135, 246–7, 264, 349
Dijon, 73
dilemma, 12, 48, 99, 162, 244, 246, 255, 285, 340
Dimitrieva, Claudia, 110, 112, 113, 196
Dimmery, Arthur, 72, 73, 350–1
'dirty hands', 12, 244
doctors, 12, 102, 107, 129, 134–5, 136, 153, 166–73
Domaille, Gerald, 82–3, 322
Dore, Owen, 73
Dorrian, Edna, 141
Dortmund, 73, 74
Doyle, Peter, 77, 78, 83–5
Duquemin, Cecil, 76–80, 82, 322
Duret Aubin, Charles, 15, 98, 155, 246, 260, 262, 268, 285

Einert, Walter, 78–80
elections, 155, 159–60, 185
Emergency Hospital, Guernsey, 101
Empire Day, 28
escapes
    from the islands, 2, 4, 5–6, 12, 68, 98, 159, 169–70, 172, 173, 184, 189, 192–3, 201, 202, 213, 215, 216, 220, 223–30, 231, 232
    from OT camps, 106, 108, 109–15, 157, 169, 172, 173, 187, 194–6
    from prison, 102, 169–70, 219–20, 230
evacuation (1940), 102, 114, 159, 161, 166, 200, 215, 224, 253–4, 262, 340, 343
Evans, Mortimer, 110, 169–70
Evening Post, Jersey, 25, 33, 103, 109, 115, 128, 159, 160, 202, 220

'fair share' principles, 245, 265–6
Falla, Clifford, 224
Falla, Frank, 1, 14, 24, 54, 74, 76, 77–81, 83, 87, 88, 266, 293, 307, 320–7, 329, 331, 351–3
Fauvic 'embarkation point', 193, 227, 228, 248
Feldgendarmerie, 30, 73, 77, 83, 84–5, 87, 225, 283, 298
Feldkommandantur, 16, 46, 66, 85, 98, 101, 103, 107, 114, 130, 189, 197–8, 252, 260, 261, 280, 286
Ferrers, Vyvyan, 30–1
Finey, Rev, 163, 164
Floyd, John, 170
Foot, M.R.D., 6, 214, 248
Foott, Louisa, 108
Forster, Ivy, 111–12, 170, 194–6
fortifications, 29, 97, 103–4, 156, 172, 192, 198, 213, 218, 221–2, 224, 225, 228, 344
Foss, Henry, 163
Foulon cemetery (Guernsey), 24
France, 6, 8, 10, 16, 30, 44, 54, 67, 71, 74, 84, 86, 98, 101, 104, 108, 141, 165, 170, 183–4, 186–7, 191–3, 197, 200, 202, 214–15, 217, 219, 223, 226–8, 230, 245, 246–8, 250, 253, 262, 264, 266, 278, 287, 295, 309, 318, 326, 340, 343, 345, 352
Frankfurt, 80, 82
Franoux, René, 110, 112
Fraser, David, 98–9, 100
Freiburg, xi, 74, 84, 85, 86
Friend, Charles, xii, 48, 280, 281, 283, 289, 292, 293, 297
Frowd, Mike, 110, 112

Gallichan, George, 71
Gallichan, Herbert, 71

Garden, Centenier, 246, 268, 285
Gaudion, Thomas, 289
Gavey, Alice, 194–5
Geheime Feldpolizei (GFP), 23, 24, 30, 35, 77, 78, 80, 84–7, 162, 261, 312, 346
Geheime Staatspolizei (Gestapo), 67, 74, 82, 89, 97, 297
General Hospital, Jersey, 72, 164, 166, 170, 171
German police records (Jersey), 84
Giffard, Harold, 100
Gill, Marjorie, 185
Gillingham, Henrietta, 79, 80, 82, 191, 329–30
Gillingham, Joseph, xii, xiii, 1, 76–9, 82, 191, 329, 330
Gladden, William, 70–1, 110, 111, 112, 113, 222, 223, 227, 232, 345
Gloucester Street prison, St Helier, 138, 159, 168, 169, 188, 196, 230, 231, 311, 326, 327
Goebbels, Josef, 67
Goldrein, Eric, xii, xiii, 290, 291, 292
Gorvel, André, 227
'go slow' attitude, 8, 72, 217
Gould, Louisa, 110–11, 112, 113, 115, 120, 194–6, 203, 328, 345
Gould, Maurice, 225
graffiti, 10, 43, 45, 46, 48, 50, 52, 53, 54, 55, 59, 192
Granville, 16, 67, 215, 226, 228
Gray, Peter, 193, 220, 316
Green, Leslie, 52, 134
Green, Maurice, 52
Green, Stanley, 52, 67, 223
Green, Winifred, 53, 58, 184
grey zone, 244, 247, 266, 280, 293, 301
Griffin, Renée, 313
Griffiths, Joseph, 161
Gross, Michael, 109
Grunfeld, Marianne, 98, 99, 101
guardians of memory, 14, 308, 320, 331, 332
Guernsey Active Secret Press (GASP), 11, 75, 83, 88, 342, 347
Guernsey Police Committee, 284, 299
Guernsey police trial (1942), 280–8
Guernsey Star, 76, 128
Guernsey Underground Barbers, 201, 220

Guernsey Underground News Service (GUNS), 1, 11, 49, 75–88, 191, 202, 293, 320, 321, 329, 330, 342, 344, 345, 347, 350
Guillemette, Louis, 46, 130, 134, 309
Guiton, Peter, 228
Guppy, Alan 35, 37, 38

Haakon VII, King, 29
Hacquoil, Dora, 194–5
Hadgetts, Nora, 145
Hague Convention, 66, 168, 250–2, 256, 319
Halle, 82
Halliwell, Arthur, 170–1, 172, 173, 219, 345
Hamon, Frank, 108
Harper, Jack, 48, 280, 284, 289, 294, 297
Harris, Francis, 220, 311, 313
Harrison, Arthur, 115, 159–60
Hartley-Jackson, Rev, 163
Hassall, Bernard, 220
Hassall, Peter, 225, 228
Hathaway, Robert, 131, 140
Hathaway, Sybil, 131, 262
Hawes, Stephen, 7
Hawkins, Miss, 100
Heller, Joseph, 285
Hensle, Michael, 88
Hepburn, Harold, 141, 143, 146, 147
Hill, Bert, 35–7, 77
Hill, Maurice, 151 n77
Hill-Cottingham, Frederick, 289, 291
historiography, 3–10, 12, 244, 247, 258
Hitler, Adolf, 20, 82, 103, 114, 127, 128, 132, 146, 187, 249, 260, 287
HMS *Charybdis*, 24, 25, 252
Hobbs, Warren, 156
Hollander, Ethan, 264
Holocaust, 102, 261, 264, 328
Home Office, 255, 261–3, 290, 292, 294, 298, 316, 319, 322
'horizontal collaboration', 200, 201–2
Houillebeq, James, 218–19
house search, 78, 84, 85, 86, 219, 282
Howlett, Alfred, 280, 281, 282, 297
Hubert, Jack, 224, 226
Huelin, Leslie, 109, 156, 157, 158, 159, 346
Hüffmeier, Friedrich, 16, 158, 223

Index

humanitarian aid, 3, 11, 101–2, 105–6, 156–7, 169–71, 173, 183, 193–6, 198, 202–3, 214, 221, 342, 343, 344, 345, 346
Hutchings, Barbara, 192
Hybrid behaviour, 247
Hyman, Edward, 154, 159

identity, 10, 31–2, 58–9, 140–2, 146, 186, 243, 311, 340, 345
illegitimate births, 201
Ingrouille, John, 217–18, 330
institutional resistance, 153, 173
intelligence-gathering, 3, 5, 7, 12, 67, 113, 156, 172, 192, 193, 202, 213, 218–23, 227, 230–2
Ivanov, Mischa, 109

Jackson, Julian, 10, 247
jail, Guernsey, 79
jail, Jersey, 52, 308, 311–19
Janvrin, Evelyn, 192–3, 317, 318
Jerovna, Michael, 109
'Jerrybags', 183, 200–2
Jersey Communist Party (JCP), 109, 111, 113, 155–9, 172, 173, 186, 202, 342, 343, 345, 346
Jersey Democratic Movement (JDM), 155, 157, 158–60, 173, 186, 341, 343, 344–5
Jersey Loyalists, 221, 223
Jersey Patriotic League, 201, 220
Jersey Progressive Party (JPP), 159–60
Jersey Scientific Society, 155
Jews, 2, 9–10, 11, 97–103, 106, 109, 111–14, 129, 135, 141, 154, 163, 165, 166, 197–8, 223, 252, 259, 330
Joanknecht, Dolly, 202
jokes, 21, 33–5, 38, 189
Journeaux, Donald, 23, 27, 28

Kaisheim, 289
Karlsruhe, 74
Kassowitz, Matthieu, 295
Kershaw, Ian, 258
Killer (Keiller), Frank, 165, 170, 196, 221, 227, 229, 231
King, Peter, 5
Kinnard, Lilian, 53
Klemann, Hein, 277

Knackfuss, Friedrich, 16, 52, 66, 71, 105, 107, 132, 168, 187, 223
Koslov, George, 109, 112, 166, 170, 194
Kosta, Siebe, 192
Kotyzova, Bozena, 103
Krokhin, Mikhail, 109
Krumpa, 81

Lainé, Abraham, 15, 98–9, 226, 262
Lainé, Adele, 27, 49, 105
Lainé, Walter, 82, 83, 322
Lambert, French consul, 106, 113, 226
Lamy, Albert, 53, 261, 279, 282–3, 293
L'Amy, J. H., 222–3, 312
Langlois, Dorothy, 22–3
Langlois, Ruby, 184
Lanyon, Hubert, 79, 330
Lanz, Albrecht, 254, 255
Larbalaster, Bernard, 228
Larbalastier, John, 228
Laufen, 29, 52, 53, 56, 67, 73, 138–40, 142, 146, 262
Laurens, A. J., 110
Leale, John, 4, 15, 46, 101, 129, 130, 131, 134, 249, 250, 254, 257, 261, 319
Le Blond, Leona, 185
Le Breton, Phyllis, 111, 113
Le Brocq, Norman, 11, 109, 156–7, 159, 160, 186, 215, 346
Le Brun, Basil, 230
Le Calvez family, 109
Le Cloche, Hugh, 227
Le Cornu, Mike, 112, 188
Le Cornu, Stanley, 112
Le Cuirot, Dennis, 226
Le Druillenec, Harold, 195, 321
Legg, Ernest, 76, 77–9, 81, 191, 322
Legg, Mabel, 192
legitimacy, 2, 8, 13, 157, 160, 244, 248, 250–2, 260, 263–4, 277, 286, 293–4, 300, 309–10, 331, 346
Le Gresley, Ernest, 107
Le Gros, Ted, 228
Le Guyader, Joseph, 56, 57
Le Marchand, Douglas, 228
Le Mottée, René, 110, 112, 113, 194–5
Le Page brothers, 226
Le Quesne, Edward, 15, 54, 106, 133, 134, 165, 188, 219, 249, 261, 267, 315, 316

Le Quesne, Wally, 158
Le Riche, Rosalie, 158, 186
Le Riche, Silver, 228
Le Ruez, Joyce, 169
Le Ruez, Nan 45, 49, 109, 113, 165
Le Sueur, Francis, 102, 227, 314
Le Sueur, John, 170
Le Sueur, Robert, 102, 110–13, 154, 157
Leuna, 82
Levi, Primo, 244, 266
Lewis, John, 134, 170
Lewis, Kenneth G., 45, 49, 167
Liberation Day, 27, 38, 43, 57, 58, 161, 327
Lieux de mémoire, 38
listening parties, 9, 11, 65–8, 72, 77, 87, 89, 155, 194, 251, 313, 319, 339, 352
Longmate, Norman, 4–5
loose talk, 83–4, 86
Lowry, Miss, 184
Luciennes, Roy, 227
Lukitch, Wasily, 109, 115

MacCartney, Rev, 164
Machon, Charles, 76–80, 191
Machon, Roy, 29–30, 50, 53, 58
Madagascar, 87
Mahy, N. W., 106, 115
Malherbe, Suzanne, 12, 88, 100, 103, 113–14, 186–90, 192, 202, 259, 312, 345
Manley, J. C. M., 222
Manley, R. H., 222
Manning, Monty, 55
Marempolski, Vasily, 194
margins, 2, 245, 253, 266, 340
Marsh, William, 72
Martel, J. E. L., 15, 280–1, 288
Martel, Philip, 255
Mayne, Richard, 224
McKinstry, Noel, 2, 11, 97, 102, 107, 109–13, 167–9, 171–3, 201, 223, 228, 232, 260–1, 346
medical board (convened to check deportees), 134
medical board (to check compensation claims for Nazi persecution), 323
Metcalfe, Augusta, 110, 112, 113, 196
MI5, 248
Michel, Henri, 5, 7, 9, 11, 340, 342

Mière, Joe, 138, 220, 224, 230, 307, 312, 314, 316, 320, 326–9, 331
military larceny, 2, 192–4, 216, 219–20, 230, 232
Miller, Percy, 80
Milward, Alan, 8
Minotaur, SS, 202, 226
Mollet, Ralph, 30, 164–5
Mont-à-L'Abbé cemetery, 25
Moore, Bob, 9–11
morale, 2–3, 7, 11, 19, 24, 38, 44, 58–9, 65, 67, 75–6, 140, 142, 157, 161, 163, 173, 187, 189, 308
Mount Bingham, 138
Mülbach, Paul, 158–9, 186
Mulholland, Desmond, 255
Müller, Erich, 71
Mylne, Clement, 161–3, 166, 191, 199, 349
Mylne, Vivienne, 191

narratives, 2, 5, 12, 65, 89, 244–8, 280, 288, 307, 319, 326, 328–9
Naumburg-on-Saale, 74–5, 80–2, 165
Neil, Michael, 228, 312
Netherlands, 21, 28–9, 99, 104, 215, 264, 342
Neuengamme, 73, 219
Neuoffingen, 289
news dissemination, 11, 71–3, 79–80, 164, 192, 317, 352
news exchange, 7, 72
news-sheets, 72–3, 75–6, 79–80, 191, 202, 344, 352
Nicolle, Hubert, 47, 214, 245, 251, 255–7, 293, 346, 350
Nicolle, John, 72–4
Noel, Peter, 228
Norman, Kathleen, 53
Normandy, 31, 215, 262, 311
Norway, 9, 20, 29, 33, 34, 66, 161, 214, 251, 264, 345

Ogier, Edward, 101
Ogier, Leonce, 221
Ogier, Richard, 221
Ord, Douglas, xii, 23–4, 27, 30, 34, 54, 65, 67, 72, 83, 88, 101, 105–6, 133–4, 136–7, 162–4, 166, 200, 214, 217, 257

Order for the Protection of the Occupying Authority (18 December 1942), 109, 246
Organisation Todt (OT), 2, 4, 10, 29, 34, 97, 102–9, 112–15, 131, 155–7, 163, 165–6, 168–70, 172–3, 183, 187, 189–90, 192–200, 216, 340
Orwell, George, 67
Osmont, Raymond, 170
'Ost Spezial' files, 84
Öttingen-Wallerstein (zu), Eugen, 286
Overy, Richard, 67
Ozanne, Beryl, 22, 106
Ozanne, Daniel, 196
Ozanne, Marie, 5, 12, 100–1, 106, 113, 133, 161–2, 165, 196–200, 203, 330–1, 339, 345

Page, Frederick, 73, 246, 268, 285
Painter, Clarence, 218–19
Painter, Peter, 218–19, 221
Paris, 58, 67, 68, 113, 197, 214, 221, 256, 279, 321
patriotic colours, 20–8, 38, 47, 56, 136, 141, 142, 144, 147, 191, 340, 341
patriotic flowers, 8, 21, 24, 25, 27, 28, 49, 56
patriotic songs, 3, 21, 33, 136, 137, 138, 145, 147, 313
People's Progressive Party, 155
Perkins, Stella, 112
Perrée, Ernest, 157
Perrin, Rose, 192
Pfeffer, Karl-Heinz, 65, 259
Picquet, Steve, 79
Pitolet, Berthe, 111, 194–5
Poignard, Clarissa, 193
Poland, 66, 101, 228
political prisoners, 14, 82, 141, 159, 168, 169, 170, 172, 189, 196, 231, 260, 267, 289, 308–20, 322, 323–4, 326–32, 345, 348, 350–1
political prisoner consciousness, 307, 311, 315, 317
Portsmouth, 73
post-war honours, 4, 9, 292, 319
Preston, Kenneth, 165
Preungesheim, 74, 80, 82
Privy Council, 13, 252, 283, 290–4, 296–7

propaganda, 20, 48, 53–4, 65, 67, 72, 89, 107, 143, 156–9, 161, 173, 189, 221, 247, 249, 262–3, 288, 296–7, 342, 349, 351

Querée, Colleen, 202, 226
Quin, William, 280, 281, 283, 289, 292, 297

radio confiscation, 2, 6, 10, 46, 53, 66–8, 70–1, 73, 87, 155, 163–5, 246–7, 251, 341–2
RAF badge, 30
Randall, C. R. J., 167
Ravensbrück, 111, 184, 196, 328, 352
Red Cross, 26, 55–7, 82, 139, 141–3, 145–6, 172, 259, 266–7, 315
Renouf, Wilfred, 34, 286
reprisal policy, 4, 43, 46, 48, 54, 56–8, 66, 113, 127, 129, 189, 214, 217, 221, 226, 243, 245, 254, 256–7, 264, 278, 308–10, 318, 332
Résistance-Fer, 278
Resistenz, 12, 258–9, 263, 264, 265
Revell, Rowan, 167, 168
Rey, Charles, 87, 164
Rheinbach, 80, 289
Richardson, Mary Erica, 99, 101–2
Ritchie, Douglas ('Colonel Britton'), 43–5, 48–50, 52, 54, 144, 286, 295–6
Romainville, 67
Rose, Alastair, 169, 226, 309
Ross, Annie ('Nan'), 108
Ross, Edward, 108
Royal Square, 47, 56, 57, 73, 165
Rozel, 192, 227
Ruaux, J. Y., 5

Saarbrücken, 73, 74
sabotage, 2–5, 7–8, 13, 43, 46, 72, 112, 113, 158, 168, 184, 189, 192, 193, 213–21, 230–2, 277–9, 287–8, 290–1, 294, 298, 310–11, 316, 319, 341–4
Sailer, Anni, 289
Salvation Army, 2, 100, 106, 133, 161–2, 196–7, 200, 330
Salzach, 73
Sanders, Paul, 10, 48, 58, 98, 99, 135, 184, 200, 308, 312, 340, 346, 349

San Sebastian, 67
Sark, 24, 45, 49, 79, 128, 129, 131, 135, 137, 139, 140, 145, 250, 330, 350
Sarre, Bill, 107, 110, 112, 115, 169
Sarre, Gwenda, 110, 112, 115, 169, 196
Schmettow (von), Rudolf, 16, 214, 259
Schumacher, Friedrich, 16, 217
Schwartz, Paula, 186
Schwob, Lucy, 12, 88, 100, 103, 108, 113–14, 186–90, 192, 200, 202, 216, 232, 259, 312, 345
Scornet, François, 217
Scott, James, 12, 13, 21
Sculpher, William, 47, 48, 197, 199, 284, 286, 290, 293, 298
security precautions, 83, 87, 194
A Self-Made Hero, 295
Semelin, Jacques, xiii, 3, 8, 11, 19, 153, 169, 172, 258
Service du Travail Obligatoire (STO), 8
Seyss-Inquart, Arthur, 21
Sheail, Una, 192
Sherwill, Ambrose, 15, 16, 47, 54, 58, 98, 214, 245, 254–7, 261–3, 266, 282, 298–9, 310, 321–2, 346
Short, Frederick, 280–1, 283
Silverman, Sydney, 290, 291
Simms, Madeleine, 75, 191
Simon, L. J. ('Tim'), 172
Sinclair, June, 184
Sinel, Leslie, 25–8, 38, 46, 53, 56, 138, 221, 225, 312, 316–17
Sirett, Eric, 55, 139, 147
Smith, Percival, 280, 281, 289, 297
social cohesion, 8–9, 11, 59, 114–15, 169–70, 340, 345
social contract, 254, 268, 346
social control, 89, 301
Sowden, George, 218, 225, 228–9
Sowerbutts, Fred, 114, 115
Soyer, Jack, 215
Spitz, Auguste, 98, 101
St. Brelades, 107, 108
St. George's Day, 28
St. Lawrence, 107, 110, 169, 196
St. Martin (Guernsey), 136, 296
St. Martin (Jersey), 70, 109–11, 113, 115, 162, 222–3
St. Ouen, 107, 109, 110, 111

St. Peter Port, xi, 24, 38, 57, 86, 99, 103, 105, 127, 162, 197, 226, 286, 326, 329
St. Saviour (Jersey), 72–3, 164, 168, 349
Stadler, Anna, 289
Stalingrad, 155, 191, 342
Steiner, Therese, 98, 101, 166
Still, Ruby, 99
Straubing, 82–3
Stroobant, Frank, 137
Sty, George Louis, 73, 87
Superior Council, Jersey, 15, 98, 100, 132–3, 154, 157, 158, 160, 165, 168, 219, 249, 340
Švejkism, 286
Sweden, 66
Switzerland, 66, 81
symbolic jewellery, 31–3
Symes, James, 47, 245, 251, 255–67, 293, 314, 346, 350
Symes, Louis, 214
Symes, William, 67, 322, 346
Symons, A. N., 15, 134, 167–8, 262

Tatam, Pat, 195
Taylor, Bill, 79
Teenagers, 6, 11, 128, 213, 216, 220, 221, 227, 312, 342, 343
Thaureux, Alice, 259
thefts, military equipment, 2, 192–4, 216, 219–20, 230, 232
Thomas, Roy, 229
thought resistance, 65, 259
Tierney, Joseph, 72–5
tip-offs, 85, 246
Tostevin, Marion, 106
Touzel, Rosanna, 192
Transport & General Workers' Union (T&GWU)
trench art, 31, 36, 52
Trubuil, Guillaume, 106
Tuck, Frank, 280, 284, 286, 289, 292, 293, 294–7
Turner, Belza, 172, 192, 313
Turpin, Bernard, 115, 230
Turpin, Henry, 224

Union Jack, 26, 27, 53, 56, 136, 141, 142, 143, 314
Utilitarianism, 48, 58, 98–9, 135, 246

Vale, Guernsey, 106, 134, 165, 197, 198, 330
V-army, 45, 49, 50, 52, 144, 145
V-badge, 29, 30
V-committee, 44
Vega, SS, 26, 57, 72
Vibert, Denis, 215, 225-6, 229
Victoria College, 27, 56, 195, 218, 231
V-Mann (informer), 77, 83
V-sign, 3, 4, 10, 11, 19, 20, 21, 26, 27, 29, 37, 39, 43-59, 66, 141, 146, 147, 191, 308, 313, 341
V-sound, 43, 44, 45

Wakeham, Arthur, 73
Wakely, Cyril, 79
Warley, Reginald, 75
weapons of the weak, 10, 13, 21
Webber, Thomas, 142
Weber, Dorothea, 103, 112-15, 196, 203, 345
Weithley, Richard, 219
Whare, Frank, 280, 283, 287, 294, 297
Wheatley, Dennis, 77

White, Miss, 100
White, Ralph, 7-8, 11
Whithy, George, 227, 315
Wilhelmina, Queen, 20, 28, 29
Williams, Alf, 29-30, 50, 51
Williams, Herbert ('Bert'), 220, 226
Willmot, Louise, 10, 138
Wolfenbüttel, 74
Wood, Alan, & Mary Seaton Wood, 4, 5, 30, 164, 193, 319, 320, 322
Woodhall, Maria, 113-14
women, 4, 5, 9-10, 11, 12, 29, 53, 58, 74, 111, 112, 139, 146, 183-203, 224, 226, 259, 289, 344-5
work education camp (Arbeitserziehungslager), 74, 165
Wurzach, 56, 139, 140, 141, 142, 143, 145, 146, 147

Yellow Star 98, 252, 259

Zöschen, 74, 165
Zweibrücken, 73

www.ingramcontent.com/pod-product-compliance
Lightning Source LLC
Chambersburg PA
CBHW070009010526
44117CB00011B/1474